T0332728

Advances in Enterprise Information Technology Security

Djamel Khadraoui
Public Research Centre Henri Toudor, Luxembourg

Francine Herrmann
University Paul Vertaine-Metz, France

INFORMATION SCIENCE REFERENCE

Hershey · New York

Acquisitions Editor:	Kristin Klinger
Development Editor:	Kristin Roth
Senior Managing Editor:	Jennifer Neidig
Managing Editor:	Sara Reed
Assistant Managing Editor:	Sharon Berger
Copy Editor:	Becky Shore
Typesetter:	Jamie Snavely
Cover Design:	Lisa Tosheff
Printed at:	Yurchak Printing Inc.

Published in the United States of America by
Information Science Reference (an imprint of IGI Global)
701 E. Chocolate Avenue, Suite 200
Hershey PA 17033
Tel: 717-533-8845
Fax: 717-533-8661
E-mail: cust@igi-pub.com
Web site: http://www.igi-pub.com/reference

and in the United Kingdom by
Information Science Reference (an imprint of IGI Global)
3 Henrietta Street
Covent Garden
London WC2E 8LU
Tel: 44 20 7240 0856
Fax: 44 20 7379 0609
Web site: http://www.eurospanonline.com

Library of Congress Cataloging-in-Publication Data

Advances in enterprise information technology security / Djamel Khadraoui and Francine Herrmann, editors.

p. cm.

Summary: "This book provides a broad working knowledge of all the major security issues affecting today's enterprise IT activities. Multiple techniques, strategies, and applications are thoroughly examined, presenting the tools to address opportunities in the field. It is an all-in-one reference for IT managers, network administrators, researchers, and students"--Provided by publisher.

Includes bibliographical references and index.

ISBN 978-1-59904-090-5 (hardcover) -- ISBN 978-1-59904-092-9 (ebook)

1. Business enterprises--Computer networks--Security measures. 2. Information technology--Security measures. 3. Computer security. 4. Data protection. I. Khadraoui, Djamel. II. Herrmann, Francine.

HF5548.37.A38 2007

005.8--dc22

2007007267

British Cataloguing in Publication Data
A Cataloguing in Publication record for this book is available from the British Library.

All work contributed to this book set is new, previously-unpublished material. The views expressed in this book are those of the authors, but not necessarily of the publisher.

Table of Contents

Section I
Security Architectures

Chapter I

Chapter II

Chapter III

Chapter IV

Chapter V

Section II
Trust, Privacy, and Authorization

Chapter VI

Section III
Threat

Section IV
Risk Management

Detailed Table of Contents

Section I
Security Architectures

Chapter I

This chapter proposes three different realistic security-level network architectures that may be currently deployed within companies. For more realistic analysis and illustration, two examples of companies with different size and profile are given. Advices, explanations, and guidelines are provided in this chapter so that readers are able to adapt those architectures to their own companies and to security and network needs.

Chapter II

GRID computing implies sharing heterogeneous resources, located in different places, belonging to different administrative domains, over a heterogeneous network. There is a great similarity between GRID security and classical network security. Moreover, additional requirements specific to grid environments exist. This chapter is dedicated to these security requirements, detailing various secured middleware systems. Finally, the chapter gives some examples of companies using such systems.

Chapter III

Fundamental security requirements of a Symbian-based mobile device such as physical protection, device access control, storage protection, network access control, network service access control, and network connection security are described in detail in this chapter. Symbian security is also evaluated by discussing its weaknesses and by comparing it to other mobile operating systems.

Chapter IV

This chapter describes in its first part the security features of IEEE 802.11 wireless local area networks and shows their weaknesses. A practical guideline for choosing the preferred WLAN configuration is given. The second part of this chapter is dedicated to the wireless radio network by presenting the associated threats with some practical defence strategies.

Chapter V

This chapter presents first a classification and a brief description of intrusion detection systems, taking into account several issues such as information sources, analysis of intrusion detection systems, response options for intrusion detection systems, analysis timing, control strategy, and architecture of intrusion detection systems. The problem of information exchange among intrusion detection systems, the intrusion detection exchange protocol, and a format for the exchange of information among intrusion detection systems is discussed. The lack of a format of the answers or countermeasures interchanged between the components of intrusion detection systems is also discussed as well as some future trends in this area.

Section II
Trust, Privacy, and Authorization

Chapter VI

This chapter presents security solutions in integrated patient-centric Web-based health-care information systems, also known as electronic health-care record (EHCR). Security solutions in several projects have been presented and in particular a solution for EHCR integration from scratch. Implementations of Public Key Infrastructure, privilege management infrastructure, role-based access control, and rule-based access control in EHCR have been presented. Regarding EHCR integration from scratch, architecture and security have been proposed and discussed.

This chapter proposes a novel interactive access control model: servers should be able to interact with clients asking for missing or excessing credentials, whereas clients my decided to comply or not with the requested credentials. The process iterates until a final agreement is reached or denied. Further, the chapter shows how to model a trust negotiation protocol that allows two entities in a network to automatically negotiate requirements needed to access a service. A practical implementation of the access control model is given using X.509 and SAML standards.

Because delegation is a concept derived from authorization, this chapter aims to put into perspective the delegation implications, issues, and concepts that are derived from a selected group of authorization schemes that have been proposed during recent years as solutions to the distributed authorization problem. It is also the analysis of some of the most interesting federation solutions that have been developed by different consortiums or companies, representing both educational and enterprise points of view. The final part of this chapter focuses on different formalisms specifically developed to support delegation services and which can be integrated into a multiplicity of applications.

This chapter introduces digital rights management (DRM) in the perspective of digital policy management (DPM), focusing on the enterprise and corporate sector. DRM has become a domain in full expansion with many stakes, which are by far not only technological. They also touch legal aspects as well as business and economic. Information is a strategic resource and as such requires a responsible approach of its management, almost to the extent of being patrimonial. This chapter mainly focuses on the latter introducing DRM concepts, standards and the underlying technologies from its origins to its most recent developments in order to assess the challenges and opportunities of enterprise digital policy management.

Section III
Threat

This chapter describes common attacks on antivirus tools and a few obfuscation techniques applied to recent viruses that were used to thwart commercial-grade antivirus tools. Similarities among different malware and their variants are also presented in this chapter. The signature used in this method is the percentage of application programming interface (APIs) appearing in the malware type.

The various ways in which phishing can take place are described in this chapter. This is followed by a description of key strategies that can be adopted for protection of end users and organizations. The end user protection strategies include desktop protection agents, password management tools, secure e-mail, simple and trusted browser setting, and digital signature. Some of the commercially available and popular antiphishing products are also described in this chapter.

This chapter describes the threat of phishing in which attackers generally sent a fraudulent e-mail to their victims in an attempt to trick them into revealing private information. This chapter starts defining the phishing threat and its impact on the financial industry. Next, it reviews different types of hardware and software attacks and their countermeasures. Finally, it discusses policies that can protect an organization against phishing attacks. An understanding of how phishers elicit confidential information along with technology and policy-based countermeasures will empower managers and end users to better protect their information systems.

This chapter provides a wide spectrum of end users with a complete reference on malicious code, or malware. End users include researchers, students, as well as information technology and security professionals in their daily activities. First, the author provides an overview of malicious code, its past, present, and future. Second, he presents methodologies, guidelines and recommendation on how an organization can enhance its prevention of malicious code, how it should respond to the occurrence of a malware incident, and how it should learn from such an incident to be better prepared in the future. Finally, the author addresses the issue of the current research as well as future trends of malicious code and the new and future means of malware prevention.

Section IV
Risk Management

This chapter provides a wide spectrum of existing security risk management methodologies. The chapter starts presenting the concept and the objectives of enterprise risk management. Some exiting security risk management methods are then presented by sowing the way to enhance their application to enterprise needs.

This chapter presents a system life cycle and suggests which aspects of security should be covered at which life-cycle stage of the system. Based on this, a process framework is presented that, due to its iterativity and detailedness, accommodates the needs for life-cycle oriented security management.

In this chapter, it is presented a study on the classification of software specification languages discussing the current state of the art regarding attack languages. Specification languages are categorized based on their features and their main purposes. A detailed comparison among attack languages is provided. We show the example extensions of the two software specification languages to include some features of the attack languages. We believe that extending certain types of software specification languages to express security aspects like attack descriptions is a major step towards unifying software and security engineering.

In this chapter, the security associated with the transfer of the content is quantified and treated as a quality of service parameter. The user is free to select the parameter depending upon the content being transferred. As dictated by the demanding situations, a minimum agreed security would be assured for the data at the expense of the appropriate resources over the network.

This chapter gives an introduction to the CORAS approach for model-based security risk analysis. It presents a guided walkthrough of the CORAS risk-analysis process based on examples from risk analysis of security, trust, and legal issues in a collaborative engineering virtual organisation. CORAS makes use of structured brainstorming to identify risks and treatments. To get a good picture of the risks, it is important to involve people with different insight into the target being analysed, such as end users, developers and managers. One challenge in this setting is to bridge the communication gap between the participants, who typically have widely different backgrounds and expertise. The use of graphical models supports communication and understanding between these participants. The CORAS graphical language for threat modelling has been developed especially with this goal in mind.

Foreword

This excellent reference source offers a fascinating new insight into modern issues of security. It brings together contributions from an international group of active researchers who, between them, are addressing a number of the current key challenges in providing enterprise-wide information technology solutions.

The general area of security has long been acknowledged as vitally important in enterprise systems design; because of the key role it has in protecting the resources belonging to the organization and in ensuring that the organization meets its objectives. Historically, the emphasis has been on protecting complete systems and hardening the communications between trusted systems against external attack. Architects have concentrated on creating an encapsulation boundary supported by a trusted computing base able to control the access to all the available resources.

However, the themes selected for this book illustrate a change of emphasis that has been in progress over recent years. There has been a steady movement during this time towards finer grain control with the introduction of progressively more subtle distinctions of role and responsibility and more precise characterization of target resources. The controls applied have also become more dynamic, with increasing emphasis on delegation of responsibility and change of organizational structure, and the need for powerful trust models to support them. At the same time there has been a blurring of the traditional boundaries, because of the need for controlled cooperation and limited sharing of resources. The protection is in terms of smaller and more specialized resource units, operated in potentially more hostile environments.

Two examples may help to illustrate this trend. On the one hand, there is a need to protect information and privileges embodied in mobile devices. A mobile phone or PDA may contain information or access tokens of considerable sensitivity and importance, and the impact of loss or theft of the device needs to be bounded by system support that resists tampering and illicit use. On the other hand, digital rights management focuses on the protection against unauthorized use of items of information, ranging from software to entertainment media, which need to be subject to access controls even when resident within the systems managed by a potential attacker. Both these situations challenge the traditional complete system view of security provision.

These examples illustrate that the emphasis is on flexibility of the organizational infrastructure and on the introduction of new styles of information use. However, this is not primarily a book about mechanisms; it is about enterprise concerns and on the interplay that is required between enterprise goals and security solutions. Even a glance at the contents makes this clear. The emphasis is on architecture and the interplay of trust, threat and risk analysis. Illustrated by practical examples and concerns, the discussion covers the subtle relationship between the exploitation of new opportunities and the exposure to new threats. Strong countermeasures that rule out otherwise attractive organizational structures represent a lost opportunity, but business decisions that change the underlying assumptions in a way that invalidates the trust and risk analysis may threaten the viability of the organization in a fundamental way.

Nothing illustrates this better than the growing importance of social engineering, or phishing, styles of attack. The attacks are based on abuse of the social relationship that must be developed between an organization and its clients, and on the ignorance of most users of the way authentication works and of the dangerous side effects of communicating with untrusted systems. Countermeasures range from education and management actions to the development of authentication techniques suitable for application between mutually suspicious systems.

One of the messages to be taken from these essays is that security must be a major consideration at all stages in the planning and development of information technology solutions. Although this is a view that experts have been promoting for many years, it is still not universally adopted. Yet we know that retrofitting security to partially completed designs is much more expensive and is often ineffectual. Risk analysis needs to start during the formulation of a business process, and the enterprise needs a well-formulated trust model as an accepted part of its organizational structure. Only in this way can really well-informed technical choices be made about the information technology infrastructure needed to support any given business initiative. The stronger integration of business and infrastructure concerns also allows timely feedback on any social or organizational changes required by the adoption of particular technical solutions, thus reducing the risk of future social attacks.

For these reasons, the section on risk management and its integration with the software lifecycle is a fitting culmination of the themes presented here. It is the endpoint of a journey from technical architectures, through trust models and threat awareness to intelligent control of risks and security responses to them.

I hope this book will stimulate a greater awareness of the whole range of security issues facing the modern enterprise in its adoption of information technology, and that it will help to convince the framers of organizational policy of the importance of addressing these issues throughout the lifecycle of new business solutions, from their inception through deployment and into service. We all know that reduction of risk brings competitive advantage, and this book shows some of the ways in which suitable security approaches can do so.

Peter F. Linington
Professor of Computer Communication
University of Kent, UK

Peter Linington is a professor of computer communication and head of the Networks and Distributed Systems Research Group at the University of Kent. His current work focuses on distributed enterprise modeling, the checking of enterprise pattern application and policy-based management. He has been heavily involved in the development of the ISO standard architecture for open distributed processing, particularly the enterprise language. His recent work in this area has focused on the monitoring of contractual behaviour in e-business systems. He has worked on the use of multiviewpoint approaches for expressing distribution architectures, and collaborated regularly with colleagues on the formal basis of such system. He was been an advocate of model-driven approaches before they became fashionable, and experimented in the Permabase project with performance prediction from models. He is currently working on the application of model driven techniques to security problems. He has performed consultancy for BT on the software engineering aspects of distribution architectures. He has recently been awarded an IBM Faculty Award to expand work on the enhancement of the Eclipse modelling framework with support for OCL constraint checking.

Preface

In the last decade information and computer security is mainly moving from the confines of academia to the enterprise concerns. As populations become more and more comfortable with the extensive use of networks and the Internet, as our reliance on the knowledge-intensive technology grows, and as progress in the computer software and wireless telecommunication increases accessibility, there will be a higher risk of unmanageable failure in enterprise systems.

In fact, today's information systems are widely spread and connected over the networks, but also heterogeneous, which involves more complexity. This situation has a dramatic drawback regarding threats, which are now occurring on such networks. Indeed, the drawback of being open and interconnected is that they are more and more vulnerable as a wide range of threats and attacks. These attacks have appeared during the last few years and are growing continuously with IP emergence and with all new technologies exploiting it (SIP vulnerabilities, phishing attacks, etc.) and also due to the threats exposing operators (DDOS) and end user (phishing attacks, worms, etc.). The Slammer and SoBig attacks are some of the examples that were widely covered in the media and broadcast into the average citizen home.

From the enterprise perspective, information about customers, competitors, products and processes is a key issue for its success. The increasing importance of information technology for production, providing and maintaining consistent security of this information on servers and across networks becomes one of the major enterprise business activities. This means that it requires a high flexibility of the organizational infrastructure and on the introduction of new ways of information usage.

In such a complex world, there is a strong need of security to ensure system protection in order to maintain the enterprise activities operational. However, this book gathers some essays that will stimulate a greater awareness of the whole range of security issues facing the modern enterprise. It mainly shows how important to have a strong interaction that is required between enterprise goals and security solutions.

OBJECTIVES

It is the purpose of this book to provide a practical survey of the principals and practice of IT security with respect to enterprise business systems. It also offers a broad working knowledge of all the major security issues affecting today's enterprise IT activities, giving readers the tools to address opportunities in the field. This is mainly because the security factors provide to the enterprise a high potential in order to provide trusted services to their customers. This book shows also to readers how to apply a number of security techniques to the enterprise environment with its complex and various applications. It covers the many domains related to the enterprise security, including: communication networks and multimedia, applications and operating system software, social engineering and styles of attacks, privacy and authorisation and enterprise security risk management.

This book gathers a best collection of papers written by many authors instead of a book that focuses on a specific approach or methodology.

Intended Audience

Aimed at the information technology practitioner, the book is valuable to CIO's, operations managers, network managers, database managers, software architects, application integrators, programmers, and analysts. The book is also suitable for graduate, master and postgraduate course in computer science as well as for computers in business courses.

STRUCTURE OF THE BOOK

The book chapters are organized in logical groupings that are akin to appropriate levels in an enterprise IT security. Each section of the actual book is devoted to carefully chosen papers, some of which reflect individual authors' experience. The strength of this approach is that it gives a benefit from a rich diversity of viewpoints and deep subject matter knowledge.

The book is organized into eighteen chapters. A brief description of each of the chapters follows:

Chapter I proposes three different realistic security-level network architectures that may be currently deployed within companies. For more realistic analysis and illustration, two examples of companies with different size and profile are given. A number of advices, explanations and guidelines are provided in this chapter so readers are able to adapt those architectures to their own companies and both security and network needs.

Chapter II is dedicated to the security requirements detailing various secured middleware systems, such as GRID computing, which implies sharing heterogeneous resources, located in different places belonging to different administrative domains over a heterogeneous network. It shows that there is a great similarity between GRID security and classical network security. Moreover, additional requirements specific to grid environments exist. At the end, the chapter gives some examples of companies using such systems.

Chapter III describes in detail the fundamental security requirements of a Symbian based mobile device such as physical protection, device access control, storage protection, network access control, network service access control, and network connection security. Symbian security is also evaluated by discussing its weaknesses and by comparing it to other mobile operating systems.

Chapter IV describes in its first part the security features of IEEE 802.11 wireless local area networks, and shows their weaknesses. A practical guideline for choosing the preferred WLAN configuration is given. The second part of this chapter is dedicated to the wireless radio network by presenting the associated threats with some practical defence strategies.

Chapter V presents first a classification and a brief description of intrusion detection systems, taking into account several issues such as information sources, analysis of intrusion detection systems, response options for intrusion detection systems, analysis timing, control strategy, and architecture of intrusion detection systems. It is then discussed the problem of information exchange among intrusion detection systems, being addressed the intrusion detection exchange protocol and a format for the exchange of information among intrusion detection systems. The lack of a format of the answers or countermeasures interchanged between the components of intrusion detection systems is also discussed as well as some future trends in this area.

Chapter VI presents security solutions in integrated patient-centric Web based healthcare information systems, also known as electronic healthcare record (EHCR). Security solutions in several projects have been presented and in particular a solution for EHCR integration from scratch. Implementations of , privilege management infrastructure, role based access control and rule based access control in EHCR have been presented. Regarding EHCR integration from scratch architecture and security have been proposed and discussed.

Chapter VII proposes a novel interactive access control model: servers should be able to interact with clients asking for missing or excessing credentials whereas clients my decided to comply or not with the requested credentials. The process iterates until a final agreement is reached or denied. Further the chapter shows how to model a trust negotiation protocol that allows two entities in a network to automatically negotiate requirements needed to access a service. A practical implementation of the access control model is given using X.509 and SAML standards.

Chapter VIII aims to put into perspective the delegation implications, issues and concepts that are derived from a selected group of authorization schemes which have been proposed during recent years as solutions to the distributed authorization problem. It is also the analysis of some of the most interesting federation solutions that have been developed by different consortiums or companies, representing both educational and enterprise points of view. The final part of this chapter focuses on different formalisms specifically developed to support delegation services and which can be integrated into a multiplicity of applications.

Chapter IX introduces digital rights management (DRM) in the perspective of digital policy management (DPM) focusing on the enterprise and corporate sector. DRM has become a domain in full expansion with many stakes, which are by far not only technological. They also touch legal aspects as well as business and economic. Information is a strategic resource and as such requires a responsible approach of its management almost to the extent of being patrimonial. This chapter mainly focuses on the latter introducing DRM concepts, standards and the underlying technologies from its origins to its most recent developments in order to assess the challenges and opportunities of enterprise digital policy management.

Chapter X describes common attacks on antivirus tools and a few obfuscation techniques applied to recent viruses that were used to thwart commercial grade antivirus tools. Similarities among different malware and their variants are also presented in this chapter. The signature used in this method is the percentage of APIs (application programming interface) appearing in the malware type.

Chapter XI describes the various ways in which phishing can take place. This is followed by a description of key strategies that can be adopted for protection of end users and organizations. The end user protection strategies include desktop protection agents, password management tools, secure email, simple and trusted browser setting, and digital signature. Some of the commercially available and popular antiphishing products are also described in this chapter.

Chapter XII describes the threat of phishing in which attackers generally sent a fraudulent email to their victims in an attempt to trick them into revealing private information. This chapter starts defining the phishing threat and its impact on the financial industry. Next, it reviews different types of hardware and software attacks and their countermeasures. Finally, it discusses policies that can protect an organization against phishing attacks. An understanding of how phishers elicit confidential information along with technology and policy-based countermeasures will empower managers and end-users to better protect their information systems.

Chapter XIII provides a wide spectrum of end users with a complete reference on malicious code or malware. End users include researchers, students, as well as information technology and security professionals in their daily activities. First, the author provides an overview of malicious code, its past, present, and future. Second, he presents methodologies, guidelines and recommendation on how an organization can enhance its prevention of malicious code, how it should respond to the occurrence of a malware incident, and how it should learn from such an incident to be better prepared in the future. Finally, the author addresses the issue of the current research as well as future trends of malicious code and the new and future means of malware prevention.

Chapter XIV provides a wide spectrum of existing security risk management methodologies. The chapter starts presenting the concept and the objectives of enterprise risk management. Some exiting security risk management methods are then presented by sowing the way to enhance their applications to enterprise needs.

Chapter XV presents a system life cycle and suggests which aspects of security should be covered at which life cycle stage of the system. Based on this it is presented a process framework that due to its iteratively and detailed ness accommodates the needs for life cycle oriented security management.

Chapter XVI presents a study on the classification of software specification languages discussing the current state of the art regarding attack languages. Specification languages are categorized based on their features and their main purposes. A detailed comparison among attack languages is provided. We show the example extensions of the two software specification languages to include some features of the attack languages. We believe that extending certain types of software specification languages to express security aspects like attack descriptions is a major step towards unifying software and security engineering.

Chapter XVII qualifies and treats the security associated with the transfer of the content, as a quality of service parameter. The user is free to select the parameter depending up on the content being transferred. As dictated by the demanding situations, a minimum agreed security would be assured for the data at the expense of the appropriate resources over the network.

Chapter XVIII gives an introduction to the CORAS approach for model-based security risk analysis. It presents a guided walkthrough of the CORAS risk analysis process based on examples from risk analysis of security, trust and legal issues in a collaborative engineering virtual organisation. CORAS makes use of structured brainstorming to identify risks and treatments. To get a good picture of the risks, it is important to involve people with different insight into the target being analysed, such as end users, developers and managers. One challenge in this setting is to bridge the communication gap between the participants, who typically have widely different backgrounds and expertise. The use of graphical models supports communication and understanding between these participants. The CORAS graphical language for threat modelling has been developed especially with this goal in mind.

Acknowledgment

The editors would like to acknowledge the help of all involved in the collation and review process of the book, without whose support the project could not have been satisfactorily completed. A further special note of thanks goes also to all the staff at IGI Global, whose contributions throughout the whole process from inception of the initial idea to final publication have been invaluable.

Deep appreciation and gratitude is due to Paul Verlaine University (Metz – France) and the CRP Henri Tudor (Luxembourg), for ongoing sponsorship in terms of generous allocation of on-line and off-line Internet, hardware and software resources and other editorial support services for coordination of this year-long project.

Most of the authors of chapters included in this also served as referees for articles written by other authors. Thanks go to all those who provided constructive and comprehensive reviews. However, some of the reviewers must be mentioned as their reviews set the benchmark. Reviewers who provided the most comprehensive, critical and constructive comments include: Peter Linington from University of Kent, Jean Henry Morin from University of Genova (Switzerland), Albin Zuccato from University Karlstad (Sweden), Muhammad Zulkernine from Queen University (Canada), Maryline Laurent-Maknavicius of ENST Paris, Fabio Massacci of University of Trento (Italy), Srinivas Mukkamala of New Mexico Tech's Institute, Fredrik Vraalsen from SINTEF (Norway), Halim M. Khelalfa of University of Wollongong in Dubai, Bogdan Hoanca of the University of Alaska Anchorage, and Hervé Guyennet of the University of Franche-Comté (France). Support of the department of computer science Metz (Paul Verlaine) University is acknowledged for the support and the archival server space reserved for the review process.

Special thanks also go to the publishing team at IGI Global. In particular to Jan Travers, who continuously prodded via e-mail for keeping the project on schedule and to Mehdi Khosrow-Pour, whose enthusiasm motivated me to initially accept his invitation for taking on this project.

In closing, we wish to thank all of the authors for their insights and excellent contributions to this book. We also want to thank all of the people who assisted us in the reviewing process. Finally, we want to thank our families (husband, wife, children and parents) for their support throughout this project.

Djamel Khadraoui, PhD, and Francine Herrmann, PhD
April 2007

Section I
Security Architectures

Chapter I
Security Architectures

Sophie Gastellier-Prevost
Institut National des Télécommunications, France

Maryline Laurent-Maknavicius
Institut National des Télécommunications, France

ABSTRACT

Within a more and more complex environment, where connectivity, reactivity and availability are mandatory, companies must be "electronically accessible and visible" (i.e., connection to the Web, e-mail exchanges, data sharing with partners, etc.). As such, companies have to protect their network and, given the broad range of security solutions on the IT security market, the only efficient way for them is to design a global secured architecture. After giving the reader all the necessary materials and explaining classical security and services needs, this chapter proposes three different realistic security-level architectures that may be currently deployed within companies. For more realistic analysis and illustration, two examples of companies with different size and profile are given. A number of advices, explanations and guidelines are provided in this chapter so readers are able to adapt those architectures to their own companies and both security and network needs.

INTRODUCTION

Today, with the increasing number of services provided by companies to their own internal users (i.e., employees), end-customers, or partners, networks are increasing in complexity, hosting more and more elements like servers and proxies. Facing a competitive business world, companies have no choice than expecting their services to be fully available and reliable. It is well known

that service disruptions might result in the loss of reactivity, performance and competitiveness, and finally a probable decreasing number of customers and loss of turnover.

To offer the mandatory reactivity and availability in this complex environment, the company's network elements are requested to be robust against malicious behaviours that usually target deterioration, alteration or theft of information. As such, strict security constraints must be defined for each network element, leading to the introduction of security elements. For an efficient security introduction into its network, a company must think about its global secured architecture. Otherwise, the resulting security policy might be weak as part of the network may be perfectly secured while a security hole remains in another one.

Defining a "single" and "miracle" security architecture is hardly ever possible. Therefore this chapter expects to give companies an overall idea of how a secured architecture can look like. In order to do that, this chapter focuses on two types of companies: A and B, and for each of them, three types of architectures are detailed, matching different security policies.

Note that those three architecture families result from a number of studies performed on realistic architectures that are currently being deployed within companies (whatever sizes).

For readers to adapt the described architectures to their own needs, this chapter appears much more as guidelines for designing appropriate security and functional architecture. Obviously, the presented architectures are not exhaustive and correspond to various budgets and security levels. This chapter explains the positioning of each network and security elements with many details and explanations, so that companies are able to adapt one of those architectures to their own needs.

Just before getting to the very heart of the matter, the authors would like to pay your attention that a company introducing security elements step by step, must always keep in mind the overall architecture, and be very careful during all deployment steps because of probable weak points until having deployed the whole solution.

Prior to describing security architectures, the chapter introduces all the necessary materials for the readers to easily understand the stakes behind the positioning of elements within the architectures. That includes system and network

elements, but also authentication tools, VPN and data security tools, and filtering elements.

When defining the overall network architecture within a company, the security constraints should be considered as well as the needs and services constraints of the company. All those elements will be detailed in the second part of this chapter, and in order to make explanations easier, two companies types will be chosen for further detailed architectures.

Finally, the next three parts of the chapter will focus on the three families of architectures, and for each of them a number of illustrations are proposed to support architectures explanations.

The first designed architecture is based on only one router that may be increased with some security functions. This is a low-budget architecture in which all the security leans on the integrity of the router.

The second architecture is a more complex one equipped with one router and one firewall. The security of the architecture is higher than the first one because a successful intrusion into the router may only affect network elements around the router, and not elements behind the firewall benefiting from its protection.

The third architecture requires two firewalls and a possible router. As the control operated by firewalls (and proxies) are much deeper than routers do, the intrusion attempts are more easily detected and blocked, so the company's network is less vulnerable. Moreover, the integrity again relies on two filtering equipments one after the other and is stronger than what is offered in the first architecture.

SECURITY BASIS

This section briefly introduces all the necessary materials for the readers to easily understand the stakes behind the positioning of elements within the architectures.

System and Network Elements

Private networks are based on a number of servers, and network level equipments including the following:

- **Dynamic host configuration protocol (DHCP)** server dynamically assigns an IP address to the requesting private network equipment, usually after booting.
- **Domain name system (DNS)** server mainly translates a domain name (URL) into an IP address, usually to enable browsers to reach a Web server only known by its URL.
- **Lightweight directory access protocol (LDAP)** server is an online directory that usually serves to manage and publish employees' administrative data like name, function, phone number, and so forth.
- **Network address translation (NAT)** performs translation between private and public addresses. It mainly serves to enable many private clients to communicate over the public network at the same time with a single public IP address, but also to make a private server directly accessible from the public network.
- **E-mail server** supports electronic mailing. A private e-mail client needing to send an e-mail requests the server, under the simple mail transfer protocol (SMTP), and if necessary, the latter relays the request to the external destination e-mail server also using SMTP; for getting its received e-mails from the server, the client sends a POP or IMAP request to the server. The e-mail server implements two fundamental functions—the e-mail forwarding/receiving and storing—which are usually separated on two distinct equipments for security reasons. The sensitive storing server next referred to as "e-mail" must be protected against e-mail disclosures and removals. The other, named "e-mail proxy" is in charge of

e-mail exchanges with the public network, and may be increased with anti-virus and antispam systems to detect virus within e-mail attachments, or to detect e-mail as a spam. **E-mails** can also be encrypted and signed with secure/multipurpose internet mail extensions (S/MIME) or pretty good privacy (PGP) protocols.

- **Anti-virus protects network** (files, operating systems…) against viruses. It may be dedicated to the e-mail service or may be common to all the private network's hosts which should contact the anti-virus server for updating their virus signatures basis.
- **Internet/Intranet/Extranet Web** servers enable employees to access to shared resources under hypertext transfer protocol (HTTP) requests from their own browser. Resources may be restricted to some persons like company's employees (Intranet server), external partners like customers (extranet server), or may be unrestricted so it is known as the public server.
- **Access points (AP)** are equipments giving IEEE 802.11 wireless equipments access to the wired network.
- **Virtual LAN (VLAN)** are designed to virtually separate flows over the same physical network, so that direct communications between equipments from different VLANs could be restricted and required to go through a router for filtering purposes.
- **Network access server (NAS)/Broadband access server (BAS)** are gateways between the switched phone network and an IP-based network. NAS is used by ISPs to give "classical" (i.e., 56K modem, etc.) PSTN/ISDN dial-up users access, while BAS is used for xDSL access.
- **Intrusion detection system (IDS)/Intrusion prevention system (IPS)** are used to detect intrusions based on known intrusion scenario signatures and then to react by dynamically denying the suspected flow.

Authentication Tools

The authentication of some entities (persons or equipments) leans either on the distributed approach, where the authentication may be performed in many equipments, or the centralized approach, where only few authentication servers have capabilities to authenticate.

The distributed approach is based on defining a pair of complementary public and private keys for each entity with the property that an encryption using one of these keys requires decrypting with the other key. While the private key remains known by the owner only, the public key must be widely distributed to other entities to manage the authentication. To avoid spoofing attacks, the public key is usually distributed in the form of an electronic certificate whose authenticity is guaranteed by a certification authority (CA) having signed the certificate. Management of certificates is known under the public key infrastructure (PKI) approach. The PKI approach is presented as distributed as any equipment having trust into the CA considers the certificate as valid and is then able to authenticate the entity. Certificates usage may be used for signing and encrypting e-mails or for securing sessions with Web servers using SSL (see section "VPN and data security protocols"). However, the remaining important PKI problem is for the entities to distinguish trusted authorities from fake authorities.

The centralized approach enables any equipment like APs, proxies to authenticate some entities by asking the centralized authentication server whether provided authentication data are correct. The authentication server may be a remote authentication dial-in user service (RADIUS) or LDAP server (Liska, 2002). The RADIUS server is widely used by ISPs to perform AAA functions (authentication, authorization, accounting), in order to authenticate remote users when establishing PPP connections, and to support extra accounting and authorization functions. Several methods are available like PAP/CHAP/EAP. In usual companies, when LDAP servers are already operational, with no need of authorization and accounting, the LDAP server solution is preferred over RADIUS to enforce authentication.

VPN and Data Security Protocols

A virtual private network (VPN) (Gupta, 2002) may be simply defined as a tunnel between two equipments carrying encapsulated and/or encrypted data. The VPN security leans on a data security protocol like IP security (IPsec) or secure socket layer (SSL). IPsec is used to protect IP packet exchanges with authentication of the origin, data encryption and integrity protection at the IP packet layer. SSL introduces the same data protection features but at the socket layer (between transport and application layers). SSL was originally designed to secure electronic commerce protecting exchanges between Web servers and clients, but the SSL protection is also applicable to any TCP-based applications like telnet, FTP. VPN solutions may also combine Layer 2 tunneling protocol (L2TP) for tunnelling management only and IPsec for security services enforcement. VPNs are based on one of these protocols, so VPNs are next referred to as IPsec VPN, L2TP/IPsec (L2TP over IPsec) VPN and SSL VPN.

VPNs may secure the interconnection between remote private networks. To do so, two VPN gateways, each one positioned at the border of each site are necessary. An IPsec tunnel (or L2TP tunnel over IPsec) is configured between the gateways. In this scenario, IPsec is preferred to SSL because IPsec affects up to the IP level and site interconnection only requires IP level equipments like routers. So the introduction of

IPsec into an existing network architecture only requires replacing the border router with a firewall or increasing the router with IPsec capacities.

In the case of nomads, to let moving users accessing private network resources like e-mail server, data basis, the VPN should be established between the nomad and the gateway at the border of the private network. Several technologies are possible but today, the most used ones are L2TP/ IPsec and SSL VPN. SSL VPN appears as a solution of choice by a number of companies because the administration of nomads is easier than in IPsec: no licence is necessary for the SSL client as the ordinary Web browser is an SSL client, and most of the services that need to be accessed by remote nomads like e-mail server or data basis, the VPN should be established.

While heavy to manage, IPsec VPN based on L2TP over IPsec gives nomads full access to the private network. The nomad is provided with one public address provided by the ISP and one private address allocated by the private network when establishing the L2TP tunnel. So the tunnel enables the nomad to create IP packets as will be received by the targeted equipment.

Note that today, when performing both IPsec and NAT, NAT should be applied first: otherwise, IPsec tunnel establishment will fail due to inconsistencies between the IP address declared when creating IPsec tunnel and the one present in the IP packets received by the IPsec endpoint.

Filtering Elements and DMZ

For private networks to remain protected from intrusions, the incoming and outgoing traffic is filtered at the border of the private network thanks to some more or less sophisticated filtering equipments like routers, firewalls, and proxies (Cheswick, 2003: Pohlman, 2002).

Routers are basic IP packet filters which analysis is limited to IP source/destination addresses, protocol number, and source/destination port numbers, and which security policy rules are known under access control list (ACL). As such, traffic may be authorized or denied according to the packet origin or destination. As routers rely on the correspondence between TCP/UDP services and port numbers, the access to some applications may be as such controlled, so the risk is to permit some traffic based on its claimed destination port number (e.g., 80) while the real encapsulated traffic (e.g., FTP) should be denied. Bypassing packet filter's policy is pretty simple using HTTP tunnelling for instance, so the solution is to proceed to a deeper analysis of the packet, as done by proxies or firewalls.

A proxy is a software between a client and a server, with the client behaving as directly connected to the server and the server to the client. Proxies in the security context are application-level filters, and commercial products include proxies for telnet, FTP, HTTP (URL proxy) or SMTP. First the client connects to the proxy and then in case of permission, the proxy establishes a second connection to the targeted server, and it relays the traffic between the two entities. The proxy may control the authenticity of the client, the client's address, and also the content of the exchanges.

Firewalls are equipments dedicated to filtering where the kernel is specialized and optimized for operating filtering. As such, application-level analysis may be performed like in proxies but with better performances because the filtering is enforced at the kernel, and does not require decapsulation of packets or TCP flow control, which are CPU and time consuming. Additionally, firewalls may support IDS/IPS functions.

A demilitarized zone (DMZ) is a restricted subnet, separated from the private and public networks, that allows servers to be accessible from other areas while keeping them protected. It also forbids direct connections from the public area to the private network, so that a successful attack requires performing two intrusions, first on the DMZ and second on the private network.

Usual equipments hosted in DMZ include proxies and Web servers.

NEEDS AND CONSTRAINTS FOR COMPANIES

The challenge for a company is to get its services fully available whatever happens: failures, or malicious behaviours that usually target deterioration, alteration or theft of information.

Note that in this context, "available" is used in a generic meaning which covers as much availability as confidentiality and integrity. Of course, there is no interest in providing an operational service if nonauthorized users can read or modify data.

The first step for a company that wants to secure its network, prior to deploying any security equipment, is to define all existing services, and expected ones in a close future. As such, a whole process must be followed in order to define the following:

- **Expected services and/or applications:**
  ○ Public Web site only
  ○ Public Web site with online secured transaction
  ○ Intranet Web site with secured access for employees
  ○ Extranet Web site with secured access for partners
  ○ Electronic mailing whether encrypted and signed. If secured, is it between end-to-end stations or e-mail servers?
  ○ Wireless network support
  ○ Content servers accessible for downloads
- **Trust levels regarding employees, partners, remote users:** Does the network request protection from external area only, or both from internal and external area?
- **Data availability for users:** Perhaps some servers will be accessible "on-site" only?

What kind of reliability for the network (equipment redundancy, link backup)?
- **Data sensitivity:** Can employees have access to all server contents; for example, can the accounting department database be accessible by any employee? Should remote users' connection be secured for setup only and/or data exchanges?
- **Privileged users:** Clearly define how many/who are privileged users. It should be fewest persons as possible, and not necessarily the general manager of the company, especially if he or she is a too busy and keeps the password on a piece of paper on his or her desk.
- **Security levels:** Does the company think that tunnelling is enough secured or does it expect that encryption is a minimum security requirement? Are layer-3 and layer-4 filterings considered as secured enough, or are e-mail content filtering and visited Web pages controls essential? (e.g., a bank that provides online accounting transactions will not expect the same security levels for its Web site than a florist will).
- **Number of sites:** Depending on how many sites the company has to manage and the capacity of its routers (e.g., products will be selected for their bandwidth and engine performance but also by the maximum number of simultaneous tunnels supported).
- **Type of users:** Internal employees only, partners' ones, remote users. If remote users, which access type is used: dial-up with 56K modem, or xDSL modem.
- **Number of users:** Depending on remote users number, choice of mechanisms and products will be impacted.
- **Quality of service requirements:** If the company needs to support voice over IP / video over IP traffic between branch offices and headquarters, traffic encryption should be avoided if possible because of the introduced latency delay that may exceed

the maximum threshold that guarantees a good quality.

- **Traffic volume:** Security measures would probably not be the same if the company wants to secure a 100 Mbps link, or a 100 kbps link.
- **Staff expertise:** Whether the company is a florist that wants to sell flowers online, or a world-wide bank, staff expertise regarding security problems will not be the same.
- **Willingness to outsource:** Many small companies would prefer to outsource their security and network management, while perhaps, huge companies would prefer to manage by themselves.
- **Budget limitation:** Companies usually plan some budgets for security investment including equipment purchasing, integration and maintenance. However, unless the company is obsessed by getting the best security level whatever the cost of the solution, companies can use the return on security investment (ROSI) indicator (Sonnenreich, 2006) in order to help the decision makers selecting the security solution appropriate to the company. The ROSI takes into account the risk exposure in terms of financial wastes, the capacity without the security solution to mitigate attacks and the cost of the security solution.

As a consequence of highlighting those above services needs and constraints within a company, a personalized architecture may be designed in terms of systems and networks with specific security constraints, then resulting in an adapted security policy. This defines security measures for each network element, leading to the introduction of security elements.

In order to give a concrete and practical point of view of security architectures, two types of companies are defined—*A* and *B*—so that, for each of them, three types of architectures, cor-responding to different security policies, are explained.

Let's start with the two companies' profiles.

A is a medium-sized company that needs to secure its existing network with the following requirements:

- *A* is set up with about 35 employees, the headquarters, and two branch offices.
- Headquarters and branch offices are connected to ISP using, respectively, 2 Mbit/s and 1 Mbit/s xDSL routers. Routers include basic functions like NAT, filtering based on access-lists.
- Employees work on-site, except ten sale managers working as remote users equipped with laptop and modem: four of them use a 56K dial-up connection, while six use an xDSL connection.
- Remote users' connections are for e-mail access only.
- Web portal on Internet (Internet Web).
- E-mail server.
- In the headquarters, IP addresses are dynamically assigned to on-site employees.
- ISP provided *A* with three static public IP addresses for the headquarters, one static public IP address per branch office, and dynamically assigned public IP addresses to remote users.
- Management servers: RADIUS for authentication, Anti-virus with e-mail proxy function, DNS server and DHCP server.
- Staff expertise is low in terms of security management: only two persons are working on system and network management, so *A* prefers to outsource its security management.
- *A* wants to be protected from external area.
- In terms of redundancy, *A* wants a minimum protection.

- For data exchanges, *A* wants to secure branch offices-to-headquarters communications and remote users' e-mail access.

B is a big-sized company that needs to secure its existing network with the following requirements:

- *B* is set up with about 300 employees, the headquarters, and about 20 branch offices.
- Headquarters are connected to ISP using a router with a 10 Mbits/s leased line.
- Branch offices are connected to ISP using, respectively, for 5 small-sized of them, a 1 Mbits/s xDSL router; 15 medium-sized routers are connected using a router with a leased line at higher rates.
- All routers include functions like NAT, IPsec, filtering based on access-lists.
- In addition to internal employees working on-site, many employees need remote access. All these remote users are equipped with laptop and xDSL access.
- Remote users' connections are for e-mail access, Intranet connection, and internal servers downloading.
- Branch offices connections are for e-mail access, Intranet connection, internal servers downloads, and multimedia over IP traffic (VoIP calls and internal TV broadcasts). Multimedia over IP is later referred to as MoIP.
- Web portal on Internet (Internet Web).
- Extranet Web server for partners, with secured connections.
- Intranet Web server for employees, with secured connections.
- E-mail server with possibility of encrypted and signed e-mails.
- Multimedia over IP (MoIP) server(s).
- Simulation server.
- In the headquarters, IP addresses are dynamically assigned to on-site employees.

- ISP provided *B* with four static public IP addresses for the headquarters, one static public IP address per branch office, and dynamically assigned public IP addresses to remote users.
- Management servers: LDAP or RADIUS for authentication, anti-virus, e-mail proxy with anti-virus / antispam functions, DNS server, DHCP server.
- Staff expertise is good in terms of security management: 15 persons are working on system and network management, and *B* wants to manage its security by itself, like 63% of the responding companies to the 2005 CSI/FBI Computer Crime and Security Survey (CSI Publications, 2005).
- *B* expects to be protected from both internal and external area. However, if not possible, it should be at least protected from the external area.
- In terms of redundancy, *B* wants a maximum protection.
- *B* wants to be alerted in case of malicious behaviours, especially if they are issued from the external area.
- For data exchanges, *B* wants to secure branch offices-to-headquarters communications, and remote users-to-headquarters connections.
- In a next future, *B* expects to equip the headquarters with a wireless network for internal users.

A MINIMAL AND LOW COST PROTECTION

The first architecture is a low-budget one, based on the existing routers that are increased with some security functions like filtering capacities of a firewall, and where several DMZ may be defined for hosting servers. Because all the security relies on a single router only, this router must be really well-protected in terms of availability (i.e., redundancy for power supply, routing engine, and fans tray appear as mandatory).

Company A Case Study for Minimal Protection

Regarding *A* company's requirements, the headquarters' network must be protected from the external area, so that the best position for most sensitive servers is within the internal area, as depicted in Figure 1.

Because of its border position, the router is highly likely to be attacked from Internet, and with its ACL configuration, only the most basic network attack attempts are blocked. As a consequence, the servers positioned in the router's DMZ are not highly protected, and should support fewer strategic functions as possible. With the condition that each router's DMZ must host machines accessible from the external area, the router's DMZ hosts at least the DNS server, Internet Web server.

The three public IP addresses allocated by the ISP for the headquarters serve as follows. The first one is assigned to the router for its external link, the second one to the Internet Web server, and the third one to the DNS server. The e-mail proxy is accessible thanks to the port redirection done by the router.

Internal users at the headquarters are protected from external area thanks to the router's ACL, which must be very strict for incoming traffic. Additionally, unidirectional NAT function enables internal users to perform outgoing connections with only one public IP address (the router's external one). With private addresses remaining hidden, internal machines are not directly reachable from the external area and are better protected.

DNS and Internet Web servers must be visible at least from the external area, so they must be located in a router's DMZ. Unlikely RADIUS, DHCP and e-mail servers are internally used only: since *A* company trusts its internal staff (see *A* company's profile in section "Needs and

Constraints for the Companies"), they are positioned in the internal area.

Anti-virus is also an important function in the network, and is required by *A* company to protect the e-mail server, in addition to its internal computers. As such, it must be separated from the internal area where the e-mail server is already located, but it must also be connected to the external area in order to download viruses' signatures updates, and to exchange e-mails with external servers. Therefore, it is located in a router's DMZ, separated from the DNS and Internet servers' one, so that all incoming e-mails go through anti-virus and next, are forwarded to the internal e-mail server thanks to the integrated e-mail proxy function of the anti-virus. in addition, the proxy may be configured so that the e-mail server is the only one authorized to initialize the connection with the proxy: this results in a better protection for the e-mail server.

For remote users' access, an SSL VPN is established between the users' laptop and the SSL gateway, and during establishment, users are authenticated by the SSL gateway thanks to the RADIUS server. In the architecture, the router supports the SSL gateway function, that is, it gets access to the e-mail server on behalf of users and relays new e-mails to the users under HTTP format.

For the branch offices, an L2TP/IPsec or IPsec tunnel is established with the headquarters between the two border routers, so that branch offices' users may access to the e-mail server and any other server as if they were connected to the headquarters.

In this kind of architecture, ACL in the router must be very restrictive, so that malicious behaviours coming from external area are blocked.

For example, incoming traffic (i.e., from external area) that is authorized is restricted to the following:

- SSL connections from remote users (users are authenticated, and traffic is encrypted using shared keys between the headquarters and the remote user),

- L2TP/IPsec or IPsec tunnels from branch offices (public IP addresses of the branch offices are well known, and routers are authenticated through IPsec tunnel),
- SMTP traffic that goes directly to anti-virus,
- HTTP traffic which is directly forwarded to Internet Web server except if the HTTP traffic is received due to a previous internal user's request,
- DNS traffic.

All other incoming traffic is forbidden.

The resulting architecture for Company *A* is given in Figure 1.

Company B Case Study for Minimal Protection

Regarding *B* company's requirements, the headquarters network must be protected both from internal and external areas. As such, the most sensitive servers should not be accessible to users, and access should be under the router's control.

The router only blocks the most basic network attack attempts, so to block malicious behaviours and protect internal staff as much as possible, its ACL configuration must be very restrictive.

The Internet/Extranet Web and the DNS server must be in the border router's DMZ because they are visible from the Internet. Similarly the MoIP server is placed in a DMZ so that exchanges with the branch offices' MoIP servers are possible through the external area. The e-mail proxy is integrated in the anti-virus server and requires access from the external area for e-mail exchanges.

All these servers are located in router's DMZ, with the idea that each DMZ hosts machines that are accessed by the same category of persons or machines, and it protects them with a specific security policy. So, the router defines four DMZ including respectively: Internet Web and DNS, anti-virus with e-mail proxy function, Extranet Web, and MoIP.

Figure 1. Company A architecture with minimal protection

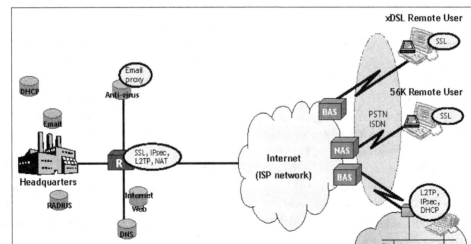

Because DHCP is only used for internal staff, and is not so sensitive, it may remain in the internal area.

Servers like intranet Web, e-mail, LDAP or RADIUS, and simulation server are too sensitive, so they are located in the internal area, but they are not protected at all from the internal staff, and misbehaviours. Because of it, this router-only-based architecture is not suitable for *B*'s security requirements.

Note that the extranet Web as well as all other internal servers accessed from Internet with no mandatory VPN connection (Internet Web, DNS, e-mail proxy) should be provided with a static bidirectional NAT translation, or port redirection, defined in the router. The four public addresses provided to *B* may be assigned to the following headquarters' equipments: external link of the router, Internet Web server, DNS server, Extranet Web server.

xDSL remote users and branch offices should connect through a L2TP/IPsec or IPsec VPN to the border router so they have access to the internal resources like e-mail, simulation server.

During VPN establishment, remote users are authenticated by the router which should contact the LDAP or RADIUS server for authentication verification. The authentication of remote routers in branch offices may be performed based on pre-shared keys or public key certificates known by the router itself. Additionally to VPN, if needed, the Intranet Web SSL protection may be activated to protect data exchange and login/password of users if they are required to authenticate to the Intranet Web.

For remote partners to get access to the Extranet Web, a specific rule into the router may be configured to permit packets with a source address belonging to the partner's address spaces (if known), the destination address of the

Figure 2. Company "B" architecture with minimal protection

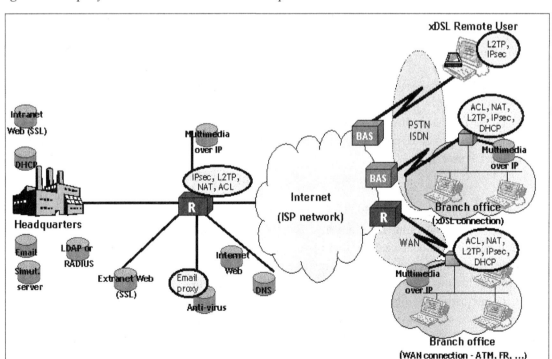

Extranet Web and the destination port number of the extranet Web. For data confidentiality reasons, during transfer, an SSL connection may be established between the partner's machine and the extranet Web. Moreover, a stronger security access to the extranet Web may be obtained by requiring authentication of partners based on login/password under the control of the LDAP/RADIUS server. As a result, access control is twofold based on the source IP addresses (done in border router) and the login/password (done in the Extranet Web).

In this architecture, ACL for authorized incoming traffic (i.e., from external area) in the router may look like the following:

- SSL connections from partners (based on IP address if known, and login/password) to extranet Web
- L2TP/IPsec or IPsec tunnel from branch offices (public IP addresses of the branch offices are well known, and routers are authenticated through IPsec tunnel)
- L2TP/IPsec or IPsec tunnel from remote users (authentication is made through tunnel)
- SMTP traffic that goes directly to anti-virus
- MoIP traffic, that goes directly to the MoIP server
- HTTP traffic, that is directly forwarded to Internet Web server except if it comes from an internal user
- DNS traffic

All other incoming traffic is forbidden.

The resulting architecture for Company *B* is given in Figure 2. In conclusion of these two case studies, the main advantage of this kind of architecture is its low cost, but all the security leans on the integrity of the router and as such this basic architecture appears as suitable for small companies only (*B* company's requirements are not achieved).

Note that in this kind of architecture, only network-layer and protocol-layer attacks are blocked. There's no way to block ActiveX or JavaCode attacks, or to filter visited Web sites, except if additional proxies are added. Even with proxies' introduction, there's no way to protect them in an efficient way within this type of architecture.

A MEDIUM-LEVEL SECURITY ARCHITECTURE

The second type of architecture equipped with one border router and one firewall, is more complex and may serve to define many DMZ to isolate servers. The security of the architecture is higher than the first one because a successful intrusion into the router may only affect network elements around the router, and not elements behind the firewall benefiting from the protection of the firewall. An intrusion into the headquarters assumes that two intrusions are successfully performed, one into the first router or router's DMZ to bypass its security policy, and a second one into the firewall ahead of the headquarters.

A firewall instead of a second router is introduced for a stronger security. The resulting security level is higher as the firewall is hardware cleanly designed equipment which additionally to routing and NAT functions may implement high-level functions like IDS/IPS and proxies, and moreover, predefined ports' behaviour with controlled exchanges in between (cf. section "Filtering Elements and DMZ"). Note that if the company chooses a software firewall product (i.e., software installed on a computer with many network cards), that can be installed with its own operating system or with the computer's existing operating system, the authors recommend to install it with its own including operating system because of possible weaknesses in the computer's existing operating system.

As previously explained, servers positioned in the router's DMZ are not highly protected, and should support non strategic functions for the company. Sensitive ones, like RADIUS, LDAP, intranet Web, extranet Web, e-mail should remain in the firewall's DMZ.

Note that the number of DMZs is generally limited because of budget savings. However, if financially affordable, the general idea that should be kept in mind when defining the architecture is each DMZ should host machines that should be accessed by the same category of persons or machines. This avoids persons from one category attempting to get access to resources of another category by realizing an attack locally to the DMZ which remains undetectable by the firewall. As such, one DMZ may be defined for the extranet, another one for the Intranet.

Note that no servers are positioned in the subnet between the firewall and the router: otherwise, a successful intrusion on that server would lead to the intruder installing a sniffing tool and so spy-ing all the traffic of the company which is going through this central link.

Company A. Case Study for Medium Protection

Internal users are better protected from the Internet attacks than in the first type of architecture with the extra firewall introduction.

The Internet Web and DNS servers have the same level of protection than in the first architecture against possible attacks from Internet area. Even if internal users are considered as trusted by company *A*, the RADIUS server positioned in a firewall's DMZ is better protected than in the first architecture as internal users have no direct access to it. On the other hand, the e-mail and DHCP servers within the internal network remain with the same level of protection against potential employees' misbehaving.

Figure 3. Company "A" architecture with medium protection

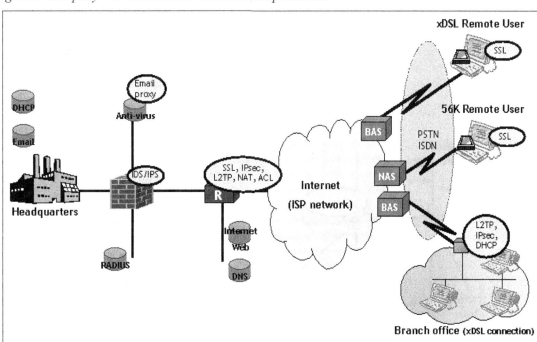

The e-mail service is well protected from Internet thanks to the router and firewall which are configured so that SMTP packets coming from Internet and addressed to the e-mail proxy are permitted.

Remote users' access and branch offices' access are achieved in the same way than in the first kind of architecture (see section "Company *A* Case Study for Minimal Protection").

Finally, for users of remote branches to get their e-mails through the VPN, one rule should be configured in the firewall to permit machines from branch offices to send POP or IMAP packets to the e-mail server.

With this kind of architecture (as depicted in Figure 3), all requirements of Company *A* are achieved and this solution can be a good value for small and medium-sized companies, both from a technical and financial point of view (i.e., it gives the best ROSI - *return on security investment*).

However the security can be improved as shown for RADIUS server. Additionally, some elements may be outsourced as requested by *A*

company, like firewall management, router management, SSL gateway.

Company B. Case Study for Medium Protection

Internal users are better protected from the Internet attacks than in the first type of architecture with the extra firewall introduction.

With the addition of the firewall (as depicted in Figure 4), sensitive servers like Intranet/Extranet Web, Simulation server, e-mail server, and LDAP/RADIUS server, three DMZ are defined on the firewall:

- One is the Intranet DMZ for hosting Intranet resources like the Intranet Web, the Simulation server, and the e-mail server.
- One is for the Extranet resources including the Extranet server.
- The latest one is for the authentication server either the LDAP or RADIUS server.

Figure 4. Company "B" architecture with medium protection

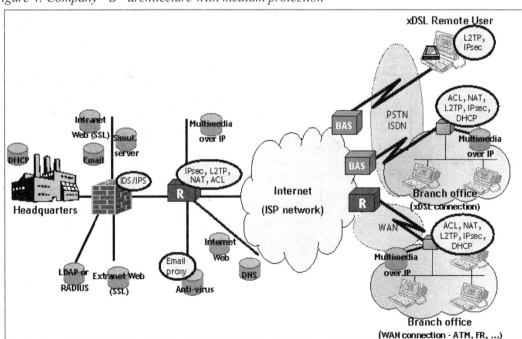

For its protection, the firewall should be configured so that communications to the authentication server are restricted to only the machines needing to authenticate users: the headquarters' border router (for remote users' authentication), the intranet Web (employees' authentication), the extranet Web (client's authentication) and the e-mail server (employees' authentication).

The extranet Web is moved to the firewall's DMZ to offer extranet partners a higher protection level. Only the DHCP server remains connected to the headquarters to ensure the dynamic configuration of internal machines.

As the firewall is unable to securely support dynamic port allocation, the MoIP server is positioned in the router's DMZ and the router only authorizes incoming MoIP calls from remote branches (based on source IP addresses).

The Internet Web, the DNS server, and e-mail proxy also remain in the border router's DMZ because they are visible on the Internet, so they may be subject to intrusions and in case of success, subverted subnets are limited to the router's DMZ, which is far from the sensitive DMZ of the firewall.

xDSL remote users' access and branch offices' access are achieved in the same way than in the first kind of architecture (see section "Company *B* Case Study for Minimal Protection").

For remote partners to get access to the extranet Web, a specific rule into the router and the firewall may be configured. Otherwise, authentication process remains unchanged compared to the previous architecture.

The security policy of Company *B*, as defined in section "Needs and Constraints for the Companies", is respected with this type of architecture. In terms of ROSI, it can be a suitable solution for classical medium to big-sized companies without critical sensitivity.

All the network or security based servers are under the firewall or router's control contrary to the first architecture, except the DHCP server which remains into the private network for functional reasons.

Servers which access is restricted to the same group of persons or machines are grouped together in the same DMZ.

Note that the present architecture assumes that a number of DMZ is available in the firewall and router. In case the firewall and/or the router is not provided with enough DMZ, or for budget savings, a first solution would be to move some of the equipments into the headquarters with the same drawbacks as described in the first architecture. A second solution is to limit the number of DMZ and to group servers together in the same DMZ, but with the risk that users benefiting from an authorized access on a server, attempts illegally to connect to another server in the same DMZ.

HIGH-LEVEL SECURITY ARCHITECTURE

The third architecture equipped with two firewalls, is the most complex one giving a maximum level of protection, with the possibilities to define many DMZ to isolate servers. The resulting security level is obviously higher as there are two firewalls implementing high-level security functions like IDS/IPS, proxies.

When defining a high-level security architecture, the more lines of defense are introduced, the more difficult the attacker will break through these defenses and the more likeliness the attacker will give up the attack. All those principles targeting delaying (rather than preventing) the advance of an attacker are better known under "defense in depth" strategy and are today widely applied by security experts.

The security of this architecture is higher than the two previous ones because a successful intrusion into the headquarters assumes that two intrusions are successfully performed, one into the first firewall to bypass its filter rules, and a second one into the firewall ahead of the headquarters.

Note that for better understanding and further references, the firewall directly connected to the external area is called "external" firewall, while the one directly connected to the internal area is called "internal" firewall.

In this kind of architecture, the fundamental idea that should be kept in mind is that the firewall products must come from different manufacturers or software editors, in order to prevent weaknesses. Within the same manufacturer/editor, common weaknesses from one product to another may result from to the same development teams using the same version of operating system

Moreover, in case a software firewall product is selected to be installed on a computer with many network cards, the best from a security point of view is to install it with its own included operating system.

Contrary to previous architectures, servers positioned in the DMZ are highly protected, so the way to choose the best DMZ for each server is to put it as close as possible to persons using it, i.e. Internet Web server should be on the "external" firewall, while Intranet Web server should be on the "internal" firewall.

Furthermore, as already explained in the other architectures, each DMZ should host machines that should be accessed by the same category of persons or machines. This avoids persons from one category attempting to get access to resources of another category by realizing a local attack within the DMZ with no detection by the firewall.

Finally, this architecture can be improved by introducing a router between the "external" firewall and external area, especially if firewall products are software ones installed on a computer (equipped with network cards), and those firewalls have been installed on the existing operating system instead of their own one. Otherwise the risk is that an intruder finds a way to shutdown the firewall process, so that the "external" firewall

is like a simple computer having only routing activated with no security rules.

Please note, that for the next following case studies, the considered architectures are based on two firewalls without any additional border router.

Company A. Case Study for High-Level Security Architecture

Internal users are better protected from the Internet attacks than in the previous type of architecture, due to the two firewalls.

The Internet Web and DNS servers are also better protected than before against possible attacks from Internet area. They are still located on a DMZ of the "external" firewall because incoming traffic addressed to these two servers comes mainly from external area.

The RADIUS server is used both for internal staff authentication, and remote offices/users' one. Considering the number of employees, it seems that the number of authentication requests seems to be higher from the internal area. Therefore, RADIUS is located on a DMZ of the "internal" firewall.

Because there are more DMZs than in the previous architecture, e-mail server can be located in a DMZ of a firewall. Considering Company *A*'s requirements, anti-virus with e-mail proxy function is moved to a DMZ of the "external" firewall, and then the e-mail server is connected to a DMZ of the "internal" firewall. Note that the e-mail server is not located on the same DMZ than the RADIUS server, because incoming requests sent to RADIUS come from unauthenticated users, and may contain malicious information like e-mail server attacks.

Because DHCP is only used by internal staff, and is not so sensitive, it can remain in the internal area.

Remote users' access and branch offices access are achieved in the same way than in the two first

16

kinds of architecture (see section "Company *A* Case Study for Minimal Protection").

With this kind of architecture (as depicted in Figure 5), all requirements of Company *A* are achieved, and intrusions attempts become really hard. However, this kind of solution is probably too much expensive regarding the targeted security requirements for small and medium-sized companies.

Company B. Case Study for High-Level Security Architecture

Internal users are better protected from the Internet attacks than in the previous type of architecture, due to the two firewalls.

The Internet Web and DNS servers are located on a DMZ of the "external" firewall because incoming traffic addressed to these two servers comes mainly from external area.

In order to improve the filtering level of some sensitive servers like intranet Web, some ad-

ditional proxies can be added. For instance, an HTTP proxy for intranet Web can be installed in the MoIP DMZ to do users' authentication but also high control on HTTP data (format and content). The "external" firewall should be configured so that HTTP traffic to Intranet Web is redirected to HTTP proxy for a first filtering. As such, the efforts required for introducing Intranet Web are really higher than before.

Anti-virus functions can be separated for e-mail server and internal staff needs, that is, the e-mail anti-virus functions remain the same as the previous architecture, while a specific anti-virus server dedicated to internal needs can be added on the intranet DMZ of the "internal" firewall.

To improve reactivity of Company *B* when malicious behaviours occur, IDS functions can be added on servers (HIDS function) or subnets (NIDS). Examples of IDS positioning may be: HIDS within the Simulation server (if it contains very sensitive data) or LDAP/RADIUS server,

Figure 5. Company A architecture with high-level protection

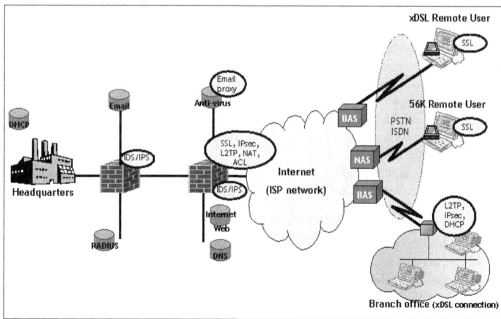

Figure 6. Company "B" architecture with high-level protection

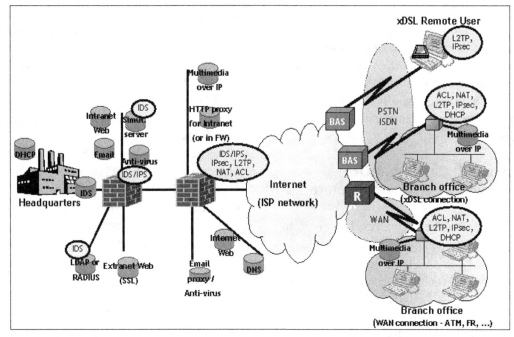

and NIDS on the internal side of the "internal" firewall.

In order to avoid direct communications between subnets of the internal network or to protect servers from users, VLANs can be defined. For example, the access to the accounting database server may be allowed for the accounts department staff only and separated from the rest of the network.

All other servers' positions remain unchanged compared to the previous architectures.

Remote users' access and branch offices' access are achieved in the same way than in the two first kinds of architecture (see section "Company *B* Case Study for Minimal Protection").

With this kind of architecture (as depicted in Figure 6), all requirements of *B* company are achieved, and beyond them, security can be improved with additional proxies capabilities or IDS external elements.

In terms of ROSI, this solution is mandatory for companies with critical sensitivity (e.g. banks),

but it can also be suitable for all classical medium to big-sized companies.

When Company *B* will introduce wireless equipments in its network (Kizza, 2005), it should first strongly control mobiles' access as they will gain access to the headquarters' network. For a higher security level, the wireless network may be considered as a specific VLAN within the "internal" network, and/or an extra DMZ hosting APs.

CONCLUSION

This chapter addresses the problematic of designing security architectures and wishes to give as much information as possible in these few pages, so it helps administrators deciding which architecture is the most suitable for them.

For more concrete explanations, two companies were considered with different sizes, and constraints. The first one, *A*, is medium-sized company with two branch offices and 35 employees: it wants to be protected from external area: it has no internal security expertise, implements a limited number of servers, and restricts remote access to e-mails. The second company, *B*, is big-sized with about 20 branch offices and 300 employees: it wants to be protected both from internal and external areas: the staff expertise is good: a number of network and security servers are implemented; access from branch offices and remote users is possible to Intranet Web, e-mail and any internal servers: it requires a highsecurity level with redundancy and alarms consideration.

For both companies, three families of architectures are studied, a low security level architecture with a router-only protection, a medium level security architecture with one router and one firewall and a high security level architecture with two firewalls. For each of these six cases, explanations or discussions are given relative to the positioning of equipments, the objectives of the DMZ, the number of DMZs, the VPN mechanism selection (L2TP/IPsec, IPsec, SSL) for a secure access by remote users and remote branches, the access control performed by proxies, firewalls and routers. Other discussions include users' authentication by LDAP/RADIUS servers, the e-mail problematic with the requirement for the open e-mail system to be reachable by any Internet machine, and to be protected so to avoid e-mail divulging, careful WiFi introduction into existing networks, VLAN usage to partition the network and limit direct interactions between machines ... Recommendations are also given for the selection of the firewall product and its installation.

To conclude, as described in this chapter, finding the appropriate architecture is a huge task as the final architecture depends on so various parameters like existing security and network architectures, security constraints, functional needs, size of companies, available budget, management of remote users or branch offices.

The idea of the authors, when writing this chapter, was to give useful guidelines to succeed in defining the appropriate architecture that reaches best compromise between companies' needs and constraints. Hope it helps.

REFERENCES

Cheswick, W. R., Bellovin, S. M., & Rubin, A. D. (2003). *Firewalls and Internet security: Repelling the wily hacker*. Addison-Wesley.

CSI Publications. (2005). CSI/FBI computer crime and security survey. Retrieved from http://www.GoCSI.com

Gupta, M. (2002). *Building a virtual private network*. Premier Press.

Kizza, J. M. (2005). *Computer network security*. Springer.

Liska, A. (2002). *The practice of network security: Deployment strategies for production environments*. Prentice Hall.

Pohlman, N., & Crothers, T. (2002). *Firewall architecture for the enterprise*. Wiley.

Sonnenreich, W., Albanese, J., & Stout, B. (2006, February). Return on security investment (ROSI)–A practical quantitative model. *Journal of Research and Practice in Information Technology, 38*(1), 99.

Chapter II
Security in GRID Computing

Eric Garcia
University of Franche-Comté, France

Hervé Guyennet
University of Franche-Comté, France

Fabien Hantz
University of Franche-Comté, France

Jean-Christophe Lapayre
University of Franche-Comté, France

ABSTRACT

GRID computing implies sharing heterogeneous resources, located in different places belonging to different administrative domains over a heterogeneous network. There is a great similarity between GRID security and classical network security. Moreover, additional requirements specific to GRID environments exist. We present these security requirements and we detail various secured middleware systems. Finally, we give some examples of companies using such systems.

INTRODUCTION

Grid technologies enable large-scale aggregation and harnessing computational, data and other resources across institutional boundaries. Fifty years of innovation have increased the speed of individual computers by an impressive factor, yet they are still too slow for many scientific problems.

A solution to the inadequacy of computer power is to "cluster" multiple individual computers. First explored in the early 1980s, this technique is now standard practice in supercomputer centers, research labs and industry. Although clustering can provide significant improvements in overall computing power, a cluster remains a dedicated resource, built at a single location. Rapid improvements in communication technologies led many researchers to consider a more decentralized approach to the problem of computing power. Several projects then saw the light of day: (Del Fabro, 2004; http://www.globus.org; http://setiathome.ssl.berkeley.edu) to name a few. Internet computing came to something much more powerful because of the ability for communities to share resources as they tackle common goals in a seemingly virtual machine. Science is increasingly collaborative and multidisciplinary, and it is not unusual for teams to span institutions, countries and continents.

GRID computing implies sharing heterogeneous resources, located in different places belonging to different administrative domains over a heterogeneous network. As GRID applications gained popularity and interest in the business world, securing business trades was not regarded lightly way. Securing information encompasses authenticating the source of a message, verifying the integrity of the message to ensure there has been no malicious modification, or protecting the confidentiality of the message being sent from prying eyes.

Because of the cross institution nature of GRID application communications, **GRID** computing has specific security needs. It has to protect a GRID community against unwanted eyes, and yet, it has to allow wider and wider access to many more identified participants. The challenge was securing these legitimate participants while not affecting local entities' authority neither the performances. The geographical dispersion of GRID participants is often unpredictable, leaving us less margin to superimpose a new constraining protocol on the existing systems.

OVERVIEW OF DISTRIBUTED SYSTEMS AND GRID COMPUTING

For several decades, researchers have tried to federate data-processing resources through networks: the first distributed systems were developed in which both data and treatment could be distributed. Parallel computing has moved from a proprietary design, centred on a supercomputer that was supported by homogeneous processors connected to an internal network, towards heterogeneous clusters of workstations distributed worldwide. The growing popularity of the Internet combined with the availability of powerful computers and high-speed networks as low cost commodity components are changing the way we do computing. These technologies enable the clustering of a wide variety of geographically distributed resources (such as supercomputers, storage systems, data sources, special devices and services that can be used as a unified resource). This new paradigm is popularly termed as "GRID" computing. The GRID is analogous to the electrical power grid and aims to couple distributed resources and offer consistent and inexpensive access to resources, irrespective of their physical location.

At the Beginning: Metacomputing

Metacomputing appeared at the beginning of the mineties. The idea was to gather within a *metacomputer* a group of small independent units equipped with calculation and storage capacities.

But network performance did not make it possible to develop such platforms on WAN. Tools were then developed to allow the installation of clusters on high performance LAN.

Parallel virtual machine (PVM) (Sunderam, 1990) was developed by Oak Ridge National Laboratory in 1990, then MPI (Message Passing Interface 1993) (Franke, 1994). These software tools simply made it possible to facilitate the programming of these applications by exchanging messages.

GRID Computing

The first appearance of the Grid goes back to 1998 (Foster, 1998). This new concept was then defined as being "*hardware and software infrastructure that provides dependable, consistent, pervasive, and inexpensive access to high-end computational capabilities.*"

A **GRID** is a software toolbox which provides services to manage distributed material and software resources. This evolution gave metacomputing a new dimension in particular by allowing the interconnection of several clusters.

Grid'5000 is a French experimental GRID linking together nine towns using optical fibres of 10Gb/s. One of the hardware objective of the platform is to reach 5,000 processors in 2007. This platform permits to deploy, to test, to improve applications, middleware, data Grid, security infrastructure.

Peer-to-Peer

An important characteristic of this family of metacomputing applications is that each site cooperates on an equal basis. The appearance of peer-to-peer (P2P) is directly related to the advent of Internet (Oram, 2001).

Compared to GRID Computing, the assets of **P2P** are:

- Choice of decentralized, and nonhierarchical organization
- Management of instability, and fault-tolerance

Indeed, P2P application is deployed to broad scale and an interruption on a node or on a network link does not endanger all the applications.

We find a wide variety of **P2P** systems (Saxena, 2003) currently used such as Nasper, Gnutella, Kazaa where peers are unaware of the total membership of nodes in the system. There are more structured P2P systems (e.g., Chord and Pastry). Most large-scale P2P systems covers more traditional, synchronous group communication systems such as SETI@Home, Totem or Horus where scalability is typically limited, and group membership requires constant online presence of each peer. Client programs such as MSN Messenger, AOL Instant Messenger allow users to exchange text, voice and files.

Users of P2P systems ask the enhancement of access control with new authentication and authorization capabilities to address users that know little about each other. P2P systems introduce other problems that require to focus the attention on protection from those who offer resources, rather than from those who want to access them, JXTA (http://www.jxta.org) provides some functionality (e.g., encryption, signatures and hashes) for the development of secure **P2P** applications. Reputation techniques allow the expression and reasoning about trust in a peer based on its behavior and interactions other peers have experienced with it (Damiani, 2002).

A Last Evolution Towards Total Computing

The last most recent evolution permits the development of GRIDs on a very large scale. New **middleware** allow data management in completely heterogeneous media, wireless and mobile. This last family tends to associate qualities of GRID computing and peer-to-peer.

The word computing is often associated with the final GRID: *GRID computing* or *global computing,* are the terms that are usually used. But these platforms are not devoted exclusively to computing; it is also possible to find Data GRID type applications. In the continuation of this chapter, we will not differentiate between the concepts of GRID and GRID computing.

SECURITY REQUIREMENTS FOR GRID COMPUTING

Security has often been a neglected aspect of most applications or systems design until a cyber attack makes it real. Oftentimes, security practitioners consider security as being a step behind electronic war. However the first step towards a better protected system is awareness. Just like many other systems and architectures, GRID computing paid little attention to securing its communications. The need was very bleak since the instigation for GRID computing emerged from a well-thinking scientific community working for a common interest. As GRID applications gained popularity and gained interest in the business world, securing business trades was not regarded in a light way. Securing information encompasses authenticating the source of a message, verifying the integrity of the message against malicious modification, or assuring the confidentiality of the message being sent against prying eyes. As electronic communication becomes pervasive, access control to privileged information became increasingly pertinent, and when new forms of attacks, such as ones not aiming at theft of information (denial of access) emerged, new protective measures needed to be put into place to ensure constant availability of service.

Traditional Security Features

There is a great similarity between GRID security and classical network security. It depends on the activity type, on the risks firms are ready to take and overall on the cost of the installation and the configuration of security systems such as firewall. All these features exist for the GRID; however, some are more important in this case. Moreover, additional requirements specific to GRID environments exist. Indeed, security policies have to protect a GRID computing platform without adding too many constraints that could seriously decrease performance in terms of calculation

power, for example. In particular, we can notice that there is a greater need for dynamicity, and greater importance of process supervision and of **rights delegation**. Classical security features have to be adapted to GRID computing environments.

Authentication, Authorization, and Auditing (AAA)

Each entity of the GRID must be able to authenticate the others. GRID entities must be authorized to communicate with other entities from the same domain or from another one. Auditing must take into account the dynamic aspect of GRID environments where component binding varies considerably and can have a short life cycle.

Confidentiality, Integrity, Availability (CIA)

Communication between GRID entities must be secure. Confidentiality must be ensured for sensitive data from the communication stage to a potential storage stage. Problems of integrity must be detected in order to avoid treatment **faults**. Availability is directly bound to performance and cost in GRID environments, and is therefore an important requirement.

Fault Tolerance

In GRID environments **fault tolerance** must be managed to ensure that a fault on a component does not cause the loss of all the work performed. Moreover, it can be important, in the particular case of the GRID, to recover a part of the work on a faulty node in order to increase global performance when a fault occurs. In the framework of fault tolerance, it is also required to supervise, to trace a process (initialization, used nodes, bindings) and to store this information.

SECURED MIDDLEWARE OF GRID COMPUTING

Whereas very few turnkey security systems exist, a lot of organizations and companies are currently trying to develop some like Global GRID Forum (GGF), Enterprise GRID Alliance (EGA), GRID Research Integration Development and Support Center (GRIDS), secured systems for GRID are presented below.

Systems Using X509 Certificates

One of the most popular security middleware for GRID is Globus using GSI [11] (GRID Security Infrastructure). GSI is based on the PKI security architecture which authenticates servers, users and processes. In order to do so, an X509 certificate signed by a certificate authority (CA) is delivered for each user and machine.

A certificate is a file which contains at least the follow information:

- The name of the authority which created the certificate

- The name and first name of the user
- Organization name
- Unit name
- E-mail address
- Public key
- Validity period
- Numeric signature

To simplify the procedure and to avoid users having to authenticate themselves each time they have to submit a calculation, a proxy is used. This is the single sign on (SSO) method.

The proxy is a new certificate with a new private/public key. This new certificate is signed by the user himself and not by the CA Figure 1.

This credential mechanism provided by the proxy implies that once someone accesses a remote system, he can give the remote system permission to use his credentials to access other systems for him. When connections are established, the SSL protocol is used to encrypt communications. Table 1 shows a comparison of X.509 public key **certificates** with a X509 proxy certificates (Welch, 2004).

Figure 1. Delegation method

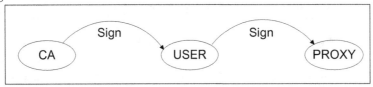

Table 1. Comparison of X.509 public key certificates and X.509 Proxy Certificates

Certificate Attribute	X.509 Public Key Certificate	X.509 Proxy Certificates
Issuer/Signer	A Certification Authority	A public key certificate or another Proxy Certificate
Name	Any as allowed by issuer's policy	Scoped to namespace defined by issuer's name
Delegation from Issuer	None	Allows for arbitrary policies expressing issuer's intent to delegate rights to Proxy Certificate bearer
Key pairs	Uses unique key pair	Uses unique key pair

A lot of middleware use GSI, to secure their system or to extend it for their own requirements like GRID Particle Physics (GRIDPP), TeraGrid. Another example is the data-exchange systems which often use GRIDftp (module of Globus) with GSI like DataGRID.

Systems Using IPSec and DNSec

GRIDSec (Le, 2002, 2003) is an architecture using **DNSSec** as a key distribution system, SSH to secure initial authentication and IPSec to protect the users communication, as illustrated in Figure 1.

DNSSec and Secure Key Management

The fundamental objectives of **DNSSec** are to provide authentication and integrity to the inherently insecure DNS. Authentication and integrity of information held within DNS zones are provided through cryptographic signatures generated through the use of public key technology

To make the secure network transport scalable, the SSH client is modified to query the DNS server for the host key of an SSH server. This key distribution server will still host the usual DNS resource records, the host key, and a signature authenticating that host key for each SSH client

of the domain. The server is transformed by the DNSSEC extensions into a local Certification Authority.

IPSec to Secure Data Transport

IPSec is a protocol suite for networking devices to communicate privately using IP. IPSec requires a secret key distribution mechanism.

Authors propose to open the architecture with the implementation of a nonproprietary certificate authority infrastructure that will allow resources to authenticate other resources directly, without appealing to a central authority like Kerberos. The security extension is used to the DNS protocol, referred to as the DNSSEC extensions.

GRIDSec Architecture

In a GRIDSec architecture, a **DNSSec** *server* is defined as a key distribution system federating several *zones*. Each zone has an *SSH server* to manage and identify each zone's key to the DNS-Sec server; each zone also has a *VPN module* to enable secure data exchange between different zones through the Internet.

The GRID system overlaid by GRIDSec has a *Resource Broker* agent to obtain and locate the resource requested by a given user (see Figure 2).

Figure 2. GRIDSec model

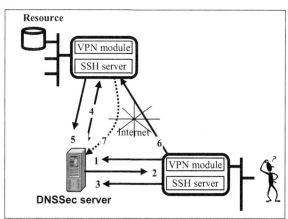

Each site participating to the GRID has a VPN module and an SSH server. An initial phase encompasses the authentication of each SSH server to a federating DNSSec server. The OpenSSH client installed on the SSH server enables the secure key exchange between each SSH server and the DNSSec server. The SSH server sends a request for registration (1) to the DNSSec server. The DNSSec server sends in return its public key (2); the requester SSH server will encrypt its own public key with that key and digitally sign it with HMAC (3). This authentication phase occurs for each zone (4) and (5).

In a second phase, secure VPN tunnels will be created between the sites (6) since IPSec can reuse the previously exchanged secret keys. At this stage, the SSH servers' keys have been gathered by the DNSSec. A user in a federated zone can request a resource located by the resource broker to be in a different zone. SSH server C will request SSH server A's public key from the DNSSec server. Using IPSec, the two sites will be able to establish pairwise VPN links.

In a third phase, when SSH servers' keys change (due to compromised keys, or security maintenance to renew keys), the DNSSec server will update its SSH keys record files (7).

Systems Using Fine Authorizations

The Legion (http://legion.virginia.edu) system provides a fine mechanism of authorization. Each resource contains a list of objects which can access it. Moreover each method of an object has an "allow" and "deny" list, which specifies the authorizations (ACL). An object will be authorized to access a method if and only if it does not appear in the deny list and does appear in the allow list.

GRIDLab focuses on the development of a flexible, manageable and robust authorization service called GAS (GAS; www.gridlab.org/gas). The main goal of GAS is to provide functionality that would be able to fulfill most authorization require-

ments of GRID computing environments. GAS is designed as a trusted single logical point for defining security policy for complex GRID infrastructures. As the flexibility is a key requirement, it is to be able to implement various security scenarios, based on push or pull models, simultaneously. Thanks to theses characteristics, GAS is also interoperable with other security toolkit like Globus.

Systems Using Sandboxing

In GRID computing relying in P2P architecture, applications are often transferred from a resource to another without having the capabilities to check mutual authenticities. In front of this difficulty to secure P2P systems, applications are more and more performed in a secure context (i.e., in a box which is an interface from and to the applications. Operations are woken up and permissions are given or refused. Permissions can mainly be applied to network, file system and system configuration. Thus, even if someone succeeds to transmit a malicious code, it is ineffectual because of permission requirements. This concept is called the "Sandboxing". Several implementations of the sandboxing exist: Java Sandboxing, Java Webstart, Gentoo Sandbox, Norman Sandbox, FMAC, Google Sandbox, S4G (Sandbox for GRID). **Figure 3** shows a simplified representation of the Java Sandbox Architecture.

Either they intercept systems calls: *strace, /proc*, allowing or refusing them; or they let the application running in a virtual context, like *chroot*.

Figure 3. Simplified Java sandbox architecture

Java Application	
Sandbox	
JVM	
OS	
Hardware	Network

HiPoP (Hantz, 2005) and XtremWEB (http://www.lri.fr/~fedak/XtremWeb) are two examples of GRID computing systems using this concept of sandboxing. HiPoP means **H**ighly dist**rI**buted **P**latform **O**f com**P**uting and is a platform entirely written in JAVA. It performs coarse grain tasks having dependences in a highly distributed way. This platform relies on a P2P architecture. On the contrary of others platforms, which use static sandbox where permissions stay the same from the beginning to the end of the execution of the deamons, HiPoP uses **HiPoP Dynamic Sandbox (HDS)** (Hantz, 2006).

Figure 4 shows an example of HiPoP permission attribution where the left part of the figure is a piece of a direced acyclic graph (DAG) to perform. When R1 has finished its execution of the task J1, it asks (1) the resource provider a reference of a resource to perform J2. Then the resource provider chooses the resource R2 and signals it (2) that R1 will contact it to perform a task. Thus R2 will accept the connection from R1. Without this query, R2 would reject all communications from all the peers. To continue, the resource provider advertises (3) R1 that it can

submit its task to R2. Finally, R1 submit (4) the task J2 to R2.

After this submission, the network permission is automatically removed and R1 will no longer access to R2.

Network permissions are just an example of permissions that HiPoP takes into account, but it also manages file permissions (tasks are only authorized to read and write files in a temporary directory identified by them). Moreover, tasks can not read information on the resource system (hostname, IP address, type of the resource, OS used) and can not modify the administration system like overload the security manager, added some additional permissions.

SECURED GRID COMPUTING IN INDUSTRY

GRID computing is developing considerably in research centres, and companies are now using this type of technique more and more. The multinationals find it difficult to face up to the complex computing infrastructures which do

Figure 4. Dynamic permission attribution

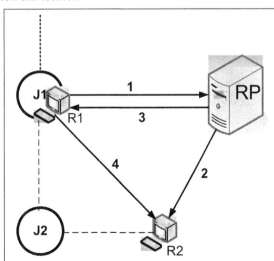

not react sufficiently quickly to the evolutions of the expectations of their activities. Currently the majority of the professional applications are managed in a rigid way. In answer to this problem, certain companies have designed an adaptable infrastructure which shares and automatically manages the system resources.

The users develop their applications on GRID architecture inside or outside the company but use machines located in other companies which are legally or financially dependent. For the moment, security techniques do not allow companies to widely use machines distributed all over the Internet.

AIM OF GRID

The aim of GRID is:

- To obtain a more efficient use of resources inside the company or inside the group by reserving unused machines
- To distribute the application load by distributing the treatments on idle or underloaded resources
- To optimize the material and software investments by having a global view and a policy at the company level and not only at the service level
- To concentrate computing power to carry out complex calculations with powerful modeling software

To reach this aim, it is necessary to solve problems of security, fault-tolerance, scheduling of tasks, data transfer and communication time. The first two problems are the most fundamental. To solve the first, a certain number of solutions exist to allow authentication, integrity, confidentiality and to maintain replay. The second problem is also significant, because in a GRID structure, machines can break down, can be moved, or can be replaced. A solution then consists in regularly saving an

image of the application to be able to recall it after having to restart due to a problem.

Examples and Domains Concerned

The main American public agencies support the Globus system: NASA, the NSF, DARPA, and in the same way, large software distributors like IBM, Sun, Cisco, Microsoft. GRIDXpert (http://www.ud.com) target 4 sectors: manufacturing, energy, biotechnology and finance. The network game domain can also be approached with Butterfly.net. Security in the GRID is directed towards the use of Web service technology. Microsoft's Passport project or Sun's Liberty Alliance were developed to solve security problems by using certificates. Research laboratories have joined the companies: lNRIA with Microsoft and Alcatel. Large Data processing companies like IBM, Sun, Microsoft, Platform, and United Devices have taken a clear turn in the direction of the GRID.

The GRID computing version of Oracle (http://www.oracle.com/technologies/grid/index.html) is a software architecture designed to pool together large amounts of low cost modular storage and servers to create a virtual computing resource which can be transparently distributed. The resources can include storage, servers, database servers, application servers, and applications. Pooling resources together offers dependable, consistent, pervasive, and inexpensive access to these resources regardless of their location and the period where they are needed.

Oracle 10g is managed by Oracle Enterprise Manager 10g GRID Control, a Web-based management console that enables administrators to manage many application servers as though they were one, thereby automating administrative tasks and reducing administrative costs. Oracle 10g supports single sign on (SSO) permitting users to be authenticated only one time to be allowed to access servers. OracleAS 10g provides a single, unified, standard based end-to-end security and identity management infrastructure based on Oracle Internet Directory, OracleAS 10g Single sign-on server and OracleAS certificate authority.

To provide a secure environment to run enterprise applications, OracleAS 10g provides a number of security enhancements including comprehensive Java2 security support; SSL support for all protocols (RMI, RMI-over-IIOP, SOAP, JMS, LDAP); a least privilege model for administrative privilege; and a comprehensive PKI-based security infrastructure.

Platform Symphony (http://www.platform. com/) is an enterprise providing GRID software for financial services. This system allows forward-thinking financial services firms to easily move to a true GRID environment where multiple users and applications share computing resources in virtual pools that dynamically adjust and scale based on the priorities and needs of the business. Platform symphony is based on the scalable platform enterprise GRID orchestrator (EGO) that sets the benchmark for GRID performance and reliability across heterogeneous enterprise environments.

DFI (http://www.d-fi.fr) proposes a technology allowing users to optimize the computing power of all the machines of a company to redistribute them to the applications which require it, according to their needs. This system relies on Oracle's GRID Control and Sun's System Manager.

On-Demand Computing

On demand computing is an approach already in use. Companies have access to a powerful calculation resource and only pay large Computer firms for the resources they actually use. The goal is to adapt the power of computing, storage and also budget. For example, the Danish company Lego (http://www.pcexpert.fr) thinks that the use of the IBM technique "on demand" will enable it to reduce management costs of its infrastructure by 30%. Indeed, it has one peak period at Christmas time when it needs very significant power over

a short period. Why thus be equipped all year long with a calculation capacity which will only be used for one month?

Datasynapse's GRIDServer (http://www. datasynapse.com/solutions/gridserver.html) creates a flexible, virtual infrastructure that enables organizations to improve application performance and resiliency by automatically sharing and managing computing resources across the enterprise. GRIDServer is adaptive GRID infrastructure software designed to virtualize compute and data intensive applications. By creating a virtualized environment across both applications and resources, GRIDServer provides an "on demand" environment to provide real-time capacity for process intensive business applications.

CONCLUSION

Computational GRID are becoming increasingly useful and powerful in the execution of large-scale and resource intensive applications. Data transit through multiple networks and their security can be put at risk. Network security is a hard-to-define paradigm in that its definition varies with the different organizations which implement it. Security is defined by the policies that implement the services offered to protect the data. These services are confidentiality, authentication, nonrepudiation, access control, integrity and to protect or to prevent against such attacks. GRID computing has its specific security requirements due to the nature of its domain distribution. We are dealing with existing and the issue of trust is very important. A certificate authority needs to identify and authenticate a legitimate GRID participant to other participants, without damaging the local entities' authority. Since Grid computing is a voluntary contribution and a trust-based relationship between different domains, it is important to establish a host-based authentication approach. Most of the time, participants speak to each other and identify themselves before engaging into such a collaboration; it cannot be an anonymous relationship.

Confined in research laboratories, GRID Computing is finally making its entrance in the business world. GRID computing has its specific security requirements due to the nature of its application domain. Large software publishers like Microsoft, Sun, IBM or HP are developing and offering GRID computing solutions. Thus far this technique is still inside the company. Indeed, it is too difficult to ensure security for Internet deployment. Therefore, GRID computing is primarily used inside companies or, when necessary, between several companies by using VPN.

REFERENCES

Damiani, E., De Capitani, S., Paraboschi, S., Samarati, P., & Violante, F. (2002). A reputation-based approach for choosing reliable resources in peer-to-peer networks. *Ninth ACM Conference on Computer and Communications Security.*

Del Fabbro, B., Laiymani, D., Nicod, J. M., & Philippe, L. (2004). A data persistency approach for the DIET metacomputing environment. *International. Conference on Internet Computing, IC'04,* Las Vegas, NV (pp. 701-707).

Foster, I., & Kesselman, C. (1998). The globus project: A status report. In *Proceedings of the IPPS/SPDP '98 Heterogeneous Computing Workshop* (pp. 4-18).

Foster, I., Kesselman, C., Tsudik, G., & Tuecke, S. (1998). A security architecture for computational grids. In *Proceedings of the Fifth ACM Conference on Computer and Communications Security Conference* (pp. 83-92).

Franke, H., Hochschild, P., Pattnaik, P., & Snir, M. (1994) An efficient implementation of MPI. *International Conference on Parallel Processing.*

Hantz, F., & Guyennet, H. (2005). HiPoP: Highly distributed platform of computing. In *Proceedingss of the IEEE Joint Internationa Conference on Autonomic and Autonomous Systems (ICAS'05) and International Conference on Networking and Services (ICNS'05).* Tahiti, French Polynesia.

Hantz, F., & Guyennet, H. (2006). A P2P Platform using sandboxing. *WSHPCS (Workshop on Security and High Performance Computing Systems) in conjunction with the 20th European Conference on Modelling and Simulation (ECMS 2006),* Bonn, Germany (pp. 736-739).

Le, V., & Guyennet, H. (2002). IPSec and DNSSEC to support GRID Application Security. *Workshop Security in the Second IEEE/ACM International Symposium on Cluster Computing and the GRID, CCGrid2002,* Berlin, Germany (pp. 405-407).

Le, V., & Guyennet, V. (2003). A scalable security architecture for grid applications. *GridSec, Second Workshop on Security and Network Architecture,* Nancy, France (pp. 195-202).

Saxena, N., Tsudik, G., & Yi, J. H. (2003). Admission control in peer-to-peer: Design and performance evaluation. *ACM Workshop on Security of Ad Hoc and Sensor Networks (SASN).*

Sunderam V. S. (1990). A framework for parallel distributed computing. *Concurrency: Practice and Experience, 2*(4), 315-339

Oram, A. (2001). *Peer-to-peer: Harnessing the power of disruptive technologies.* O'Reilly.

Welch, V., Foster, Y., Kesselman, C., Mulmo, O., Pearlman, L., Tuecke, S., et al. (2004). X.509 proxy certificates for dynamic delegation. *Third Annual PKI R&D Workshop.*

Chapter III
Security of Symbian Based Mobile Devices

Göran Pulkkis
Arcada Polytechnic, Finland

Kaj J. Grahn
Arcada Polytechnic, Finland

Jonny Karlsson
Arcada Polytechnic, Finland

Nhat Dai Tran
Arcada Polytechnic, Finland

ABSTRACT

Security issues of Symbian-based mobile computing devices such as PDAs and smart phones are surveyed. The evolution of Symbian OS architecture is outlined. Security threats and problems in mobile computing are analyzed. Theft/loss of the mobile device or removable memory cards exposes stored sensitive information. Wireless connection vulnerabilities are exploited for unauthorized access to mobile devices, to network, and to network service. Malicious software attacks in form of Trojan horses, viruses, and worms are also becoming more common The Symbian OS is open for external software and content which makes Symbian devices vulnerable for hostile applications. Embedded security features in Symbian OS are: a cryptographic software module, verification procedures for PKI signed software installation files, and support for the communication security protocols IPSec and TLS. The newest version 9.3 of Symbian also embeds a platform security structure with layered trusted computing, protection capabilities for installed software, and data caging for integrity and confidentiality of private data. Fundamental security requirements of a Symbian based mobile device such as physical protection, device access control, storage protection, network access control, network service access control, and network connection security are described in detail. Symbian security is also evaluated by discussing its weaknesses and by comparing it to other mobile operating systems. Current availability of add-on security software for Symbian based mobile devices is outlined in an appendix. In another appendix, measurement results on how add-on security software degrades network communication performance of a Symbian based mobile device are presented and analyzed as a case study.

INTRODUCTION

Users of the Internet have become increasingly more mobile. At the same time, mobile users want to access Internet wireless services demanding the same quality as over a wire. Emerging new protocols and standards, and the availability of WLANs, cellular data and satellite systems are making the convergence of wired and wireless Internet possible. Lack of standards is however still the biggest obstacle to further development. Mobile devices are generally more resource constrained due to size, power and memory. The portability making these devices attractive greatly increases the risk of exposing data or allowing network penetration.

Mobile handheld devices can be connected to a number of different kinds of networks. Such wireless networks are cellular networks, personal area networks (PANs), local area networks (LANs), metropolitan area networks (MANs) and wide area networks (Satellite-based WANs). Network services needed for transferring data to and from a mobile device include among others e-commerce, electronic payments, WAP and HTTP services. The network connection of a mobile device can be based on a dial-up connection through a cellular network (GSM, UMTS), be based on packet communication through a cellular network (GPRS), be a WLAN or a Bluetooth connection, or be an infrared link (IrDA). Network connection examples are e-mailing (pop3, pop3s, imap, imaps, smtp, smtps), web browsing (http, https), synchronization with a desktop computer (HotSync, ActiveSync, SyncML), network

monitoring/management (snmp), reception of video/audio streams, and communication of any installed application.

Realization of data services over mobile devices offers interesting new features for the user, but also a threat to security. A mobile device optimized for data services requires that the terminal becomes an open platform for software applications, i.e. the mobile device becomes more vulnerable to attacks. Mobile computing also requires operating systems supporting mobile environments. Such a widely used operating system is Symbian OS.

Symbian is a common operating system for mobile communication devices. The most important requirements are multitasking/threading, real-time operation of the cellular software, effective power management, small size of the operation system itself, ease of developing new features, reusability, modularity, connectivity and robustness (DIGIA Inc., 2003). The world's top mobile phone manufacturers with the largest market share have chosen Symbian. According to many analysts, the major part of operation systems for mobile communication devices of the future will rely on Symbian or on Windows.

In this chapter, security issues of Symbian based mobile devices are surveyed.

BACKGROUND

Mobile computing device types are pocket PC, also called personal digital assistant (PDA), and smart phone. Symbian is the leading operating system for smart phones currently available on the market. Symbian was founded as a private independent company in June 1998 by Ericsson, Matsushita, Motorola, Nokia and Psion. Currently, Symbian is owned by BenQ, Ericsson, Panasonic, Nokia, Siemens AG, and Sony Ericsson. There are both open and closed platforms based on Symbian OS. Examples of open platforms are the Nokia platforms UIQ, Series 60, Series 80, and Series 90 and examples of closed platforms are the platforms developed for NTT DoCoMo's FOMA handsets. The most recent version of Symbian OS is Symbian OS v9.3. (Symbian OS Version 9.3, 2006)

During recent years, security has become a very important issue when Symbian OS platforms and applications are developed and designed. The security threats related to data stored in the devices, network communication, and software installation have increased in parallel with the evolution of the Symbian device platforms and the increasing use of Symbian devices. Symbian devices are becoming more commonly used also by corporate employees for storing confidential data. Such data are easily physically accessed if the device is lost or stolen. Confidential data sent to and from Symbian devices over various wireless network connections can be captured "from the air" by intruders. Malware attacks are also an increasing threat against Symbian devices. The first Symbian worm, Cabir, was detected in 2004. Today, there are already several known Symbian viruses and malware threatening smart phone users.

Security solutions for Symbian devices are currently under ongoing development. The Symbian OS provide embedded security features i.e. underlying support for secure communications protocols, such as TLS/SSL, and authentication of installable software using digital certificates. Security solutions are also developed by several third party companies. Such solutions include anti-virus software, personal firewalls, memory card encryption, and access control systems.

SECURITY THREATS AND PROBLEMS FOR MOBILE DEVICES

Today's mobile devices offer many benefits to enterprises: access to e-mail/Internet, to customer's information, and to vital corporate data. These benefits are however associated with risks such as loss/theft of device, malicious software, unauthorized access to data or device, hacking, cracking, wireless exploit, etc.(de Haas, 2005)

Modern mobile devices, such as smart phone and PDA computers, are small, portable and thus easily lost and stolen. In addition they have connection interfaces to several types of wireless networks such as general packet radio service (GPRS), wireless local area network (WLAN), infrared data association (IrDA), and Bluetooth. Unfortunately only few such devices are presently equipped with firewalls or anti-virus software. Moreover, many mobile devices lack credible physical and electronic access control. These features make mobile computing devices targets of security attacks such as (Olzak, 2005):

- Theft/loss of the device and removable memory cards
- Malicious code
- Exploit of wireless connection vulnerabilities

The most serious security threats with mobile devices are unauthorized access to data and credentials stored in the memory of the device.

Theft/Loss of Information/Device

Obviously, by design modern mobile computers and other types of portable devices have a higher risk of being stolen than a nonportable device. Many users are carrying around confidential corporate or client data on mobile devices without any protection. Often such devices cause security risks if stolen. Often bigger loss comes from the loss of the data than the loss of the device itself when the device is stolen.

Most platforms for mobile devices only offer simple software-based login schemes. Such schemes can however easily be bypassed by reading the information from the device without login. Accordingly, critical and confidential unencrypted data stored in the device memory is an easy target for an attacker who has physical access to the device. Encryption and authentication are therefore strongly recommended solutions in order to avoid loss of data confidentiality, if a mobile device is lost or stolen. (Symantec, 2005; Hickey, 2005)

Malicious Software

Malware have constituted a growing threat for mobile devices since the first Symbian worm (Cabir) was detected in 2004. Malware is still not a serious threat, but the continuous increasing number of the mobile device users worldwide is changing the situation. In the near future the threat might become similar to the problems encountered in the PC world today. Most likely the development of malware makes especially companies to face completely new kinds of attacks such as Trojan horses in games, screensavers and other applications, which attempt to make false billing, delete and transfer data. Malicious software does not only cause serious threats for the mobile device itself, it may also cause a threat for the network which the mobile device is connected to. (F-Secure, 2004; Hicks, 2005)

Viruses are easily spread to an internal computer network and there are several methods by which a mobile device can be infected. Malware can be received manually via MMS, Bluetooth, infrared or WLAN, or by downloading and installing from the Web. Current malware is primary focused on Symbian OS and Windows based devices. Malware may result in (Olzak, 2005):

- Loss of productivity
- Exploitation of software vulnerabilities to gain access to recourses and data
- Destruction of information stored on a SIM card
- Hi-jacking of air time resulting in increased costs

Wireless Connection Vulnerabilities

Handheld devices are often connected to the Internet through wireless networks such as cellular mobile networks (GSM, GPRS, and UMTS), WLANs, and Bluetooth networks. These networks are based on open air connections and are thus by their nature easy to access. Furthermore, confidential data transmitted over an unprotected wireless network can easily be captured by an eavesdropper. Transmitting data over wireless networks are open doorways for hackers, outsiders and causes a remarkable security risk. Data transmitted over the air can be easily exploited, if the networks are unprotected.

Despite the mentioned security risks, many Bluetooth networks and especially WLANs are still unprotected even today. WLANs have earlier been associated with serious security vulnerabilities because of the lack of user authentication methods. However, today WLANs fulfill secure user authentication requirements, when solutions based on the recently ratified security standard 802.11i are implemented.

For any wireless connectivity, the most effective way to ensure end-to-end security is to set up a Virtual Private Network (VPN) channel. The data channel is then encrypted. In addition to avoid security risks, users should disable all wireless network connections, including Bluetooth, infrared and WLAN whenever these connections aren't needed. (Taylor, 2004; Ye & Cheang, 2005)

SYMBIAN OS ARCHITECTURE

The Symbian OS is implemented and used in several different user interface platforms, both open and closed. Notable is that "open" doesn't in this case mean that the Symbian OS source code is publicly available. It rather means that the APIs are publicly documented and anyone is able to develop software for Symbian OS devices. The latest version of Symbian is Symbian OS v9.3. The architecture, visualized in Figure 1, has five layers (Siezen, 2005):

- User interface (UI) framework
- Application services
- OS services
- Base services
- Kernel services and hardware interface

UI Framework

The user interface (UI) framework consists of the UI application framework subsystem and internationalization support. The main objective of the graphical user interface (GUI) framework is to minimize UI designer constraints by defining as little policy as possible. This makes porting of application user interfaces between different Symbian phones easier. Internationalization sup-

port provides i.e. operating system compatibility for various input languages.

Application Services

The application services provide application engines for the central mobile phone applications with the purpose to ensure compatibility between different Symbian devices. Application services include:

- **Personal information management (PIM) services:** Applications such as agenda, to-do, and contacts
- **Messaging services:** Short message service (SMS), enhanced message service (EMS), and e-mail (including support for both POP3 and IMAP4 protocols)
- Content management services
- **Internet and web application support:** HTTP transport framework and WAP stack
- **Data synchronization services (OMA):** Providing the OMA (SyncML) data synchronization client
- **Provisioning services (OMA):** Enables the network operator to deliver settings to the mobile device using a technique based on the Nokia Ericsson over-the-air (OTA)

Figure 1. Symbian OS architecture overview

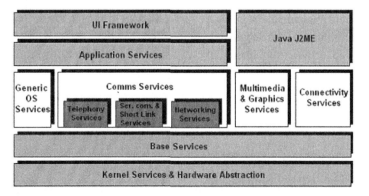

specification and the Nokia smart messaging specification.

Java

The Symbian OS provides a Java application execution environment which is optimized for mobile devices and mobile applications. This provides compatibility with mobile device Java applications and advanced Java applications able to make use of capabilities of a Symbian device. Symbian OS versions 9.1 and later support J2ME MIDP 2.0 and CLDC 1.1.

OS Services

The OS services level is the heart of the Symbian OS. These services provide important OS infrastructure components such as multimedia and graphics subsystems, networking, telephony, short link protocols, security services, and PC connectivity infrastructure.

Multimedia and Graphics Services

Multimedia and graphics services consist of multimedia, OpenGL ES, and the graphics subsystem. Multimedia services include multimedia framework (MMF), media support library (MSL), image conversion library (ICL), and camera support.

OpenGL for Embedded Systems (OpenGL ES) is a subset of the OpenGL 3D graphics API specially designed for embedded devices such as mobile phones.

The graphics subsystem implements the graphics device interface (GDI) and provides i.e. shared access for Symbian OS applications to components such as the screen, keyboard and pointing devices input, bitmap fonts, and scalable fonts.

Security Services

Symbian OS v9 provides extended platform security in form of capability control of installed applications. This ensures the integrity of the Symbian devices and the network, and still enables an open environment for third party applications. Other embedded security features are data confidentiality, integrity, and authentication realized by providing underlying support for secure communication protocols such as TLS/SSL and IPSec. The Symbian OS security services also support authentication of installable software using digital signatures. Embedded security features in Symbian OS are surveyed in more detail in a later section

Comms Services

Networking, telephony and short link protocols are actually subsystems of the "Comms Services" of the Symbian OS services. The purpose of the Comms services is to provide key frameworks and system services for communication and networking.

The networking services contain the key frameworks and system services for wide area communication. Various communication protocols can be implemented through a socket interface. Both IPv4 and IPv6 are supported using a dual IP stack. A plug-in architecture is provided for the IP stack allowing licensees to implement extensions, such as IPSec for secure network communication.

The telephony subsystem provides a multimode API for the clients. An abstraction layer for cellular networks is provided including support for GSM, GPRS, EDGE, CDMA (IS-95), 3GPP2, CDMA2000 1 x RTT, and 3GPP W-CDMA.

The Symbian OS services provide support for point to point communications through the short link services. Supported short link technologies include Bluetooth, serial, USB, and infrared (IrDA).

Connectivity Services

The connectivity services implements the connection manager and the connectivity framework. The connection manager handles connections between a PC and a Symbian OS device including both PC side and mobile device side components. Standard TCP/IP protocols are used for data transfer.

The connectivity framework implements the PC Connectivity toolkit. Features of this toolkit are:

- PC and mobile device synchronization
- Software install from PC
- Backup and restore
- Remote file management.

Base Services

The base system services provide the programming framework for all other components, than the above mentioned. The main elements visible for the user are the file system and the common user libraries.

Kernel Services and Hardware Abstraction Interface

The main functionality of the kernel services and the abstraction interface is to ensure Symbian OS robustness, performance, and efficient power management. These are all essential in a mobile phone. The kernel services and hardware abstraction interface include also logical device drivers. The kernel is the core of the system and performs i.e. memory allocation, power management, owns device drivers, and implements the scheduling policy. The logical device drivers provide drivers and/or software controllers for devices such as DTE serial port, DCE serial port, USB client 1.1, keyboard, Ethernet, etc. For more details about the architecture of Symbian OS v9.1, see (Siezen, 2005).

EMBEDDED SECURITY FEATURES IN SYMBIAN

Original embedded security feature in Symbian OS are:

- Cryptographic module with:
  - implementations of symmetric algorithms (DES, 3DES, RC2, RC4, and RC5) and asymmetric cryptographic algorithms (RSA, DSA, and DH)
  - Implementations of hash functions (MD5, SHA1, and HMAC)
  - A pseudo-random number generator for cryptographic key generation
- Certificate management module
- Password locking of contents of multimedia-card (MMCs) and other removable memory cards
- Installation packet signing, see (Symbian Signed, 2006).

IPSec and VPN support were added in Symbian OS v6.0. SSL/TLS support and a content security feature, a digital rights management (DRM) API, were introduced in Symbian OS v6.0. platform security features were embedded in Symbian OS v9.1:

- To control access to sensitive operations and to sensitive APIs.
- To provide confidentiality of private data in a Symbian device.
- To protect the hardware and software integrity of a Symbian device. (Symbian OS, 2006)

Installation Packet Signing

Developers of Symbian applications should follow the Symbian Signed procedure described in (Symbian Signed, 2006):

- An application developer request and gets from VeriSign a publisher ID on a X.509 certificate for a signature key pair.
- The developer creates a SIS file and signs it with the private key of the certified key pair.
- The developer sends the application to a Symbian Test House.
- If test criteria are met, then the VeriSign certified signature is removed and replaced by a signature created by the Symbian Root certified private key.
- The Symbian Signed SIS file is returned to the developer for distribution to Symbian device users.

The Symbian Software Installer:
- Stores the Symbian Root Certificate on the Symbian device if it isn't already stored.
- Tries to verify the SIS file signature with the public key on the Symbian Root Certificate.
- Installs the SIS file only if the signature is verified.

Certificate Management

The Certificate Management module:
- Stores WTLS certificates and X.509 certificates. Certificates are used for authentication of application developers, web servers, and Symbian device users.
- Nerifies trust in stored certificates.
- Checks certificate revocation using the online certificate status protocol (OCSP). Certificate management is implemented by methods of the CcertStore class. (Symbian OS, 2006)

Platform Security

Platform security is based on the following concepts: (EMCC Software, 2005; Shackman, 2005; Heath, 2006):

- **Unit of Trust:** The kernel, file system and the software installer are part of a trusted computing base (TCB) and have unrestricted access to the device's resources. The TCB is responsible for maintaining integrity of the device. Other system components surrounding the TCB comprise a trusted computing environment (TCE).
- **Capability Model:** A capability is an entity of protection. Functionality in Symbian OS is implemented by a set of application programming interfaces. An API needing protection is associated with a capability. Applications must be authorized by the Symbian Software Installer to access the capabilities they wish to use. Only authorized applications are trusted to use capability protected APIs.
- **Data caging:** Data caging is a filing system facility for protection of private data.

Permissions

Authorization of an application can give the application either 'Blanket' permission or 'Single shot' permission to a Symbian API. 'Blanket' permission grants a capability until the application is uninstalled or re-installed. 'Single shot' permission requires end-user permission each time the application is started. 'Single shot' permission can be given to all unsigned applications and to some Symbian Signed applications.

Capabilities

Capabilities requested by an application are listed in its project definition file (MMP). Capabilities are grouped in three sets for authorization by the Symbian Software installer:

- "Unsigned-Sandboxed" set consisting of the capabilities
  ○ Nonclassified APIs
  ○ 'LocalServices' and 'UserEnvironment' with 'Blanket' permission

- ° 'Network Services', 'ReadUserData', and 'WriteUserData' with 'Single shot' permission
- "Basic" set consisting of the capabilities 'Network Services', 'ReadUserData', and 'WriteUserData' with 'Blanket' permission
- "Extended" set consisting of the capabilities 'NetworkControl', 'PowerMgmt', 'Trusted-UI', 'SwEvent', 'ProtServ', 'MultimediaDD', 'ReadDeviceData', 'WriteDeviceData', 'DRM' and 'SurroundingsDD'.

Applications in the "Basic" and "Extended" sets are all Symbian Signed. The most powerful capabilities:

- **AllFiles:** Granting read access to entire file system and write access to private directories of other processes.
- **CommDD capability:** Granting access to communicating device drivers.
- **DiskAdmin capability:** Granting access to specific disk administration operations.
- **TCB capability:** Granting unrestricted access to all hardware and software, including write access to executables and shared read-only resources are however not included in the "Extended Set".

A Symbian process will always get the capabilities of the executable file. Capabilities cannot change during execution. A library module can be loaded dynamically only if it has equal or more capabilities than the calling process.

Data Caging

Data caging implements a protected directory structure in Symbian OS:

- Sstem critical file and executable files are stored in \Sys, which can be modified only

by the Symbian OS Kernel, File Server, and Software Installer. Executable files are stored in \Sys\bin, which is the only place from which C++ programmed software can run. A locally unique security identifier (SID) must be contained in every executable file.
- Read-only resource files shared by all applications are stored in \Resource, which can be modified only by the Symbian OS Software Installer.
- Private data for all installed programs is stored in \Private by the Symbian OS Software Installer. Only the process of running the executable file with SID=<SID> has access to its private data in the subdirectory \Private\<SID>\.

Other directories than \Sys, \Resource, and \Private are not protected by data caging.

Other Platform Security Features

Security options for client/server communication are available. Every Symbian OS server process can define and check what capabilities, which SID, and which VID (Vendor Identifier) are required from the calling client process. The calling client process can check the name of the server process.

A new secure backup and restore functionality is implemented. Also file capabilities are backed up and restored. Private data files are backed up and restored in cooperation with the owning process.

The data-sharing mechanism in earlier Symbian OS versions has been replaced by a Central Repository for secure storage of structured data. Central Repository is implemented as a Symbian OS server process, which manages the data storage.

PHYSICAL PROTECTION

Physical security involves safekeeping systems from theft, physical and electromagnetic damage, and preventing unauthorized access to those systems (Rittinghouse & Ransome, 2004). Today, device theft is more attractive to thieves as mobile devices become smaller and more powerful (Grami & Schell, 2005). When a stolen device is reported, location technology can be employed to help track down the thief. All employees should be held responsible for taking every reasonable precaution to ensure the physical security of their mobile devices from theft, abuse, avoidable hazards, or unauthorized use.

Protection of stored content against power failures and other functional failures and possibilities to recover stored content after damage, after a functional failure or after a not prevented intrusion attack are highly important security measures. Shielding the mobile device from unwanted wireless communication, protection of stored content in case of theft or other loss of the mobile device and visible ownership information for return of a lost or stolen mobile device are other essential security measures. When a mobile device is misplaced or stolen, it can be used to purchase items, enabling thieves to easily commit fraud. There are no safeguards against theft of electronic cash on such devices (Hong, 2005). In the near future, when many mobile devices are used in home automation, for instance to remotely lock/unlock doors, insufficient physical protection of mobile devices is also a threat to the owner's home security.

DEVICE ACCESS CONTROL

It is highly important to implement reliable access control mechanisms for Symbian devices in order to protect the data stored in memory, since physical access control mechanisms are ineffective due to the small size and easy portability of such devices. There are currently no widely adopted standards for access control in Symbian based mobile devices. Access control services are mostly provided by third party companies, see section 'Add-on Security Software' for examples.

Access control on a mobile device can be implemented using a combination of the following security services and features (Perelson & Botha, 2004):

* Authentication service
* Confidentiality service
* Nonrepudiation service
* Authorization

The principle of access control in a mobile device is shown in Figure 2.

Figure 2. The principle of access control in mobile devices

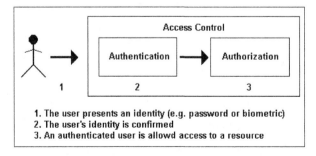

40

Authentication

An authentication service is a system confirming that a user, trying to access the mobile device, is the owner of or is permitted access to the device. There are several methods in which a user can authenticate to a handheld device. For Symbian devices at least the following authentication methods are available:

- Passwords/PINs
- Visual login
- Biometrics

Visual login and biometrics are, however, only available as add-on security hardware and software, see Appendix 1.

PIN and Password Authentication

PIN and password authentication means protection of the device's system using a numeric (PIN) or alphabetic (password) combination of digits/characters which is to be entered by the user in order to access the system. The PIN is typically four digits of length and is entered by the user from a ten-digit (0-9) numerical keypad. However, PINs are susceptible to shoulder surfing or to systematic trial-and-error attacks due to their limited length and alphabet. Passwords are more secure than PINs since they support a larger alphabet and increase the number of digits in the password string. (Jansen, 2003)

In Symbian based mobile phones the user is normally by default authenticated to the SIM and no password/PIN protection is activated for the device itself. This means that the whole system of the device can be accessed by removing the SIM and starting the device in "offline mode". Most mobile phones, however, provide a system lock function. This function locks the system if the SIM is removed or changed. This lock code typically consists of more digits than standard

PINs, e.g. Nokia Series 60 phones use a five digit numerical lock code.

Visual Login

An example of a visual login method is picture passwords. A picture password system can be designed to require a sequence of pictures or objects matching a certain criteria and not exactly the same pictures. For example, the user must find a certain number of objects with four sides. Shoulder surfing of a picture password is much more difficult than shoulder surfing passwords or PINs. (Duncan, 2004)

Biometrics

Biometric user authentication is based on a technology which measures and analyzes physical or behavioral characteristics of a human. Examples of physical characteristics utilized for user authentication to Symbian devices include fingerprint, voice, and face (Biometrics, 2006; Yoshihisa, 2005). Biometric user authentication based on behavioral characteristics can for example be a system analyzing the movement of the person carrying the device (Karkimo, 2005). Biometric user authentication systems are becoming more and more common in Symbian devices and such systems are currently provided by several third party companies.

Authorization

Hitherto, user authorization has generally not been considered to be important for Symbian based mobile devices. These devices are typically personal and the authentication process infers that the user is authorized. It has also been assumed that all data stored on a device is owned by only one person who is the device owner. It is, however, becoming more common that handheld devices replace desktop and notebook computers in companies. This means that a single device, owned by the company, may be used by several employees and may contain confidential company information. Thus, the need for proper user authorization services is becoming more important. Needed user authorization features for mobile devices include (Perelson & Botha, 2004):

- **File masking:** Certain protected records are being prevented from being viewed by unauthorized users.
- **Access control lists:** Such a list defines permissions for a set of particular objects associated with a user.
- **Role based access control:** Permissions are defined in association with user roles.

STORAGE PROTECTION

Storage protection of a mobile device means:

- Online integrity control of all stored program code and all stored data
- Optional confidentiality of stored user data
- Protection against unauthorized tampering of stored content

Protection should include all removable storage modules used by the mobile device.

The integrity of:

- The operating system code
- The program code of installed applications
- Dystem and user data

can be verified when being used by traditional tools like checksums, cyclic redundancy codes CRC, hashes, message authentication codes (MAC, HMAC), and cryptographic signatures. Only hardware base security solutions for protection of verification keys needed by MACs,

HMACs and signatures provide strong protection against tampering attacks, since a checksum, a CRC, and a hash of a tampered file can easily be updated by an attacker. Online integrity control of program and data files must be combined with online integrity control of the configuration of a mobile device. This is needed to give sufficient protection against attempts to enter malicious software like viruses, worms and Trojans. Malicious software can be stored in the file system of a tampered configuration.

Confidentiality required for user data can be granted by file encryption software. This software also protects the integrity of the stored encrypted files, since successful decryption of an encrypted file is also an integrity proof.

NETWORK ACCESS CONTROL

Symbian devices support various wireless network connections. Typical networks are cellular networks such as 2G, 2.5G, and 3G, wireless local area networks (WLANs), and local connectivity networks such as Bluetooth and IrDA.

Identification Hardware

Identification hardware contains user information and cryptographic keys used to authenticate users to mobile devices, applications, networks, and network services. Common identification hardware used in Symbian devices include:

- Subscriber identity module (SIM)
- Public key infrastructure SIM (PKI SIM)
- Universal SIM (USIM)

SIM

A basic SIM card is a smartcard securely storing an authentication key identifying a GSM network user. The SIM card is technically a microcomputer, consisting of a CPU, ROM, RAM, EEPROM and

Input/Output (I/O) circuits. This microcomputer is able to perform operations based on information stored inside it, such as performing cryptographic calculations with the individual authentication key needed for authenticating the subscriber. The SIM card also contains storage space for i.e. Short message services (SMS) messages, multimedia messaging system (MMS) messages, and a phone book. The use and content of a SIM card is protected by PIN codes (Rankl & Effing, 2003).

PKI SIM

A PKI SIM card is a basic SIM with PKI functionality. A RSA coprocessor is added which performs public key based encryption and signing with private keys. The PKI SIM card contains space for storing private keys and certified public keys needed for digital signatures and encryption (Setec, 2006).

USIM

A USIM card is a SIM used in 3G mobile telephony networks, such as UMTS. The physical size of a USIM card is the same as a basic 2G GSM SIM card, but USIM is based on a different type of hardware. USIM is actually an application running on a UICC (Universal Integrated Circuit Card). The USIM stores a pre-shared secret key as the basic SIM (Lu, 2002).

Cellular Networks

2G and 2.5G

User authentication in 2G (Second Generation, GSM) and 2.5G ("Second and a half" generation, GPRS) networks is handled by a challenge/re-

Figure 3. GSM authentication and key agreement

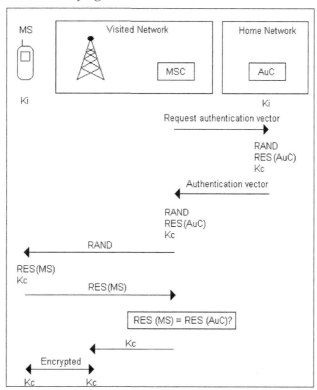

sponse based protocol. Every mobile station (MS) shares a secret key Ki with its home network. This key is stored in the SIM card of the MS and the authentication centre (AuC) of the home GSM network. Ki is used to authenticate the MS to the visited GSM network and for generating session keys needed for encrypting the mobile communication. The authentication process, shown in Figure 3, is started by the mobile switching centre (MSC) which requests an authentication vector from the AuC of the home network of the MS. The authentication vector, generated by the AuC, consists of a challenge/response pair (RAND, RES) and an encryption key Kc. The MSC of the visited network sends the 128-bit RAND to the MS. Upon receiving the RAND,

the MS computes a 32-bit response (RES) and an encryption key Kc using the received RAND and the Ki stored in the SIM. The calculation is processed within the SIM. The MS sends the RES back to the MSC. The MSC verifies the identity of the MS by comparing the received RES from the MS with the received RES from the AuC. If they match, authentication is successful and the MSC sends the encryption key Kc to the base station serving the MS. Then the MS is granted access to the GSM network service and the communication between the MS and the base station is encrypted using Kc (Meyer & Wetzel, 2004).

2G and 2.5G networks provide reasonably secure access control mechanisms. However, lack of mutual authentication is a considerable

Figure 4. UMTS authentication and key agreement

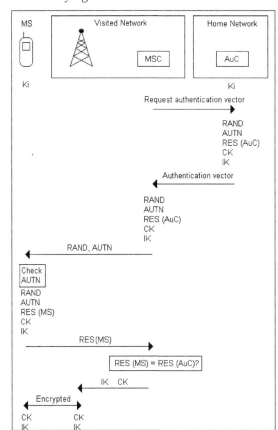

vulnerability. An attacker could setup a false base station and imitate a legitimate GSM network. As a result, i.e. the Ki could be cracked and the attacker could impersonate a legitimate user. (GSM, 2006)

3G

The authentication and key management technique used in 3G (third generation/UMTS) networks is based on the same principles as in GSM networks, see Figure 4. A secret authentication key is shared between the network and the MS. This key is stored on the USIM of the MS and in the AuC of the home network.

Unlike in GSM networks, UMTS networks provide mutual authentication. This means that not only the MS is authenticated to the GSM network but the GSM network is also authenticated to the MS. This protects the MS from attackers trying to impersonate a valid network to the MS. Network authentication is provided by a so called authentication token AUTN. The MSC (Mobile Switching Centre) of the visited network sends the AUTN together with the authentication challenge to the MS during the authentication process. Upon receiving the AUTN, containing a sequence number, the MS checks whether it is in the right range. If the sequence number is in the right range the MS has successfully authenticated the network and the authentication process can proceed. The MS computes an authentication response, here called RES, and encryption and integrity protection keys, called CK and IK, and send these back to the MSC. The MSC verifies the identity of the MS by checking the correctness of the received RES.

Upon successful authentication, the MSC sends the encryption key CK and integrity key IK to the UMTS base station. The MS is now able to communicate with the UMTS network and the communication between the MS and the base station is encrypted with CK and the integrity is protected with IK. (Meyer & Wetsel, 2004).

Local Connectivity Networks

IrDA

Symbian includes three different APIs for IrDA (Infrared Data Association) connections:

- IrDA Sockets for socket based communication
- IrDA Serial for serial communication
- IrTranP for communication with digital cameras and printers.

The IrDA standard doesn't specify any access control or other security features. However, since infrared connections work with the line-of-sight principle, access is easily controlled by physical security measures. (Symbian OS, 2006)

Bluetooth

Bluetooth is a technique providing a wireless medium for transmitting data and voice signals between electronic devices over a short distance. The specification is defined by the Bluetooth SIG (Special Interest Group). SIG involves a Bluetooth Security Experts Group, which is responsible for the security issues. The security is based on three different services, authentication, authorization, and encryption. The Bluetooth devices can be set in one of three different security modes:

- **Security mode 1:** No security measures
- **Security mode 2:** Security measures based on authorization
- **Security mode 3:** Authentication and encryption

Bluetooth performs device authentication (not user authentication) based on a challenge/response process which can be either unidirectional or mutual. The devices are authenticated using secret keys called link keys. These keys are generated either dynamically or through a process called pairing. When dynamical generation of the link key is used, the user is required to enter a passkey each time a connection is established. The same passkey must be entered in both connecting devices. When pairing is used, a long-term, stored link key is generated from a user entered passkey, which can be automatically used from several connection sessions between the same devices.

Bluetooth access control also provides an authorization service. The authorization service allows a Bluetooth device to determine whether or not another device is allowed access to a particular service. Authorization includes two security concepts: trust relationships and service security levels. Three different levels of trust between devices are allowed by the Bluetooth specification: trusted, not trusted, and unknown. By using combinations of authentication and authorization, Bluetooth provides three service levels as shown in Table 1.

A major weakness in Bluetooth access control is the lack of support for user authentication. This means that a malicious user can easily access network resources and services with a stolen device. Furthermore, PIN codes are often allowed to be short which is susceptible to attacks. However, the coverage range of a Bluetooth network is very short. This means that malicious access to a Bluetooth network can mostly be prevented by use of physical access control measures.

For more detailed information about access control in Bluetooth networks, see the official Bluetooth wireless info site (Bluetooth, 2006).

WLAN

WLANs provide wireless high speed Internet connections and are supported by some Symbian smart phones. Implementation and use of secure access control mechanisms is essential in order to protect WLANs from unauthorized network access, since WLANs are by their nature easy to access and are unable to protect by physical security measures. WLANs were earlier associated with serious security vulnerabilities. One of the most significant concerns has been the lack of proper user authentication methods. Today, WLANs provide acceptable security through the recently ratified security standard 802.11i.

Access Control Mechanisms Defined in the 802.11 Standard

The authentication mechanisms defined in the original WLAN standard 802.11 are weak and not recommended. The 802.11 standard only provides device authentication in form of the use of static shared secret keys called wired equivalent privacy (WEP) keys. The same WEP key is shared between the WLAN access point and all authorized clients. WEP keys have turned out to be easily cracked with cracking software, which is widely available in Internet. If a WEP key is cracked by an intruder, the intruder gets full access to the WLAN.

WEP authentication can be strengthened using MAC filters and by disabling SSID broadcasting on the access point. These measures, however,

Table 1. Bluetooth service levels

	Authorization	Authentication	Encryption
Service Level 1	Yes	Yes	Yes
Service Level 2	No	Yes	Yes
Service Level 3	No	No	Yes

still don't provide needed level of security. SSIDs are easily determined by sniffing probe response frames from an AP. MAC addresses are easily captured and spoofed.

Access Control Mechanisms Defined in the 802.11i Standard

The recently ratified WLAN security standards WPA and WPA2 address the vulnerabilities of WEP. WPA, introduced at the end of 2002, is a subset of the 802.11i standard, and WPA2, ratified in the summer 2004, provides full 802.11i support. The difference between WPA and WPA2 is the way how the communication is encrypted. Furthermore, WPA2 provides support for ad-hoc networks which is missing in WPA. User authentication in WPA and WPA2 are based on the same techniques. WPA is currently supported in a few available Symbian smart phone models. WPA2, however, is presently supported only in the most recent model of Nokia Communicators, Nokia 9300i (Wi-Fi, 2006).

Access Control Based on Pre-Shared Keys

802.11i provides two security modes: home mode and enterprise mode. 802.11i home mode is as WEP based on a shared secret string, here called pre-shared key (PSK). The difference compared to WEP is that the PSK is never used directly as an input for data encryption algorithms. 802.11i home mode is suitable for small WLAN environments, such as small office and home WLANs where the number of users is low.

802.1X Port Based Access Control

For large enterprise WLAN environments 802.11i enterprise mode is recommended. This security mode utilizes the 802.1X standard for authenticating users. IEEE 802.1X is a standard, originally designed for LANs, to address open network access. 802.1X has three different components involved: supplicant (client), authenticator (WLAN AP) and authentication, authorization, and accounting (AAA) server. The supplicant is a user or client who wants to be authenticated. The supplicant accesses the network via the authenticator which is, in case of a WLAN, a wireless AP. The AAA server, typically a remote authentication dial-in user service (RADIUS) server, works as a backend server providing authentication service to an authenticator. The AAA server validates the identity and determines, from the credentials provided by the supplicant, whether the supplicant is authorized to access the WLAN or not.

During the authentication process, the authenticator works as an intermediary between the

Figure 5. 802.1X authentication in unauthorized state

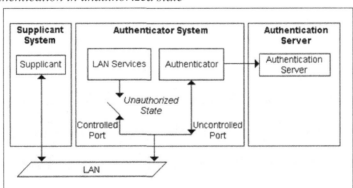

supplicant and the AAA server passing authentication information messages between these entities. Until the supplicant is successfully authenticated on the AAA server, only authentication messages are permitted between the supplicant and the AAA server through the authenticator's uncontrolled port. The controlled port, through which a supplicant can access the network services, remains in unauthorized state, see Figure 5. As a result of successful authentication, the controlled port switches to authorized state, and the supplicant is permitted access to the network services, see Figure 6.

802.1X binds the extensible authentication protocol (EAP) protocol which handles the transportation of authentication messages between the

Figure 6. 802.1X authentication in authorized state

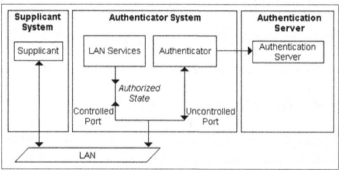

Figure 7. EAP authentication exchange messages

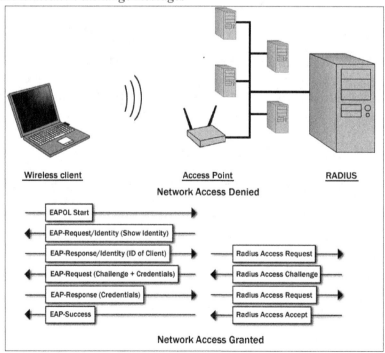

supplicant and the AAA server. The authentication message exchange is performed over the link layer, using device MAC addresses as destination addresses. A typical EAP authentication conversation between a supplicant and an AAA server in a WLAN is shown in Figure 7.

EAP supports the use of a number of authentication protocols, usually called EAP types. The following EAP types are WPA and WPA2 certified (Wi-Fi, 2006):

- EAP-transport layer security (EAP-TLS)
- EAP-tunneled transport layer security (EAP-TTLS)
- Protected EAP version 0/EAP-Microsoft challenge authentication protocol version 2 (PEAPv0/EAP-MSCHAPv2)
- PEAPv1/EAP-Generic Token Card(PEAPv1/EAP-GTC)
- EAP-SIM

EAP-TLS, EAP-TTLS and EAP-PEAP are based on PKI authentication. EAP-TTLS and EAP-PEAP however only use certificate authentication for authenticating the network to the user. User authentication is performed using less complex methods, such as user name and password. EAP-TLS provides mutual certificate based authentication between wireless clients and authentication servers. This means that a X.509 based certificate is required both on the client and authentication server for user and server authentication.

EAP-SIM is an emerging EAP authentication protocol for WLANs and is recently supported by several WLAN Hotspot environments. This standard is still an IETF draft. EAP-SIM is based on the existing GSM mobile phone authentication system and the SIM. A WLAN user is thus able to authenticate to the network using the secret key and algorithms embedded on the SIM card. In order to implement EAP-SIM authentication in a WLAN, a RADIUS server supporting EAP-SIM and equipped with a GSM/MAP/SS7 (GSM/Mobile Application Part/Signalling System 7) gateway is needed. Additionally the WLAN client software must support the EAP-SIM authentication protocol. During the EAP authentication process, the RADIUS server contacts the user's home GSM operator through the GSM/MAP/SS7 gateway and retrieves the GSM triplets used to authenticate the user. The triplets are sent to the wireless client, via the AP, and if the supplicant and the user's SIM card are able to validate the GSM triplets, the RADIUS server requests the AP to grant the client network access.

For further reading about WLAN access control and security (see Pulkkis, Grahn, Karlsson, Martikainen, & Daniel, 2005).

ACCESS CONTROL FOR APPLICATIONS AND NETWORK SERVICES

Typical network services transferring confidential data to and from a Symbian devices are E-commerce and electronic payments. These services normally run over HTTP and WAP connections. This section concentrates on access control in such connections as well as local applications handling confidential data.

Local Applications

Symbian OS doesn't support individual user accounts and has no concept of user logon at operating system level. Mobile applications, handling confidential data, should thus require user authentication before access to the application is granted. Applications should also support "session timeout" for the case that a mobile device is lost or stolen, while the device user is logged in to an application. This means that a limited time is specified for which an application can be inactive before re-authentication is required (DevX, 2006).

Client/server Applications

Symbian OS provides the possibility to develop tailor made client/server applications based on socket communication. SSL sockets are supported providing mutual certificate authentication. X.509 based certificates are supported in Symbian devices and a certificate management application and certificate validation module is embedded in the operating system (Siezen, 2005).

Typical client/server applications are WAP and HTTP services. The communication between the WAP/HTTP browser residing on the Symbian device and the WAP/HTTP server consists of two parts:

1. The wireless connection between the mobile device and its mobile carrier
2. The Internet connection between the mobile device and the Internet host/server via the mobile carrier

The security of the first mentioned connection is based on hardware level security, and cannot be affected by application developers. The second mentioned connection is, however, to be secured at the application level.

WAP Connections

Wireless application protocol (WAP) is an open standard for applications residing on mobile devices. The protocol is currently widely used in Symbian smart phones, also for confidential data transmissions. Thus, security is an important issue for the WAP protocol. WAP security protocols and specifications are being developed by the WAP Forum (Open, 2006). The evolution of WAP security specifications is shown in Figure 8.

WTLS

The security in WAP versions 1.0 and 1.1 mainly relies on the wireless transport layer security (WTLS) protocol. This protocol is designed to provide privacy, data integrity and authentication between two communicating WAP applications. WTLS is derived from transport layer security (TLS) and optimised for low-bandwidth bearer networks with relatively long latency. WTLS provides similar functionality as TLS 1.0 and adds new features such as datagram support, optimised handshake and dynamic key refreshing. WTLS offers three levels of security:

Figure 8. The development of WAP security specifications

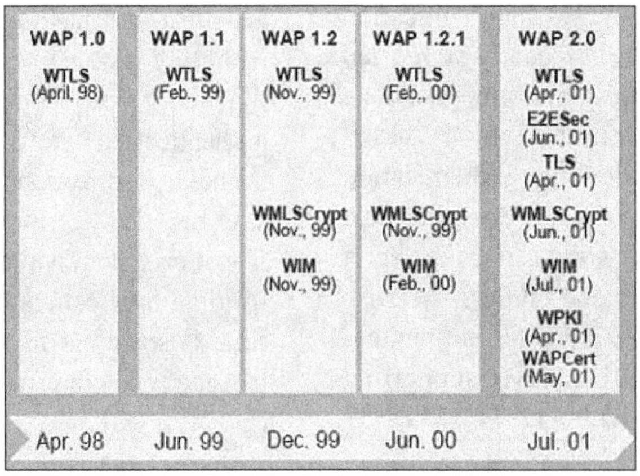

- **WTLS class 1:** An encrypted channel is used, but no authentication takes place.
- **WTLS class 2:** Certificate authentication of the server is used but the client is authenticated using alternative means, such as username/password.
- **WTLS class 3:** Both client and server are authenticated using certificates. (Open, 2006)

WMLScript and WIM

WAP Forum introduced two new initiatives in WAP version 1.2 to address the lack of both nonrepudiation services and real end-user authentication in earlier WAP versions:

- WMLScript (wireless markup language script) Crypto Library
- WAP identity module (WIM)

WMLScript provides cryptographic functionality of a WAP client (WAP Forum WMLScript, 2001). It defines a signature interface to digitally sign application data with mobile devices.

WIM is used in WTLS and in application level security functions (WAP Forum, 2001). The main function of WIM is to store and process user identification and authentication information, such as private keys. An example of a WIM implementation is a combination with SIM (Subscriber Identity Module) of a mobile phone. This combined SIM and WIM is called S/WIM.

TLS/SSL

SSL/TLS are security protocols for secure communication in Internet based client/server applications. WAP 2.0 adopts TLS as security protocol and supports the tunnelling of SSL/TLS sessions through a WAP proxy. TLS/SSL in WAP 2.0 replaces the WTLS protocol.

WPKI

Wireless Public Key Infrastructure (WPKI) is a PKI specification for mobile environments. This specification is supported since WAP version 2.0. WPKI mainly describes the establishment and maintenance of authentic bindings between entity identifiers and public keys (Open, 2006).

HTTP Connections

For HTTP-based client/server applications the SSL protocol is a simple and secure way for providing mutual authentication. Examples of applications and systems using SSL are:

- Web browsers for secure communications with web servers (HTTPS)
- E-mail client software for secure reading of e-mail messages on e-mail servers
- Secure electronic transactions (SET), a protocol for secure financial transactions and secure use of credit cards on the Internet

SSL supports mutual authentication based on X.509 certificates. The Symbian operating system integrates support for this protocol. Browsers supporting HTTPS connections are available also in Symbian devices.

NETWORK CONNECTION SECURITY

Connection security means (Markovski & Gusev, 2003):

- Availability of data communication
- Mutual authentication of communicating partners
- Integrity of data communication
- Possibility of confidential data communication

- Intrusion prevention/detection
- Malware rejection

Essential for fulfilment of all these security requirements in a mobile device are security settings and commitment to security policy rules controlled by centralized security management software.

Availability of data communication to/from a mobile device is achieved if the connection network is operational and can reject denial-of-service (DoS) attacks.

Mutual authentication of communicating partners can be achieved by:

- Using SSH, VPN or SSL software
- Using IEEE 802.1X/EAP-TLS in WLAN connection networks
- USIM cards in UMTS cellular networks

Integrity and confidentiality of data communication is achieved by:

- Using SSH, VPN or SSL software
- Security protocols WPA and WPA2 in WLAN connection networks
- SIM, USIM, PKI SIM, ISIM cards in cellular mobile networks (GSM, GPRS, UMTS)

Intrusion prevention/detection is achieved by:

- A traffic filtering firewall
- Logging of connection attempts
- Security audits based on communication event logging, analysis of logged information, alerts and alarms
- Control of remote synchronization (Palm OS/HotSync, Windows CE & Windows Mobile/ActiveSync, Symbian OS/SyncML based)
- Shielding the mobile device from unwanted wireless communication with electro-

magnetic shielding bag. (MobileCloak™, 2006)

Malware rejection is achieved by using anti-virus software and anti-spyware.

Basic Communication Security

Basic communication security of a mobile device can be defined as intrusion prevention and malware rejection. The basic intrusion prevention tool is a configurable firewall with communication event logging and alert messaging. The basic malware rejection tools are anti-virus and anti-spyware with suspicious event alarming features. The core of a malware rejection tool is a malware recognition database. Malware rejection tool providers constantly update this database and the updated malware recognition database is available to malware rejection tool users through some network connection. An installed malware rejection tool should always use the latest update of the malware recognition database. Anti-virus software for mobile devices is delivered for example by (Symantec Corporation, 2006) and (Kaspersky, 2005).

Authentic Data Communication

Authentic data communication is based on mutual authentication of communicating parties. In 2G cellular networks (GSM Data) authentication is unidirectional. The mobile device is authenticated to the cellular network by use of the shared secret key in the SIM card. Mutual authentication, for example based on public key certificates, is however possible for packet data communication in GSM networks (GPRS) in addition to PIN based GSM authentication. In 3G cellular networks, like UMTS, authentication is mutual, the mobile device and the network are authenticated to each other by the authentication and key agreement (AKA) mechanism. (Cremonini, Damiani, de Vimercati, Samarati, Corallo, & Elia, 2005)

In a WLAN authentication is mutual for WPA and IEEE 802.11i (WPA2). The authentication of a mobile client is based on presented credentials and information registered in an AAA server. The authentication protocol, EAP, also requires authentication of the AAA server to the mobile client. (Pulkkis, Grahn, Karlsson, Martikainen & Daniel, 2005). Also a Bluetooth connection can be configured for mutual authentication. The default security level of a Bluetooth service is:

- **Incoming connection:** Authorisation and Authentication required,
- **Outgoing connection:** Authentication required. (Muller, 1999)

Integrity and Confidentiality of Data Communication

Confidentiality and integrity of all data communication to and from cellular mobile networks (GSM, GPRS, and UMTS) is provided by the security hardware of SIM/USIM/PKI SIM/ISIM cards in mobile devices. For data communication through other network types (WLAN, Bluetooth, IrDA) connection specific security solutions must be installed, configured, and activated. Alternatively, end-to-end security software like VPN and SSH must be used. Available PDA VPN products are referred to in (Taylor, 2004, Part IV).

For WLAN connections available solutions for confidentiality and integrity of all data communication are WEP, WPA, and IEE 802.11i (WPA2). WEP security is however weak, since WEP protection can be cracked from recorded WEP protected data communication (WEPCrack, 2004).

For Bluetooth connections link level security corresponding to security mode 3 should be used (Sun, Howie, Koivisto & Sauvola, 2001).

Connection Security Management

Security settings and commitment to security policy rules should be controlled by centralized security management software. Security audits based on:

- Communication event logging
- Analysis of logged information
- Alerts and alarms

should be performed with timed and manual options. When necessary, a mobile device should be shielded from unwanted wireless communication with an electromagnetic shielding bag.

Special attention should be paid to control of remote synchronization (Palm OS/HotSync, Windows CE & Windows Mobile/ActiveSync, Symbian OS/SyncML based). Remote synchronization should be disabled when not in use. Also mobile devices should have basic communication security features like:

- Personal firewalls
- Antimalware protection software with updated malware recognition data
- Latest software patches installed

Use and attempts to use remote synchronization ports (see Table 2) should be logged and alerts and alarms should be triggered by unauthorized use or usage attempts. Passwords

Table 2. TCP and UDP port used by synchronization software

	TCP Ports Used	UDP Ports Used
ActiveSync	990, 999, 5678, 5679	
HotSync	14237, 14238	14237
SyncML based	80 (http)	

used by synchronization software in desktop and laptop computers should resist dictionary attacks and the PC/Windows option to save connection passwords should not be used.

ADD-ON SECURITY SOFTWARE

Several security products are available for solving security problems associated with Symbian OS based mobile devices. The security products are designed to solve individual or more comprehensive security problems. Following list of the product groups reveal versatility of Symbian OS based smart phone security solutions (Taylor, 2004, part III; Douglas, 2004):

- Authentication solutions
- Encryption software
- Anti-virus and firewall software
- VPN software
- Forensic analysis software
- Wireless security software
- Multifunctional software

Add-on security software products for Symbian OS are presented in Appendix A.

EVALUATION OF SYMBIAN SECURITY

This section concentrates on evaluating the security of the Symbian OS by discussing its weaknesses and by comparing Symbian to other mobile device operating systems. A case study with security software performance measurements for Symbian OS is presented in Appendix B.

Security Weaknesses

Symbian based mobile devices do not provide all the security features required by corporate security policies. Major weaknesses include:

- Lack of user authorization
- No access controls in the file system
- Insufficient protection against malicious applications

Symbian devices are designed to be personal and it is thus assumed that all the data stored on the devices is owned by the person using it. This causes problems when the device is owned by a company and it is used by many employees. In order to meet corporate access control requirements, Symbian devices should provide authorization features such as file masking, access control lists, and role-based access control. These authorization features are however currently missing (Perelson & Botha, 2004).

Malicious software is a growing threat for Symbian devices. Although Symbian provide an application signature feature (Symbian Signed) it does not provide a complete protection against malicious code. Viruses and other malicious software are usually transmitted to a mobile phone as SIS installation files. If the installation file is not digitally signed by a trusted third party, the system will notify the user about it. Nevertheless, in case the user chooses to install the application anyway, the Symbian OS provides no protection against it after it has been installed. An installed application has full access to delete or change any file in the file system. A Symbian application signed by a trusted authority is neither 100% secure. The installation and the application file are tested by the authority by analyzing the functionality, but the authority has no access to the source files. Malicious functions of an application can thus be programmed to be activated after a certain time period. As a result, these functions will not be discovered during the test phase (Smulders, 2004).

Comparison to other Mobile Device Operating Systems

Symbian, Palm OS, and Windows Mobile are currently the most common mobile device operating systems. In this section the main security features of these operating systems are briefly discussed and compared. In the comparison, only inherent security features are compared. Add-on security software is not taken into account.

Windows Mobile

Windows Mobile is an operating system combined with a suite of basic applications for mobile devices based on the Microsoft Win32 API. The Windows Mobile OS runs mainly on two different kinds of devices: Pocket PCs and Smartphones. The main security features of Windows Mobile include (Microsoft, 2006):

- Authentication functionality
- Data encryption
- Application-level encryption
- Information service encryption
- Network-level encryption

Authentication Functionality

Windows Mobile supports 4-digit device passwords and in Pocket PC also a strong password option with 7 or more alphanumeric and punctuation characters. Windows Mobile authentication functionality also provide SIM lock for GSM devices, SSL and PCT for secure Web site authentication, CHAP, MS-CHAP and PAP protocols for VPN authentication, WTLS class 2 for secure WAP, and file signing for code/application authentication. The local authentication subsystem (LASS) is a new feature since Windows Mobile 5.0. It is an OS feature that separates user authentication from the application and its authentication method. LASS provides plug-in modules for additional authentication methods such as biometric and smartcard authentication. Windows Mobile also provides a unique security feature known as Role-Based Access Control. This feature, however, doesn't provide any organizational roles for users. The role-based access control is used for assigning roles for over-the-air (OTA) messages and determine which Windows Mobile device resources the messages has access to.

Data Encryption

In Windows Mobile handheld devices sensitive data can be stored in a relational database (SQL Server CE). The stored data is protected with 128-bit encryption and a password. This feature is only supported in Pocket PC.

Application Level Encryption

For application and network communication protection, the Windows Mobile platform provides various encryption algorithms including:

- **Stream-based encryption algorithms:** RC2 and RC4
- **Block cipher encryption algorithms:** DES and 3DES
- **One-way hashing algorithms:** MD2, MD4, MD5, SHA-1, MAC, and HMAC
- Digital signature encryption using RSA public-key algorithm

A library called CryptoAPI also support the use of 128-bit encryption by developers for integrating encryption into their applications and communications.

Information Service Encryption

The Microsoft Exchange software with integrated Server ActiveSync provides technology for encrypting e-mail, calendar, and contacts data and for synchronizing such data between the Windows Mobile device and the server. Microsoft Exchange also provides WTLS encrypted browsing over the Internet when using a WAP-enabled browser. The method used for protecting data synchronization is SSL 128-bit end-to-end encryption.

Network-Level Encryption

Windows Mobile provides the following types of network-level encryption for protecting data transmitted over the Internet and wireless networks:

- **VPN protocol support:** PPTP, IPSec, and IPSec/L2TP
- **Secure access to Web sites:** SSL (HTTPS) and PCT
- **Secure access to WAP sites:** WTLS class 2
- **Secure wireless LAN connectivity:** VPN, WEP, and WPA

Palm OS

Palm OS is a compact operating system designed for PDAs. The current latest version is Palm OS Cobalt 6.1. Main security features of Palm OS are (PalmSource, 2006):

- Authorization and authentication manager
- Cryptography provider manager (CPM)
- Secure communication
- Data synchronization and backup

Authorization and Authentication Manager

The authorization and authentication manager provides access control to the Palm OS devices. The authorization manager provides a file masking feature. This feature enables applications to specify a set of rules that must be met in order to access data on the device. As a result any stored data, application code, or kernel resource can be protected.

The authentication manager handles tokens used for verifying device access such as: passwords, PINs, or pass-phrases. Authentication manager also provides an option for developers to incorporate advanced authentication methods such as biometrics (handwriting, voice recognition, fingerprints, etc.) and smart cards. A code signing feature is also supported. Code signing ensures that only applications with a valid digital signature can access certain data and resources.

CPM

The CPM provides a system-wide suite of cryptographic services for securing data and resources on a Palm OS device. The encryption services are available to any written application which needs to take advantage of these services. 128-bit encryption is a standard feature of the CPM. Palm OS has a partnership with RSA Security (one of the leading encryption providers in the security industry) and through the partnership Palm OS includes RC4, SHA-1, and signature verification using RSA-verify. The CPM also incorporates a plug-in cryptographic architecture, allowing developers to incorporate other encryption algorithms such as AES through a suite of APIs.

Secure Communication

For extending encryption services to communication, networking, and e-commerce applications Palm OS incorporates SSL/TLS providing secure end-to-end connections over the Internet using 128-bit SSL encryption. The RC4 encryption algorithm is a standard feature in Palm OS and it is used for encrypting data transmissions. Palm OS also support unique device identification, based on the Flash ID, mobile access number (MAN), and electronic serial number (ESN), for network access. Access to VPN networks and WPA secured WLAN access is possible through the use of third party client software.

Analysis

Symbian OS has several security features in common with Palm OS and Windows Mobile. They are all based on a modular design which enables mobile device manufacturers to choose what OS features they want to implement. The operating systems provide basic security services such as authentication and encryption while user authorization is not considered to be important. The most important security features of Symbian, Palm OS, and Windows Mobile are presented in Table 3. (Perelson & Botha, 2004)

FUTURE TRENDS

The growth of the Internet, e-commerce and m-commerce has dramatically increased the amount of personal and corporate information that can be captured or modified. In the near future ubicomp systems will accentuate this trend. An increase in privacy and security risks is expected, not only with the emergence of mobile devices, but also with sensor-based systems, wireless networking and embedded devices.

Within the mobile field, emerging technologies like RFID (Radio Frequency IDentification), ZigBee, Wireless USB (Universal Serial Bus), Wireless UWB (Ultra Wide Band), cellular mobile fourth generation (4G) systems, location determi-

nation, adaptive modulation and coding (AMC), digital signal compression, biometrics, Internet protocol (IPv6), mobile ad-hoc networks, multiple-input multiple output (MIMO), orthogonal frequency division multiplexing (OFDM), turbo codes, data encryption technologies among others will have a severe impact on the deployment of ubicomp systems and on their security features. These emerging technologies will impose new security features and the information society of the future will be much more difficult to keep secure. As an example of an emerging application we mention digital rights management (DRM). DRM is any of several technologies used by publishers to control access to digital data and hardware in order to handle usage restrictions.

Ubicomp technologies will probably suffer from the same sorts of unforeseen vulnerabilities that met the Internet society. In the ubicomp world existing security models will be obsolete. In comparison to the Internet the burden of security and privacy is increasingly falling on the user (Hong, 2005).

Privacy, security and trust issues are and will be of major importance. Collection of personal data, usage tracking and sharing of knowledge about a user's location with third parties are typical examples of privacy violation that need to be prevented. Personal information collected by business corporations and governments is already strictly regulated in many countries.

Table 3. Inherent security features of the major mobile device operating systems

	Windows Mobile	Symbian OS	Palm OS
Passwords	X	X	X
Biometrics	X		X
Auto Logout	X	X	X
File Masking			X
Access Control Lists			
Role-Based Access Control	X		
Encryption	X	X	X
Synchronisation	X	X	X

The success of many services like m-commerce is dependent on the underlying mobile technology. Enhanced wireless security requires technological improvements like higher computing speed and higher data rates of the mobile devices in order to compensate for additional overhead and increased complexity. On a more general level, both active and passive security threats need to be prevented by a combination of proactive and reactive methods. A proactive method attempts a priori to prevent an attack in the first place and a reactive method detects security threats and reacts accordingly (Grami & Schell, 2005).

The adoption of many mobile services like m-commerce will not be realized until the level of user trust will rise. Typical examples that have an impact on the wireless service performance and on the level of trust are dropped calls, busy signals and dead spots (Grami and Schell, 2005). Issues of health and safety due to electromagnetic radiation in mobile devices will also affect the level of trust. All reliability and security risks in ubiquitous computing systems cannot be avoided but better security models and interaction techniques can be developed to prevent and minimize foreseeable threats.

CONCLUSION

The popularity of Symbian based mobile computing devices is constantly growing in both corporate and private use. Smart phones and PDAs are in many companies replacing desktop and laptop computers. As a result, it is becoming more and more common that confidential data is stored in mobile devices. Symbian devices have also interfaces for various wireless network types. Wireless network access can be based on a dial-up connection to a cellular network (GSM, UMTS), on packet communication to a cellular network (GPRS), on a WLAN connection, on a Bluetooth connection, or on an infrared link (IrDA). With these network connections Symbian devices can use several network service types such as web services (HTTP or HTTPS), WAP services, e-commerce, and electronic payment services.

In parallel with the growing popularity, security threats against Symbian devices and against data communication to and from Symbian devices have also been constantly growing. The most serious security issues are related to protecting data and user credentials stored in the mobile devices. Due to the small size and portability of the Symbian devices access control is difficult to manage physically. Furthermore, Symbian does not provide proper user authentication systems at the OS level. Symbian devices do not provide all the security features required by corporate security policies. They where originally designed for private use, and thus lack proper user authorization mechanisms such as file masking, access control lists, and role-based access control. Symbian devices also face threats due to openness. Open means in this case that the operating system is open for external software and content. Malicious software, such as Trojan horses, viruses, and worms has also started to emerge. A comparison study shows that Symbian provides quite similar security features than its most important competitor operating systems, Windows Mobile and Palm OS. Neither the security features nor the security flaws significantly differ from each other within these operating systems.

The security threats must be seriously taken into account when mobile applications are designed and when mobile devices are used for storing and transmitting sensitive data. Some security features are provided by Symbian OS. These features do not cover all security needs, even though Symbian devices implement many security standards and protocols for wireless networking. There are, however, several add-on security solutions available for Symbian OS. Sufficient security can be reached by supplementing the scarcity of embedded security features with add-on security solutions.

REFERENCES

Biometrics Research homepage. (n.d.). Retrieved February 5, 2006, from http://biometrics.cse.msu.edu/

Bluetooth SIG. (2006). *The official Bluetooth wireless info site.* Retrieved February 5, 2006, from http://www.bluetooth.com

Cremonini, M., Damiani, E., De Capitani di Vimercati, S., Samarati, P., Corallo, A., & Elia, G. (2005). Security, privacy, and trust in mobile systems and applications. In M. Pagani (Ed.), *Mobile and wireless systems beyond 3G: Managing new business opportunities.* USA: IRM Press.

de Haas, J. (2005, Septemeber15-16). *Symbian phone security.* Presentation on T2'05 Conference, Helsinki, Finland. Retrieved October 9, 2005, from http://www.symternals.com/downloads/T2-Symbian-Security-v1.1.pdf

DevX Portal. (2006). *Wireless application security: What's up with that?* Retrieved February 6, 2006, from http://www.devx.com/Intel/Article/18013/0/page/1

DIGIA Inc. (2003). *Programming for the series 60 platform and Symbian OS.* UK: Wiley.

Douglas, D. (2004). *Windows mobile-based devices and security: Protecting sensitive business information.* Retrieved October 9, 2005, from http://download.microsoft.com/download/4/7/c/47c9d8ec-94d4-472b-887d-4a9ccf194160/6.%20WM_Security_Final_print.pdf

Duncan, M. V., Akhtari, M. S., & Bradford, P. G. (2004). Visual security for wireless handheld devices. *JOSHUA, 2.*

EMCC Software. (2005). *Symbian OS v9 - Advances in Symbian OS.* Retrieved October 12, 2005, from http://www.newlc.com/article.php3?id_article=959

F-Secure. (2004, December). *The malware attack against mobile phones is mounting.* Retrieved December 19, 2005, from http://www.f-secure.com/news/items/news_2004122200.shtml

Grami, A., & Schell, B. H. (2005). *Future trends in mobile commerce: Service offerings, technological advances and security challenges.* Retrieved January 15, 2005, from http://dev.hil.unb.ca/Texts/PST/pdf/grami.pdf

GSM Security Portal. (2006). Retrieved February 5, 2006, from http://www.gsm-security.net/

Heath, C. (2006). *Symbian OS platform security: Software development using the Symbian OS security architecture.* UK: Wiley.

Hickey, R. A. (2005, November). *Loss, theft still no. 1 threat to mobile data.* Retrieved December 17, 2005, from http://searchmobilecomputing.techtarget.com/originalContent/0,289142,sid40_gci1143983,00.html

Hicks, S. (2005). *Mobile and malicious.* Retrieved December 17, 2005, from http://www.ciostrategycenter.com/darwin/Threat/threat_strategies/mobile_malicious/

Hong, J. I. (2005, December). Minimizing security risks in ubicomp systems. *Computer, 118-119.*

Intoto Inc. (2005), *iGateway SSL-VPN.* Retrieved January 21, 2006, from http://www.intoto.com/product_briefs/iGateway%20SSL%20VPN.pdf

Jansen, W. A. (2003, May 12-15). *Authenticating users on handheld devices.* The 15th Annual Canadian Information Technology Security Symposium (CITSS), Ottawa, Canada. Retrieved July 11, from http://csrc.nist.gov/mobilesecurity/publications.html#MD

Karkimo, A. (2005, October 13). Kännykkää tunnistaa kantajansa askelista. *Tietokone computer science magazine on-line news.* Retrieved February 1st, 2006, from www.tietokone.fi

Kaspersky Security for PDAs. (n.d.) Retrieved June 30, 2005, from http://anti-virusi.com/kaspersky/kaspersky_pda.html

Lu, W. W. (2002). *Broadband wireless mobile, 3G and beyond.* USA: Wiley.

Markovski, J., & Gusev, M. (2003, April). Application level security of mobile communications (pp. 309–317). In *Proceedings of the 1ˢᵗ International Conference Mathematics and Informatics for Industry MII 2003.* Thessaloniki, Greece.

Meyer, U., & Wetzel, S. (2004, September 5-8). *On the impact of GSM encryption and man-in-the-middle attacks on the security of interoperating GSM/UMTS networks.* The 15ᵗʰ IEEE International Symposium on Personal, Indoor and Mobile Radio Communications (PIMRC 2004), Barcelona, Spain. Retrieved February 5, 2006, from http://www.cdc.informatik.tu-darmstadt.de/~umeyer/UliPIMRC04.pdf

Microsoft. (2006). *Network Security for the Windows Mobile Software Platform.* Microsoft White Paper. Retrieved July 17, 2006, from http://www.microsoft.com

MobileCloak™ Portal. Retrieved July 20, 2006, from http://www.mobilecloak.com/

Muller, T. (1999). *Bluetooth Security Architecture.* White Paper. Retrieved July 20, 2006, from http://www.bluetooth.com/Bluetooth/Apply/Technology/Research/Bluetooth_Security_Architecture.htm

Olzak, T. (2005). *Wireless Handheld Device Security.* Retrieved October 12, 2005, from http://www.securitydocs.com/pdf/3188.PDF

Open Mobile Alliance (2006). *WAP Forum.* Retrieved February 6, 2006, from http://www.wapforum.org/

PalmSource, Inc. (2006). *PalmSource portal.* Retrieved July 17, 2006, from http://www.palmsource.com.

Perelson, S., and Botha, R. (2004). *An Investigation Into Access Control for Mobile Devices.* In H. S. Venter (Ed.), J. H. P. Eloff (Ed.), L. Labuschagne (Ed.), M.M. Eloff (Ed.), ISSA 2004 Enabling Tomorrow Conference. *Peer-reviewed Proceedings of the ISSA 2004 Enabling Tomorrow Conference. Information Security South Africa* (ISSA).

Pulkkis, G., Grahn, K., Karlsson, J., Martikainen, M., & Daniel, D.E. (2005). Recent Developments in WLAN Security. In Pagani, M. (Ed.), *Mobile and Wireless Systems Beyond 3G: Managing New Business Opportunities.* USA: IRM Press.

Rankl, W., & Effing, W. (2003). *Smart Card Handbook* (3ʳᵈ ed). USA: John Wiley & Sons.

Rittinghouse, J.W., & Ransome, J.F. (2004). *Wireless Operational Security.* Amsterdam. Elsevier Digital Press.

Setec Portal. (2006). Retrieved February 5, 2006, from http://www.setec.fi

Shackman, M. (2005). *Platform Security: A Technical Overview.* Retrieved October 11, 2005, from http://www.symbian.com/developer/techlib/papers/plat_sec_tech_overview/platform_security_a_technical_overview_v1.1.pdf

Siezen, S. (2005). *Symbian OS Version 9.1, Product Description.* Retrieved July 20, 2006, from http://www.symbian.com/files/rx/file6965.pdf

Smulders, T. H. (2004). *Security threats of executing malicious applications on mobile phones.* Masters thesis. Technische Universiteit Eindhoven, Department of Mathematics and Computer Science, Netherlands. Retrieved July 20, 2006, from http://www.win.tue.nl/~ecss/internships/reports/TSmulders2004.pdf

Sun, J., Howie, D., Koivisto, A., & Sauvola, J. (2001). Design, implementation, and evaluation of Bluetooth security. In *Proceedings IEEE International Conference on Wireless LANs and Home Networks*, Singapore (pp. 121-130).

Symantec. (2005). *Wireless handheld and smartphone security.* Retrieved December 16, 2005, from http://enterprisesecurity.symantec.com/Products/products.cfm?MenuItemNo=2&productID=663&EID=0

Symantec Corporation. (2006). *Symantec mobile security for Symbian.* Retrieved January 15, 2006, from http://www.symantec.com/Products/enterprise?c=prodinfo&refId=921 and http://eval.veritas.com/mktginfo/enterprise/fact_sheets/ent-factsheet_mobile_security_for_symbian_04-2005.en-us.pdf

Symbian. (2006). *Symbian OS: The mobile operating system.* Retrieved January 26, 2006, from http://www.symbian.com

Symbian OS: Overview to Security (2006). Version 1.1, Retrieved January 26, 2006, from http://sw.nokia.com/id/5e713b29-fe0e-488d-8fc6-b4dd1950f3c2/Symbian_OS_Overview_To_Security_v1_1_en.pdf

Symbian OS Version 9.3 (2006). Retrieved July 20, 2006, from http://www.symbian.com/files/rx/file7999.pdf

Symbian Signed Portal. Retrieved January 30, 2006, from http://www.symbiansigned.com

Taylor, L., (2004-2005). *Handheld Security, Part I-V.* Retrieved October 9, 2005, from http://www.firewallguide.com/pda.htm

WEPCrack. Retrieved March 3, 2004, from http://webcrack.sf.net

Wi-Fi Alliance Portal. (2006). Retrieved February 5, 2006, from http://www.wi-fi.org

Ye, T. S. and Cheang, A.. (2005, September). *The Mobility Threat.* Retrieved December 18, 2005, from http://cio-asia.com/ShowPage.aspx?pagetype=2&articleid=2535&pubid=5&issueid=63

Yoshihisa, I., Miharu, S., Shihong, L., Masato, K. (2005, Oct 15-21). Face Recognition on Cellular Phone. Demo *Proceedings of the 10th IEEE International Conference on Computer Vision (ICCV2005)*, Beijing, China. Demo Nr 13.

APPENDIX A:
ADD-ON SECURITY SOFTWARE PRODUCTS FOR SYMBIAN OS

Authentication Solutions

Unauthorized access has not always been recognized as a security risk especially among private users, even though mobile devices such as smart phones are small, portable and easily lost or stolen. These features lead to a high risk of vital data loss. From this point of view it is easy to understand the necessity of authentication.

There are several authentication methods (Douglas, 2004, p. 13):

- Signature recognition based authentication
- Picture based password authentication
- Fingerprint authentication
- Voice authentication
- Face recognition authentication
- Smartcard based authentication
- Legacy host access

Overviews of authentication software for Symbian OS-based smart phones are presented in Tables A1-A3.

Signature Recognition Based Authentication

Signature recognition based authentication has several benefits. It provides high level of security and a signature is, from the user's point of view, a simple password which cannot be forgotten. The main problem is that the biographic signature is varying from time to time, which causes the possibility of access denial.

Communication Intelligence Corp. provides "Sign-On™ for Symbian OS" software, which enables device access through the use of dynamic biometric signature verification. Sign-On™ for Symbian OS is an authentication system, which verifies a real-time signature drawing. A signature is easy to recreate and test against an encrypted template of user data created during an enrollment phase. All signature data and templates are encrypted with the 3DES encryption algorithm (Communication Intelligence Corp., 2005).

There are not many available biometric signature authentication solutions for Symbian OS based mobile phones. However, Wacom, which is a Symbian Platinum Partner and Softpro have announced that they develop in co-operation a signature recognitions based authentication solution. Combination of Wacom's Penabled™ pen-based interface technology and Softpro's handwriting verification and authentication technology will deliver a complete solution for capturing and automatically authenticating a biometric signature to enable secure authorization of mobile transactions. The product consists of Wacom's display and pen and Softpro's signature verification technology. Penabled™ technology captures dynamic features of a signature, such as the speed of writing, pen pressure, letter shape and the writing rhythm. The signature is then managed and analyzed by Softpro's verification system (WACOM Technology Corp. 2005).

Available signature recognition based authentication software for Symbian based mobile devices are summarized in Table A1.

Fingerprint Based Authentication

Fingerprint based identification is the oldest method of the biometric techniques. The uniqueness of human fingerprint prevents effectively forgery attempts. The security level of fingerprint authentication is depending on such factors as the quality of scanning and the visual image recognition (ROSISTEM, 2005).

Users, who are interested in using biometric fingerprint authentication solution, should choose a Symbian OS based mobile phone with an integrated fingerprint sensor, because it is difficult to find separate solution including both software and hardware. Unfortunately most of them do not have integrated sensor for fingerprint authentication even nowadays. Several different effective fingerprint authentication sensors are presently available and these sensors could be applicable in Symbian OS based mobile phones. However, fingerprint sensors are mostly used in PCs and notebook computers. Fingerprint authentication to mobile phones will probably be more common in a near future.

Presently, for example Fujitsu produces mobile phones with an integrated biometric fingerprint sensor for secure access to the phone and to stored data. The FOMA F900i series of 3G FOMA i-mode® mobile phones uses a fingerprint sensor for access security and synchronization with a PC. See Table A2 (NTT DoCoMo Inc., 2004).

Picture Based Password Authentication

Picture based password authentication or graphical login software can as fingerprint authentication software be categorized as an unusual solution offered by few providers. Pointsec® for Symbian OS includes PicturePIN technology, which is a picture based authentication method. Presently the PicturePIN

Table A1. Signature recognition based authentication software

Company	Product Name	Feature / Function
Communication Intelligence Corp.	Sign-On™ for Symbian OS	Authentication system which verifies a real-time signature or repeatable drawing or annotation against an encrypted template of user data created during an enrollment phase. The software uses 3DES encryption.
WACOM Technology Corp. and Softpro in co-operation.	Wacom's Penabled™ and Softpro's handwriting verification	Biometric signature verification solution. The product is currently under development.

Table A2. Fingerprint authentication software

Company	Product Name	Feature / Function
Fujitsu	F900i	The mobile phone, F900i with an integrated fingerprint sensor to secure access and data on the device.

technology is patent pending. Pointsec allows users to select a password consisting of a combination of icons, see Figure A1. The positions of Pointsec's password icons change each time the mobile device is switched on. This feature makes it highly difficult for shoulder surfers to recognize passwords. Even the scratches on the screen could not reveal the passwords. See Table A3 (Pointsec Mobile Technologies, 2006).

Face Recognition Authentication

Face recognition authentication is based on captured images, which can be static digital pictures or dynamic pictures i.e. video clips. Authentication software measures and compares key features of the observed picture to the picture or series of pictures stored in the mobile device. Some systems are even

Table A3. Picture based password authentication software

Company	Product Name	Feature / Function
Pointsec Mobile Technologies	Pointsec® for Symbian OS	Encryption software for Symbian OS-based mobile phones, including picture based authentication functionality.

Figure A1. Pointsec's PicturePIN picture based authentication

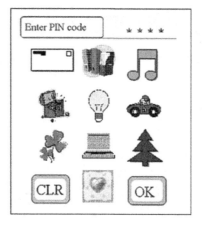

able to recognize a face from a crowd. The ability to recognize and verify the authenticity of the user through face recognition is meant to contribute to greater security and safety for mobile devices and the information they contain.

A face recognition authentication solution for Symbian OS based mobile phones is "OKAO Vision Face Recognition Sensor", provided by OMRON Corporation. This technology has been presented at the "Security Show Japan 2005". See Table A4. Camera equipped mobile phones can use "OKAO Vision Face Recognition Sensor" without additional hardware requirements. Users register their own face image to their phones by taking their own photo with the camera. There is no need to adjust the camera position when taking the photo. After the registration, the "OKAO Vision Face Recognition Sensor" will automatically detect the user and unlock the mobile phone. In addition the sensor will detect the owner automatically if the face is included in the photo. According to OMROM's tests, The registered mobile device owner is recognized with a probability of 99% or higher. This face recognition technology supports besides Symbian OS also BREW, embedded Linux, and ITRON OS (OMRON Corporation, 2005; Biometric Watch 2005).

Encryption Software

A simple method to protect sensitive data is encryption. Pointsec for Symbian OS provides a solution for real time encryption of data on Symbian OS based mobile devices, on different types of memory cards such as Memory Stick Duo, and on MMC (multimedia cards) without any user interaction. Pointsec for Symbian OS uses strong 128 bit AES encryption to protect information stored on the device and on memory cards with no noticeable reduction in speed or in other performance measures. Data can be accessed or decrypted only with proper authentication (Pointsec Mobile Technologies, 2006).

Also Ultimaco's SafeGuard PDA 4.0 provides an authentication and encryption solution for Symbian OS based mobile devices. This solution includes user authentication to the device by password, symbolic or numeric PIN. Forgotten passwords or PINs can be easily reset centrally via SafeGuard's emergency mechanism. SafeGuard PDA for Symbian support encryption for files, for directories, and for internal databases used in PIM (Personal Information Management) such as e-mails, SMS, tasks and events. Configuration, encryption and security rules can also be centrally managed by administrators. Currently SafeGuard PDA 4.0 supports Symbian Series 80 (Nokia Communicator 9300/9500), Symbian UIQ 2.1 (Sony-Ericsson P900/P910i) and Windows mobile 2003 devices (Utimaco Safeware AG., 2005).

Security software for Symbian OS based mobile devices mostly commercial. FreEPOC's FreeCrypt 1.02 and jRC4 software are examples of freeware for encryption purposes. Both security software solu-

Table A4. Face recognition authentication software

Company	Product Name	Feature / Function
OMRON Corporation	OKAO Vision Face Recognition Sensor	A face recognition authentication method. The system compares the captured image to the user's image stored in the mobile device.

Table A5. Encryption software

Company	Product Name	Feature / Function
Pointsec Mobile Technologies	Pointsec® for Symbian OS	Authentication and encryption software for Symbian OS based mobile phones.
Utimaco Safeware AG.	SafeGuard PDA 4.0	Authentication and encryption software for Symbian OS based mobile devices
FreEPOC	FreeCrypt 1.02	Freeware encryption software for Communicator 92xx, which uses RC4 algorithm.
FreEPOC	jRC4	Freeware encryption software for Symbian UIQ 1.01 (Sony Ericsson P800), which uses RC4 algorithm.

tions encrypt data with the RC4 algorithm. FreeCrypt is available for Nokia Communicator 92xx and jRC4 for Symbian UIQ 1.01 (for example Sony Ericsson P800) mobile devices (FreEPOC, 2006).

Available encryption software for Symbian based mobile devices is summarized in Table A5.

Anti-Virus and Firewall Software

F-Secure Mobile Anti-Virus™ protects mobile devices against harmful content, for example viruses, worms, and Trojans. The software has been available for most Symbian Series 60, 80 and 90 mobile devices. To prevent infection all files are scanned automatically and transparently during modification, synchronization or transference of data, without any need of user intervention. Also all files on memory cards are automatically scanned. When an infected file is detected, the file is immediately quarantined to protect all other data in the system. In addition, the virus recognition database in the mobile devices is automatically updated over a secure HTTPS connection or with SMS messages. The software supports automatic detection of data connections (for example GPRS, WLAN, UMTS) for updates.

F-Secure recently announced 'F-Secure Mobile Security for Symbian Series 80', a combination of integrated anti-virus functionality and a firewall (F-Secure Corporation, 2005).

Symantec provides solutions with integrated anti-virus and firewall capabilities, called Symantec™ Mobile Security Corporate Edition for Symbian. This software is available for Symbian OS Series 60 and 80. The software has almost the same functionality as F-Secure's Mobile Security for Symbian. The LiveUpdate Wireless feature from Symantec™ Mobile Security Corporate Edition for Symbian enables users to download virus definitions and software updates directly to their mobile device via an available wireless Internet connection. The key feature of this version is centralized management via a third-party mobile device. This functionality enables administrators to configure, lock and enforce security policies either remotely or locally (Symantec Corporation, 2006).

Available anti-virus and firewall software for Symbian based mobile devices is summarized in Table A6.

VPN (Virtual Private Network) Software

Transmitting data over wireless networks causes a remarkable security risk, because the transmitted data over air can be easily exploited by outsiders. Secure VPNs use cryptographic tunneling protocols to ensure sender authentication, as well as the confidentially and integrity of data.

In an IPSEC VPN environment a mobile device requires preinstalled VPN client software to authenticate and connect to the VPN gateway. When the application on the user's mobile device attempts to communicate, the network traffic from these requests is tunneled through the VPN connection

Nokia Mobile VPN is an example of a third party VPN solution for Symbian devices. The components of Nokia Mobile VPN include Nokia Mobile VPN Client and Nokia Security Service Manager (SSM). Nokia Mobile VPN Client is an IPSec based VPN application. It allows a user to authenticate and connect to an enterprise VPN and as a result data can be securely transferred between the mobile client and the VPN network. Key features of the Nokia Mobile VPN Client are:

- Provides a user the possibility to securely access any network services in a remote network
- Support for Nokia Series 60 and Series 80 Symbian smart phones
- Supports legacy and PKI based authentication
- DES (Data Encryption Standard), 3DES, and AES for encryption
- SHA-1 (Secure Hash Algorithm 1) and MD5 (Message Digest 5) for data integrity
- Uses Nokia SSM for automatic provisioning of VPN settings, policy updates, and certificate enrollment

The Nokia SSM is the core of a scalable mobile VPN solution. It extends VPN to the mobile domain using the Nokia Mobile VPN Clients and supported gateways. Key features of the Nokia SSM include:

- The cornerstone for rapid, large scale Mobile VPN deployments
- Integrates with management systems, VPN policy, and external authentication servers
- Enables trust creation between a user and a corporate infrastructure
- Provides secure provisioning of VPN configuration automatically over the air
- Provides PKI services for mobile devices (Nokia, 2006)

Table A6. Anti-virus & firewall software

Company	Product Name	Feature / Function
F-Secure Corporation	Anti-Virus™	Anti-virus software for Symbian Series 60, 80 and 90.
F-Secure Corporation	F-Secure Mobile Security for Symbian Series 80	Anti-virus and firewall software for Symbian Series 80.
Symantec Corporation	Symantec™ Mobile Security Corporate Edition for Symbian	Anti-virus and firewall software for Symbian Series 60 and 80.

Compared to the more common VPN, which uses IPSec technology, the modern VPN with SSL (secure sockets layer) cryptographic protocol makes it easier for administrators and users to set-up and manage secure communication on the Internet. SSL VPN uses SSL technology to enable secure remote access. The benefit of using SSL VPN instead of IPSec VPN is that users do not need any VPN client software installed on the mobile device. Users can also quickly and easily connect to the SSL VPN gateway via a web browser and on any compatible device or computer. SSL protocol is widely supported on most Web browsers (Ferraro, 2003; WIKIPEDIA, 2005).

Intoto's iGateway SSL-VPN allows users to access enterprise Intranet services securely from mobile devices. iGateway SSL-VPN makes it possible for users to create a secure encrypted virtual tunnel from any standard web browser. Users of iGateway SSL-VPN can choose authentication methods according to their preferences from following alternatives: RADIUS (Remote Authentication Dial In User Service), LDAP (Lightweight Directory Access Protocol), Active Directory, Windows NTLM (NT LAN Manager) and digital certificates. The software provides end-point security controls i.e. features such as: filtering, anti-virus, personal firewall, registry, file-system entries and browser traces removal, etc. (Intoto Inc., 2005; ZDNet India News, 2005).

Available VPN software for Symbian based mobile devices is summarized in Table A7.

Forensic Analysis Software

While a large variety of forensic analysis software is available for personal computers, the range of solutions is much more limited for mobile devices, especially for Symbian OS based mobile devices. The problem is not only fewer software solution for Symbian OS, but also that available solutions operate only in most common series of Symbian OS based mobile devices.

Forensic analysis software has three main functionalities: acquisition, examination and reporting. Only available solutions have all these functionalities. Often several software solutions must be acquired for a full forensic examination process. The forensic analysis software need full access to a mobile device in order to start acquisition of data. If the examined mobile device is protected with some authentication method, then cracking software is needed.

Oxygen Software delivers software for police departments, law enforcement units and all government services for investigation purposes. The Oxygen Phone Manager II (Forensic version) secures phone data to remain unchanged during extraction and exporting. This forensic version allows users to read data from mobile phone and export this data in any supported formats (Oxygen Software, 2006).

Table A7. VPN software

Company	Product Name	Feature / Function
Nokia	Nokia Mobile VPN	Nokia Mobile VPN Client is an IPSec based VPN application for Symbian devices.
Intoto Inc	iGateway SSL-VPN	SSL VPN solution, which enables users to create a secure encrypted virtual tunnel from any standard web browser.

Paraben Corporation has developed tools to assist law enforcement, corporate security and digital investigators. Paraben's PDA Seizure offers forensic analysis tools for Symbian OS, Windows CE/Pocket PC, Windows Mobile, and RIM BlackBerry. The version for Symbian OS allows forensic examiners to acquire, examine and analyze data. Both physical and logical acquisition of data is possible. Physical acquisition means complete bit-by-bit copying from physical storage, for example from a disk drive. Logical acquisition means exact copying of logical storage objects, i.e., files and folders. PDA Seizure has a built-in searching function on acquired data and also a book-marking function to help users to organize data. Moreover, the tool supports HTML reporting on findings.

Paraben Corporation provides another software solution, Cell Seizure, for forensic data acquisition. A **forensic acquisition** is carried out on all data stored on **GSM SIM cards** including deleted data (Paraben Corporation, 2006; Ayers & Jansen, 2004, p.14).

Available forensic analysis software for Symbian based mobile devices is summarized in Table A8.

Multifunctional Software

Multifunctional software is developed to solve comprehensively all security needs of mobile devices. From an administrators point of view such software is appealing, since a lot of resources can be saved in terms of effective central administration.

Table A8. Forensic analysis software

Company	Product Name	Feature / Function
Oxygen Software	The Oxygen Phone Manager II (Forensic version)	Solutions for police departments, law enforcement units and all government services for investigation purposes. The software keeps phone data unchanged during extraction and exporting.
Paraben Corporation	PDA Seizure	Tools to assist law enforcement, corporate security and digital investigators. The software allows forensic examiners to acquire, examine and analyze data.
Paraben Corporation	Cell Seizure	Carries out forensic acquisition on all data stored on GSM SIM Cards including deleted data.

The key function of Pointsec® for Symbian OS software is encryption. This feature ensures high security level, because all data can be automatically and immediately encrypted before being stored or transferred and decrypted automatically by an authenticated user. Recipients of encrypted data files do not need the same kind of software to open the encrypted data. Recipients can open files with a valid password. Pointsec® for Symbian OS encrypts automatically all data stored on 'Pointsec for Symbian OS' protected devices and on memory cards, such as Memory Stick Duo and MMC (Multimedia Cards) without any user interaction.

Trust Digital 2005 encrypts data on Symbian OS based mobile devices and PDA devices. Before data can be decrypted, users are required to authenticate themselves to the devices. Data can be encrypted based on administrator and user preferences.

Both Pointsec® for Symbian OS software uses the Advanced Encryption Standard (AES) algorithm, the US government approved cryptographic standard, based on the "Rijndael" algorithm with a 128-bit encryption key to encrypt data. Trust Digital 2005 provides six different selectable encryption algorithms, including the Advanced Encryption Standard (AES). In addition Trust Digital 2005 uses MD5 hash algorithm to protect passwords stored on the device.

One of the most important features of multifunctional software is the central management possibility. Pointsec® for Symbian OS enables administrators to create, deploy and manage their organization's security policy for mobile devices from one central location. The central management system ensures that the security policy is enforced. End-users cannot uninstall the software from their mobile devices. Trust Digital 2005 can be centrally managed from a "Policy Editor" or from a "Trusted Mobility Server", which allows administrators to create, push and manage a security policy for each device. The access policies for the device can also be managed.

Trust Digital 2005 together with Encryption Plus products makes a powerful combination, which provides end-to-end data access control and encryption.

Pointsec for Symbian OS enables users to securely regain access via "Remote Help", when a PIN or a password is forgotten. The number of failed authentication attempts is restricted and access to the

Table A9. Multifunctional software

Features / Function	Company: Pointsec Product: Pointsec® for Symbian OS	Company: GuardianEdge Technologies Product: Trust Digital 2005
Central Administration	X	X
Remote Help	X	
FIPS 140-2 certified, AES algorithm with 128 bit encryption key	X	X
Automatic and immediate encryption	X	X
Memory card encryption	X	X
Picture-based passwords authentication	X	
Alphanumeric password authentication	X	X
End-to-end data access control		X

mobile device is denied without authentication. Administrators can assist users via a secure challenge/response procedure, which helps user to regain access to the device and resets the PIN or password (Pointsec Mobile Technologies, 2006; GuardianEdge Technologies, 2005).

Two multifunctional security software solutions for Symbian based mobile devices are compared in Table A9.

REFERENCES

Ayers, R., & Jansen, W. (2004). PDA forensic tools: An overview and analysis. Retrieved July 6, 2005, from http://csrc.nist.gov/publications/nistir/nistir-7100-PDAForensics.pdf

Biometric Watch. (2005). Face recognition, coming to a cell phone or PDA near you. Retrieved January 6, 2006, from http://www.biometricwatch.com/BW_20_issue/BW_20.htm

Communication Intelligence Corp. (2005). Sign-On™ True Verification comes to the handheld. Retrieved February 3, 2006, from http://www.cic.com/products/signon/

Ferraro, C. I. (2003). Choosing between IPSec and SSL VPNs. Retrieved January 16, 2006, from http://searchsecurity.techtarget.com/qna/0,289202,sid14_gci940324,00.html

F-Secure Corporation. (2005). F-Secure mobile security for Series 80. Retrieved January 15, 2006, from http://www.f-secure.com/download-purchase/manuals/docs/manual/fsmavs80/avfws80.pdf

FreEPOC. (2006), FreEPOC's software. Retrieved February 2, 2006, from http://www.freepoc.org/software.php

GuardianEdge Technologies. (2005). Trust digital 2005. Retrieved February 4, 2006, from http://www.guardianedge.com/products/PDASecure/index.html

Nokia. (2006). Nokia mobile VPN. Retrieved January 20, 2006, from http://www.europe.nokia.com/nokia/0,0,77172,0.html

NTT DoCoMo, Inc. (2004). NTT DoCoMo to market F900i, first model of 3G FOMA 900i series. Retrieved January 3, 2006, from http://www.nttdocomo.com/presscenter/pressreleases/press/pressrelease.html?param[no]=415

OMRON Corporation. Face recognition sensor for mobile phone. Retrieved January 5, 2006, from http://www.omron.com/ecb/products/mobile/okao.html

Oxygen Software. (2006), Oxygen phone manager II for Symbian OS phones. Retrieved January 22, 2006, from http://www.oxygensoftware.com/en/products/

Paraben Corporation. (2006), Handheld digital forensics. Retrieved January 22, 2006, from http://www.paraben-forensics.com/handheld_forensics.html

Pointsec Mobile Technologies. (2006). Pointsec® for Symbian OS. Retrieved January 10, 2006, from http://www.pointsec.com/_file/SymbianOS_LTR_72dpi_ENG_v0506.pdf

ROSISTEM. (2005). Biometric education » Fingerprint. Retrieved January 19, 2006, from http://www.barcode.ro/tutorials/biometrics/fingerprint.html

Symantec Corporation. (2006). Symantec mobile security for Symbian. Retrieved January 15, 2006, from http://www.symantec.com/Products/enterprise?c=prodinfo&refId=921

Utimaco Safeware AG. (2005). [SafeGuard® PDA] enterprise edition. Retrieved January 12, 2006, from http://www.utimaco.com/content_pdf/SG_PDA_40_en.pdf

WACOM Technology Corp. (2004). Softpro joins Wacom's Dynamic signature initiative to deliver secure mobile commerce. Retrieved January 20, 2006 from http://www.wacom-components.com/english/news_and_events/nw0021.asp

Wikipedia. (2005), Secure sockets layer (SSL) and transport layer security (TLS). Retrieved January 16, 2006, from http://en.wikipedia.org/wiki/Secure_Sockets_Layer

ZDNet India News. (2005), Intoto introduces multi-service security software. Retrieved January 21, 2006, from http://www.zdnetindia.com/news/pr/stories/121012.html

APPENDIX B: SECURITY SOFTWARE PERFORMANCE MEASUREMENTS FOR SYMBIAN OS

This case study presents performance measurements for the security software Pointsec for Symbian OS. The purpose was to measure the influence of Pointsec on data communication performance of Symbian OS. Pointsec is presented in more detail in the section Add-on Security Software. According to Pointsec Mobile Technologies, the Pointsec security software should not reduce speed or other performance measures even when the strong 128-bit AES encryption is used to protect the information in the device and in memory cards.

Measurements

However, security solutions may reduce data communication performance measures of mobile operating systems, such as download speed and connection times. These performance measures were measured for a Pointsec security software installation in a Nokia Communicator 9500 for:

- Downloading a 4.92 MB file
- Connection to an e-mail server (penti.arcada.fi) with imaps based e-mail client software
- Connection to a www site (www.nokia.com)
- Connection to a ssh server (penti.arcada.fi) with a putty ssh client

All four performance measures were measured six times with and without installed Pointsec security software for two different access network types, WLAN and GPRS. The network bandwidths were 11 Mbit/s for the WLAN and 56 Kbit/s for GPRS. Measurement results are presented in Tables B1 through B4.

Table B1. Download speed measurements (download times for a 4.92 MB file)

With "Pointsec for Symbian OS"		Without "Pointsec for Symbian OS"	
WLAN (11 Mbit/s)	*GPRS (56 Kbit/s)*	*WLAN (11 Mbit/s)*	*GPRS (56 Kbit/s)*
1 min	16 min 33 s	59.62 s	21 min 1 s
57 s	20 min 54 s	58.28 s	19 min 52 s
59 s	18 min 16 s	59.14 s	18 min 2 s
1 min 2 s	19 min 25 s	1.0 min	18 min 42 s
1min 3 s	20 min 40 s	59.61 s	18 min 14 s
59.2 s	19 min 48 s	1 min 1 s	19 min 3 s
Average 60.03 s	**Average** 19 min 16 s	**Average** 59.61 s	**Average** 19 min 9 s
Standard Deviation 2.174093 s	Standard Deviation 97.912206 s	Standard Deviation 3.253739 s	Standard Deviation 67.337954 s
		Average +0.42 s with Pointsec	**Average +7 s** with Pointsec

Usefulness of Measurement Results

Condition cannot be assumed to be equal for different measurements since the download speed and connection times were measured for data communication through the public Internet. The utilization of Internet during a measurement session is not deterministic. Measurement results have been considered to be useful if standard deviation is less than 10% of the calculated average for measurements with the same mobile device configuration. Standard deviation exceeded 10% of calculated average only in one measurement case, GPRS connection to an e-mail server without Pointsec security software installed, being about 15% of calculated average; see Table B2.

Table B2. Connection time measurements (to mailbox on e-mail server)

With "Pointsec for Symbian OS"		Without "Pointsec for Symbian OS"	
WLAN (11 Mbit/s)	*GPRS (56 Kbit/s)*	*WLAN (11 Mbit/s)*	*GPRS (56 Kbit/s)*
31.62 s	36.96 s	24.29 s	35.91 s
32.23 s	40.70 s	25.16 s	32.07 s
32.17 s	37.11 s	26.21 s	33.88 s
31.86 s	38.42 s	25.34 s	31.30 s
31.19 s	39.71 s	25.45 s	43.76 s
32.42 s	42.51 s	25.46 s	30.14 s
Average 31.915 s	**Average** 39.235 s	**Average** 25.31833 s	**Average** 34.51 s
Standard deviation 0.454962 s	Standard deviation 2.165777 s	Standard deviation 0.618948 s	Standard deviation 4.965360 s
		Average +6.60 s with Pointsec	**Average +4.72 s** with Pointsec

Measured Degradation of Data Communication Performance Caused by Pointsec

The influence of Pointsec was considered to be noticeable if the intervals defined by measured average and standard deviation do not overlap with and without Pointsec for otherwise the same mobile device configuration. Noticeable performance degradation was measured only for connection time to a Web site, about twice as long for a GPRS connection and about 17 % longer for a WLAN connection; see Table B3. However, the influence of the traffic load in Internet and the load on the selected web server during carried-out performance measurements is unfortunately unknown.

The measurements can thus be considered to support the view of the provider of Pointsec security software, that the performance degradation from this security software is insignificant on a Symbian device; see Table B4.

Table B3. Connection time measurements (Web site www.nokia.fi)

With "Pointsec for Symbian OS"		Without "Pointsec for Symbian OS"	
WLAN (11 Mbit/s)	*GPRS (56 Kbit/s)*	*WLAN (11 Mbit/s)*	*GPRS (56 Kbit/s)*
22.68 s	58.68 s	21.55 s	27.17 s
26.70 s	57.65 s	22.27 s	28.98 s
27.62 s	59.06 s	23.24 s	29.20 s
31.47 s	56.06 s	24.58 s	29.76 s
27.87 s	59.03 s	22.94 s	30.43 s
25.14 s	58.23 s	23.31 s	30.11 s
Average 26.91333 s	**Average** 58.11833 s	**Average** 22.98167 s	**Average** 29.275 s
Standard deviation 2.942419 s	Standard deviation 1.140341 s	Standard deviation 1.028308 s	Standard deviation 1.165345 s
		Average + **4.93 s** with Pointsec	**Average** +**28.84 s** with Pointsec

Table B4. Connection time measurements (to a SSH server)

With "Pointsec for Symbian OS"		Without "Pointsec for Symbian OS"	
WLAN (11 Mbit/s)	*GPRS (56 Kbit/s)*	*WLAN (11 Mbit/s)*	*GPRS (56 Kbit/s)*
<1 s	4.85 s	<1 s	4.9 s
<1 s	4.65 s	<1 s	4.71 s
<1 s	4.62 s	<1 s	4.13 s
<1 s	4.79 s	<1 s	4.61 s
<1 s	4.86 s	<1 s	4.42 s
<1 s	4.80 s	<1 s	4.52 s
Average <1 s	**Average** 4.761667 s	**Average** <1 s	**Average** 4.548333 s
Standard deviation < 1 s	Standard deviation 0.102258s	Standard deviation <1 s	Standard deviation 0.263015 s
		Average +**0.21 s** with Pointsec	

Chapter IV
Wireless Local Area
Network Security

Michéle Germain
ComXper, France

Alexis Ferrero
RTL, France

Jouni Karvo
TKK, Finland

ABSTRACT

Using WLAN networks in enterprises has become a popular method for providing connectivity. We present the security threats of WLAN networks, and the basic mechanisms for protecting the network. We also give some advice on avoiding the threats.

INTRODUCTION

The ease of deploying wireless local area network (WLAN) systems and the abundance of affordable IEEE 802.11 WLAN-based products on the market makes the idea of a wireless office luring. Offices using laptops as workstations can benefit from the ease of bringing a laptop to the meeting and preserving network connectivity. The WLAN connectivity can also be used for salesmen and executives who are on a tour to communicate with the office when residing within hot-spot areas. This ease and flexibility comes with a price–wireless local area networks are inherently insecure when compared to the wired networks.

There are various applications of wireless networks. The first of them is the hot spot, which provides in a public (or private) place, an open radio infrastructure that allows everyone to get an Internet connection or to join the Intranet of his enterprise. A second application is the enterprise WLAN, which completes or replaces a legacy wired network. This has also place in the SoHo or domestic environment for sharing an ADSL connection between several users. WLAN provide also nice network possibility in areas where cabling is impossible or restricted. A last case is the constitution of wireless bridges between nets or subnets.

Such wireless networks present specific vulnerabilities due to the radio media and are subject to specific threats from the hackers. The object of this paper is to identify them and to explain how to avoid them.

The WLAN connections are based on a radio connection in unlicensed 2.4 or 5GHz radio band, depending of the WLAN type. The radio waves broadcast, and most antennae of a typical WLAN equipment are not designed to produce directed radio beams, but they transmit freely to all directions. Thus, in addition to the intended receiver, any other receiver that is close enough can receive the signal. This is fundamentally different from the wired networks, such as Ethernet, where in order to listen to the traffic, one needs to get physical access to the networking equipment, or at least cabling.

The transmission for typical WLAN equipment ranges up to the order of 50 m. Even if the range is short, low-level signal can be received at a longer distances, of even some kilometres, using illicit antennae and high sensitivity receivers. Walls, ceilings and other such constructions reduce the transmission ranges significantly–depending on the materials that are on the radio signal's way.

Thus, there are several concerns on the accessibility of the radio signal. First, the signal may easily be heard outside the premises of the office. Second, the guests visiting the offices are often able to carry in a laptop, thus being able to listen and even connect to the company's network without being suspicious, unless the network is properly protected.

The security of WLAN is a major concern of Network Administrators, on the one hand because

multiple (true or false) weaknesses have been reported and amplified by the papers and on the other hand because it is a new technology with multiple new aspects to take in consideration. From the network administrator's point of view, it is not conceivable to deploy a radio network in complement of his existing network if it introduces vulnerability. To avoid this, standardisation bodies and forums, in particular the IEEE, as well as manufacturers, have worked to develop security mechanisms well suited to this kind of networks. This chapter describes the security features of IEEE 802.11 wireless local area networks, and shows their weaknesses. We present the associated threats with some practical defence strategies.

Scope

This chapter deals with wireless LAN's built on wired infrastructures that support one or more radio bases, so-named "access points" (AP). The infrastructure may also support fixed stations. Mobile stations take service from the access points (see Figure 1).

The following is mainly for Wi-Fi technology based on the 801.11 standard of the IEEE, which is presently the most commonly used one. Other technologies will be mentioned later. Wi-Fi is an interoperability label for 802.11 equipment, delivered by the Wi-Fi Alliance (previously WECA).

Ad-hoc networks that operate without any kind of infrastructure and in which routing is performed by the mobile stations (that act both as routers and as terminals) are not taken into consideration here.

BACKGROUND

IEEE 802.11 wireless LAN networks come in many varieties. The original standard, IEEE 802.11 from 1997 specifies data rates of 1 to 2 megabits per second and has radio and infrared

Figure 1. General WLAN architecture

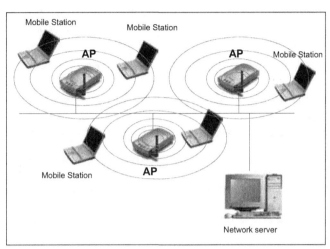

connectivity as options. The standard includes authentication and association procedures, and support for privacy. Several standard versions have since emerged, each pushing the limits in data rates (11Mbps for 802.11b, 54 Mbps for 802.11a and 802.11g, all using radio transmission for communications) or new features for QoS (802.11e), network management (802.11h) or security features (802.11i). In common parlance, all the different versions are just called IEEE 802.11 wireless local area network.

There are also other local area network technologies, such as the ETSI HiperLAN, but the IEEE 802.11 WLAN products have an overwhelming market position, and is a de-facto standard. The WLAN network equipment is common and cheap, and while the cellular networks have also security holes that can be misused, the abundance of available radio equipment for WLAN networks makes them much more vulnerable to attacks.

There can be different objectives for securing a company's WLAN network, such as:

- Preventing unauthorized use. For example, preventing sending mass e-mail from the company's network or preventing attempts

to attack other institution's computer infrastructure from the company's network.

- Protecting the company's sensitive information. For example, protecting industrial property rights, tender documents, etc.

Each of these objectives may require different priorities for security measures.

The Threats

The main threats to WLAN networks are

- **Radio waves:** The major threats are relative to the radio aspect, since radio waves broadcast and respect neither walls nor other limit. Without precaution, a hacker can accede to a network from the street. Another threat comes from the user who, when using a laptop in a public place is exposed to inquisitive glances, or worse, exposed to spurious connections issued from neighbouring hackers. In such a wild environment, encryption and authentication have a major importance.

- **Denial of service (DoS):** The purpose is to make the network ineffective. Protections do not exist but it is possible to apply local corrective actions, eventually with the help of tools.

- ○ **Jamming:** It is relatively easy to jam a radio network, using a high power emitter on the same frequency. This attack does not present any risk of intrusion but the network becomes unusable.
- ○ **Rush access:** This consists to overload the network with malicious connection requests. Tools are able to detect this kind of traffic and to provide information to help the network administrator to identify and locate the origin.
- ○ **Spoofed de-authentication frames:** The purpose is to send malicious frames that force the de-authentication of a station and to make it unable to connect again. A variant is to broadcast such frames in order to attack any mobile station in range.
- **Intrusions:** In opposition with the DoS, hacker's purpose is get access to the network, may be just to get a free Internet connection or worse, to read–or modify–the information stored in the network stations.
  - ○ **Client intrusion:** This is the most common attack that aims to intrude the network via a client station. Protections are the same as for wired networks (firewall).
  - ○ **Network intrusion:** This is the most critical attack that aims to take the control of network resources of the enterprise. Wi-Fi dedicated intrusion detection systems (IDS) are efficient against such attacks.
- **Falsification of access points:** With these attacks, the hacker uses false access points to fetch the traffic on the network. Such attacks are discovered by detecting abnormal radio transmission in unexpected areas.
  - ○ **Fake AP:** The hacker's station presents the characteristics of a network access

point, using appropriate software applications. From his laptop, the hacker can intercept user's connections for man in the middle attacks, can catch passwords on a Web page identical to the one of the authentication server, or simply can get into a station to read or modify station data.

- ○ **Rogue AP:** This attack consists of connecting a pirate access point on the network infrastructure. This AP broadcasts in the area where the hacker stays. Naturally, this attack needs some complicity within the enterprise, but it may be innocently provoked by an employee who installs by him- or herself an AP in his or her office, just for improving the working environment. These AP are particularly dangerous because they open the enterprise network (that may be a wired one) to the Wi-Fi world, generally with poor protections.
- ○ **Inversed honey pot:** In the network area, the hacker installs an AP that transmits with a high radio level and that appears like a network AP. By this means, the hacker observes the connection sequence and reproduces it for a man in the middle attack.
- **Spoofing:** The purpose is to take the place of a mobile station in order to accede to network services. The attack is achieved using the MAC address of a mobile station. It could be the consequence of a Fake AP attack.
- **Probing and network discovery:** This is the first step of an attack: to know that a network exists before attacking it.

Operations of wardriving are done by hackers that move (in a car, by foot, by plane) using a radio mobile station to locate radio networks. Using a GPS receptor improves the localisation of detected networks. Wardriving software's are available from the Internet and the equipment is easy to get or to do (some cookies boxes provide excellent antennas). Warchalking consists of tagging the place of available networks (may be with a chalk).

Some tools are able to detect wardriving attacks.

- **Sensible network information fetching:** This concerns the information that the hacker needs to be able to accede to the attacked network and the information that constitutes the enterprise property.
  - ○ **Intrusion by sniffing:** This attack is the same as for an ethernet network. It requires a radio sniffer that intercepts session opening messages and catches login/password. As hackers just receive and never transmit, the operation is undetectable. After, a hacker accedes to the network as any authorised user and can send false commands and viruses. A characteristic of this attack is that it can be managed far from the

enterprise, for example on the laptop of an employee that joins his or her Intranet from an airport hot spot.
  - ○ **Eavesdropping:** This consists of observing the traffic on the network. The main protection against eavesdropping is encryption.
- **Rebound attack:** In this case, the hacker uses the ad-hoc networking facility to accede to the network via an authorised mobile station. It has just to set up an ad-hoc connection with the attacked station. The attacked station is mobile or fixed with the Wi-Fi option enabled (see Figure 2).

It is recommended to disable the Wi-Fi option on mobile stations when unused and to forbid ad-hoc connections.

Basic Defences

Naturally, most of security protections of wired networks can be applied to wireless networks. However, as seen before, some specific attacks are due to the radio aspect and need adapted tools and defences described hereafter.

Figure 2. Rebound attack

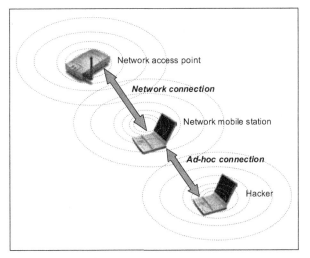

- **Network Monitoring:** A good defence is to observe the network in order to be informed if "something strange" occurs.
  - ° **The IDS:** An intrusion detection system (IDS) especially designed for wireless, is generally used against network intrusions. An IDS correlates several suspect events, and tries to determine if they could be due to an intrusion. The IDS is integrated in the Wi-Fi switch and works in real time. It monitors all exchanges and Wi-Fi flows in order to detect as soon as possible any risk or abnormal event. In case of detection, it alerts the network administrator.

    Enhanced systems are able to detect weak WEP, Rogue AP's and wireless bridges. They can also locate devices responsible of DoS attacks and detect spoofing or ASLEAP (tool used to crack LEAP) attacks. These functions are based on information hold by the Wi-Fi switch, enhanced by each occurring event: connection, authentication, roaming or modification of equipment characteristics.

  - ° **Traffic monitoring:** A particularly efficient prevention against spoofing is to observe in permanence the Wi-Fi traffic and the traffic on the wired network in order to detect any inconsistent situation. The goal is to detect an unforeseen device–access point or station–or the duplication of a station or access point, or the changing of location of an access point. To do that, a solution is to check that the traffic generated by well-known Wi-Fi stations goes through the appropriate LAN's. Another mean is joining the indication of radio link level to the MAC address of each mobile station: if a MAC address appears at a same time with two different levels, the mobile is

quarantined and an alert is sent to the network administrator.

Devices that supervise communication flows check that communications issued from AP do not reach the network by an illicit circuit–typically a Rogue AP. Conversely, they check that these communications appear on the wired network after having crossed the protection equipment (firewall or switch) and are not diverted to a pirate network via a Fake AP.

  - ° **Radio monitoring:** Wi-Fi working mode imposes that an AP can just operate on the radio channel at which it has been attached and, consequently, it cannot supervise other channels. To do that, passive monitoring access points, in reception only, scan all radio channels in order to check the correct operation of neighbouring access points. Monitoring AP's are able to detect and monitor low-level signals issued from relatively far devices. Thus, they cover a larger range than active AP's. The traffic of monitoring AP is carried to the switch that checks that no mobile station is connected to an unreferenced AP.

    Radio monitoring ensures also the protection of wired networks against illicit radio communications (Rogue AP). In this case, the Network Administrator deploys a radio network just to detect illicit Wi-Fi transmissions.

  - ° **Forced detachment:** A frequently used defence is to force the detachment of suspect stations or stations attached to a suspect AP. The Wi-Fi network is not reachable again by pirate stations that are unable to set up a complete connection. This feature brings an efficient protection but the problem must be definitively solved by an intervention on the station or AP origin of the danger. Tools facilitate the localisation of involved devices.

- ○ **Audit of radio coverage:** When installing the access points, it is important to check that the radio coverage does not spread in a long range from the required area, even if this does not completely prevent from hackers who use amplifiers that provide them radio signal far beyond the nominal coverage. Adequate location of access points and antennas provides an optimal coverage. This coverage must be periodically checked afterwards, to make sure that no pirate access point has been added to the network (Rogue AP). This precaution is also for wired networks. Some users having had the surprise to discover a radio coverage that they never installed.

- • **Network Engineering**
  - ○ **The switch:** If the access points are connected on a hub and not on a switch, any data directed to any fixed or mobile station is broadcasted on the radio network and thus, can be intercepted by a sniffer. It is strongly recommended to deploy WLAN's on switches instead of hubs and to control the traffic between the mobile stations and the wired network.

    There are two types of WLAN architectures:
    - ▪ The first one is based on a standard switch. Access points integrate radio networking and security functions. The switch manages both fixed and mobile stations.
    - ▪ The second one is based on a WLAN-dedicated switch that manages radio, networking and security functions. Access points

are used just as emitters/receptors. This second configuration has a better resistance against Rogue-AP attacks, because adding an AP needs an intervention on the switch.

Note that ideally the WLAN switch should manage several queues to provide flow control with QoS, typically for the transmission of voice over IP.

- ○ **Firewall:** As for wired networks, the best protection is to install a firewall between the WLAN and the wired network. When present, it is integrated in the WLAN switch. This firewall shall manage protections at addressing level, provide filters, log connections, manage access control list (ACL) used for access filtering, monitor the connections (« stateful » characteristic), in order to maintain the same security level as on a wired network. All devices in relation with the wireless network (in and out of the enterprise) shall be considered as insecurity points. They must be installed in a DMZ and VPN authentication and encryption mechanisms activated.

- ○ **VLAN:** A precaution is to split the network in order to isolate strategic data from the radio network. For that, the WLAN is deployed on a dedicated virtual LAN (VLAN) structure. The network may contain several VLAN's, each of them associated to a WLAN subnet with its own SSID.

  Radio subnets are installed in the De-Militarized Zone (DMZ) of a firewall that controls the transactions between the radio network and the wired network.

  It is strongly recommended to connect all VLAN's on the WLAN switch, even if no traffic has to transit through the switch. By this means, the switch locates all devices, updates its network description database and detects abnormal flow or equipment on a segment where it should not appear.

- **Honey pot:** The WLAN configuration may integrate honey pots made by access points with a poor protection that can just give access to insignificant data. They will attract hackers and keep them out of the protected network.
- **VPN:** The Virtual Private Network (VPN) provides a ciphered tunnel that constitutes an efficient protection, in particular for users in unsecured areas, like public hot spots. A VPN protects the link in the same way as done for a wired nomad station via a telephone modem. The VPN ensures encryption and mutual authentication and protects the traffic between the client station and the Wi-Fi switch. This last one manages the end point of all clients VPN and delivers a safe traffic to the LAN at which it is connected.

- **Mobile station configuration**
  - **Forbid « ad hoc » networking:** Mobile stations, as well as fixed ones equipped with Wi-Fi option, shall be configured for rejecting ad-hoc connections, that is, forbid direct connections that do not go through a network access point. This prevents from hackers who would try a rebound attack. This is a major precaution for users who are used to join their enterprise from a public hot spot. Fixed stations are invited to disable their Wi-Fi option when unused.
  - **Firewall:** It is strongly recommended to use a personal firewall on nomad stations in order to filter unexpected input accesses and to limit output connections.

- **Radio throughput control:** This is a usual protection against Fake AP's that are located at some distance from the enterprise and thus are received with a low radio level (and consequently transmit with a low bitrate). It consists to forbid mobile stations to connect under a given bitrate (i.e., 1 or 2 Mbps), because it is a priori inconsistent with network engineering design.

- **Radio defences**
  - **Lures:** This kind of defence, specific to Wi-Fi networks, is a reaction against Wardriving (« Fake AP » of Black Alchimy). This consists to broadcast a large number of false frames with random SSID's (network identifiers), MAC addresses and channel numbers. Wardrivers detect a vast of networks and are unable to find the right one.

- **Security at application level:** An application software supports the security of carried data without having to protect the association between the mobile station and the access point. The information can be intercepted but it is unusable.
  - **Encryption:** Standard protocols like transport layer security (TLS) may be used in this scope.
  - **Authentication by Web server:** This is well suited to hot spot type connections. When connecting, the user is directed to a Web portal resident in the WLAN switch. Authentication is done by a login/password sequence. The link between the client and the server is secured by TLS and the authentication is done via a local authentication database. In return, the server assigns a category that defines user's VLAN, rights, etc. For example, if the user is known but has no more credit, he will be redirected to a page that invites him to renew his subscription. For a complete security

of communications authenticated by Web server, it is recommended, after the authentication phase, to set up a VPN client, which can be downloaded (Dialer VPN).

IEEE 802.11 SECURITY FEATURES

Basic Protocol Mechanisms

When a mobile node, such as a laptop, connects to the WLAN network is a process called association. To be able to do this, the mobile node needs to find a suitable access point (AP). The access points are identified using the network name (Basic Service Set IDentifier BSSID or Extended Service Set IDentifier ESSID, or short: SSID).

The access points can be configured using two methods. The first option is that the access point sends periodically the SSID in plaintext, and the mobile terminals can then decide to ask for association with this access point. Manufacturers provide equipment pieces with a standard SSID. Naturally, lists of manufacturer's SSID are available from the Internet. A first precaution is to change it into another one.

It is recommended to configure the access point to be mute, and just to listen to requests for associations from the mobile nodes. The first level imposes the client station to send a connection request to know the networks in range. When receiving it, AP's in range send their SSID. This is a good precaution, but a poor protection. Hackers have just to wait for the arrival of a mobile station: offices opening hour is a very nice time for SSID interception. The second level imposes that AP's do not answer to broadcasts sent by mobile stations that request for access. In this case, mobile stations must know the SSID to attach the network.

This may seem secure at the first glance, but the added feeling of security is futile: an attacker can get the necessary information by passively listening to the network traffic, and as soon as the first legitimate association request is heard, it can find out about the network identifier, which will be present in the request as plaintext. Even worse—the attacker may force a legitimate node to disassociate from an access point by sending a disassociation request to it. Then the legitimate node will try to reassociate immediately, thus revealing the network name.

Note: The inhibition of SSID exchange can block the attachment of some NIC's (network interface card) whose implementation requests for this step in their connection process.

Changing and hiding the SSID is better than nothing, but not enough!

- **MAC addresses filtering:** The second non-cryptographic security feature in the IEEE WLANs is MAC filtering. This method uses the unique link layer (MAC) address of the WLAN network card to identify legitimate users. The system administration uses network configuration tools to give to the access points a list of valid MAC addresses called ACL: access control list. The access points refuse to answer to any messages received from network cards that are not listed in the ACL. This security feature is also easy to bypass: just listen for a while network traffic, and when a legitimate node leaves the network, set your network card to use its MAC address instead, for impersonating as a legitimate node. This constitutes also a constraint for the network administrator because the introduction of a new station needs an intervention on the network. Address filtering is usable only if the park of stations is limited and stable.
  MAC addresses filtering it is better than nothing, but not perfect!
- **Encryption with WEP:** There are several security features that are based on cryptography. The original and most widely deployed is called wired equivalent privacy (WEP).

It was defined in the initial IEEE 802.11 standard. WEP can be used in conjunction with the aforementioned noncryptographic features, or as such. WEP provides authentication and encryption with 40 to 128 bit key length. The system is based on a shared key that is configured both to the mobile node and to the access point. Using this key, the mobile node is authenticated when it associates to the access point. The access point is not authenticated. One problem with this authentication is that since the WEP key is the same for all nodes, the nodes cannot be distinguished from each other in authentication. WEP uses data encryption on the radio link for providing confidentiality and integrity. The integrity mechanism uses a linear CRC algorithm where an attacker is able to flip bits in the packet without the risk of being detected.

The weaknesses of WEP arise from the following factors:

- The pseudo-random sequence is computed by a linear algorithm and thus, is easily predictable.
- The key is static and common to all access points and mobile stations.
- The integrity control is weak and does not efficiently filter frame alterations.
- Sequences are not numbered; this facilitates replay attacks.
- The pseudo-random sequence is initialised by the means of a 24-bit vector transmitted in clear on the air interface and thus, easily intercepted by sniffing.

Fluhrer, Mantin, and Shamir (2001) described an attack (FMS) that allows finding the secret key used in WEP in reasonable time. The WEP algorithm uses the RC4 stream cipher in a mode where the actual key used consists of two parts–a known part called initialization vector (IV), which is concatenated with the secret key. The RC4 algorithm uses a key generation algorithm that generates a pseudo-random bit sequence from the concatenation of IV and the key, and uses the generated bit sequence for encrypting the actual data by a simple "exclusive or" operation. The problem is that the algorithm for generating the bit stream carries some patterns of the original key to the resulting bit stream.

The reason for the initialization vectors is that the RC4 algorithm produces an identical bit stream each time it is used with the same key. This would lead to a situation where knowing one bit in plaintext for one packet would mean the corresponding bit would be known for all packets, and thus reducing the strength of the algorithm considerably. Using IVs is supposed to prevent this, but the downside is that the first 24 bits of the key are now known. And since the standard format of an IP packet is also known, this can be used to guess more bytes in the key. This repetition of IVs can be used for decrypting messages even without knowing the key–if the attacker can inject traffic to the WLAN from the fixed network and collect the packets encrypted by the access point, it can get the necessary information for decrypting traffic (see, e.g., Barken, 2004).

The attack was first implemented by Stubblefield, Ioannidis, and Rubin (2001) and is now available in common cracking tools, such as Air-Snort and WEPCrack. The attack requires several millions of packets to be captured, afterwards the actual cracking is done in seconds. Even if the FMS attack requires capturing a huge number of packets, it can be done quite fast if the attacker can inject packets to the network, and capture them encrypted.

In practice, cracking the WEP needs less than two hours and some hackers boast to do it in fifteen minutes! In order to facilitate hacker's task, it exists some dictionaries of pseudo-random sequences, depending on the values of the initial vector. Excellent software's for WEP cracking are also available from the Internet (e.g., Airsnort or Netstrumbler).

- **Key renewal:** Since the keys can be compromised in a reasonable time, a mechanism has to change keys within a considerable short time. The problem in WEP is that all the nodes share the same unique ciphering key, which is static. The key should be changed in all nodes (laptops, etc.) and in the access points, simultaneously and frequently. The 802.11 protocol does not contain key updating mechanisms. Thus, this must be done manually and simultaneously on all radio devices. Even if it could be done on very small networks, in practice keys are never changed.

  Key renewing is good, but not realistic!

- **Authentication:** Since a WLAN using WEP does not authenticate the access point, the attacker can also impersonate as an access point. To launch a man-in-the middle attack, he may force network nodes to reassociate by sending deassociation frames to it, and then let the node to associate with the attacking node. This is easy if the attacker can position himself or use such equipment so that it can overpower the access point. With modified antennae it is easy to gain transmitting power, but they may look suspicious. Here,

we have a conflict with leaking radio signal outside the premises and making man-in-the-middle attack easier–for example Wi-Fi Alliance (2003) recommend low power for access points in order to reduce leaking the radio outside company premises. Several enhancements have been introduced in order to solve some of these weaknesses. Among them, the dynamic WEP with TKIP that makes frequently the key changed. This will be included in the 802.11i standard described next.

WEP using is better than nothing, but not enough!

WiFi Protected Access

Conscious of WEP weakness, the IEEE has designed a complementary protocol so-named 802.11i, which was ratified in July 2004, and known as WPA 2 (Wi-Fi Protected Access 2). Before that, WPA 1.0 with TKIP was introduced as a first step, considered as a subpart of 802.11i (see Figure 3).

802.11i relies on TKIP and 802.1x features with increased key-length, MIC integrity code and packet sequencing. However, the major innovation

Figure 3. Key dates for 802.1x security

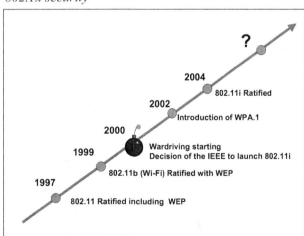

is the particularly efficient AES encryption that is also compatible with QoS requirements.

- **WPA 1.0:** WPA 1.0 is based on IEEE 802.1x that refers to a remote authentication dial-in user service (RADIUS) authentication server. The WLAN switch looks like a modem concentrator (RAS or BAS) in a traditional architecture. WPA 1.0 uses temporal key integrity protocol (TKIP) that manages key generation and dynamic exchange above WEP. In brief:

  ○ 802.1x is a network access protocol that applies to any type of LAN, radio or wired. It defines a frame for WEP or AES implementation.

  ○ EAP, initially designed for PPP, is an authentication transport protocol, authentication carried by an upper layer application on a RADIUS server.

  ○ RADIUS is a client/server protocol that manages user's account and access rights in a centralised way. It supports various authentication mechanisms, including EAP.

  ○ The RADIUS server is an authentication, authorisation and accounting (AAA) server whose communications with the clients are managed by the RADIUS protocol.

WiFi protected access (WPA) was originally called WEP2, created in the IEEE 802.11i working group. It aims at correcting the security flaws in WEP while preserving as much as possible from the original WEP mechanism, so that a simple firmware update would suffice for updating equipment. There are two main differences: encryption uses TKIP for generating RC4 keys, instead of the old secret key + IV mechanism, and a new access control mechanism (IEEE 802.1X).

- **Encryption with TKIP:** Keeping the WEP design model, TKIP brings mechanisms to enhance the resistance against attacks; in particular, it solves the problem of key cyclic reusing:

  ○ The common key shared by mobile stations and access points is changed every 10.000 packets.

  ○ Common keys are renewed by a dynamic distribution.

  ○ The MAC address of the station is introduced in the generation of key sequences, thus each station has its own sequence.

  ○ The initial vector is incremented with each packet thus it is possible to reject packets replayed with an old packet number.

  ○ An integrity code ICV (computed according to a MIC algorithm, so named MICHAEL) introduces a notion of "ciphered CRC".

Upgrading WEP equipment needs just a software evolution. Note also that all WAP 1.0 products are ascendant compatible with 802.11i. As WPA 1.0 is compatible with the WEP, WEP and WPA 1.0 devices are interoperable, but with the WEP protection level.

Temporal key integrity protocol (TKIP) is used for generating per-packet keys for the RC4 ciphering used. The way of using RC4 in WEP is problematic due to the way keys are used. TKIP solves this by using a key mixing mechanism that creates a new key from three sources: a Temporal key, which is shared between the node and the access point, but is not necessarily the same for all users. This key is called "temporal" since it is changed frequently. The temporal key is combined with the sender's MAC address using the exclusive OR-operation, thus resulting using different keys for upstream and downstream transmissions, and then with a sequence number for the packet. This sequence number replaces the initialization vector, making each transmission use a different key, but the mixing is done differently. While WEP just concatenates the IV and the key, WPA uses the mixed Temporal key and sender's MAC for encrypting the sequence number, producing a 128bit key of which the first three bytes are given to the original WEP algorithm as the IV and the rest as the user's key. As a result, it is not possible to use the FMS attack to crack the key, as it is different for each packet.

There are two modes for TKIP key management. The first one uses a pre-shared key (PSK) from which the temporal keys are derived. PSK needs to be remembered by the user. To ease this, the PSK is created from a pass-phrase using a hashing algorithm. The problem of the approach is that the pass-phrase needs to be sufficiently long in order to give any real protection against an attack. The attacker can use a short denial of service attack to disconnect temporarily a legitimate node and record the re-association procedure. Then the attacker can just use a dictionary or brute force attack to the captured packets for getting the key.

- **Access control:** The second option is to use IEEE 802.1X and the extensible authentication protocol (EAP) for providing both the mobile node and the access point the key during association. When using this mode, the access point blocks access to the network until the node has authenticated with an authentication server (a RADIUS server). The authentication is mutual, and if successful, the authentication server and the mobile node both generate a key pairwise master key. This key is new for each session, so the attacker does not benefit much even if he is able to get this key. This key can then be used in the access point for generating temporal keys (for privacy and integrity) and key encryption keys for enabling rekeying later.

  Several layers are defined over EAP to support security polices (in increasing security order):
  - ° EAP-MD5 uses a RADIUS server that just checks a hash-code of the mobile station password and does not manage

mutual authentication. This protocol is not recommended for radio networks, because the mobile station can be connected to a honey pot.
  - ° LEAP, developed by CISCO, provides a better protection against the knowledge of passwords by an unauthorised third party, but it is vulnerable to dictionary-type attacks.
  - ° PEAP and EAP-TTLS use a RADIUS server and are based on the exchange of certificates. RADIUS servers that support PEAP and EAP-TTLS may use external databases (e.g., Domain Windows or LDAP directories). They are particularly resistant to dictionary-type attacks.
- EAP-TLS is the most recommended standard for WLAN security. It uses a RADIUS authentication server. Mobile stations and the server must mutually authenticate, using certificates. The transaction is secured by the means of a ciphered tunnel. It is also particularly resistant to dictionary-type attacks.

  Even this type of key management has a problem: reauthentication with the authentication servers will be too slow for supporting handovers with real-time traffic (such as VoIP). This would require the access points being able to pass keys with each other.
- **Integrity:** TKIP also uses a different checksum algorithm than WEP. The WEP CRC algorithm is not cryptographically secure, so a new message integrity code (MIC) algorithm, Michael was developed. Michael uses a MIC key, and the sender's and receiver's MAC addresses as keys, and results in a 64bit message integrity code which is appended to the plaintext before ciphering. The effective security level of Michael is assumed around 20bits, meaning that the attacker could make an active attack against Michael, and succeed in around

2^{20} messages, which might be possible in a couple of minutes. In order to prevent this, TKIP uses a mechanism where a node disassociates from the network and deletes its keys if it finds out two failed forgeries within a second. It will reassociate with the network after a minute.

In addition, a mechanism against replay attacks is implemented: a sequence number is used for each packet. If a packet with a lower sequence number than used earlier is found, it is discarded.

WPA 2 is the result of 802.11i standardisation process that has been ratified in June 2004. It relies on most of the improvements of WPA 1 but uses the more powerful advanced encryption standard (AES) encryption, which is a block ciphering algorithm using symmetrical keys with 128, 192 or 256 key length. The processing power needed by AES requires a coprocessor already present (as a reserve for the future) on equipment pieces delivered with WPA 1.0. Older WEP equipment needs a hardware modification to be upgraded to WPA 2. Even if these algorithms and protocols do protect the wireless network from unauthorized use or eavesdropping, the nature of the network makes it prone to Denial of Service type attacks. It is easy for an attacker to jam the frequency band, or more cleverly inject traffic to the access points so that the network is not able to serve legitimate users.

THE SECURITY OF WIRELESS RADIO NETWORKS

Application

Lets us forget the old WEP and take just WPA in consideration. The security level depends on the usage.

- **For the enterprise:** WPA Enterprise needs a RADIUS server with EAP-TLS, EAP-TTLS and PEAP, plus a network controller. This costly solution provides high-level security for large–and small–networks. In this implementation, a VPN is not useful, even not recommended if the network supports VoIP because it degrades the quality of service.
- **For residential and Soho usage:** WPA personal does not need a RADIUS server but uses a pre-shared key (PSK) distributed to the access points and mobile stations. This constitutes a flexible and cheap solution for small networks, in particular for Soho and domestic usage.
- **Hot spots:** In order to facilitate the access, no security mechanism is implemented on public hot spots. In particular, there is no authentication of the Wi-Fi network, because the user does not know what it is when connecting and vice versa. In this case, authentication is done by a Web portal. The user has to manage its own protection by VPN, by ciphering at application level and by configuring properly his station in order to reject intrusions from others.

OTHER TECHNOLOGIES

Bluetooth

Bluetooth is well known for point-to-point applications, rather than for WLAN realisation, even if this is technically possible. Even if Bluetooth integrates performing security mechanisms, those are rarely used. The short range (10 meters) of a Bluetooth link is seen as protection against most intrusions, but do not forget that in a public hot spot, users are generally less than 10 meters from each other's. On another hand, Bluetooth standard foresees several transmission power levels: 10 mW that is the most frequently used for wireless connections, and 100 mW that transmits in a range comparable to Wi-Fi. Some 100 mW devices are available, in particular for building small size WLAN's that are as much vulnerable as Wi-Fi WLAN's.

Vigilance is particularly recommended when using a Bluetooth wireless keypad: keyboarded codes, in particular passwords, go though the radio link and can be detected in the range of Bluetooth transmission. A new form of spamming has appeared, named « Blue Jacking », that seems promised to a great future. It consists to send spam's on the screen of bistandard GSM-Bluetooth mobile phones that are in range of the spammer. The short range is not a limitation because the spammer is also mobile.

Another Bluetooth attack involves bi-standard mobile phones and nomad stations. It takes advantage of a weakness of Bluetooth that makes possible to fetch remotely the information stored in a handy. Attacks are generally done in public areas. By this means, the hacker gets the coordinates of the service provider and the login/password that a victim close from him has just received by SMS. A precaution is to inhibit the Bluetooth option of the mobile phone when unused.

HiperLAN/2

HiperLAN/2 is an ETSI standard concurrent of 802.11a that has no commercial issue at this time. HiperLAN/2 integrates basically efficient mechanisms of encryption, authentication and dynamic key assignment.

2G/2,5G/3G Networks

GSM uses strong security mechanisms that can be attacked (Barkan et al., 2003), but UMTS networks use improved mechanisms, that can be considered reliable. They ensure user's authentication as well as the confidentiality of user's identity, signalling and exchanged information.

Security is managed at three places:

- **In the SIM card:** Personal security information (authentication key, algorithms for authentication and key generation, PIN)
- **In the terminal:** Ciphering algorithm
- **In the network:** Ciphering algorithm, authentication server.

The terminal identifier is hidden and replaced by a temporary identifier allocated when registering on a relay. This constitutes an efficient protection against interception.

FUTURE TRENDS

- **802.11 technology:** The 802.11 technology is now mature and its variant 802.11g with 54 Mbps throughput is largely distributed. The standard is enhanced by protocol extensions: 802.11i brings a high level of security and 802.11e provides QoS (Quality of service) for transmitting video and voice in the best conditions.
  The IEEE is still working on other evolutions of the 802.11 standard, in particular for high-speed data (> 100 Mbps) and meshed networks without wired infrastructure.
- **Ad-hoc networks:** On the other hands, researches are undertaken in the domain of ad-hoc networks, in particular in the scope of public safety and defence, in order to provide broadband communication means at the place of an intervention or in case of a major disaster when communication infrastructures have been destroyed. Ad-hoc networks are new targets for new attacks. The fact that routing is done by node terminals makes these networks particularly vulnerable.
- **WiMAX:** WiMAX is the commercial name for of IEEE 802.16, and an interoperability label from the WiMAX forum.

WiMAX can support throughputs of 70 Mbps in a range of some tenths of kilometres in line of sight. This makes WiMAX well suited for metropolitan networks and in particular, it could be an alternative to the Internet distribution in low-density areas.

The first step of WiMAX 802.16a is just for radio connected fixed stations. The next step 802.16e, recently ratified, integrates mobility.

In opposition with Wi-Fi, stations must be registered in the system to be allowed to accede to the WiMAX network. This feature does not facilitate hacker's attacks.

Authentication uses certificates and an asymmetrical ciphering. Encryption uses a key generated during the authentication sequence and a 3-DES algorithm.

- **802.20:** The 802.20 standard will address WAN structures for mobile users. In opposition with 3G networks designed for voice and data, 802.20 networks will be dedicated to mobile Internet with an asymmetrical throughput, like the ADSL.

Mutual authentication uses certificates with RSA signature. Symmetric encryption keys are exchanged during the authentication.

At the present time, 802.20 is under study at the IEEE. No date of ratification is foreseen.

CONCLUSION

WLAN networks are insecure, and attacking a poorly configured WLAN network is easy. There are plenty of different security solutions for WLAN networks, having their weaknesses. Even if the network can be protected against intrusion attempts, the attacker has always the possibility to launch a denial of service attack to shut down the network operation. There are two possible main paths for the system to choose:

- To accept that the WLAN network is insecure, and to treat is as it were a public hot spot, using VPN solutions for the mobile nodes. This has the advantage that it is possible to provide access to the Internet for the visitors.
- To set up a full authentication, encryption and key management infrastructure with WPA or WPA2. With this option, it is essential to drop support of legacy equipment not being able to use the full set of security options. Providing compatibility means opening security holes.

Both of these approaches require that the essential IT infrastructure is in a wired network to counter for the ease of denial of service attacks against WLANs.

One can say that wireless technologies meet the requirements of nomad users that aim to obtain the same level of service and security than in their office. Even if the security has been a great concern in the past, we may consider now that, using appropriate technologies and engineering, wireless networks are as safe as traditional wired networks.

REFERENCES

Barkan, E., Biham, E., & Keller, N. (2003). Instant ciphetext-only cryptoanalysis of GSM encrypted communication. *CRYPTO 2003*, 600-616.

Barken, L. (2004). *How secure is your wireless network?* Upper Saddle River, NJ: Prentice Hall.

Fluhrer, S., Mantin, I., & Shamir, A. (2001). Weaknesses in the key scheduling algorithm of RC4. In S. Vaudenay & A. Youssef (Eds.), *Selected areas in cryptography* (pp. 1-24). Springer.

Germain, M., & Ferrero, A. (2006). English translation Michèle Germain. Les réseaux particuliers

– La sécurité des réseaux sans fil. In La Sécurité à l'usage des décideurs (pp. 154 to 166). Paris: © Éditions tenor 2006.

IAIK. (2005). *AES lounge.* Retrieved from http://www.iaik.tu-graz.ac.at/research/krypto/AES/

Stubblefield, A., Ioannidis, J., & Rubin, A. (2001). *Using the Fluhrer, Mantin, and Shamir attack to break WEP.* (Tech. Rep. TD-4ZCPZZ). AT&T Labs.

Wi-Fi Alliance. (2003). *Enterprise solutions for wireless LAN security.*

Chapter V
Interoperability Among Instrusion Detection Systems

Mário M. Ferire
University of Beira Interior, Portugal

ABSTRACT

This chapter addresses the problem of interoperability among intrusion detection systems. It presents a classification and a brief description of intrusion detection systems, taking into account several issues such as information sources, analysis of intrusion detection systems, response options for intrusion detection systems, analysis timing, control strategy, and architecture of intrusion detection systems. It is also discussed the problem of information exchange among intrusion detection systems, being addressed the intrusion detection exchange protocol and a format for the exchange of information among intrusion detection systems, called by intrusion detection message exchange format. The lack of a format of the answers or countermeasures interchanged between the components of intrusion detection systems is also discussed as well as some future trends in this area.

INTRODUCTION

Security incidents are becoming a serious problem in enterprise networked systems. Due to this problem, intrusion detection systems (IDS) are attracting an increasing commercial importance. This kind of systems is used in enterprise network security to attempt the identification and tracking of attacks to the networked systems. Nowadays, several commercial and free intrusion detection systems are available. Some of them are intended for detecting intrusions on the network, others are intended for host operating systems, while still others are intended for applications. Tools of these categories may have very different strengths and weaknesses. Therefore, it is likely that network and systems administrators deploy more than a one kind of IDS, and administrators may want to analyse the output of these tools from different systems. Therefore, the existence of a standard format for reporting may simplify this task. Moreover, intrusions frequently occur in several organizations or in several sites of the same organization, which may use different IDS. Therefore, it would be very helpful to correlate such distributed intrusions across multiple sites and administrative domains. Thus, it is required the existence of a common format in order to allow an easy interconnection of different IDS.

Due to these reasons, recently, the group Intrusion Detection Working Group (IDWG) of Internet Engineering Task Force (IETF) has carried out standardization activities regarding IDS whose objective is to define data formats and exchange procedures for sharing information among intrusion detection and response systems, systems. As result, it was specified a new protocol and a format for the exchange of information among IDS. The specified protocol is called by intrusion detection exchange protocol (IDXP) (Buchheim, Erlinger, et al., 2001; Feinstein, Matthews, & White, 2002) and the specified data format is called by intrusion detection message exchange format (IDMEF) (Debar, Curry, & Feinstein, 2005; Wood & Erlinger, 2002).

The model specified by the IDWG group does not define the format of the answers or countermeasures interchanged among the components of IDS. Without the definition of a common format for the exchange of answers, it is not possible to get total interoperability between IDS of different manufacturers. Moreover, use of the incident object description exchange format (IODEF) for incident handling should also be considered regarding real time network defense. This chapter will provide an overview of intrusion detection systems and will discuss how information regarding the detection of an intrusion may de shared with other intrusion detection systems.

INTRUSION DETECTION SYSTEMS

Early work on intrusion detection was reported by Anderson (1980) and Denning (1987) and, since then, it has been subject of intense research activities from both academia and industry. Early intrusion detection systems were based either on the use of simple rule–based techniques to detect very specific patterns of intrusive behaviour or on the analysis of historical activity profiles to confirm legitimate behaviour. Nowadays, intrusion detection systems may use data-mining and machine-learning techniques for the dynamic collection of new intrusion signatures, which allows for relatively general expressions of what may constitute intrusive behaviour. Other modern intrusion detection systems may use a mixture of sophisticated statistical and forecasting techniques to predict what is legitimate activity (Almgren & Jonsson, 2004; Abad et al., 2003; Carey, Mohay, & Clark, 2003).

In the context of computer security, an intrusion can be defined as any set of actions that attempt to compromise the integrity, confidentiality or availability of a resource. An intruder can be internal or external. External intruders do not have any authorized access to the system they attack while internal intruders have some kind of authority and therefore some legitimate access, but seek to gain additional ability to take action without legitimate authorization (Jones & Lin, 2001). Intrusion detection is the process of monitoring the events occurring in a computer system or network and analyzing them for signs of intrusions. Intrusion detection systems (IDS) are software or hardware tools that automate this monitoring and analysis process and reports any anomalous events or any known patterns indicating potential intrusions (Bace & Mell, 2001; Wan & Yang, 2000).

There are several types of IDS currently available, which are characterized by different monitoring and analysis approaches. Most of the currently available IDS can be classified according three fundamental functional components: information sources, analysis and response (Bace & Mell, 2001). Nevertheless, there are other issues that may also be taken into account for the classification of IDS (Kazienko & Dorosz, 2004). An overview of the classification of IDS is presented in Figure 1. In the following, a brief description of some categories, in which IDS may be classified, is presented.

Information Sources

The most common classification of IDS is based on the kind of information source used to determine whether an intrusion has occurred. Most common information sources are network, host, and application monitoring (see Figure 1; Bace & Mell, 2001; Coull, Branch, Szymanski, & Breimer, 2003; Feng et al., 2004; Gopalakrishna, Spafford, & Vitek, 2005; Lindqvist & Porras, 2001; Kruegel, Valeur, Vigna, & Kemmerer, 2002; Rubin, Jha, & Miller, 2004, 2005; Shankar & Paxson, 2003).

The larger part of commercially available IDS is network-based. This kind of IDS analyzes network packets, captured from network backbones or local area network (LAN) segments, in order to detect attacks. Network-based IDS (NIDS) often consist of a set of single-purpose sensors or hosts placed at suitable points in a network. These sensors monitor network traffic, performing local analysis of that traffic and reporting attacks to a central management console. Since the sensors only support the IDS, they can be more easily secured against attacks and may also be configured to run in a stealth mode, in order to make more difficult to determine their presence and location in the network. These systems are usually designed to work as passive devices for monitoring the network traffic without interference with the normal operation of the network

(Bace & Mell, 2001). However, NIDS have some limitations: they may be unable to analyze, without network performance degradation, all the packets in a large or busy network or under very high speed operation at LAN interfaces. Moreover, as we move from shared topologies to switched-per-port LAN topologies, most switches limit monitoring range of a NIDS to a single host, provided that the switch does not provide universal monitoring ports. Besides, NIDS are unable to analyze encrypted information, becoming in a particular problem in the case of using Virtual Private Networks (VPNs).

Host-based IDS (HIDS) analyze information sources generated by the operating system or application software, trying to find an intrusion. Application-based IDS (AIDS) are a special subset of host-based IDS. HIDS can analyze activities with great reliability and precision, determining

Figure 1. Classification of intrusion detection systems

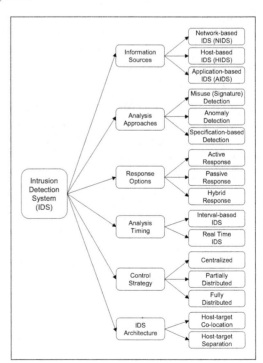

exactly which processes and users are involved in a particular attack on a given operating system. Moreover, unlike NIDS, HIDS can see the outcome of an attempted attack, as they can directly access and monitor the data files and system processes usually targeted by attacks. HIDS usually use two types of information sources: operating system audit trails, and system logs. Operating system audit trails are normally generated at the kernel of the operating system, and are therefore more detailed and better protected than system logs. However, system logs are much less imperceptive and much smaller than audit trails, and are furthermore far easier to understand. Some host-based IDS are designed to support a centralized IDS management and reporting infrastructure that can allow a single management console to track many hosts. Others generate messages in formats that are compatible with network management systems (Bace & Mell, 2001). Due to the ability to monitor events in the host, HIDS may detect attacks that cannot be detected by NIDS. Furthermore, unlike NIDS, HIDS are not directly dependent of the evolution form shared topologies towards switched per port topologies and HIDS can often operate in networked environments with encrypted traffic, namely when host-based information is generated before data encryption and/or after data decryption in the destination host. On the other hand, HIDS only read network packets destined to that host and therefore they are unsuitable for network surveillance. Moreover, configuration and management of HIDS are more difficult and they can be disabled during an attack. Besides, HIDS make use of host computing resources, which lead to a performance cost and, when operating system audit trails are used, additional storage capability may be required due to huge volume of information.

As referred above, application-based IDS (AIDS) are a special subset of host-based IDS. The most common information sources used by AIDS are the transaction log files of applications. The ability to interface with the application directly, with significant domain or application-specific knowledge included in the analysis engine, allows application-based IDS to detect suspicious behavior due to authorized users exceeding their authorization. This is because such problems are more likely to appear in the interaction between the network administrator, the data, and the application (Bace & Mell, 2001).

AIDS can monitor the interaction between user and application, which often allows them to trace unauthorized activity to individual users. Moreover, AIDS can often work in encrypted environments, since they interface with the application at transaction endpoints, where information is sent in an unencrypted form. On the other hand, AIDS may be more vulnerable than host-based IDS to attacks as the applications logs are not as well protected as the operating system audit trails used for host-based IDS. In any case, as AIDS often monitor events at the user level of abstraction, they usually cannot detect Trojan Horses or other similar attacks. Therefore, it is advisable to use application-based IDS jointly with host-based and/or network-based IDS.

IDS Analysis

Nowadays, there are three main intrusion detection approaches: the behavioural approach, also called anomaly detection, and the signature analysis, also called misuse detection and specification-based detection (Ko, 2000). Anomaly detection is based on statistical description of the normal behaviour of users or applications. The purpose is to detect any abnormal action performed by these users or applications. The second approach, called "misuse detection," is based on collecting attack signatures in order to store them in an attack base. The IDS then parses audit files to find patterns that match the description of an attack stored in the attack base. On the other hand, specification-based techniques detect deviation of executing programs from their valid program behaviour. Misuse detection is the most used technique by commercial systems. Anomaly detection has been subject to intense research activities and is used in limited form by a number of IDS. None of these approaches is fully satisfactory, since they may generate many false positives, corresponding to false alerts, false negatives, corresponding to nondetected attacks, and the alerts are too elementary and not enough accurate to be directly managed by a security administrator. There are strengths and weaknesses associated with each approach, and it appears that the most effective IDS use mostly misuse detection methods with a smattering of anomaly detection components (Cuppens & Miège, 2002; Ko, 2000; Kruegel et al., 2003; Li & Das, 2004; Mutz, Vigna, & Kemmerer, 2003; Tombini, Debar, Mé, & Ducassé, 2004; Vigna, et al., 2004; Wu et al., 2003; Wu & Shao, 2005).

Misuse detectors analyse system activity, looking for events or sets of events that match a predefined pattern of events that describe a known attack. Since the patterns corresponding to known attacks are called signatures, misuse detection is sometimes referred to as signature-based detection. The most common form of misuse detection used in commercial products specifies each pattern of events corresponding to an attack as a separate signature. However, there are more sophisticated approaches to doing misuse detection, called state-based analysis techniques that can force a single signature to detect groups of attacks.

Anomaly detectors identify abnormal unusual behaviour (anomalies) on a host or network. They function on the assumption that attacks are different from normal (legitimate) activity and can therefore be detected by systems that identify these differences. Anomaly detectors construct profiles representing normal behaviour of users, hosts, or network connections. These profiles are constructed from historical data collected over a period of normal operation. The detectors then collect event data and use a variety of measures to determine when monitored activity deviates from the norm.

Specification-based techniques detect the deviation of executing programs from their correct behaviour and they assume that penetrations often cause privileged programs to behave differently from their intended behaviour, which, for most programs, are fairly regular and can be written concisely. They lead to a very low false alarm rate and are able to explain why the deviation is an intrusion. Specification-based techniques are promising for detecting previously unseen attacks. However, specifications need to be written by system or security experts for every security-critical program. Nevertheless, specification-based approaches take advantage from techniques that automate the development of specifications (Ko, 2000).

Response Options for IDS

The response of an IDS is the set of actions that the system takes once it detects intrusions (Bace & Mell, 2001; Kazienko & Dorosz, 2004). They are typically grouped into active and passive measures, with active measures involving some automatic actions while passive measures involve the reporting of intrusion detection findings to network administrators, who are expected to take action based on those reports. Though researchers and some network administrators are tempted to underestimate the importance of good response functions in IDS, they may be very important. In fact, commercial IDS support a wide range of response options, often categorized as active responses, passive responses, or some mixture of both kinds of responses.

Active responses are automatic reactions taken after the detection of some types of intrusions. Active responses may be classified into three categories (Bace & Mell, 2001): collect additional information, change the environment, and take action against the intruder. A brief description of these three categories follows.

Collect additional information is the most inoffensive active response, although sometimes the most productive, which is based on the collection of additional information about a potential attack. This is generally associated with the increase of the level of information sources sensitivity (e.g., increasing the number of events logged by an operating system audit trail, or increasing the sensitivity of a network monitor in order to analyse more packets). The collection of additional information may be of interest. For instance, the additional information collected can help decide the detection of the attack. The gathered information may be further used to support investigation and criminal and civil legal actions (Bace & Mell, 2001).

Changing the environment is another active response, which is based on the stop of a possible an attack in progress with subsequent block of attacker access. Typically, IDS block Internet protocol (IP) addresses identified as the origin of the attack. Although it is difficult to block a particular attacker, IDS can often prevent attacks through the following actions (Bace & Mell, 2001): (1) injecting TCP reset packets into the attacker connection to the victim system, leading to a close of the connection; (2) reconfiguring routers and firewalls to block IP packets from the attacker apparent location; (3) reconfiguring routers and firewalls to block the network ports, protocols, or services being used by an attacker, and (4) in extreme cases, reconfiguring routers and firewalls to separate and cut all connections that use specific network interfaces.

Although an attack to the attacker may be considered, this active option can represent a larger risk than the attack it is intended to block due to civil legal responsibilities. Besides, generally, attacks are carried out from false network addresses, or from zombies. Moreover, this approach may lead to an escalade of the attack (Bace & Mell, 2001).

Passive response approaches are based on information made available to network administrators, leaving to administrators the decision to be taken based on that information. A large

number of commercial IDS only rely on passive response approaches. These approaches can be alarms and notifications or relay on SNMP Traps and Plug-ins (Bace & Mell, 2001).

When an IDS detects an attack, it generates alarms and notifications to inform network administrators that an attack was detected. Most commercial IDS allow a large degree of freedom regarding how and when alarms are generated and to whom they are displayed. The information included in the alarm message may range from a simple notification saying that an intrusion has taken place to extremely detailed messages including IP addresses of the source and target of the attack, the specific attack tool used to obtain access, and the result of the attack. Another set of options that may be helpful to large or multi-site organizations are those involving remote notification of alarms or alerts. These allow organizations to configure the IDS so that it sends alerts to cellular phones or pagers carried by incident response teams or system security personnel. E-mail messages are avoided because attackers may monitor network traffic and block e-mail messages (Bace & Mell, 2001).

Some commercial IDS generate alarms and alerts to network management systems, which use SNMP traps and messages to send alarms and alerts to central network management consoles, where they can be analyzed by network administrators. This reporting scheme may lead to several benefits such as the ability to adapt the entire network infrastructure to act in response to a detected attack, the ability to move the processing load associated with an active response to a another system that is not under attack, and the capability to use common communications channels (Bace & Mell, 2001).

Analysis Timing

Analysis timing is concerned with the elapsed time between the occurrence of events and the analysis of those events. It can be classified into interval based IDS and real time IDS (Bace & Mell, 2001; Kazienko & Dorosz, 2004). In the first approach, the information is not sent continuously from monitoring systems to analysis engines. Audit trail (event log) analysis is the most common method used by systems operated periodically. Real time IDS are designed for on-the -fly processing and are the most common approach used by network-based IDS.

Control Strategy

Control strategy refers to the way the elements of an IDS are controlled and how input and output is managed. Control strategy may be classified into three classes: centralized systems, partially distributed systems, and fully distributed systems (Bace & Mell, 2001). In the first strategy, all monitoring, detection and reporting functions are controlled by a central location. In partially distributed systems, monitoring and detection functions are controlled by local node, but reporting is done hierarchically to one or more central locations. In fully distributed systems, monitoring and detection functions are performed through an agent-based approach, being response decisions taken at the point of analysis.

Architecture

The architecture of an IDS is devoted to the organization of the functional components of a given IDS. The architecture of an IDS includes the host, the system in which the IDS software is running, and the target, which is the system to be monitoring by the IDS. The architecture of an IDS may be categorized into two classes: host-target co-location and host-target separation (Bace & Mell, 2001). Most of early IDS were of the first type, in which the IDS ran on the systems they protected. However, this architecture presents a security problem, since, after a successful attack to the target, the attacker could disable the IDS. This architecture was typically used several years ago

in scenarios dominated by mainframes, in which the high cost of computers prohibited the use of a separated IDS system. With the widespread use of workstations and personal computers, the architecture was changed in order to running the IDS control and analysis systems on a separate system. Therefore, the IDS host and the target are separated systems. This approach makes much more easy to hide the IDS from attackers.

INFORMATION EXCHANGE AMONG INTRUSION DETECTION SYSTEMS

As referred previously, nowadays, there are a lot available IDS with very different strengths and weaknesses. Even within each category it is possible to find IDS with different characteristics. For the case of NIDS, which are very popular nowadays, a web site devoted to the most important network intrusion detection systems was made available by (Computer Network Defence, 2006). This web site provides details about several NIDS and links to the products provided by manufacturers. As may be seen in this site, there are IDS with very different characteristics, being likely that network administrators may deploy more than a single IDS in order to complement their scopes. Due to these reasons, a standard format is required for reporting events among intrusion detection systems. Besides, the existence of a common format should allow components from different IDS to be integrated more easily, namely when different IDS are deployed in multiple organizations or in multiple sites within the same organization. Recently, it was specified a new protocol, called by intrusion detection exchange protocol (IDXP) (Buchheim, Erlinger, et al., 2001; Feinstein et al., 2002), and a format for the exchange of information among IDS, called by intrusion detection message exchange format (IDMEF) (Debar, Curry, & Feinstein, 2005; Wood & Erlinger, 2002).

The Intrusion Detection Working Group (IDWG) of Internet engineering task force (IETF) has made two assumptions about the deployment configuration of an IDS. First, it was assumed that only analyzers create and communicate ID alerts. These alerts contain information stating that an event occurred, but they may contain more detailed information about the event, in order to make easy an informed action or response by the receiving party. The same system may act as both an analyzer and a manager, but these will be two separate ID entities. This assumption is associated with the second, since analyzers and managers can be separate components that communicate pair wise across a TCP/IP network. These assumptions distinguish between creation and consumption of ID alerts, and allow the acts of alert creation and consumption to occur at different IDS components on the network. These assumptions also affect the transfer protocol, since alerts will be transferred from one component to another component over TCP/IP networks, which must be done in a secure way (Buchheim, Erlinger, et al., 2001).

Messages sent between IDS elements must get through and be acknowledged, namely under difficult network conditions. The severity of an attack, and therefore the relevance of a prompt response, may be revealed by the number and frequency of messages generated by IDS analyzers, being desirable to achieve a reliable transmission in order to avoid duplication of messages. Therefore, the IDWG has specified that the protocol for exchange of intrusion detection information be based on the transmission control protocol (TCP).

The first attempt of the IDWG to meet IDWG transport protocol (IDP) requirements for communicating IDMEF messages was the development of the intrusion alert protocol (IAP) (Buchheim, Feinstein, Gupta, Matthews, and Pollock, 2001). The design of IAP was based on the hypertext transfer protocol (HTTP). In HTTP, the HTTP client is the party that initiates the TCP connection. In IDP, a passive analyzer should act as a client even though it receives the TCP connection.

Nevertheless, IAP still borrows many of HTTP headers and response codes (Buchheim, Erlinger, at al., 2001). However, IAP presents some limitations, namely, regarding security issues.

In order to overcome the limitations of IAP, it was proposed the blocks extensible exchange protocol (BEEP) (Rose, 2001), a new IETF general framework for application protocols. Then, the intrusion detection exchange protocol (IDXP) was designed and implemented within the BEEP framework, that fulfills the IDWG requirements for that transport protocol. BEEP is a generalized framework for the development of application-layer protocols, since it is located above TCP in the TCP/IP architecture. BEEP offers asynchronous, connection-oriented, and reliable transport. Therefore, an application level transport protocol such as IDP can be implemented using the BEEP framework.

Overall, BEEP supports higher-level protocols by providing the following protocol mechanisms (Buchheim, Erlinger, et al., 2001):

- **Framing:** How the beginning and ending of each message is delimited
- **Encoding:** How a message is represented when exchanged
- **Reporting:** How errors are described
- **Asynchrony:** How independent exchanges are handled
- **Authentication:** How the peers at each end of the connection are identified and verified
- **Privacy:** How the exchanges are protected against third-party interception or modification

The intrusion detection exchange protocol (IDXP) is an implementation, as a BEEP profile, of the IDWG application level transport protocol. Therefore, BEEP provides the protocol while the IDXP profile specifies the BEEP channel characteristics necessary for implementation of the IDP requirements. IDXP can be split into four main phases: connection provisioning, security setup, BEEP channel creation, and data transfer. Details about IDXP implementation are given in (Buchheim, Erlinger, et al., 2001).

The model specified for IDWG group does not define the format of the answers or countermeasures interchanged between the components of IDS. Without the definition of a common format for the exchange of answers, it is not possible to get complete interoperability between different IDS. Therefore, recent work has been focused towards a solution for this problem. Recently, Silva, and Westphall (2005) proposed a model for interoperability of answers in intrusion detection systems. This model of data and architecture is compatible with works accomplished by IDWG group related with the interoperability between IDS. More details regarding the development and tests of their model can be found in Silva and Westphall (2005).

FUTURE TRENDS

Recent work has been focused in the specification and development of a transport protocol and message formats. A first model for the format of the answers or countermeasures interchanged between the components of IDS has also been reported. Some research issues still open are the detection of intrusions in high-speed network environments and the share of information regarding attacks under high-speed operation.

CONCLUSION

This chapter provided an overview of intrusion detection systems and the way this kind of systems may exchange information regarding attacks. It was briefly discussed the Intrusion detection exchange protocol and the intrusion detection message exchange format and a data model for interoperability of answers among different IDS.

This model is compatible with the model of alerts already developed for IDWG group, in order to make possible the integration of both models.

REFERENCES

Abad, C., Taylor, J., Sengul, C., Yurcik, W., Zhou, Y., & Rowe, K. (2003). Log correlation for intrusion detection: A proof of concept. In *Proceedings of the 19th Annual Computer Security Applications Conference (ACSAC 2003)*. Los Alamitos, CA: IEEE Computer Society Press.

Almgren, M., & Jonsson, E. (2004). Using active learning in intrusion detection. In *Proceedings of the 17th IEEE Computer Security Foundations Workshop (CSFW'04)*. Los Alamitos, CA: IEEE Computer Society Press.

Anderson, J. P. (1980). *Computer security threat monitoring and surveillance* (Tech.l Rep.). Fort Washington, PA: James P. Anderson.

Bace, R., & Mell, P. (2001). *Intrusion detection systems.* NIST special publication in intrusion detection systems. Retrieved from http://csrc.nist.gov/publications/nistpubs/800-31/sp800-31.pdf

Buchheim, T., Erlinger, M., Feinstein, B., Matthews., G., Pollock, R., Betser, J., et al. (2001). Implementing the Intrusion detection exchange protocol. In *Proceedings of 17th Annual Computer Security Applications Conference (ACSAC'01)* (pp. 32-41). IEEE Press.

Buchheim, T., Feinstein, B., Gupta, D., Matthews, G., & Pollock, R. (2001). *IAP: Intrusion alert protocol, Internet engineering task force, draft-ietf-idwg-iap-05.*

Carey, N., Mohay, G., & Clark, A. (2003). Attack signature matching and discovery in systems employing heterogeneous IDS. In *Proceedings of the 19th Annual Computer Security Applications Conference (ACSAC 2003)*. Los Alamitos, CA: IEEE Computer Society Press.

Computer Network Defence Ltd. (2006). *Network intrusion detection systems product descriptions.* Retrieved from http://www.networkintrusion. co.uk/N_ids.htm. Last access: 2006/07/13

Coull, S., Branch, J., Szymanski, B., & Breimer, E. (2003). Intrusion detection: A bioinformatics approach. In *Proceedings of the 19ᵗʰ Annual Computer Security Applications Conference (AC-SAC 2003).* Los Alamitos, CA: IEEE Computer Society Press.

Cuppens, F., & Miège, A. (2002). Alert correlation in a cooperative intrusion detection framework. In *Proceedings of the 2002 IEEE Symposium on Security and Privacy (S&P 2002).* Los Alamitos, CA: IEEE Computer Society Press.

Debar, H., Curry, D., & Feinstein, B. (2005). *The intrusion detection message exchange format, IETF, RFC Draft, draft-ietf-idwg-idmef-xml-14.*

Denning, D. E. (1987). An intrusion-detection model. *IEEE Transactions on Software Engineering, 13*(2).

Feinstein, B., Matthews, G., & White, J. (2002). *The Intrusion detection exchange protocol (IDXP), Internet engineering task force, RFC Draft, draft-ietf-idwg-beep-idxp-07.*

Feng, H. H., Giffin, J. T., Huang, Y., Jha, S., Lee, W., & Miller, B. P. (2004). Formalizing sensitivity in static analysis for intrusion detection. In *Proceedings of the 2004 IEEE Symposium on Security and Privacy (S&P'04).* Los Alamitos, CA: IEEE Computer Society Press.

Gopalakrishna, R., Spafford, E. H., & Vitek, J. (2005). Efficient Intrusion detection using automaton inlining. In *Proceedings of the 2005 IEEE Symposium on Security and Privacy (S&P'05).* Los Alamitos, CA: IEEE Computer Society Press.

Jones, A. K., & Lin, Y. (2001). Application intrusion detection using language library calls. In *Proceedings of 17ᵗʰ Annual Computer Security*

Applications Conference (ACSAC'01). Los Alamitos, CA: IEEE Computer Society Press.

Kazienko, P., & Dorosz, P. (2004). *Intrusion detection systems* (IDS) Part 2 – Classification; methods; techniques (White paper).

Ko, C. (2000). *Logic induction of valid behavior specifications for intrusion detection.* Los Alamitos, CA: IEEE Press.

Kruegel, C., Valeur, F., Vigna, G., & Kemmerer, R. (2002). Stateful intrusion detection for high-speed networks. In *Proceedings of the 2002 IEEE Symposium on Security and Privacy (S&P.02).* Los Alamitos, CA: IEEE Computer Society Press.

Kruegel, C., Mutz, D., Robertson, W., & Valeur, F. (2003). Bayesian event classification for intrusion detection. In *Proceedings of the 19ᵗʰ Annual Computer Security Applications Conference (AC-SAC 2003).* Los Alamitos, CA: IEEE Computer Society Press.

Li, Z., & Das, A. (2004). Visualizing and identifying intrusion context from system calls trace. In *Proceedings of the 20ᵗʰ Annual Computer Security Applications Conference (ACSAC'04).* Los Alamitos, CA: IEEE Computer Society Press.

Lindqvist, U., & Porras, P. A. (2001). *eXpert-BSM: A Host-based intrusion detection solution for Sun Solaris.* Los Alamitos, CA: IEEE Press.

Mutz, D., Vigna, G., & Kemmerer, R. (2003). An experience developing an IDS Stimulator for the black-box testing of network intrusion detection systems. In *Proceedings of the 19ᵗʰ Annual Computer Security Applications Conference (ACSAC 2003).* Los Alamitos, CA: IEEE Computer Society Press.

Rose, M. (2001). RFC 3080: The blocks extensible exchange protocol core. *Internet Engineering Task Force.*

Rubin, S., Jha, S., & Miller, B. P. (2004). Automatic @sis of NIDS attacks. In *Proceedings of the 20ᵗʰ Annual Computer Security Applications Conference (ACSAC'04).* Los Alamitos, CA:. IEEE Computer Society Press.

Rubin, S., Jha, S., & Miller, B. P. (2005). Language-based generation and evaluation of NIDS signatures. In *Proceedings of the 2005 IEEE Symposium on Security and Privacy (S&P'05).* Los Alamitos, CA: IEEE Computer Society Press.

Shankar, U., & Paxson, V. (2003). Active mapping: Resisting NIDS evasion without altering traffic. In *Proceedings of the 2003 IEEE Symposium on Security and Privacy (SP.03).* Los Alamitos, CA: IEEE Computer Society Press.

Silva, P. F., & Westphall, C. P. (2005, July, 17-20). A model for interoperability of answers in intrusion detection systems. *CD-ROM Proceedings of the Advanced International Conference on Telecomunications (AICT 2005),* Lisbon, Portugal.

Tombini, E., Debar, H., Mé, L., & Ducassé, M. (2004). A serial combination of anomaly and misuse IDSes applied to HTTP traffic. In *Proceedings of the 20th Annual Computer Security Applications Conference (ACSAC'04).* Los Alamitos, CA: IEEE Computer Society Press.

Vigna, G., Gwalani, S., Srinivasan, K., Belding-Royer, E. M., & Kemmerer, R. A. (2004). An intrusion detection tool for AODV-based ad hoc wireless networks. In *Proceedings of the 20ᵗʰ Annual Computer Security Applications Conference (ACSAC'04).* Los Alamitos, CA: IEEE Computer Society Press.

Wan, T., & Yang, X. D. (2000). *IntruDetector: A software platform for testing network intrusion detection algorithms.*

Wood, M., & Erlinger, M. (2002). *Intrusion detection message exchange requirements, IETF, RFC Draft, draft-ietf-idwg-requirements-10.*

Wu, Q., & Shao, Z. (2005). Network anomaly detection using time series analysis. In *Proceedings of the Joint International Conference on Autonomic and Autonomous Systems and International Conference on Networking and Services (ICAS/ICNS 2005).* Los Alamitos, CA: IEEE Computer Society Press.

Wu, Y.-S., Foo, B., Mei, Y., & Bagchi, S. (2003). Collaborative intrusion detection system (CIDS): A framework for accurate and efficient IDS. In *Proceedings of the 19ᵗʰ Annual Computer Security Applications Conference (ACSAC 2003).* Los Alamitos, CA: IEEE Computer Society Press.

Section II
Trust, Privacy, and Authorization

Chapter VI
Security in
E-Health Applications

Snezana Sucurovic
Institute Mihailo Pupin, Serbia

ABSTRACT

This chapter presents security solutions in integrated patient-centric Web-based health-care information systems, also known as electronic healthcare record (EHCR). Security solutions in several projects have been presented and in particular a solution for EHCR integration from scratch. Implementations of Public key infrastructure, privilege management infrastructure, role based access control and rule based access control in EHCR have been presented. Regarding EHCR integration from scratch architecture and security have been proposed and discussed. This integration is particularly suitable for developing countries with wide spread Internet while at the same time the integration of heterogeneous systems is not needed. The chapter aims at contributing to initiatives for implementation of national and transnational EHCR in security aspect.

INTRODUCTION

E-health has become the preferred term for healthcare services available through the Internet. While the first generation of e-health applications comprises educational and informational Web sites, at present e-health has grown into national and transnational patient centric healthcare record processing. A patient centric healthcare record, also called electronic healthcare record (EHCR) and electronic patient record (EPR), enables a physician to access a patient record from any place with Internet connection and give a new face to integration of patient data. Such integration can improve healthcare treatment and reduce the cost of services to a large extent. Benefits are based on extended possibilities for collaboration through sharing data between a physician and a patient and between physicians. In such large scale information systems, which spread over different domains, standardization is highly required. The second paragraph describes the main issues in e-health security as well as the results of EU projects EUROMED and TRUSTHEALTH, while the third paragraph presents MEDIS prototype of national healthcare electronic record suitable especially for developing countries where the Internet is widespread and healthcare information systems are not developed to large extent and therefore integration from scratch is proposed.

EXISTING SOLUTIONS

In general, the following lines of development for healthcare information system were considered as important (Reichertz, 2006): (1) the shift from paper-based to computer-based processing and storage, as well as the increase of data in health care settings; (2) the shift from institution-centered departmental and, later, hospital information systems towards regional and global HIS; (3) the inclusion of patients and health consumers as HIS users, besides health care professionals and administrators; (4) the use of HIS data not only for patient care and administrative purposes, but also for health care planning as well as clinical and epidemiological research; (5) the shift from focusing mainly on technical HIS problems to those of change management as well as of strategic information management; (6) the shift from mainly alpha-numeric data in HIS to images and now also to data on the molecular level; (7) the steady increase of new technologies to be included, now starting to include ubiquitous computing environments and sensor-based technologies for health monitoring.

As consequences for HIS in the future, the need for institutional, national, and international HIS-strategies is first seen; second, the need to explore new (transinstitutional) HIS architectural styles is needed; third, the need for education in

Figure 1. Degree of sophistication in healthcare information systems. Note. From Information Systems, Sao Paolo University Technical Report, 2006)

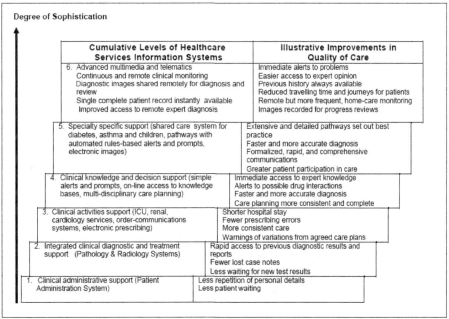

health informatics and/or biomedical informatics, including appropriate knowledge and skills on HIS are needed. As these new HIS are urgently needed for reorganizing health care in an aging society, as last consequence the need for research around HIS is seen. Research should include the development and investigation of appropriate transinstitutional information system architectures, of adequate methods for strategic information management, of methods for modeling and evaluating HIS, the development and investigation of comprehensive electronic patient records, providing appropriate access for health-care professionals as well as for patients (e.g., including home care and health monitoring facilities). All these requirements have implications on security issues. See Figure 1 for an example of the degree of sophistication in healthcare information systems.

Security is a very complex issue related to legal, ethical, physical, organizational, and technological dimensions defined as security policy. In that context, security addresses human, physical, system, network, data, or other aspects.

Legal Issues

Hipocrate's oath contains the obligation of keeping health data secret as a part of professional ethics «What I may see or hear in the course of the treatment or even outside of the treatment in regard to the life of men, which on no account one must spread abroad, I will keep to myself, holding such things shameful to be spoken about". As far as today's practice is concerned, several countries have adopted acts on medical data privacy protection, and especially on privacy protection of the electronic form of medical data. One among such documents is European Directive on the Protection of Individuals with Regard to the Processing of Personal Data and on the Free Movement of such Data of September 25, 1995, intended for privacy protection in data processing systems. Medical data privacy protection is presented in Section 3 of paragraph 2 «Special

Processing Categories», whose article 1 states that member countries should forbid the processing of personal data on political attitudes, religious and philosophic beliefs, racial and ethnic origin as well as medical data unless they satisfy particular, precisely specified conditions. For medical data, these conditions are as follows:

- When data processing is performed for purposes of preventive medicine, medical diagnostics, the provision of medical treatment and management of medical protection services where these data are processed by health professionals who are bound to keep professional secrecy by national laws or rules established by competent bodies or by some other persons subject to an equivalent obligation.
- Persons to which these data refer have given an explicit consent to the processing of such data.
- Processing is required for protecting the vital data of the person to which these data pertain or of some other persons, when the person in question is physically or legally incapable of giving a consent.
- Processing of data relating to persons which have committed a criminal act or to persons which may violate safety is performed under the supervision of authorized officials.

Section 4 of paragraph 2 «Information to be submitted to a person» states the conditions under which a person has to be given the information on the processing of that person's private data, and especially the informataion about forwarding these data to a third party.

Section 5 of paragraph 2 of this Document «A subject's right to access his own data» states a person's rights to access his personal data in data processing systems.

Paragraph 3 of this document says that member countries should ensure for each person, which considers that he/she has suffered a loss because of illegal processing of his/her data, to be entitled to a compensation.

Results of EUROMED Project

All European Commision funded e-health projects are in compilance with EU directive. One of first implemented was EUROMED (Katsikas,1998). This projects (started in 1997) examines use of trusted third party (TTP) services in distributed healthcare information systems. A trusted third party (TTP) is an entity which facilitates inter-actions between two parties who both trust the third party; they use this trust to secure their own interactions. One of TTPs is a certificate authority (CA). CAs are defined in X. 509 standard (ITU-T Standard, 1997).

X.509 standard defines a framework for the authentication service which a directory provides to all interested users. A directory is taken to mean that part of the system which possesses authentic information on system users. A dirctory is implemented as a certificate authority (CA) which issues certificates to users. X.509 defines two authentication levels:

- Simple authentication, which uses a pass-word for identity verification
- Strong authentication, which involves credentials—additional means of identification obtained by cryptographic

Strong authentication is based on an asymmetric cryptosystem involving a pair of keys: a public and a private key. The standard does not prescribe mandatory usage of a particular crypto system (DSA, RSA, etc.) and thus supports modifications in methods to be brought about by the development of cryptography.

Each user should have a unique distinguished name. A naming authority is responsible for assigning a name.

A user is identified by proving that he/she possesses a private key. To be able to verify a private key, a user–partner in the communication process must possess a public key. The public key is available on the directory.

A user should be given a public key from a trusted source. Such a source is a CA which uses its own public key to certify a user's public key and produces a certificate in this way. A certificate has the following properties:

- Each user having the access to a CA's public key can disclose the public key on which a certificate has been created.
- No party, except for the CA, can make a modification to a certificate without such a modification being detected. Owing to this property certificates may be stored on a directory with no need for additional protection efforts.

A certificate is obtained by creating a digital signature on a set of information about a user, such as a unique name, a user's public key and additional information about a user. This set of information also contains a certificate's validity period. This period includes the interval during which the CA has to keep the information about certificate status, i.e., publish an eventual certificate revocation. A certificate is presented in the ASN.1 notation as follows:

```
Certificate      ::= SIGNED {SEQUENCE{
version          [0]        Version DEFAULT
v1,
      serialNumber        CertificateSerial
      Number,
      signature           AlgorithmIdentifier,
      issuer              Name,
      validity            Validity,
      subject             name,
      subjectPublicKeyInfo  SubjectPublicKey-
Info,
      issuerUniqueIdentifier    [1]      I M -
PLICIT UniqueIdentifier OPTIONAL,
      subjectUniqueIdentifier   [2]      I M -
```

PLICIT UniqueIdentifier OPTIONAL

```
    extensions      [3]      Extensions OP-
TIONAL  }}

Validity            ::=      SEQUENCE {
    notBefore                Time,
    notAfter                 Time
}

SubjectPublicKeyInfo ::=     SEQUENCE {
    algorithm                AlgorithmI-
dentifier,
    subjectPublicKey         BIT STRING
}
Extensions           ::=     SEQUENCEOF
Extension
```

Three types of strong authentication are described in the standard:

a. **One-way authentication:** Includes only one transfer from a user A to an intended user B

b. **Two-way authentication:** Includes a reply from B to A as well

c. **Three-way authentication:** Includes an additional transfer from A to B

An example of using two-way authentication is given in CEN ENV 13729 standard which prescribes the use of strong authentication in health information systems.

CEN ENV 13729 has defined local and remote two way strong authentication using X509 standard.

EUROMED-ETS provides integrity, authentication and confidentiality services using measures such as:

• Digital signatures to ensure data integrity
• Encryption to provide confidentiality

TTP sites were established in four different locations in Europe: Institute of Computer and Communication Systems - ICCS (Athens-Greece), University Hospital Magdeburg - UHM (Magdeburg-Germany), University of the Aegean - UoA (Samos-Greece), and University of Calabria - Uni-CAL (Calabria-Italy).

Among the functions performed by the Certification Authority are: initialisation, electronic registration, authentication, key generation and distribution, key personalisation, certificate generation, certificate directory management, certificate revocation, CRL generation, maintenance, distribution storage and retrieval.

The Directories have served in that way as a repository for identification and authentication information; this information was utilised automatically by the EUROMED-ETS pilot Secure Web Servers to identify potential users and grant or deny to them rights; this identification information was also accessible anonymously through the Internet by the use of LDAP search tools.

Figure 2. Challenge-response authentication protocol using X.509 public key certificates

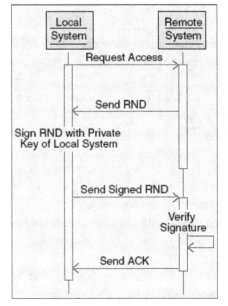

Figure 3. Remote strong authentication according to CEN ENV 13729

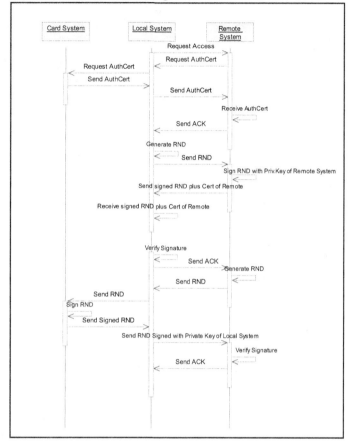

Results of Trusthealth Project

«Trustworth Health Telematics 2» (Blobel, 2001) project was started in June 1998 under the auspices of the European Commission. The aim of the project is to create a national infrastructure that would provide the security on the communication and application level of health information systems in: Belgium, France, Germany, Norway, Sweden and Great Britain and the focus is on interstate interoperability. The implementation of Trusthealth I Project, which took part from 1996 to 1997 involved the introduction of:

- The use of Health Professional Cards (HPC), microprocessor cards used in the authentication process
- Card reader services
- Services of Trusted Third Party which manages certificates

Within TH-1 the following services have been provided:

- Sending of a physician's report with all relevant data to a central register.
- Execution of prespecified and freely formed SQL queries relating to a patient's EHCR.

- Statistical analyses by various criteria, also by making a SQL query
- Exchange of any information, including HL7 messages, images, etc.

A TTP involves several independent organizations responsible for defining TTP services. TTP components may be:

- Key generation instance
- Naming authority
- Registration authority
- Directory service authority

In the TrustHealth Project the public key registration authority (PKRA) is an entity that identifies, in a unique way, a user requiring the provision of a digital signature service. The professional registration authority (PRA) is an entity registering an individual as a physician, i.e. as a medical care professional. The naming authority (NA) is an entity assigning to users a unique name to be used in certificates. The NA may be involved in assigning unique names to classes within the medical profession (e.g., internal medicine) and subclasses (e.g. nephrology). The public key Certification Authority (PKCA) is an entity certifying the relation between a user's unique name and public key by issuing a public key certificate with a PKCA digital signature. The PKCA is also responsible for revoking and repeated issuance of a certificate with a public key, whereas the professional Certification Authority (PCA) certifies the relation between a user's unique name and professional status, after having created a digital signature on these data. The PCA is also reponsible for revoking and repeated issuance of professional certificates. The card issuing system (CIS) is an entity issuing microprocessor cards that must contain a private key and may contain certificates as well. The generation of a private-public key pair may be performed using a local or a central key generator (LKG), an entity that may be located locally (with a user or PKRA) or

centrally (with the PKC or CIS). Certificates have to be stored on the certificate directory (DIR). The DIR is an entity that isues, on a request, certificates with a public key, professional certificates, revoked certificate lists as well as other information about users. In the TrustHealth Project the TTP services (NA, PRA, PCA, LKG, PKRA i DIR) are proposed to be implemented in institutions such as the chamber of physicians.

In this project the NA is implemented so as to assign a unique name to a user by using the name of a state, a unique number assigned to each physician on a state level and a physician's name. The RA is implemented so as to certify a user's identity and attributes such as profession or qualification. On a user's request, relevant information is verified, associated to a distinguish name – DN and sent online to a certification entity. The RA uses the information provided by the qualification authentication authority (QAA) or by the profession authentication authority (PAA). The former instance may be a university, for example, while the latter may be a chamber of physicians. In the part of TrustHealth Project implemented in Magdeburg, the chamber of physicians of the state of Saxony-Anhalt has implemented a majority of TTP services. The chamber of physicians has also included QAA services such as qualification, specialization, etc. All these pieces of information have been transmitted online to a certification body.

Based on data obtained from the RA, the Certification Authority creates certificates. Certificates that associate a user's distinguish name and the remaining relevant information to a user's public key are referred to as public-key certificates. Certificates that associate information about profession, qualification are attribute certificates. The first service is provided by the CA and the second by the PCA. CA Management Toolkit from the SECUDE package is used for X509v3 certificate creation and management in the TrustHealth Project.

The DIR directory service includes the publication and revocation of certificates using public directories. An X.500 compatible solution implemented in the SECUDE package is used in the TrustHealth Project. In this Project DIR maintains both public-key and attribute certificates. It is planned to use the Lightweight directory access protocol (LDAP) server later.

Results of PCASSO Project

The Patient Centered Access to Secure Systems Online (*http://medicine.ucsd.edu/pcasso/index. html*) was developed in 1997-2000 at the University of California San Diego School of Medicine. It is intended primarily to permit patients and health care providers to access health information, including sensitive health data. Access control is achieved by combining role-based access control (RBAC), mandatory access control (MAC) and discretionary access control (DAC). PCASSO is patient-centered and all data are stored on a single server in the current project stage.

According to DAC, when a user requests accessing an object, it is checked whether there is a rule allowing that user to access that object in a given mode. If there is, access is allowed, otherwise it is forbidden. Such an approach is viewed as very flexible and has found a wide usage, especially in commercial and industrial environments. Its shortcoming is the lack of information flow control. It is thought that it is easy to avoid access restrictions imposed by authorization (a set of rules stating which subject is allowed to access a particular object and in which mode). For example, when a user has read some data once, he/she may forward them to an unauthorized user without data owner's knowledge. In contrast to this, information flow from a higher-level object to a lower-level one is prevented in the MAC approach.

In MAC access rights are based on the classification of subjects and objects in the system. A particular protection level is assigned to each subject and each object. The protection level assigned to an object reflects data sensitivity level. The protection level assigned to a subject reflects the level of confidence in that subject that it will not forward accessed information to persons that do not have such rights. These levels are arranged in a hierarchy where each protection level dominates lower levels. A subject has the right of access to an object only if there is a particular relation between the protection level belonging to that subject and the protetcion level belonging to that object. One among such relations is the following: the protection level belonging to the subject has to dominate the protection level belonging to the object. MAC is used in defense and governmental departments.

Some researchers have expressed a view that DAC and MAC approaches cannot satisfy many practical requirements. The MAC approach is suitable for a military environment, whereas DAC is suitable for communities where cooperative work predominates, such as academic institutions. This is why a number of alternatives have been offered. Role based access control (RBAC) is the most widely used among them. RBAC controls a user's access right on the basis of user's activities performed in the system. A role may be defined as a set of activities and responsibilities relating to a particular activity. The advantages of RBAC approach include:

- Simpler authorization control. Authorization specification is divided into two stages: assigning roles to users and assigning object access rights to roles.
- Role hierarchy is easy to create, which is suitable for many systems
- Roles permit a user to work with a minimal-privilege role and use only exceptionally a role having maximal privileges. Error occurrence possibilities are reduced in this way.
- Separation of duties. It is possible to provide that not a single person can autonomously

abuse the system. An example is the introduction of ... : each person performs only a portion of an operation instead of the entire operation.

In PCASSO users may have one of the following roles: patient, primary care provider (PCP), secondary care provider (SCP) or Emergency Caregiver. Information and functionalities available to a user depend on the role belonging to her/him. PCASSO employs the following security policy:

- The system controls all accesses to data for each single user.
- Primary care providers are allowed to access all parts of a patient's EHCR.
- PCP is privileged to mark some data in an EHCR as accessible to or forbidden for a patient or other care providers.
- A patient is allowed to access all parts of an EHCR except for those marked as "patient deniable"
- Care providers marked as PCP may change protection attributes in a patient's record. PCPs may authorize and give rights to consultants referred to as Secondary care providers. A patient's PCP may declare a SCP to be a PCP for a particular time period, after the expiration of which a previous role is resumed.
- A possibility is given to care providers to deny access to a part of a child's EHCR to parents.
- In emergency cases care providers may have an unlimited access (reading only) to a patient's EHCR.

PCASSO distinguishes 5 patient data protection levels: Patient-deniable, Parent/Guardian-deniable, Public-deniable, Standard and Low. A user will be allowed to access data having the same or a lower label (protection level) compared with the user's label (MAC approach) and belong,

at the same time, to the group having the right of access to that piece of data (DAC approach).

EHCR ARCHITECTURE - CEN ENV 13 606 STANDARD

All EU transnational projects are in compliance with CEN ENV 13 606 standard.

The Comité Européen de Normalisation European Standard (CEN ENV 13606, 2002) "EHCR Communication" is a high level template which provides a set of design decisions which can be used by system vendors to develop specific implementations for their customers.

It contains several parts:

- **Part 1. Extended Architecture:** Defines component-based EHCR reference architecture.
- **Part 2. Domain Term List:** Defines terms which are used in extended architecture.
- **Part 3. Distribution Rules:** Defines data structures which are used in distribution and shared access to EHCR.

Communication as an act of imparting or exchanging information is the primary concern of this standard. In its Part 1 the standard defines an EHCR Communication View as the reuse of stored clinical data in a different context. There can be many such Communication Views and they provide presentation of information in a chronological order , "problem-oriented" manner or some other convention. This is provided by use of architectural components which are rich enough to be able to communicate data by a combination of components. There are a root component, which contains basic information about a patient, on one hand, and, on the other hand, a record component established by original component complexes (OCCs), selected component complexes (SCC), data items (DI) and link items (LI). An OCC comprises (according to data homogeneity) four basic components: folders, compositions, headed sections and clusters. A SCC contains a collection of data representing an aggregation of other record components that is not determined by the time or situation in which they were originally added to the EHCR. It may contain a reference to a set of search criteria, a procedure or some other query device whereby its members are generated dynamically (for example "current medication"). A Link Item is a component that provides a means of associating two other instances of architectural component and specifying the relationship between them ("caused by", for example). A data item is a record component that represents the smallest structural unit into which the content of the EHCR can be broken down without losing its meaning.

As a result of cooperation of CEN Technical Committee 251 and Australian Good Electronic Health Record (GEHR) project, CEN ENV 13606 Part 1 was revised in 2002. The revised standard adopted the GEHR concept in which object-oriented EHCR architecture is distinguished from a knowledge model. A knowledge model contains specifications of clinical structures named archetypes. There are many benefits of that two-layer model and one is that archetypes can be developed by clinicians at the same time when IT specialists develop EHCR object oriented architecture. In the revised CEN standard architectural components

contain an identifier of archetype (for example "vitals", "blood pressure" etc.).

In part 2 CEN ENV 13 606 standard defines a list of terms, such as category names for Compositions ("Notes on Consultations", "Clinical Care Referrals" etc.) and Headed Sections ("Former Patient History", "Ongoing Problems & Lifestyle" etc.).

According to part 3 of CEN ENV 13606 standard, each Architectural Component has a reference to a Distribution Rule. A Distribution Rule comprises When, Where, Why, Who and How classes. Class Why is mandatory, i.e. one of its attributes has to be "not null". Instances of these classes define When, Where, Why, Who and How is allowed to access that component (see Figure 4).

IMPLEMENTING SECURE DISTRIBUTED EHCR: MEDIS EXAMPLE

The MEDIS project aims at developing a prototype secure national healthcare information system. Since clinical information systems in Serbia and Montenegro have not been implemented to a large extent, we have focused our efforts on integration itself from the very beginning, instead of on studying how to integrate various

Figure 4. Distribution rule (CEN ENV 13606 Part 3)

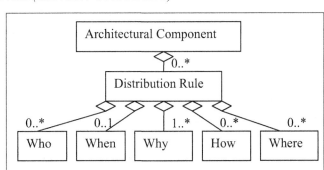

Table 1. Projects' characteristics

	EUROMED	TRUSTHEALTH	PCASSO	MEDIS
Internet based architecture	X	X	X	X
Component based architecture	X	X		X
Public key infrastructure	X	X	X	X
Privilege management infrastructure		X		X
Web service security				X
Role based access control	X	X	X	X
Rule based access control				X

systems. In recent years Internet has become widespread in our country and using Internet to implement a shared care paradigm is becoming a reality. MEDIS is based on CEN ENV 13606 standard and follows a component-based software paradigm in both EHCR architecture and software implementation. MEDIS has been implemented as a federated system where the central server hosts basic EHCR information and clinical servers contain their own part of patients' EHCR. CEN ENV 13 606 requirements have been strictly fulfilled in clinical servers as well as in the central server. In our opinion the user interface has to be standardised and we give our proposal for standardisation. As for the security aspect, MEDIS implements achievements from recent years, such as Public Key Infrastructure and privilege management infrastructure, SSL and Web Service security as well as pluggable, XML based access control policies. Table 1. presents characteristics of EUROMED, TRUSTHEALTH and MEDIS projects.

MEDIS Architecture

Since the MEDIS project refers to integration from the very beginning, EHCR reference architecture has been followed in defining the database model. Data have been stored in a hierarchical manner, where architectural components contain pointers to a supercomponent, linked components and also a selected component complex.

MEDIS has been implemented as a federated system. Architectural components are created in compliance with CEN ENV 13606 and stored there where they are created – at hospitals and clinics and are accessed via a central server which contains a root component and the addresses of the clinical and hospital servers. Architectural components that are hosted on the clinical and hospital servers have pointers to supercomponents and linked components (see Figure 5). User interface has been standardised in the following way. HTML pages are created on the central server and contain five frames: the required architectural component (AC) in the right frame, links to subcomponents and linked components in the upper left frame, links to selected component complex (actually distributed queries) in the lower left frame, the AC position in the hierarchical structure of EHCR in the upper frame and information about a user in the lower frame (see Figure 6). A physician can define the position in EHCR (and therefore HTML page) which will appear when he requests EHCR for a patient.

Currently, in the MEDIS architecture there are two types of selected component complex. Firstly, there are SCCs given as a union of queries on all clinical servers such as «current medication» or «current diagnosis». Search criteria are made according to the identifier of archetype.

Figure 5. System architecture

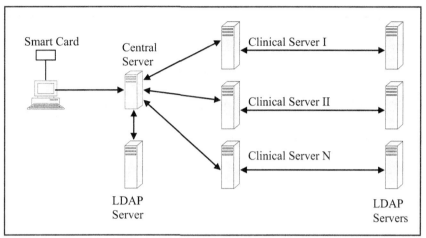

Secondly, there are SCCs related to architectural components on clinical servers and they contain search criteria for architectural components on that clinical server.

In MEDIS there is an authentication applet (Sucurovic, 2005) which is processed in a browser and, after successful authentication, a HTML page has been generated using JSPs on the central server. The clinical servers tier has been implemented in Java Web Services technology using Apache Axis Web Service server and Tomcat Web Server. Business logic has been implemented in reusable

Figure 6. CEN ENV 13 606 Composition Component example

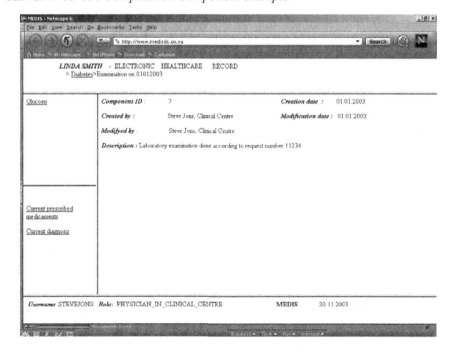

Figure 7. MEDIS access control components

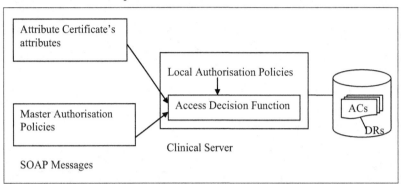

components–Java Beans. Authorisation policy is decomposed into components which can be plugged in Beznosov (2004) (see Figure 7).

Implementing Security

Using a password as a means of verification of claimed identity has many disadvantages in distributed systems. Therefore, MEDIS implements CEN ENV 13 729 (CEN ENV, 2000) which defines authentication as a challenge-response procedure using X.509 public key certificates. Solutions related to attribute certificates management have also been implemented (Sucurovic, 2006). Originally, X.509 certificates were meant to provide nonforgeable evidence of a person's identity. Consequently, X.509 certificates contain information about certificate owners, such as their name and public key, signed by a certificate authority (CA). However, it quickly became evident that in many situations, information about a person's privileges or attributes can be much more important than that of their identity. Therefore, in the fourth edition of the X.509 Standard (2000), the definition of an attribute certificate was introduced to distinguish it from public-key certificates from previous versions of the X.509 Standard (ITU-T, 2000).

In the MEDIS project X.509 PKCs are supposed to be generated by the public certificate authority, while ACs are supposed to be generated by the MEDIS attribute authority. The

public key certificates are transferred to users and stored in a browser (Sucurovic, 2005). The attribute certificates are stored on LDAP server (Sucurovic, 2006), because they are supposed to be under control of the MEDIS access control administrator. In the MEDIS approach, attribute certificates contain user's attributes as XML text. There are two types of public key and attribute certificates: the Clinicians' and a Patients' as distribution rules contain a flag which denotes if the architectural component is allowed to be read by a patient. Patients will be granted reading the architectural component if physicians set a corresponding flag.

Access Control

In a complex distributed system, such as MEDIS, access control is consequently very complex and has to satisfy both a fine grained access control and administrative simplicity. This can be realised using plugable, component based authorisation policies (Beznosov, 2004). An authorisation policy is the complex of legal, ethical, social, organisational, psychological, functional and technical implications for trustworthiness of health information system. One common way to express policy definition is an XML shemadata. These schemas should be standardised for interoperatibility purposes (Blobel, 2004). The MEDIS project aims at developing the authorisation policy definitions, using XML schemadata (MEDIS Tech. Report, 2005), which are based on CEN ENV 13 606 Distribution rules attributes (CEN ENV, 2002).

Distribution rules define the attributes of architectural components related to access control (CEN ENV, 2002). A distribution rule comprises Who, When Where, Why and How objects (see Table 2). The object Why is mandatory, i.e. one of its attributes has to be "not null". The attributes and entities contained within the objects Who, When, Where, Why and How shall be processed as ANDs. If, however there is more than one Who, How, Where, When or Why object present in a distribution rule, the occurrences of each of those object types shall be processed as ORs.

The MEDIS project has adopted XML as the language for developing constrained hierarchical role based access control and, at the same time, has its focus on decomposing policy engines into components (Beznosov, 2004; Blobel, 2004; Chadwick et al., 2003; Joshi et al., 2004; Zhou, 2004).

The MEDIS project authorisation policy has several components (MEDIS Technical Report, 2005). First, there is an XML schema of user attributes that corresponds to the attribute certificate attributes. Second, there are distribution rules attached to each architectural component (see Figure 4). Third, there are local authorisation policies on local LDAP servers. Fourth, there are Master Authorisation Policies on central LDAP server. There are several types of policies:

- Authorisation policy for hierarchy. It defines hierarchies of How, When, Where, Why and Who attributes (hierarchy of roles, professions, regions etc). In that way, a hierarchical RBAC can be implemented, with constraints defined by security attributes (software security, physical security rating etc.) and nonsecurity attributes (profession, specialisation etc.).
- Authorisation policy for hierarchy combinations. It defines which combination of,

Table 2. Distribution Rule objects [1]

Classes	Attributes	Type
Who	Profession Specialization Engaged in care Healthcare agent	String String Boolean Class
Where	Country Legal requirement	String Boolean
When	Episode of care Episode reference	Boolean String
Why	Healthcare process code Healthcare process text Sensitivity class Purpose of use Healthcare party role	String String String Class Class
How	Access method (read, modify) Consent required Signed Encrypted Operating system security rating Physical security rating Software security rating	String Class Boolean Boolean String String String

for example, role hierarchy and profession hierarchy is valid.

- Authorisation policy for DRs. It defines which combinations of attributes in a Distribution Rule are allowed.

There is an enable/disable flag, which defines whether the policy is enabling or disabling. There are in fact, two administrators: one on the clinical server and another on the central LDAP server. In that way, this approach provides flexibility and administrative simplicity. Our future work is to explore the best allocation of these policies between the central server and local servers.

Encryption

The MEDIS project implements Web Service security between the clinical and central server and SSL between the central server and a client (Microsoft, IBM, 2004). We use Apache's implementation of the OASIS Web Services Security (WS-Security) specification–Web Service Security for Java (WSS4J) (W3C Recommendation, 2002). WSS4J can secure Web services deployed in most Java Web services environments; however, it has specific support for the Axis Web services framework. WSS4J provides the encryption and digital signing of SOAP messages. The RSA algorithm has been chosen for signing and the TripleDES for encryption. Communication between the browser and Web Server has been encrypted using SSL. Currently, Netscape 6 browser and Tomcat 5.0 Web Server are used and the agreed chiper suite between them is SSL_RSA_WITH_RC4_128_MD5.

FUTURE WORK

If an application has a large number of users and requires a large number of roles and fine-grained

access control at the same time, a formal verification of security policy properties is needed. Secondly, MEDIS project is going to develop a powerful search engine based on intensive use of distributed queries with corresponding security questions solved. MEDIS is a medical record and we are planning to make it a multidisciplinary and multiprofessional record. Nowadays, integration in electronic record comprises the integration of previously introduced HIS using a communication protocol, such as HL7, and Web Services. Hospitals and clinics are connected in grids with protocols similar to Web Services SOAP protocol.

CONCLUSION

Regarding the basic requirements of secure communication and secure cooperation in distributed systems based on networks, basic security services are required. These services have to provide identification and authentication, integrity, confidentiality, availability, audit, accountability (including nonrepudiation), and access control. Additionally, infrastructural services such as registration, naming, directory services, certificate handling, or key management are needed. Especially, but not only in health care, value added services protecting human privacy rights are indisputable. This paper presents existing solutions in transnational electronic healthcare records and also gives a proposal for EHCR architecture and EHCR security solutions in developing countries with widespread Internet.

ACKNOWLEDGMENT

The author would like to thank Mrs. Vesna Zivkovic, PhD, Director of Institute Mihailo Pupin, Computer Systems, for her overall support.

REFERENCES

Beznosov, K. (2004). *On the benefits of decomposing policy engines into components.* Third Workshop on Adaptive and Reflect Middleware, Toronto, Canada.

Blobel, B. (2001). The European TrustHealth project experiences with implementing a security infrastructure. *International Journal of Medical Informatics, 60,* 193-201.

Blobel, B. (2004). Authorisation and access control for electronic health record system. *International Journal of Medical Informatics, 73,* 251-257.

Blobel, B., Hoepner, P., Joop, R., Karnouskos, S., Kleinhuis, G., & Stassinopoulos, G. (2003). Using a privilege management infrastructure for secure Web-based e-health applications. *Computer Communication, 26*(16), 1863-1872.

Chadwick, D., et. al. (2003, March-April). Role based access control with X.509 attribute certificates. *IEEE Internet Computing*, 62-69.

Commite Europen de Normalisation ENV 13606 Standard. (2002). *Extended architecture.*

Commite Europen de Normalisation ENV 13729 Standard. (2002). *Secure user identification.*

ITU-T Standard X. 509. (1995, October 24). *Information technology. Open systems interconnection-The directory: Public-key and attribute certificate frameworks.* Directive of the European Parliament and of the Council of 1995 on the protection of individuals with regard to the processing of personal data and on the free movement of such data. Retrieved January 10, 2006, from http://www.dsv.su.se/jpalme/society/eu-personal-privacy-directive.html

Information Systems and Information Technology Solutions. (n.d.). *Sao Paolo University report.* Retrieved June 10, 2006, from http://www.virtual.epm.br/material/healthcare/B01.pdf

Joshi, J., et. al. (2004, November–December). Access control language for multidomain environments. *IEEE Internet Computing*, 40-50.

MEDIS technical report. (n.d.). Retrieved September 28, 2005, from http://www.imp.bg.ac.yu/dokumenti/MEDISTechnicalReport.doc

Microsoft and IBM white paper. (2005). *Security in Web service world: A proposed architecture and roadmap.* Retrieved September 28, 2005, from http://www-128.ibm.com/developerworks/webservices/library/ws-secmap

Katsikas S., Spinellis D., Iliadis J., Blobel B., 1998, Using trusted third parties for secure telemedical applications over the WWW: The EUROMED-ETS approach. *Intern. Journal of Medical Informatics, 49,* 59-68

Reichertz, P. (in press). Hospital information systems: Past, present, future. *International Journal of Medical Informatics.*

Sucurovic, S., & Jovanovic, Z. (2005, February). *Java cryptography & X.509 authentication.* San Francisco: Dr. Dobb's Journal.

Sucurovic, S., & Jovanovic Z. (in press). *Java cryptography & attribute certificate management.* San Francisco: Dr. Dobb's Journal.

Wei, Z., & Meinl, Z. (2004). *Implement role based access control with attribute certificates, ICACT 2004.* International Conference on Advanced Communication Technology, Korea.

Chapter VII
Interactive Access Control and Trust Negotiation for Autonomic Communication

Hristo Koshutanski
University of Trento, Italy

Fabio Massacci
University of Trento, Italy

ABSTRACT

Autonomic communication and computing is the new paradigm for dynamic service integration over a network. In an autonomic network, clients may have the right credentials to access a service but may not know it; equally, it is unrealistic to assume that service providers would publish their policies on the Web so that clients could do policy evaluation themselves. To solve this problem, the chapter proposes a novel interactive access control model: Servers should be able to interact with clients asking for missing credentials, whereas clients may decide to comply or not with the requested credentials. The process iterates until a final agreement is reached or denied. Further, the chapter shows how to model a trust negotiation protocol that allows two entities in a network to automatically negotiate requirements needed to access a service. A practical implementation of the access control model is given using X.509 and SAML standards.

INTRODUCTION

Recent advances of Internet technologies and globalization of peer-to-peer communications offer for organizations and individuals an open environment for rapid and dynamic resource integration. In such an environment, federations of heterogeneous systems are formed with no central authority and no unified security infrastructure. Considering this level of openness, each server is responsible for the management and enforcement of its own security policies with a high degree of autonomy.

Controlling access to services is a key aspect of networking and the last few years have seen the domination of policy-based access control. Indeed, the paradigm is broader than simple access control, and one may speak of policy-based self-management of networks (see, e.g., IEEE Policy Workshop series; Lymberopoulos, Lupu & Sloman, 2003; Sloman & Lupu, 1999). The intuition is that actions of nodes controlling access to services are automatically derived from policies. The nodes look at events, requested actions and credentials presented to them, evaluate the policy rules according to those new facts and derive the actions (Sloman & Lupu, 1999; Smirnov, 2003). Policies can be "simple" iptables configuration rules for Linux firewalls (see http://www.netfilter.org) or complex logical policies expressed in languages such as Ponder (Damianou, Dulay, Lupu, & Sloman, 2001) or a combination of policies across heterogeneous systems as in OASIS XACML framework (XACML, 2004).

Dynamic coalitions and autonomic communication add new challenges: A truly autonomic network is born when nodes are no longer within the boundary of a single enterprise, which could deploy its policies on each and every node and guarantee interoperability. An autonomic network is characterized by properties of self-awareness, self-management and self-configuration of its constituent nodes. In an autonomic network nodes are like partners that offer services and lightly integrate their efforts into one (hopefully coherent) network. This cross enterprise scenario poses novel security challenges with aspects of both trust management and workflow security.

From trust management systems (Ellison et al., 1999; Li, Grosof, & Feigenbaum, 2003; Weeks, 2001) we take the credential-based view. Since access to network services is offered by autonomic nodes and to potentially unknown clients, the decision of grant or deny access can only be made on the basis of credentials sent by a client.

From workflow access control systems (Atluri, Chun, & Mazzoleni, 2001; Bertino, Ferrari, & Atluri, 1999; Georgakopoulos, Hornick, & Sheth, 1995; Kang, Park, & Froscher, 2001) we borrow all classical problems such as dynamic assignment of roles to users, dynamic separation of duties, and assignment of permissions to users according to the least privilege principle.

In an autonomic communication scenario a client might have all the necessary credentials to access a service but may simply not know it. Equally, because of privacy considerations, it is unrealistic to assume that servers will publish their security policies on the Web so that clients can do a policy combination and evaluation themselves. So, it should be possible for a server to ask a client on-the-fly for additional credentials whereas the client may disclose or decline to provide them. Next, the server reevaluates the client's request, considering the newly submitted credentials and computes an access decision. The process iterates between the server and the client until a final decision of grant or deny is taken. We call this modality interactive access control.

Part of these challenges can be solved by using policy-based self-management of networks, but not all of them. Indeed, if we abstract away the details on policy implementation, one can observe that the only reasoning service actually used by nowadays policy-based approaches is *deduction*: given a policy and a set of additional facts, find out all consequences (actions or obligations) from the policy according to the facts. We simply look whether granting the request can be deduced from the policy and the current facts. Policies could be different (Bertino et al., 2001; Bertino, Ferrari, & Atluri, 1999; Bonatti & Samarati, 2002; Li, Grosof & Feigenbaum, 2003), but the kernel reasoning service is the same.

Access control for autonomic communication needs another less-known reasoning service, taken from AI domain, called abduction (Shanahan, 1989). Loosely speaking, we could say that abduction is deduction in reverse: Given a policy and a request to access a network service, we want to know what are the credentials (facts) that would grant access. Logically, we want to know whether there is a (possibly minimal) set of facts that added to the policy would entail (deduce) the request.

If we look again at our intuitive description of the interactive access control it is immediate to realize that abduction is the core service needed by the policy-based autonomic servers to reason for missing credentials.

We can also use abduction on a client side so that whenever a client is requested for missing credentials it can perform evaluation on its policy and counter-request the server for some evidences in order to establish confidence (trust) to disclose the originally requested credentials.

Chapter Scope

This chapter targets readers who want to put into a practical framework security policies for access control. As a chapter outcome, the readers will be able to understand the logical reasoning services of deduction and abduction, and how to use them to model a practical access control framework. Furthermore, the readers will be able to model interactive access control between two entities,

each of them running its own deduction and abduction algorithms, thus allowing a bilateral exchange of access requirements until an agreement is reached or denied.

For those readers with practical background, the chapter presents how to implement and integrate the interactive access control model with the security standards such as X.509 and SAML. Readers should be familiar with either logic programming or answer set programming or datalog, as a prerequisite to the chapter's content.

A PRIMER ON INTERACTIVE ACCESS CONTROL

Motivation by Example

Let us consider a shared overlay network Planet-Lab between the University of Trento and Fraunhofer institute in Berlin in the context of the E-NEXT project. For the sake of simplicity assume that there are three main access types to resources: *disk* – read access to data residing on the Planet-Lab machines; *run* – execute access to data and possibility to run processes on the machines; and *configure* – including the previous two types of access plus the possibility of configuring network services on the machines.

Members of the two labs are classified in a hierarchy shown in Figure 1. The partial order of roles is indicated by arcs where higher the role in the hierarchy is more powerful it is. A role *dominates* another role if it is higher in the hierarchy and there is a direct path between them.

The access policy of the Planet-Lab network specifies that:

- *Disk* access is allowed to any request coming from the two institutions.
- *Run* access is allowed to any request coming either from specific machines at the two institutions or from any machine at the two

Figure 1. Joint hierarchy model

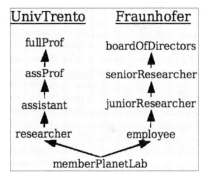

institutions accompanied with a membership certificate.

- *Configure* access is allowed to anybody that has run access to the network resources and is at least researcher at University of Trento or junior researcher at Fraunhofer institute. Additionally, configure access is also granted to associate professors or senior researchers with the requirement of accessing the Planet-Lab network from the respective country domains of Italy or Germany. The least restrictive access is granted to full professors or members of board of directors obliging them to provide the appropriate credential attesting their positions.

Let us have the scenario where Alice is a senior researcher at Fraunhofer and daily she needs to get run access to resources at Planet-Lab network. So, whenever she is at her office and she wants to execute some services she sends her employee certificate to the system. According to the access policy, run access is granted to Alice because as an employee she is a member of the Planet-Lab hierarchy model (see Figure 1).

Now, examine the case in which Alice wants to have access to the system from his home place (in Munich) presenting her employee certificate assuming that it is potentially enough to get run access to certain services. But, according to the policy rules the system should deny the request because run access requests coming from domains different than University of Trento or Fraunhofer institute are allowed only to associate professors or senior researchers or higher role positions.

So, the natural question is, "is it the behavior we want from the system?" Shall we leave Alice with only "access denied" decision and being idle for the whole day simply because she did not know or just has forgotten that access to the system outside Fraunhofer needs another certificate?

An answer like "sorry, we also need a credential for being at least a senior researcher" would be more than welcomed by most employees. At the same time, servers want to be sure to ask this additional credential only to employees.

Protecting Sensitive Policies

Practical access control policies like those protecting companies' resources, EU project sensitive documents etc, may leak valuable business information when revealed to public. Furthermore, an access control policy sometimes may disclose the entire business strategy of a company or an institution. Consider the following examples:

Example 1 *(Seamons, Winslett, & Yu, 2001) Suppose a Web page's access control policy states that in order to access documents of a project in the site, a requester should present an employee ID issued either by Microsoft or by IBM. If such a policy can be shown to any requester, then one can infer with high confidence that this project is a cooperative effort of the two companies.*

Example 2 *(Yu & Winslett, 2003) McKinley clinic makes its patient records available for online access. Let r be Alice's record. To gain access to r a requester must either present Alice's patient ID for McKinley clinic ($C_{AliceID}$), or present a California social worker license (C_{CSWL}) and a release-of-information credential (C_{RoI}) issued to the requester by Alice.*

Knowing that Alice's record specifically allows access by social workers will help people infer that Alice may have a mental or emotional problem. Alice will probably want to keep the latter constraint inaccessible to strangers. However, employees of McKinley clinic ($C_{McKinleyEmployee}$) should be allowed to see the contents of the policy.

To summarize, we have identified the following two issues:

- Provide additional information on missing credentials back to clients in case they do not have enough access rights.

- Protect access policies and their requirements from unnecessary disclosure.

How to approach the above cases is the subject of the next section.

Interactive Access Control vs. Current Approaches

In this section we introduce step-by-step the novel contribution of interactive access control model by evolving the existing access control frameworks.

Let us start with the traditional access control. A server has a *security policy for access control* P_A that is used when taking access decisions about usage of services offered by a service provider. A user submits a set of credentials C_p and a service request r in order to execute a service. We say that policy P_A and credentials C_p entail r (informally for the moment, $P_A \cup C_p \models r$) meaning that request r should be granted by the policy P_A and the presented credentials C_p.

Figure 2 shows the "traditional" access control decision process. Whether the decision process uses RBAC (Sandhu et al, 1996), SDSI/SPKI (SPKI), RT (Li & Mitchell, 2003) or any other trust management framework it is immaterial

at this stage: they can be captured by suitably defining P_A, C_p and the entailment operator ($\models$). This approach is the cornerstone of most logical formalizations (De Capitani di Vimercati & Samarati, 2001): If the request r is a consequence of the policy and the credentials, then access is granted; otherwise it is denied.

A number of works has deemed such blunt denials unsatisfactory. Bonatti and Samarati (2002) and Yu, Winslett and Seamons (2003) proposed to send back to clients some of the rules that are necessary to gain additional access. Figure 3 shows the essence of the approaches.

Both works have powerful and efficient access control establishment mechanisms. However, they merge two different security issues: policy for governing access to server's own resources and policy for governing the disclosure of foreign credentials.

Both approaches require policies to be flat: A policy protecting a resource must contain all credentials needed to allow access to that resource. As a result, it calls for structuring of policy rules that is counter-intuitive from the access control point of view. For instance, a policy rule may say that for access to the full text of an online journal article a requester must satisfy the requirements for browsing the journal's table of contents plus some additional credentials. The policy detailing access to the table of contents could then specify another set of credentials.

Further, constraints that would make policy reasoning nonmonotone (such as separation of duties) are also ruled out as they require to look at more than one rule at a time. So, if the policy is not flat and it has constraints on the credentials that

Figure 2. Traditional access control

1. check whether P_A and C_p entail r,
2. if the check succeeds then *grant* access
3. else *deny* access.

Figure 3. Disclosable access control

1. check whether P_A and C_p entail r,
2. if the check succeeds <u>then</u> *grant* access
3. else
   - (a) find a rule $r \leftarrow p \in PartialEvaluation(P_A \cup C_p)$, where p is a (partial) policy protecting r,
   - (b) if such a rule exists <u>then</u> *send* it back to the client else *deny* access.

can be presented at the same time (e.g., separation of duties) or a more complex role structure is used, those formalisms would not be complete.

Bonatti and Samarati's approach has further limitations on the granularity level of disclosure of information. In their work governing access to a service is composed in two parts: a prerequisite rule and a requisite rule. Prerequisite rules specify the requirements that a client should satisfy before being considered for the requirements stated by the requisite rules, which in turn grant access to services. Thus, prerequisite rules play the role of controlling the disclosure of the service requisite rules. In this way their approach does not decouple policy disclosure from policy satisfaction, as already noted by Yu and Winslett (2003), which becomes a limitation when information disclosure plays crucial role.

The work by Yu and Winslett (2003) overcomes this latter limitation and proposes to treat policies as fist class resources, i.e., each policy protecting a resource is considered as a sensitive resource itself whose disclosure is recursively protected by another policy. Still they have the same flatness, unicity and monotonicity limitations. These limitations are due to a traditional viewpoint: the only reasoning service one needs for access viewpoint is deduction, i.e., check that the request follows from the policy and the presented credentials.

Intuition 1: We claim that we need another less-known reasoning service, called *abduction*:

check which missing credentials are necessary so that the request can follow from the policy and the presented credentials. Thereupon, we present the basic idea of interactive access control in Figure 4.

The "compute a set C_M such that ..." (Step 3a) is exactly the operation of abduction. Essential part of the abduction reasoning is the computation of missing credentials that are solution for a request and at the same time consistant with the access policy. The consistency property gives up strong guarantees for the missing set of credentials when applying the algorithm on nonmonotonic policies.

This solution raises a new challenge: how do we decide the potential set of missing credentials? It is clearly undesirable to disclose all credentials occurring in the access policy and, therefore, we need a way to define how to control the disclosure of such a set.

As we have already noted, Yu and Winslett (2003) addressed partly this issue by protecting policies within the access policy itself. The authors distinguish between policy disclosure and policy staisfaction. It allows them to have control on when a policy can be disclosed from a policy is satisfied.

However, this is not really satisfactory as it does not decouple the decision about access from the decision about disclosure. Resource access is decided by the business logic whereas credential access is due to security and privacy considerations.

Figure 4. Basic idea of interactive access control

1. check whether P_A and C_p entail r,
2. if the check succeeds then *grant* access
3. else
(a) compute a set C_M such that:
- P_A together with C_p and C_M entail r, and
- P_A together with C_p and C_M preserve consistency.
(b) if C_M exists then *ask* the client for C_M and iterate
(c) (c) else *deny* access.

Intuition 2: We claim that we need two policies: one for granting access to one's own resources and one for disclosing the need of foreign (someone else's) credentials. Therefore, we introduce a *security policy for disclosure control* P_D. The policy for disclosure control is used to decide credentials whose need can be potentially disclosed to a client. In other words, P_A protects partner's resources by stipulating what credentials a requestor must satisfy to be authorized for a particular resource while, in contrast, P_D defines which credentials among those occurring in P_A are disclosable so, if needed, can be demanded from the requestor.

We give a new refined algorithm for interactive access control with controlled disclosure shown in Figure 5.

Yu and Winslett's policy scheme determine s whether a client is authorized to be informed of the need to satisfy a given policy. While, in our case, having a separate disclosure policy allows us to have a finer-grained disclosure control, i.e., determine whether a client is allowed to see the need of single credentials. Control the disclosure of (entire) policies as a finest-grained unit as well as the disclosure of single credentials composing those policies separately and independently from the disclosure of the policies themselves.

Now, let us look at Yu and Winslett's own example (Example 2) formalized as two logic programs:

Example 3

$$P_D \quad \begin{array}{|l} C_{AliceID} \leftarrow \\ C_{CSWL} \leftarrow C_{McKinleyEmployee} \\ C_{RoI} \leftarrow C_{McKinleyEmployee} \end{array} \qquad P_A \quad \begin{array}{|l} r \leftarrow C_{AliceID} \\ r \leftarrow C_{CSWL}, C_{RoI} \end{array}$$

The disclosure control policy is read as the disclosure of Alice's ID is not protected and potentially released to anybody requesting. The need for credentials California social worker license C_{CSWL} and release-of-information C_{RoI} is released only to users requested for, and that have pushed their McKinley employee certificates $C_{McKinleyEmployee}$.

The access policy specifies that access to r is granted either to Alice or to California social workers that have a release-of-information credential issued by Alice.

We note that the disclosure requirement for $C_{McKinleyEmployee}$ cannot be captured via the service accessibility scheme by Bonatti and Samarati (2002) and refer to Yu and Winslett (2003) for details. We also point out (as in Yu & Winslett, 2003) that having $C_{McKinleyEmployee}$ does not allow access to *r* but rather is used to unlock more information on how to access *r*. We also emphasize that the disclosure control on *r*'s policy $\{C_{CSWL}, C_{RoI}\}$ can be further split down on controlling the disclosure of the single credentials constituting it.

There are still tricky questions to be answered such as:

Figure 5. Interactive access control with controlled disclosure

> 1. check whether P_A and C_p entail *r*,
> 2. if the check succeeds then *grant* access
> 3. else
>   (a) compute the set of disclosable credentials C_D entailed by P_D and C_p,
>   (b) compute a set C_M out of the disclosable ones ($C_M \subseteq C_D$) such that:
>   - P_A together with C_p and C_M entail *r*, and
>   - P_A together with C_p and C_M preserve consistency.
>   (c) if C_M exists then *ask* the client for C_M and iterate
>   (d) else *deny* access.

- How do we know that the algorithm terminates? In other words, can actually arrive to a grant? For example, can we assure that the server will not keep asking Alice for a UNITN full professor credential which she does not have while never asking for a FOKUS senior researcher credential, which she has?
- How do we know that if a client gets granted then he has enough credientials of the resource.
- On the other hand, if a client has a solution for a resource then he will be granted the resource?

We will show how to fix the details of the algorithm later in the chatper so that all answers are positive.

So far, we have considered the access control process taking part on a server side. Then one would ask what about protecting clients from unauthorized disclosure of missing credentials. One can use the interactive access control algorithm also on the client side so that the client can do policy evaluation itself to determine whether the requested credentials can be disclosed to (granted, to be seen by) servers. And, alternatively, what additional information the servers should provide in order to see the requested credentials. In this way the interactive access control model can be used on client and server sides allowing them to automatically negotiate missing credentials until an agreement is reached or denied. The full evolvement of the negotiation model is described later in the chapter.

This is enough to cover stateless systems. We still have a major challenge ahead: How do we cope with stateful systems? Stateful systems are systems where the access decisions change depending on past interactions or past presented credentials. Such systems can easily become inconsistent with respect to the client's set of presented credentials mainly because access policies may forbid the presentation of credential

if another currently active credential has been presented in the past.

Past requests or services usage may deny access to future services as in Bertino, Ferrari and Atluri (1999) centralized access control model for workflows. Separation of duties means that we cannot extend privileges by supplying more credentials. For instance a branch manager of a bank clearing a cheque cannot be the same member of staff who has emitted the cheque (Bertino, Ferrari & Atluri, 1999, p. 67). If we have no memory of past credentials then it is impossible to enforce any security policy for separation of duties on application workflow. The problems that could cause a process to get stuck are the following:

- The request may be inconsistent with some roles, actions or events taken by the client in the past.
- The new set of presented credentials may be inconsistent with system requirements and constraints such as separation of duties.

Intuition 3: To address the problem of inconsistency, we need to extend the stateless algorithm in a way that it allows a service provider to reason of not only what missing credentials are needed to get a service, but also to reason on what conflicts credentials have to be deactiviated that make the access policy inconsistent.We need a procedure by which if a user has exceeded his privileges he has the chance to revoke them.

The algorithm for interactive access control for stateful systems is shown in Figure 6. Steps 1 to 3d are essentially the basic interactive access control algorithm.

The part for stateful systems comes when we are not able to find a set of missing credentials among the disclosable ones (Step 3d).

In this case there are two reasons which may cause the abduction failure when computing C_M. The first one could be that in C_D there are not enough disclosed credentials to grant r – case in

Figure 6. Interactive access control for stateful systems with controlled disclosure

1. check whether P_A and C_p entail r,
2. if the check succeeds then *grant* access
3. else
    (a) compute the set of disclosable credentials C_D entailed by P_D and C_p,
    (b) compute a set of missing credentials C_M out of the disclosable ones ($C_M \subseteq C_D$) such that:
        -   P_A together with C_p and C_M entail r, and
        -   P_A together with C_p and C_M preserve consistency.
    (c) if a set C_M exists then *ask* the client for C_M and iterate
    (d) else
        i. compute a set of *excessing credentials* C_E among the client's presented ones ($C_E \subseteq C_p$) such that:
            A) P_A together with $C_p \backslash C_E$ preserve consistency, and
            B) it exists $C_M (\subseteq C_D)$ such that:
                -   P_A together with $C_p \backslash C_E$ and C_M entail r, and
                -   P_A together with $C_p \backslash C_E$ and C_M preserve consistency.
        ii. if a set C_E exists then *ask* the client to present C_M and revoke C_E, and iterate
        iii.   else *deny* access.

which we should deny access (Step 3(d)iii), or, the second one, there might be credentials in the client's set of presented credentials C_p that make the policy state inconsistent—case in which any solution among the disclosable credentials cannot be found by the abduction.

The latter reason motivates Step 3(d)i. In this step, first, we want to find a set of conflicting credentials C_E, called excessing, among the presented ones C_p such that removing them from C_p preserves the access policy consistent, Step 3(d)iA. Second, on top of the not conflicting credentials it must exist a solution set that entails the service request, Step 3(d)iB. The second requirement assures that there is a potential solution for the client to get access to the requested service.

We refer the reader to (Koshutanski, 2005) for full details on the stateful model.

Interactive Access Control and Current Policy-Based Approaches

Having introduced the reasoning services and the respective access control algorithms does not completely show the advantages of the interactive access control model. This section describes how current logic-based approaches suit our interactive model.

The logical model, as presented so far, abstracts from a specific policy language and presents an executional framework for reasoning about access control. As such, the model fills an important gap between policy language specification and policy language enforcement and evaluation.

We skip here the classical access control models, (see De Capitani di Vimercati & Samarati, 2001) for a comprehensive survey) and concentrate on the current logic-based access control approaches cited in the literature.

The work by Li, Mitchell, and Winsborough (2002) introduces a model for distributed access control, called RT (Role-based Trust management). The core idea of the model is the way it classifies principles in a distributed manner. Basically, the model classifies each entity's local attributes (roles) and how other entities relate to those attributes. It classifies how each entity's attributes relates to other entities' attributes (attribute mapping from one domain to another). It also defines attribute-based delegation of attribute authority, i.e., the ability to delegate authority to strangers whose trustworthiness is determined based on their own certified attributes.

A later approach (Li, Li, & Winsborough, 2005) extends the RT framework to cope with different cryptographic schemes (e.g., zero-knowledge proof of attributes, oblivious signature envelope, hidden credential etc.) that are used to improve the privacy protection and effectiveness during a process of bilateral negotiation. The authors proposed a new language, called attribute-based trust negotiation language (ATNL), that specifies fine-grained protection of resources and their policies.

Another interesting logic-based approach is (Ruan, Varadharajan, & Zhang, 2003). In contrast to what we have seen, this work presents an authorization model that supports both positive and negative authorizations. The model introduces variety of rules that define different authorization and delegation statements, as well as, rules for conflict resolutions. This work targets another type of polices where explicit negation is needed to express the policy requirements.

All of the above described approaches are good candidates for an underlying policy language as the interactive access control model is data-driven by the abduction and deduction reasoning services. So, we will not target a particular policy language throughout the chapter as it is immaterial to the metalevel access control process.

Winsborough and Li (2004) postulate an important property concerning trust negotiation called safety in automated trust negotiation. During a negotiation process a sensitive credential is disclosed when its policy is satisfied by the negotiator. So, the problem comes from the fact that although a sensitive credential itself is not transmitted unless its associated policy is satisfied, the behavior of a negotiator differs based on whether he has the attribute or not. One can reveal additional information about the content of the credential by monitoring the opponent's behavior.

Since the interactive access control model enforces a metalevel negotiation process one can address the safety property requirement by properly defining the structure of access and disclosure control policies.

POLICY SYNTAX AND SEMANTICS

Syntax

Access policies are written as normal logic programs (Apt, 1990). These are sets of rules of the form:

$$A \leftarrow B_1, \ldots, B_n, not\ C_1, \ldots, not\ C_m, \quad (1)$$

where A, B_i and C_j are (possibly ground) predicates. A is called the head of the rule, each B_i is called a positive literal and each *not* C_j is a negative literal, whereas the conjunction of the B_i and *not* C_j is called the body of the rule. If the body is empty the rule is called a fact. A normal logic program is a set of rules.

In our framework, we also need constraints that are rules with an empty head.

$$\leftarrow B_1, \ldots, B_n, not\ C_1, \ldots, not\ C_m \quad (2)$$

The intuition is to interpret the rules of a program P as constraints on a solution set S (a set of ground atoms) for the program itself. So, if S is a set of atoms, rule (1) is a constraint on S stating that if all B_i are in S and none of C_j are in it, then A must be in S. A constraint (2) is used to rule out from the set of acceptable models situations in which B_i are true and all C_j are false.

One of the most prominent semantics for normal logic programs is the stable model semantics proposed by Gelfond and Lifschitz (1988) (see also Apt, 1990, for an introduction). In the following we formally define the reasoning services intuitively introduced in the motivation section.

Definition 1 (Deduction and Consistency) *Let P be a policy and L be a ground literal. L is de-*

ducible of P (P ⊨ L) if L is true in every stable model of P. P is consistent (P ⊭ ⊥) if there is a stable model for P.

Definition 2 (Security Consequence) *A resource r is a security consequence of a policy P if (i) P is consistent and (ii) r is deducible of P.*

Definition 3 (Abduction) *Let P be a policy, H a set of ground atoms (called hypotheses or abducibles), L a ground literal (called observation) and ≺ a partial order (p.o.) over subsets of H. A solution of the abduction problem <L, H, P> is a set of ground atoms E such that:*

1. $E \subseteq H$,
2. $P \cup E \vDash L$,
3. $P \cup E \nvDash \bot$,
4. *any set E' ≺ E does not satisfy all conditions above.*

Traditional partial orders are subset containment or set cardinality.

Definition 4 (Solution Set for a Resource) *Let P be a policy and r be a resource. A set of credentials C_S is a solution set for r according to P if r is a security consequence of P and C_S, i.e. P $\cup C_S \vDash r$ and $P \cup C_S \nvDash \bot$.*

Definition 5 (Monotonic and Nonmonotonic Policy) *A policy P is monotonic if whenever a set of statements C is a solution set for r according to P (P $\cup$ C ⊨ r) then any superset C'⊃C is also a solution set for r according to P (P $\cup$ C' ⊨ r). In contrast, a nonmonotonic policy is a logic program in which if C is a solution for r it may exist C'⊃C that is not a solution for r, i.e. $P \cup C' \nvDash r$.*

Formalization of the Example

Following is the full formalization of the example introduced at the beginning of the chapter. The predicate *authNet(IP, DomainName)*. It is a tuple with first argument the IP address of the authorized network endpoint (the client's machine) and the second argument the domain name where the IP address comes from.

For any resource in the system the user is considered to have *disk*, *run* or *configure* access rights. We represent variables with staring capital letter (e.g., Holder, Attr, Issuer) while constants with starting small case letters (e.g., planetLab-Class1SOA, institute, juniorResearcher). A variable indicates any value in its field.

Figure 7 shows the formalization of the Planet-Lab policies. Following is the functional explanation of the policies.

The access policy says:

- Rules (1), (2), and (3) classify issuers (SOAs) in different logical categories used by the access control logic. Example, Rule (1) categorizes planetLabClass1SOA as a system level SOA.
- Rules (4) and (5) give disk access to the shared network content to everybody from the University of Trento and Fraunhofer institute, regardless the IP and roles at these institutions.
- Rule (6) gives disk access to anybody who has a run access permission.
- Rules (7) and (8) allow run access for those machines that are internal to the two institutions (dedicated only for Planet-Lab access) and distinguished by their fixed IPs.
- Rules (9), (10), and (11) relax the previous two and allow run access from any place of the institutions to those users which present either a Planet-Lab membership certificate or a role-position certificate at one of the two institutions.

- Rule (12) gives run access to anybody who has a configure access permission.
- Rules (13) and (14) give configure access right if a user has a disk access and is at minimum assistant, attested (issued) by a trusted university's SOA, or at minimum junior researcher attested by a trusted institutional SOA.
- Rules (15) and (16) relax the previous two and give configure access to associate professors and senior researchers provided that requests come from the respective country domains.
- Rules (17) and (18) give configure access regardless the geographical region only to

members of board of directors and to full professors.

The disclosure policy says:

- Rules (1), (2), (3) and (4), disclose the need of specific authorization networks the request should come from. The need of specific authorization domains is disclosed to any potential client.
- Rules (5), (6) and (7), disclose the need for an employee, researcher and PlantLab member certificates to any potential client.
- Rules (8) and (9) disclose (upgrade) the need of higher role-position certificates than those provided either by a client or (disclosed) by other rules of the policy.

Figure 7. Planet-lab access and disclosure control policies

Access Policy:
(1)   classify(planetLabClass1SOA, system).
(2)   classify(fraunhoferClass1SOA, institute).
(3)   classify(unitnClass1SOA, university).
(4)   grant(disk) ← authNet(*, *.unitn.it).
(5)   grant(disk) ← authNet(*, *.fraunhofer.de).
(6)   grant(disk) ← grant(run).
(7)   grant(run) ← authNet(193.168.205.*, *.unitn.it).
(8)   grant(run) ← authNet(198.162.45.*, *.fraunhofer.de).
(9)   grant(run) ← grant (disk), credential(Holder, memberPlanetLab, Issuer), classify(Issuer, system).
(10)   grant(run) ← grant(disk), credential(Holder, Attr, Issuer), classify (Issuer, university), Attr ≻ researcher.
(11)   grant(run) ← grant(disk), credential(Holder, Attr, Issuer), classify (Issuer, institute), Attr ≻ employee.
(12)   grant(run) ← grant(configure).
(13)   grant(configure) ← grant(disk), credential(Holder, Attr, Issuer), classify(Issuer, university), Attr ≻ assistant.
(14)   grant(configure) ← grant(disk), credential(Holder, Attr, Issuer), classify(Issuer, institute), Attr ≻ juniorResearcher.
(15)   grant(configure) ← authNet(*, *.it), credential(Holder, Attr, Issuer), classify(Issuer, university), Attr ≻ assProf.
(16)   grant(configure) ← authNet(*, *.de), credential(Holder, Attr, Issuer), classify(Issuer, institute), Attr ≻ seniorResearcher.
(17)   grant(configure) ← credential(Holder, Attr, Issuer), classify(Issuer, university), Attr ≻ fullProf.
(18)   grant(configure) ← credential(Holder, Attr, Issuer), classify(Issuer, institute), Attr ≻ boardOfDirectors.

Disclosure Policy:
(1)   authNet(*, *, it)
(2)   authNet(*, *, de)
(3)   authNet(*, *, unitn.it)
(4)   authNet(*, *, fraunhofer.de)
(5)   credential(Holder, memberPlantLab, planetLabClass1SOA)
(6)   credential(Holder, employee, unitnClass1SOA)
(7)   credential(Holder, researcher, fraunhoferClassISOA)
(8)   credential(Holder, AttrX, unitnClass1SOA) ← credential(Holder, AttrY, unitnClass1SOA), AttrX ≻ AttrY
(9)   credential(Holder, fraunhoferClass1SOA) ← credential(Holder, AttrY, fraunhoferClass1SOA), AttrX ≻ AttrY

THE INTERACTIVE ACCESS CONTROL ALGORITHM

Below we summarize all the information we have recalled (policies, credentials, etc.) to this extend.

- P_A security policy governing access to resources.
- P_D security policy controlling the disclosure of foreign (missing) credentials.
- C_p the set of credentials presented by a client in a single interaction.
- C_P the set of active credentials that have been presented by a client during an interactive access control process.
- C_N the set of credentials that a client has declined to present during an interactive access control process.

Now, we have all the necessary material to introduce our interactive access control algorithm, shown in Figure 8.

The intuition behind the algorithm is the following. Once the client has initiated a service request r with (optionally) a set of credentials C_p, the interactive algorithm updates the client's profile C_P and C_N (lines 1: and 2:). C_P is updated with the newly presented credentials C_p while C_N is updated with the set difference of what the client was asked in the last interaction (C_M) and what he presents in the current one (C_p). Next, the algorithm consults for an access decision (line 3:). The first step of the access decision function checks whether the request r is granted by P_A according to the client's set C_p (Step 1). If the check fails, the starting point of the interactive framework, then in Step 2a the algorithm computes all credentials disclosable from P_D according to C_p and from the resulting set removes all already declined and already presented credentials. The latter is used to avoid dead loops of asking something already declined or presented. Then, the algorithm computes (using the abduction reasoning) all possible subsets of C_D that are consistent with the access policy P_A and, at the same time, grant r. Out of all those sets (if any) the algorithm selects the minimal one.

Example 5 *A senior researcher at Fraunhofer institute FOKUS wants to reconfigure an online service for paper submissions of a workshop. The service is part of a big management system hosted at the University of Trento's network that is part of the Planet-Lab network, formalized in the previous section. For doing that, at the time of access, she presents her employee certificate, issued by a Fraunhofer certificate authority, presuming that it is enough as a potential employee. Formally speaking, the request comes from a domain fokus. fraunhofer.de with an attribute credential for an employee. The set of credentials is:*

{authNet(198.162.193.46, fokus.fraunhofer. de), credential(AliceMilburk, employee, fraunhoferClass1SOA)}

According to the access policy the credentials are not enough to get configure access (see rule 14 in Figure 7). Then, the algorithm (Step 2a in Figure 8) computes the set of disclosable credentials from the disclosure policy and the user's set of active credentials C_p. In our case, C_p is the set of credentials mentioned above. Next, the algorithm computes C_D as the need of all roles higher in position than memberPlanetLab (see Figure 7, Disclosure Policy part) and the abduction Step (Figure 8 Step 2b), with criterion minimal set cardinality, computes the following missing sets that satisfy the request:

{credential(AliceMilburk, juniorResearcher, fraunhoferClass1SOA)},

{credential(AliceMilburk, seniorResearcher, fraunhoferClass1SOA)},

{credential(AliceMilburk, boardOfDirectors, fraunhoferClass1SOA)}

Then, using role minimality *criterion, the algorithm returns back the need for {credenti al(AliceMilburk, juniorResearcher, fraunhofer-Class1SOA)}.*

In the next interaction, since Alice is a senior researcher, she declines to present the requested credential by returning the same query but with no entry for presented credentials ($C_p = \varnothing$). So, the algorithm updates the user's profile marking the requested credential credential(AliceMilburk, juniorResearcher, fraunhoferClass1SOA) declined.

The difference comes when the algorithm recomputes the disclosable credentials as all disclosable credentials from the last interaction minus the newly declined one. Next, abduction computes the following sets of missing credentials that satisfy the request:

{credential(AliceMilburk, seniorResearcher, fraunhoferClass1SOA)},
{credential(AliceMilburk, boardOfDirectors, fraunhoferClass1SOA)}

According to role minimality criterion, the algorithm returns the need for a credential {credential(AliceMilburk, seniorResearcher, fraunhoferClass1SOA)}. On the next interaction, Alice presents a certificate attesting her as a senior researcher and the algorithm grants the requested service.

Remark 1 *Using declined credentials is essential to avoid loops in the process and to guarantee successful interactions in presence of disjunctive information.*

Technical Guarantees

In the following we show the summary of the technical results that the access control algorithm provides. We refer the reader to (Koshutanski, 2005) for full details on the theoretical framework.

Following are the basic guarantees that the interactive framework provides:

Figure 8. Interactive access control algorithm

```
Input: r, C_p
Output: grant/deny/ask(C_M)
iAccessControl(r, C_p){
 1: C_P = C_P ∪ C_p;
 2: C_N = C_N ∪(C_M\C_P), where C_M is from the last interaction;
 3: result = iAccessDecision(r, P_A, P_D, C_P, C_N );
 4: return result;
}

iAccessDecision(r, P_A, P_D, C_P, C_N ){
       1.   check whether r is a security consequence of P_A and C_p , namely
                 -   P_A ∪C_P |= r, and
                 -   P_A ∪C_P |≠ ⊥.
       2.   if the check succeeds then return grant else
            (a)   compute the set of disclosable credentials C_D as
                  C_D = {c | c credential that P_D ∪C_P |= c} \ (C_N∪C_P) ,
            (b)   use abduction to find a set of missing credentials C_M (⊆C_D) such that:
                 -   P_A ∪C_P ∪C_M |= r, and
                 -   P_A ∪C_P ∪C_M |≠ ⊥.
            (c)   if no such set exists then return deny
            (d)   else return ask(C_M).
}
```

- **Termination:** The interactive access control algorithm always terminates, that is, in a finite number of interactions either grant or deny is returned by the algorithm (resistant against DoS attacks).
- **Correctness:** If a client gets grant for a service then he has a solution for the service, that is, the algorithm does not grant access to unauthorized clients.
- **Completeness:** If a client has a solution for a service request then the algorithm will grant him access.

The most important thing, also the most difficult, is to model and prove that a client who has the right set of credentials and who is willing to send them to the server will not be left stranded in our autonomic network and will get grant.

First we need to define what would be a reasonable client our framework aims to provide the guarantees for.

Definition 6 (Powerful client) *A powerful client is a client that whenever receives a request for missing credentials returns all of them.*

Definition 7 (Cooperative client) *A cooperative client is a client that whenever receives a request for missing credentials returns those of them that he has in possession.*

Defining the notion of good clients with respect to the interactive algorithm is still not enough to state the practical relevance of the access control model. We need to introduce the notion of fairness reflecting the access and disclosure control policies. We define the following two properties:

Definition 8 (Fair Access) *A fair access property guarantees that whenever there is a request for a service it exists a solution in the access control policy which unlocks (grants) the service.*

In other words, for each resource protected by the access policy there should exist a set of credentials (a solution) that grants the resource according to the policy. Fair access property avoids cases where the policy specifies a solution for a service but the solution itself makes the policy state inconsistent, so that even a client with the right set of credentials for the service cannot get it.

Definition 9 (Fair Interaction) *A fair interaction property guarantees that if a solution for a service request exists (according to the access policy) then this solution should be disclosable by the disclosure control policy.*

In other words, any solution for a service should be potentially disclosable to a client requesting the service. In an autonomic scenario, where a service is potentially accessible by any client, fair interaction property would disclose a solution for a service to potentially any client requesting it. So, on one side, we want to be fair and disclose solutions to clients but, on the other side, we want to protect and restrict the disclosure of information only to selected clients (not to anybody). To approach this problem we introduce the notion of hidden credentials.

Informally speaking, a credential is hidden if an access control system needs it for taking an access decision, but does not disclose the need to anybody. Thus, an autonomic server can dynamically protect the privacy of its policies by specifying which credentials are hidden and which are not. This allows a server to restrict access to certain services only to selected clients.

Now we can define a client with hidden credentials.

Definition 10 (Client with Hidden Credentials for a Service) *A client with hidden credentials for a service is any client that has in possession the hidden credentials for that service and knows that these are to be pushed to the server initially.*

Now, we have to redefine the fair interaction property with respect to hidden credentials.

Definition 11 (Fair Interaction with Hidden Credentials) *If a solution for a service exists and there are hidden credentials for that solution then all credentials from the solution set which are not hidden must be disclosable by the disclosure policy and the set of hidden credentials.*

So far, we have introduced all we need to formulate the main guarantees showing the practical relevance of the access control framework.

Completeness for a cooperative client: If access and disclosure control policies guarantee fair access and interaction, respectively, then if a cooperative client has a solution for a service request then he will get grant with the interactive access control algorithm.

We can postulate the same claim per a cooperative client with hidden credentials for a resource.

IMPLEMENTING THE ACCESS CONTROL FRAMEWORK

This section emphasizes on the practical relevance of the access control framework and, particularly, on how the access control model can be of practical use.

There are two main points relevant to the implementation of the framework. This first one is how to cope with the implementation of the interactive access control algorithm and the second one is how to integrate the logical model with the current security standards widely adopted by IT companies.

For the first point, we will use a logical-based reasoning system, called DLV (see *http://www. dlvsystem.com*) and, particularly, how to employ DLV in order to perform the basic computations of abduction and deduction. As for the second one, we will show how to integrate the logical model with X.509 certificate framework and OASIS SAML standard.

Figure 9. Implementation of the basic functionalities of deduction and abduction

```
iAccessDecision(r, P_A, P_D, C_P, C_N){
1: if doDeduction(r, P_A∪C_P) then return grant
2: else
3:   C_D = {c | P_D∪C_P |= c} \ (C_N ∪C_P );
4:   result = doAbduction(r, C_D, P_A∪C_P );
5:   if result == ⊥ then return deny
6:   else return ask(result);
}

doDeduction(R: Query, P: LogProgram){ check for P |= R?
1: run DLV in deduction mode with input: P , R? ;
2: check output: if R is deducible then return true else return false;
}

doAbduction(R: Observation, H: Hypotheses, P : LogProgram){
1: run DLV in abduction diagnosis mode with input: R, H, P ;
2: DLV output: all sets C_i that (i) C_i ⊆ H, (ii) P ∪C_i |= R, (iii) P ∪C_i |≠ ⊥;
3: if no C_i exists then return ⊥
4: else select a minimal C_min and return C_min;
}
```

Integration with the Automated Reasoning Tool DLV

For the implementation of the interactive access control algorithm we use the DLV system (a disjunctive datalog system with negations and constraints) as a core engine for the basic functionalities of deduction and abduction. The disjunctive datalog front end (the default one) is used for deductive computations while the diagnosis front end is used for abductive computations. Figure 9 shows the implementation using the DLV system. The input of the function *i*AccessDecision is the requested service r, the policy for access control P_A, the policy for disclosure control P_D, the set of active credentials C_P and the set of declined credentials C_N. Step 1 uses the DLV's deductive front end. It specifies as input the service request r marked as a query over the models (r?) computed on $P_A \cup C_P$. The output of this step are those models in which r is true.

If it exists a model in Step 1 that satisfies r then the system returns grant (Step 1). If no model for r exists then we use the DLV's deductive front end with input $P_D \cup C_P$ (Step 3). In this case, DLV computes all credentials disclosable from $P_D \cup C_P$. Then from the computed set we remove all credentials that belong to C_N and C_P.

Once the disclosable credentials are computed then, in Step 4, we use the abductive diagnosis front end with the input: the requested service r stored in a temporary file with extension .obs (observations), the just computed set of disclosable credentials C_D stored in a temporary file with extension .hyp (hypotheses or also called abducibles) and the third argument is the access policy together with the active credentials $P_A \cup C_P$. The two input files (.hyp and .obs) have particular meaning for DLV system in the abductive mode.

The output of that computation are all possible subsets of the hypotheses that satisfy the observations. In that way we find all possible missing sets of credentials satisfying r. Then we filter them according to some minimality criteria and select the minimal set out of them.

The automated reasoning tool depends on the one's own choice. It can be used any other tool that supports the basic reasoning services (see for example, *www.tcs.hut.fi/spyware/smodels*).

Integration with X.509 and SAML Standards

The framework described so far processes credentials on a high (abstract) level: defines what can be inferred and what missing is from partner's

Figure 10. X.509 identity and attribute certificates structure

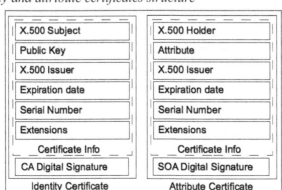

access policy and user's set of credentials. There is a need of a suitable certificate infrastructure for describing participant's identities and access rights. A good choice is the widely adopted certificate standard X.509 (X.509, 2001).

There are two certificate types considered by the standard: identity and attribute certificates. Figure 10 shows the structures of the two certificates.

X.509 identity certificate is used to identify entities in a network. The main fields of the certificate's structure are the subject information, the public key identifying the subject (corresponding to the subject's private key), the issuer information and the digital signature on the document, signed by the issuer (with its private key).

X.509 attribute certificate has the same structure like the identity one with the difference that instead of a public key field there is a field for listing attributes and the Subject field is called Holder (of the attributes).

Referring to the message level, one can adopt to use the OASIS SAML standard (SAML) for having standard semantics for authorization statements among participants in an autonomic network. SAML offers a standard way for exchanging authentication and authorization information between on-line partners.

The basic SAML data objects are assertions. Assertions contain information that determines whether users can be authenticated or authorized to use resources. The SAML framework also defines a protocol for requesting assertions and responding to them, which makes it suitable when modeling interactive communications between entities in a distributed environment.

We list below the SAML request/response protocol and how we employ it in the interactive access control framework.

- **SAML Request:** Use the authorization decision query statement for expressing access decision requests. Specify the resource and

action in the respective standard fields of the access statement.

Once an access decision is taken use the SAML response part.

- **SAML Response:** Use the authorization decision statement
  - **Permit / Deny:** When explicit grant/deny is returned by the *i*AccessControl protocol.
  - **Indeterminate:** When ask(C_M) is returned. In this case, list the missing credentials in the standard SAML attribute fields, for example,

    <attribute name=``MISSING_CREDENTIAL''>Employee ID</attribute>
    <attribute name=``MISSING_CREDENTIAL''>Full Professor</attribute>

To make the access decision engine Web Services compatible we also adopted the W3C SOAP (see *http://www.w3.org/TR/soap*) as a main transport layer protocol. SOAP is a lightweight protocol for exchanging structured information in a decentralized, distributed environment. It has an optional Header element and a required Body element. Informally, in the body we specify what information is directly associated with the service request and in the header additional information that should be considered by the end-point server.

So, to request for an access decision on a message level we have to:

  - First, attach X.509 Certificates in the SOAP Header using WS-Security (WS-Security) specification for that,
  - Then, place the SAML Request in the SOAP Body thus making it an input to the decision engine being invoked.

Having the needed technologies in hands, the next section describes how the just introduced standards and protocols can be integrated into one architecture.

System Architecture

Figure 11 shows the architecture of a prototype that has been developed, called *i*Access. The bottom most layer in the figure comprises the integration of the prototype with Tomcat (see *http://tomcat.apache.org*) application server. We perform all requests over SSL connection. Thus, assuring message confidentiality and integrity on the transport layer.

Once an access request is received by the Tomcat server, it invokes the *i*Access engine for an access decision. As shown in the figure, first, the engine parses the SOAP envelope, containing the body and the header elements. Then, it extracts X.509 (see X.509 technology provider: *http://*

www.bouncycastle.org) identity and attribute certificates, and the SAML (see SAML technology provider: *http://www.opensaml.org*) request protocol. Next, the engine performs validation and verification of the certificates: first for expiration dates and second for trustworthiness. The latter is performed according to local databases listing the trusted identity issuers and, respectively, the trusted attribute issuers (their public keys). The two databases are domain specific.

Remark 2 *We point out that the check for trusted CAs and SOAs is to filter out those certificates that are issued by unknown (distrusted) certificate authorities. The fine-grained verification on trusted attributes and identities is performed on the logical level and according to the access policy.*

Figure 11. iAccess architecture

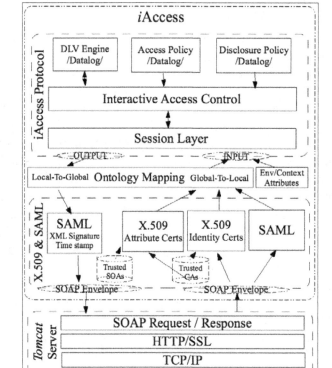

Once the certificates are validated and verified, *i*Access invokes an ontology conversion module for mapping the global certificate information to a local, provider specific, representation. The same mapping is also performed for the SAML request protocol information.

The ontology module semantically transforms global-to-local and local-to-global the following information:

- Certificate attributes
- Certificate issuers
- Resource names (service requests)
- Service actions

The *conversion* module transforms certificates' information and SAML request to predicates suitable for the logical model, as described below.

- Identity certificates are transformed to certificate(subject, Issuer: *i*) predicates,
- Attribute certificates are transformed to credential(holder, Attr: *a*, Issuer: *i*) predicates,
- SAML access request to grant(Resource: *r*, Action: *p*).

These transformations leverage access control management on the logical level because on this level there is local (domain specific) syntax for the representation of the above items.

After the transformation is performed *i*Access invokes the *i*AccessControl module for an access decision.

Once an access decision is taken (returned by the *i*AccessControl protocol), *i*Access maps the information grant, deny or additional credentials to their global representation and then generates the respective SAML Response protocol. After that, *i*Access places a time-stamp for validity period on the access decision statement and then digitally signs it to ensure integrity of the infor-mation. Next, Tomcat server returns the SAML decision to the entity requested for it.

TRUST NEGOTIATION

In an autonomic network scenario servers must have a way to find out what credentials are required for clients to get access to resources. Clients, once asked for missing credentials, may be unwilling to disclose them unless the server discloses some of its credentials first, that is, negotiate the need of sensitive credentials.

If we merge the two frameworks we have the following open problems:

1. Alice wants to access some service of Bob
2. Alice does not know exactly what credentials Bob needs, so
   (a) Bob must compute what is missing and ask Alice,
   (b) Alice must send to Bob all credentials he requested.
3. In response to 2b, Alice may want to have some credentials from Bob before sending hers, so
   (a) She must tell Bob what he needs to provide,
   (b) Bob must have a policy to decide how access to his credentials is granted.
4. In response to 2a, Bob may not want to disclose all that is missing at once but may want to ask Alice first some of the less sensitive credentials, so
   (a) Bob must have a way to request in a stepwise fashion the missing creden-tials.

To combine automated trust negotiation and interactive access control we assume that both clients and servers have the three logical security policies:

1. P_{AR} a policy for access to *own* resources on the basis of *foreign* credentials,
2. P_{AC} a policy for access to *own* credentials on the basis of *foreign* credentials,
3. P_D a policy for disclosure the need of (missing) *foreign* credentials.

Technically speaking we could merge 1 and 2 into a flat policy for protecting sensitive resources as in (Yu & Winslett, 2003; Yu, Winslett, & Seamons, 2003). However, the structured approach is better because the criteria behind and likely the administrator of each policy are different. Resource access is decided by the business logic whereas credential access is due to security and privacy considerations.

For example the negotiation of a sensitive credential may require activation of credentials that are not considered from the business logic for the actual access control process and even they may be inconsistent with the business logic rules. Thus, forcing separation between policies P_{AR} and P_{AC} we free the access policy P_{AR} to be arbitrarily complex with almost everything that is on the (Datalog) access control market (say with negation as failure, constraints on separation of duties, or other credentials such as those by Li and Mitchell (2003)).

Rather, the policy for access to own credentials P_{AC} we restrict to be monotonic because of its particular nature: once the need for a credential is disclosed (granted), it is disclosed! In contrast, a credential needed to access a resource may come and go due to separation of duty or other access control constraints.

The Negotiation Protocol

This sections shows how one can bootstrap from the simple security policies a comprehensive negotiation protocol that establishes proper trust relationships via bilateral exchange of credentials.

We introduce a new set notation O indicating a set of own credentials with respect to a negotiation opponent.

Now, let us recall the interactive access control protocol with the following modification. Instead of returning the set of missing credentials C_M we will transform it into a sequence of single requests each requesting for a foreign credential from the missing set. Figure 12 shows the new version of the protocol.

Figure 12. The core of the negotiation protocol

```
Session vars: C_P and C_N. Initially C_P=C_N = ∅;.
iAccessNegotiation(r, C_p){
  1: C_P = C_P∪C_p;
  2: repeat
  3:   result = iAccessDecision(r, P_A, P_D, C_P, C_N);
  4:   if result == ask(C_M) then
  5:     for each c ∈ C_M do
  6:       response = invoke iAccessNegotiation(c, ∅)@Opponent;
  7:       if response == grant then
  8:         C_P = C_P ∪ {c};
  9:       else
  10:        C_N = C_N ∪ {c};
  11:   done
  12: fi
  13: until result == grant or result == deny.
  14: return result;
}
```

We extended the protocol to work on client and server sides so that they automatically request each other for missing credentials. Step 1 of the protocol updates the set of active (foreign) credentials with those presented at the time of request. Those presented credentials are typically pushed by the opponent when initially requests for a service. After the initial update we go in a loop where *i*AccessDecision algorithm is run for an access decision.

The purpose of the loop is to keep asking the opponent new solutions (missing credentials) until a final decision of grant or deny is taken. The technicality of the protocol is in Step 6 where we represent the request for a missing credential as a remote invocation of the *i*AccessNegotiation protocol on the opponent side. In this way, the new protocol has the same functionality as *i*AccessControl protocol.

Step 6 invokes *i*AccessNegotiation protocol with an empty set of presented own credentials.

One can slightly modify the protocol by introducing a function PushedCredentials(*c*) that decides what own credentials an opponent has to present (O_{push}) when requesting for a foreign credential *c*.

To approach bilateral negotiation first we have to take into account the following two issues:

- Each request for a credential spurs a new negotiation thread that negotiates access to this credential.
- During a negotiation process parties may start to request each other credentials that are already in a negotiation. So, the notion of suspended credential requests must be taken into account.

Figure 13 shows the updated version of the *i*AccessNegotiation protocol. With its new version, whenever a request arrives it is run in a new thread that shares the same session variables C_p,

Figure 13. The negotiation protocol with suspended credentials

```
Session vars: C_p and C_N and O_neg. Initially C_p =C_N = O_neg = ∅;.
iAccessNegotiation(r, C_p){ runs in a new thread
 1: C_p = C_p ∪ C_p;
 2: if r ∈ O_neg then
 3:   suspend and await for the result on r's negotiation;
 4:   return result when resumed;
 5: else
 6:   O_neg = O_neg ∪ {r};
 7:   repeat
 8:     result = iAccessDecision(r, P_A, P_D, C_p, C_N);
 9:     if result == ask(C_M) then
10:       for each c ∈ C_M do
11:         response = invoke iAccessNegotiation(c, ∅)@Opponent;
12:         if response == grant then
13:           C_p = C_p ∪ {c};
14:         else
15:           C_N = C_N ∪ {c};
16:       done
17:     fi
18:   until result == grant or result == deny.
19:   O_neg = O_neg \ {r};
20:   resume all processes awaiting on r with the result of the negotiation;
21:   return result;
22:elseif
}
```

C_N and O_{neg} with other threads running under the same negotiation process. The set O_{neg} keeps track of the opponent's own credentials that have been requested and which are still in a negotiation.

Now, if a request for a credential, which is already in a negotiation, is received the protocol suspends the new thread until the respective negotiation thread finishes (Step 3). Then, when

the original thread returns an access decision the protocol resumes all threads awaiting on the requested credential and informs them for the final decision (Step 20).

Figure 14 shows the full-fledged negotiation protocol. The *iAccessDispatcher* module manages the negotiation session information. Its role is to

Figure 14. The negotiation protocol

```
Session vars: C_P, C_N and O_neg. Initially C_P = C_N = O_neg = ∅;.
iAccessDispatcher{
OnReceiveRequest: iAccessNegotiation(r, C_p)
1: if isService(r) then
2:   reply response = iAccessNegotiation(r, C_p); in a new negotiation session process.
3: else
4:   reply response = iAccessNegotiation(r, C_p); in a new thread under the original negotiation session.
OnSendRequest: <r, O_p>
1: if isService(r) then
2:   result = invoke iAccessNegotiation(r, O_p)@Opponent; in a new negotiation session process.
}
iAccessNegotiation(r, C_p){
1: C_p = C_p ∪ C_p;
2: if r ∈ O_neg then
3:   suspend and await for the result on r's negotiation;
4:   return result when resumed;
5: else
6:   O_neg = O_neg ∪ {r};
7:   repeat
8:     if isService(r) then
9:       result = iAccessDecision(r, P_AR, P_D, C_P, C_N);
10:    else
11:      result = iAccessDecision(r, P_AC, P_D, C_P, C_N);
12:    if result == ask(C_M) then
13:      AskCredentials(C_M);
14:   until result == grant or result == deny.
15:   O_neg = O_neg \ {r};
16:   resume all processes awaiting on r with the result of the negotiation;
17:   return result;
18:elseif
}
AskCredentials(C_M){
1: parfor each c ∈ C_M do
2:   response = invoke iAccessNegotiation(c, ∅)@Opponent;
3:   if response == grant then
4:     C_p = C_p ∪ {c};
5:   else
6:     C_N = C_N ∪ {c};
7: done
8: await untill all responses are received (await until C_M ⊆ C_p ∪ C_N);
}
```

dispatch (assign) to each request/response the right negotiation process information. It works in the following way. Whenever a request for a service is received the dispatcher runs *i*AccessNegotiation in a new session process and initializes C_p, C_N and O_{susp} to an empty set (Step 2). Then each counter-request for a credential is run in a new thread under the same negotiation process (Step 4).

On the other hand, whenever an entity requests a service r at the opponent side, presenting initially some own credentials O_p, the *i*AccessDispatcher module invokes *i*AccessNegotiation (at the opponent side) and creates a new session process so that any counter-request from the opponent is run in a new thread under the new negotiation process.

The intuition behind the negotiation protocol is the following:

1. A client, Alice, sends a service request r and (optionally) a set of own credentials O_p to a server, Bob.

2. Bob's *i*AccessDispatcher receives the requests and runs *i*AccessNegotiation(r, C_p) in a new process. Here $C_p = O_p$ with respect to Bob.

3. Once the protocol is initiated, it updates the over all set of presented foreign credentials with the newly presented ones and checks whether the request should be suspended or not (Steps 1 and 2).

4. If not suspended, then Bob looks at r and if it is a request for a service he calls *i*AccessDecision with his policy for access to resources P_{AR}, his policy for disclosure of foreign credentials P_D, the set of foreign presented credentials C_p and the set of foreign declined credentials C_N (Step 9).

5. If r is a request for a credential then Bob calls *i*AccessDecision with his policy for access to own credentials P_{AC}, his policy for disclosure of foreign credentials P_D, the set of presented foreign credentials C_p and the

set of declined foreign credentials C_N (Step 11).

6. In the case of computed missing foreign credentials C_M, Bob transforms it into requests for credentials and awaits until receives all responses. At this point Bob acts as a client, requesting Alice the set of credentials C_M. Alice runs the same protocol with swapped roles.

7. When Bob receives all responses he restarts the loop and consults the *i*AccessDecision algorithm for a new decision.

8. When a final decision of grant or deny is taken, the respective response is returned back to Alice.

Technicality in the protocol is in the way the server requests missing credentials back to the client. As indicated in the figure, we use the keyword parfor for representing that the body of the loop is run each time in a parallel thread. Thus, each missing credential is requested independently from the requests for the others. At that point of the protocol, it is important that each of the finished threads updates presented and declined sets of foreign credentials properly without interfering with other threads. We note that after a certain session time expires each credential request that is still awaiting on an answer is marked as declined.

Also an important point here is to clarify the way we treat declined and not yet released credentials. In a negotiation process, declining a credential is when an entity is asked for it and the same entity replies to the same request with answer deny. In the second case, when the entity is asked for a credential and, instead of reply, there is a counter request for more credentials, then the thread, started the original request, awaits the client for an explicit reply and treats the requested credential as not yet released. In any case, at the end of a negotiation process a client either supplies the originally asked credential or declines it.

Example 6 *Figure 15 shows an example of Alice's and Bob's interactions using the negotiation protocol on both sides. The policies for access to resources and access to sensitive credentials are in notations like in Yu, Winslett and Seamons (2003) where the Alice's local credentials are marked with subscript "A" and Bob's with "B", respectively. Bob's access policy P_{AR} says that access to resource r_1 is granted if $\{C_{A1}, C_{A2}\}$ are presented by Alice. To get access to r_2 Alice should either present $\{C_{A1}, C_{A3}\}$ or satisfy the requirements for access to r_1 and present C_{A4}. To get access to r_5 Alice should either satisfy the requirements for r_2 and present C_{A7} or satisfy the requirements for r_1 and present C_{A6}.*

Bob's disclosure policy discloses the need for credentials $C_{A1}, C_{A2}, C_{A3}, C_{A5}, C_{A6}$, and C_{A7} to potentially any client. But in contrast, the need for a credential C_{A4} is never disclosed but expected when r_2 is requested. It is an example of a hidden credential that must be pushed.

Analogously, Bob's P_{AC} says: to grant access to Bob's C_{B1} Alice must present C_{A5} and to grant access to Bob's C_{B2} Alice must present C_{A7}.

Following is the negotiation scenario. Alice requests r_5 to Bob presenting empty set of initial credentials. Alice's TN Dispatcher detects the request and creates a new session process awaiting on Bob's reply. Next, Bob runs the interactive algorithm on his P_{AR}. The outcome of the algorithm is the set of missing credentials $\{C_{A1}, C_{A3}, C_{A7}\}$ (computed as the minimal one). Then, Bob transforms the missing credentials in single requests and asks Alice for them.

Alice's TN Dispatcher receives the requests and runs them in three new threads for each of them, respectively. Next, Alice runs the interactive access control algorithm on her P_{AC} for each of the requests and returns grant C_{A1}, deny C_{A3} and counter request for Bob's C_{B2}. Bob replies to the request for C_{B2} with a counter request for Alice's C_{A7}. Since C_{A7} has been already requested by Bob, now Alice suspends the new request and awaits on the original one to finish its negotiation.

If we look again in the sequence of requests we recognize than the original thread depends on the outcome of the suspended one and we come to a recursive loop (interlock). Since Alice's suspended

Figure 15. Example of interoperability of the negotiation protocol

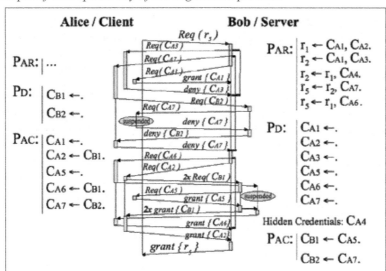

thread has a session timeout, so after it expires Alice returns to Bob a decision deny. At this point Alice can choose (automatically) to extend her session time to allow the negotiation to continue and eventually to successfully finish.

Next, Bob recalls its interactive access control for a new decision for r_5. The next set of missing credentials is $\{C_{A2}, C_{A6}\}$ which Bob transforms to single requests. The rest of the scenario follows analogously.

After Alice and Bob successfully negotiate on Bob's requests for missing credentials, Bob grants access to the service request r_5.

However, we have not solved the problem of stepwise disclosure of missing foreign credentials yet. The intuition here is that Bob may not want to disclose the missing foreign credentials all at once to Alice but, instead, he may want to ask Alice first some of the less sensitive credentials assuring him that Alice is enough trustworthy to disclose her other more sensitive credentials and so on until all the missing ones are disclosed. Here we point out that the stepwise approach may require a client to provide credentials that are not directly related to a specific resource but needed for a fine-grained disclosure control.

To address this issue we extend the negotiation protocol with an algorithm for stepwise disclosure of missing credentials. The basic intuition is that the logical policy structure itself tells us which credentials must be disclosed to obtain the information that other credentials are missing. So, we simply need to extract this information automatically. We perform a step-by-step evaluation on the policy structure. For that purpose we use a one-step deduction over the disclosure policy P_D to determine the next set of potentially disclosable credentials. We refer the reader to (Koshutanski & Massacci, 2007) for details on the stepwise algorithm.

Implementing the Trust Negotiation Framework

Figure 16 shows the architecture of the trust negotiation framework. JBOSS application server (see *http://www.jboss.org/products/jbossas*) uses TCP/IP sockets to send/receive information. The functionality of the server has been extended with the possibility to transform high-level credential/service requests, understandable by the TN Dispatcher, to low-level raw data requests suitable for transmission over TCP/IP connections.

Whenever the TN Dispatcher is initially run it internally runs the JBOSS application server. The TN Dispatcher it resides active in the memory awaiting for new requests. Once the JBOSS server receives a request it transforms the request it

Figure 16. The architecture of the negotiation framework

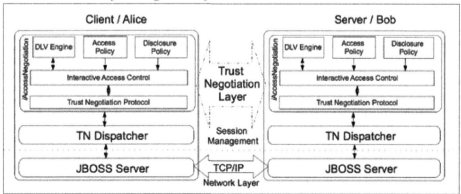

from raw data to a high-level representation and automatically redirects it to the dispatcher.

On each received request the TN Dispatcher analyzes the session data from the request against its local database, and acts as following. If no session data is specified in the request then the dispatcher generates new session information (new session data sets, see Figure 14) and runs the negotiation protocol with the new session info. If it exists a session ID in the request and the session ID correctly maps to the corresponding one in the dispatcher's local database then the dispatcher runs the negotiation protocol under the existing session. We not that any negotiation protocol instance is always run in a new parallel thread that it internally updates the session information. The trust negotiation protocol uses the JBOSS server methods to send/receive requests.

CONCLUSION

In this chapter we presented a framework on policy-based access control for autonomic communications. The framework is grounded in a formal model with the stable model semantics. The key idea is that in an autonomic network a client may have the right credentials but may not know it and thus an autonomic server needs a way to interact and negotiate with the client the missing credentials that grant access.

We have proposed a solution to this problem by extending classical access control models with an advanced reasoning service: abduction. Building on top of this service, we have presented the key interactive access control algorithm that, in case service request fails, computes on-the-fly missing credentials that entail the request. We have also introduced the notion of disclosable and hidden credentials. The distinction allows servers to dynamically protect the privacy of their policies by specifying which credentials are hidden and which are not and notifying selected clients for that.

We have identified the interactive access control model as a way for protecting security interests with respect to disclosure of information and access control of both server and client sides. We have proposed a protocol for leveraging trust negotiation between two entities involved in an autonomic communication. The protocol communicates and negotiates the missing credentials until enough trust is established and the service is granted or the negotiation fails and the process is terminated. The protocol is run on both client and server sides so that they understand each other and automatically interoperate until a desired solution is reached or denied.

One of the advantages of the approach is that we do not pose any restrictions on partner's policies because the basic computations of deduction and abduction, performed on the policies, do not require any specific policy structure. We have also presented an implementation of the framework using X.509 and SAML standards.

Open Problems and Future Work

Future work is in the direction of characterizing the complexity of the framework. Proving which guarantees the protocol can offer in terms of interoperability, completeness and correctness when applied to a practical policy language is still an open process and will be a subject of future research.

In the direction of mutual negotiation, future work is to explore the interoperability of the negotiation framework with the TrustBuilder prototype (Yu, Winslett, & Seamons, 2003). We believe that this is an important step toward building a secure open computing environment.

ACKNOWLEDGMENT

This work was partly supported by the projects: 2003-S116-00018 PAT-MOSTRO, 016004 IST-FP6-FET-IP-SENSORIA, 27587 IST-FP6-

IP-SERENITY, 038978 EU-MarieCurie-EIF-iAccess, 034744 EU-INFSO-IST ONE, 034824 EU-INFSO-IST OPAALS.

REFERENCES

Apt, K. (1990). Logic programming. In J. van Leeuwen (Ed.), *Handbook of theoretical computer science*. Elsevier.

Atluri, V., Chun, S. A., & Mazzoleni, P. A (2001). Chinese wall security model for decentralized workflow systems. In *Proceedings of the Eighth ACM conference on Computer and Communications Security* (pp. 48-57).

Bertino, E., Catania, B., Ferrari, E., & Perlasca, P. (2001). A logical framework for reasoning about access control models. In *Proceedings of the Sixth ACM Symposium on Access Control Models and Technologies (SACMAT)* (pp. 41-52).

Bertino, E., Ferrari, E., & Atluri, V. (1999) The specification and enforcement of authorization constraints in workflow management systems. *ACM Transactions on Information and System Security (TISSEC), 2*(1), 65-104.

Bonatti, P., & Samarati, P. (2002). A unified framework for regulating access and information release on the Web. *Journal of Computer Security, 10*(3), 241-272.

Damianou, N., Dulay, N., Lupu, E., & Sloman, M. (2001). The Ponder policy specification language. In *Proceedings of the International Workshop on Policies for Distributed Systems and Networks (POLICY)* (pp. 18-38).

De Capitani di Vimercati, S., & Samarati, P. (2001). Access control: Policies, models, and mechanism. In R. Focardi & F. Gorrieri (Eds.), *Foundations of security analysis and design - Tutorial lectures* (vol. 2171 of LNCS). Springer-Verlag.

Ellison, C., Frantz, B., Lampson, B., Rivest, R., Thomas, B. M., & Ylonen, T. (1999, September). SPKI certificate theory. *IETF RFC,* 2693.

Gelfond, M., & Lifschitz, V. (1988). The stable model semantics for logic programming. In R. Kowalski & K. Bowen (Eds.), *Proceedings of the Fifth International Conference on Logic Programming (ICLP'88)* (pp. 1070-1080).

Georgakopoulos, D., Hornick, M. F., & Sheth, A. P. (1995, April). An overview of workflow management: From process modeling to workflow automation infrastructure. *Distributed and Parallel Databases 3*(2), 119-153.

Kang, M. H., Park, J. S., & Froscher, J. N. (2001). Access control mechanisms for interorganizational workflow. In *Proceedings of the Sixth ACM Symposium on Access Control Models and Technologies* (pp. 66-74).

Koshutanski, H. (2005). *Interactive access control for autonomic systems*. Unpublished doctoral dissertation, University of Trento, Italy.

Koshutanski, H., & Massacci, F. (2007). A negotiation scheme for access rights establishment in autonomic communication. *Journal of Network and System Management (JNSM), 15*(1), 117-136.

Li, J., Li, N., & Winsborough, W. H. (2005). Automated trust negotiation using cryptographic credentials. In *Proceedings of the 12th ACM Conference on Computer and Communications Security* (pp. 46-57).

Li, N., Grosof, B. N., & Feigenbaum, J. (2003). Delegation logic: A logic-based approach to distributed authorization. *ACM Transactions on Information and System Security (TISSEC), 6*(1), 128-171.

Li, N., & Mitchell, J. C. (2003). RT: A role-based trust-management framework. In *Proceedings of the Third DARPA Information Survivability Conference and Exposition (DISCEX III)* (pp. 201-212).

Li, N., Mitchell, J. C., & Winsborough, W. H. (2002). Design of a role-based trust management framework. In *Proceedings of IEEE Symposium on Security and Privacy (S&P)* (pp. 114-130).

Lymberopoulos, L., Lupu, E., & Sloman, M. (2003). An adaptive policy based framework for network services management. *Plenum Press Journal of Network and Systems Management, 11*(3), 277-303.

Ruan, C., Varadharajan, V., & Zhang, Y. (2003). A logic model for temporal authorization delegation with negation. In C. Boyd & W. Mao (Eds.), *Proceedings of the Sixth International Conference on Information Security (ISC), 2851* (pp. 310-324).

SAML. (2004). *Security assertion markup language (SAML).* Retrieved from http://www.oasis-open.org/committees/security

Sandhu, R., Coyne, E., Feinstein, H., & Youman, C. (1996). Role-based access control models. *IEEE Computer, 39*(2), 38-47.

Seamons, K., Winslett, M., & Yu, T. (2001). Limiting the disclosure of access control policies during automated trust negotiation. In *Network and Distributed System Security Symposium.* San Diego, CA.

Shanahan, M. (1989). Prediction is deduction but explanation is abduction. In *Proceedings of IJCAI'89* (pp. 1055-1060). Morgan Kaufmann.

Sloman, M., & Lupu, E. (1999). Policy specification for programmable networks. In *Proceedings of the First International Working Conference on Active Networks* (pp. 73-84).

Smirnov, M. (2003). Rule-based systems security model. In *Proceedings of the Second International Workshop on Mathematical Methods, Models, and Architectures for Computer Network Security (MMM-ACNS)* (pp. 135-146).

SPKI. (1999). SPKI certificate theory. *IETF RFC,* 2693. Retrieved from, http://www.ietf.org/rfc/rfc2693.txt

Weeks, S. (2001). Understanding trust management systems. *IEEE Symposium on Security and Privacy.*

Winsborough, W., & Li, N. (2004). Safety in automated trust negotiation. In *Proceedings of the IEEE Symposium on Security and Privacy* (pp. 147-160).

WS-Security. (2006). *Web services security* (WS-security). Retrieved from http://www.oasis-open.org/committees.wss

X.509. (2001). The directory: Public-key and attribute certificate frameworks. *ITU-T Recommendation X.509:2000(E) | ISO/IEC 9594-8:2001(E).*

XACML. (2004). *eXtensible Access Control Markup Language (XACML).* Retrieved from http://www.oasis-open.org/committees/xacml

Yu, T., & Winslett, M. (2003). A unified scheme for resource protection in automated trust negotiation. In *Proceedings of the IEEE Symposium on Security and Privacy* (pp. 110-122).

Yu, T., Winslett, M., & Seamons, K. E. (2003). Supporting structured credentials and sensitive policies through interoperable strategies for automated trust negotiation. *ACM Transactions on Information and System Security (TISSEC), 6*(1), 1-42.

Chapter VIII
Delegation Services:
A Step Beyond Authorization

Isaac Agudo
University of Malaga, Spain

Javier Lopez
University of Malaga, Spain

Jose A. Montenegro
University of Malaga, Spain

ABSTRACT

Advanced applications for the Internet need to make use of the authorization service so that users can prove what they are allowed to do and show their privileges to perform different tasks. However, for a real scalable distributed authorization solution to work, the delegation service needs to be seriously considered. In this chapter, we first put into perspective the delegation implications, issues and concepts derived from authorization schemes proposed as solutions to the distributed authorization problem, indicating the delegation approaches that some of them take. Then, we analyze interesting federation solutions. Finally, we examine different formalisms specifically developed to support delegation services, focusing on a generalization of those approaches, the Weighted Delegation Graphs solution.

INTRODUCTION

Information and network security are related to the Internet more than ever before. As a consequence, the use of the Internet has produced variations in security software. A number of these changes focus on the way users are authenticated by Internet applications and how their rights and privileges are managed.

One of the most widely used controversial security services is *Access Control*. Lampson (2004) defines access control as the composition of two services, *authentication* and *authorization*. But Internet applications require distributed solutions for the access control service; thus, accordingly, authentication and authorization services need to be distributed, too.

As it is widely known, by using an authentication service, users can prove their identity. More formally, ITU-T (International Telecommunications Union-Telecommunication Standardization Sector) defines authentication as *"the process of corroborating an identity. Authentication can be unilateral or mutual. Unilateral authentication provides assurance of the identity of only one principal. Mutual authentication provides assurance of the identities of both principals."*

However, new applications, particularly in the area of e-commerce, need an authorization service to describe what the user is allowed to do and privileges to perform tasks should be also considered. Additionally, according to ITU-T, authorization is *"the granting of rights, which includes the granting of access based on access rights. This definition implies the rights to perform some activity (such as to access data); and that they have been granted to some process, entity, or human agent."*

For instance, when a company needs to establish distinctions among their employees regarding privileges on resources, the authorization service becomes important. Different sets of privileges on resources (either hardware or software) will be assigned to different categories of employees. In those distributed applications where company resources must be partially shared over the Internet with other associated companies, providers, or clients, the authorization service becomes an essential part.

Because authorization is not a new problem, different solutions have been used in the past. However, "traditional" authorization solutions are not very helpful for many Internet applications. In order to achieve a real scalable distributed authorization solution, the *Delegation* service

needs to be seriously considered. Again, ITU-T defines delegation as *"conveyance of privilege from one entity that holds such privilege, to another entity."*

Delegation is quite a complex concept, both from the theoretical point of view and from the practical point of view. In this sense, the implementation of an appropriate delegation service has been one of the cornerstones of Internet applications since a few years ago.

Because delegation is a concept derived from authorization, the second section aims to put into perspective the delegation implications, issues and concepts that are derived from a selected group of authorization schemes which have been proposed during recent years as solutions to the distributed authorization problem. In the third section, we analyze some of the most interesting federation solutions that have been developed by different consortiums or companies, representing both educational and enterprise points of view. The final section focuses on different formalisms that have been specifically developed to support delegation services and which can be integrated into a multiplicity of applications.

DELEGATION (MIS)PERCEPTIONS IN AUTHORIZATION-BASED SCHEMES

As mentioned previously, in this section we analyze some of the most interesting authorization schemes proposed in the literature to date. In fact, and because of the many solutions that can be found on this topic, we mainly focus on those that have been supported by international bodies or organizations, or that have special implications for commercial products in the information security market. In the different subsections, we review each of the solutions, explaining in certain detail their operational foundations from the authorization perspective while at the same time analyzing the delegation perceptions, and in some cases, misperceptions associated with those solutions.

PolicyMaker and Keynote

Blaze, Feigenbaum, and Lacy introduced the notion of *Trust Management* in Blaze, Feigenbaum, Ioanndis, and Krromytis (1999). In that original work, they proposed the PolicyMaker scheme as a solution for trust management purposes. PolicyMaker is a general and powerful solution that allows the use of any programming language to encode the nature of the authority being granted as well as the entities to whom it is being granted. It addresses the authorization problem directly, without considering two different phases (one for authentication and another for access control).

PolicyMaker encodes trust in assertions. They are represented as pairs (f,s), where s is the issuer of the statement, and f is a program. Additionally, it introduces two different types of assertions: *certificates* and *policies*. The main difference between them is the value of the *Source* field. To be more precise, the value is a key for the first one (certificates), and a label for the second one (policies).

It is important to note that, in PolicyMaker, negative credentials are not allowed. Therefore, trust is monotonic; that is, each policy statement or credential can only increase the capabilities granted by others. Moreover, trust is also transitive. This means that if *Alice* trusts *Bob* and *Bob* trusts Carol, then *Alice* trusts *Carol*. In other words, all authorizations are delegable. Indeed, delegation is implicit in PolicyMaker; thus, it is not possible to restrict delegation capabilities. This is the reason why delegation is uncontrolled in this scheme.

Keynote (Blaze, Feigenbaum, & Lacy, 1996) is a derivation of PolicyMaker, and has been supported by IETF. It has been proposed and designed to improve two main aspects of PolicyMaker. First, to achieve standardization and secondly, to facilitate its integration into applications.

KeyNote uses a specific assertion language that is flexible enough to handle the security policies of different applications. Assertions delegate the authorization to perform operations to other principals. Like PolicyMaker, KeyNote considers two types of assertions. Also, as in PolicyMaker, these two types of assertions are called *policies* and *credentials*, respectively:

- **Policies:** This type of assertion does not need to be signed because they are locally trusted. They do not contain the corresponding *Issuer* of PolicyMaker.
- **Credentials:** This type of assertion delegates authorization from the issuer of the credential, or *Authorizer*, to some subjects or *Licensees* (see later for details). Assertions are valid or not valid depending on *action attributes*, which are attribute/value pairs such as resouce == "database" or access == "read."

KeyNote assertions are composed of five fields:

- **Authorizer:** If the assertion is a credential, then this field encodes the issuer of that credential. However, if the assertion is a policy, then this field contains the keyword **POLICY**.
- **Licensees:** It specifies the principal or principals to which the authority is delegated. It can be a single principal or a conjunction, disjunction or threshold of principals.
- **Comment:** It is a comment for the assertion.
- **Conditions:** It corresponds to the "program" concept of PolicyMaker, and consists of tests on action attributes. Logical operators are used in order to combine them.
- **Signature:** It is the signature of the assertion. This field is not necessary for policies, only for credentials. Further description on how KeyNote uses cryptographic keys and

signatures can be found in (Blaze, Ioannidis, & Keromytis, 2000).

Figure 1 shows an example of assertion. It states that an RSA key *12345678* authorizes the DSA keys *abcd1234 1234abcd* with read and write access in the database.

Given a set of action attributes, an assertion graph is a directed graph with vertex corresponding to principals. An arc exists from principal *A* to principal *B* if an assertion exists where the *Authorizer* field corresponds to *A*, the *Licensees* field corresponds to *B* and the predicate encoded in the *Conditions* field holds for the given set of action attributes. A principal is authorized, within a given set of action attributes, if the associated graph contains a path from a policy to the principal. We conclude then that all authorized principals are allowed to re-delegate their authorizations. Thus, there is no restriction on delegation.

KeyNote has been used in several contexts, like Network-layer Access Control, Distributed Firewalls, Web Access Control, Grid Computing, and so forth (Blaze, Ioannidis, & Keromytis, 2003), which gives some idea of its flexibility.

SDSI/SPKI

This solution is a unification of two similar proposals, simple distributed security infrastructure (SDSI) and simple Public Key Infrastructure (SPKI). SPKI was proposed by the IETF working group and, in particular, by Carl Ellison (Ellison, Frantz, & Lacy, 1996). SDSI, designed by Ronald L. Rivest and Butler Lampson (Rivest & Lampson, 1996), was proposed as an alternative to X.509 public-key infrastructure.

The *SPKI/SDSI* certificate format is the result of the SPKI Working Group of the IETF (Ellison, 1999). The main feature of SDSI/SPKI is that its design provides a simple Public Key Infrastructure which uses linked local name spaces rather than a global, hierarchical one. All entities are considered analogous; hence, every principal can produce signed statements. The data format chosen for SPKI/SDSI is *S-expression*. This is a LISP-like parenthesized expression with the limitations that empty lists are not allowed and the first element in any S-expression must be a string, called the "type" of the expression.

In this subsection, we detail the SDSI solution and the integrated solution SDSI/SPKI, as the development of the SPKI solution is similar to the integrated solution. The subsections detail the certificates of each proposal and explain how delegation is implemented.

SDSI

SDSI establishes four types of certificates: *Name/Value, Membership, Autocert* and *Delegation*.

Figure 1. KeyNote assertion

```
KeyNote-Version: 2
Authorizer: "rsa-hex:12345678"
Licensees: "dsa-hex:abcd1234" || "dsa-hex:1234abcd"
Comment: Authorizer delegates read and write access
   to either of the licensees
Conditions:  (resource == "database" &&
(access == "read") || (access == "write"))
Signature: "sig-rsa-md5-hex:abcd1234"
```

- **Name/Value Certificates:** These certificates are used to bind principals to local names. Every certificate must be signed by the issuer, using his/her public key (see Figure 2).
- **Membership Certificates:** These provide principals with the membership to a particular SDSI group.
- **Autocert Certificates:** These are a special kind of self-certificate. Every SDSI principal is required to have an *Autocert* (see Figure 3).

- **Delegation Certificates:** These are the mechanisms for implementing the Delegation in SDSI, (see Figure 3). SDSI provides two types of delegation, based on the structure of the delegation certificate:
  1. A user (issuer) can delegate to someone by adding that person as a member of the group which they control. *A* issues a delegation certificate to *B*. Therefore, *B* will have the same privileges as group.
  2. A user (issuer) can delegate to someone so that this person is able to sign objects of a certain type on the user's behalf. The "certain type" is defined by using the template form.

Integrated Solution: SPKI/SDSI

SPKI/SDSI unifies all types of SDSI certificates into one single type of structure. The SPKI/SDSI certificate contains at least an *Issuer* and a *Subject*, and it can contain validity conditions, authorization and delegation information. Therefore, there are three categories: ID (mapping <name,key>),

Figure 2. Name-value certificates

```
(Cert:
(Local-Name: user1 )
(Value:
       (Principal:
           (Public-Key:
           (Algorithm: RSA-with-SHA1 )
           ......
           )))
       (Signed: ...))
```

Figure 3. Autocert and delegation certificates

```
(Auto-Cert:                              (Delegation-Cert:
(Local-Name: user1 )                     (Template: form )
   (Public-Key: ....)              (       Group: group1 )
       (Description: temporal user)   (Signed: ...))
       (Signed: ...))
```

Figure 4. ID and authorization certificates

```
(cert                                  (cert
(issuer <principal>)                   (issuer <principal>)
(subject <principal>)                  (subject <principal>)
(valid <valid>))                       (propagate)
                                       (tag <tag>)
                                       (valid ))
```

Attribute (mapping <authorization,name>), and Authorization (mapping <authorization,key>).

The structure of Figure 4 represents the *ID certificate* and the *authorization certificate*. The *attribute certificate* has the same structure as authorization certificates.

The field *propagate* is (the field) used to perform the delegation. As it was desirable to limit the depth of delegation, initially, SPKI/SDSI had three options for controlling this: no control, boolean control and integer control. Currently, these options have been reduced to boolean control only. In this way, if this field is true, the Subject is permitted by the Issuer to further propagate the authorization.

Privilege Management Infrastructure (PMI)

A wide-ranging authentication service based on *identity certificates* proposed by ITU-T in its X.509 Recommendation is possible by using a *public-key infrastructure* (PKI) (ITU-T, 1997). A PKI provides an efficient and trustworthy means to manage and distribute all certificates in the system. At the same time it supports encryption, integrity and nonrepudiation services. Without its use, it is impractical and unrealistic to expect that large scale digital signature applications can become a reality.

Similarly, ITU-T has defined the a*ttribute certificates* framework for authorization services. It defines the foundation upon which a *privilege management infrastructure* (PMI) can be built (ITU-T, 2000). PKI and PMI infrastructures are linked by information contained in the identity and attribute certificates of every user. The link is justified by the fact that authorization relies on authentication to prove who users are (see Figure 5).

Although linked, both infrastructures can be autonomous, and managed independently. Creation and maintenance of identities can be separated from PMI, as the authorities that issue

Figure 5. ITU-T identity and attribute certificates

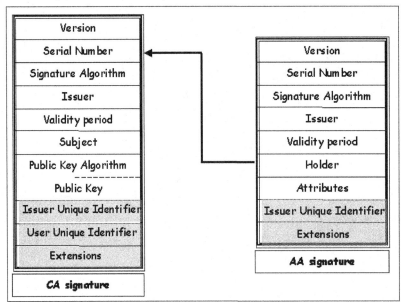

certificates in each infrastructure are not necessarily the same ones. In fact, the entire PKI may be existing and operational prior to the establishment of the PMI.

One of the advantages of an attribute certificate is that it can be used for various purposes. It may contain group membership, role, clearance, or any other form of authorization. Yet another essential feature is that the attribute certificate provides the means to transport authorization information to decentralized applications. Moreover, many of those applications deal with delegation. In fact, ITU-T defines PMI models for different environments, among them, one specific for delegation, as shown in the following:

- **Control model:** Describes the techniques that enable the privilege verifier to control access to the object method by the privilege asserter, in accordance with the attribute certificate and the privilege policy.
- **Roles model:** Individuals are issued *role assignment certificates* that assign one or more roles to them through the role attribute contained in the certificate. Specific privileges are assigned to a role name through *role specification certificates*, rather than to individual privilege holders through attribute certificates.
- **Delegation model:** When delegation is used, a privilege verifier trusts the SOA to delegate a set of privileges to holders, some of which may further delegate some or all of those privileges to other holders.

Regarding the delegation model, there are four components: the privilege verifier, the *source of authorization* (SOA), the *attribute authorities* (AAs), and the privilege asserter. The SOA, the initial issuer of certificates, is the authority for a given set of privileges for the resource and can impose constraints on how delegation can be done. The SOA assigns privileges to intermediary AAs, which further delegate privileges to other

entities but obviously not more privilege than they hold. A delegator may also further restrict the ability of downstream AAs. If the privilege asserter's certificate is not issued by that SOA, then the verifier shall locate a delegation path of certificates from that of the privilege asserter to one issued by the SOA. The validation of that delegation path includes checking that each AA had sufficient privileges and was duly authorized to delegate those privileges.

DELEGATION CONSIDERATIONS IN FEDERATION SOLUTIONS

In this section we analyze some of the most interesting federation solutions that have been developed by different consortiums or companies. We focus on two significant solutions such as *Shibboleth, and .Net Passport*. These selected solutions represent both educational and enterprise points of view. Shibboleth represents academia solutions, although there are other solutions like *PAPI* and *Athens*. On the other hand, we chose *.Net Passport* as the representative of companies' solutions, although its opponent *Liberty Alliance* is growing in popularity, mainly due to the relevance of the partners that form the consortium.

The general definition of *federation* is the act of establishing a trust relationship between two or more entities or, more specifically, an association comprising any number of service providers and identity providers. Therefore, federation should be understood as delegation of services where the service providers delegate the security management to identity providers.

Microsoft Passport

At the end of the 90's, as part of its .NET initiative, Microsoft introduced a set of Web services that implement a so-called user-centric application model, and which are collectively referred to as *.NET My Services*. At the core of *Microsoft .NET*

My Services is a password-based user authentication and Single Sign-In service called *Microsoft .NET Passport* (Microsoft 2002, 2004). The fundamental component of a federation Solution is *single sign-in (SSI)* Service, therefore *Microsoft .NET Passport* could be considered as the first partial Federation Solution.

Microsoft .NET Passport users are uniquely identified with an e-mail address (usually hotmail and MSN accounts) and all participating sites are uniquely identified with their DNS names. A Passport account has four parts. The first is a *Passport unique identifier (PUID)*, assigned to the user when he/she sets up the account. This *PUID* is a 64-bit number that is sent to the user's site as the authentication credential when a Passport user signs in, being used in representation of the user for the administrative operations. The second is the user profile, containing the user's phone number or e-mail address, user's name and demographic information. The third part of a Passport account is the credential information such as the password or security key used for a second level of authentication. The wallet is the fourth element that enables users to digitally store credit card numbers, expiration dates, and billing and shipping addresses.

Passport use a series of cookies to store the authentication information and to assist the sign-in functionality in the user computer. The cookies are obtained by using HTTP redirections and are appended as elements in the transferred URI. Passport uses two different types of cookies:

- **Domain authority cookies:** None of these cookies can be directly accessed by the user's site. They are written only to the domain by authority's domain (e.g., Passport.com).
- **Participant cookies:** These cookies are written in the domain of the participating site and enable the user to sign in at any Passport participating sites during a browser session.

Passport is composed mainly of two processes, the *registration process* and the *authentication process*. A button named "Sign In" is the only modification needed in the site to interact with *Passport* service.

- **Registration process:** Occurs when the user has not an account in the system.
  1. The user browses to the Site and clicks on the "Sign In" button.
  2. The user is redirected to a co-branded registration page displaying the registration fields that were chosen by Site. The minimum number of fields required is two: e-mail name and password.
  3. The user reads and accepts terms of use (or declines, and the process ends), and submits the form.
  4. The user is then redirected back to Site with the encrypted authentication ticket and profile information attached.
  5. Site *A* decrypts the authentication ticket and profile information and continues the registration process, or grants access to their site.

- **Authentication process:** A registered user attempts to use a protected service and the sign-in process is activated.
  1. User browses to a/the participating site. User clicks on the "Sign In" button or link.
  2. User is redirected to Passport.
  3. Passport checks if the user has a *ticket granting cookie* (TGC) in the browser's cookie file. If one is found, it skips to Step 4 and never sees the Passport login UI. If the TGC does not satisfy the time limit conditions since the last sign in requested by Site, then Passport removes information that Site passed on the query string, and redirects the user to a page that asks for the currently signed-in users' password. This new page has a short URL in the Passport.

net domain. If the user enters the correct information, the process continues.

4. The user is redirected back to Site with the encrypted authentication ticket and profile information attached.

5. Site decrypts the authentication ticket and profile information, and signs the customer into the site.

6. User accesses the page, resource, or service they requested from Site.

During the early years, there were numerous security failures. The work by Kormann (Kormann & Rubin, 2000) enumerates a series of Passport flaws. The security issues are related to: User Interface, Key management, Cookies and Javascript, Persistent cookies and Automatic credential assignment.

In 2003, IBM, Microsoft, BEA, RSA and Verisign published a competing identity management framework called *Web Services Federation Language*, or *WS-Federation* which was intended to be the direct competitor of Liberty (Liberty, 2003), although at this moment IBM, BEA, RSA and Verisign are part of the Liberty consortium.

Shibboleth

Shibboleth is an Internet2/MACE project. The purpose of the proposal is to determine if a person using a web browser has permission to access a target resource based on information such as being a member of an institution or a particular class. It is implemented using federated administration.

Usually in federated administration, a resource provider leaves the administration of user identities and attributes to the user's origin site. Therefore, users are registered only at (their origin) this site, but not at each resource provider. Moreover, the system is privacy preserving in the sense that it does not use identity information. Therefore, it is necessary to associate a *handle* with the user. This handle stores the security information without exposing the identity of the user.

Consequently, Shibboleth is a system for securely transferring attributes about a user, from the user's origin to a resource provider site. Two principal components are in charge of performing the attribute transference, the *attribute authority (AA)* on the user side and the *Shibboleth attribute requester (SHAR)* on the resource side. These components interchange authorization information by exchanging *SAML* (Cantor, 2005) messages using any shared protocol that supports the required functional characteristics. These messages are named *attribute query message (AQM)* and *attribute response message (ARM)*, and their complete syntax depends on the protocol used, but all protocols must share the core *AQM/ARM* syntax and semantics. The *AQM* is sent by a *SHAR* to an *AA*, whereas the *ARM* is the response to an *AQM* sent. Guidance on usage of the schema definition by Shibboleth components is explained in details in (Erdos & Cantor, 2002).

Besides the *SHAR* and *AA*, Shibboleth needs other support components. *Shibboleth Indexical Reference Establisher (SHIRE)* is the component responsible for intercepting an HTTP request to a protected resource and associating it with a handle. Therefore, this is the component that triggers the Shibboleth system. *Handle service (HS)* establishes a secure context for communication about the user that will later occur between the *SHAR* an *AA*, preserving user's anonymity. *Where are you from? (WAYF)* component assists *SHIRE* to locate the *HS* associated to the user. These elements are used in the following process, as is shown in Figure 6:

1. The user makes an initial request for a resource protected by a *SHIRE*.

2. The *SHIRE* obtains the *URL* of the user's *HS* (Step 5), or redirects the user to a *WAYF* service for this purpose (Step 3).

3. The *WAYF* asks the *HS* to create a handle for this user, redirecting the request through the user's browser.

4. The *HS* returns a *handle* for the user that can be used by the *SHAR* to get attributes from the appropriate *AA* at the origin site.

5. *SHIRE* passes on the *handle* (and *AA* information, and organization name) to the *SHAR*.

6. The *SHAR* asks the *AA* for attributes via an *AQM* message.

7. It receives attributes back from the *AA* via an *ARM* message.

8. Finally, *SHAR* passes the attributes to the HTTP Server.

The process shown in Figure 6 explains the complete scenario, where the *SHIRE* does not have a previous *handle* associated to the user. In other case, Steps 2, 3 and 4 are not accomplished.

SPECIFIC DELEGATION SCHEMES

In this section we focus on different formalisms that have been specifically developed to support delegation services and that can be integrated into a multiplicity of applications. Those schemes will be explained and analyzed but, in addition, we show how to include the solutions on existing working frameworks, which facilitates the introduction of users' delegation operations into final applications.

Logic Frameworks

Logic programming offers a powerful mechanism to represent authorization and access control decisions (Barker, 2000; Bertino, Bonatti, & Ferrari, 2001; Crampton, Loizou, & O'Shea, 2001). In this context, authorizations are represented as predicates and decisions are based on formulae verification.

There are many solutions for formulae verification but the most widely known is probably PRO-LOG (Nilsson & Maluszynski, 2000), which has several implementations for different platforms (Windows, Linux, Macintosh, etc,). Having this number of different implementations, most of them provided with some kind of free license, it is easy to implement authorization decision systems based on formulae verification.

When looking for a suitable logic language to represent an authorization system and its authorization rules, one decision to be taken is

Figure 6. Shibboleth components and flow for complete scenario

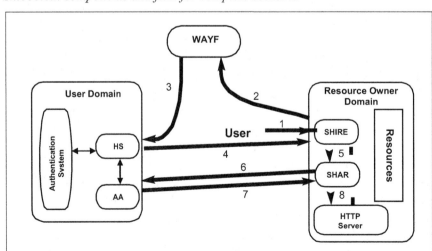

whether authorization must be explicitly denied. Depending on the available information, i.e. complete or incomplete, it is possible to choose an explicit negation approach or a negation as failure approach.

Let us see the differences of those approaches with an example. If we look at a railway timetable, all trains are included in this table. There are no exceptions, so any other train one could think about is implicitly disallowed. This is negation by failure as the failure of finding a positive conclusion leads to a negative conclusion. Now suppose the booking center says that there is a train at 16:00 and another one a 17:50. Could we infer that there are no more trains between 16:00 and 17:50? There may be more, but without free seats. Therefore the information obtained is incomplete and it can not be inferred that there are no trains between 16:00 and 17:50. In order to find out, one may ask the booking center and get an explicit negative statement or a positive one.

Specifically, in this section, we focus our attention on two solutions. One of them implements the explicit negation: the *delegatable authorization program (DAP)* scheme. The other one implements negation by failure: the *role based trust management framework (RT)*. We describe the foundations of each of them and elaborate on the way they manage delegation.

Delegatable Authorization Program (DAP)

Ruan et al. proposed in Ruan, Varadharajan, and Zhang (2002) a logical approach to model delegation. They base their approach on extended logic programs (Gelfond & Lifschitz, 1991) so they allow explicit negation (denial) of authorization. Their language is based on the following concepts:

- **Subjects:** These are the grantors and grantees of authorizations. There is an special subject, the security administrator, denoted by #, which is the responsible for all authori-

zation in the system. Any authorization must be derived from one of the administrator authorizations.

- **Objects:** They are the target of authorizations, that is, available system resources.

- **Access rights:** The same object can be accessed in several ways. For example, a file can be accessed in read-only mode or in read-write.

- **Authorization Type:** DAP considers three authorization types: *negative* authorization (-), *positive* authorization (+) and *delegatable* authorization (*). A negative authorization specifies the access that must be forbidden, while a positive authorization specifies the access that must be granted. Finally, a delegable authorization specifies the access that must be delegated as well as granted.

DAP defines three partial orders $<_S$, $<_O$, $<_A$ to represent inheritance hierarchies of subjects, objects and access rights, respectively. We find examples of these partial orders in a classical UNIX system:

- *Subjects* are the system users. As the *root* user is the administrator, any authorization issued to any user is also issued to the *root*. This translates into $any-user <_S root$;

- Files and folders are *Objects*, and the fact that the files of a folder are accessible if the folder is accessible, is translated into *folder* $<_O$ *file-insider-folder*;

- In a UNIX system there are three authorization types for files: *read (r), write(w), execute(x)* and the combination of them, an example order relation is the following $rw <_A r$ which represents that when granting *read-write (rw)* access we are also granting *read-only (r)* access.

In DAP, *predicates* consist of a set of ordinary predicates defined by users, and one built-in predicate symbol, *grant*, for delegatable authorization. The later is a 5-term predicate symbol with type $S \times O \times T \times A \times Z$, where the first argument is the grantee, the second one is the object, the third is the authorization type, the fourth is the access right and, finally, the fifth argument is the grantor of this authorization. Intuitively, $grant(s,o,t,a,g)$ means s is granted by g the access right a on object o with authorization type t. $grant$ is called *authorization predicate*. There are two special predicates named *cangrant* and *delegate*, of type $S \times O \times A$ and $S \times S \times O \times A$, respectively, that are used to model delegation. $cangrant(s,o,a)$ means subject s has the right to grant access a on object o to other subjects, while $delegate(g,s,o,a)$ means subject g has granted to subject s access a on object o with access type *.

In order to define a DAP rule the definition of the following concepts is necessary:

- **Term:** A parameter in predicates. It could be a variable or a constant, but not a function.
- **Atom:** An atomic predicate. It is a construct of the form $p(t_1,...,t_n)$ where each t_i is a term.
- **Literal:** Either an atom p or the classical negation of an atom $\neg p$.

Then, a DAP consists of a finite set of rules of the form:

$$b_0 \leftarrow b_1,...,b_k, not\, b_{k+1},...,not\, b_{k+m}, m \geq 0,$$

where each b_i is a literal and *not* is the negation as failure symbol .

Once the administrator defines the DAP corresponding to the system, it has to be transformed in order to be consistent with special predicates *cangrant* and *delegate*. This is done by adding the following rules to the DAP and by doing some transformations on those rules in which the head (the leftmost element) is an authorization predicate.

- d_1. *cangrant (#, o, a)* $\leftarrow$
- d_2. *Cangrant (s, o, a)* $\leftarrow$ *grant (s, o,*, a, g)*
- d_3. *delegate (g, s, o, a)* $\leftarrow$ *grant (s, o,*, a, g)*
- d_4. *delegate (s, s$_1$, o, a)* $\leftarrow$ *delegate (s, s$_2$, o, a)*, *delegate (s$_2$, s$_1$, o, a)*

The previous rules are self-explanatory but we translate them to natural language anyway: d_1 means that the security administrator # can issue authorization regarding any object and access right; d_2 means that the grantee of a delegable authorization can issue new authorization regarding the granted object and access right; d_3 means that the grantee of a delegable authorization has been delegated the respective access right on the respective object; d_4 is used to chain delegations.

In (Ruan, 2003), Ruan et al. extend their model with temporal capabilities by adding a new temporal parameter to predicates. They add two new elements to the system: *time points* and *time intervals*. Every authorization (*grant* predicate) is associated with a time interval and new rules have to be added to make the system consistent.

Once there is a consistent DAP, it would be possible to ask if a particular authorization predicate p is true trying to infer p from the rules of the DAP. As there are both positive and negative authorizations in a DAP, there could be conflicts among authorization, i.e. contradictory authorization predicates. DAP proposes several methods for solving conflicts:

- **Using delegation relation:** If the predicate *delegate (g, s, o, a)* holds then all the authorization issued by g override the ones issued by s.
- **Using grantee inheritance:** When the grantors of two conflicting authorizations are the same, then we use the partial order on subjects to compare the grantees, if $s <_s s_0$, then the authorization with s_0 as grantee will override the inherited one with s as grantee.

- **Using object inheritance:** When both the grantor and grantees are the same we use the partial order in object to discard the authorization with the "lower" object.

- **Using access right inheritance:** When all grantors, grantees and objects are the same, we discard the authorization with the "lower" access right.

- **Using time:** We may also define an order relation between time intervals (inclusion is one easy example, but not the only one) and then, when all grantors, grantees, objects and access rights are the same, we discard the authorization with the "lower" interval.

RT Framework

Contrary to DAP, RT (Li, Mitchell, & Winsborough, 2002) does not support negative statements, so RT does not have to worry about conflict resolution. It is based on a subset of Prolog, Datalog (Abiteboul & Hull, 1988; Ullman, 1988, 1989), which is a language of facts and rules. Datalog is a logic-based query language for the relational model that has been mainly used in the field of knowledge discovery but also in some other fields. One of the more attractive properties of DATALOG, regarding its tractability, is the absence of function-symbols as arguments in the predicates. This is the main reason for DATALOG having efficient procedures for answering queries.

Li et al. (2003) proposed logic programming as a way to model authorization and delegation relations. They use *Roles* for this purpose and they define a full general framework, RT for *role based trust management*. It is composed of different languages, each of them with different characteristics. Roles can be interpreted as privileges or attributes. In DAP, resources are universal objects, known for all entities and are the same for each entity, but in RT, as it uses local names, each user could have his/her own roles (resources) or name them in a different way. The same role name could be used by two different users for different purposes. This is done by placing the name of the user before the role name, separated by a dot (e.g., *A.Director* is different from *B.Director*). The only way to relate different roles is by means of credentials, which will be defined later on.

As in the previous proposal, the RT framework defines a partial order in roles, establishing how rights can be inherited. Partial orders are used to represent other concepts too. Let u, p, r denote users, rights and roles, respectively; then:

- $r_1 \geq r_2$, is read as r_1 *dominates* r_2, and means that r_1 has all the rights r_2 has. It can also be read as r_2 contains r_1. As an example, if we define two roles: *Director* and *SubDirector*; then clearly *Director* $\geq$ *SubDirector*

- $u \geq r$ assigns role r to user u. If *Bob* is the Director of the company, this can be expressed with the predicate *Bob* $\geq$ *Director*

- $r \geq p$ assigns right p to role r. This is the only way to relate resources and access rights with roles. If *SignContract* represents the right of signing contracts, then *Director* $\geq$ *SignContract*

RT defines several types of credentials, an analogous concept to *DAP* predicates. The basic credentials are:

1. **A.R←D:** This credential is issued by A (like all the others) and it means that D is a member of A's role R. In the attribute-based view, this credential can be read as D *has the attribute A.R*, or equivalently, *A says that D has the attribute R*.

2. **A.R←B.R₁:** It means that the role A.R includes all members the role $B.R_1$. In the attribute-based view, this credential can be read as *if B says that an entity has the attribute R_1, then A says that it has the attribute R*.

3. **A.R←A.R₁. R₂:** The expression on the right is called a *linked role*. It means that A.R

contains $B.R_2$ for all B in $A.R_1$. The attribute-based reading of this credential is: *if A says that an entity B has the attribute R_1, and B says that an entity D has the attribute R_2, then A says that D has the attribute R.*

4. $A.R \leftarrow B_1.R_1 \cap B_2.R_2 \cap ... \cap B_n.R_n$: This credential means that if an entity is a member of $B_1.R_1$, $B_2.R_2$, and $B_k.R_k$, then it is also a member of $A.R$. The attribute-based reading of this credential is *A believes that anyone who has all the attributes $B_1.R_1,...,B_k.R_k$ also has the attribute R.*

The following is an example of the use of the previous rules. The first rule describes how a student gets a degree if and only if he/she passes the final exam and also completes the practical work. The second rule establishes that the practical work can be evaluated by the companies provided by the Subject. The third rule defines *Bank1* as a valid company to evaluate the practical work. The last rule defines *Bob* as having passed the final exam and also as having completed the practical work in *Bank1*.

Subject.pass $\leftarrow$ Subject.passExam $\cap$ Subject.passPract
Subject.passPract $\leftarrow$ Subject.company.pract
Subject.company $\leftarrow$ Bank1
Bank1.pract $\leftarrow$ Bob
Subject.passExamn $\leftarrow$ Bob

The previous are rules defined from RT_0, which is the basic language of the *RT framework*, but there are more languages in *RT*. We will elaborate a little more on RT_1, for a detailed description of the rest of the languages see Li et al. (2002).

RT_1 allows the use of constants and variables or parameters in the definition of roles and credentials. In a credential, when we use the same variable in more than one role, we are linking the value of this variable for each role, so it has to be the same throughout the credential. When the same role has both a constant and a variable in

different credentials, in order to combine them, the variable should take the value of the constant. This language allows the previous example to be refined, adding marks to the subject. One way of adding grades to the previous example is by modifying the first and the last credential in the following way:

Subject.pass(x) $\leftarrow$ Subject.passExam(x) $\cap$ Subject.passPract
Subject.passExamn(B) $\leftarrow$ Bob

In this way, the conclusion will be that Bob gets the degree subject with grade B.

Graph Frameworks

Although logic programming offers a powerful mechanism to model authorization and delegation relationships and it is also very suitable for decision taking, it is not so easy to understand and has an obscure transcription; therefore there is a need for extensive training before being able to use it.

In order to close the gap between the user and the computer, there are graphical solutions that are thought to be less powerful but more expressive and more understandable. A graphical solution may be based on the use of directed graphs to model the authorization and delegation process. Basically, this maps each predicate to a directed arc in a graph. Arcs go from the issuer of the authorization or delegation statement to the subject who is authorized or granted privileges. There are as many different arcs as there are different authorization/delegation statements to consider.

In this way, all the authorization and delegation relationships are represented in the same chart, making it easier for an inexperienced user to understand how the system is defined. Diagrams are always the first step in the process of software engineering and, similarly, they should also be in the field of security and authorization.

Normally, an initial approach to the system is defined in a graphical way and then translated to a hard formalism in which authorization is decided. The problem of this approach is that the response of an authorization query can not be presented in a graphical way. If we use a powerful and simple graphical language to define our system, both queries and responses are expressed in a graphical way, allowing human interaction in the decision taking process.

We usually model authorization and delegation in the same chart but there could be scenarios in which only authorization or delegation is required. If we use a directed edge to represent each authorization or delegation statement, we get a graph in which all the paths come from the owner of the resource we are reasoning about. This graph looks like a tree (see Figure 7).

The root of the tree is the owner (administrator) of the resource. With such a tree it is possible to study the relationships among entities in the system in a graphical way.

Varadharajan and Ruan have proposed two solutions to represent authorization and delegation using directed graphs. In Ruan and Varadharajan (2003) they present a first approach to the problem. This approach considers three types of authorizations: negative authorization, positive authorization and delegatable authorization, a cross arrow represents a negative authorization, a dashed arrow represents a positive authorization and a simple arrow represents a delegatable one.

In Ruan and Varadharajan (2004), the same authors proposed a new approach, *weighted graphs*. In that proposal, each authorization is associated with a weight given by the grantor, representing the degrees of certainty about the authorization grants. The weight is a nonnegative number, and a smaller number represents a higher certainty. When considering both negative and positive authorizations, conflicts result if the same subject is issued a negative and a positive authorization. In this case, we need to define a conflict resolution method that allows us to decide which of them has

to be considered. These authors follow the idea of predecessor-take-precedence. However, there are still some conflicts which they do not solve.

One example is when two contradictory paths exist, with the same weight; in this case their approach can not provide any help. Their proposal has other limitations; in particular, owners of resources can not define more restrictive authorization policies. For some critical resources, the mere non existence of conflicts may not be enough. One possible solution is to require the existence of paths with at least a given weight for granting authorization.

An evolution of this solution which overcomes some of the limitations mentioned, is *weighted trust graph (WTG)* (Agudo, Lopez, & Montenegro, 2005), that aims to generalize the previous approaches. In fact, WTG supports the previous proposal as a particular case. Additionally, WTG allows defining more complex policies. Even if in other solutions a delegation statement is usually

Figure 7. Delegation and authorization graph

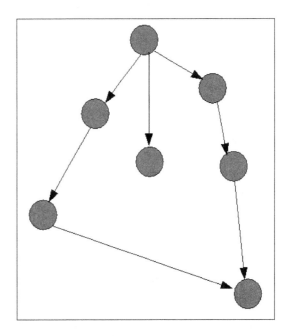

issued together with an authorization statement, our solution can use both of them separately and independently, allowing us to introduce the notion of negative delegation.

WTG assigns a weight to each authorization that, together with the security level policy, allows many conflicts to be avoided. In the case that weights are the same, WTG follows a predecessor-take-precedence principle with some refinements; that is, a new conflict resolution method called *strict-predecessor-take-precedence*.

This principle can also be used as a stand alone policy, where the owner of the resource establishes a hierarchy of subjects by assigning appropriate weights to their delegations, and any of the further delegations made for these subjects must preserve this hierarchy. For instance, if *A* gets from *S* the higher priority in the hierarchy, all *A*'s delegation or authorization statements will take preference over all the others.

Then, in case contradictory paths exist, we compare them edge by edge until a difference is detected, and in this case, the path with the greatest weight in this edge will override the others.

If we had the following scenario in the proposal from Ruan et al. (see Figure 8), we would get no response when asking for an authorization decision, but applying the *strict-predecessor-take-*

precedence (changing greater for lower, because in the Ruan approach the greater the weight of the path is, the worse is the path) the path ACD would be chosen and therefore, D would not be authorized. This is because AC has a greater trust level than AB.

The main security policy is the *mean policy*. In this case, the weights of all paths connecting the two entities (the grantor and the grantee) are computed, and the mean of those values is calculated. If the mean is included in a given interval then the user is authorized, and otherwise the authorization is denied. There are some important details that have to be taken into account in order to calculate a correct mean. These details are described in (Agudo et al., 2005). Apart from the *mean policy*, there are other two simpler policies: the *lower policy* and the *higher policy*. In this case, the administrator or owner of the resource defines a lower bound in a way that an authorization is denied if the lower/higher weight within all the paths is lower than the defined bound. The last tool provided by WTG to control delegation, is the *security level policy* in which a lower bound is imposed for credentials (not paths as before) to be valid. In this case, edges or credentials with a weight lower than the given one, will not be taken into account when forming authorization paths. This policy permits discarding nonrelevant credentials.

All the previously defined authorization and delegation policies can be combined and owners of resources are in charge of defining their own custom combination of policies.

WTG defines a graphical representation for the four types of credentials supported:

a. **Positive delegation statement:** It means that the issuer trusts the subject about his/her positive authorizations or delegations. Depending on the system, we may define this credential to be interpreted as a *b* or *c* credential.

Figure 8. Example of unresolved scenario applying Ruan's policy

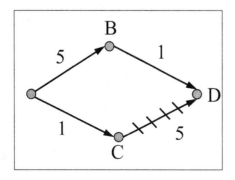

b.   **Positive authorization statement:** It means that the issuer authorizes the subject to access the resource.

c.   **Negative delegation statement:** It means that the issuer trusts the subject about his/her negative authorizations or delegations.

d.   **Negative authorization statement:** It means that the issuer denies access to the subject over the resource.

The weight is placed over the edges in the graph. The different edges that WTG support are represented in Figure 9.

Prototypes of Integration

The implementation of the X.509 PMI Control and Roles models are feasible tasks, though not free of complexity. However, the case of the Delegation model is substantially different because of the intrinsically difficult problems of the delegation concept. In this section, we discuss the implementation of the Delegation model using our WTG solution in combination with attribute certificates.

As mentioned previously, a typical PMI will contain a SOA, a number of AAs and a multiplicity of final users. As regarding our scheme, we will represent the previous elements as the nodes of the graph. The SOA will be the first node that outflows initial arcs. AAs will be the intermedi-

Figure 9. Different arcs supported in WTG

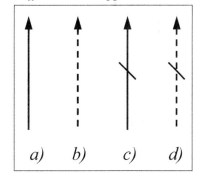

ary nodes while the final users will be the leaf nodes (that is, the nodes that do not outflow arcs but inflow authorization arcs only).

One of the fields of the attribute certificate which is essential for the practical implementation of our proposal is the extensions field. This field allows us to include additional information into the attribute certificate. The X.509 standard provides the following predefined extension categories:

*   **Basic privilege management:** Extensions to convey information relevant to the assertion of a privilege.
*   **Privilege revocation:** Extensions to convey information regarding location of revocation status information.
*   **Source of authority:** These certificate extensions relate to the trusted source of privilege assignment by a verifier for a given resource.
*   **Roles:** Extensions that convey information regarding location of related role specification certificates.
*   **Delegation:** Extensions that allow constraints to be set on subsequent delegation of assigned privileges.

We focus on the Delegation extension category that defines different extension fields. Among them, the ITU-T Recommendation includes:

*   **Authority attribute identifier:** In privilege delegation, an AA that delegates privileges shall itself have at least the same privilege and the authority to delegate that privilege. An AA delegating privileges to another AA or to an end-entity may place this extension in the AA or end-entity certificate that it issues. The extension is a back pointer to the certificate in which the issuer of the certificate containing the extension was assigned its corresponding privilege. The extension can be used by a privilege verifier to ensure

that the issuing AA had sufficient privilege to be able to delegate to the holder of the certificate containing this extension.

That extension is close to our goals. However, it does not define the weight associated to the arc between the issuer and the holder of the certificate. Therefore, we define our own extension, in ASN.1, based on the authority attribute identifier one (see Figure 10).

This new extension determines a sequence between the SOA and the holder. Each sequence

includes another sequence, *ArcsId*, where the information of the arcs in the graph, weight of the arc, origin node, and boolean information about statements, delegation and sign. The destination node must coincide with the serial number of the attribute certificate.

The proposal allows the design of authorization and delegation statements in a graphical mode which can later be automatically turned into X.509 attribute certificate chains.

Figure 11 shows the graphical design of delegation statements (normal line) and authoriza-

Figure 10. Attribute certificate and weight path identifier extension

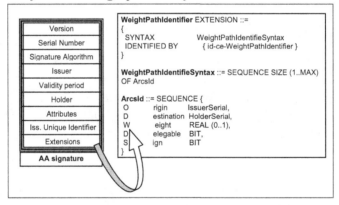

Figure 11. Design of statements and its corresponding certificate chains

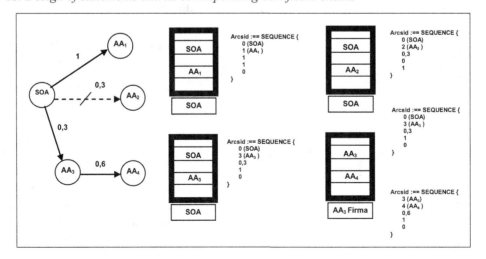

tion statements (dotted line) and its equivalent representation using attribute certificates. Each attribute certificate store, in the extension field, the graphical information.

CONCLUSION

A real scalable distributed authorization scenario can no exist without the use of a delegation service. However, the inappropriate use of that service and the delegation statements that it encompasses can become a very serious security threat because users may erroneously get privileges (over a resource) that go beyond their real entitlement. In this chapter, our goal has been, in a first stage, to study the delegation implications of a group of schemes that have been proposed as solutions for distributed authorization problems. On the one hand, PolicyMaker and KeyNote, and on the other hand, SDSI/SPKI, have been put into perspective, followed by the PMI solution that, to our understanding, provides a broader mechanism for delegation, mainly due to its delegation model. Then, we have analyzed two interesting federation solutions: .Net Passport, as a representative of companies-oriented solutions, and Shibboleth, as a representative of academia-oriented solutions. Finally, we have focused on formalisms that have been specifically developed to support delegation services. That is the case of the logic frameworks and the graph frameworks, which are in some cases oriented to the integration into applications, like we have shown in the case of Weighted Trust Graphs that, based on PMI and on the use of the extension fields of the attribute certificate, provides a solution for controlled delegation.

REFERENCES

Abiteboul, S., & Hull, R. (1988). Data functions, datalog and negation. In *Proceedings of the ACM-SIGMOD Conference.*

Agudo, I., Lopez, J., & Montenegro, J. A. (2005, December). A representation model of trust relationships with delegation extensions. *Lecture Notes in Computer Science, 3477,* 116-130.

Blaze, M., Feigenbaum, J., Ioannidis, J., & Keromytis, A. (1999). The KeyNote trust-management system version 2. *RFC,* 2704.

Blaze, M., Feigenbaum, J., & Lacy, J. (1996). Decentralized trust management. In *Proceedings of the IEEE Symposium on Security and Privacy,* 164-173.

Blaze, M., Ioannidis, J., & Keromytis, A. (2000). DSA and RSA key and signature encoding for the KeyNote trust management system. *RFC,* 2792.

Blaze, M., Ioannidis, J., & Keromytis, A. (2003, May). Experience with the KeyNote trust management system: Applications and future directions. In *Proceedings of the First International Conference on Trust Management,* 284 - 300.

Barker, S. (2000). Data protection by logic programming. *Lecture Notes in Computer Science, 1861,* 1300-1314.

Bertino, E., Bonatti, P. A., & Ferrari, E. (2001). TRBAC: A temporal role-based access control model. *ACM Trans. on Information and System Security, 4*(3), 191-233.

Cantor, S., Kemp, J., Philpott, R., & Maler, E. (2005). *Security assertion markup language (SAML V2.0).* Retrieved March 15, 2005, from http://docs.oasis-open.org/security/ saml/v2.0/

Crampton, J., Loizou, G., & O'Shea, G. (2001). A logic of access control. *The Computer Journal, 44,* 54-66.

Ellison, C. (1999). *SPKI Certificate Theory, RFC, 2693.*

Ellison, C., Frantz, B., & Lacy, J. (1996). *Simple public key certificate.* Internet draft available online from draft-ietf-spki-cert-structure-06.txt

Erdos, M., & Cantor, S. (2002) *Shibboleth-architecture.* Retrieved May 2, 2002, from http://shibboleth.internet2.edu/docs/draft-internet2-shibboleth-arch-v04.pdf

Gelfond, M., & Lifschitz, V. (1991) Classical negation in logic programs and disjunctive databases. *New Generation Computing, 9,* 365-385.

ITU-T Recommendation X.509. (1997, June). *Information technology–*Open systems interconnection–The directory: Authentication framework.

ITU-T Recommendation X.509. (2000, March), *Information technology–*Open systems interconnection–The directory: Public-key and attribute certificate frameworks.

Kormann, D., & Rubin, A. (2000). Risks of the Passport single signon protocol. *Computer Networks, 33,* 51-58.

Lampson, B. (2004). Computer security in the real world. *IEEE Computer Society Press, 37*(6), 37, 46.

Li, N., & Mitchell, J. C. (2003) Datalog with constraints: A foundation for trust management languages. In *Proceedings of the Fifth International Symposium on Practical Aspects of Declarative Languages.*

Li, N., Mitchell, J. C., & Winsborough, W. H. (2002). Design of a role-based trust management framework. In *Proceedings of the 2002 IEEE Symposium on Security and Privacy,* 114\u2013130.

Liberty Alliance Project. (2003). *Liberty Alliance & WS-Federation: A comparative overview* (White Paper). Retrieved October 14, 2003, from http://www.liberty.org

Microsoft. (2002). *NET Passport: Balanced authentication solutions.* Retrieved December 1, 2002, from http://www.passport.com

Microsoft. (2004). *NET Passport review guide.* Retrieved January 1, 2004, from http://www.passport.com

Nilsson, U., & Maluszynski, J. (2000). *Logic, Programming and prolog* (2nd ed.).

Rivest, R., & Lampson, B. (1996). *SDSI -A simple distributed security infrastructure* (Working document). Presented at CRYPTO '96.

Ruan, C., Varadharajan, V., & Zhang, Y. (2002) Logic-based reasoning on delegatable authorizations. In *Proceedings of the 13th International Symposium on Methodologies for Intelligent Systems,* 185-193.

Ruan, C., & Varadharajan, V. (2003). A formal graph based framework for supporting authorization delegations and conflict resolutions. *International Journal of Information Security, 1*(4), 211-222.

Ruan, C., Varadharajan, V., & Zhang, Y. (2003). A logic model for temporal authorization delegation with negation. *LNCS, 2851,* 310–324, 2003.

Ruan, C., & Varadharajan, V. (2004). A weighted graph approach to authorization delegation and conflict resolution. *Lecture Notes in Computer Science, 3108,* 402-413.

Ullman, J. D. (1988). *Principles of database and knowledge-base systems: Vol. I.* Computer Science Press.

Ullman, J. D. (1989). *Principles of database and knowledge-base systems: Vol. II.* Computer Science Press.

Chapter IX
From DRM to Enterprise Rights and Policy Management:
Challenges and Opportunities

Jean-Henry Morin
Korea University Business School, Korea

Michel Pawlak
University of Geneva—CUI, Switzerland

ABSTRACT

This chapter introduces digital rights management (DRM) in the perspective of digital policy management (DPM) focusing on the enterprise and corporate sector. DRM has become a domain in full expansion with many stakes which are by far not only technological. They also touch legal aspects as well as business and economic. Information is a strategic resource and as such requires a responsible approach of its management, almost to the extent of being patrimonial. Digital rights and policy management is now well established mainly in two distinct sectors sharing the same fundamental underlying technical principles: on the one hand, the entertainment and media industry, and on the other hand, the enterprise sector. This chapter mainly focuses on the latter, introducing DRM concepts, standards, and the underlying technologies from its origins to its most recent developments in order to assess the challenges and opportunities of enterprise digital policy management.

INTRODUCTION

Digital rights and policy management has become a domain in full expansion with many stakes, which are by far not only technological. They also touch legal aspects as well as business and economic as described in Becker, Buhse, Günnewig, and Rump (2003) and Rosenblatt, Trippe, and Mooney (2001). Information is a strategic resource and as such requires a responsible approach of its management almost to the extent of being patrimonial.

Let us mention as an example some recent cases such as the loss by UPS of a parcel containing the information of 3.9 million clients of a Citigroup company (Ewalt, 2005). Or the loss of personal data of 600,000 current and former Time Warner employees while in physical transport (Silver, 2005; TimeWarner, 2005). These only represent a couple of recent examples of known cases of information theft, leakage, or disclosure that most companies would have rather not disclosed. This is probably not new, but what changed in recent years and "forced" disclosure of such information lies in the obligation to comply with emerging regulatory frameworks. An interesting chronology and up-to-date monitor of such events can be found on the Privacy Rights Clearinghouse Web site (Privacy Rights Clearinghouse, 2005).

Digital rights and policy management is now well established mainly in two distinct sectors sharing the same fundamental underlying technical principles: the entertainment and media industry and the enterprise sector. This chapter mainly focuses on the latter while sketching the broader challenges and opportunities of this industry.

The overall objective of this chapter is essentially twofold. First, it is a plea for raising awareness on the strategic nature of using digital rights management technologies in the corporate environment for digital policy management. To this end we present a basic guiding framework for corporate policy management. Second, assuming this awareness, we argue the corporate information systems landscape is on the verge of a profound transformation by which systems will have to factor in persistent protection, governed usage and managed content. In other words, to become "rights and policy enabled." A key challenge facing the DRM industry still remains to be tackled with interoperability issue both at functional and semantic levels. Proprietary incompatible solutions could represent a major legacy and problem

for the future. It is thus critical to both address the interoperability issue and the strategic dimension of digital policy management.

Specific objectives include understanding the background and fundamental concepts of DRM including standards in this industry, providing a clear view of the stakes and challenges facing the corporate and enterprise sector with respect to DRM and persistently managed information, raising the debate to the level of global corporate policy management, understanding that the issues are strategic and not technological and finally to provide some insights on future trends.

This chapter is organized as follows; after a brief introduction, the second section presents the background, the fundamental underlying concepts, and the evolution of DRM. Particular attention is given to picture more recent initiatives and trends with respect to standards. We then focus on the corporate and enterprise sector, presenting the issues of regulatory frameworks, compliance, risk and corporate governance and how these relate to DRM technology. Shortcomings of traditional approaches are then discussed, thus setting the ground for opportunities to considering a broader approach of digital policy management. The following section discusses future trends and leads before conclusions.

BACKGROUND: ORIGINS AND EVOLUTION OF DRM

In order to better grasp this field and its evolution from its inception to its recent developments, let us review some of the key concepts and contributions in this field. This will allow to shed some light on current issues in this industry considering challenges and opportunities.

What is DRM and Where is it Used?

DRM is the acronym for digital rights management, it represents a technology allowing to cryptographically associate usage rules, also called policies, to digital content. These rules govern the usage of the content they are associated to. They have to be interpreted by an enforcement point prior to any access in order to determine whether or not access can be granted or denied. In the former case, the content is decrypted and rendered in a trusted interface (e.g., browser, application, sound or video device). The content being itself encrypted using strong cryptographic algorithms, it becomes persistently protected at all time and no matter where it resides.

The general DRM scenario can be decomposed in the following four main steps and illustrated in Figure 1:

1. **Content preparation and packaging:** This step requires the content owner to securely package the content by encrypting it together with its usage rules. The rules are also cryptographically attached to the content thus allowing superdistribution. To be noted that the rules could also be dynamically acquired provided the only attached rule is

to acquire these. This is particularly useful to retain some control on the rules.

2. **Content distribution (and superdistribution):** From thereon, the content may be freely distributed (and superdistributed) through any media (Web, CD, DVD, e-mail, ftp, removable storage, streaming, etc.) since it is persistently protected.

3. **Content usage:** This step involves a consumer trying to access and render the content. It typically involves acquiring a license (from a license server) based on the interpretation of the rules attached to the content. If successful the license is granted and returned to the users DRM enforcement point for decryption and rendering of the content in a trusted interface. To be noted that the license server is not necessarily the content owner, this role may be outsourced to external actors such as content "clearing houses." This activity is of great importance as it will provide the usage data and metering information to the content owners for marketing and market analysis purposes.

Figure 1. General steps of a DRM scenario

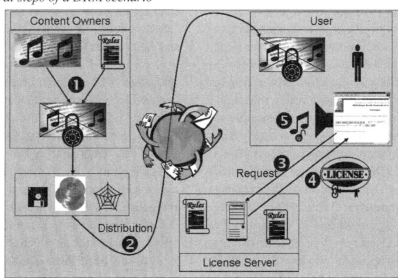

4. Settlement, clearing of transactions and usage metering: Finally, this step concerns the financial clearing and settlement of the completed transactions. It is mostly back office and is based on the collected data from the license acquisition request transactions.

In order to better illustrate the issue and before delving further in to this chapter, let's consider a few examples of widely available systems currently using DRM technology followed by some common usage situations.

iTunes is probably the most popular example averaging between 60 and 80 percent of the worldwide online music market. This platform offers legal downloading of music protected by the FairPlay DRM technology. Although very basic and easy to circumvent it is often considered sufficient by the content industry compared to an economically viable risk. It basically allows non technology users to enjoy the digital music experience. It does however suffer from major limitations and problems, especially with respect to interoperability issues such as space shifting, described in further details later in this chapter.

Another wide spread system using DRM is integrated in the Microsoft Office 2003 productivity suite. It allows through a simple interface to apply DRM rules to Office documents (e.g., Word, Excel, Outlook, PowerPoint). Possible rules include the ability to restrict content access to specific people, in read only or read write mode; to restrict printing, forwarding of e-mails, to copy/paste content or even to set an expiry date to the content, thus preventing its access after a given date. The DRM technology used is called information rights management (IRM) and is accessible to anyone using Office 2003 by clicking on the no-way sign of the toolbar. It relies on the underlying DRM technology called RMS (Rights Management Services) for Windows Server 2003 (RMS, 2003) and is based on XrML (XrML, 2000) as the underlying rights expression language.

Common examples of enforceable rules include for example to restrict the number of transfers to CDs, an e-mail recipient cannot forward, print or copy the content of an e-mail, a document expires September 30 and can only be accesses by board members provided an audit trace is logged or explicit authorization is given by the chairman, the CEO delegates to the CCO the right to manage policies provided audit traces are logged. These more or less complex examples are common in everyday situations.

DRM technology is essentially used in two distinct domains nowadays. Initially in the media and entertainment industry for multimedia content and more recently in the corporate and enterprise sector to address issues of information protection, intellectual property, corporate governance, compliance related for example to corporate scandals. This chapter essentially focuses on the latter trying to place the debate at the strategic level rather than the pure technology.

Even though the underlying technologies and principles are the same, the characteristics of these two domains are radically different. The first emerged thanks to three converging factors: global information networks and broadband, the MP3 audio compression format, and peer-to-peer architectures and protocols. This industry is dominated by powerful media and entertainment giants and their lobbies (music Majors, MPAA, RIAA, IFPI, etc.) facing a market where consumers are characterized by irrational attitudes ranging from intellectual property and copyright fanaticism to utopia of "information wants to be free."

The second domain appears at first sight to be slightly less "emotional" in the sense employees will have a much more rational attitude with respect to issues dealing with corporate information and policies they are expected to comply with. However the challenge is not therefore simpler given the issues at stake which are inherently strategic. As will be further discussed in this chapter, the issues touch upon corporate governance and are therefore under the responsibility of the top management. It is precisely in this context that the notion of digital policy management takes its full strategic dimension, thus dissociating from the primarily technological and instrumental aspects of DRM which only represent the means for their partial implementation.

Superdistribution

The concept of superdistribution, as coined by Ryoichi Mori in 1987 and described in a paper published in 1990 (Mori & Kawahara, 1990), is probably among the most prominent pieces of background work for DRM. Initially, this idea was first invented by Mori in 1983 and known as the software service system (SSS; Mori & Tashiro, 1987).

The aim was to solve the crucial problem of software distribution enforcing fair compensation to software producers and protection of the software against modification with the least possible burden from the user's point of view. Mori observed that while trying to detect whether software was copied (i.e., software piracy) was particularly difficult, it was much easier or almost trivial for a program to detect and monitor its own use. From there on, Mori proposed a model where programs were encrypted prior to their release, thus enabling and allowing widespread and uncontrolled copying and distribution without any problem of piracy, since compensation was bound to usage rather than to acquisition of the software. Mori described a set of four properties for software superdistribution:

- Software products are freely distributed without restriction. The user of a software product pays for using that product, not for possessing it.
- The software vendor can set the terms and conditions of its use and the schedule of fees, if any, for its use.
- Software products can be executed by any user having the proper equipment, provided that the user adheres to the conditions of use set by the vendor and pays the fees charged by the vendor.
- The proper operation of the superdistribution system, including the enforcement of the conditions set by the vendor, is ensured by tamper-resistant electronic devices as digitally protected modules.

The resulting proposed superdistribution architecture relies on three principal functions:

- Administrative arrangements for collecting accounting information on software usage and fees for software usage.
- An accounting process that records and accumulates usage charges, payments and the allocation of usage charges among different software vendors.
- A defense mechanism, utilizing digitally protected modules, that protects the system against interference with its proper operation.

In Mori's design, computers are equipped with devices he calls Superdistribution Box (S-box). Computers equipped with such devices become S-computers. These boxes are to be understood as tamper resistant devices embodying microprocessors, RAM, ROM and a real-time clock intended for storage, processing, and management of sensitive elements such as deciphering keys and other aspects of the superdistribution system. It is noteworthy to mention with respect to this specific issue that current trends in electronic commerce and security still follow this interesting idea of tamper resistant secure device for smart card readers and cryptographic devices. The resulting encrypted software together with its usage terms and conditions is called an S-program. Its permanent encrypted state has the very nice property of enabling it to be transmitted over untrusted and insecure communication channels. This is the exact property which is needed for communicating over today's open networks like the Internet. Furthermore, since programs are encrypted they can be copied and distributed by anybody without causing any prejudice.

From an operational point of view, the S-box holds a metering program called the software usage monitor (SUM) in charge of enforcing usage terms and conditions set by software vendors and of tracking the fees (i.e., software usage units called S-credits) owed to each vendor. The S-box then generates payment files which are encrypted and sent through the network to collection agencies which in turn transmits payments to vendors. A clearinghouse, which may be a credit card company, keeps track of funds transfers in the superdistribution system.

In doing so, Mori turns a major drawback into a major asset. Namely, the inherent nature of software that allows it to be copied and distributed in a marginal, cost-effective way, turns out to be a real asset. In this scope, users become themselves "legal" redistributors of software they like and use most. Based on this work, two prototype S-box systems were built. The first one based on a NEC9801 personal computer in 1987. The second prototype built as a co-processor for a Macintosh in 1990.

It so happens that apparently Mori was not the only one working on similar ideas. Brad Cox claims to also have been a pioneer in the field of superdistribution. In 1984, Cox came up with a similar design without knowledge of Mori's work. This design was documented in a notarized patent workbook which he never filed for reasons explained in his book (Cox, 1996). Cox gave it the name of CopyFree Software in the sense that software could be copied and distributed for free, but revenue collection would be based on usage. Later on, in an article published in Wired Magazine, Cox (1994) describes superdistribution (meterware) as a possible foundation of a new networked economy. In 1996, Cox published *Objects as Property on the Electronic Frontier* (Cox, 1996) a book on superdistribution, compar-

ing the challenge faced by electronic goods in the information age to the pony express days of the Wild West of America. He calls this challenging process of hauling goods made of bits rather than atoms in an emerging networked economy: taming the electronic frontier.

From the Rise and Fall of the Dotcoms to Corporate Scandals

The 1990s witnessed massive expansion of information and communication technologies thanks to the Web. It gave rise to new business practices and models, new trades and, consequently, new needs. E-commerce was born, and with it came naturally all the issues facing intellectual property and copyright. The United States, under the pressure of the media and entertainment industry, even passed a law (DMCA 1998a, 1998b) by which it became illegal to analyze or try to circumvent technical protection measures, including for cryptography researchers.

In this context, DRM found a natural ground for its growth in the media and entertainment industry. It was easy for large companies and startups to raise funding for projects and initiatives in this field. Among the most significant initiatives were InterTrust with DigiBox (Sibert, Bernstein, & Van Wie, 1995; Van Wie, Sibert, & Horning, 1997), IBM with Cryptolope (Kaplan, 1996; Kohl, Lotspiech, & Kaplan, 1997) and Xerox PARC with the work on digital property rights language (DPRL), developed per Mark Stefik (1996). These systems and works were essentially oriented towards copyright protection, media content marketing and usage metering. All these systems and approaches suffered from a major limitation in the sense they would lockup the customer in proprietary noninteroperable solutions. Moreover, the underlying business model was to take a share of each individual transaction as a revenue stream. Consequently, new intermediaries appeared in the form of content clearing houses positioning themselves in the middle of the transaction to act as gateways between the incompatible solutions and to manage the actual transaction clearing among the parties. A host of solutions appeared at this time, most of them have disappeared today. Also, it is during this period that many patents were filed and granted thus further contributing to blocking this industry's progress due to many lawsuits and patent infringement claims. More recently, it was through industrial consortiums (e.g., Coral) that companies gathered in patent pools to be able to move forward.

The story then unfolds around the technology bubble explosion and the financial scandals which particularly struck corporate America (e.g., Enron, Martha Stewart), thus destabilizing investor trust and confidence in the financial markets. It is in this context that emerged initiatives, aiming at regulating accounting practices and financial reporting of publicly traded companies. These have materialized through regulatory frameworks defining very precisely the practices and responsibilities of corporate managers with respect to accounting and financial procedures, operational risk management, traceability, disclosure of security problems, and so forth. The most famous example is the Sarbanes Oxley Act 2002. The most notable difference with the prior situation lies in the criminal liability of corporate managers (CEO, CFO, COO, etc.). It also corresponds to the increase in responsibility of what was formerly known as internal control which is now part of the top management as Chief Compliance Officer (CCO).

At the same time, the technology landscape also witnessed important concentration, acquisition and intellectual property and patent valorization (e.g., Acquisition of InterTrust by Sony and Philips and lawsuit against Microsoft). It is also at this time that Microsoft enters the missing sector of enterprise rights management with rights management services (RMS) relying on XrML from Contentguard (Xerox spin-off) partially held by Microsoft. Rights expression languages became more popular to express rules; several standards appeared including ISO standards.

DRM Standards

One of the major problems that hampered broader and faster adoption of DRM was the lack of standards and the totally incompatible proprietary solutions made available by companies like Microsoft, InterTrust, ContentGuard, IBM, Real-Networks, Apple, and so forth. Recent progress in this field is extremely encouraging in particular with respect to standards. Although current standardization efforts are often sector bound, they are needed in order to go towards DRM interoperability. In this section we will explore some of these standards and related technologies, highlighting their interesting properties.

From Sector-Bound Standards to Global DRM Standards

In this first part, we focus on covering main DRM standards and initiatives. Presented standards go from sector-bound approaches to more global ones, providing more or less flexibility and interoperability.

The eXtensible rights markup language (XrML) is the result of the research done by the Xerox Palo Alto Research Center (PARC) (XrML, 2000). Governed by Contentguard Inc, this language provides a method for specifying and managing rights and conditions which can be securely assigned at different levels of granularity to authenticable individuals and groups of individuals and be associated with any kind of resources be it digital content or even services. XrML is designed to be used in either single tier or multitier channels of distribution and provides means to specify the trust environment in the language in order to maintain the integrity of chosen rights and conditions. XrML is fully extensible and compatible with XML namespaces by using XML schemas, which allow designing extensions for specific industries. To ensure authentication and protection of the rights expressions, XML Signature and XML Encryption standards are used (XrML, 2002).

XrML is currently used in commercially deployed solutions such as Microsoft DRM solutions. While still supporting it, ContentGuard has frozen the release of XrML at Version 2.0 and gave governance and control of XrML to the international standards community, making it available to any standards organization seeking a rights language. Changes as well as updates to the XrML Version 2.0 Core are now directly issued by Moving Picture Experts Group (MPEG) and OASIS (1993; Organization for the Advancement of Structured Information Standards) standard bodies, consistent with the XrML architecture and design intent. These releases are built on a common XrML core and standard extensions, while specific extensions meeting specific requirements are released by each standard body.

For instance, the MPEG-21 group uses XrML as a basis for MPEG-REL, their rights expression language. This group aims at providing a normative open multimedia framework for use by all actors in the multimedia delivery and consumption chain. It defines the technology needed to "*support users to exchange, access, consume, trade and otherwise manipulate digital items in an efficient, transparent and interoperable way*" (MPEG-21, 2002). This framework includes two parts directly related to digital rights management: a rights expression language (MPEG-REL, 2004), a machine-readable language that can declare rights and permissions and a Rights Data Dictionary (MPEG-RDD, 2004), defining the terms used by the rights expression language and which addresses the issue of rights interoperability and semantics. Both MPEG-REL and MPEG-RDD have been ratified as ISO standards. Such initiatives are instrumental in this field and represent a prerequisite for broader adoption and interoperability.

The open digital rights language (ODRL, 2002) initiative is an international effort aimed at developing open standards for digital rights management. The initiative is intended to provide flexible and interoperable means to handle rights enabled content. Thus, like MPEG-21's standards, the ODRL specification provides an extensible language and data dictionary language allowing the expression of content usage conditions, constraints, permissions, offers and agreements with rights holders, while providing interoperability. Nevertheless, unlike MPEG-21 standards which are strongly related to the multimedia sector, the ODRL information model, in order to cover a large community base, is based on prior research and analysis of requirements of multiple sectors. ODRL uses two XML schemas to express both the rights expression language and the rights data dictionary.

The secure video processor (SVP, 2004) Alliance launched by NDS, STMicroelectronics, and Thomson aims at defining an open standard for hardware-based digital video content protection for a large variety of digital devices. SVP includes a rights expression language allowing content owners to control rights in a similar way MPEG-REL or ODRL offers, named content segment license (CSL) (OCP, 2005). CSL offers interesting features such as the capability to define domains of validity for created licenses. These domains can be for instance a home network, or a set of devices.

The open mobile alliance (OMA) is an organization set up by the mobile industry in order to facilitate global user adoption of mobile data services by specifying market driven mobile service enablers that ensure service interoperability across devices, locations, operators, networks and service providers (OMA, 2002). It aims at providing open global standards protocols and interfaces not locked to proprietary technologies and independent of operating systems. The particularity of OMA is that the specifications it delivers are based on mobile service use cases and open standards. Further, all key segments of the industry, are involved into the specification process.

OMA has published two releases of its specifications. The release 1.0 specifications (OMA, 2004) provided some fundamental building blocks for a DRM system, but lacked the complete security necessary for a robust, end-to-end DRM system that considers the need for secure distribution, authentication of Devices, revocation and other aspects. The main feature of this first release was its ability to prevent users from forwarding digital content to others. The release 2.0 specification (OMA, 2006) addresses missing aspects of the first version of OMA DRM and is much more powerful and flexible as it is designed for full featured multimedia mobile devices such as handsets. It covers all aspects of rights protection such as rights object acquisition, key management, certificate checking, content protection, capability signaling, etc. OMA has adopted ODRL to define the rights expression language of OMA DRM. The goal of the OMA REL is to take into account the special requirements and characteristics of the mobile domain to express consumption rights over DRM Content (OMA, 2006b).

The Coral Consortium (CORAL, 2004) is a cross-industry consortium consisting of content providers, service providers, and consumer electronics manufacturers. Its founding members include Hewlett-Packard, Intertrust, Philips, Panasonic, Samsung, Sony and the Twentieth Century Fox Film Corp. It focuses on creating an open technology framework that enables interoperability between different and disparate content formats, devices, and content distribution services. The goal of the Coral Consortium is to provide consumers with a set of DRM-agnostic service protocols for interoperability between DRM systems and standards and other content distribution technologies while simultaneously meeting the content protection and management needs of content providers and other participants in the content distribution value chain.

InterTrust is contributing multiple technologies (Intertrust, 2005) to the Coral Consortium, among others NEMO and Octopus. The First one, NEMO (Networked Environment for Media Orchestration) (Bradley & Maher, 2004), is a service provider architecture that achieves interoperability among a wide range of devices, formats, networks, and types of services. The idea underlying the NEMO approach stipulates that as long as it is possible to obtain rights to use content, people should not be prevented from doing it, whatever device they own. Thus, NEMO provides a media services framework allowing nodes to find each other on a peer-to-peer network, and interact, while allowing communication between different DRM technologies through wrappers or gateways. The second technology, Octopus (Intertrust, 2004), is a DRM lightweight client and toolkit for building DRM engines designed for rapid DRM deployment on a large variety of devices and operating systems. It is an open specification enabling the DRM-enhancement of existing systems and providing flexibility to Octopus users by allowing them to freely choose cryptography solutions, implementation, and business model. The architecture of Octopus is made up of basic building blocks that can be used to protect digital content, expressing content usage rules and evaluating those rules.

Consumer-Oriented DRM

In this second part we focus on DRM standards and approaches that do not only consider rights management from a content owner's perspective, but also from a consumer's point of view. Such standards are extremely important as they ensure rights balance as they take into consideration user's rights and what users can expect from DRM systems.

Digital rights management raises issues having to deal with heterogeneous interests and multiple requirements of existing actors in the value chain. While current DRM solutions are content provider centric and are meant to protect their rights, there has been little attention given to the consumer side of managing rights. In order to raise awareness, help to reconcile these interests and to support the emergence of a common European position with regard to consumer and user issues of DRM solutions, the INformed DIalogue about Consumer Acceptability of DRM Solutions in Europe Project, INDICARE (INDICARE, 2004) was launched. It aims at investigating issues like consumer acceptability of DRM systems, their interface and functionality, as well as policy issues linked to privacy and access to information. The INDICARE project maintains and stimulates discussions about consumer and user issues of DRM by providing quality input such as news information and profound analyses.

The disruption of rights balance between content can be illustrated with the fact that currently most widespread DRM solutions bind content to hardware devices; while such an approach provides straight-forward security for content owners, it limits content usage by forbidding often legitimate behaviors such as space shifting. To tackle this issue, Sun Microsystems introduced Project DReaM (DRM everywhere available) (Sun Microsystems, 2005), a project to create an open-source standard for interoperable DRM that relies on user authentication alone and not devices anymore. Project DReaM includes the DRM-OPERA architecture and makes it available in the form of an open-source community Java development project.

DRM-OPERA is an open DRM architecture (EURESCOM P1207 OPERA, 2003) aiming at enabling the interoperability between different DRM systems. It has been specified and prototyped within project OPERA of the Eurescom organization. Among other activities, the OPERA project has produced an overview of state-of-the art DRM systems and standardization activities as of 2002 (EURESCOM P1207 OPERA, 2002). The DRM-OPERA architecture offers two interesting features that differentiate it from other solutions. First, it makes usage licenses independent of the underlying DRM system by offering its own license management. Then, usage licenses are bound to users instead of, as it is common with existing solutions, to devices. The architecture provides interoperability through a lowest common denominator approach. Indeed OPERA is built above existing DRM systems and provides its own users authentication and licensing, hiding details of underlying systems. To operate, OPERA only needs a play once license from these systems.

While DRM future was discussed in silos across the industry be it consortiums like Coral or standard initiative like DMP (DMP, 2003), there was no place where the whole community of all of the digital content stakeholders could come to discuss, define, and develop the future of digital content and DRM. To tackle this issue, Sun Microsystems decided in August 2005 to provide a virtual meeting place for all those contributing to this effort by creating the open media commons (OMC, 2005), an open source community project, and a tool by sharing the internal project DReaM with the community under the OSI-approved common development and distribution license (CDDL). The aim of the Open Media Commons community is threefold. First, OMC aims at developing an open-source, royalty-free solution for the distribution of digital content, focused on authenticating people and roles, not just devices. Then it aims at addressing the application of DRM technology to a wide range of content and situations, such as personal rights management, the privacy of health records and compliance management for businesses dealing with Sarbanes-Oxley. Finally it aims at creating an open environment where creators, content owners, consumers, network operators, technology providers and consumer electronics device manufacturers can work together to address the technical problems associated with DRM (OMC, 2006a).

In March 2006 (OMC, 2006b), Open Media Commons released two draft specifications – DReaM-CAS (Conditional Access System) and DReaM-MMI (Mother May I) as well as the source code for a prototype implementation of DReaM-CAS. DREAM-CAS defines a complete open conditional access system that enables delivery and consumption of protected content over Internet Protocol networks while DREAM-MMI defines a message protocol, a message transport and a list of profiles required to ascertain rights by a DRM client from a rights server in order to allow clients to negotiate for rights through standardized protocols rather than downloading a license with an embedded expression of rights.

The Marlin Joint Development Association (Marlin, 2005), is a consumer electronics industry technology development alliance formed by Intertrust Technologies, Matsushita Electric Industrial (Panasonic), Royal Philips Electronics, Samsung Electronics, and Sony Corporation that aims at creating a set of specifications for an open standard interoperable DRM platform for consumer electronics. In order to provide interoperability of content whatever distribution mode, DRM technology and standard are used, Marlin JDA specifications aim at providing a single technology toolkit to build DRM functions into their devices to support commonly used content distribution modes and thus avoid conflicts due to proprietary DRM technologies and standards. A key feature of Marlin's design is that it is consumer-oriented. Indeed Marlin authentication is user-based: it defines that user should be able to use content on any device they own and thus that content be tied to user identities and not device identities. While hiding issues such as content and device ownership that will need to be tackled, such a design is a step towards the copyright balance as defined previously. Marlin JDA is closely related to the Coral Consortium and as such, Marlin-based devices will be able to interoperate with Coral-enabled DRM systems even if those systems do not use Marlin DRM components. It relies on Intertrust's NEMO and Octopus technologies.

The digital media project (DMP, 2003) is an independent standards initiative lead by Dr. Chiariglione, the founder of MPEG, aiming at tackling specific issues of DRM environment mainly related to the balance between content owner and consumer rights. The DMP defines its mission as being to "*promote continuing successful development, deployment and use of Digital Media that respect the rights of creators and rights holders to exploit their works, the wish of end users to fully enjoy the benefits of Digital Media and the interests of various value-chain players to provide products and services*" (DMP, 2003). The project standardizes appropriate protocols aiming at supporting the functions value-chain users need to execute and provides an interoperable DRM platform (IDP) specification (DMP, 2005) derived from MPEG-21 standards and including an extended subset of MPEG-REL. The IDP is based on requirements that have been derived from three sources, and which the platform has to be able to represent. The first one, traditional rights usages (TRUs) covers usages exercised by media users and enjoyed in the pre digital era. The second one, digital enabled usages (DEU), are usages either not possible or not considered in the analog domain. Finally the digital media business models (DMBM) is a set of TRUs and DEUs assembled to achieve a goal.

THE CORPORATE AND ENTERPRISE SECTOR

Nowadays, enterprise information systems orchestrate complex processes requiring fine grained business engineering skills and competencies in order to deliver, in a sound, accurate and cost-effective way, the dynamically evolving services they need. Therefore, this sector is about to witness one of its most profound and significant transformation from the point of view of information management and its organizational and information systems impact.

Currently, information protection still mainly relies on perimeter based security and access control approaches whether in the local Intranet or through a VPN using secure communication channels. However, outside these boundaries it remains a critical issue rarely taken into consideration. This is all the more significant given the broad availability and use of mobile and external storage devices such as USB keys, CD, DVD, PDA, removable hard drives, etc. All things considered, from the moment information leaves the perimeter or any form of secured extension, and by any means, it is as if it were in clear on the Web. Consequently, the established relationships among parties are based on trust. From a Corporate point of view, this simple form of trust relationship is becoming increasingly insufficient simply considering the incurred risk and the strategic nature of information.

Policy management nowadays also suffers major gaps. It has now become common to receive e-mails or electronic documents having an up-front statement in bold reading the policy under which it is provided, or a statement saying *"CONFIDENTIAL, DO NOT FORWARD UNDER ANY CIRCUMSTANCES, PLEASE"*. Wishful thinking with close to zero effect. Forwarding risks, whether intentional or not, are non negligible. This simple example sows by itself, while we have definitely passed the point of no return of using electronic mail, at what point organizations are left without means in such situations. Corporate policies still mainly reside in dusty handbooks often provided to employees upon starting the job. In their most advanced form, these are documented on the corporate Intranet basically for ease of maintenance and update reasons. In most cases, corporate policies are split among common sense and on the job experience of employees. Rare are those companies having instrumented policies by systems enforcing them, and none to this date and to the best of our

knowledge, have full fledged global corporate digital policy management in place. This is a major issue and challenge we have to face in the coming years for this sector.

A Few Facts and Figures

In order to further assess some of the key motivations of this domain, let us consider a few facts, figures and trends. According to the 2001 FBI Crime Survey, information theft has caused the greatest financial damage of all security related problems. A 2002 PriceWaterhouseCoopers report revealed that 32% of the worst security problems are caused by insiders. The Gartner G2 revealed in 2003 that most companies loose intellectual property through employees, whether intentionally or by inadvertence. The META Group estimated in 2004, that by 2006 about 20% of the global 2000 companies would use digital rights management technologies. These are a few quotes which are representative of a growing uneasiness in the field of enterprise and corporate security. This uneasiness materializes a fear facing a security phenomenon which is still by far embryonic: the strategic importance of Information as a resource and asset, as well as the mitigation of its associated risk.

Information: A Strategic Resource

Information has become a strategic resource for corporations. It has become critical and increasingly considered as an asset in digital form: "digital asset". The term asset reveals its financial and business value dimension requiring it to be managed accordingly.

It concerns every corporate functions whether it is HR, legal, accounting and finance, sales, suppliers, customers, budget and planning, production, marketing, design, R&D, competition, analysis and simulations, tax reporting, internal control and compliance, and the list goes on and on. None of these functions whatsoever escapes this rule of requiring to be considered as a corporate asset. They all handle more or less sensitive information, be they static or dynamic, requiring various levels of protection and rules governing their use at all time and no matter where they reside.

When mentioning dynamic information, we are referring explicitly to all the dynamically generated data by application portals, ERP systems, databases, line of business applications, etc. often ending up in spreadsheets or files, thus escaping any form of control and protection allowing them to be freely transferred to removable storage devices or worse sent by e-mail to a personal address to further work at home.

Regulatory Frameworks, Compliance, Risk and Corporate Governance

The economy and the corporate world have been recently under heavy pressure due to several scandals thus raising major concerns for investors and markets. It is in this context that several regulatory frameworks emerged defining principles of practices, responsibilities (now criminal) as well as the duties of publicly traded companies.

Among the most striking example was probably the Sarbanes–Oxley Act governing the integrity of financial and accounting data. Another example in the banking industry is the Basel II agreements requiring banks to comply by 2007 in order to minimize as much as possible the level of their reserves.

By now, there are many such regulatory frameworks either sector based, or by type of risk, and so forth. These issues now have a direct impact on corporate governance in the sense that compliance is not only mandatory and bound in time, but must also be audited on a regular basis. The cost of not complying is crippling and may even lead to sever penalties, fines and jail or even stop the business with disastrous consequences on reputation and image. DRM technologies can

help up to a certain point in managing these issues and thus mitigate such risks.

Among the most widely known regulatory frameworks which were or still are on the compliance agenda, we find, classified by activity:

- **Financial services**
  Graham-Leach-Bliley (1999) Title V – confidentiality of customer banking data
  Sarbanes-Oxley (2002) – integrity of financial and accounting data
  NASD 2711 (2002) – relation between research analysts and investment banks
  Bale II – (2007) level of reserves based on operational risks
- **Health**
  HIPAA (1996) – confidentiality of patient records
  FDA 21 CFR Part 11 (1997) – data integrity of drug clinical studies
- **Other**
  California SB 1386 (2003) – confidentiality of personal data
  ISO 17799 (2000-2) – best practices for information security
  Etc.

It is noteworthy to mention that the compliance issue is a sustainable problem which is here to stay, having a recurring audit activity in order to prove and assess compliance on a permanent basis. It is therefore vital for corporations to place this issue high on the agenda not only from specific risk mitigation point of views but also and more importantly at the strategic level of corporate governance. This requires a consistent approach which is global to the enterprise, involving everyone at all levels, as well as defining the most accurate management dashboards for its continuous monitoring. Thus, digital policy management becomes a strategic project under the supervision and responsibility of the top management. It will be only at this price that companies will be able to cope seamlessly with such issues in a cost effective way. Thus allowing to capture not only the evolution of the existing regulatory frameworks but also the emerging and future ones we cannot anticipate but are bound to appear on a regular basis.

Digital Rights Management: A Help Rather than a Constraint

Let us mention here that it is not a question of adopting a paranoid attitude aiming to the total and absolute control of everything aka "big brother." It is rather a responsible and aware attitude and clear general policy with respect to information management representing one of its most invaluable assets and intellectual property.

Given such a context, DRM technologies can provide a more pleasant and safe work environment substantially reducing numerous risks of unintentional errors. It represents a help providing potential risk detection and mitigation.

Let us consider a particularly striking example to illustrate this. It is now common to work on several projects involving many people and partners. Moreover, it is also not uncommon to be allocated to different projects at the same time. E-mail remains a widely spread and used tool for communication and coordination among the project members. Now, how many times do we diligently and carefully check the recipient list when doing a "reply all"? The most frequent and honest answer is "almost never". However, it is possible that some people leaving for a few days decide to use another more convenient personal address to keep in touch with the project. Now consider one of these persons be fired with immediate notice while away.

Well, in such a situation, if no one pays attention this person will continue to receive e-mails on his personal address until someone realizes it, if ever. Thus having access to information he is no longer entitled to receive he could easily disclose it to the competition or the media.

Moreover, if this person still holds work related data on mobile or removable devices he will still be able to access it freely.

This is exactly one among many information risk situations, for which DRM technologies can provide significant help in applying and verifying dynamically corporate policies applicable to specific situations. Moreover, by applying consistently those policies to work documents, an employee leave would immediately trigger the revocation of his rights in a centralized way thus preventing further access to held documents provided the policy required some form of online license acquisition.

DRM technology represents the technical means to manage digital assets and define the rules governing their use in a persistently protected way. It relies on the basic following principles common to all sectors where DRM is used:

- Superdistribution (Cox, 1994, 1996 ; Mori & Kawahara, 1990; Mori & Tashiro, 1987)
- Persistent protection
- Definition and expression of rules governing usage and access to digital assets using rights expression languages (Stefik, 1996)
- Direct or indirect association of these rules to the digital asset

What can DRM Do—and Not Do—in the Corporate Environment

DRM technology can address and help solve a number of issues becoming increasingly critical in the corporate environment. In particular, it represents a solution for the digital management of rights and policies governing content usage as well as the processes and electronic services. Most common examples are among the following:

- Enables a responsible management and use of digital assets within and outside the corporate perimeter.

- Helps in managing classifications (e.g., company confidential, board of directors, projects).
- Helps instrument compliance management with respect to regulatory frameworks and corporate policies at large (e.g., Sarbanes-Oxley, HIPAA, NASD2711).
- Helps in managing retention policies (e.g., e-mails, documents).
- Provides the means to manage issues facing traceability, monitoring, tracking, usage metering, audit trails, etc.
- Provides a centralized management of revocation and granting (e.g., new employee, employee leave).

However, DRM technology does not and never will provide total "military grade" security. The issue is to find the right balance between security and a commercially viable risk level. Or, in other words, security stops where the marginal cost of implementing it is disproportionate to the risk one is trying to mitigate. Moreover, technology cannot provide any protection against analog attacks like reading information over the phone, taking a picture or hand copying. Such cases are however clear and leave no doubts on the malicious intentions, thus allowing to take legal or disciplinary measures.

A Framework for Corporate Policy Management

A possible approach to addressing this issue at the strategic level proposes a general framework for studying, analyzing and defining corporate policy management towards its partial digital instrumentation (Morin & Pawlak, 2005a). The starting point is a basic layered architecture commonly found in the enterprise by which security issues are categorized by infrastructure, application and content. These three layers traditionally fall under the responsibility of IT and IS involving the CTO, CIO and CSO.

Another layer is then introduced for corporate policy management, under the responsibility of the top management including CEO, CFO, CCO and COO. To be noted that the compliance officer (CCO) has moved from traditionally known "internal controls" to a top management position and responsibility, mainly in the light of compliance issues. This layer is strategic and focuses mainly

Figure 2. General framework for corporate policy management

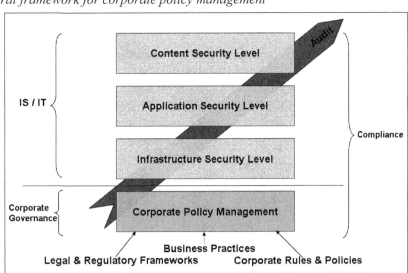

on corporate governance. In the scope of corporate policy management, we identified three main sources of inputs in two distinct categories. The first category is internal and deals with internal corporate rules and policies. The second category is external and has two sources. The business practices commonly applicable for the activity sector and the legal and regulatory frameworks the company must comply with.

Now, across these four layers, the three technology ones and the strategic one runs a recurring audit activity to monitor and assess compliance. Traditionally undertaken by external auditors, it is also the case that such activities are fundamental from inside the enterprise for corporate governance reasons using management dashboards and indicators. Figure 2 illustrates this general framework for corporate policy management.

Given such a framework, it provides the means to analyze those policies in order to determine the ones that can be partially or fully digitally instrumented by technologies such as DRM at IT and IS level. To be noted that definitely not all policies can map to technical solutions. A good example of this would be the notion on "intention" when accessing a report for example within NASD 2711.

Intentions will hopefully remain hard to calculate in the future. Nevertheless, part of the corporate policy management will be instrumented and the remaining will stay under the control of traditional measures. The instrumented part will provide the means to answer questions such as: who, what, when where, traces, delegations, and so forth. Figure 3 places corporate policy management with respect to its sources and its potential digital instrumentation using digital rights and policy management technologies.

FUTURE TRENDS AND CONCLUSION: THE ROAD AHEAD, KEY CHALLENGES AND OPPORTUNITIES

To conclude, we highlight some key issues and their challenges in this industry for the years ahead. It appears clearly that the various actors in this ecosystem have each tried to put themselves in the center of the picture, thus trying to align the others. History has shown through market sanction that on the one hand the approach was wrong and on the other hand that if there should

Figure 3. Positioning of corporate policy management

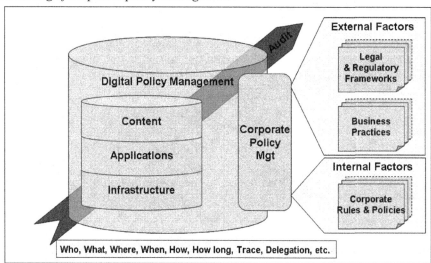

be a central actor it should definitely be the customer who happens to be the end user. This is something the technology vendors and content holder have a hard time understanding.

More recently, this market has somewhat stabilized around a few big players and vendors upon which some integrators rely to provide often sector specific solutions as added value. However, standards are a critical success factor in this domain for the growth of this industry. In a global massively interconnected society, it is definitely not reasonable to be locked in proprietary noninteroperable solutions. Likewise, in the media and entertainment industry, one cannot reasonably assume users will carry/hold as many consumer electronic rendering devices as there are incompatible competing DRM technologies.

As a result, technical and semantic interoperability represents one, if not the most important challenge in this industry. Likewise, exception management in the context of DRM enabled systems is another key issue and challenge whereby all usage situations cannot reasonably be anticipated. For example, many laws still rely on often contradictory national or territorial specificities (Morin & Pawlak, 2005b).

The evolution in the field of trusted computing, especially at the operating system level, is likely to be a key critical factor maybe complemented by a DRM chip as discussed for many years now.

Identity management is also a domain in full expansion that integrates well in the context of digital rights and policy management.

Finally, the emergence of digital policy management in the corporate and enterprise sector is not arguable. It represents a major challenge and work to be accomplished on the corporate agenda for the years ahead.

Digital rights and policy management represents a founding technology and a major strategic issue in the light of a responsible, sustainable, cost effective and perennial approach to modern information systems. DRM technologies encompass the instrumental dimension of the issue (i.e.,

the means) while digital policy management (DPM) cover the strategic dimension consisting in capturing, analyzing, specifying, representing, evolving, and managing internal and external policies before instrumenting those that can be through DRM technologies.

In this context, emerging frameworks for studying, analyzing and defining corporate policy management towards its partial digital instrumentation are being studied. Such issues and approaches still represent ongoing work requiring much further work to refine, validate and implement the necessary models and tools at the corporate policy level to capture, design, define technical requirements to be implemented by underlying technologies, monitor, evolve, assess, audit and manage corporate policies. Current leads considered for further work include investigating the recent evolution in the ISO/IEC 15504 standard towards a general process oriented framework. Other relevant frameworks (e.g., COBIT, ITIL) should also be studied from the point of view of alignment, risk management, corporate governance and business value. Links with enterprise architecture frameworks also have to be investigated and requirements engineering techniques could prove to be particularly useful in initial phases of defining and formalizing policies from unstructured heterogeneous sources. Finally, let us stress that in such a perspective rights and policy enabling the corporate information system represents a mandatory major challenge for the years ahead.

ACKNOWLEDGMENT

This work was supported by the Swiss Secrétariat d'Etat à l'éducation et à la Recherche SER under grant No. 03.0391-1 within INTEROP Network of Excellence (IST-508011), Task Group 7 on Interoperability Challenges of Trust, Confidence/Security, Policies and NFA.

REFERENCES

Becker, E., Buhse, W., Günnewig, D., & Rump, N. (Eds.). (2003). Digital rights management, technological, economic, legal and political aspects. *LNCS, 2770.*

Bradley, W. B., & Maher, D. P. (2004). The NEMO P2P service orchestration framework. In *Proceedings of the 37th Hawaii International Conference on System Science.*

CORAL. (2004). Coral consortium corporation. Retrieved January 26, 2006, from http://www.coral-interop.org/

Cox, B. (1994, September). Superdistribution. *Wired Magazine,* pp 89-92.

Cox, B. (1996). *Superdistribution objects as property on the electronic frontier.* Addison-Wesley.

DMCA. (1998a). *H.R.2281 Digital Millennium Copyright Act (enrolled as agreed to or passed by both house and senate).* Retrieved January 26, 2006, from http://thomas.loc.gov/cgi-bin/query/z?c105:H.R.2281.ENR:

DMCA. (1998b). *The Digital Millennium Copyright Act of 1998 - U.S. copyright office summary.* Retrieved January 26, 2006, from http://www.copyright.gov/legislation/dmca.pdf

DMP. (2003). *Digital media project.* Retrieved January 26, 2006, from http://www.dmpf.org/

DMP. (2005). *Digital media project (Approved document No 3).* Retrieved January 26, 2006, from http://www.dmpf.org/open/dmp0653.zip

EURESCOM P1207 OPERA. (2002). *Overview of state-of-the art DRM systems and standardisation activities.* Retrieved January 26, 2006, from http://www.eurescom.de/public/projectresults/P1200-series/P1207-TI.asp

EURESCOM P1207 OPERA. (2003). *An open DRM architecture.* Retrieved January 26, 2006, from http://www.eurescom.de/public/projectresults/P1200-series/P1207-D2.asp

Ewalt, D. M. (2005). *Citigroup blames UPS for customer data loss.* Retrieved January 26, 2006, from http://www.forbes.com/facesinthenews/2005/06/06/0606autofacescan09.html

INDICARE. (2004). *The Informed dialogue about consumer acceptability of DRM solutions in Europe.* Retrieved January 26, 2006, from http://www.indicare.org/

Intertrust. (2004). *Octopus principles of operation* (Internal memo).

Intertrust. (2005). *Reference technology.* Retrieved January 26, 2006, from http://www.intertrust.com/main/research/reference.html

Kaplan, M. A. (1996). *IBM cryptolopesTM, superdistribution and digital rights management.* Retrieved December 1996, from http://www.research.ibm.com/people/k/kaplan

Kohl, U., Lotspiech, J., & Kaplan, A. (1997). *Safeguarding digital library contents and users protecting documents rather than channels.* Retrieved from http://www.dlib.org/dlib/september97/ibm/09lotspiech.html

Marlin, J. D. A. (2005). *CE and DRM technology leaders to create a DRM toolkit for consumer devices.* Retrieved January 26, 2006, from http://www.intertrust.com/main/news/2003_2005/050119_marlin.html

Mori, R., & Kawahara, M. (1990, July). Superdistribution: The concept and the architecture. *Transaction of the IEICE, E73*(7), 1133-1146.

Mori, R., & Tashiro, S. (1987, January). The concept of software service system (SSS). *Transaction of the IEICE, J70*(D1), 70-81.

Morin, J.-H., & Pawlak, M. (2005a, December 11). Towards a global framework for corporate and enterprise digital policy management. In

Proceedings of the SoftWars Conference on Protecting the Intangible Organizational Assets, Las Vegas, NV.

Morin, J.-H., & Pawlak, M. (2005b, December 10). A credential based approach to managing exceptions in digital rights management systems. In *Proceedings of Fourth Pre-ICIS Academic Workshop AIM on New trends in IT and New Challenges in IT Regulation, Las Vegas, NV.*

MPEG-21. (2002). *MPEG-21 multimedia framework.* Retrieved January 26, 2006, from http://www.chiariglione.org/mpeg/standards/mpeg-21/mpeg-21.htm

MPEG-RDD. (2004). *Multimedia framework (MPEG-21)–Part 6: Rights data dictionary.* Retrieved January 26, 2006, from http://www.iso.ch/iso/en/CombinedQueryResult.CombinedQueryResult?queryString=21000-6

MPEG-REL. (2004). *Multimedia framework (MPEG-21)–Part 5: Rights expression language.* Retrieved January 26, 2006, from http://www.iso.ch/iso/en/CombinedQueryResult.CombinedQueryResult?queryString=21000-5

OASIS. (1993). *Organization for the advancement of structured information standards.* Retrieved March 28, 2006, from http://www.oasis-open.org/

OCP. (2005). *The secure video processor (SVP) initiative–SVP open content protection system: Technical overview.* Retrieved January 26, 2006, from http://www.svpalliance.org/docs/e2e_technical_introduction.pdf

ODRL. (2002). *The open digital rights language (ODRL) initiative.* Retrieved January 26, 2006, from http://www.odrl.net/

OMA. (2002). *Open mobile alliance.* Retrieved January 26, 2006, from http://www.openmobile-alliance.org/

OMA. (2004). *Open mobile alliance.* Retrieved January 26, 2006, from http://www.openmobilealliance.org/release_program/drm_v1_0.html

OMA, (2006a). *Open mobile alliance.* Retrieved January 26, 2006, from http://www.openmobilealliance.org/release_program/drm_v2_0.html

OMA. (2006b). *Open mobile alliance.* Retrieved January 26, 2006, from http://www.openmobilealliance.org/release_program/drm_v2_0.html

OMC. (2005). *Open media commons.* Retrieved March 28, 2006, from http://www.openmediacommons.org/

OMC. (2006a). *Open media commons FAQ's.* Retrieved March 28 , 2006, from http://www.openmediacommons.org/faqs.html

OMC. (2006b). *Open media commons releases specifications and source code for open, royalty-free digital rights management.* Retrieved March 28, 2006, from http://www.openmediacommons.org/news/03212006-omcworkshop_press_release.html

Privacy Rights Clearinghouse. (2005). *A chronology of data breaches reported since the ChoicePoint incident.* Retrieved May 31, 2006, from http://www.privacyrights.org/

RMS. (2003). *Microsoft Windows rights management services (RMS) for Windows server 2003.* Retrieved May 31, 2006, from http://www.microsoft.com/rms

Rosenblatt, B., Trippe, B., & Mooney, S. (2001). *Digital rights management: Business and technology.* New York: Hungry Minds/Wiley.

Sibert, O., Bernstein, D., & Van Wie, D. (1995, July 11-12,). The DigiBox: A self-protecting container for information commerce. In *Proceedings of First USENIX Workshop on Electronic Commerce,* New York.

Silver, C. (2005). *Time Warner employee data missing.* Retrieved January 26, 2006, from http://money.cnn.com/2005/05/02/news/fortune500/security_timewarner/?cnn=yes

Stefik, M. (1996). Letting loose the light: Igniting commerce in electronic publication. In M. Stefic (Ed.), *Internet dreams: Archetypes, myths and metaphors.* Cambridge, MA.

Sun Microsystems. (2005). *Sun Microsystems president Jonathan Schwartz shares project dream.* Retrieved January 26, 2006, from http://www.sun.com/smi/Press/sunflash/2005-08/sunflash.20050822.2.html

SVP. (2004). *The secure video processor (SVP) initiative.* Retrieved January 26, 2006, from http://www.svpalliance.org/

TimeWarner. (2005). *Time Warner statement on lost employee data tapes.* Retrieved January 26, 2006, from http://www.timewarner.com/corp/newsroom/employee_data_tapes/press_release.html

Van Wie, D., Sibert, O., & Horning, J. (1997, October 7-10). Panel on the InterTrust commerce architecture. In *Proceedings of the 20th National Information Systems Security Conference,* Baltimore.

XrML. (2000). *eXtended rights markup language.* Retrieved March 28, 2006, from http://www.xrml.org/

XrML. (2002). XrML 2.0 (Technical Overview Version 1.0). Retrieved March 28, 2006, from http://www.xrml.org/Reference/XrMLTechnicalOverviewV1.pdf

Section III
Threat

Chapter X
Limitations of Current Anti-Virus Scanning Technologies

Srinivas Mukkamala
New Mexico Tech, USA

Antonins Sulaiman
New Mexico Tech, USA

Patrick Chavez
New Mexico Tech, USA

Andrew H. Sung
New Mexico Tech, USA

ABSTRACT

Malware has become more lethal by using multiple attack vectors to exploit both known and unknown vulnerabilities and can attack prescanned targets with lightning speed. In the future, it is important that the scanners are capable of detecting polymoraphic (obfuscated or variant) and metamorphic (mutated or evolved) versions of malware, however current scanning techniques for malware detection have serious limitations. Simple software obfuscation a general technique that is used to protect the software from reverse engineering techniques can circumvent the current detection mechanisms (anti-virus tools). In this chapter, we describe common attacks on anti-virus tools and a few obfuscation techniques applied to recent viruses that were used to thwart commercial grade anti-virus tools. Similarities among different malware and their variants are also presented in this chapter. The signature used in this method is the percentage of application programming interface (APIs) appearing in the malware type. The hypothesis is that mutants and variants will not stray far from the original. Table 5 shows serious limitations of commercial grade anti-virus scanners in detecting simple obfuscation attacks. Table 6 shows the percentages of similarity of a particular malware when compared to others. One important thing to note is that even the polymorphic ZMist uses the same set of APIs on all three variants.

INTRODUCTION

The circle of attack and defense in the world of **malicious software** is one that never ends. Anti-virus companies are competing to devise their best scanning technology, while the malware writers are devising every possible way to defeat the scanners. So the war against malware continues.

Internet worms, Trojans, and backdoors are now a significant growing threat, alongside EXE infectors and macro-viruses. Increasingly, the term **malware** is used to encompass all threats. A **malware** or **malicious code** is a piece of code that can affect the secrecy, integrity, data and control flow, and functionality of a system. Therefore, detection is a major concern within the research community as well as within the user community. As malicious code can affect the data and control flow of a program, static analysis may naturally be helpful as part of the detection process (Christodorescu & Jha, 2003).

Malicious software is classified broadly based on the payload and propagation mechanism. In this work, we are classifying malware based on their behavioral pattern. By doing this, we can use our techniques, which are based on similarities to the known malware **signature**. The main goal here is to find a **similar pattern** for each class that we can use to identify future malware based on that class. So our next section will briefly introduce the malware classifications that we use for our purpose.

Malware categorization based on the behavioral patterns is described further in this chapter. Considering that we want to be able to detect future malware, especially malware variants, we also present obfuscation techniques that can be used to generate variants. These techniques can be seen on a lot of malware variants on the field. We also use the same techniques to produce our own brand of variants for our purpose. Such techniques are presented later in this chapter.

Our collection of malware samples originated from e-mails we received, malware that attacked our servers, and from various places on the internet that provide such contents. Some of the experimental data will be discussed in a later section. In order to be able to create our own variants, we must peep into how anti-virus software works: Which parts are taken into consideration when creating a signature and which bytes determine an executable is malicious. We discuss the methods used to thwart the commercial anti-virus scanners.

Figure 1. Malware taxonomy

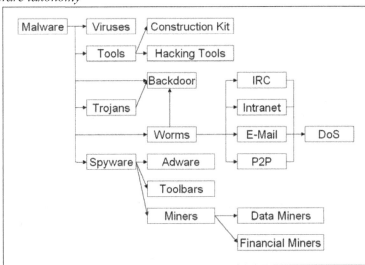

Similarity analysis of different types of malware is described, as is the behavior analysis of malware. We conclude the chapter with a summary of our results and conclusions.

MALWARE CLASSIFICATIONS

Our analysis set consists of around 700 latest **malware** and their variants. From these samples, we have analyzed and characterized them according to their behavioral patterns. Figure 1 shows the full breakdown of our categories.

From the full set of malware in our collection, we divided them based on their functionalities. We collected all mass-mailing **worms** into one category and **Trojans** into another. There may be overlaps between each category since a malicious program may be a Trojan and a mass mailer at the same time. We also put the normal programs into one category so that we can be certain that the **snippets** we find do not appear in normal programs.

We first divided up **malware** as viruses, tools, backdoors, **Trojans, worms,** and **spyware**. This categorization is based on the basic functionality of the malware:

- **Viruses:** Viruses (vital information resource under siege) are software programs that interfere with computer operations by attaching themselves to files, usually executables, so that they are run whenever the hosts are run.
- **Tools:** Tools can be further categorized into hacking tools and construction kit. Tools are programs that can be used to create malware. These programs by themselves are not malicious.
- **Hacking tools:** Hacking tools are programs used primarily to create, manipulate, modify, or analyze other programs, such as a compiler, an editor, or a cross-referencing program.

- **Construction kits:** There are four kinds of construction kits in our database: C1, C2, C3, and C4. Each has different functionalities. They may not be malicious by themselves, but they can be used to create malicious programs.
- **Backdoor:** These are malicious codes designed to connect to the authors/distributors Web site to download various files.
- **Trojan:** It is a destructive program that masquerades as a benign application. Unlike viruses, Trojan horses do not replicate themselves but they can be just as destructive. One of the most insidious types of Trojan horse is a program that claims to rid your computer of viruses but instead introduces viruses onto your computer. Since Trojans can be used as a backdoor, we have some Trojans that have backdoor capability incorporated in them (Webopedia, 2005).
- **Worms:** Worms are software programs deliberately designed to interfere with computer operations, records, corrupt, or delete data, or spread themselves to other computers and throughout the Internet, often slowing things down and causing other problems in the process (F-Secure, 2005c). Rather than injecting itself to another program like viruses, worms are stand-alone programs that are designed to propagate (Whalley et al., 2000). Worms are further characterized based on their propagation method: IRC, intranet, e-mails, or P2P. We also included worms that propagate using two or more methods. We call this type proxy worms.
- **IRC worms:** IRC (Internet Relay Chat) is a special protocol, which was elaborated for communications between Internet users. Powerful and branched IRC clients' command system and scripts allow creating malware, which spread via IRC networks, that we call "IRC worms." The first report about IRC worms was registered at the end of

1997 from mIRC users (Whalley, 2000).

- **Mass-mailers:** A mass-mailing worm is designed to trick recipients into opening a malicious program attached to the message. If a recipient opens the attachment, the worm sends itself to all of the contacts in the e-mail program's address book. An example of a mass-mailer is Beagle. A (Kaspersky, 2005).

- **Intranet worms:** An Intranet worm is usually a standalone program that tries to copy itself to other computers connected to the same local area network (LAN). Such worms travel from one computer to another using shares. A share is a media (hard drive for example) or part of it that can be accessed by everyone or only by users with specific access rights.

- **P2P:** These worms spread via file-sharing networks. They either use peer-to-peer (P2P) file-sharing networks, such as Kaazaa or Morpheus, as a means to infect innocent victims, or they use P2P technology to construct worms that can communicate with one another (F-Secure, 2005b).

- **Denial of service:** A "denial-of-service" attack is characterized by an explicit attempt by attackers to prevent legitimate users of a service from using that service. An example of this is attempts to "flood" a network, thereby preventing legitimate network traffic. A lot of our worms are included in this category (CERT, 2005).

- **Spyware:** Spyware are programs that spy on the users' behavior. A lot of spyware are piggy-backing other seemingly legitimate programs. Spyware can be further divided based on their appearance as adware, toolbars, and miners: both data miners and financial miners (I Am Not a Geek, 2005).

- **Adware:** Adware is software that is installed on your computer to show you advertise-ments. Adware can slow your PC by using RAM and CPU cycles. Adware can also slow your Internet connection by using bandwidth to retrieve advertisements (Wieslander, Boldt, & Carlsson, 2003).

- **Data miners:** A data miner is a software application that monitors and/or analyzes the activities of a computer, and subsequently its user, for the purpose of collecting information that typically will be used for marketing purposes (Ars Technica, 2005).

- **Financial data miners:** A financial data miner is similar to the data miners, except that it is concerned with online financial data of the user.

- **Toolbars:** Toolbars plug into internet browsers such as Internet Explorer to provide additional functionalities such as search forms or pop-up blockers. Google and Yahoo! toolbars are probably the most common legitimate examples. Malicious toolbars often attempt to emulate their functionality and look. Malicious toolbars almost always include characteristics of the other malware categories, which is usually what gets it classified as malware (F-Secure, 2005a).

We also included a special category called **Polymorphic**. This is the type of malware that can change its appearance code-wise so that anti-virus software cannot detect them. This rather interesting functionality can be applied to any of the malware categories we mentioned earlier. So, we included in this category any malicious codes from any categories that have this capability. A worse category of Polymorphic is called **Metamorphic**. This type of malware can change its functionality to do even more damage as it mutates. We only have a limited number of samples of Metamorphic. Hence, we decided to combine the two categories into one for the time being.

OBFUSCATION

In its simplest form obfuscation is obscuring some information such that another person cannot construe its true meaning. This is certainly true for code obfuscation where the objective is to hide the underlying logic of a program.

Code **obfuscation** has been compared to code optimization where code optimization is some transformation that will minimize a program's metric, such as execution time or execution size, while code obfuscation has the additional requirement that the code transformation also maximizes obscurity (Collberg & Thomborson, 2002). When we optimize for speed we generally try to take advantage of hardware pipelines, memory buffers, and such on while leaving the program essentially the same. Any optimization that changes the program's functionality or logic cannot be applied blindly and is generally avoided.

Obfuscation has also been applied to program watermarking and is a well known technique to prevent reverse engineering (Collberg, Thomborson, & Low, 1997). In general, obfuscating a program to prevent reverse engineering is similar to a classic cryptography game: You try and make reversing your obfuscation hard enough such that it is impractical to attack. Given enough time and resources any obfuscation can be reversed but as long as it takes 100,000 years it is considered

pretty secure. By obfuscating you can prevent another individual from gaining knowledge about your program. With respect to **malware**, code obfuscation is an appealing technique to hinder detection. A simple obfuscation technique may render a known virus completely invisible to conventional scanners with very little effort on the part of the virus writer.

Applying an obfuscation transformation to a program has the advantage that it is essentially self-decrypting encryption. The code is rendered incomprehensible while still remaining a viable program.

Classification

For simplicity we have separated the obfuscation techniques into six general categories. Because of the complexity in implementing and detecting pointer aliases we gave them their own category. As a general rule the complexity and robustness of the technique increases the greater the type. Straight control flow obfuscation is (in general) not as robust as both data and control flow obfuscation together. These types assume a low level language such as x86 assembly.

Type 0—None
Program is left unmodified and functions exactly the same as before.

Table 1. Null operations obfuscation

Original code			After transformation	
mov	eax, -44(ebp)		Mov	Eax, -44(ebp)
mov	-44(ebp), ebx		Mov **Nop**	-44(ebp), ebx
sub	12, esp			
lea	-24(ebp)		Sub	12, esp
push	Eax		Lea	-24(ebp)
			Nop	**Null Operation**
			Push	Eax

Type 1—Null Pperations

NOPs are inserted into the code. There is virtually no modification to data or control flow. An example of a Type 1 transformation is presented in Table 1. On the left is the original code and on the right is the modified code with null operations inserted every second operation.

Inserting null operations is essentially the same as inserting white space in a document: it may take longer to read but the content is exactly the same.

Type 2—Data

Some data obfuscation transformation is applied, such as string splitting or variable type replacement. For example, we could replace a Boolean variable with two integers. If they are equal, the statement is true, otherwise it is false. In the example in Table 2, x is a Boolean variable and a and b are integers. The code on the left is the

original control flow and the code on the right performs exactly the same but has a different signature.

Type 3—Control Flow

Control flow transformations are applied. Code is swapped around and jump instructions are inserted. For example, we could copy the contents of a subroutine to another location in the file and add jumps to and from the subroutine. The code would function exactly the same but look quite different. In Table 3, three lines of code have been shifted to some location (denoted as **[shift]**) and helper code has been inserted.

Type 4—Combination of 2 and 3

We pull out all the stops and combine data and control flow transformations. At this level, junk code is inserted and variables can be completely replaced with large sections of needless code. For

Table 2. Null operations obfuscation

Original code and meaning			Transformed code and meaning		
cmpb	0, x	if (x == true)	mov	a, eax	if (a < b)
je	.sub	goto sub	cmpl	b, eax	goto sub
			jge	.sub	

Table 3. Control flow obfuscation

Original code			After transformation	
Cmp	24, eax		**Jmp**	**[shift]**
Jne	.sub		**Nop**	**Helper Code**
Sub	12, eax		**Nop**	
Push	eax		Push	eax **Original execution path resumes**
			Cmp	24, eax
			Jne	.sub – [shift]
			Sub	12, eax
			Jmp	**-[shift]Helper Code**

Table 4. Combination of null operations and control flow obfuscation

Original code			After transformation	
cmp	24, eax	**jmp**	**[shift]**	
jne	.sub	**nop**	**Helper Code**	
sub	12, eax	**nop**		
push	eax	push	eax	
			Original execution path resumes	
		mov	24, eax **Data obfuscation**	
		cmpl	b, eax **Data obfuscation**	
		jle	.dead_code	
		jne	.sub – **[shift]**	
		sub	12, eax	
		jmp	**-[shift]Helper Code**	

example, we can modify all integer variables as above and transpose the program's entry point as in Table 4.

Type 5—Pointer Aliasing

The final step is to introduce pointer aliasing. Variables are replaced with global pointers and functions are referred to by arrays of function pointers. This type of transformation is relatively easy to implement using high level languages that allow pointer references but tricky (at best) using assembly languages. Pointer aliasing can be as simple as changing *a = b* into **a = **b* or as complex as converting all variables and functions into an array of pointers referenced by pointers to pointers.

MALWARE USED FOR ANALYSIS

Listed below are some experimental data worth mentioning from the seven hundred malware in our collection because of their popularity in the wild, causing the most damage. Our collection ranges from malware for Windows, DOS, and Linux. We also have spyware and adware included in our collection. While some of these so-called legitimate software may not do dam-

age, they are at the very least a nuisance and the technology they provide can be used for a more devastating result.

- **W32.Beagle:** Beagle is a mass mailing worm blended with a back door. The worm contains large scale e-mail extensions as WAB, HTM, XML, CFG, ASP and etc (Symantec Corporation, 2005). Uses its own SMTP engine, TCP port 2745 to spread and also tries to spread via file sharing networks like Kaazaa infects all Windows systems.

- **W32.Blaster:** W32.Blaster.Worm is a worm that exploits the DCOM RPC vulnerability using TCP port 135. The worm targets only Windows 2000 and Windows XP machines. The worm also attempts to perform a denial of service (DoS) on the Microsoft Windows Update Web server (*http://windowsupdate. microsoft.com/*). The purpose of the virus is to spread to as many machines as possible. By exploiting an unplugged hole in Windows, the virus is able to execute without requiring any action on the part of the user (Symantec Corporation, 2005).

- **W32.Blebla** This worm arrives with one of several different subject lines and has two attachments named Myjuliet.chm and

196

Myromeo.exe. Once you read the message, the two attachments are automatically saved and launched. When launched, this worm attempts to send itself out to all names in the Microsoft Outlook address book using one of several Internet mail servers located in Poland. Otherwise this worm does no harm to the infected system (Symantec Corporation, 2005).

- **W32.Klez:** Klez is a mass-mailing e-mail worm that also attempts to copy itself to network shares. The worm exploits vulnerability in Microsoft Outlook in an attempt to execute itself when you open or even preview the message in which it is contained. The worm attempts to disable some common anti-virus products and has a payload which fills files with all zeroes (Symantec Corporation, 2005).

- **W32.MyDoom:** MyDoom is a worm that spreads over e-mail and Kaazaa P2P network. When executed, the worm opens up Windows' Notepad with garbage data in it. In e-mails, it uses variable subjects, bodies and attachment names. It also performs a Distributed Denial-of-Service attack on www.sco.com. It attempts to send e-mail messages using its own SMTP engine (Symantec Corporation, 2005).

- **W32.SirCam:** Sircam contains its own SMTP engine, and propagates in a manner similar to the W32.Magistr.Worm. Due to what appears to be a bug, W32.Sircam. Worm@mm does not replicate under Windows NT, 2000, or XP (Symantec Corporation, 2005).

- **W32.Wozer:** Wozer is a worm that spreads through network shares and IRC. It also attempts to spread through e-mail by sending itself as an attached .zip file, which, however, is corrupt and will not spread the worm (Symantec Corporation, 2005).

- **WNT.Energy:** This is an e-mail worm. It runs under Windows NT and 2000 only.

The worm runs as a service and copies its code into running processes. It hooks the MAPISendMail function and adds itself as Setup.exe to any RAR archives in outgoing mail (Symantec Corporation, 2005).

- **Backdoor.HackDefender:** It is a backdoor Trojan component that hides processes, services, and files (Symantec Corporation, 2005).

- **AirCop:** AirCop is a master boot record (MBR)/Boot Sector infecting virus. It only infects floppy diskettes. Upon infection, the virus becomes memory resident at the top of high system memory. AirCop hooks interrupt 13. Once AirCop is memory resident, any nonwrite protected diskettes accessed are infected (Symantec Corporation, 2005). AirCop copies the original disk boot sector to sector 719 (Side 1, Cylinder 39, Sector 9 on a normal 360K 5.25" diskette) and then replaces the boot sector at sector 0 with a copy of the virus.

- **Badboy:** These are harmless memory resident parasitic encrypted viruses. They hook INT 21h and write themselves at the beginning of COM-files are executed. These viruses use System File Table on infection. They are divided on nine blocks of code and data (installation block, data block, INT 21h block, etc.). When the virus installs itself into the memory, eight of these nine blocks can be rearranged in any order depending on the system timer (Symantec Corporation, 2005).

- **Stoned:** The Stoned virus, also known as the New Zealand or the Marijuana virus, is another of the most common PC-DOS viruses. The Stoned is a boot-sector infector; it infects diskette boot sectors, and "master" boot sectors on hard disks (Symantec Corporation, 2005). When a machine is booted from an infected diskette, the virus first infects the hard disk, and then installs itself in memory. Any diskette used in the A: drive thereafter is likely to be infected.

- **180SA:** 180 Search Assistant is generally installed by some other piece of spyware. This not only displays ads but logs your browsing habits to send back to 180 servers (Symantec Corporation, 2005).
- **Ebates.MoneyMaker:** MoneyMaker not only displays pop-up ads but it interferes with many programs that try to prevent it from working properly. On top of this it also hijacks your browser and redirects you to sites where it can make money off of you (Symantec Corporation, 2005).
- **Gator.GMT:** Gator tracks the sites that users visit and forwards that data back to the company's servers. Gator sells the use of this information to advertisers and generates ads pop up at certain moments, such as when specific words appear on a screen. It also lets companies launch a pop-up ad when users visit a competitor's Web site (Symantec Corporation, 2005).

NORMAL PROGRAMS

Normal programs are used in the experiments to enable us to find false positives. The main goal of creating a detection algorithm is to find **malware** and to leave the normal programs alone. When a detection algorithm detects a normal program as a malware, it is called a false positive. Normal programs are executables that are known not to have any malicious code in them. Included in this set are several hundred programs, executables and libraries:

- **System programs:** These are the executables and libraries that reside in Windows\ System32 folder.
- **Windows programs:** These are the executables that are installed with Windows; for example, Notepad and Paint.

- **Program Installers:** These are packages of downloaded programs; for example, Acrobat Reader and WinZip. Some installers may be in the scale of several megabytes.
- **Office programs:** These are pre-installed programs, not the installer; for example, Excel, Word, and Photoshop. The executables for these programs may get very large.
- **Games:** These include the games that are installed with Windows and several home-made games.
- **OpenGL programs:** These are home-made programs using OpenGL that were used in one of our classes.

OBFUSCATION USED FOR DEFEATING COMMERCIAL SCANNERS

In our research, we discovered that most **commercial virus scanners** could be defeated with very simple **obfuscation** techniques (Rabek, Lewandowshi, Khazan, & Cunningham, 2003; Sung, Xu, Chavez, & Mukkamala, 2004). For example, simple program entry point modifications consisting of two extra jump instructions effectively defeated most scanners. Therefore, we only used the bare minimum level of obfuscation needed to prevent detection. Our goal was to show how trivial it is to modify recent malware to defeat existing scanning techniques using only the compiled executable and a few tools. The **obfuscation** process is presented in Figure 2. The binary code is disassembled into a more readable format so that we may understand what the program is doing. Someone with foreknowledge about the **malware** need not spend so much time analyzing the program. Once we have the disassembled program and have given it study we pick out an area to attack. The first target when applying a control flow transformation is to attack the program's entry point but when using a data transformation we generally have to take a guess.

We decide where and what modifications need to be performed and change the binary file directly, using the disassembled version as a guide or map. Once all modifications have been made, the file is examined using the anti-virus scanners.

All variants with the exception of the *MyDoom* virus were generated using off-the-shelf hex editing tools. We were fortunate enough to have a copy of the *MyDoom.A* source code and made all our modifications using the *Microsoft Visual* development suite. The *Hackman* hex editing utility was used to generate all other variants.

The **obfuscation** techniques used to produce the **polymorphic** versions of different **malware** tested in the experiments include control flow modification (e.g., Mydoom V2, Beagle V2), data segment modification (e.g., Mydoom V1, Beagle V1), and insertion of dead code (e.g., Bika V1).

SIMILARITY ANALYSIS OF MALICIOUS EXECUTABLES (SAME)

The goal of SAME is to find shared characteristics between all the malicious codes. To get the application program interface (**API**) **snippets**, we first divided the programs we have in our collection into two categories: malware and normal programs. In **malware** category, we put everything that can be considered malicious, such as viruses, Trojans, worms, spyware, and so forth.

API is a set of routines or protocols to build applications. A set of APIs is available for most operating systems. Since our focus is on Windows, the APIs mentioned in this work are **Windows APIs**. These APIs are provided in the form of **dynamically linked libraries** (DLL). The most commonly used library is kernel32.dll (Microsoft, 2005).

Figure 2. Obfuscation attack process on commercial scanners

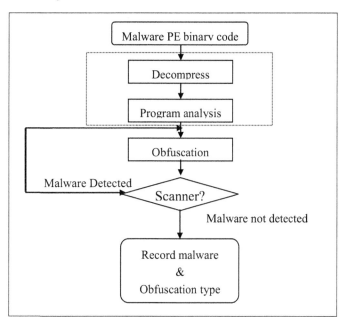

Table 5. Limitations of commercial anti-virus scanners to obfuscation attacks

	N	M[1]	D	P	K	F	A
Mydoom.A	✓	✓	✓	✓	✓	✓	✓
Mydoom.A V1	✗	✓	✗	✗	✓	✓	✗
Mydoom.A V2	✓	✗	✗	✗	✗	✗	✗
Mydoom.A V3	✗	✗	✗	✗	✗	✗	✗
Mydoom.A V4	✗	✗	✗	✗	✗	✗	✗
Bika	✓	✓	✓	✓	✓	✓	✓
Bika V1	✗	✗	✓	✗	✓	✓	✓
Bika V2	✗	✗	✓	✗	✓	✓	✓
Beagle.B	✓	✓	✓	✓	✓	✓	✓
Beagle.B V1	✓	✓	✗	✗	✓	✓	✗
Beagle.B V2	✓	✗	✗	✗	✗	✗	✗
Blaster	✓	✓	✓	✓	✓	✓	✓
Blaster V1	✗	✓	✓	✓	✓	✓	✗
Blaster V2	✓	✓	✗	✗	✓	✓	✗
Aircop	✓	✓	✓	✓	✗	✓	✗
Aircop V1	✗	✗	✓	✗	✓	✗	✗
Aircop V2	✗	✗	✓	✗	✗	✗	✗
Badboy	✓	✓	✓	✓	✗	✗	✗
Badboy V1	✗	✓	✓	✗	✓	✗	✗
Badboy V2	✗	✗	✗	✗	✗	✓	✗
Phalcom	✓	✓	✓	✗	✓	✗	✗
Phalcom V1	✗	✓	✗	✗	✗	✓	✗
Phalcom V2	✗	✗	✗	✗	✗	✓	✗
Stoned	✓	✓	✓	✓	✓	✗	✗
Stoned V1	✗	✗	✓	✓	✗	✗	✗
Stoned V2	✗	✗	✗	✗	✗	✗	✗
Dos (com virus)	✓	✓	✓	✓	✓	✓	✓
Dos (com virus) V1	✗	✗	✗	✗	✗	✗	✗

Note. N = Norton, M = McAfee, D = Dr. Web, P = Panda, K = Kaspersky, F = F-Secure, A = Anti Ghostbusters.

Table 6. Percentage of similarity based on the APIs used in the malware

	Bagle.A	Bagle.I	Bagle.O	Bagle	Klez.E	Klez.H	MyDoom.A	MyDoom.E	MyDoom.F	Wozer.C	Wozer.E	ZMist.C1	ZMist.C2	ZMist.C3
Bagle.A	-	100	80.81	100	32.48	32.77	42.39	43.68	43.68	33.33	48.19	15.94	15.94	15.94
Bagle.I	100	-	80.81	100	32.48	32.77	42.39	43.68	43.68	33.33	48.19	15.94	15.94	15.94
Bagle.O	95.24	95.24	-	94.2	36.75	36.97	46.74	48.28	48.28	33.33	50.6	21.74	21.74	21.74
Bagle	82.14	82.14	65.66	-	23.08	23.53	36.96	37.93	37.93	27.78	42.17	15.94	15.94	15.94
Klez.E	45.24	45.24	43.43	39.13	-	98.32	51.09	54.02	54.02	51.85	53.01	12.32	12.32	12.32
Klez.H	46.43	46.43	44.44	40.58	100	-	53.26	55.17	55.17	53.7	54.22	12.32	12.32	12.32
MyDoom.A	46.43	46.43	43.43	49.28	40.17	41.18	-	97.7	97.7	31.48	43.37	14.49	14.49	14.49
MyDoom.E	45.24	45.24	42.42	47.83	40.17	40.34	92.39	-	100	33.33	44.58	15.22	15.22	15.22
MyDoom.F	45.24	45.24	42.42	47.83	40.17	40.34	92.39	100	-	33.33	44.58	15.22	15.22	15.22
Wozer.C	20.24	20.24	17.17	20.29	23.08	23.53	18.48	20.69	20.69	-	60.24	12.32	12.32	12.32
Wozer.E	38.1	38.1	34.34	42.03	29.91	30.25	30.43	32.18	32.18	75.93	-	11.59	11.59	11.59
ZMist.C1	26.19	26.19	30.3	31.88	14.53	14.29	21.74	24.14	24.14	33.33	25.3	-	100	100
ZMist.C2	26.19	26.19	30.3	31.88	14.53	14.29	21.74	24.14	24.14	33.33	25.3	100	-	100
ZMist.C3	26.19	26.19	30.3	31.88	14.53	14.29	21.74	24.14	24.14	33.33	25.3	100	100	-

Our initial analysis shows stunning **similarities** of the APIs used between variants of a particular malware. Table 6 shows the percentages of APIs used in a particular malware when compared to others. One important thing to note is that even the polymorphic ZMist uses the same set of APIs on all three variants. This result is what prompted us to include APIs as part of the detection process.

We propose a technique that may be helpful as part of the detection process for current and future threats. With the increasing number of **malware** let loose monthly, anti-virus static scanning may not be enough to stop unidentified threats. We have to find different methods to detect such threats. Our technique is one of those methods. Since a significant number of malware target the Windows operating system, we choose to focus on detection in this operating system. The goal here is to create the **signature** sets based on the **APIs** generally used by malware. In other words, we want to find **API snippets** that exist in most **malicious codes**. However, these snippets should not exist in normal programs. The existence of these snippets in normal programs would generate false positives, where normal programs are identified as malicious. So, we make certain that

the snippets we find in malware do not occur in normal programs, or at least occur only in a minimal number.

BEHAVIOR ANALYSIS OF VICIOUS EXECUTABLES (BRAVE)

The goal here is to find shared characteristics between all the **malicious codes**. These characteristics must be over 75% available throughout the malicious codes. However, they must not appear in normal programs to be considered unique to malware.

In order to find shared characteristics between **malware** from each category shown in Figure 1, we also run the same algorithm for each category. To get the **API snippets** of one category, we first need to find shared characteristics between all the **malicious codes** of that particular malware category. These characteristics should be available throughout most of the **malicious codes** used in the experiments. The same condition applies: they must not appear in normal programs.

A bag of APIs only shows all APIs that a PE may call during its lifetime. An API call in a bag

Figure 3. Creating snippets list for each malware in a category

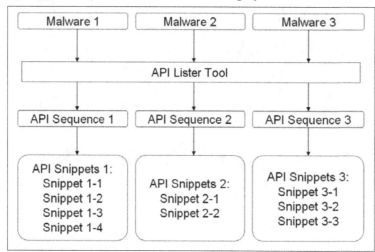

Figure 4. Flowchart to get sequences of five APIs in a category (left) and flowchart of comparing sequences of five to other malware (right)

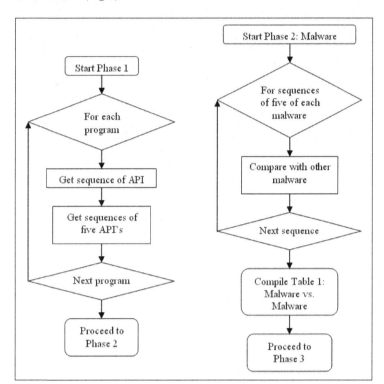

is only shown once. However, a sequence shows a list of all the API calls being made. An API call in a sequence can be made more than once. Hence, a sequence may show a particular API call over and over again.

For our first step, we looked at one category. Using the API Lister Tool, we can get the **sequence of APIs** for each program under this category. For example in Figure 3, we have three malicious programs that we put through the API tool. Each program will yield an API sequence. From each sequence, we can get the snippets. Figure 3 is not based on any of our samples.

During our experiments, we assembled a sequence of two APIs, three APIs, up to ten APIs. We found that two APIs yield more false positives while ten APIs yield almost no similarities. We decided to use only five APIs in the sequence and

started gathering our snippets. From the full API sequence, we cut it up and assemble much shorter sequences consisting only of five APIs each.

In the next step, we compared malware *A* with other malware to see if any of these **sequences** exist in other malware. Once we finished with malware *A*, we moved on to the next malware and proceeded with the same method until all the malware in the collection are compared with one another. We labeled a sequence of five APIs as 1 if it exists in a program and 0 otherwise.

After we have compared the **sequences** with all the **malicious programs**, we compiled a table of sequences against malware. We analyzed this table and picked out the ones that are "common" to most malware. A sequence is considered "common" if the said sequence exists in most malware. In other words, we have ones across the table.

Table 7: Process to find "common" malicious snippets

Process #1	Malware 1	Malware 2	Malware 3
Malware 1:			
• **Snippet 1-1**	1 (Found)	1 (Found)	1 (Found)
• **Snippet 1-2**	1 (Found)	0 (Not Found)	0 (Not Found)
• **Snippet 1-3**	1 (Found)	1 (Found)	1 (Found)
• **Snippet 1-4**	0 (Not Found)	0 (Not Found)	1 (Found)
Malware 2:			
• **Snippet 2-1**	1 (Found)	1 (Found)	1 (Found)
• **Snippet 2-2**	0 (Not Found)	1 (Found)	0 (Not Found)
Malware 3:			
• **Snippet 3-1**	1 (Found)	0 (Not Found)	1 (Found)
• **Snippet 3-2**	0 (Not Found)	0 (Not Found)	1 (Found)
• **Snippet 3-3**	1 (Found)	1 (Found)	1 (Found)

Figure 5. Flowchart of comparing sequences (malware with normal programs)

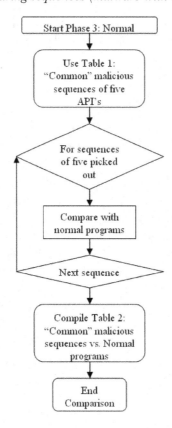

These "common" sequences are collected in a file to be used in the next step (see Figure 5).

For example in Table 8, we have snippets 1-1, 1-3, 2-1, and 3-3 that have all ones across the table, because these **snippets** exist in all these malware in the category. These are the snippets that we carry on to the next process.

Next, we looked at the normal programs. Using the same method, we get a sequence of APIs for each normal program. Using the file containing the "common" sequences we gathered from the malware, we performed another comparison similar to the one we did earlier. The difference is that this time we compared the "common" malicious sequences with the sequences of normal programs. We also labeled a sequence as one if it exists in a program and compiled a table of sequences against normal programs.

Our analysis this time involves **sequences** that are only "common" in malware. We picked out sequences that do not exist in normal programs. In other words, we have zeroes across the table. These are the **API snippets** that exist only in malware.

We repeat this process for each **malware** category to reveal **snippets** for each. The same snippets may occur in different categories as malware in different categories may use the same functions at one time or another.

BRAVE RESULTS

After performing the analysis on normal programs, we get the following **API snippets** that are "common" to malware and are "uncommon" to normal programs. The malware used in the analysis includes the traditional viruses, worms, Trojans, and samples of popular spyware/adware.

Sequence #1:
KERNEL32.DLL.GETFILESIZE
KERNEL32.DLL.GETSTDHANDLE
KERNEL32.DLL.RAISEEXCEPTION
KERNEL32.DLL.READFILE
KERNEL32.DLL.RTLUNWIND
KERNEL32.DLL.SETENDOFFILE
KERNEL32.DLL.SETFILEPOINTER

The *GetFileSize* function retrieves the size of the specified file. The file size that can be reported by this function is limited to a DWORD value. The *GetStdHandle* function retrieves a handle for the standard input, standard output, or standard error device. The *RaiseException* function raises an exception in the calling thread. The *ReadFile* function reads data from a file, starting at the position that the file pointer indicates. The *RtlUnwind* function initiates an unwind of procedure call frames. This function may not be

Table 8. Process to find "common" malicious snippets that are "uncommon" to normal programs

Process #2	Normal 1	Normal 2	Normal 3
Malware 1:			
• **Snippet 1-1**	0 (Not Found)	0 (Not Found)	0 (Not Found)
• **Snippet 1-3**	0 (Not Found)	1 (Found)	0 (Not Found)
Malware 2:			
• **Snippet 2-1**	1 (Found)	0 (Not Found)	0 (Not Found)
Malware 3:			
• **Snippet 3-3**	0 (Not Found)	0 (Not Found)	0 (Not Found)

Table 9. Comparison of API snippets, to find which sequences are available across all the malware

	CloseHandle	CreateFileA	GetFileType	GetFileSize	GetStdHandle	RaiseException	ReadFile	RtlUnwind	SetEndOfFile	SetFilePointer	LeaveCriticalSection	DeleteCriticalSection	EnterCriticalSection	LeaveCriticalSection	EnterCriticalSection	LeaveCriticalSection	User32.dll.CharNextA	User32.dll.CharNextA
WNT.Energy				✓	✓	✓	✓	✓	✓	✓				✓	✓	✓	✓	✓
												✓	✓	✓	✓	✓		
											✓	✓	✓	✓	✓			
	✓	✓	✓	✓	✓						✓	✓	✓	✓	✓			
W32.Wozer														✓	✓	✓	✓	✓
												✓	✓	✓	✓	✓		
											✓	✓	✓	✓	✓			
				✓	✓	✓	✓	✓	✓	✓	✓	✓	✓	✓	✓			
W32.Sircam												✓	✓	✓	✓	✓		
				✓	✓	✓	✓	✓	✓	✓	✓	✓	✓	✓	✓			
W32.Blebla												✓	✓	✓	✓	✓		
				✓	✓	✓	✓	✓	✓	✓	✓	✓	✓	✓	✓			
Backdoor.Hack Defender				✓	✓	✓	✓	✓	✓	✓				✓	✓	✓	✓	✓
			✓	✓	✓	✓	✓						✓	✓	✓	✓		
		✓	✓	✓	✓	✓						✓	✓	✓	✓	✓		
	✓	✓	✓	✓	✓						✓	✓	✓	✓	✓			

available in future Windows. The *SetEndOfFile* function moves the end-of-file (EOF) position for the specified file to the current position of the file pointer. The *SetFilePointer* function moves the file pointer of an open file.

Sequence #2:
KERNEL32.DLL.LEAVECRITICALSEC-TION
KERNEL32.DLL.DELETECRITICALSEC-TION
KERNEL32.DLL.ENTERCRITICALSEC-TION
KERNEL32.DLL.LEAVECRITICALSEC-TION
KERNEL32.DLL.ENTERCRITICALSEC-TION

The *EnterCriticalSection* function waits for ownership of the specified critical section object. The function returns when the calling thread is granted ownership. The *LeaveCriticalSection* function releases ownership of the specified critical section object. The *DeleteCriticalSection* function releases all resources used by an unowned critical section object.

This sequence indicates that a lot of malicious codes rely on critical sections. Critical sections protect a piece of code from being used by another thread. However, we found that this particular sequence also exists in a lot of system libraries. As a result, we cannot rely on this sequence to detect malware in system folders.

Sequence #3:
USER32.DLL.GETKEYBOARDTYPE
USER32.DLL.GETKEYBOARDTYPE
USER32.DLL.GETKEYBOARDTYPE
ADVAPI32.DLL.REGOPENKEYEXA
ADVAPI32.DLL.REGQUERYVALUEEXA

The *GetKeyboardType* function retrieves information about the current keyboard. The *RegOpenKeyEx* function opens the specified

registry key. The *RegQueryValueEx* function retrieves the type and data for a specified value name associated with an open registry key.

This sequence indicates the part where malicious codes may log the keyboard activity to provide the authors with private information.

Sequence #4:
KERNEL32.DLL.GETLASTERROR
KERNEL32.DLL.WRITEFILE
KERNEL32.DLL.GETLASTERROR
KERNEL32.DLL.CLOSEHANDLE
KERNEL32.DLL.GETLASTERROR

The *GetLastError* function retrieves the calling thread's last-error code value. The last-error code is maintained on a per-thread basis. Multiple threads do not overwrite each other's last-error code. The *WriteFile* function writes data to a file at the position specified by the file pointer. The *CloseHandle* function closes an open object handle.

Table 9 lists the **API snippets** that are "common" to malware and are "uncommon" to normal programs. BRAVE provides the basis to reduce false positives and false negatives by omitting all the common API snippets that occur in common executables. It helps in detecting Zero day attacks that share same behavior of a known malware which current scanners can not provide with out a signature.

CONCLUSION

Because malware can conceivably become more lethal (so-called fourth-generation worms), use multiple attack vectors to exploit both known and unknown vulnerabilities, and spread even faster by attacking prescanned targets with lightning speed) in the future, it is important that the **scanners** are capable of detecting **polymorphic** (obfuscated, or variant) and **metamorphic** (mutated or evolved versions) versions of known malware. The currently available **scanners**, however, are inadequate since they are not able to detect even slightly **obfuscated** versions of known malware.

A number of observations and conclusions are drawn from the experimental results:

1. Our obfuscation is based on executables (and not on assembly code or high-level source code that is usually not available).
2. Our results are based on some of the latest malware targeting current OS platforms–not dated malware intended for now legacy systems.
3. As all of our detection methods are able to detect variants better than the commercial anti-virus, these methods have a tremendous potential and can be used as a foundation to a more-robust detection method based on the behavioral pattern of a malware.
4. The main use of this analysis is to warn users of suspicious executables that may be malicious. Based on the information a user is given on the likelihood of a program is malicious, he or she then can decide whether to continue executing that suspected program.
5. Our technique has a tremendous potential and can be used as a foundation to a more robust detection method based on its **behavioral patterns**.

The presented results clearly reveal the alarming deficiency of current scanning techniques and the tremendous potential of our approach. In view of the serious looming threat of future generation malware, the following topics will need to be investigated:

1. **Development of signatures for different types of malware:** Even though the sequence of API system calls provides a potentially effective basis for defining the signature, more sophisticated (statically constructed) signatures must be investigated to deal with polymorphic versions of known malware.
2. **Development of tools for malware scanning:** Since for each malware the signature is different, it is useful to have a tool that assists in the (static and dynamic) analysis of malware code and the development of effective signatures.
3. **Metamorphic malware:** Mutated or evolved versions of malware are even more difficult to detect since their functionality has changed from the original. Signature based detection again provides the best hope and we will investigate static techniques for detection.

REFERENCES

Ars Technica. (2005). *Malware: What it is and how to prevent it.* Retrieved October 2005 from http://arstechnica.com/articles/paedia/malware.ars/1

CERT. (2005). *Denial of service attacks.* Retrieved October 2005 from http://www.cert.org/tech_tips/denial_of_service.html

Christodorescu, M., & Jha, S. (2003, August). *Static analysis of executables to detect malicious patterns.* Proceeds of the Usenix Security Symposium.

Collberg, C. & Thomborson, C. (2002, August). Tamper-proofing, and obfuscation - tools for software protection. *IEEE Transactions on Software Engineering,* 701-746.

Collberg, C., Thomborson, C., & Low, D. (1997, July). *A taxonomy of obfuscating transformations* (Tech. Rep. 148).

F-Secure. (2005a). *F-secure virus description database.* Retrieved November 2005 from http://www.f-secure.com/v-descs/

F-Secure. (2005b). *F-Secure virus description: P2P worm.* Retrieved October 2005 from http://www.f-secure.com/v-descs/p2pworm.shtml

F-Secure. (2005c). *F-Secure virus description: Worm.* Retrieved October 2005 from http://www.f-secure.com/v-descs/worm.shtml

I Am Not A Geek. (2005). *Spyware removal guides.* October 2005 http://www.iamnotageek.com/a/spyware.php

Kaspersky. (2005). *IRC worms.* Retrieved October 2005 from http://www.avp.ch/avpve/worms/irc.stm

Microsoft. (2005, November) *Microsoft developer network library.* Retrieved November 2005 from http://msdn.microsoft.com/library/

Rabek, C., Lewandowski, M., Khazan, I. & Cunningham, K. (2003). Detection of injected, dynamically generated, and obfuscated malicious code. In *Proceedings of the 2003 ACM Workshop on Rapid Malcode.*

Sung, A. H., Xu, J., Chavez, P., & Mukkamala, S. (2004). Static analyzer for vicious executables (SAVE). In *Proceedings of 20th Annual Computer Security Applications Conference (ACSAC)* (pp. 326-334).

Symantec Corporation. (2005). *Symantec security response.* Retrieved November 2005 from http://securityresponse.symantec.com/avcenter/

Webopedia, (2005). *Trojan horse.* Retrieved October 2005 from http://www.webopedia.com/TERM/T/Trojan_horse.html

Whalley, I. Arnold, B., Chess, D., Morar, J., Segal, A., & Swimmer, M (2000). *An environment for controlled worm replication & analysis (Internet-inna-box).* Retrieved from http://www.research.ibm.com/anti-virus/SciPapers/VB2000INW.pdf

Wieslander, J., Boldt, M., & Carlsson, B. (2003). Investigating spyware on the Internet. *In Proceedings of the Seventh Nordic Workshop on Secure IT Systems,* Norway.

Chapter XI
Phishing:
The New Security Threat on the Internet

Indranil Bose
The University of Hong Kong, China

ABSTRACT

Phishing is a new form of online crime where the unsuspecting user is tricked into revealing his/her personal information. It is usually conducted using social engineering or technical deceit–based methods. The various ways in which phishing can take place are described in this chapter. This is followed by a description of key strategies that can be adopted for protection of end users and organizations. The end user protection strategies include desktop protection agents, password management tools, secure e-mail, simple and trusted browser setting, and digital signature. Among corporate protection strategies are such measures as e-mail personalization, mail server authentication, monitoring transaction logs, detecting unusual downloading activities, token based and multifactor authentication, domain monitoring, and Web poisoning. Some of the commercially available and popular anti-phishing products are also described in this chapter.

INTRODUCTION

Phishing is an identity theft that scams a user into surrendering private information such as credit card numbers, account user names and passwords, and social security numbers by way of fraudulent e-mails and fake Web sites that falsely claim to be from an established legitimate enterprise (Lininger & Vines, 2005). The number of phishing attacks is escalating and becoming more sophisticated every day and the total financial losses resulting from phishing is estimated to be around US$137 million (Goth, 2005). Phishing attacks target millions of e-mail addresses around the world in the hope that a percentage of owners will fall victim to the trick. About 5% of fraudulent e-mail recipients do respond to e-mails or provide personal information to fake Web sites whose addresses are obtained from the e-mails (Knight, 2005). According to the Anti-Phishing Working Group (2005), the number of phishing Web sites reached 4,630 in November 2005, which is a 205% increase over the number reported for November 2004. Financial Institutions, retail companies, and Internet service providers remain the frequent target or "phish." The latest statistics show that phishing has become a global issue because over 10 countries have suffered from phishing. The United States is in the top location for hosting phishing sites (over 32.96%), followed by Korea (11.34%) and China (8.04%).

THE MECHANICS OF PHISHING

Phishing attacks use both social engineering and technical deceit to steal consumers' personal identity data. Phishers lure the victim to perform a series of actions so that they can obtain confidential data about the victim. Two types of techniques are used for phishing and these are social engineering–based or technical deceit–based.

Social Engineering–Based Techniques

"Social engineering" refers to the act of obtaining secure data by conning an individual into revealing secure information. It usually uses "spoofed" e-mails to lead consumers to counterfeit Web sites designed to trick recipients into divulging sensitive personal data. The most successful means of social engineering based phishing attacks are initiated by e-mail. In a typical case, a phishing attack occurs in the following stages.

Figure 1. A phishing e-mail received by the author

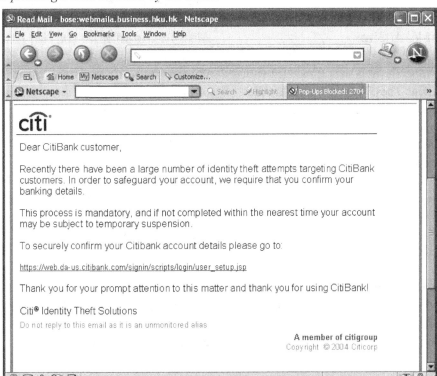

First, an attacker generates an e-mail that appears legitimate and requests the recipients to perform certain actions. Second, the attacker sends the e-mail in a way that obscures the true source to the recipients. Third, the recipients respond to the e-mail by opening a malicious attachment, filling out a form, or visiting a phony Web site. Finally, the attacker records the victims' personal information by asking them to update their account information or to provide information for verification purposes. A common tactic used is to inform the recipient that they have won a large sum of money that they can transfer to their bank account. As soon as the recipient tries to transfer the money, the sensitive bank account information is recorded by the phisher.

Technical Deceit-Based Techniques

In addition to social engineering factors, phishers can use technical means to deceive the victims or intercept communication between the victim and a legitimate organization.

Fraudulent Web Site

Phishers may operate Web sites embedded with malicious content. These Web sites contain codes that intentionally intrude into end users' systems without permission and cause harm. First, phishers may include HTML disguised links and fake advertising banners in public areas of renowned Web sites or bulletin boards to lure customers to fraudulent sites. Second, the Web sites will expose customers to vulnerabilities by installing software like key-loggers, adware, spyware, Trojan horses, and dialers into their computers. Third, phishers may use pop-up or frameless windows to hide actual URL of malicious Web sites. This is possible due to the presence of loopholes in most Web browsers for handling pop-up windows. Fourth, the Web sites may modify a user's

browser settings, bookmarks, homepages, or operating systems' configurations. Figure 1 shows an example of a fraudulent Web site referred to in a phishing e-mail.

Malicious Code

Malicious code attacks are increasingly prevalent in the Internet world. Phishers make use of Internet Relay Chat or Instant Messaging to send fake information to would-be victims. Spyware and keyloggers are common examples of malicious code that intercept the communications between a user and a legitimate organization. They are surveillance software which collect information about the users' activities including keystrokes, and visited Web sites and record them in a log file. Phishers also use BOT applications in communication channels to convert machines into BOT networks so that they can anonymously lure users to fraudulent Web sites. The BOT network can also trigger Distributed Denial of Service attacks or serve as spam relays.

Man-in-the-Middle (MITM) Attacks

Phishers may get between the sender and receiver of information and sniff any information being sent without the knowledge of the sender or the receiver (Slewe & Hoogenboom, 2004). This type of attack is effective for both HTTP and HTTPS communications. MITM is difficult to overcome because all features used by the user to authenticate with the legitimate server can be repeated by the phisher. According to research conducted by NGS Consulting, MITM may be carried out through transparent proxies, DNS Cache Poisoning, URL obfuscation, and browser proxy configuration. Many of the phishing attacks succeed because they can trick the recipient to follow a deliberately designed hyperlink (URL) to the attacker's server.

Cross Site Scripting (CSS) Attacks

The dynamic content of Web sites are prone to suffer from cross site scripting attacks which maliciously alter the URL of a valid Web site by use of a custom URL or code injection into a Web application (Geer, 2005). This attack is caused by the lack of validation of the client's input before sending the page to the client's browser. In cross site scripting a phisher forces a legitimate Web server to send a page containing malicious Javascript to a victim's browser. The malicious script runs on the victim's browser while enjoying the privileges of a legitimate script originating from the legitimate Web server. For example, if you are interested to view more items listed by an auctioner on an auction site you will click on the auctioneer's screen name. Although no other items may be actually listed on the auction site the auctioner may trick you to a page that looks exactly same as the auction site but contains details about items that are actually not on auction but are set up there to record your account information.

PHISHING DETECTION AND PREVENTION

As mentioned in the previous section, there are numerous ways for a phisher to trigger an attack on an unsuspecting customer. Therefore, there is no single solution capable of combating all types of attacks. Some researchers have remarked that anti-phishing should be conducted in five stages: education, preparation, avoidance, intervention, and treatment (Merwe, Loock, & Dabrowski, 2005). The best strategy to deal with phishing is to deploy a combination of security solutions. These may be grouped into end user protection strategies and organization protection strategies.

End User Protection Strategies

Desktop Protection Agents

These days most end users have installed protection software such as anti-virus software on their desktop computers to provide basic protection. Desktop computers can be easily configured to install personal firewalls, personal intrusion detection systems, personal antispam, and spyware detection software. In addition to preventing inbound spam e-mails, these solutions can block unauthorized outbound connections from installed software and can detect anomalies in network traffic profiles. Implementing these solutions helps provide an overlapping protection so that a failure or security lapse in one product may be defended by another.

Password Management Tools

With the prevalence of e-commerce activities users tend to use different passwords for different Web sites. Since it becomes quite difficult to remember so many passwords often users allow their computer systems to store passwords in cookies and fill up the login and password information automatically at e-commerce sites. If phishers get hold of such information the user accounts can be compromised. One way to handle this is to use software that will add IP-specific characters to the password field. The software will append IP-specific characters automatically after the password is supported by the user. This can prevent a phisher from stealing the account information of customers because users are only aware of partial password information. PwdHash is an Internet Explorer plug-in that converts a user's password into a domain specific password (Kirda & Kruegel, 2005). Pvault is a password management tool that requests domain name and IP address of current

Web site from three different DNS and generates a warning for the user if any of them return a different IP address (Jammalamadaka, Mehrotra, & Venkatasubramanian, 2005).

Secure E-Mail

Since many phishing attacks are done through HTML based e-mail, it is in the interests of the users to check if their e-mail applications can obfuscate the true destination of links. If this functionality is not available to users, they should at least disable the HTML functionality. E-mails will then be delivered in plain text. While the visual appeal of the received e-mails will be lessened due to this, the security will be improved. End-users should also use e-mail applications with "dangerous" attachment-blocking functions that prevent users from quickly executing or viewing malicious attached content and getting infected with malicious software. The basic blocking function should block all attachments with .exe extension.

Simple and Trusted Path Browser Settings

If Web browser can be configured properly, it can be a good defense against phishing attacks. Normally, for an average user without sophisticated needs there is no need for a browser with many fascinating features. As long as a page can be displayed properly by a browser, it should fulfill the users' needs. To prevent phishing attacks, the Web browser should disable all window pop-up functionalities, Java runtime support, ActiveX support, all multimedia and auto-execute extensions, and prevent the storage of cookies. Another key step towards preventing phishing attacks is to ensure the use of secure sockets layer (SSL). However it is possible for a phisher to create an impression that the browser has already displayed signals that are characteristic of genuine SSL.

Users can be protected from this kind of Web spoofing by using synchronized random dynamic (SRD) boundaries that allow users to differentiate between genuine status of messages from the browser itself and malicious content from the server (Ye, Smith, & Anthony, 2005). An extension of Mozilla Firefox called "Dynamic Security Skins" has been proposed that uses pictures that can be verified by humans only to visually determine if a trusted path exists or not (Dhamija & Tygar, 2005).

Digital Signature

Using public key cryptography to digitally sign an e-mail is a common measure to verify the integrity of the message content. This avoids the alteration of the message content during transit. Users can make use of their private key to decrypt the content of the message which is signed digitally by the public key. The message signature is a sophisticated hash value. Users can make use of the public key to verify the hash value and confirm the integrity of the message. Authentication using digitally signed e-mail is considered to be a strong measure of protection against phishing (Garfinkel et al., 2005).

Organization Protection Strategies

E-Mail Personalization

Average customers usually lack simple means by which they can verify the authenticity of received messages. The simplest way to increase the integrity of an e-mail is to embed the customer's name as in "Dear Mr. Smith" instead of "Dear Sir" in the outgoing e-mail. However, if the e-mail address already contains the recipient's name, it is possible for phishers to know how to address the recipient. A more personalized e-mail can include a portion of the recipient's account number, or a sequence number can be added to each e-mail.

The sequence number will be easily verifiable by the recipient and will be incremented by one when a new e-mail is sent.

Mail Server Authentication

The sender's e-mail address can be validated by resolving the sender's domain and IP address. If the sender's IP address does not match with the authorized address for the e-mail domain, the e-mail will automatically be filtered by the main server. Secure SMTP can alternatively be used to provide an encrypted, private, and authenticated communication over the Internet. This gives SMTP agents the ability to protect some or all of their communication from eavesdroppers. When the sender's mail server communicates with the recipient's mail server, certificates are exchanged to identify a trusted sender.

Monitoring Transaction Logs

Most financial institutions monitor the transactions of their customers to identify suspicious activities. In the context of phishing this becomes even more important. Of particular concern is increased frequency of transactions from a particular IP address. This could indicate that a phisher has obtained access to a user account and is attempting to transfer funds from the user account. The financial organizations also need to watch out for transactions of large amounts taking place at a location which is different from the user's residence location or the typical location for user transactions. If such an activity is detected the organization needs to suspend the user account and contact the user immediately to notify him/her about the action and warn him/her about possible fraudulent activity in the account. This may sometimes lead to false alarms and hence inconvenience for users but it is a good protective measure.

Detecting Unusual Downloading Activities

In order to build bogus Web sites, phishers tend to download company logos and trademarks from corporate Web sites. The log files of a corporate Web site contains information about such activities and so they need to be examined from time to time to see if a large amount of downloading of images from corporate Web pages is occurring from a particular IP address. The Corillian Fraud Detection System is an example of a software that searches for suspicious access patterns from Web-log files (Geer, 2005). Although downloading logos or trademarks cannot be categorized as a fraudulent activity but it should definitely be treated as a cause for concern. The particular IP address can be black listed and any further download requests from that particular IP address should be closely monitored to find out what files are being downloaded. If necessary, the IP address can also be reported to the legal authorities so that further investigation can be conducted.

Token-Based and Multifactor Authentication

Phishing aims to retrieve sensitive information from ignorant customers. If the customers themselves do not know that information, it would be hard for phishing to take place. Secure token authentication is based on the idea that the users should not know the authentication information. Secure token is a physical device such as key fob or smartcard that generates a strong one time password that cannot be repeatedly used to access a Web site or an application. Due to the one time feature, it does not matter even if a phisher obtains that value. Since this solution requires high set up and maintenance cost, it is unlikely that all companies can distribute tokens to every user. Most organizations will possibly distribute tokens only to valuable customers. However, it has been stated that token based two factor authentication schemes may not work for MITM and Trojan attacks (Schneier, 2005). Multifactor authentication is an extension of two factor authentication and combines knowledge-based authentication with possession based authentication, and biometrics based authentication (Zviran & Erlich, 2006). Biometric based authentication can include finger print recognition, face recognition, hand geometry, iris scanning, retina scanning, voice recognition, among others (Boukhonine, Krotov, & Rupert, 2005).

Domain Monitoring and Web Poisoning

Managed service providers deploy agent based solutions to monitor URLs and Web content. The solution actively searches for all instances of an organization's logo, trademark, or major Web content. The client organization will provide a white list of authorized users of logo, trademark, and major Web content to the service provider. A methodology for comparing the visual similarity between two Web sites has been suggested that can be used for this purpose (Liu et al., 2005).

Table 1. Individual consumer and organizational strategies to prevent phishing

Protection strategies	Tasks
End user protection	
Desktop protection agents	• Install anti-virus software • Install antispam software • Install spyware detection software
Password management tools	• Append IP specific characters automatically to password fields • Convert user password to a domain specific password
Secure e-mail	• Prevent obfuscation of link destinations in e-mail • Disable HTML in incoming e-mail
Simple and trusted browser setting	• Disable window pop-up • Disable ActiveX support • No storage of cookie • Use Synchronized Random Dynamic Boundaries • Use Dynamic Security Skins
Digital signature	• Use Public Key cryptography
Corporate protection	
E-mail personalization	• Use customer name in body of e-mail • Include partial customer account number or any personal details of customer in e-mail • Use sequence number for e-mail
Mail server authentication	• Filter e-mail if there is a mismatch between domain name and IP address of sender
Monitoring transaction logs	• Detecting multiple transactions within short time • Detecting large value transactions from unusual locations
Detecting unusual downloading activities	• Analyze Web logs for download of logos and trademarks from same IP address
Token based and multi-factor authentication	• Distribute token to customers • Instruct customers about use of token • Renew token at regular intervals • Use biometric authentication
Domain monitoring and Web poisoning	• Create a black list of domains that make unauthorized use of trademarks and logos • Overwhelm suspected phishing Web sites by sending fake customer information to them

If the agent-based solution detects unauthorized use of the logos, trademarks, and major Web content, remediation actions will be taken by the client. The client can send a large amount of fake customer related information to the suspected phishing Web site. This can serve two purposes. First, it can dilute the true customer information that has been collected by the phishing Web site and second, it can occupy the bandwidth of the connection to the fake Web site so that unsuspecting customers are not able to reveal any more confidential information.

Table 1 summarizes the various measures that can be adopted by an individual consumer and by a corporation for preventing phishing attacks.

ANTI-PHISHING PRODUCTS

In order to prevent phishing, security companies have launched different anti-phishing solutions to protect corporations and individual users. VeriSign, Inc., has launched a comprehensive Anti-phishing and Identity theft solution that emphasizes prevention, detection, response and recovery. For phishing prevention, VeriSign provides a VeriSign Multipurpose Next-Generation Token that can generate dynamic one time passwords and store digital certificates and smart card information (Verisign, 2005). VeriSign's

authentication services can enable digital signatures for outgoing e-mails so that recipients can confidently validate that e-mails originated from credible sources. In February 2005, Bank of America selected the VeriSign Unified Authentication solution to support its deployment of strong two-factor authentication.

Entrust, a Canadian security company, developed an identity theft solution called IdentityGuard that provides username/password authentication and physical form of authentication based on the assorted characters on a card. In addition to providing username and password, the user must enter the digit that appears in three or four cells (see Figure 2). The different random coordinates used in each subsequent login can ensure that users are in possession of the appropriate card (Wildstrom, 2005). This solution provides users with two factor authentication that is resistant to phishing. Even if the phishers steal the login name and password, they cannot use them on the legitimate site as they do not have the IdentityGuard grid card. The generation of the random number is based on Entrust FIPS 140-2 certified cryptographic algorithm and the probability of a person successfully tampering the content of the card is small.

ActivCard delivers a solution aimed at thwarting phishing and it is called ActivCard Token-Protected Online Consumer Banking. The solu-

Figure 2. IdentityGuard by Entrust Note (Adapted from Wildstrom, 2005)

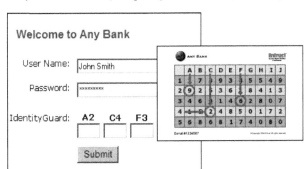

Figure 3. VASCO's Digipass token used by HSBC

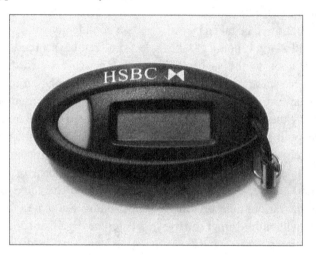

tion targets the online banking and e-commerce market. ActivCard sets a time limit on passwords so that it is effective for a short time period within which the customers can access their account information (ActivCard, 2005). With this method, it provides two-factor authentication to prevent phishers from using captured data to gain access to customer account.

Another Token-Protected One Time Password solution is provided by VASCO. VASCO's Digipass is a token solution like that of VeriSign and ActivCard, and it generates one-time passwords when the owner makes a request by entering PIN code or pressing a button on the token. As the verification of passwords is done in real time, this reduces the time for fraudsters to act, due to expiration of password (VASCO, 2005). Currently, more than 370 financial institutions are using VASCO's Digipass products to secure their internet banking and other e-commerce activities. In 2005, HSBC in Hong Kong became the first bank in the Greater China area to offer Digipass GO3 authentication device to all its retail Internet customers (see Figure 3).

CONCLUSION

The aforementioned strategies are mostly concerned with technical solutions that can detect and prevent phishing. But a common criticism against them is that they are difficult to implement within a short time and require substantial knowledge about Internet technologies. However, it is heartening to know that the use of anti-phishing products is on the rise among informed consumers and corporations. We hope that as ideas of anti-phishing become common knowledge even unsophisticated computer users will be prompted to adopt one or more measures to make their transactions on the Internet stable and secure. An important step in preventing phishing includes educating users about the dangers and techniques of phishing and also measures of anti-phishing. Financial institutions and shopping portals need to play a key role in protecting users and making them aware of the dangers of phishing. This will require continued support from top management, active research in the field of anti-phishing and information security, and allocation of significant amount of budget for adoption of cutting-edge measures.

Phishing has already become a global menace but with cooperative, conscious, and calculated efforts of customers and organizations the threats of phishing can be minimized in future.

REFERENCES

ActivCard. (2005). *How to catch a phish*(White paper). Retrieved July 1, 2006, from http://wp.bitpipe.com/resource/org_975950994_468/Phishing_WP.pdf

Anti-Phishing Working Group. (2005, November). *Phishing activity trends report.* Retrieved July 1, 2006, from *ht*tp://antiphishing.org/reports/apwg_report_Nov2005_FINAL.pdf

Boukhonine, S., Krotov, V., & Rupert B. (2005). Future security approaches and biometrics. *Communications of AIS, 16*(48), 937-966.

Dhamija, R., & Tygar, J. D. (2005, July 6-8). The battle against phishing: Dynamic Security Skins. In *Proceedings of the 2005 Symposium on Usable Privacy and Security,* Pittsburgh, PA.

Garfinkel, S. L., Margrave D., Schiller, J. I., Nordlander, E., & Miller, R. C. (2005, April 2-7). How to make secure e-mail easier to user. In *Proceedings of the ACM Conference on Human Factors in Computing Systems,* Portland, OR.

Geer, D. (June 2005). Security technologies go phishing. *IEEE Computer, 38*(6), 18-21.

Goth, G. (2005, January). Phishing attacks rising, but dollar losses down. *IEEE Security & Privacy Magazine, 3*(1), 8.

Jammalamadaka, R. C., Mehrotra, S., & Venkatasubramanian, N. (2005, November 11). Pvault: A client server system providing mobile access to personal data. In *Proceedings of the 2005 ACM International Workshop on Storage Security and Survivability,* Fairfax, VA.

Kirda, E., & Kruegel, C. (2005, July, 26-28) Protecting users against phishing attacks with AntiPhish. In *Proceedings of the 29th Annual International Conference on Computer Software and Applications,* Edinburgh, Scotland.

Knight, W. (2005, July). Caught in the net. *IEE Review, 51*(7), 26-30.

Lininger, R., & Vines, R. D. (2005). *Phishing: Cutting the identity theft line.* Indianapolis, IN: Wiley.

Liu, W., Guanglin, H., Liu, X., Zhang, M., & Xiaotie, D. (2005, May 10-14). *Detection of phishing Web pages based on visual similarity.* Special Interest Tracks and Posters of the 14th International Conference on World Wide Web, Chiba, Japan.

Merwe, A. V. D., Loock, M., & Dabrowski, M. (2005). Characteristics and responsibilities involved in a phishing attack. In *Proceedings of the Fourth International Symposium on Information and Communication Technologies* (pp. 249-254).

Schneier, B. (April 2005). Two-factor authentication: Too little, too late. *Communications of the ACM, 48*(4), 136.

Slewe, T., & Hoogenboom, M. (2004, May). Who will rob you on the digital highway? *Communications of the ACM, 47*(5), 56-60.

VASCO. (2005, December). *Avoid phishing – Use strong authentication.* Retrieved July 1, 2006, from http://www.firewalls.com.au/docs/nophishing.pdf

VeriSign. (2005, December). *Unified authentication tokens.* Retrieved July 1, 2006, from http://www.verisign.com/products-services/security-services/unified-authentication/usb-tokens/index.html

Wildstrom, S. H. (2005, March 3). New weapons to stop identity threat. *Businessweek.*

Ye, Z., Smith, S., & Anthony, D. (2005). Trusted paths for browsers. *ACM Transactions on Information and System Security, 8*(2), 153-186.

Zviran, M., & Erlich, Z. (2006). Identification and authentication: Technology and implementation issues. *Communications of AIS, 17*(4), 90-105.

Chapter XII
Phishing Attacks and Countermeasures:
Implications for Enterprise Information Security

Bogdan Hoanca
University of Alaska Anchorage, USA

Kenrick Mock
University of Alaska Anchorage, USA

ABSTRACT

The field of information security has realized many advances in the past few decades. Some of these innovations include new cryptographic techniques, network protocols, and hardware tokens. However, the weakest link in information security systems, human gullibility, remains extremely vulnerable. Even the strongest cryptographic algorithms are useless if a user is fooled into disclosing their authentication information. This chapter describes the threat of phishing in which attackers generally sent a fraudulent e-mail to their victims in an attempt to trick them into revealing private information. We start by defining the phishing threat and its impact on the financial industry. Next, we review different types of hardware and software attacks and their countermeasures. Finally, we discuss policies that can protect an organization against phishing attacks. An understanding of how phishers elicit confidential information along with technology and policy-based countermeasures will empower managers and end users to better protect their information systems.

INTRODUCTION

Following many decades of advances in information security, the one component of the information system that has remained almost as vulnerable as ever is the human element. Advances in technology have made software, hardware, networks, and databases increasingly more secure. If anything, technology has only made users more vulnerable to attacks. Because of this, according to the 2005 annual IBM "Security Threats and Attack Trends Report," computer criminals are expected to focus increasingly on targeting workers and customers (the human element) (IBM Report, 2006).

One reason why users are still the weakest link is the increased use of e-commerce. More and more employees and customers of any organization have access to information systems. Each new user with access to a subset of the company data is a potential entry point for attackers. It is difficult to make sure all users are trained sufficiently well to resist such attacks.

Another reason why users are the weakest link is the fact that most information systems are vulnerable to the so-called replay attacks. In such attacks, the assailant first tricks an authorized user into disclosing his or her password. The attacker then "replays" the password later, thereby authenticating to the information system protected by the password. The success of the replay attack hinges on the fact that a valid user name and password will give the attacker the access level of the user whose credentials are being used.

This chapter focuses on one particular type of replay attack, the e-mail-based phishing attack. In such attacks, the user receives an e-mail requesting him or her to go to a Web site to provide authentication or personal information, supposedly for verification purposes. The Web site is a fake, masquerading as a legitimate corporate Web site, and is set up by attackers to collect the authentication information from the user. The information is later used to transfer money or to gain access to computing resources.

Phishing attacks are only the latest technique in the family of social engineering attacks, a general term for exploiting human credulity to get a user to disclose confidential information, for example, a password. Using techniques originally developed by spammers, e-mail messages are sent by large networks of compromised computers, controlled remotely by the attacker. The compromised computers are individually known as "zombies" or collectively referred to as "botnets." The use of botnets allows phishers to reach a large number of potential victims with minimal effort and associated costs. Using Web pages to collect the authentication information automates the collection of phishing data, since the user input can be captured and stored into databases without any effort on the part of the phisher.

This chapter will start by defining the phishing threat and quantifying its impact on the financial industry in particular as well as on IS security in general. We will review both hardware and software replay attacks, and then present hardware and software measures to counteract such attacks. Most of the chapter will focus on software-based counter measures, including one-time passwords, challenge-response, and zero-knowledge protocols. We will also discuss policies that can safeguard an organization against phishing attacks and against replay attacks in general. We conclude the chapter with a perspective on the future of phishing.

BACKGROUND: PHISHING AND SIMILAR ATTACKS ON INFORMATION SYSTEMS

The most common phishing attack involves sending an e-mail message to a list of e-mail addresses, often acquired from a spammer organization. The message urges the recipient to go to a Web site and submit personal or authentication information. The claimed reason is a need to verify this information. The e-mail may also threaten the user with account closure or legal action (e.g., from the Department of Homeland security for accessing illegal Web sites). Alternatively, the phishing e-mail may offer the user one last chance to make changes to the account (to cancel an undesired change made automatically or to sign up for a limited time highly desirable offer).

The phishing Web site is a spoofed copy of a corporate Web site, most often of a financial or e-commerce organization. It is usually online for a limited time (a matter of hours or a few days), after which it is taken offline either by the phisher (to limit exposure) or by the spoofed organization (as a counter-phishing measure). Using the authentication information acquired on the phishing site, criminals access the victim's accounts for personal gain, for example transferring money out of the victim's account. The process is shown in Figure 1.

The term *phishing* is celebrating a decade of existence online as of this writing. According to WordSpy (WordSpy-Physhing, n.d) the term was first mentioned in a hackers' newsgroup, alt.2600, in January 1996, although it had probably been used in the print version of the group's newsletter before that date. The term *phishing* is derived from the word *fish,* hacker slang for a computer account that has been compromised. Hackers' spelling that uses "ph" instead of "f" is credited to John Draper, who also coined the term *phone phreaking* in reference to making pirated long

distance calls using a small toy whistle. The initial phished accounts were America Online accounts. Hackers used to trade user names and passwords for these "phish" as online currency, for example to purchase software (Origins of the Word, n.d.).

The first phishing e-mail attacks were as blatant as to request user authentication in a response message; even the most naïve users today know that no confidential information is safe if sent via e-mail. The next step was to direct the user to a Web site via a phishing attack. The early phishing Web sites were also crude and easy to spot, but the most recent mailings are sophisticated enough to confuse even expert users (MailFrontier, 2005). Lately, carefully crafted e-mail messages and the professionally designed Web sites replicate the corporate look of the spoofed organization by duplicating company insignia from the real Web site.

Phishing works because of several limitations of protocols and procedures in use on the Internet. Widespread use of single-factor user authentication, difficulty in verifying the sender

Figure 1. Basic phishing attack

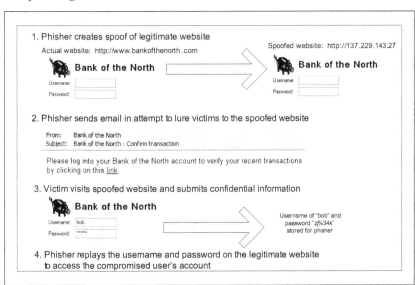

of an e-mail message, and difficulty of verifying the validity of a Web site are the main reasons, which are explained in more detail later in this chapter. Such attacks that exploit several vulnerabilities simultaneously are often called "blended attacks."

Limitations Due to User Authentication Procedures

The security of information systems is based on user authentication (verifying the identity of a user) using one or more of the following: (a) something you have (a hardware token, e.g., ATM card); (b) something you know (a password); and (c) something you are (a biometric trait, e.g., fingerprint or retinal scan). The first and the last types of authentication require the use of special hardware, which makes them more expensive and less well-suited for e-commerce applications. As such, most information systems use single-factor, password-based authentication. Multifactor authentication (using a combination of two or more independent authentication mechanisms) is much more robust, but also more complex and expensive, hence usually reserved for critical applications. In particular, remote access to corporate networks is most often based on two-factor authentication, usually a combination of password and hardware token or of password and biometric data.

Most e-commerce transactions for business to consumer applications are only protected by passwords, a single-factor authentication, highly vulnerable to phishing attacks. Once an attacker has captured the user password (through a phishing Web site or through the use of a Key Logger), the attacker has full access to the user's account.

Key Loggers can be hardware devices or software programs that can be delivered to the victim's computer via viruses, Trojan horse programs, or direct break-in. Most often, users receive software Key Loggers in spam messages and install them by opening attachments. Software Key Loggers can also be installed when users visit certain Web sites that use ActiveX or JavaScript. Hardware Key Loggers are more difficult to install, because they require physical access to the target computer, but once installed are less likely to be detected. Some hardware devices include sufficient memory to store up to a year's worth of Key Logging data (e.g., see *www.keyghost.com/sx*). Manufacturers of custom keyboards offer keyboard models with integrated Key Loggers to replace any existing keyboard on the market. Graphical analogs of Key Loggers are devices that can capture screen shots of mouse click locations, useful for logging access on graphical interfaces (APWG, 2005).

A recent guidance document released by the Federal Deposit Insurance Corporation (FDIC) finds *"single-factor authentication, when used as the only control mechanism, to be inadequate for high-risk transactions involving access to customer information or the movement of funds to other parties"* (FFIEC Guidance, 2005). The document recommends that financial institutions deploy security measures that are commensurate with the potential risks associated with the company's line of products. The FFIEC calls for wider deployment of two-factor authentication by the end of 2006. Although multifactor authentication will decrease the risk of phishing as it exists today, it will take time to implement widely, and it will most likely not eliminate it completely.

Limitations in E-Mail Protocols

E-mail is the preferred vehicle for delivering phishing attacks. It is used to deliver Key Loggers, as well as to direct victims to connect to phishing Web sites. E-mail is widely used and the costs to send large volumes of e-mail are minimal to the sender. Most interestingly for phishers, it is extremely easy to spoof the identity of the e-mail sender, as each e-mail server relaying a message only verifies the identity of the preceding server along the delivery path. Using open relay servers, a phisher can pretend to be sending from any desired address.

Additionally, the widespread use of HTML based e-mail messages makes it easy for the phisher to include in the message links that display the correct URL of a legitimate institution but instead link to a different location where the phisher Web site is located. The HTML syntax <A href="http://phishing_site.com/"> www.real_site.com</A> displays as *www.real_site.com* but when clicked it takes the user to *www.phishing_site.com*. Additional disguises are required to avoid the user's noticing the different URL than the one expected after clicking on the link.

Limitations Due to Lack of Web Site Verification

Phishing e-mail messages must look convincing enough for the recipient to follow the link to the spoof Web site and surrender the personal information. The look of the Web site and its address must also look credible. Copying the look of a Web site is trivial, but disguising the address requires a bit more ingenuity.

The most basic disguises of a Web site address involve using an IP address instead of a company name in the URL of the site. Users are unlikely to know the IP address of the legitimate site. Successful in the early days of phishing, using IP addresses is less likely to trick today's users, who are more aware of phishing techniques.

Phishers also use slightly misspelled URL's (sometimes referred to as "cousin domains," e.g., citibanc.com instead of citibank.com) or URL's that seem to indicate the correct affiliation (e.g., visa-fraud.com may imply a relationship to VISA) but are in fact registered to the phishers. This technique works, if only on the less careful users.

A modified URL can also be disguised by using special unprintable characters; special characters that are not displayed in the URL or by using a floating JavaScript window that covers the actual URL and displays the one the user expects to see

Figure 2. DNS attacks. (A) Normal DNS. (B) Redirect to fake DNS. (C) Compromised DNS Server

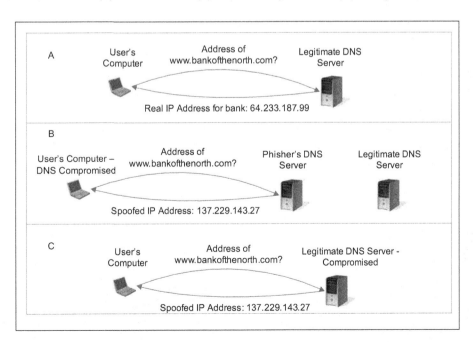

on the legitimate Web site (see reports on the *www. anti-phishing.org* Web site). Such techniques are able to trick even advanced users.

Limitations Due to Name Translation

A whole family of DNS-based attacks is also used for phishing purposes. DNS or domain name service translates between human-friendly URL's like *www.yahoo.com* and the IP addresses of servers (see Figure 2a). The basic attack involves changing the mapping of domain names to link to the phisher Web site. The user might type the address *www.real-bank.com* in a browser and will see the correct address displayed, but the Web site will in fact be the phishing site (see Figure 2b). DNS attacks can occur at several levels. Phishers can attack the hosts file that provides the first level of DNS lookup on the user's computer. This can be achieved using Trojans or viruses, but also via scripts that get activated when the user visits certain Web sites. Another level of DNS attack is when phishers redirect the DNS server for the user's machine to a spoofed DNS server. This requires making changes on the TCP/IP settings on the user's computer, and is achievable using some of the viruses and Trojans that circulate on the Internet. Finally, the most technically challenging DNS attacks involve hacking into a legitimate DNS server and changing the entries to point to the phishing site (also known as "pharming"; see Figure 2c). All of these attacks are virtually undetectable by users, for whom the DNS lookup process is fully transparent. On the other hand, DNS-based attacks are easily spotted by any means that involve checking the IP address of visited sites.

Other Types of Attacks Related to Phishing

Although the technical limitations listed are often blamed for the success of phishing, they are not the only ones. Other types of attack mechanisms are related to phishing, yet different enough to be mentioned on their own.

We already mentioned that phishing is a special type of social engineering. Tricking users is not limited to using e-mail and Web sites as in traditional phishing attacks. An entire class of attacks is based on attracting users to Web sites that offer unbelievably good deals, without trying to impersonate an existing online brand. Such exceptional deals could include financial products (with interest rates much higher than legitimate banks) or technology products at deep discounts. To complete a transaction, the customer must provide a credit card number. After collecting the credit card information, the process is identical with that on any other phishing site. Such attacks are less common today, but might become more common when the technology improvements will limit the easier phishing techniques in use today.

Probably the most difficult attack to defend against is the man–in–the–middle attack (see Figure 3). In such attacks, the assailant is able to intercept and modify the communication between the user and the authentication server. To mount such an attack, one would have to interpose a device between the sender and receiver, making sure that all data packets travel through this device. The attack would commence when a user is trying to connect to a secure site, and the attacker would simply pass messages back and forth between the user and secure site. To the secure site, the attacker will look just like the user he or she is impersonating and will be granted access to the secure site. To the victim, the attacker will look just like the legitimate site to which he or she is connecting. In July 2006, the *Washington Post* reported a man-in-the-middle phishing attack targeted at Citibank (Krebs, 2006).

The man-in-the-middle attack is usually carried out at the network layer but could involve higher layer protocols or even human users. A well-known security expert, Bruce Schneier, cites the case of a woman carrying out a "woman in

Figure 3. Man-in-the-middle attack

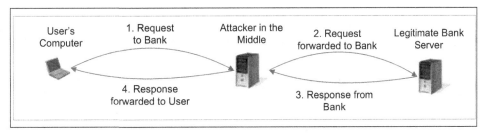

the middle" attack impersonating nannies. She would place an ad in the paper seeking nanny services, ask for references, then turn around and advertise nanny services giving the other nannies' names and references (*Nanny,* 2004). Having thus impersonated another nanny, she would proceed to rob the houses where she was babysitting.

With Web-based phishing, a man-in-the-middle attack could direct the user to a fake Web site, and use scripts on the fake site to submit the user's credentials to the legitimate site. Once the user is authenticated, the attacker has already witnessed the password and can use it later for a replay attack. But even if the system is designed to defend against replay attacks, the man in the middle can take control of the communication after the user has authenticated, and freely transact with the secure site. The analogy with a bank ATM would be, no matter how secure the ATM authentication is, once the user has signed on, an attacker could step in, put a gun to the user's head, and proceed with transferring or withdrawing any amount of money available in the account.

Man in the middle attacks are notoriously difficult to prevent. In particular, there is very little that can be done to prevent such attacks on users that log on from computers in public places (Burkholder, 2002).

DIRECT AND INDIRECT COSTS OF PHISHING

According to the Anti-Phishing Working Group (APWG) reports at *www.antiphishing.org,* the number of unique phishing reports increased from 176 in January 2004 to 12,845 in January 2005. The number of new phishing sites increased from 1,142 in October 2004 to a high of 5,259 in August 2005. The growth is flattening out somewhat, probably because of reaching saturation of the user population. Another reason for the flattening of the growth is the strategy of the attackers, who are keeping a lower profile, to avoid media attention, according to the 2005 IBM's "Security Threats and Attack Trends Report" (IBM Report, 2006).

Losses of the order of billions of dollars per year are reportedly occurring due to phishing attacks (Wetzel, 2005). Gartner estimates that a couple of million of Americans have already fallen prey to phishing attacks (Gartner Study, 2004) and that losses for 2003 were of the order of $1.2 billion. The Gartner study estimates that 3% of the users receiving phishing e-mails gave personal information to phishers.

For enterprise users, phishing can lead to two types of losses: direct losses, through attacks that harvest corporate passwords from employees, and indirect losses that target the customers of the company, by impersonating the corporate image. Through direct attacks phishers obtain user names and passwords that allow them access to documents internal to companies. Little is published about phishing for industrial espionage, although the process would be similar with that of phishing for financial purposes. This type of attacks is less likely to succeed, if a company has strong defenses, not the least being well-trained employees, less likely to fall prey to social engineering attacks. On the other hand, the damage inflicted by a successful direct attack can be considerable, just like robbing a bank is more difficult, but also more lucrative than robbing people in the street.

Indirect phishing attacks use the corporate image to phish the company's customers for personal information. This can lead to financial losses for the customers. These losses, in turn, are likely to be passed back to the company. This is because liability for losses is limited by federal laws, and the company must reimburse the customer for any losses exceeding the limit.

Additionally, phishing is likely to lead to an erosion of the trust of customers in e-commerce. A Gartner report estimates that phishing along with other online attacks will reduce e-commerce growth by 1 % to 3% over the next 3 years (Litan, 2005). As more and more incidents of spoofed phishing sites are reported, the public will have a more difficult time differentiating between legitimate and spoofed sites. The same way spam is diminishing the usefulness of e-mail, phishing impacts the efficiency and security of e-commerce. In turn, a decrease in customer trust can lead to loss of market share, or if this loss of trust occurs industry wide, it can lead to an increase in customer service costs and of operating costs in general. Customers distrusting e-commerce will be forced to conduct business in person, by mail or by telephone; the cost of such transactions is higher than the cost of e-commerce-based transactions.

Finally, organizations that are targets of phishing attacks can also experience denial of service type of attacks, as an unintended consequence of the phishing attack. Often a phisher will use a corporate return address in the baiting e-mail and will send this e-mail to a spammer's list. Many of the recipients on spammers' list are not valid e-mail addresses. As the receiving servers bounce the undeliverable messages, these get sent to the corporate reply-to address, which can be overwhelmed with their number. One tell-tale sign of an organization being subjected to a phishing attack is a large number of bounced e-mail messages from the spam mailing—from all the invalid addresses triggering error messages to the return address.

COUNTERMEASURES TO PHISHING ATTACKS

Many companies outsource anti-phishing solutions to vendors who provide turnkey solutions. According to an article in InfoWorld, Symantec is one of the vendors offering anti-phishing solutions (Roberts, 2004). The company establishes spam traps that are able to detect when the initial spam message is sent, then notifies the client company. The client company can then contact one of the services available to take down the phishing Web site. Client companies using the vendor's Internet filtering products can also filter out the spam messages identified as phishing related. Another vendor, VeriSign (see *www.verisign.com*) offers help with prevention, detection, response, and post incident forensics and reporting. In addition to monitoring spam traps, the phishing detection includes the more general Brand Monitoring which identifies unauthorized use of corporate content and insignia online.

Although outsourcing is a simple solution, defending against phishing attacks is within the range of capabilities of most financial institutions with an online presence. Given the way e-mail and Web-based phishing attacks are carried out,

228

three main defense techniques can be used against phishers: spam control, using multiple-factor authentication techniques, and educating users.

Spam control solutions remove the bait before it can reach the user. To the extent to which they can actually filter out phishing e-mail, spam control solutions can be highly effective against e-mail and Web-based phishing. To some extent, spam control can also prevent key loggers from reaching the users' computers, because many key loggers are delivered via e-mail. Spam filtering is not effective against social engineering attacks (often carried out by phone), against DNS-based attacks (especially not effective against pharming attacks but can be effective against attacks directed to the user's computer) and also not effective against man in the middle attacks. To the extent to which it can reduce the volume of spam, any spam-control technique can be effective in reducing phishing related risks. Unfortunately, none of the existing spam control solutions is satisfactory, and there is little hope for a major breakthrough in the future (Hoanca, 2006).

User education is also very effective. In fact, the most critical measures a company can take to protect from direct phishing attacks are to (a) hire trustworthy employees, (b) educate employees about the dangers of social engineering, (c) limit physical access to the corporate servers inside the company, and (d) deploy multiple-factor authentication for employees who have remote access to sensitive data.

For indirect attacks (on customers of the company), education is a low-cost and highly effective approach, as long as customers are willing to be educated. Many companies include extensive information on their Web sites, helping customers understand the dangers of phishing, the ways to protect against phishing attacks, as well as ways to recover from phishing attacks (e.g., at *www.citibank.com,* a company that has been target of a large number of phishing attacks).

User education can be very effective against social engineering, as well as against phishing attacks. Educated users are less likely to engage in potentially dangerous activities that might lead to the download of Key Loggers. Unfortunately, education has limited effectiveness against pharming attacks as well as against man-in-the-middle attacks, unless the users are highly technical and use complex defenses.

As a simple aid to educating customers, a company can advise them to use one of the many anti-phishing toolbars freely available online. SpoofStick is a toolbar that displays prominently the actual URL of the site accessed. It is available at *www.corestreet.com.* Google, Earthlink, eBay, and Netcraft also make available toolbars that can warn about known phishing sites, give danger ratings of the site accesses, display the true URL's (to prevent spoofs of URLs covered by JavaScript windows), or even go as far as to block access to dangerous sites. Phishing aware browsers like Netscape 8.1, Internet Explorer 7, and Firefox 2.0 are also available to alert users when they are accessing a dangerous site, to block blacklisted sites, or to turn off ActiveX and JavaScript on such sites. The main problem with such approaches is that they are not able to prevent DNS-based attacks. Moreover, many users either do not notice toolbar warnings, or if they do notice warnings they often discount or even ignore them (Wu, Miller, & Garfinkel, 2006). Browsers are also starting to offer capabilities in detecting spyware and Key Loggers installed on the user's computer.

The third anti-phishing tool involves special authentication techniques. Multiple factor authentication is effective against e-mail based phishing, because phishers have a much more difficult task in acquiring hardware based tokens or user biometrics as compared to acquiring passwords. In the remainder of this section, we review the small number of phishing-resistant single-factor authentication techniques reported in the literature.

Internal (nonremote) systems may only require a password, but they can only be accessed from within the organization. The fact that the user must be inside the organization's building to access internal systems makes authentication on these systems in effect be a two-factor authentication. The two factors are the user password and the ability to enter the organization's premises. For this reason, an organization can more easily protect against the direct losses, those targeting the employees.

Indirect losses, due to attacks on the customers of an organization are more difficult to prevent, because of the widespread use of single-factor authentication for online transactions. The reasons for using single-factor authentication are cost and convenience: two-factor authentication is likely to be too expensive, and also inconvenient for the customers (Litan, 2005a). For example, USB tokens are small and relatively inexpensive flash memory devices that could be practical for e-commerce applications. They do not require special hardware, because most computers today have several USB ports. However low, costs increase if users need to carry multiple such devices (one for each online financial institution). Additionally, if the token is used from a public computer, it is possible for an attacker to sniff the hardware token and password and to replay both data later on to authenticate. Establishing secure, encrypted communication is not always an option when using such public terminals. The use of smart cards with microchips embedded for extra security has similar promises and drawbacks with those of USB tokens; an added requirement is the card reader, currently not standard on consumer computers.

Until multiple-factor authentication becomes more feasible, researchers have attempted to modify existing single-factor authentication procedures to make them more secure to phishing attacks. The basic problem is that the user password is fixed. (Good password management requires users to change their password periodically. The time between changes is 1 to 3 months, and is intended to reduce the risk of dictionary attacks, where the attacker attempts an exhaus-

tive search of the password space. These monthly changes do nothing to protect against replay attacks, where the attacker knows the password and can use it within days of getting the password.) Once an attacker has witnessed the user enter the password, via a Key Logger, via a phishing site or via shoulder surfing (direct observation of the user's screen by an attacker trying to steal the password), the attacker has all the information needed for a replay attack. By entering the same password at a later time, the attacker will gain as much access to the information system as the authorized user whose password was entered. By making the password a moving target, a phisher will no longer be able to use a replay attack with such a password, because the password will likely have "expired" after it was harvested. We review some of these solutions, as well as their limitations in the next section.

PASSWORD-BASED AUTHENTICATION RESISTANT TO PHISHING ATTACKS

PassMark "Two-Factor, Two-Way" Authentication

One approach newly introduced by several banks is the two-way, two-factor authentication of Pass-Mark Security, Inc. (PassMark, n.d.); one bank working on incorporating this scheme is Bank of America (n.d.). The two-way nature involves not just the customer authenticating to the financial institution (via a password) but also the bank authenticating itself to the customer, by displaying a textual passphrase and an image that the customer has chosen in the initial registration process. The customer is instructed not to submit information on a Web site unless the correct passphrase and image are displayed to authenticate the site.

The two-factor element involves the password as one factor and the physical address of the user's computer as the second factor. The user can only access the site from a registered computer, with an address registered with the financial institution. The address of the computer is recorded in the initial registration session. A phisher who has the user name and password information would not be able to log on, because it is using a different computer than the one registered by the user. Access from unregistered IP addresses requires successfully answering a challenge question set up during registration.

Although this sounds simple, there are several hidden complications. First the process of registering with the bank to access one's account online is more complex. Second, the technique is only successful if users notice the absence of the passphrase and image when presented with a phishing attack. Finally the phisher can still retrieve the user's password, albeit not in a single step. Instead, the phisher will need to conduct a two step attack, first retrieving the secret image and text passphrase, then retrieving the user password by displaying the secret image to the user. The secret image can be retrieved relatively easily by the attacker by setting up a phishing site that first queries the user with the challenge question. Once the answer to the challenge question has been entered by the user, the phishing site can retrieve the proper image and passphrase from the financial institution. This is in effect a man-in-the-middle attack. In the case of attacks using Key Loggers or visual observation, the two-factor authentication proposed by the banking industry has little advantage over the simple password authentication currently in use. The Key Logger will record the entire registration session, which will allow the attacker to register a new computer to access the secure site once the answer to the challenge question can be determined.

One-Time Passwords

Another type of authentication resistant to phishing is the use of one-time passwords (OTP, 1998). As the name indicates, these are "disposable passwords" that are used only once. An attacker who may witness and capture a password will find it useless for authentication the next time. One time password schemes are more complex than traditional passwords. OTP require additional hardware tokens that generate the password on the fly, or a list of passwords that the user is required to memorize or to carry with her. The password list can be generated in advance (if printed or memorized) and shared between the user and the authentication server, or can be generated on the fly as a pseudo random sequence using a seed number or a timer that is shared between the user and the server. If the list is printed or embedded in a hardware token, the OTP scheme effectively becomes a limited two-factor authentication.

For the case of the list, the customer uses each password on the list in sequence. Each password is used a single time. Three problems are known for one time passwords. First, if the user loses a list, there must be a way for the user to cancel an entire list of passwords. Secondly, the user must have multiple password lists, in case one of them gets lost. Third, if a session is abandoned or otherwise not completed, it might not be clear whether a certain password should be considered as used or not. As such, the user must be able to synchronize the list with the password expected by the authentication server.

Similar considerations apply to one-time hardware-based passwords (also a two-factor technique). These passwords are generated by a token that the user carries with him. The token can be timer-based, or can have a sequence of passwords synchronized with the sequence on the authentication server, just like the list described in the previous paragraph. As with the list, if the authorized user loses the token, the security of the access is compromised.

One time passwords are also vulnerable to phishing. In 2005 the Scandinavian bank Nordea was targeted by phishers and the bank temporarily shut down its Web site. The phishers sent e-mail directing users to a bogus site that asked the recipients to enter their account details and the next password from their list of one-time passwords issued by the bank (Finextra.com, 2005). The scheme is also vulnerable to the man in the middle attack (Krebs, 2006).

Challenge Response Systems

Another type of hardware or software authentication is the challenge response approach. As before, the user has a list of passwords or a token that can generate passwords. This time, the authentication system generates a challenge, a random code. For the list, the user must look up the password that corresponds to the code, and enter that as the response to the challenge. For the case of the token, the user enters the challenge in the token, then enters the output from the token as the response. This approach is very similar with the one time passwords described previously, except that the list of passwords or the token is used to look up the challenge presented by the server. As for one time passwords, if the list or the token are lost, the finder gets access to the protected resources. For this reason, the use of one time passwords or challenge response systems could be combined with the use of a secret password. A phisher must obtain both the list or hardware token and

the password to gain access to the information system.

Password Hashing

Another anti-phishing scheme, proposed by a group at Stanford University, takes a fixed user password and makes it site dependent (Ross et al., 2005). The idea is to hash the user password with a salt element derived from the domain of the site where the user is entering the password. Ideally, a phishing site will not receive the clear text password, but only the hashed value, calculated based on the phishing site, and hence useless at the legitimate site being phished for (see Figure 4). The solution is elegant, based on browser extensions that are installed once and that operate transparently for the user. The user experience is unchanged from the usual case of no password hashing. Moreover, the user can safely use the same clear text password for multiple sites, knowing that the transmitted (hashed) password will be different for each site (due to the different salt used).

A clever use of special characters allows the user to choose between hashed and unhashed passwords. Still, because the salt is using the DNS entry of a Web site (e.g., www.yahoo.com), the

Figure 4. Hashing scheme

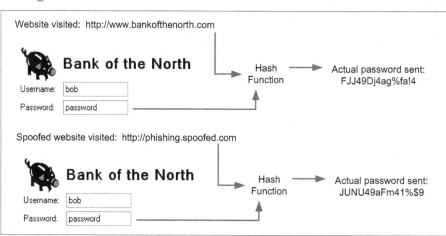

scheme will do nothing to protect against DNS-based attacks. The password at the phishing site will be valid without hashing at the legitimate site. Second, client side phishing software running outside the browser (Key Loggers, screen capture programs, or network packet capture) will not be deterred either. Finally, the user may sometimes need to access the same Web site with a browser where she cannot install extensions (e.g., a browser on a computer at work), in which case the password will not operate correctly (or the hash will need to be computed manually).

Single-Factor Challenge Response

Other phishing-resistant schemes are based on the challenge response idea, but the response is generated in the user's mind. There are no lookup lists or hardware tokens to be lost. The user must combine information from the random challenge and the shared secret by mentally computing a hashing function (Hoanca & Mock, 2005; Hopper & Blum, 2000; Man, Hong, Hayes, & Matthews, 2004; Man, Hong, & Matthews, 2003; Matsumoto, 1996; Sobrado & Birget, 2002, 2005). Such protocols are part of the class of shared secret protocols. The strength of such protocols is that a malicious observer that records an authentication session does not obtain enough information to be able to authenticate successfully in place of the user.

One of the first ideas in this class was that of Sobrado and Birget (2002). The authors proposed a scheme that is resistant to shoulder surfing. The password is a string of graphic symbols from a set of such symbols. At log on, the entire set of symbols are displayed in random order on the screen. The user selects his password by entering information about three symbols at a time. Instead of selecting the three symbols directly, which would reveal them to the attacker, the user must click inside the convex hull of the triangle formed by the three symbols. Because of the relatively

large number of possible triplets associated with any click, an attacker will have a difficult time determining what the authentication triplet was. The initial idea had several shortcomings. First, different screen regions have unequal probabilities of containing the click location, making it more likely for an attacker to "guess" right by clicking in the center of the screen. Additionally, users have difficulty in distinguishing among some of the symbols (especially users with perception difficulties). Finally, the authentication session is time-consuming, requiring careful observation of several screens of graphical symbols. Over time, the authors and others cited in the previous paragraph have evolved techniques that address the problems of the initial idea, but have a similar approach to hiding the password.

Probably the most fundamental limitation of single-factor challenge response approaches is the fact that some small but nonzero amount of information is released to an observer any time a user authenticates with this method. Over time, sometimes over as few as three observations, the attacker can gather sufficient data to recover the user's password. On a phishing site, this is not an acceptable situation, because the user can be induced to re-enter the password a few times (by issuing fake error messages).

Zero-Knowledge Protocols

Only the most secure protocols, the ones in the family of zero-knowledge protocols can overcome the limitation of repeated observations. The attacker does not receive any information by observing an authentication session employing a zero-knowledge protocol. These protocols tend to be either highly mathematical or based on fantasy (magical) features. A classical example is a story involving the secret to Ali Baba's magical cave door (Quisquater et al., 1990). Unlike the character in *Arabian Nights*, Quisquater's Ali Baba can prove that he can open his magical cave door without actually revealing the password.

Although this is a good allegoric illustration of zero-knowledge protocols, it is of little practical use in building a secure authentication system. Zero-knowledge protocols are a theoretical and somewhat idealized construct. The story mentioned above focuses on how Ali Baba could prove to a Verifier that he knows the secret without disclosing anything about it. The technique is so powerful that a third party eavesdropping on the authentication process cannot even tell whether (a) Ali Baba actually knows the secret or (b) Ali Baba and the Verifier are colluding. Something like this would be the perfect solution for phishing attacks, where the phisher would never be able to infer the user's password. Practical zero-knowledge protocols are yet to be developed.

POLICIES FOR PREVENTING E-MAIL-BASED PHISHING

In closing, several types of policies can be adopted by organizations to prevent or reduce the losses due to phishing. Detailed information on how to prepare for and to handle phishing attacks can be found in several recent publications on phishing, which devote more extensive space than this chapter allows (Emigh, 2005; Lininger & Vines, 2005). In this chapter, we focus on actions and policies that enterprise users can and should take, leaving out other tools and techniques that are more appropriate for individual users.

Since e-mail is currently the leading vehicle for delivering phishing threats, e-mail policies are essential. Organizations that send e-mail to customers should allow customers to elect to receive plain-text e-mail. HTML e-mail can more easily hide phishing links than simple text e-mail. Distributed spam filters or spam traps can help filter out spam and can give indication of when phishing attacks are launched. Authenticated e-mail is expected to greatly reduce the spam problem, and along with it the phishing problem.

However, authenticated phishing e-mails may still be sent from compromised systems, such as those infected by a phisher's virus.

User education is a continuing requirement for any organization whose customers are likely to be targets of phishing attacks. Establishing how the company will contact users, establishing two-way authentication mechanisms like the PassMark scheme described above, and communicating closely with the customer before, during and after a phishing attack are also important. Information about preventing phishing attacks can be posted on the company site or sent in e-mail mailings to the customers.

Internally, organizations must continue to educate their employees, to make sure they do not fall prey to phishing attacks and disclose authentication information to unauthorized persons. On the other hand, policies must be adopted for limiting access to information on a need to know basis, limiting employees' ability to install software (whether with malicious intents or having fallen prey to an attack), and limiting employees' access to potentially dangerous Web sites outside the company. A new threat to information security comes from the increasing use of blogs, on which sometimes employees post company confidential information (IBM Report, 2006).

Finally, organizations must have policies about detecting and responding to phishing threats and attacks. We have seen that multiple e-mail bounces might indicate errors due to a phishing spam mailing. Monitoring HTTP requests for links to images is another telltale sign, as phishers link from the e-mail message to logos and hyperlinks on the site they are trying to spoof. Monitoring Web sites with closely spelled names could indicate when one of them is used for phishing. Also, a drop in traffic from the usual levels might indicate a DNS-based phishing attack, because the traffic is redirected to the phishing site. Finally, monitoring anti-phishing groups is also a good policy to get early warning of potential phishing attacks.

After detecting an attack, responding to it in a timely manner, communicating to customers and employees throughout the process and restoring access to any compromised resources is key to minimize the impact of a phishing attack.

Layered Approach to Security

Authentication techniques described here can be combined with other technologies to further reduce the risk of phishing. Out of band authentication require transactions to be confirmed via a different medium (by a phone call or fax to a registered phone number, or even to a person who needs to provide a password to validate the transaction). Geo-location information can also be used to provide additional security factors, similar with the requirement for physical access to a company premises in order to access internal information systems (Authentication Guidance, 2005).

A best practices approach to any security application, including anti-phishing defenses, includes several layers of countermeasures. As Table 1 shows, no single defense approach is able to handle all types of attacks related to phishing. Some defenses could in an ideal situation be 100% effective against one or more attacks, but in practice the effectiveness is much more reduced. Effectiveness is increased by deploying a layered defense approach. For anti-phishing efforts, a three pronged approach includes customer and employee education, combined with judicious deployment of multiple-factor or other phishing resistant authentication, and with spam monitoring and filtering. This approach is taken by most vendors, including companies like Symantec and Microsoft. In addition, well thought out policies and procedures should be in place for before, during and after an attack.

THE FUTURE OF PHISHING

Phishing is already changing. As more and more phishing-related stories are broadcast on the news, users become more aware of the phishing threat and of ways to fight back, but attackers adapt and invent new techniques. Personalization, extensively used in marketing, is making inroads into the phishing world as well. By sending highly personalized targeted e-mails (technique known as "spear-phishing"), the attack is more likely to succeed. Such attacks are more likely to be directed at corporate targets, for example pretending to be sent by the IT manager or by a functional manager the person reports to. Spear phishing attacks will continue to target customers of financial institutions as well (one of the authors of this chapter received a phishing e-mail credible

Table 1. Effectiveness of the three main anti-phishing approaches to the main phishing type threats. Note: (-) stands for no effect, (+) for some improvement and (++) for possible cure.

Attack Type	Defense Approach		
	Spam control	User education	Phishing-resistant authentication
Social engineering	-	++	-
Traditional e-mail + Web site phishing	++	++	++
Use of Key Loggers	+	++	++
DNS-based attacks	-	-	++
Man-in-the-middle	-	-	-

enough to make him go and change his password on a bank Web site, although of course, not by following the link in the e-mail).

Another trend is "puddle phishing," which goes after customers of smaller financial institutions (here, referred to as "puddles"). As the larger institutions have already been subject to phishing attacks and have mounted defenses, smaller targets are becoming attractive to the phishers. The puddle phishers have a well defined audience, and might personalize their attack to the audience. A recent community announcement in the *14850 Online*, an online newspaper for Ithaca, New York, warns readers of a phishing attack targeting the local community. The target company is the Cornell Finger Lakes Community Credit Union, a small credit union with locations in Ithaca and nearby Cortland (CFCU, 2005).

A more sinister but less well-known side of phishing is that it has attracted organized crime. The IBM Report (2006) on security trends cites a reduction in the overall information security threat level the company reported for 2005 as compared with 2004, but cites concern regarding the intensity of the attacks and the targeting of the human element instead of the usual software vulnerabilities. The report also attributes the decrease in reported incidents to the increased ability of the phishers to cover their tracks.

At the same time, a legal framework is developing for handling phishing related crimes. While phishers may already be prosecuted under statutes of wire fraud or identify theft, these prosecutions likely take place only after someone has been defrauded. In the United States, the Anti-Phishing Act proposed in March of 2005 will make it illegal to knowingly send phishing e-mail and host phony Web sites with the intent of committing a crime. The bill proposes a 5-year prison sentence and/or fine up to $250,000 for individuals who commit phishing fraud. However, even if passed, it remains to be seen if the bill can be enforced. Many phishing attacks originate outside of the

United States and enforcement of the bill may be difficult.

CONCLUSION

It is difficult to forecast how phishing attacks will evolve, even in the near term. As we pointed out, they are expected to be more targeted and personalized, and to be directed increasingly at enterprise users. Enterprises will continue to educate their employees and customers, and to deploy multiple-factor authentication solutions. In response, attackers may move increasingly towards using DNS and man in the middle types of attacks. In the meantime, as new online technologies arise, attackers will gravitate towards those new areas where larger numbers of users with limited skills make for good prey.

REFERENCES

APWG. (2005, July). *APWG phishing activity report*. Retrieved October 7, 2005, from http://anti-phishing.org/APWG_Phishing_Activity_Report_Jul_05.pdf

Authentication Guidance. (2005, October). *Authentication in an Internet banking environment*. Retrieved January 26, 2006, from ww.ffiec.gov/pdf/authentication_guidance.pdf

Bank of America. (n.d.). *Here's how sitekey works*. Retrieved September 29, 2005, from http://www.bankofamerica.com/privacy/passmark/

Burkholder, P. (2002). *SSL man-in-the-middle attacks (SANS report)*. Retrieved January 30, 2006, from http://www.sans.org/rr/whitepapers/threats/480.php

CFCU. (2005, January 24). *CFCU credit union says customers received "phishing" scam e-mails*. Retrieved January 26, 2006, from http://today.14850.com/0124cfcuscam.html

CipherTrust. (n.d.). *Sender policy framework statistics*. Retrieved January 29, 2006, from http://www.ciphertrust.com/resources/statistics/spf_stats.php

Emigh, A. (2005). O*nline identity theft: Phishing technology, chokepoints and countermeasures (ITTC report on online identity theft technology and countermeasures)*. Retrieved on July 14, 2006, from http://www.anti-phishing.org/Phishing-dhs-report.pdf

FFIEC Guidance. (2005, October 12). *Authentication in an Internet banking environment (FIL-103-2005)*.Retrieved January 25, 2006 from http://www.fdic.gov/news/news/financial/2005/fil10305.pdf

Finextra.com (2005). *Phishers target Nordea's one-time password system*. Retrieved January 24, 2006, from http://www.finextra.com/fullstory.asp?id=14384

Gartner Study. (2004). *Gartner study finds significant increase in e-mail phishing attacks*. Retrieved January 17, 2006, from http://www.gartner.com/5_about/press_releases/asset_71087_11.jsp

Hoanca, B. (2006, Spring). How good are our weapons in the spam wars? A systems analysis of spam fighting techniques. *IEEE Technology and Society Magazine, 25*(1), 22-30.

Hoanca, B., & Mock, K. (2005, June 20-24). *Screen oriented technique for reducing the incidence of shoulder surfing*. Paper presented at Security and Management (SAM'05), Las Vegas, NV.

Hopper, N., & Blum, M. (2000). *A secure human-computer authentication scheme (CMU Tech. Rep. CMU-CS-00-139)*. Retrieved October 5, 2005, from http://reports-archive.adm.cs.cmu.edu/anon/2000/CMU-CS-00-139.pdf

IBM Report. (2006). *IBM Report: Surge in CRIMINAL-DRIVEN CYBER ATTACKS Anticipated in 2006*. Retrieved January 26, 2006, from http://www-03.ibm.com/press/us/en/press-release/19141.wss

Krebs, B. (2006). *Citibank phish spoofs 2-factor authentication*. Retrieved July 23, 2006, from http://blog.washingtonpost.com/securityfix/2006/07/citibank_phish_spoofs_2factor_1.html

Lininger, R., & Vines, R. D. (2005). *Phishing: Cutting the identity theft line*, Hoboken, NJ: Wiley.

Litan, A. (2005a). *Findings from Credit Reporting Agency: Authentication Practices* (Gartner Rep. G00136618).

Litan, A. (2005b). *Increased phishing and online attacks cause dip in consumer confidence* (Gartner Rep. G00129146).

MailFrontier. (2005). *MailFrontier Phishing IQ Test II*. Retrieved October 5, 2005, from http://survey.mailfrontier.com/survey/quiztest.html

Man, S., Hong, D., & Matthews, M. (2003). A shoulder-surfing resistant graphical password scheme – WIW. In *Proceedings of the International Conference on Security and Management,* 105-111.

Man, S., Hong, D., Hayes, B., & Matthews, M. (2004). A password scheme strongly resistant to spyware. In *Proceedings of the International Conference on Security and Management,* 94-100.

Matsumoto, T. (1996, March). Human-computer cryptography: An attempt. In *Proceedings of the Third ACM Conference on Computer and Communications Security,* 68-75.

Nanny. (2004, March 18). *Police investigation of nanny widens*. Retrieved January 30, 2006, from http://www.sfgate.com/cgi-bin/article.cgi?file=/chronicle/archive/2004/03/18/BAG6S5MUEO1.DTL

Origins of the Word. (n.d.). *Origins of the word "phishing."* Retrieved January 5, 2006, from http://www.antiphishing.org/word_phish.html

OTP. (1998). RFC 2289 - *A one-time password system.* Retrieved October 5, 2005, from http://www.faqs.org/rfcs/rfc2289.html

PassMark. (n.d.). *PassMark security: Two-factor two-way authentication.* Retrieved September 29, 2005, from http://www.passmarksecurity.com/main.jsp

Quisquater, J-J., Quisquater, M., Quisquater, M., Quisquater, M., Guillou, L. Guillou, M. A., et al. (1990). How to explain zero-knowledge protocols to your children. In G. Brassard (Ed.), *Advances in cryptology* (vol. 435, pp. 628-631). Springer-Verlag.

Roberts, P. (2004, September 13). *Symantec launches antiphishing service.* Retrieved January 25, 2006, from http://www.infoworld.com/article/04/09/13/HNsymantiphishing_1.html

Ross, B., Jackson, C., Miyake, N., Boneh, D., & Mitchell, J. C. (2005). Stronger password authentication using browser extensions. In *Proceedings of the 14th Usenix Security Symposium.*

Sobrado, L., & Birget, J.-C. (2002). *Graphical passwords.* Retrieved April 14, 2005, from http://rutgersscholar.rutgers.edu/volume04/sobrbirg/sobrbirg.htm

Sobrado, L., & Birget, J.-C. (2005). *Shoulder surfing resistant graphical passwords.* Retrieved October 5, 2005, from http://clam.rutgers.edu/~birget/grPssw/srgp.pdf

Wetzel, R. (2005, February). Tackling phishing. *Business Communications Review*, pp. 46-51.

WordSpy-Phishing. (n.d.). *Phishing.* Retrieved January 23, 2006, from http://www.wordspy.com/words/phishing.asp

Wu, M., Miller R. C., & Garfinkel, S. L. (2006). *Do security toolbars actually prevent phishing attacks?* Retrieved July 14, 2006, from http://groups.csail.mit.edu/uid/projects/phishing/chi-security-toolbar.pdf

Chapter XIII
Prevention and Handling of Malicious Code

Halim Khelafa
University of Wollongong in Dubai, United Arab Emirates

ABSRACT

The purpose of this chapter is to provide a wide spectrum of end users with a complete reference on malicious code or malware. End users include researchers, students, as well as information technology and security professionals in their daily activities. A particular effort aims at educating users about malware, enhancing organization capabilities for preventing as well as handling malicious code incidents when they occur, and preparing them for tomorrow's new types of malware, as well as the new types of safeguards they should consider. First, the author provides an overview of malicious code, its past, present, and future. Second, he presents methodologies, guidelines and recommendation on how an organization can enhance its prevention of malicious code, how it should respond to the occurrence of a malware incident, and how it should learn from such an incident to be better prepared in the future. Finally, the author addresses the issue of the current research as well as future trends of malicious code and the new and future means of malware prevention.

INTRODUCTION

The information age has revolutionized all sectors of human activity: business, health care, education, even entertainment. However, this has come with a price; these enhancements bring about new threats from an ever technically sophisticated group of hackers. Stevens (2006) distinguishes four major types of attacks: network intrusions, viruses, worms, rootkits, and poisoning of the Domain Name Service. Tremendous losses can result from suck attacks. According to the FBI computer crime and security survey of 2005, losses due to viruses accounted for US$42,787,667 out of a total loss of US$130,104,542. In addition, the respondents to the survey have consistently put *viruses* as the type of attacks with the highest occurrences (more than 70%). Virus is a concept used by the general public. A more appropriate description would be malicious code or malware. Even though, some authors make a difference between malware and malicious code, the terms will be used interchangeably because of the convergence of the different malware vectors.

The term *malicious code* is a recent term in the taxonomy of information security. It can be defined as any program or piece of code that in-

terferes with the proper operation of a computer or a network. The categories of malicious code are no longer restricted to viruses, worms, and Trojan horses, but new breeds of malicious code have emerged with the development of the Internet in general and online business activities in particular. Hoefemeyer (2004) asserts that malicious code attacks are quite similar to biological ones, with one crucial difference: the propagation of malware infections is significantly faster than biological ones thanks to the Internet. In matters of hours,

Figure 1. Financial impact of malware estimated in billions of U.S. dollars (Anonymous, 2005)

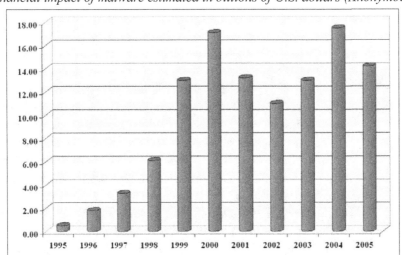

Figure 2. Percentage of financial impact of malware (Anonymous, 2005)

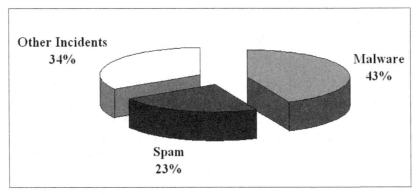

the infection can spread over continents. Recently researchers have noticed a convergence between spam and viruses (Erbeschloe, 2005; Sunner 2005; Viveros, 2005). Virus, worms, and the like are no longer a nuisance, nor a teenager's bad habit. Malicious code is more and more sophisticated, with evidence that it is the work of groups of greedy experts seeking to tap on the huge opportunities offered by the Internet in general, and online business in particular.

Indeed, Internet has revolutionized the way we conduct business. Internet has given people the opportunity to run businesses 24 hours a day, 7 days a week, while cutting on operating costs; a privilege enjoyed only by few large corporations a few years ago. Today, Internet is a necessary sale method for businesses (Egan, 2005). However, security threats in general, and threats based on malicious code are becoming significant impediments to businesses. The following graphs (see Figure 1 and Figure 2) illustrate how the impact of malware on businesses is becoming more and more alarming (Anonymous, 2005).

The same article reports that although it is the first time since 2002 that there is a decline in financial losses due to malware, the alarming news is that increasingly malware attacks are more and more covert, and more focused on particular business sector. This later finding corroborates results from more recent researches (Barwinski, 2005). Moreover, today malware is proliferating in an almost idealistic breeding ground (Savage & Voelker, 2004). Malware writers see the combination of homogeneous software along with the ever-ubiquitous communication model as a blessing. Infections propagate in matter of seconds and even less. Traditional protections are ineffective to fight the new trends in malware. For example, most organization relied on the concept of a security perimeter to keep out rogue software. This is no longer true. Mobile users take their laptop home or along with them on business trips, connect to unsecured networks, then eventually use a VPN to connect to the corporate network, or bring back

the lap top and hook it to the company network. Continuously evolving technology is making networking use more and more affordable. For business and governments, very often it is not a choice but a necessity to use networking as the underlying infrastructure of the company or the agency. Hence, malware is an inescapable problem, a business problem (Gordon, 2006).

The purpose of this chapter is to provide a wide spectrum of end users with a practical reference on malicious code or malware. A particular effort aims at educating users about malware, enhancing organization capabilities for preventing as well as handling malicious code incidents when they occur, preparing them for tomorrow's new types of malware as well at the type of safeguard they should consider.

BACKGROUND

This chapter may be divided into thee sections. The first section is an overview of malicious code, its past, present, and future. A second one, provides methodology, guidelines and recommendation on how an organization can enhance its prevention of malicious code, how it should respond to the occurrence of a malware incident, and how it should learn from such an incident to be better prepared in the future. Finally, a third section addresses the issue of the future trends of malicious code and the new and future means of malware prevention. The rest of this first section overviews the different types of malware and presents a set of criteria or characteristics (Heiser, 2004) that can be used in categorizing the different types of malware.

Definition of Malicious Code

The concept of malicious code or malware has evolved over the years. A ninth-grade student, Rich Skrenta, wrote the very first viral code in 1982 (Heiser, 2004). When using his school's Apple II computer, Rich would add some extra code to the operating system before leaving. According to Rich, if the next student in line to use the Apple II did not reboot the computer prior to using it, get his/her floppy would carry whatever code Rich intended to propagate (Paquette, 2000). Of course, Fred Cohen created the first replicating code in 1983.

But what is exactly malware nowadays? Heiser (2004) describes malware as any type of unwanted code, whose writer meant it to be installed without the explicit authorisation of the system owner or administrator. Heiser provides also an economic definition of malware. Malware can be seen as any piece of code that organization will pay money to get rid of it or prevent it form reaching their systems.

A Simple View of Malicious Code

The following is an overview of the major categories of malicious code. It is based largely on the NIST classification (Mell, 2005); nevertheless the reader should bear in mind that in today's world, different categories of malware or malicious code that historically operated in isolation are now combined as a response to the implementation by organization of better security practices (Heiser, 2004). The main categories are:

- **Viruses:** A virus is a malicious code designed to reproduce potentially an evolved version of it, and multiply without the knowledge or the consent of the user of the machine (Szor, 2005).
- **Worms:** Worms have been defined as network viruses because they multiply over a network. They differ from viruses in that they usually do no need the intervention of the user to propagate. Even though this may not be true for mailers and mass mailers (Slade, 2005; Szor, 2005).
- **Trojan horses:** Named after the horse of the Greek mythology. A Trojan horse is a

program intended to lure users by appealing to them, pretending to perform a genuine and benign function while performing unwanted tasks without the knowledge or consent of the user.
- **Malicious mobile code:** Mobile code is software sent through a network, from one computer to another computer, where it will execute without the user's explicit interaction. (NIST SP800-83; Primode 2005, Wikipedia, 2005)
- **Blended attacks:** It is a type of malware that can multiply and spread itself in more than one way, using different techniques. It uses several distribution methods including: E-mail, unsecured Windows file shares, vulnerable Web servers and Web Clients, Instant messaging Severs, and peer-to-peer file sharing services (Duham, 2006; Gilliland, 2006; Park, 2005).
- **Spyware:** A broad definition of spyware would be any software that subverts a computer for the benefit of a third party. Brawinski (2005) stresses the difficulty security professionals have in defining spyware. The definition may vary according to the intent of the spyware writer. As Microsoft (2005) defined it: "Spyware is a general term used for software that performs certain behaviours such as advertising, collecting personal information, or changing the configuration of your computer, generally without appropriately obtaining your consent."
- **Attacker tools:** NIST considers this category as malicious code that enables attackers to use the resources and data of an infected system. Major categories of attacker tools include: backdoors, keystroke loggers, rootkit, malicious web browser's plugins, and e-mail generators.
- **Backdoors:** Backdoor software requires two components: a client program in the attacker machine and a server in the infected

machine. The client program performs hostile actions on the infected machine such as unauthorized file transfer, resource usage, information stealing. Some are used for more dangerous activities such as:

a. *Zombies,* which are program installed on systems that will be used as a base for launching attacks on other systems. The most common use is for Distribute denial of service attacks (DDoS).

b. *RAT or Remote Administration Tools* sometimes called remote access trojans. The attacker is able to gain full control of the system resources and data, including even such devices as a web cam.

- **Keystroke logger:** Monitoring software that record ever keystroke made on a computer. It will record e-mails, messages, document, source code, passwords, usernames, creditcards, Web pages visited, and so forth.

- **Rootkit:** It is a set of files and attack tools a hacker installs on a machine after gaining root or administrator access to that machine. The attacker can alter the configuration functionality of the machine and even the behaviour of the kernel.

- **Malicious Web browser plugins:** Attackers use malicious plugins to take control of a user browser.

- **E-mail generators:** Malicious program placed on infected machine then used for spam related activities such as mass mailing without permission of machine owner.

Compiled vs. Interpreted Viruses

Viruses are either compiled or interpreted (Mell, 2005). Compiled viruses are executed by operating systems while interpreted viruses are executed only by a specific application or service. There are three types of compiled viruses: file infectors, boot-sector infectors, and multipartite viruses. A file infector attaches itself to an executable file

such as .exe and .com in Windows-run machines. A classic example of file infector virus is Jerusalem. A boot sector infects the master boot sector of a hard drive or boot sector portion of a booting media such as a floppy diskette. Examples of boot-sector viruses include Brain, Michelangelo, and Stone. A multipartite virus is a type of virus that infects files and boot sectors. Nowadays, a multipartite virus is a virus that can infect more than one type of objects, and that can also multiply in more than one way. Examples include: Junkie, One Half, and Telefonica.

Interpreted viruses fall into two categories: macro-viruses and script-viruses. Macro-viruses take advantage of the fact that many Microsoft applications use macros to free users from tedious and repetitive commands. Macro-viruses infect application documents like word processing files and spreadsheets. When such an infection occurs, the template, such as MS Word Normal.dot, used by the program to open and create files is also infected. Hence, the program will infect all documents using that template. Melissa, Marker, and Concept are examples of such a type of virus. Scripting viruses differ from macro-viruses only in that a macro-virus is written in a programming language specific to a particular application while a scripting virus is written in a language that can be executed by an interpreter. Love letter is an example of a scripting virus.

Virus writers use several obfuscation techniques. The more complex the obfuscation the harder it is to detect the virus; thus the easier it will spread. The following is a compilation by NIST of the main virus obfuscation techniques:

- **Self-encryption and decryption:** The objective is to hide the virus code from direct examination. Such viruses may use several layers of encryption, or choose the cryptographic key randomly at each encryption, making each instance of the virus appear different from the others. The first virus of this type is Cascade.1701.

- **Polymorphism:** This is an improved form of encryption. The decryption code is made more robust. An example is the 1260 virus.
- **Metamorphism:** Instead of hiding its content via encryption, a polymorphic virus changes its body content. Metamorphic viruses create a new generation of viruses that look different from their creators. Code alteration may include adding unneeded instructions, or modifying the sequencing of the different parts of the code.
- **Stealth:** This type of viruses tries to conceal the occurrence of an infection. Stealth viruses manipulate the data returned to a function call. For example, it will manipulate the system call requesting the listing of files on a machine by altering the size of the infected file. The displayed file size would correspond to the size of the original file, not the infected one. Examples include: Brain, Read Stealth, and Number_of_the_Beast.
- **Armoring:** This type of virus aims at preventing human expert and automated tools from analysing its code. The basic methods used by armoured viruses are to make tasks such as disassembly and debugging more difficult.
- **Tunnelling:** This type of virus installs itself in the lower layers of the operating system as to be able to take control of the interrupt handler, modifying it so that control is first passed to the virus in the event of a system call or interrupt. The virus can defeat any attempt of monitoring activity. One of the first tunnelling viruses is the Eddie virus or Dark_Avenger.1800.A.

Classification of Malware

In the early 1980, malware referred to viruses, worms, and Trojans. This is no longer the case today (Licari, 2006). Today's malware is very sophisticated compared to its ancestors. There is no easy way to classify malware using a tree-like structure. Heiser (2004) distinguishes several characteristics in describing malware:

- **Lifecycle:** It describes the behaviour of the malicious code. It has a very important role in the different forms the code may take.
- **Reproduction:** Malware can either reproduce or it cannot reproduce.
- **Autonomy:** The code can require human cooperation or not.
- **Infection mechanisms:** Infection means that the malicious code should access a target and infect it. However it needs to use a medium to do so. There are three ways of infection: manual installation by a human (accidental or malicious), use of removable storage media such as CD's, use of social engineering, automated infection (via a network).
- **Viral capacity:** Malware can complete executable on its own, or it can be embedded in another piece of code.
- **Defence mechanism:** Malware needs to use protective methods in order to survive; they include the following four strategies, in chronological order of creation and sophistication:
  a. **A stealth strategy:** Hiding, controlling and modifying system calls to give a false view of the system activities.
  b. **Evading detection strategy:** Encryption and polymorphism modify the code perception without changing its functions.
  c. **Disabling detection strategy:** Anti-viruses are targeted themselves by the malware.
  d. **Redundancy strategy:** Not only the superficial view of the malware changes as with polymorphism, but virus writers are creating muted forms of the malware to fight efforts of anti-virus companies.

- **Parasitism:** Characteristics of the new forms of malware. Examples include stealing network connectivity, CPU cycles, and information such as password.

Malware Growth and Propagation

According to Manfred Hung (Cybersecurity, 2004), and Alfred Huger (Avar, 2003), malicious threats have been evolving in number and in complexity. In addition, the contagion timeframe of malicious code keeps decreasing. While the contagion timeframe was measured in terms of months in the 1990's, nowadays it is expressed in minutes, and the trend shows that it will keep decreasing (see Figure 3).

Drawing an analogy with biology, Heiser (2004) remarks that two main factors contribute to the spread and propagation of malware: the size of a population and the complexity of its environment. In terms of computer, this translates into:

- The size of a population, the degree of intimacy between members of the population, and the number of common properties or characteristics.
- The more complex (and large) a code is the more prone it is to contain bugs. In addition the higher a piece of code interacts with network the more likely it is to be targeted by malware.

THE NIST RECOMMENDATIONS ABOUT MALWARE HANDLING

This part will draw from several sources with an emphasis on the Guide to malware authored by the NIST, US National Institute of Standards and Technology (Mell, 2005). The guide produces security guidelines and procedures that are vendor independent; thus weeding out any commercial conflict of interest. NIST approach to malware

Figure 3. Evolution in malware propagation time

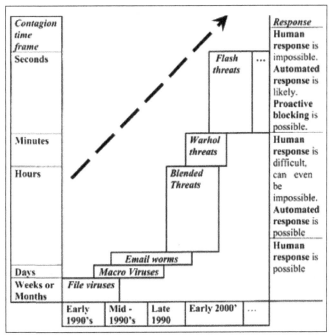

handling is based on the prevention of malware incidents, and the recovery from malware incidents. The following issues will be covered:

- Recommendations for the preventions of malicious code.
- Recommendation concerning the contingency planning process to malicious code incidents.

Malware Incident Prevention

As stated earlier, preventing malware incidents requires three complementary actions:

- Elaborating and enforcing a security policy supporting specifically the prevention of malware incidents.

- Conducting awareness and training for the end users and information technology (IT) staff.
- Mitigating vulnerabilities and threats related to malware incidents.

Security policy: An information security policy is the cornerstone on any successful information security programs. NIST recommends that the following issues be considered while elaborating an information security policy.

- Do the current security policies of the enterprise provide for preventing malicious code incidents? Both issue specific and system specific security policies should be analysed (Whitman, 2004)

Table 1. Checklist for malware prevention policy

Yes/No	Checklist for Malware Prevention Policy
	Do you scan media from outside the organization for malware before using its contents?
	Do you save e-mail file attachments, including compressed files to a local media?
	Do you then scan them before opening them?
	Do you block certain files (.exe) from being sent/received through e-mail?
	Do you block temporarily other types of files in response to impending malware threats?
	Do you restrict or limit the use of unneccessary software: • User applications (personal use of external IM, peer-to-peer file sharing services, desktop-based search engines?) • Unneeded services, services duplicating services provided by the company?
	Do you restrict the use of administrative-level privileges by users?
	Do you restrict the use of removable media particularly on systems that are high risk of infection? • Floppy • CDs • USB flash Drives
	Do you specify the type of software required for each type of system and application?
	Do you list the high-level requirements for software configuration and maintenance? • How often software is updated? • System scan scope and frequency?
	Is access to other networks, including Internet, possible only via organization-approved and secure mechanisms?
	Do you require approval through a formal process to any firewall configuration changes?
	Do you specify which types of mobile code can be used from various sources? • Internal web servers • Other organizations' Web servers

- Which categories of malicious code are presently covered by the security policies?
- What systems are covered by the malicious code policy?
- Are contractors, consultants, and business partners covered?
- Is remote access to the corporate network covered?
- Is the policy specific enough in terms of intent and scope?
- Is it general enough to allow flexibility in policy implementation?

While building your system specific policy, the following checklist (see Table 1) can be helpful when addressing malware.

Awareness: Establishing and maintaining a Information Security Education Training and Awareness (SETA) program is essential to ensure that management, end- users, and IT staff are fully aware of malware, that management and end-users are properly educated about safe use of computers, and IT staff are properly trained to recognize, prevent, and respond to malware incidents. NIST SP800-83 suggests that the following issues are investigated when designing a SETA program.

- Does the company have a (SETA) program?
- Does it cover malicious code?
- Are users aware of how malicious code spreads?
- Are users trained to prevent malicious code incidents?
- Are they trained on how to report a malware incident?
- Are all types of users covered?
- Are telecommuters covered?
- Are travelling employees in hotels, coffee shops covered?
- Are employees covered potentially use other external locations?
- Does the training and awareness program cover the security policy and procedures relative to malware?

Table 2. Recommendations for end users

Rules	Common Sense recommendations
1	Do not open suspicious e-mails attachments from unknown senders
2	Do not click on suspicious Web browser popup windows
3	Do not visit Web sites that are least somewhat likely to contain malicious code
4	Do not open files with extensions that are potentially associated with malware, example: .bat, com, ...exe, .pif. vbs
Rules	**Recommendations against phishing**
5	• Do not give financial or personal informaton to e-mail requests • Organizations should not ask for such information by e-mail. A hostile party may be monitoring the mail • You should rather call the relevant organization at their legitimate phone number, or type the organization's known Web site in a browser
6	• Do not provide **PIN** numbers or other access codes to e-mail requests • Do not provide **PIN** numbers or other access codes to suspicious or unsolicited popup windows • Provide this information into the organization legitimate Web site
7	• Do not open suspicious e-mail file atachments, even if the sender seems to be known to you • If such an e-mail is received, contact the sender, use another means of cummunication than e-mail, and confirm that he attachment is legitimate
8	• Do not answer any suspicious or unwanted e-mails • If you ask that your e-mail address be removed from a suspicious mailing list it will only confirm that your e-mail address is active, allowing the hostile party to target you with further attacks.

- Are the users trained on how to report a potential infection?
- What steps should they take to help in preventing malware incident—such as updating their antimalware software, scanning their systems regularly?
- Are users trained how they will receive notices about major malware incidents? How to distinguish between an authentic notice and a hoax?
- Are they familiar with the possible changes to the working environment such as the temporary suppression of certain services, or the blocking of certain type of e-mail attachments?

In addition, users should be provided with the following recommendations (see Table 2):

Vulnerability mitigation: The number of vulnerabilities has been steadily increasing over the years as reported by the CERT diagram (CERT, 2005), and vulnerabilities are used extensively in malware attacks. Vulnerability mitigation is crucial especially now that the time between the announcement of a new vulnerability and the first exploit keeps shrinking. According to NIST, vulnerabilities can be mitigated through patches, reconfiguration, and policies. Does the enterprise have policies, processes, procedures and tools to mitigate system potential vulnerabilities to malicious code attacks as well as reducing the threats of such attacks? What procedures, processes, and tools are used? Which should be recommended? Is the security side of applications taken into consideration?

The organization should have a vulnerability management program to answer the many challenges posed by the ever-increasing number of vulnerabilities. This is very important, because, the only element that the organisation can full controls is managing vulnerabilities; you will not be able to manage hackers, or threats; the recommendation is to mitigate threats so that malware will not exploit those vulnerabilities. NIST ap-

Table 3. NIST approaches to vulnerability management

Patch management:
 • Most frequently used mitigating approach
 • Patch management process involves several phases:
    a. Assessment if the patch is critical for your organization
    b. Analysis of the impact of applying or not applying such a patch
    c. Testing the patch
    d. Applying the patch in a controlled environment
 • Increasingly, it is difficult to deploy a patch. On one hand, the time from the announcement of a vulnerability to an attack has been reduced to a matter of days. On the other hand, testing a patch thoroughly may take weeks.
 • Patches cannot be deployed immediately organization wide. A patch has to be tested thoroughly. Deploying it may cause some systems to crash.
 • Even then, you still have to make sure that the patch is deployed on all the machines of the organization, including remote users.

Least privilege   The idea is to grant the strict minimum rights to users, processes and hosts, so that in case an incident occurs, any attempt by the malware to acquire administration privileges will be greatly reduced. It is applied on all orgainzation servers and network devices. It can also be applied to user's desktops and laptops, removing administration privileges from those systems. As a consequence, users will not be able to an update of the OS or of software applications.
Other Hardening Measures   Other measures that might reduce further malware incidents from occurring include: • Eliminate unsecured files shares; worms use them   • Disable or remove unneeded services: They may be vulnerable   • Remove and change default user ID and passwords for OS and applications: can be exploited for unauthorized accesses

Table 4. Recommendations for anti-virus selection

Tool Name: Anti-virus
- Most commonly used tool for malware mitigation
- Has become a standard rather than an option in terms of system protection
- Offered by several vendors, usually with similar features

Recommended Features	Examples
1. Scanning critical elements	• Start-up files, BIOS, boot records
2. Real-time monitoring, Dectecting suspicious activites	• Scanning all e-mails (both sent and received) for known viruses • Real-time scanning of each file that is downloaded, opened, or executed
3. Monitoring common applications	• E-mail clients. Web browsers, file transfer programs, instant messaging • Applications most commonly used to infect or to spread malware to other systems

4. Scanning files for known viruses	• Anti-software configuration should:
	  a. Scan all hard drives regularly
	  b. Provide option to scan all types of storage media
	  c. Allow the user to perform manual or on demand scanning

5. Identity all types of malware	• Viruses, worms, Trojans, malicious mobile code, blended threats, spyware • If spyware capabilities are not present, anti-spyware software must be acquired
6. Disinfecting and quarantining files	• Malware infected files are isolated for disinfections or examination • Disinfections should be the first choice • If disinfections is not possible in real-time, file should be quarantined for later disinfections

Type of malware and attack vectors addressed:
- Viruses, worms, trojans, malicious mobile code, blended threats
- Malware can spread via different ways: Storage media, network protocols, and services (e-mail, file flip, web browsing, peer-to-peer)

Methods used for detection:
- Signature identification for all known malware
- Heuristics for unknown malware, risk of false positive, false negative

Table 5. Recommendations for the implementation of anti-virus software.

Recommendations and guidelines for implementation
1. Anti-virus should be installed (with the latest signatures and anti-viruses patches) right after the operating system (OS) installation
2. Full scan should be performed right after that
3. For managed organization, redundancy and capacity planning are important
4. Solutions include: multiple anti-virus servers, preferably, OS platforms of anti-virus servers should be different from servers and workstations commonly used in organization
5. Using anti-virus products from different manufacturers for most exposed systems like e-mail servers, some vendors may deliver an anti-virus much earlier than another one
6. If multi products are used, they should be installed on separate machines as to avoid crashing problems when installed on same machine
7. Malware can spread via different ways: storage media, network protocols, and services (e-mail, file ftp, web browsing, peer-to-peer)
8. Use both network based (e-mail, and firewall scanners) and server based anti-viruses

Table 6. Recommendations for anti-virus configuration and maintenance

Recommedation and guidelines for configuration
• **Managed organizations:**
    a. Central control of anti-virus software by administrators
    b. Acquiring, testing, approving of anti-virus software, delivery of signatures, and updates are performed only by administrator
    c. The administrator periodically checks for updates and configuration settings
    d. Users not allowed modifying administrator setting of anti-virus
• **Unmanaged organization**
    a. If users have full controls of their machines, high risk of inconsistency in implementation and maintenance
    b. User's awareness is crucial: sending periodic update reminders, providing step-by-step procedures on how to keep a system up to date, on how to acquire signatures
    c. Users should be notified when new threats call for software updates
    d. Users should be encourage to automate anti-virus updates

Recommendations and guidelines for maintenance • Anti-virus software should automatically check for updates, download them, and install them
Weaknesses and shortcomings • Running more than one anti-virus product on a single system may lead to crashes • Anti-virus cannot detect unknown viruses • Window of vulnerability between the discovery of a new threat and the deployment of a new signature • Activity involving new applications may not be analyzed by anti-virus software • Activities outside the control of the organization cannot be monitored for virus activities (business partners, employees using home computers with modem or VPN Connections)

Table 7. Recommendations for anti-spyware selection

Tool Name: Spyware detection and removal Designed to identify spyware, quarantine or remove spyware files	
Features (recommended)	**Examples**
1. Monitoring applications that are most eligible to be targeted to introduce spyware	Web browsers, e-mail clients
2. Scanning periodical scans for spyware	Files, memory, configuration file
3. Identification of different types of spyware	Spyware, malicious code, tracking cookies
4. Quarantining and removing spyware	Disinfections cannnot be applied to most spyware
5. Preventing spyware installation	Popup adds, tracking cookies, browser plugins, browser hijacking
Type of malware and attack vectors addressed	Detects known threats and their variants
Methods used for detection	Use spyware signatures
Recommendations and guidelines for implementation	Use the most up to date signatures and software updates
Recommendations and guidelines for configuration	Use in combination with other antimalware tools like anti-viruses
Recommendations and guidelines for maintenance	Tools must be kepts up-to-date
Weaknesses and shortcomings	• There is no centralized management or monitoring • Some tools lack the ability for automated spyware checking or automated downloading of updates; reply on the user

Table 8. Recommendations for the selection of network-based intrusion prevention systems

Tool Name: Network-based Intrusion Prevention System (IPS) Differs from Intrusion detection systems (IDS) in that, an IPS can stop malicious activity, while an IDS cannot	
Features	• Detects attacks on networks, before they stop their targets • Sniffs packets, tantalizes them, then either allows them in or blocks them out • DDoS attack mitigation
Types of malware and attack vectors addressed	• Stops known malware threats-network service worms, e-mail borne worms, viruses • Might stop unknown threats through analysis of applications protocols
Methods used to detection	• Uses a combination of signatures and analysis of network protocol and applications
Recommendation and guidelines for implementation	• Deploying network based IPS's along the network perimeter can reduce the load generated by malware like network service worms • Should be used in combination with anti-virus software
Recommendation and guidelines for configuration	• Limiting the maximum bandwidth of network devices helps mitigate DDoS • By default Network based IPS's can detect only a few instances of malware • Administrators should use the IPS customization feature to write new attack signatures
Weaknesses and shortcomings	• Cannot stop malicious mobile code or Trojan • False positive and false negative

Table 9. Recommendations for firewall selection

Tool Name: Network firewall	
Features	**Protects from external threats**
Type of malware and attack vectors addressed	• Stops network service worms • Stops worm infections to spread from internal network to external networks
Methods used for detection	Set of rules (rule-set) dictates which traffic is allowed in/out or not
Recommendations and guidelines for implementation	Use the deny by default approach
Recommendations and guidelines for configuration	Ensure both egress and ingress filtering are activated
Recommendations and guidelines for maintenance	Firewall rule-set should be reviewed periodically
Weaknesses and shortcomings	• Peer-to-peer file sharing services and instant messaging services may not be blocked if they use port numbers dedicated to other services • Blocking port numbers may result in denial of legitimate services

proach to vulnerability mitigation is a defence in depth strategy that includes three main approaches (see Table 3): patch management, least privilege, and other hardening measures.

Threat mitigation: This activity aims at thwarting malware threats by either blocking them or detecting them. NIST recommends using the following types of security tools and procedures:

- Anti-virus software (see Tables 4, 5, and 6)
- Spyware detection and removal software (see Table 7)
- Intrusion prevention systems (see Table 8)
- Firewalls and routers (see Table 9)
- Application settings (see Table 10)

Incident Response

According to NIST (Grance, 2004), incident response handling is a set four processes aimed at:

a. Preparation or anticipation for an incident
b. Detecting and analysing an incident
c. Containing, eradicating, and recovering from the impact of incident
d. Post-incident actions.

Preparing for an incident: For an effective response to a malware incident, NIST recommends the following actions:

- Develop a set of procedures and policies specific to handling malware incidents.

Table 10. Recommendations for application settings

Common applications: Web browsers, e-mail, word processors	
Recommendations and guidelines for implementation	• In non managed environments, users's awareness is essential • In manged environments, problem related to exceptions to application setting may arise, approval is required

Recommendations and guidelines for configuration	• Usually configured by default top privilege functionality over security
	• Unneeded features should be disabled
	• Identify applications that are prone to be used by malware, applications should be configured to filter content, and block malicious looking activity
	• Specific examples:
	  a. Restrict Web browser cookies
	  b. Block Web browser popup windows
	  c. Disallow software installation in Web browsers
	  d. Block suspicious e-mail attachments
	  e. Filter Spam
	  f. Filter Web site content
	  g. Disallow automatic/loading of e-mail images
	  h. Modify file association
	  i. Limit mobile code execution
	  j. Restrict macro use
	  k. Disallow open relaying of e-mail

Recommendations and guidelines for maintenance	• Periodic review of exceptions to application settings
Weaknesses and shortcomings	• Exceptions to application settings

- Design, develop and schedule periodic exercises and training.
- Because, exposure to malware varies according to your organization specific industry, a traditional incident response team may not be enough. You should consider forming a small incident response team specifically for malware handling.
- Plan for additional secure and reliable communication channels for time of crisis so that communication and coordination amongst management, users, members of the malware incident handling team, and IT staff are maintained at an operational level.

Detecting and analysing an incident: Early detection and validation of a malware incident is crucial for an organization. On one hand, early detection will minimize the risk of a widespread infection especially with today's means of mal-

Table 11. Most likely indications of malware (Source: NIST SP800-83 (Mell, 2005))

Indications	Malware Type						Attacker Tool Type				
	Multipartite Virus	Macro Virus	Network Service Worm	Mass Mailing Worm	Trojan Horse	Malicious Mobile Code	Backdoor	Keystroke Logger	Rootkit	Malicious Browser Plug-Ins	E-mail Generators
Security Tools											
Antivirus software alerts	√	√	√	√	√	√	√	√	√	√	√
Spyware detection and removal utility alerts					√	√				√	
Network-based intrusion prevention alerts			√	√			√				
Host-based intrusion detection alerts for changes to files					√				√		
Firewall and router log entries			√				√				
Observed Host Activity											
System cannot boot	√								√		
Error message displayed during system boot	√								√		
System instability and crashes occur		√	√		√		√		√		
Programs start slowly, run slowly, or do not run at all	√	√	√		√				√	√	
Unknown processes are run at system startup					√		√	√			√
Unusual and unexpected ports open							√				
Sudden increase occurs in the number of e-mails being sent and received		√		√					√		
Changes are made in templates for word processing documents, spreadsheets, etc.		√									
Web browser configuration is changed, such as different home page and new toolbars						√				√	
Files are deleted, corrupted, or inaccessible	√	√			√				√		
Unusual items appear on the screen, such as odd messages, graphics, and overlapping or overlaid message boxes		√				√			√		√
Unexpected dialog boxes appear, requesting permission to do something						√				√	
Observed Network Activity											
Significantly increased network usage			√	√			√				√
Port scans and failed connection attempts targeted at the vulnerable service (e.g., open Windows shares, HTTP)			√				√				
Network connections between the host and unknown remote systems			√		√	√	√	√	√	√	√

ware propagation. On the other hand validation of malware incident will weed out or lessen the effects of false alerts. Both actions aim at minimizing the recovering effort and shortening the damage and down time for the organization. Having a skilled and up-to-date malware-handling team will increase the success of such an endeavour. NIST recommends the following actions:

- Monitoring malware advisories
- Reviewing data from primary sources
- Constructing trusted toolkits on removable media
- Establishing a set of prioritisation criteria

Several events can signal the potential presence of a malware incident. They can be divided into precursors and indications of malware incidents.

Precursors are signs leading to the possibility of occurrence of a malware incident in the future. To keep abreast of the latest malware threats, members of the malware incident handling team should subscribe to advisories mailing list from anti-virus vendors and organizations like the CERT- Computer Emergency Response team of Carnegie Mellon University, SANS, NPIC, National Infrastructure Protection Centre, CVE computer vulnerabilities and exposures of Mitre's corporation, etc. In some cases, the organization may also decide to pay a premium price in order to get knowledge of malware threats before the information is released to the general public.

Indications are signs leading to the conclusion that a malware may be currently occurring. Indications of malware incident are numerous and may be caused by other reasons than malware. Members of the malware team should have the necessary skills and training to review several indications of malware from several sources, correlate the data, and quickly decide if a malware incident has occurred. Indication main sources are: the users, the IT staff, and the various security tools used by the organization. Compiling these sources

into indications is not easy. The following table (Table 11) from NIST gives the most probable indications of malware incidents.

Containment of malware: There are two main issues in malware containment: stopping malware from spreading, and preventing infected systems from more damage. It is recommended that organizations establish procedures and strategies so that decisions of containment can be made as quickly as possible while taking into consideration the level of risk deemed acceptable by the organization. This is usually reflected in the decision to discontinue certain vital machines to prevent further damage and malware spreading, and to continue offering basic services to the organization customers.

NIST divides containment methods into four types:

a. Containment based on users
b. Containment based on automated detection
c. Containment based on loss of services
d. Containment based on loss of connectivity

Incident handlers should use a combination of these methods. Sound containment decisions call for the establishment of policies that state clearly who can make major containment decision, and also rules that specify under which conditions a given set of actions can be taken.

Eradication: The most commonly used eradication techniques include: anti-virus software, spyware detection and removal programs, and patch management software. NIST recommends automated methods over using manual methods such as walking in into the office where the infected system is, and using a CD with the disinfections software. Nonetheless, user participation is also recommended. If step-by-step instructions are periodically provided to users on new malware threats, the load on IT staff especially during major malware crisis will be reduced significantly.

Recovery: Recovery from a malware incident involves restoring the infected systems to their normal state of operation, and lifting any temporary containment measures taken during the incident. The restoration process should have a detailed procedure that would state how systems would be recovered, who will conduct the recovery task, who would estimate the number of labour hours that would be needed, what would be the priorities?

Lifting the temporary containment measures can be very challenging. Incident handlers must keep the containment measure in place until the number of unpatched systems and infected machine drops under such a level that any potential malware incident will have only a negligible effect. An alternative may be to use another containment measure as to continue the containment of the incident while lessening the impact on the normal operations of the organization.

The decision to restore systems as well as to lift containment measures take in consideration on one hand the risk of further damage by the malware and on the other hand the business risk associated with less functionality and less operations. Management will make the final decisions based on the technical recommendations of the malware incident handling team.

Lessons learned from malware incidents: A major malware incident may demand for the incident-handling team to work continuously on the matter for several days without rest. Even though, after the incident the major actors are drained, and would rather recuperate before writing reports on the incident, it is recommended that a review meeting be held right away while incident is still fresh. One of the main objectives of the review is to determine what lessons have been learned from the incident. They may lead to:

- Modifying the current security policies to be able to handle such incidents.
- Software may need to be reconfigured according to changes in security policies.
- Acquisitions and installation of new malware detection tools.
- Reconfigure existing malware detection tools.

FUTURE TRENDS

The previous section presented a methodology for the handling of malware. This section is dedicated to the most recent developments in malware, the future trend in malware as well as how the information security community is addressing the problem.

Professionals agree that malware is no longer produced by bragging teenagers or nerd hackers. There is an evolution towards more sophistication and skills from the hackers as well as greed. The reaction time to new vulnerabilities is a matter of days if not hours, and will eventually be measured in terms of minutes and seconds. New methods of protection such as new patch procedures and signature deployment methods are needed. In addition, recent research (Barwinski, 2005) in the field has shown that malware attackers are targeting less organizations or field of activities. But the bad news is that they are concentrating on a few fields they feel more worthwhile and lucrative. With a financial impact in the order of ten of billions, malware is no longer a nuisance or a problem on company discipline. Organizations should incorporate in their policies, issues concerning reporting malware actives to law enforcement. This section reviews the most recent trends in malware, the issues involved and how organization can fight back.

According to Nevis Network (2006), network scanning worms and mass e-mail worms and viruses have been the most forms of attacks of the last few years. Instant Messenger (IM) worms have been making their way to the top-ten list (Mannan & van Oorschot', 2005). There is a bit of good news: the ubiquitous laptop, and the ever-expending use of wireless networks (Milito, 2006). Milito describes today's enterprise as a piece of swiss cheese. The good old days of a security perimeter are gone. The trend is towards deperimeterisation (Price, 2005; Waker, 2005; Plamer, 2005). A choke point at the entrance of the network will not be able to detect wireless users accessing the corporate network through improperly configured access points, an executive connecting to the corporate office through a VPN just after a connection to an insecure network, a user bringing his laptop Monday morning after having used a public IM during the weekend, an invited speaker connecting her own laptop to your network for a crucial business deal. Worms, viruses and other types of malware would roam through your network even if you have the most expensive firewall.

In this section, we will develop a two-ladder answer to control and manage the problem: a technological answer and a human-factor answer.

A Technology-Based Answer

As we stated earlier, wireless technology and ubiquity have killed the old concept of security perimeter. Security must be based on a multilayered defence. Network worms can bypass the choke point, propagate inside the corporate network and launch attacks on other corporate networks. This brings about two issues: detection of worm propagation inside the corporate network, and their containment (Milito, 2006).

Worm detection is based on:

a. The location of the detector
b. The method used

The detector can act at the host level or the network level. It can use a set signatures to detect know worms; this approach is not effective against unknown worms. A current approach to detect unknown worm is based on behaviour of network. Such approaches look for abnormal activities within the network. They also rely on the multi-layer defense. In order to minimize the false alarms, network based worm detectors can be placed in various locations (Milito, 2006):

a. At the Internet access point (outer firewall).
b. At the internal firewalls of the enterprise.
c. Next to the hosts.

The closest the detector is to a host the more visible is the traffic generated by that host. The multilayered security approach has led to a set of solutions called UMT or Unified Management solutions to security (Bailey, 2006; Everett, 2005, Stevens, 2006). A UMT solution combines several functions into one; they include: firewall capabilities, VPN, URL filtering, spam protection, spyware protection, intrusion protection, worm protection, and intrusion prevention. In addition a UMT facility centralizes management, monitoring, and logging, simplifying the threat management task. However, this comes at a price: currently UMT is a single point of failure. In addition, many UMTs combine different security functions from different vendors into a unified application. This does not often guarantee optimal performance. Precious processor time may be wasted by processing information unnecessarily several times by different security functions since there is prior mean of communicating pertinent information from one function to the other. Another issue worth watching is how performance of a UMT is specified. Very often, no overall index is given, but rather the performance of the individual functions measured on a stand-alone basis. Most recent research, drawing again from biology, is using the concept of *Artificial Hygiene* (Talukder, 2005; Talukder, Rao, Kapoor, & Sharma, 2004) in order to detect, contain, and even eradicate malware.

A Human-Factor Answer

For Luo (2006), spyware threats are a business strategic problem whose solution not only calls for technical safeguards and procedures but also nontechnical or managerial solutions. The behaviour of end users can play an important role in minimizing the risk of being the breach through which malware enters the corporate network. Users' behaviour cannot be controlled even if by the best armada technology can offer. Eventually a user will receive e-mail messages, opens them up, read them, open attachments, surf the web, connect his wireless machine to an unsecured access point, download files, access peer-to-peer networks from home, disable his laptop firewall or anti-virus in order to get connected easily (Fulton, 2006). More recently we have seen an outbreak in IM worms. Restricting or disallowing certain Internet services during normal times can be counterproductive for the enterprise. Very often, users do not intend any harm in their risky behaviour. The sad truth is that they most probably are unaware of the risks. Some users even may think that security is not their concern. Theirs is to get the job done; security is a task for IT or for the INFOSEC team. This is the conclusion of a survey from Deloit Touche Tohmatsu (Fulton, 2006). The survey showed that a combination of sophisticated threats and lack user's awareness led to exploitable vulnerabilities.

An awareness program for end-user should aim at the following:

- Make users fully aware of what the enterprise information security and privacy policy states so that they adjust their behaviour and computing activities to comply with the policy or rather to avoid violating the policy.
- Make users become responsible on how to surf the internet, and on what types of software reside on their computer.

- Make users willingly refrain from downloading software from unknown Web sites.
- Make users willingly avoid using peer-to-peer programs.

CONCLUSION

This chapter presented the current guidelines to the handling of malware incidents. It covers three main aspects of malware incidents: the prevention of malware incidents, the recovery from malware incidents, and the future trends in malware. Preventing malware incidents is based on three main actions: elaborating a security policy specific to preventing the occurrence of malicious incidents, establishing awareness programs for the end-users and the IT staff, and establishing a robust incident response capability to handle malware. The recovery process includes four phases: preparation, detection and analysis, containment, recovery, and post incident analysis. Recommendations drawn from the guidelines developed by NIST were summarized and highlighted for an easier application by professional on the field. Current trends in malicious code show that the information security community should be more proactive than ever in its battle with malware writers who are becoming more and more sophisticated technically, and also greedier than ever.

REFERENCES

Anonymous. (2005). *Malware report: The impact of malicious code attacks.* Retrieved on July 7, 2006, from http://www.computereconomics.com/article.cfm?id=1090

Bailey, D. (2006). Versatile appliance guards branches. *IT Week, 9*(4), 27.

Barwinski, M. A. (2005). *Taxonomy of spyware and empirical study of network drive-by-down-*

load. Unpublished doctoral dissertation, Naval Postgraduate School, Monterey, California.

Crutchfield, S. (n.d.). Outsmarting the malware. *EDPACS, 2006*(33), 18-20.

Duham, K. (2006). The problem with P2P. *EDPACS, 2006*(33), 9-13.

Egan, M. (2005). *The executive guide to information security.* Indianapolis, IN: Addison-Wesley.

Erbeschloe, M. (2005). *A computer security professional's guide to malicious code.* Oxford, England: Elsevier.

Everett, C. (2005). Ready for take-off? *Infosecurity Today, 2*(6), 44-5.

Fulton, J. (2006). Saving users from themselves. *EDPACS, 2006*(33), 20-21.

Gilliland, A. (2006). Understanding the IM security threat. *EDPACS, 2006*(33), 1-7.

Gordon, S. (2006). Fighting spyware and adware in the enterprise. *EDPACS , 2006*(33), 14-18.

Grance, T. (2004). *Computer security incident handling guide* (Special Publication 800-61). U.S. Department of Commerce, National Institute of Standards.

Hoefelmeyer, R. (2004). Malicious code: The threat, detection and protection. In H. F.Tipton & N. Krause (Eds.), *Information security management handbook.* Raton, FL: CRC Press.

Kay, J. (2005). Low volume viruses: New tools for criminals. *Network Security, 2005*(6), 16-18.

Landesman, M. (2005, November). Best defenders. *PC World.*

Licari, J. (2006). Protecting the information workplace. *EDPACS , 2006*(33), 13-20.

Mannan, M., & van Oorschot' (2005, November). On instant messaging worms, analysis and coun-termeasures. In *Proceedings of the 2005 ACM Workshop on Rapid Malcode.*

Microsoft. (2005).Retrieved on July 7, 2006, from http://www.microsoft.com/athome/security/spy-warewhat.msx

Milito, R. A. (2006). The inside-out approach to infection control. *EDPACS, 2006*(33), 9-14.

Nevis Network. (2006). *Stopping malware spread from untrusted hosts.* Retrieved July 7, 2006, from http://www.nevisnetworks.com

Paquette, J. (2000). *A history of viruses.* Retrieved July 7, 2006, from http://www.securityfocus.com/infocus/1286

Park J. S. (2005). Security analyses for enterprise instant messenger (EIM) systems. *EDPACS, 2005*(32), 8-24.

Peter, M. (2005). *Guide to malware incident prevention and handling* (Special Publication, pp. 800-83). U.S. Department of Commerce, National Institute of Standards.

Plamer, G. (2005). De-peremetrization: Benefits and limitations. *Information Security Technical Report 2005*(10), 189-203.

Price, G. (2005). Editorial: The security perimeter. *Information Security Technical Report, 2005*(10), 185.

Primode. (2005). *Information security glossary.* Retrieved July 7, 2006, from www.primode.com/glossary.html

Savage, S., & Voelker, G. M. (2004). *NSF cybertrust center proposal: Center for Internet epidemiology and defenses.*

Slade, R. M. (2004). Malware and computer viruses. In H. F. Tipton & N. Krause (Eds.), *Information security management handbook.* Raton, FL: CRC Press.

Stevens, M. (2006). UTM: One-stop protection. *Network Security, 2006*(2), 12-14.

Sunner, M. (2005). E-mail security best practice. *Network Security, 2005*(12), 4-6.

Szor, P . (2005). *The art of computer virus research and defense.* Upper Saddle River, NJ: Addison-Wesley.

Talukder, A. K. (2005). Clean and tidy. *Communications Engineer, 3*(4),38-41.

Talukder, A. K., Rao V. B., Kapoor, V., & Sharma, D. (2004). Artificial hygiene: A critical step towards safety from e-mail viruses. In *Proceedings of the IEEE INDICON 2004,* 484-489.

Viveros, S. (2005). Changing malware threats-AV vendors's view. *Network Security, 2005*(12), 16-18.

Waker, J. (2005). The extended security perimeter. *Information Security Technical Report, 2005*(10), 220-227.

Whitman, M. E., & Mattord, H. J. (2004). Management of information security. *Course Technology.*

Wikipedia. (2005). The free encyclopedia. Retrieved on July 7, 2006, from http://en.wikipedia.org/wiki/Mobile_code

Section IV
Risk Management

Chapter XIV
Security Risk Management Methodologies

Francine Herrmann
University of Metz, France

Djamel Khadraoui
CRP Henri Tudor, Luxembourg

ABSTRACT

This chapter provides a wide spectrum of existing security risk management methodologies. The chapter starts presenting the concept and the objectives of enterprise risk management. Some exiting security risk management methods are then presented by showing the way to enhance their applications to enterprise needs.

INTRODUCTION

Enterprise **risk management** is the total process of identifying, measuring, and minimizing the uncertain events that can affect the enterprise resources. This implies the process of bringing management as a remedial action, and control into the risk analysis. A main element of risk assessment and analysis is the concept of **vulnerability**. The **vulnerability** is a weakness in any information system, system security procedure, internal controls, or implementation that an attacker could potentially exploit. It can also be a weakness in

a system, such as a coding bug or design flaw. An attack occurs when an attacker with a reason to strike takes advantage of a **vulnerability** to **Threat**en an enterprise **Asset**. The second most important element in risk assessment is the concept of a **Threat**, which is any circumstance or event with the potential to adversely impact an information system through unauthorized access, destruction, disclosure, modification of data, or denial of service. We can define risk as the possibility that a particular **Threat** will adversely impact an information system by exploiting a particular **Vulnerability**. The third element in the risk analysis is the **Countermeasure** or lack thereof. A **Countermeasure** is an action, device, procedure, technique, or other measure that reduces risk to an information system. Consequently, the residual risk is the portion of risk remaining after a **Countermeasure** is applied. Residual risk could be of none if a perfect **Countermeasure** exists.

The enterprise information systems security requires controlling the whole techniques and methods used to reduce the risks on the potential related vulnerabilities and **Threat**s. The risks analysis consists in decreasing those on an acceptable level in order to be supported by the enterprise. Successful risk analysis is however nothing more than a business-level decision-support tool, which is a way of gathering the requisite data to make a good judgment call based on knowledge about vulnerabilities, **Threat**s, impacts, and probability.

The risk analysis must thus be coordinated within a well-defined strategy. An organization can reduce the risk to an acceptable level by enhancing its security as well as by sensitizing the personnel and the trade partners as for their responsibilities with regard to the underlined strategies. Security may also contribute to the results of an enterprise insofar as the customers appreciate the reliability of a supplier.

To solve these issues, the answer is not only by mastering the technical solutions that ensure, for instance, system and data confidentiality and integrity, maintaining the safety of networks (firewall, IDS, etc.), controlling the security of the Web applications, updating protections against the attacks and to ensuring the personnel training and sensitizing. These technical skills are essential and must be planned, organized and be structured by using **risk management** methodologies. The concept and objectives of these are presented in the following.

ENTERPRISE SECURITY RISK MANAGEMENT: CONCEPTS AND OBJECTIVES

As a corpus, traditional methodologies are varied and view risk from different perspectives. Examples of basic approaches include the following:

- Financial loss methodologies that seek to provide a loss figure to balance against the cost of implementing various controls.
- Mathematically derived "risk ratings" that equate risk with arbitrary ratings for **Threat**, probability, and impact.
- Qualitative assessment techniques that base risk assessment on anecdotal or knowledge-driven factors.

Each basic approach has distinctly different merits, but they almost all share some valuable concepts that should be considered in any risk analysis. We can capture these commonalities in a set of basic definitions:

- The **Asset**, or object of the protection efforts, can be a system component, data, or even a complete system.
- The risk, the probability that an **Asset** will suffer an event of a given negative impact, is determined from various factors: the ease of executing an attack, the attacker's motivation and resources, a system's existing vulnerabilities, and the cost or impact in a particular business context.
- The **Threat**, or danger source, is invariably the danger a malicious agent poses and that agent's motivations (financial gain, prestige, and so on). **Threat**s manifest themselves as direct attacks on system security.
- The **vulnerability** is a defect or weakness in system security procedure, design,

implementation, or internal control that an attacker can compromise. It can exist in one or more of the components making up a system, even if those components aren't necessarily involved with security functionality. A given system's **vulnerability** data are usually compiled from a combination of OS and application level **vulnerability** test results, code reviews, and higher-level architectural reviews. Software vulnerabilities come in two basic flavors: flaws due to the design-level problems, or bugs related to the implementation level problems. Automated scanners tend to focus on bugs, since human expertise is required for uncovering flaws.

- The **Countermeasure**s or safeguards are the management, operational, and technical controls prescribed for an information system that, taken together, adequately protect the system's confidentiality, integrity, and availability as well as its information. For every risk, a designer can put controls in place that either prevent or (at a minimum) detect the risk when it triggers.

- The impact on the organization, were the risk to be realized, can be monetary or tied to reputation, or it might result in the breach of a law, regulation, or contract. Without a quantification of impact, technical **vulnerability** is hard to handle, especially when it comes to mitigation activities.

- Probability is the likelihood that a given event will be triggered. In most cases, probability calculation is extremely rough. Although they start with these basic definitions, risk methodologies usually diverge on how to arrive at specific values. Many methods calculate a nominal value for an information **Asset**, and attempt to determine risk as a function of loss and event probability. Others rely on checklists of **Threat**s and vulnerabilities to determine a basic risk measurement.

The calculation of the financial impact of the disasters or incidents is not carried out in the majority of the cases; the security return on investment (ROI) is often not calculated. Some organizations that want to calculate the ROI would in addition be confronted with a lack for indicators, rigorous methodologies, standards and tools of benchmark and simulation. Consequently, it is then necessary to improve the processes of management and control of the risks related to the assurance in the enterprises by the following some recommendations like described in the following:

- Define a security policy and a security charter.
- Compare the estimated losses in case of disaster with regard to the cost of the implemented continuity plan that has to be defined and validated.
- Supervise the security level and define the indicators and rigorous methodologies of control.

The **risk management** is the first stage that has to be realized in the development of the security policy. The actual enterprise security management requires the ability to:

- Applying the ISO 17799 (ISO17799, 2000) standard that recommends that the risk analysis should be undertaken in order to determine the needs for security and to choose the security measures to be implemented;
- Using the methodological approaches based on the **risk management** and mainly the risk analysis ones.
- Mastering the audit methodologies.
- Building the continuity plans.
- Take into account of the legal risks related to the information system.

RISK MANAGEMENT METHODOLOGIES

The **risk management** is defined by the ISO (ISO/IEC Guide, 2002) as a whole of a coordinated activities aiming to control an organization with respect to the risk. We mainly have three finalities regarding the enterprise information system **risk management**:

- Improving the security of the information system.
- Justifying the budget allocated with the security of the information system.
- Proving the credibility of the information system using the analyses carried out.

Bosworth (2002) considers that the risks can be divided into five categories as described in the following:

- The risks that have a weak occurrence and impact are neglected.
- The risks having a strong occurrence and an important impact should not exist, otherwise there is actually a big problem concerning the enterprise business activities.
- The risks that have a strong occurrence and a weak impact that are accepted, the related cost is generally included in the operational costs of the organization (acceptance of the risk).
- The risks having a weak occurrence and a heavy impact should be transferred.
- The other risks, that represent most of the cases, are treated on a case-by-case basis and are in the center of the **risk management** process; the objective is basically to decrease the risks by mitigating the risk using necessary controls.

Example risk-analysis methodologies for software usually fall into two basic categories: commercial (including Microsoft's STRIDE, Sun's ACSM/SAR, Insight's **CRAMM**, and Cigital's SQM) and standards based (from the National Institute of Standards and Technology's **ASSET** or the Software Engineering Institute's (**OCTAVE**, 1999), or (**EBIOS**, 2004), and (**MEHARI**, 2004). An in-depth analysis of all existing methodologies is beyond the scope of this chapter, but we'll give a short description of some of them looking at basic common features, and at potentially some relative strengths and weaknesses.

The objective of any risk analysis is the identification and the estimate of each component of the risk (**Threat**/**vulnerability**/impact), in order to evaluate the risk and to appreciate its level, in order to take the adequate measures. The risk identification process is achieved either by carrying out an audit of the system and its various actors (as recommended in (**OCTAVE**, 1999), or starting from the existing knowledge bases (like in (**EBIOS**, 2004) and in (**MEHARI**, 2004).

Some of these methodologies will be presented in the following sections.

CRAMM

General information

The CCTA risk analysis and management method (**CRAMM**) method has been created by the UK government and is commonly used in commonwealth countries and within NATO (**CRAMM**).

Description of the Method

Today most current risk analysis methodologies start with identifying and valuing **Asset**s, followed by identifying **Threat**s likely to occur to them with related vulnerabilities. Finally risk is determined for combinations of identified **Asset**s, **Threat**s and vulnerabilities to propose appropriate **Countermeasure**s.

During this process two different measurement schemes can be applied to risk elements; quantitative or qualitative. Quantitative approach articulates risk in numerical terms, i.e. expected monetary loss and probability (e.g., annual loss expectancy, or ALE). Qualitative approach has no numeric value and is usually opinion based. Results are summarized in words like "low", "medium" and "high."

CRAMM is a qualitative risk analysis associated with a management tool. The tool, which has undergone major revisions (currently in Version 4), is later commercialized and now distributed by a UK firm, Insight Consulting, as "**CRAMM** Manager" (alongside the U.K. Security Service).

The essential elements of data collection, analysis and output results that should be present in an automated risk analysis tool are covered in the three stages of a **CRAMM** review:

- Identifying and valuing **Asset**s.
- Identifying **Threat**s and vulnerabilities, calculating risks.
- Identifying and prioritizing **Countermeasure**s.

Identification and Valuation of Assets

Asset values to an organization are central in determining the risks and the required security level. Three types of **Asset**s are identified: data, application software and physical **Asset**s (i.e., equipment, buildings, staff; assessed with locations where appropriate). With **CRAMM** all interrelated **Asset**s, including end user services to differentiate the processing of data (e.g., e-mail, interactive session, Web browsing), can be defined in **Asset** models, which can reflect business processes. Modeling is one of the most critical issues in using the tool, since too fine granularity here may unnecessarily extend the review process, while a too coarse one may miss important **Asset**s causing misleading results. The valuation of information **Asset**s is regarded sometimes as a speculative activity, since it depends on who (e.g., sensitive information in hands of a competitor or a script-kiddie) and when (e.g., expiring passwords) possesses them. In **CRAMM** the reviewer conducts interviews with "data owners" (e.g., business unit managers) to value data **Asset**s, which raises the level of organizational acceptance of the review. This part of valuation is more difficult, since it may be hard to identify data (or business process) owners or the interviewees may need some guidance for estimations, which may also be regarded as an awareness process.

Values are derived from the impacts of breaches of confidentiality, integrity, availability and nonrepudiation, the widely accepted principles of information security. The interviewees describe reasonable worst-case scenarios and outline the

Figure 1. CRAMM method steps

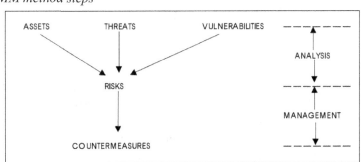

possible consequences of data being unavailable (e.g., for several time frames between "less than 15 minutes" and "2 months and over"), destroyed (e.g., loss of data since last backup), disclosed (to insiders, contracted service providers or outsiders) or modified (e.g., keying errors, misrouting, insertion of false messages).

The defined severity of impacts is then compared to an appropriate guideline (e.g., "financial loss/disruption to activities") provided by the tool to derive an **Asset** value within the scale of 1 to 10. The customizable range of values (e.g., "1" for "losses of $1000 or less", "2" for "losses of between $1000 and $10,000", etc.) defined in the guidelines avoids the difficulty of making single-point estimates. For financial loss scenarios, the actual financial loss can also be assessed.

Threat and Vulnerability Assessment

In addition to **Asset** values, the other two key components of a **CRAMM** risk analysis are levels (likelihoods of occurring) of **Threat** and **vulnerability**. **Threat**s and vulnerabilities are investigated against selected **Asset** groups, which are put together to stay in reasonable review time frames. **CRAMM** has predefined tables for **Threat/Asset** group and **Threat**/impact combinations. An exhaustive assessment of every **Threat** to every **Asset** group does not make sense and is not feasible, so the reviewer chooses here suitable **Threat**s and **Asset**s according to customer needs. On the **vulnerability** front, it should be noted that **CRAMM** is targeting a managerial level risk assessment, thus detailed technical, system specific vulnerabilities which may be identified by **vulnerability** scanners are not addressed by the tool.

There are two ways to assess **Threat**s and vulnerabilities: 'full' and 'rapid' risk assessment. In the recommended full risk assessment, **Threat**s and vulnerabilities are identified by asking questions to support personnel (e.g., system or network administrators) from structured questionnaires and entering the answers in the tool, after which **CRAMM** calculates levels of **Threat** to **Asset**s on a five point scale of "Very Low, Low, Medium, High or Very High" as well as levels of **vulnerability** to **Threat**s on a scale of "Low, Medium or High". The likelihood element is implied in the questions for assessing **Threat**s and vulnerabilities.

Risk Calculation

CRAMM calculates risks for each **Asset** group against the **Threat**s to which it is vulnerable on a scale of 1 to 7 using a risk matrix with predefined values by comparing **Asset** values to **Threat** and **vulnerability** levels. On this scale, "1" indicates a low-level baseline security requirement and "7" indicates a very high security requirement.

The system can report the findings that should be presented to the management for agreement and approval to proceed to the **risk management** phase. At that stage a review meeting with the management should concentrate on major findings like high **Threat/vulnerability** areas (which should be reviewed before for discrepancies, e.g., with "backtrack" facility of the tool-based on estimation or input errors), which also contributes to awareness.

Risk Management

Based on the findings of the risk analysis, **CRAMM** produces a set of **Countermeasure**s applicable to the system or network that are considered necessary to manage the identified risks. The recommended security profile will then be compared to the existing **Countermeasure**s to identify areas of weakness or over provision.

CRAMM's large selection of **Countermeasure**s (almost 4,000) are collected together in groups and subgroups, which have the same 'security aspect' as hardware, software, communications, procedural, physical, personnel and environment. They are also arranged in a hierarchical structure, being in three different categories, from high-level security objectives to detailed examples of implementation.

This way one of the critics against this generation of tools, i.e., the ignorance of cost and efficiency evaluation of **Countermeasure**s while focusing on **Asset** value, is covered by **CRAMM** to some degree (a traditional cost/benefit analysis is not offered, as regarded not applicable due to the intangible nature of risk).

This way one of the critics against this generation of tools, i.e., the ignorance of cost and efficiency evaluation of **Countermeasure**s while focusing on **Asset** value, is covered by **CRAMM** to some degree (a traditional cost/benefit analysis is not offered, as regarded not applicable due to the intangible nature of risk).

EBIOS

General Information

EBIOS is a French acronym meaning Expression of Needs and Identification of Security Objectives (**EBIOS**, 2004). The method formalizes an approach for assessing and treating risks in the field of information systems security. It has been created by the French INFOSEC agency (DCSSI) and is commonly used for the analysis of French military and governmental information systems.

Presentation of the Approach

The method is performed in five steps, shown in Figure 2.

Step 1. Context Study
The purpose of this essential step is to identify the target system in global terms and position it in its environment so that the target of the security study can be accurately determined.

In particular, it allows the issues at stake for the system to be specified, together with the con-

Figure 2. EBIOS method steps

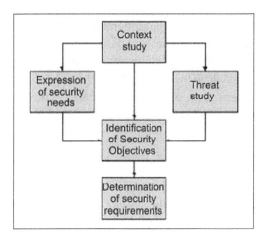

text in which it is used, the missions or services it must provide and the means used. It is also the stage at which all the information required for planning the study is collected.

After this step, the field of investigation for the study is clearly marked out, the assumptions, obligations and constraints are identified and the subjects to be dealt with are known.

Step 2. Expression of Security Needs
This step contributes to risk estimation and definition of risk criteria. It also allows system users to express their security needs for the functions and information they handle.

The expression of security needs results from the operational requirements of the system, independently of any technical solution.

It is based on the preparation and use of a scale of needs and the detection of impacts that are unacceptable for the organization.

The expression of needs is also used to define system's operating mode, i.e. the general manner in which system users are managed.

Step 3. Threat Study
This step contributes to risk assessment. Its purpose is to determine the **Threat**s affecting the

system. These **Threat**s are formalized by identifying their components: the attack methods to which the organization is exposed, the **Threat** agents that may use them, the vulnerabilities exploitable on the system entities and their level.

The **Threat**s highlighted through this step are specific to the system. Their characterization is independent of the security needs, information processed and functions supported by the system.

Step 4. Identification of Security Objectives

The purpose of this step is to evaluate and treat the risks affecting the system.

The comparison of **Threat**s with security needs highlights the risks to be covered by the security objectives. These security objectives constitute the security specifications for the target system and its environment. They must be consistent with all the assumptions, constraints, regulatory references and security rules identified during the study. The level of security objectives and the assurance level must also be determined during this step.

Step 5. Determination of Security Requirements

The purpose of this step is to determine how to achieve the security objectives, i.e. how to treat the risks affecting the system. This requires determining: the security functional requirements describing the required security behavior and designed to satisfy the security objectives as formulated in the previous step, and the security assurance requirements forming the grounds for confidence that the product or system satisfies its security objectives. These requirements are established especially on the basis of functional and assurance components proposed by ISO 15408 (2004).

OCTAVE

General Information

The Operationally Critical **Threat**, **Asset**, and **Vulnerability** Evaluation (**OCTAVE**, 1999) is a **risk-management** approach proposed by the Software Engineering Institute that is popular in the United States.

Description of the Method

The **OCTAVE** method is a human centric approach that looks on the organizational and technical aspects to derive the security risks and the subsequent security needs of an organization. The core investigation mechanism within OCATVE are workshops where:

a. Various members of the organization discuss security problems.
b. Or the analysis teams condense, complete and interpret the results derived in the previous case (a).

During the workshops human knowledge about the organizational **Asset**s, **Threat**s, vulnerabilities and subsequent risks is derived. The workshops build on checklists included in the OCATVE method with a clear emphasis on the importance of human creativity to complete these checklists and in that way to cope with variation and dynamics common in modern organizations. To be able to make decisions qualitative values are elucidated during workshops. Those values are used to calculate risk values and derive a security strategy.

To overcome the problem of a snapshot view on the organization's security risks, which is inherent in all common evaluation methods,

OCTAVE assumes that a continuous management cycle of the form: Identify → Analyze → Plan → Implement → Monitor → Control is used. **OCTAVE**, however, covers only the first three phases of this cycle.

Process

The approach is a three-phases process with a dedicated preparation phase – see Figure 3. We will briefly describe each phase. It is important to note that **OCTAVE** is assumed to be non linear and requires an iterative approach where initial decisions are revisited. In that way **OCTAVE** supports stepwise refinement during evaluation to handle complexity via multiple feedback loops.

Preparation

In the beginning senior management sponsorship is sought. Then the analysis team is formed, the scope of evaluation defined and suitable participants for the organizational inputs selected.

Phase 1. Build Asset-Based Threat Profiles
The first three activities in this phase are meant to derive knowledge from senior management,

middle management and staff. The purpose is to identify **Asset**s and their priority, identify security requirements for the critical **Asset**s and learn the used security practices. In the fourth activity the analysis team consolidates and refines this information to create a common **Threat** profile.

Phase 2. Identify Infrastructure Vulnerabilities
This phase starts with investigating the technical infrastructure to identify critical components for which technical weaknesses have to be evaluated. The next activity is to evaluate these components by means of tests (with **vulnerability** evaluation tools) and reviews to learn the security vulnerabilities.

Phase 3. Develop Security Strategy and Plans
Based on the results of the previous phases a risk analysis is conducted as the first activity. For that purpose the impacts of **Threat**s to critical **Asset**s are identified and evaluated. This risk information serves as input for the development of the protection strategy. Subsequently this information is presented to the sponsoring senior management.

Figure 3. The octave method [Alberts02]

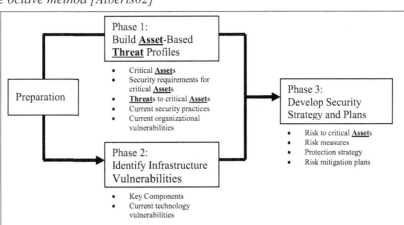

MEHARI

General Information

MEHARI is derived from two other methods of analysis of risks (MARION and MELISA). **MEHARI** is maintained in France by the CLUSIF (French Information System Security Club) (**MEHARI**, 2004).

Aims of MEHARI

MEHARI provides a pattern, methods and an important knowledge bases in order to be able to answer the following fundamental questions:

- What are my major stakes?
- What are my vulnerabilities?
- What are my risks and what is their gravity level?
- What should I develop to drive my security?

Based on several risk evaluation methods developped in the 80s, **MEHARI** followed the evolution of the IT world towards openess, and focuses not only on **vulnerability** discovery but on the correlation between the identified risks and the impact of any exploit of a **vulnerability**.

The **MEHARI** method evaluates each **vulnerability** in regards to the danger and focusses on the more dangerous (risky) one from a business perpective.

This concept is highlighted in Figure 4 extracted from **MEHARI** documentation.

The MEHARI Process

The process consists of three phases, summarized in Figure 5. Each substep corresponds to a **MEHARI** module that can be applied separately if needed. The method is formal and based on ISO 13335 model for **risk management**. The compatibility with the ISO 17799:2000 is claimed.

ENTERPRISE SECURITY MANAGEMENT RECOMMENDATIONS

We highlight here recommendations that will be able to improve the usage of enterprise security management methodologies.

Auditing

The audit is one of the important steps that have to follow in the perspective of enhancement of

Figure 4. Vulnerabilities and impacts correlation

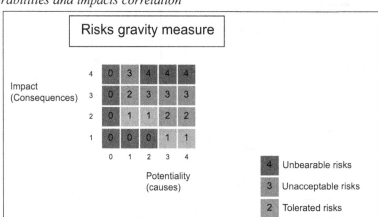

Figure 5. The MEHARI process

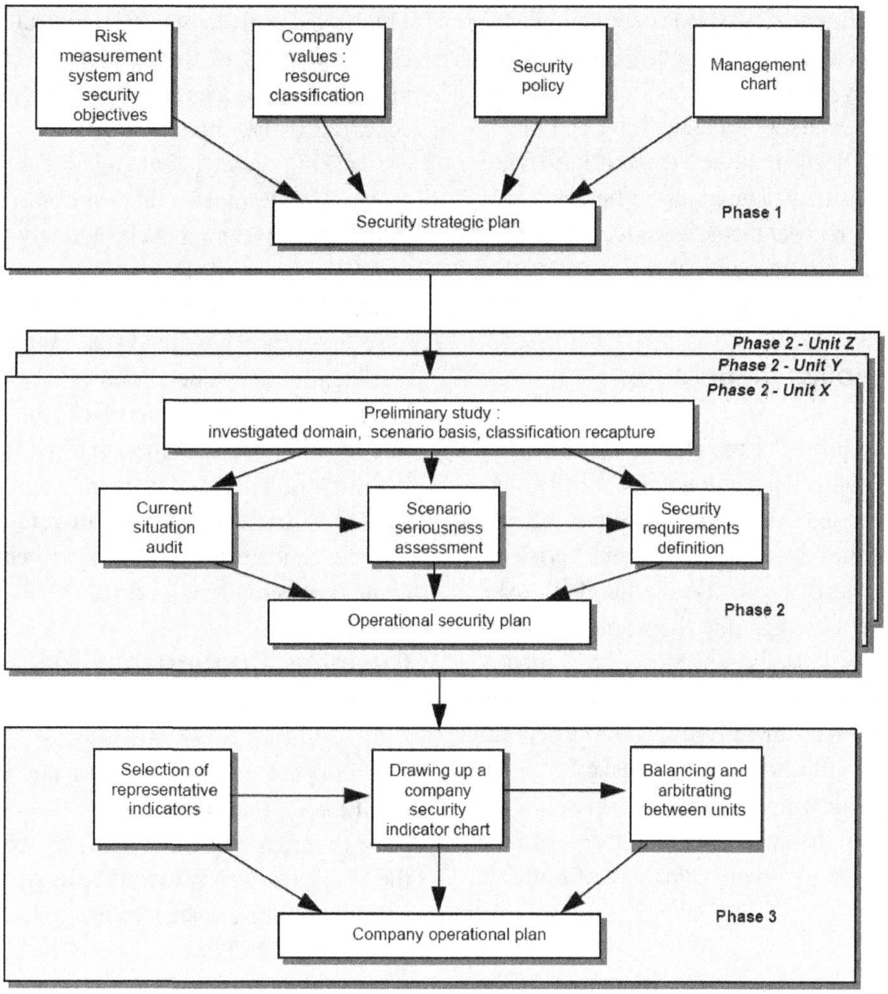

security management of the enterprise. Actually, all risk-analysis methods presented here in this chapter help to lead detailed security audits. The aim of the audits elaboration is to be able to identify the security level of the system, as well as the vulnerabilities of its components. These security audits are generally carried out by specialized organizations external to the enterprise.

We distinguish here two main types of audits: technical and organizational. The technical security audit permits to have a complete view

of the security at the technical level (system requirements, vulnerabilities of the networks, etc.). This is mainly known as preventive audit, which is very useful, for instance, when making online a Web site or when making a company network into production. This kind of audit includes also programs source code of online applications of whatever programming language used. The organizational audit permits to evaluate the general security of the organization including the physical security, organizational security, the achievements, the production, the exploitation, as well as the communications in more general.

Based on the audit, two basic of recommendations have to be established in order to make the information system more secure by highlighting its strengths and its weaknesses. The first one is related to the security policy elaboration and to the setup of security monitoring and supervision, which should respect the actual security policy. The second recommendation is mainly related to the business contingency plan elaboration.

Security Policy Elaboration

The security policy is basically a document of some pages describing the general security policy of the enterprise. This written document should clearly state the engagement of the enterprise regarding the way that security solutions have to be implemented with regard to the wanted security level to apply. This also shows to the company that there is an accepted risk taken in relationship to the estimated business values of the system for which the security policy is established.

The document must be written in close cooperation with the management of the corporate because it gathers some valuable information such as:

- Stakes of the enterprise with respect to the information systems (availability of IS, given confidential or sensitive, risk of public image).
- Existing **Threat**s (related to the business, the regulation, etc.) and induced risks.
- Main security measures taken (sensitizing and training, organizational and technical actions, continuity of activity, etc.).

This document has to enclose the security charter in how using the information security of the company. This has to integrate the rights and duties of each employee and the sanctions, incurred in case of nonrespect of these rules.

Monitoring and Supervising Security

This is basically a security control activity of IT components of the enterprise. This is very important to manage security by monitoring and checking if the implemented security solutions are working correctly with respect to the security policy. The attempts of intrusion and attack to the information system must be actively supervised. Moreover, most of the attacks are not explicitly visible. In fact, monitoring security is a way to have assurance on the system and gives more confidence. The supervision of an environment gives the best chances to detect the attacks but this requires the definition and the follow-up in real time of security levels indicators. It is also needed to use specialized software application in order to identify any improper behaviors that could correspond to the risk.

Business Contingency Plan Elaboration

The purpose of the business continuity plan (**BCP**) is to guarantee the survival of the enterprise by preparing in advance the continuity of the activities already identified as strategic to the enterprise. The disaster recovery plan (**DRP**) is a subset of the **BCP**, which covers the IT resources. It guarantees the functioning (after incident) of critical IT components in a fixed minimum time, with a fixed minimum loss of information data. To be able to define these plans, it is crucial for the company to identify the objectives of continuity related to the crucial activities and the critical operations, which will not have to be stopped. It is then necessary to define the procedures of the **BCP**, which will have to be carried out by specifying the necessary IT and human resources. This mainly requires an establishment of a hierarchical representation of the critical operations and a definition of the priorities specifying the order of restoring the system and data. It is also essential to regularly test and maintain the **BCP** and the

DRP so that they will be fully operational when the incident event occurs.

CONCLUSION

Risk analysis is, at best, a good general-purpose by which we can judge an enterprise information systems security. Because most of security problems are the result of design flaws, performing a risk analysis is an important part of a solid information-system security. The risk-analysis process is continuous and applies to many different levels, at once identifying system-level vulnerabilities, assigning probability and impact, and determining reasonable mitigation strategies. By considering the resulting ranked risks, business stakeholders can determine how to manage particular risks and what the most cost effective controls might be.

REFERENCES

Bosworth, S., & Kabay, M. E. (2002). Computer security handbook (4th ed.). Wiley.

CRAMM. *CCTA risk analysis and management method (version 5)*. Retrieved from http://www.cramm.com/

EBIOS. (2004, February). *Expression of needs and identification of security objectives*. Retrieved from http://www.ssi.gouv.fr/fr/confiance/ebio-spresentation.html

ISO 15408. (2004). *Information technology—Security techniques—Evaluation criteria for IT security (Common Criteria), International Organization for Standardization (version 2.2, ISO 15408)*. Retrieved from http://www.commoncriteriaportal.org

ISO 17799. (2000). *Code of practice for information security management* (ISO/IEC 17799:2000). International Organization for Standardization.

ISO/IEC. (2002).Risk management–Vocabulary–Guidelines for use in standards. *ISO/IEC Guide, 73*.

MEHARI. (2004, December). *Harmonized method for risks analysis: Principles and mechanisms (CLUSIF, version 3)*. Retrieved from http://www.clusif.asso.fr/fr/production/mehari

OCTAVE. (1999, June). *Operationally critical threat, asset and vulnerability evaluation (version 2.0)*. Retrieved from http://www.cert.org/octave/methods

Chapter XV
Information System
Life Cycles and Security

Albin Zuccato
University of Karlstad, Sweden

ABSTRACT

Organizations are required by legal provision to include information system security into their day-to-day management activities. To do this effectively and efficiently, it is necessary that information security management integrates into the overall system life cycle. Here I will present a system life cycle and suggest which aspects of security should be covered at which life cycle stage of the system. Based on this, I will present a process framework that due to its iterativity and detailedness accommodates the needs for life cycle oriented security management.

INTRODUCTION

Organizations have become more and more dependent on their information processing system. This fact is also acknowledged by recent legal regulations (e.g., BASEL II, 2005; Sarbanes-Oxley Act, 2002), and these legal provisions therefore mandate that organizations deal (among others) with the security of their information-processing systems. It is commonly agreed that it is better to build security into the system from the beginning and not add it to the running system (ISO17799, 2000). Many people assume that this makes it easier to achieve more effective and efficient security because it smoothly integrates into the overall system and builds a natural whole. To achieve built-in security, which satisfies the regulative demands, it is necessary to integrate security considerations into the system life cycle. It is important to note that it is not sufficient to integrate security only in the development but in all phases of the system life cycle.

I have used the concept of system, which is unfortunately not unambiguous, and a further discussion is therefore needed in order to clarify what I mean by a system. According to Schoderbek, Schoderbek, and Kefalas (1990), a system is *"a set of objects together with relationships between the objects and between their attributes connected or related to each other and to their environment in such a manner as to form an entirety or whole."* An information processing system not only contains the technical objects (i.e., the computers and the software) but also includes the organizational objects (i.e., structures and procedures); only together do they form the whole, which is necessary to process the information. As the definition also suggests, the object-interdependencies are of great importance and have to be cared for actively.

Such a system is inherently complex due to the large number of objects and object relations. To deal with the complexity, it is necessary to have structured processes that can handle different objects and their relation as well as specifically provide for complexity management. In addition, the process has to deal with the high degree of uncertainty due to environmental changes, which are common in modern IT-based systems. According to PMI (2000) it is thus common to divide the process into smaller phases that together form the life cycle. This allows for easier management by following the "divide and conquer" philosophy.

Subsequently, I will suggest a security-management life cycle for information-processing systems and indicate the specific security needs in each life cycle phase. This security-management life cycle has to be understood as a part of the overall life cycle and not as an add-on that runs parallel. Based on this understanding of the system life cycle, I will present a process that suggests detailed workflows to achieve security in correlation with the system life cycle. Finally,

I will present an analysis of the process and conclude the work.

SECURITY MANAGEMENT LIFE CYCLE

In most security literature (e.g., BS7799-2, 1999; Lipner & Howard, 2005), the life cycle primarily focuses on the development (elaboration, design and construction) and the operation of the system. This focus seems too narrow for the management of system security as the beginning and the end of the system life cycle are not included in this view. Grance, Stash, and Stevens (2004) expands this by including the disposal of the system into the life cycle. In addition to disposal, also a start phase is crucial for the system life cycle because here the rational for the system is derived (purpose motivation and feasibility of security). Based on business administration (PMI, 2000) and software engineering (Jacobson, Booch, & Rumbaugh, 1999) findings I therefore include an inception which starts the life cycle.

We would also like to add, based on the unified process (Jacobson, Booch, & Rumbaugh, 1999), an additional phase between construction and operation. This phase should be called transition and reflects the specific need to deploy and validate the system security (i.e., gain assurance). Note that Lipner and Howard (2005) include a "release" phase that matches with the here suggested transition phase in respect to security assurance purpose.

A six-phase security management life cycle (Figure 1) is suggested that contains: inception, elaboration, construction, transition, operation, and retirement.

Figure 1. Security management life cycle

| Inception | Elaboration | Construction | Transition | Operation | Retirement |

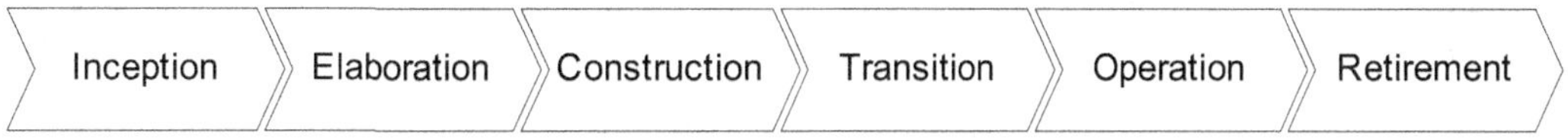

It is important to achieve tight integration between the security-management life cycle and the system life cycle. This is especially important for the technical development activities, because here various life cycle models (see Figure 1) are common.

Due to their chronological order, each of the six phases puts emphasis on specific security aspects, which I discuss below. Although the subsequent presentation might give the impression that system security is sequentially achieved it is important to note that in reality this is achieved iteratively. However, each life cycle stage focuses more on certain aspects than on others.

Inception

During Inception the focus of security management is to provide the business case for securing the system. The two major tasks here are to provide motivation for the organization to invest into security and to investigate the feasibility. In that way the scope for security of the system is established.

Security Motivation

State of the art is to motivate security with risk analysis. The aim with risk analysis is to argue that it is cheaper to proactively invest into information security. However, recent trends have led to a refocusing by identifying additional factors that motivate an investment into information security. I think that the following three aspects should be used in today's environments.

- **Security as a resource protection mechanism:** One function of information system security is to protect the resources of the company, its customers and suppliers (or rather, everyone who shares data with the organization). Protection of resources can also be seen as insurance. As with insur-

ance it is possible to calculate the benefits and costs of the security investment (i.e., the financial motivation). Motivation here is financially induced.

- **Security as a regulative/moral obligation:** I have argued earlier that regulations require an investment in security. In addition, information security has also become a moral obligation and the seriousness of an organization is judged by its security behavior. Motivation here has become externally induced on the organization.

- **Security as a business enabler:** Another function of security is to enable business. Customer acceptances of services (especially e-commerce services) depend on the visible availability of information security. Therefore, security becomes a business enabler because customers decide whether to use/buy a product depending on how secure they perceive it to be. Motivation here is based on aim to provide products that find market acceptance or have a competitive advantage.

Together these factors justify why it is necessary to invest into information security and tell the purpose of security. Commonly the findings are documented in a security vision and incorporated in the corporate security policy.

Feasibility

Based on the findings why security is needed for the system the next step is to investigate if the organization has the capabilities to handle security. For that purpose it is important that the organizational and the knowledge prerequisites are identified and compared to the actual capabilities. The result will reflect to business risks in respect to system security and provides the base for adequate management. This should result in a formal kick-off for the development of security.

Elaboration

When the elaboration phase of the system life cycle is reached there is commonly a good understanding why the system and security is needed on a high level. To operationalize the motivation (i.e., bring the system into a state so that it satisfies the needs) it is necessary to transform the needs into security requirements towards the system which have a higher granularity. Due to the large number of requirements, a selection of the most important ones has to be made during elaboration.

To prepare for the construction later, in elaboration, the security for the system is conceptualized. It is important to preserve holism during this phase by not solely relying on technical solutions but investigate what safeguards accommodate the requirements best.

Security Requirements

To accommodate the various sources that motivate investment in security the security requirements have to be holistic. It is therefore necessary to derive those requirements not only from risk analysis but to include more dimensions. I identified the business process and stakeholders/environmental domains as additional sources (see Zuccato, 2004).

A special property of security requirements is that they not only reflect needs towards the systems but also restrictions that are imposed on the system.

Construction

The primary focus during construction is to build the system. During this phase not only the technical components but, among others, also organizational security structures and procedural guidelines are implemented.

In parallel to the implementation activities in this life cycle phase a demand for assurance[a] has to be satisfied. Therefore this phase has to focus on security tests and reviews as assurance techniques. Important to note is that during this stage, the assurance demand is primarily internal, and therefore it does not necessarily have to fulfill formal evaluation requirements (although reusable documentation could/should be crafted).

Transition

Transition aims to deploy the system security and assure it (i.e., prove it working). It is commonly assumed that although the technical deployment is complex, the real challenge is the organizational deployment. Organizational behavior research indicates ways of how the transition in organizations can be achieved and how it should, after adaptation to security, be applied.

Figure 2. Security requirement sources

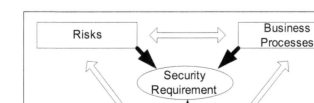

In the motivation for a transition phase I have argued that such a phase is necessary due to assurance demand of information security. I assume therefore that during this phase, the majority of the efforts will be dedicated to gain assurance by checking the system. In contrast to construction this will be more formal and also externally oriented. However, this does not mean that it is necessarily a third-party evaluation but mainly that the assurance evidence is for external stakeholders (primarily customers).

Operation

After the system is deployed it enters the operational phase. Here the system is maintained to preserve the intended security. This life cycle phase is by far the longest and most heterogeneous. Commonly two major focus areas are commonly identifiable.

The first focus is to monitor the system for possible security breaches to prevent harm to the organization. This focus is reactive in nature and requires high awareness and alertness.

The second focus aims to proactively prevent security problems by re-adjusting (i.e., maintaining and patching) the system to accommodate environmental changes.

Retirement

When the system or parts of it reaches the end of its usefulness it/they will be disposed. From a security point of view it is important that the disposal happens in a way that sensitive information is not compromised.

In addition most systems/components have a successor and the aim of this phase is therefore to transfer the data to the new system/component in a secure way. Especially important is that context information (e.g., purpose of collected personal data, log files, etc.) is preserved.

SECURITY MANAGEMENT PROCESS

The life cycle presented above correlates security needs with the different life cycle phases of the system. From a security point of view it is important to be able to show that the different life cycle needs are considered. From the quality assurance area (ISO9000, 1999; Paulk, Curtis, Chrissis, & Weber, 1993) we know that such a demonstration of need consideration, although difficult to achieve, could be done by a well documented process. More specific for security the common criteria (ISO 15048, 1999) advocate that it is crucial to follow a process to gain confidence in IT security and similar claims are supported by (SSECMM, 2003).

Given the intention of having a well documented process, from our point of view primarily monolithic[2] processes have to be used. The reason is that agile processes with their philosophy of "do only what is needed to finish the current iteration" conflict in our view with the requirement of security for proactiveness and the subsequent need for the systemic overview ("big picture"). Another problem of agile processes is that they frequently do not cover more than the construction part of the system life cycle.

The following holistic security-management framework (except the disposal) was developed during a doctoral thesis (Zuccato, 2005). Due to space restrictions, only an overview is presented whereas the mentioned thesis contains a more in-depth description of the process and its subactivities. Important to note is that as such a process framework has to be adapted to the organization in which it is applied.

Holistic Security Management

Security management has to apply mechanisms that can deal with the inherent complexity and dynamic in the modern information processing systems. To achieve this state-of-the-art system/software life cycle approaches commonly split each phase into multiple iterations. The advantage with iterations is that they allow for timely correction and adoption to changed environmental circumstances (i.e., changed security requirements).

For all the iterations, a generic workflow can be described. Given the iterations timely position (i.e., in which life cycle stage the iteration is) different emphasis is put on activities. However, it is to note that all activities should be executed (see Figure 3). Note that the disposal activities are not part of Figure 3 as they primarily happen at the end of the system life cycle (with the exception of very small but continuous efforts in destroying sensitive media, which we see as part of maintenance).

Business Modeling

This workflow starts the security management processes and is triggered by the organizational

system. The workflow produces the base on which the secure system is built. In the first iteration the framework is tailored to the needs for the particular security management tasks for the system at hand. In addition the security vision, a project specific terminology and the business/project risks for the system are crafted. Those will be refined in subsequent iterations.

For all iterations this workflow requires the development of the security-enhanced business model for the iterations relevant business functions. In this model the organization defines how the business model should be enhanced by security and which security functions are expected to generate business benefit.

Security Planning

In the previous workflow a security domain specific business model of the systems and a corresponding vision should have been developed. All the created domain information has to be analyzed and formalized in a way that the result can be used for the secure system construction. This workflow

Figure 3. Holistic security management framework

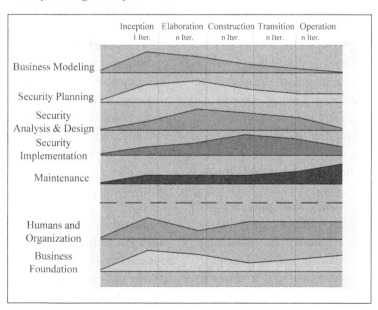

aims to develop plans how to incorporate security into the operative business.

For this purpose, the security needs that the system has to satisfy must be codified into security requirements. To conform with the holistic intend of this framework the requirement gathering process has to take multiple sources into account. An important activity in security requirement engineering is the compilation of the requirements from the different sources into one set of requirements. This involves the harmonization of requirements, the resolution of contradictions and conflicts between requirements and the exploitation of synergies of different requirements with the ultimate goal of best possible security.

In addition the operative orientation of the system under consideration requires a codification of the organizational security assumptions and constrains in a product policy. Such a product policy should be a refinement of the overall security policies.

Security Analysis and Design

What we have seen until now are activities with the goal of preparation on an abstract level. When conducting a security project we should, by now, be aware of the position of security in the organization and know what we require from the security system and how we plan to realize it by means of a security analysis and design workflow.

Now it is time to connect this information to achieve an understanding of how a secure system can be realized. Therefore we need to prioritize the requirements according to their importance and feasibility.

After knowing the important requirements for the iteration, the goal of security analysis is to overcome redundancy, ambiguity, and incompleteness of security requirements (due to their customer-oriented nature) by translating them into an analysis which is in the language of the developers. In due course it is also the goal to reduce redundancy and to achieve completeness. Furthermore, to reduce complexity in subsequent activities (design, implementation and maintenance) the analysis can be used to organize the requirements into a structure that reflects similarity.

After that a security design, dealing solely with security and not the underlying software, can be performed. The security design aims to describe how the security has to be implemented by describing security relevant objects[3], interfaces and interaction in the system. Based on that the security functions are described so that implementation can start.

Security Implementation

In the course of the implementation workflow the analyzed and designed requirements are put into reality. This chain should allow traceability from an implemented security function to its underlying requirements. It is again important to recall that this is a holistic activity which has to encompass the business, social, and technical dimensions.

This workflow covers the technical (software and infrastructure) and organizational implementation. The social implementation, on the other hand, is done in the humans and organization workflow as it has different preconditions.

This workflow also emphasizes quality control of the implementation and deployment to achieve an acceptable degree of assurance that the plan is implemented as intended and the expected security protection achieved. We suggest performing tests (module, integration, and system), penetration tests and inspections/reviews for this purpose.

Maintenance

Maintenance is by far the most heterogeneous workflow in the framework. It covers all the three dimensions (business, social and technical) in equal share. This is also reflected in the varying focus of the involved sub-activities.

It ranges from the heavily technologically focused "technical maintenance[4]" over the all-inclusive "system monitoring" and "external and internal audit" to the business-specific "business foundation" and the socially focused "humans and organization".

Another important characteristic is the continuous nature of maintenance. It never stops until the system is "retired".

Disposal

During the disposal workflow a set of activities aims to identify critical information and decide what to do with it. Some of the information has to be stored for documentary purpose (i.e., legal obligations), some information has to be transferred to other systems and the remaining information (including eventual information in the hardware) destroyed in an irrecoverable way.

In parallel to these activities during disposal also the organizational connections of the system have to be closed. This includes the elimination of internal adaptation of the organization as well as the closeout of external contracts.

Humans and Organization

The purpose of this workflow is to enable people and introduce activities to enable them for a more effective and efficient treatment of information security. The support character of this workflow implies that the activities are conducted whenever a demand for their results is perceived.

Important subworkflows concern the educational aspects of security with the goal to increase the awareness for security and its importance for the organization's future and create security literacy for individuals dependent on their role in the organization. Another aspect is to provide motivation for security (from a social viewpoint) and to enable communication between individuals and the organizational unit.

Business Foundation

The ultimate goal of this workflow is to motivate and control the economic viability of the security investment. Therefore this workflow aims to integrate and connect the security management process with the organization's overall management process.

A stronger focus on information security is applied when it comes to information security risk analysis, control and monitoring/measurement. Information security risk analysis, in this context, aims to support both technical security risk management and the organizational risk management. The security specific control and monitoring/measurement aim at collection and analysis of data for technical and process improvement aspects.

EVALUATION WITH SSE-CMM

The "Systems Security Engineering Capability Maturity Model" (SSECMM 2003) is intended to classify the capabilities of an organization in performing a security engineering process. The model is based on the "Capability Maturity Model" for software development (Paulk et al., 1993).

SSE-CMM makes some basic assumptions concerning a security engineering process. It divides security engineering into three areas (risk, engineering and assurance) which work together. The "risks" are the means to derive requirements which are designed and implemented in "engineering". "Assurance" is continuously applied to produce confidence that the planned security is attained.

These assumptions are reflected in an architecture which comprises a two-dimensional model formed by the domain dimension and the capability dimension.

The domain dimension comprises 129 base practices, which are organized into 22 process areas. About half of these domain practices (organized into 11 process areas[5]) address security engineering. The other half are inherited from the standard CMM model and focus on project and organizational aspects[6].

The capability dimension comprises 0 + 1–5 capability levels with the corresponding generic practices (see Figure 4).

This two-dimensional structure is used when the "capability evaluation" is conducted. In this case for each (applicable) process area the capa-

bility level is evaluated. The generated data are then used to form a capability matrix representing the maturity of the process areas. Note that it is not the overall process but the process areas that have a maturity assigned.

Evaluation

Inspired by Paulk et al. (2001), who conducted an evaluation of extreme programming (XP) accord-

Figure 4. SSE CMM capability levels

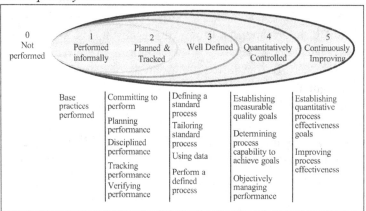

Figure 5. Process area capability chart of HSMF

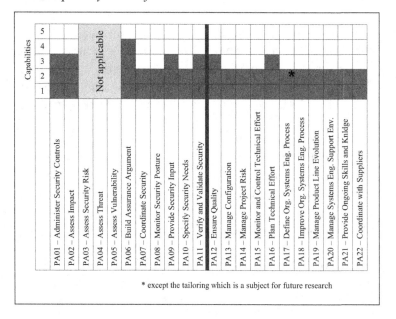

ing to CMM, I analyzed the HSMF framework with SSE-CMM to indicate what level could be achieved. Note that due to the tailorable character of HSMF, this evaluation[7] is conducted with the assumption that all defined activities are performed (see Figure 5).

As already mentioned in the description, SSE-CMM is risk centered. The evaluation therefore marks certain areas which are specific for risk analysis as ``not applicable'' instead of assigning 0.

The aforementioned evaluation indicates that an "out-of-the-box" application of HSMF generically is "planned and tracked" (SSE-CMM level 2). In addition certain process areas are already "well defined" (SSE-CMM level 3). We think that further tailoring the process to the organization will lead to an overall "well defined" process.

CONCLUSION

To include security into information system seems a natural choice in today's environment. To do this efficiently and effectively, it is necessary to organize the security efforts similar to the system's life cycle. The security life cycle presented in this paper is a combination of life cycles from system engineering, software engineering, and security engineering. Due to the combination, I think that the life cycle presented here can smoothly integrate in the other life cycles and help to build in security more efficiently and effectively.

To give more ideas what to do in the different life cycle phases we presented the security needs that should be accommodated in the different life phases of a system. A process framework was then suggested that should help organizations to seamlessly integrate the security efforts into their overall system life cycle management. In the analysis, it was shown that commonly expected security properties can be achieved by applying the process framework. This is a great benefit

because it allows a system life cycle–oriented security management that satisfies today's best.

REFERENCES

Basel II. (2005). *International convergence of capital measurement and capital standards: A revised framework.* Basel Committee on Banking Supervision.

BS7799-2:1999. (1999). *British standard - Specification for information security management system.*

Grance, T., Hash, H., & Stevens, M. (2004). *Security considerations in the information development life cycle* (NIST Special Publication 800-64 Rev.1). National Institute of Standards and Technology.

ISO/IEC 9000:2000. (1999). *Quality management systems–Fundamentals and vocabulary.* ISO/IEC 9000:2000, International Organization for Standardization.

ISO 15048. (1999). *Information technology–Security techniques–Evaluation criteria for IT security* (common criteria). International Organization for Standardization.

ISO17799. (2000). *Code of practice for information security management.* International Organization for Standardization.

Jacobson, I., Booch, G., & Rumbaugh, J. (1999). *The unified software development process.* Addison Wesley Longman.

Lipner, S., & Howard, M. (2005). *The trustworthy computing security development lifecycle.* MSDN Library, Microsoft.

Paulk, M. (2001). Extreme programming from a CMM perspective. *IEEE Software, 18*(6), 19-26.

Paulk, M. C., Curtis, B., Chrissis, M. B., & Weber, C. V. (1993). *Capability maturity model* (SE, version 1.1). Software Engineering Institute.

PMI. (2000). *A guide to the project management body of knowledge*. Author.

Schoderbek, P., Schoderbek, C., & Kefalas, A. (1990). *Management systems–Conceptual considerations* (4th ed.). Irwin.

Sommerville, I. (2004). *Software engineering* (7th ed.). Addison Wesley.

Sarbanes-Oxley Act of 2002, 116 Stat. 745 (2002).

SSE-CMM Project. (2003). *Systems security engineering capability maturity model* (version 3.0).

Zuccato, A. (2004). Holistic security requirement engineering for electronic commerce, *Computers & Security, 23*(1), 63–76.

Zuccato, A. (2005). *Holistic information security management framework for electronic commerce*. Unpublished doctoral dissertation, Karlstad University Studies, Sweden.

ENDNOTES

[1]   Means here the certainty that the security functionality is implemented and working as specified.

[2]   In contrast to agile processes like eXtreme Programming, Scrum …

[3]   Object here means "a thing that forms an element of or constitutes the subject matter of an investigation or science." Mirriam-Webster Online Dictionary, http://www.m-w.com, Nov. 2005

[4]   Dependent on the type (corrective, adaptive and perfective (Sommerville04)) and scope (amount of required effort) of the improvement it is either covered within the maintenance phase of the process (for smaller modifications) or for more extensive modifications an own instance of the framework (most likely tailored to the scope) is started.

[5]   Security Engineering Process Areas: Administer Security Controls; Assess Impact; Assess Security Risk; Assess Threat; Assess Vulnerability; Build Assurance Argument; Coordinate Security; Monitor Security Posture; Provide Security Input; Specify Security Needs; Verify and Validate Security

[6]   Project and Organizational Process Areas: Ensure Quality; Manage Configuration; Manage Project Risk; Monitor and Control Technical Effort; Plan Technical Effort; Define Organization's Systems Engineering Process; Improve Organization's Systems Engineering Process; Manage Product Line Evolution; Manage Systems Engineering Support Environment; Provide Ongoing Skills and Knowledge; Coordinate with Suppliers

[7]   For a detailed evaluation of all the activities see (Zuccato 2005)

Chapter XVI
Software Specification and Attack Languages

Mohammed Hussein
Queen's University, Canada

Mohammad Raihan
Queen's University, Canada

Mohammad Zulkernine
Queen's University, Canada

ABSTRACT

General-purpose software specification languages are introduced to model software by providing a better understanding of their characteristics. Nevertheless, these languages may fail to model some nonfunctional requirements such as security and safety. The necessity for simplifying the specification of nonfunctional requirements led to the development of domain-specific languages (e.g., attack description languages). Attack languages are employed to specify intrusion detection related aspects like intrusion signatures, normal behavior, alert correlation, and so forth. They provide language constructs and libraries that simplify the specification of the aforementioned intrusion detection aspects. Attack languages are used heavily due to the rapid growth of computer intrusions. The current trend in software development is to develop the core functionalities of the software based on the requirements expressed in general-purpose software specification languages. Then, attack languages and other security mechanisms are used to deal with security requirements. However, using two sets of languages may result in several disadvantages such as redundant and conflicting requirements (e.g., usability vs. security). Moreover, incorporating security at the latter stages of a software life cycle is more difficult and time consuming. Many research works propose the unification and reconciliation of software engineering and security engineering in various directions. These research efforts aim to enable developers to use the current software engineering tools and techniques to specify security requirements. In this chapter, we present a study on the classification of software specification languages and discuss the current state of the art regarding attack languages. Specification languages are categorized based on their features and their main purposes. A detailed comparison among attack languages is provided. We show the example extensions of the two software specification languages to include some features of the attack languages. We believe that extending certain types of software specification languages to express security aspects like attack descriptions is a major step towards unifying software and security engineering.

INTRODUCTION

Software requirements specification is an intermediate step between requirements elicitation and implementation. Software specification languages (SSL) are used to model software systems to gain better understanding of the software. The outcome of such modeling is a design which can be verified against the user requirements. Specifications can also help in code and test case generation. Several studies exist in the literature that compare a number of SSL based on different properties (Clements, 1996; Ostroff, 1992; Jin & Nahrstedt, 2004; Wieringa, 1998). Although SSL are powerful, developers face difficulties when using them to model nonfunctional requirements. Complex models, lack of language constructs, and libraries are examples of such difficulties. These difficulties lead to the presence of domain-specific languages (e.g., attack languages). Attack languages are employed to specify intrusion detection related aspects like intrusion signature, normal behavior, and alert correlation.

Software play a key role in every strata of our life. For example, they are being used in financial institutions, government agencies, health sectors, and power-control systems to store and process security critical information. As the world is becoming more dependent on such software systems, the need for developing secure software is becoming more evident. Computer attacks or intrusions are increasing since the knowledge required for launching them is becoming more available. According to Computer Emergency Response Team (CERT) statistics (CERT, 2005), the number of

incidents reported to CERT in 2001 was 52,658, while in 2002, the number was 82,094. In 2003, 137,529 incidents were reported. which is more than the number in both 2001 and 2002 together. The current trend in the software industry is to wait till the main functionalities of the software are implemented, and then to add security aspects by using special languages for security.

However, using two sets of languages may cause several disadvantages. First, designing the system without considering security at the early stages of the software development life cycle (SDLC) increases the number of vulnerabilities that must be dealt with in the latter stages. Second, incorporating security aspects within an existing design leads to redundant and conflicting development efforts. Third, delaying security issues imposes higher development cost and produces less maintainable software.

Unifying software and security engineering, on the other hand, is a promising solution to the above mentioned problems. The unified engineering approach is called Software Security Engineering (Zulkernine & Ahamed, 2005). It provides developers with a more concrete view of security requirements which helps in avoiding conflicting design decisions due to the requirements. Moreover, the unification enables the developers who are not expert in security engineering to build secure software. Software security engineering also helps in anticipating the cost of developing security aspects of the system at the early stages of the SDLC. Many research directions have been explored for the purpose of unification such as new frameworks for software development, extensions of process models, and extensions of software specification languages (SSL). For example, in Lipner and Howard (2005), a software development framework for handling security issues during each phase of the SDLC is proposed. It has shown how security issues can be incorporated in the requirement, design, implementation, integration, testing, and verification phases of the SDLC.

This chapter presents a study on software specification languages and attack description languages. The study provides an overview of the history of SSL and classifies SSL based on their main purposes. State of the art of attack languages and their features are also discussed in this study. However, the aim of the study is not to rank the presented SSL or attack languages. The aim is to present an overview of SSL and attack languages and explore the directions of extending SSL for handling security requirements and unifying the two sets of languages. The incorporation of the features provided by attack languages into certain types of software specification languages helps to unify the two types of languages. This unification, in our point of view, is an important step towards unifying software engineering and security engineering.

The remaining of this chapter is organized as follows. The next section provides an overview and a classification of SSL based on their purpose. After that, we discuss the state of the art of attack languages and their features. An overview on the extensions of the SSL for security specification is presented afterwards. Finally, we conclude with the chapter summary and some future work.

SOFTWARE SPECIFICATION LANGUAGES (SSL)

Prior to 1970, software were described either in plain natural languages or in programming languages code. While descriptions in natural languages were ambiguous and produced piles of

documents, programming languages code were too detailed and difficult to be communicated even among developers. When software engineering started to gain its popularity after the 1968 NATO Software Engineering Conference (Naur & Randell, 1969), researchers began to propose process models and frameworks which had guided developers in developing software systems. The common basis of all these process models and frameworks was to facilitate the specifications of software at different levels of abstraction. To achieve this goal, new languages were proposed to enable the development of software to be carried out in step-wise refinements, where each step produced a more detailed design of the software. The outcome was a design that enabled developers to explore one characteristics of software. In general, these characteristics defined the structure, behavior, and constraints of the software. The design of the software was then transformed into programming languages code. The languages which facilitated the specifications of software characteristics were called software specification languages (SSL).

Influenced by the early pioneers of computer science in which their vast majority were mathematicians, SSL were based on mathematical models and notations. Algebra, temporal logic, and state-machines were the basis of several SSL such as Actor Model (Hewitt, Bishop, & Steiger, 1973), B (Abrial, 1996), Vienna Development Method Specification Language (VDM-SL; Larsen & Pawlowski, 1995), and Z (Bowenm, 1996). The common feature of those languages was that they were formally defined. The software specified in these languages could be easily tested against their user requirements. One of the problems of those languages was that they were difficult to be communicated to customers. A strong mathematical background was needed to understand the software specifications. In the 1980s, new SSL such as Jackson structured design (JSD) (Jackson, 1983) started to appear that provided graphical notations to make the specifications more understandable.

Inheritance and other features of object oriented software engineering were the rationale behind the development of many SSL like common algebraic specification language (CASL) (Bidoit & Mosses, 2003) and language of temporal order specification (LOTOS; Van Eijk, Vissers, & Diaz, 1989). Old languages were also extended to support object oriented features and to provide graphical notations, that is, Object-Z (Smith, 2000). In the 1990s, object oriented languages (Wieringa, 1998) grew rapidly and researchers combined the features of several of these languages to produce stronger ones. However, each SSL had its own strengths and weaknesses. In 1997, a new language was released that was the combination of three well-known object oriented languages, The Booch Method (Booch, 1991), object oriented software engineering (OOSE) (Jacobson, Christerson, Johnsson, & Overgaard, 1992), and object modeling technique (OMT) (Rumbaugh et al., 1991). This language has been called the unified modeling language (UML) (Booch, Rumbaugh, & Jacobson, 1999). Since then, the popularity of UML has been increasing an it has become a de-facto standard for software development. The reasons behind the popularity of UML include the presence of graphical notations, the support for object oriented features, and the ability to specify different constraints and behavioral and structural characteristics of the software.

Generally, SSL can be classified based on two aspects: the features they provide and their purpose. The focus of this section is on SSL in general, while the next section focuses on one type of SSL, that is, attack languages.

Feature-Based Classification of SSL

Several studies classify or evaluate SSL based on the features they provide (Clements, 1996; Jin & Nahrstedt, 2004; Ostroff, 1992; Wieringa, 1998). The SSL features included in these studies are level of formalism, support for object oriented features, graphical notations, paradigms, concurrency, executability, support for validations and verifications, and specification methods. In Wieringa (1998), over 20 object oriented and structured SSL are compared based on the techniques and methods used in the specification of software communication, external behavior, decomposition into objects, and object functions and behavior. Many SSL for real-time systems are described in (Ostroff, 1992), where these languages are compared based on their notations, paradigms, and executability. In Jin and Nahrstedt (2004), SSL for the specification of quality of service are classified and evaluated based on their expressiveness, extensibility, and reusability. Architecture refinement, validation, analysis, and scope are used to compare several architectural SSL in (Clements, 1996).

Purpose-Based Classification of SSL

The early SSL were aimed towards specifying the general structures, behaviors, and constraints of the software. Such languages were denoted as general-purpose SSL (Van Deursen, Klint, & Visser, 2000) (e.g., B, VDM-SL, OMT, and UML). General-purpose SSL were successfully used to specify software characteristics. However, as software complexity grew and nonfunctional requirements started to gain attention, many problems of general purpose SSL started to arise to the surface. The software specifications produced by those SSL became complex, and in some cases those SSL were not able to specify the new characteristics or requirements (e.g., safety, security, quality of service, and other nonfunctional requirements). Driven by the necessity of simplifying software specifications, new SSL were introduced. Many SSL are proposed to facilitate the specification of domain specific properties. STATECHARTS (Gabrielian & Franklin, 1988) and RT-ASALN (Auernheimer, 1987) are the examples of such languages which specify real-time characteristics of the software. Those new languages were denoted as domain specific SSL (Van Deursen et al., 2000).

A Purpose-Based Classification Tree for SSL

Based on their main purpose, SSL can be classified as general purpose and domain-specific. Figure 1 shows a classification tree which categorizes SSL based on their main purpose into general-purpose SSL (GPL) and domain-specific SSL (DSL). The leaves of the tree are the examples of SSL under the parent nodes. GPL are divided into the following categories: behavior, structure, constraint, and multipurpose. Behavior specific languages specify the behavior and dynamic aspects of the system. B and Z are examples of such languages. The techniques employed to specify software behavior include algebra, temporal logic, state-machines, activity diagrams, collaboration diagrams, and their variations. Structure specific languages specify the structure and static aspects of the systems. Several techniques are employed to

specify software structure like entity-relationship diagrams, class diagrams, and their variations (Wieringa, 1998). The languages that specify constraints on software such as the object constraint language (OCL) (OMG, 2005) form the constraint category. However, most of the GPL which constitute the multipurpose category have the ability to model software behavior, structure, and constraints. Booch, LOTOS, OOSE, OMT, UML, and most of the other object oriented specification languages fall into this category.

On the other hand, DSL can be further categorized into area-specific and requirement specific. Area-specific languages deal with the requirements of a specific type of software such as real-time, embedded, multimedia, games, drivers, Web-services, database systems, and so forth. This category is also classified into behavior, structure, constraint, and multipurpose. Well-established areas of software have languages to specify the behavior, structure, and constraints of the software. Multipurpose refers to the languages that specify more than one aspect of software (i.e., behavior, structure, and constraints). STATECHARTS is

Figure 1. Purpose-based classification of SSL

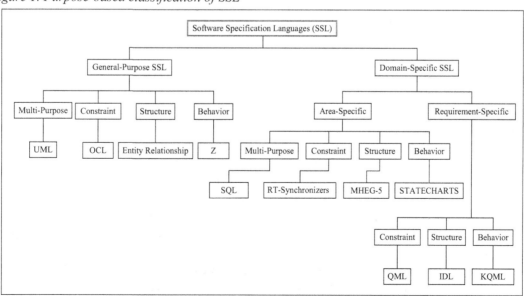

used to specify the behavior of real-time systems; Multimedia Hypermedia Experts Group (MHEG-5) (Hofmann, 1996) is employed to specify the data structures for multimedia applications; RT-Synchronizers (Nielsen et al., 1998) is used to specify constraints on real-time systems; and structured query language (SQL) (Chamberlin et al., 1974) is utilized to specify relational database applications. SQL is considered as a multipurpose SSL because it is employed to specify the behavior, structure and constraints.

The multipurpose categories of general-purpose and area-specific SSL share a common feature which is the ability of specifying software structure, behavior, and constraints. The only difference is that area-specific SSL are intended to specify a particular type of software. The languages that are designed for specific type of requirements are called requirement-specific SSL. The languages in this category describe specific type of requirements (behavior, structure, or constraint) without being specific to a particular type of software (i.e., real-time, embedded). For instance, architectural description languages such as Wright (Allen & Garlan, 1996) describe software architectures. Similarly, interface description languages such as interface definition language (IDL) (OMG, 2004) describe software interfaces. Knowledge query and manipulation language (KQML) (Finin, Fritzon, McKay, & McEntire, 1994) is an example language used to specify communications and messages, whereas quality of service modeling language (QML) (Frolund & Koistinen, 1998) is a language utilized for defining quality of service attributes of software systems. Since this category deals with specific type of requirements, it does not have a multipurpose category.

Classifying Example SSL

Almost any SSL should have a place in the classification tree of Figure 1. The following paragraphs describe how three example languages (IDL,

RT-Synchronizers, and UML) are classified using the tree. Interface definition language (IDL) from the Object Management Group (OMG) is a language for specifying the interfaces that the implemented objects provide and client objects use. Each interface defines name, parameters, return values, and other information related to the operations. Since this language deals with one of the structural aspects of software (i.e., interfaces), it should fall into one of structure categories shown in Figure 1. The reason that prevents this language from falling into the GPL structure category is that it deals only with interfaces. Interfaces are not intended to use for the software of one specific area; therefore, IDL is considered part of the structure category of the requirement-specific languages.

RT-Synchronizers is a language for specifying constraints on real-time systems such as timing constrains. This language deals with the constraint aspects of software, therefore, this language should fall into one of the constraint categories shown in Figure 1.

UML is a de-facto standard for software development. UML is used for the specification of software structure and behavior, whereas constraints are specified using the OCL of UML. Since UML is not designed for a particular domain, UML falls into the multipurpose category of GPL.

STATE OF THE ART OF ATTACK LANGUAGES

Attack languages are used to describe patterns (also known as attack signatures) that are used by intrusion detection systems (IDS) to identify intrusions in the audit data stream. IDS are playing a major role complementary to the available preventive mechanisms (e.g., access control and password protection) in securing computer systems. They monitor events (like system audit records and network packets) that are taking place in the system, analyze the events, and generate alerts whenever they detect any suspicious or illegal activities as defined in the security policy. Therefore, IDS are able to detect security violations such as break-ins, penetrations, and abuse of the system resources. To detect several attacks of the same type taking place simultaneously, IDS need to instantiate a separate instance of the attack signature. The instances differ from each other by some particular features of the attack signature; for example, IP address of the victim machine.

Attack languages are being used by both pattern matching anomaly detection systems and misuse detection systems which are two broad approaches to intrusion detection (Axelsson, 2000). An anomaly detection system builds a normal behavioral profile of an application and attempts to identify any deviation from the normal profile by comparing it with the current usage patterns. The normal behavioral profile can be built by performing some statistical analysis on the historical data of the applications (Javits & Valdes, 1994). It can also be constructed by using rule-based approaches (Ko, Ruschitzka, & Levett, 1997; Sekar & Uppuluri, 1999; Vaccaro & Liepins, 1989; Porras & Neumann, 1997) or immunology-based methods (Forrest & Longstaff, 1996). Some of the features used in anomaly detection systems are CPU activity, number of network connections within a time period, or access to restricted system resources. Anomaly detection systems do not require the knowledge about the security flaws in order to detect the attacks. They can detect novel attacks (attacks that have not been seen before). However, anomaly detection systems suffer from high false positive rates as they are based on the assumption that an intrusion can be identified by detecting abnormal system behavior, which is not true in all cases. Moreover, it cannot detect all types of intrusions, as some intrusions may not exhibit abnormal behavior. Setting the anomaly threshold level for the system is also a challenging task in this domain. On the other hand, the IDS based on misuse detection principle encode knowledge about the known intrusion patterns in some representations which are known as attack signatures. These signatures are matched with the current system activity in an attempt to identify the attacks. Misuse detection systems are simpler to implement and configure, and generate less number of false positives than anomaly detection systems. However, misuse IDS cannot detect novel attacks, since it is not possible to specify attack signatures for unknown attacks. Like anti-virus software, the efficiency of misuse detection systems heavily depends on the database of attack signatures. The primary approaches to misuse detection (Kumar & Spafford, 1994) are expert systems (Habra, Charlier, Mounji, & Mathieu, 1992; Porras & Neumann, 1997), state transition analysis (Crosbie et al., 1996; Ilgun, 1993; Porras & Neumann, 1992), and model-based reasoning systems (Garvey & Lunt, 1991).

Anomaly detection systems define the intended or expected behavior through attack languages to build the application behavioral profile (Ko et al., 1997; Porras & Neumann, 1997; Sekar & Uppuluri, 1999; Vaccaro & Liepins, 1989). On the other hand, misuse detection systems employ attack languages to encode the undesirable events that should not take place in the system (Crosbie et al., 1996; Habra et al., 1992; Ilgun, 1993; Porras & Kemmerer, 1992; Porras & Neumann, 1997). Attack languages are also used to analyze the relationships among different attacks and to simulate the attacks for testing the systems (Vigna, Eckmann, & Kemmerer, 2000).

Features of Attack Languages

Attack languages differ in the set of attack signatures that can be described. Some aspects that can be expressed in one language cannot be specified in another. They differ in the expressiveness and are suitable in different domains. Some of the desirable characteristics of attack languages are summarized in the following paragraphs.

- Able to express variants of an attack scenario by defining the event parameters on which they differ. For example, the same attack can be carried out by different attackers at the same time (like the same attack scenario with different user names, IP addresses, or port numbers). This could be possible by defining variables in the attack specifications.

- Able to express the temporal ordering of the events. Moreover, it should be expressive enough so that it can cover possible re-ordering of the events. For example, assume an attack scenario that requires three events to take place: *a, b,* and *c,* where the events *a* and *b* could be taking place in any order, followed by the occurrence of event *c.* Thus it will be able to detect both the orderings: *a, b, c* and *b, a, c.* Moreover, it should be able to express the iterations over events. For example, event *c,* in the above scenario, has to occur five times in order for the attack to be successful.

- Should be easy to introduce changes to an attack scenario. For example, in the above scenario, assume that we want to incorporate a new event *d* that is functionally equivalent to event *a.* After the incorporation of this new event, it is able to detect all the possible orderings of the events: *<b, a, c>, <a, b, c>, <b, d, c>, <d, b, c>.*

A Comparative Study of the Current Attack Languages

This section compares and contrasts a number of attack languages. The attack languages are compared to each other in terms of a number of criterions: *language class,* the *type of IDS* that uses that attack language, *the approach* the language has adopted to represent attack scenarios, *performance evaluation,* and finally the way the attack language specification has been translated to operational signatures (*interpretation of attack*

specification). Table 1 presents a comparative view of the attack languages. The following sections provide a brief discussion on each of the criterions used in making the comparison.

Attack Language Classes

In Vigna et al. (2000), attack languages have been categorized into six classes: event languages, response languages, reporting languages, correlation languages, exploit languages, and detection languages. In the following paragraphs, we incorporate a brief description of each of these language classes.

- **Event languages.** IDS perform analysis on the system events represented by event languages. Basic security module (BSM) audit records (Sun Microsystems Inc, 1991), tcpdump packets (McCanne, Leres, & Jacobson, 1998), and Windows audit log records (Microsoft, 2003) are some of the examples of event languages.

- **Response languages.** Response languages are used to define the actions to be taken by the IDS upon detecting intrusions. Currently, most IDS use C or Java library functions for this purpose. However, in (Michel & Mé, 2001), ADeLe language is proposed for the specification of the responses to intrusions.

- **Reporting languages.** Reporting languages are used to define the format of alert messages generated by IDS. It specifies the information about attacks such as type of attack, the attacker, the victim, the severity of the attack, the events that caused the attack to be successful, the software vulnerabilities that are exploited by the attack, *etc.* Two examples of reporting languages are the common intrusion specification language (CISL) (CIDF Working Group, 1999) and the intrusion detection message exchange format (IDMEF) (Curry, 2000).

Table 1. A comparison between attack languages

Attack Language / IDS	Language Class	Type of IDS	Approach	Attack Pattern Encoding Scheme	Performance Evaluation			Interpretation of Attack Specification
					Time	Mem	Detection	
RUSSEL / ASAX	Detection	Anomaly	Procedural	Rule-based expert system	N	N	N	Interpreted by RUSSEL inference engine
IDIOT language / IDIOT	Detection	Misuse	Procedural	Colored Petri-net	N	N	N	Compiled to C/C++ code
N-Code / NFR	Detection	Misuse	Procedural	N programming language	N	N	N	Compiled to byte code
P-BEST / EMERALD	Correlation	Anomaly and Misuse	Procedural	Rule-based expert system	N	N	N	Interpreted by P-BEST inference engine
DPEM language / DPEM	Detection	Anomaly	Procedural	Parallel environment grammar	N	N	Y	Interpreted by specification manager
CASL /	Exploit	N/A	Procedural	Scripting language	N/A	N/A	N/A	Interpreted by CASL interpreter
BRO language / BRO	Detection	Misuse	Declarative	Regular expressions	Y	Y	N	Interpreted to build FSM
Snort language / Snort	Detection	Misuse	Declarative	Snort rules	N	N	Y	Interpreted as Rules
REE / IDS based on REE	Detection	Anomaly and Misuse	Declarative	Regular expressions	Y	Y	Y	Compiled to C/C++ code
Lambda / IDS based on Lambda	Exploit, Detection, and Correlation	Misuse	Declarative	Algebraic	N	N	N	Not provided
NASL /	Exploit	N/A	Procedural	Scripting language	N/A	N/A	N/A	Interpreted by NASL interpreter
Logweaver language / Logweaver	Detection	Misuse	Declarative	Linear temporal logic	N	N	Y	Model checking
ADeLe / GnG	Exploit, Detection, Correlation, and Response	Misuse	Procedural	Algebraic	Y	N	Y	Interpreted to build FSM
Sutekh / IDS based on Sutekh	Detection	Misuse	Declarative	Algebraic	N	N	N	Translated to RUSSEL and P-BEST rules
SHEDEL / HEIDI	Detection	Misuse	Declarative	Algebraic with state transition diagram	N	N	N	Not provided
STATL / STAT	Detection	Misuse	Procedural	State transition diagram	N	N	N	Translated to RUSSEL and P-BEST rules
CAML / IDS based on CAML	Correlation	Misuse	Declarative	Library of predicates	Y	N	N	Translated to P-BEST rules
CISL /	Reporting	N/A	N/A	N/A	N/A		N/A	N/A

- **Correlation languages.** These languages are used to define the relationships between attacks, and they attempt to detect coordinated intrusions. Some example correlation languages are P-BEST (Lindqvist et al., 1999), correlated attack modeling language (CAML) (Cheung, Lindqvist, & Fong, 2003), ADeLe (Michel & Mé,, 2001), Lambda (Cuppens & Ortalo, 2000), and JIGSAW (Templeton & Levitt, 2000).
- **Exploit languages.** Exploit languages are used to define the steps of an attack. Both GPL like C, C++, Perl, Python, and attack scripting languages like custom attack simulation language (CASL) (Ptacek, 1998), Nessus attack specification language (NASL) (Deraison, 2000), ADeLe (Michel & Mé, 2001), Lambda (Cuppens & Ortalo, 2000) are being used for this purpose.
- **Detection languages.** Detection languages define how to detect attacks. Some examples of detection languages are P-BEST (Lindqvist & Porras, 1999), STATL (Eckmann, Vigna, & Kemmerer, 2002), N-Code (Ranum et al., 1997), the language used by Bro (Paxson, 1998), Snort (Roesch, 1998) and intrusion detection in our time (IDIOT) (Crosbie et al., 1996), RUSSEL (Habra et al., 1992), regular expression over events (REE) (Sekar & Uppuluri, 1999), the language used by distributed program execution monitor (DPEM) (Ko et al., 1997), ADeLe (Michel & Mé, 2001), simple hierarchical event description language (SHEDEL) (Meier, Bischof, & Holz, 2002), Lambda (Cuppens & Ortalo, 2000), and Sutekh (Pouzol & Ducassé, 2001).

Types of Intrusion Detection Systems

Attack scenarios written in the attack languages of the IDS are interpreted by the corresponding IDS. Attack languages can be classified based on the type of IDS. Every IDS has its own language in order to represent attack patterns. Some of the attack languages are used by misuse detection systems (Habra et al., 1992), while the rest are utilized by anomaly detection systems (Crosbie et al., 1996).

Approaches of Attack Languages

There are two main approaches that attack languages follow to represent attack scenarios. One is declarative approach and the other one is procedural approach. In the declarative approach, an attack language specifies what to detect by specifying the events of interests and their orderings as well as the conditions that need to be satisfied to carry out a successful attack. On the other hand, the procedural approach not only specifies what to detect but also mentions how to detect the scenario (like creating a new instance and updating state variables). The latter approach makes writing attack signatures more difficult, especially when representing complex attack scenarios. In contrast, the scenarios written in the declarative approach are easier to read and to make changes to the existing attack specifications.

Attack Pattern Encoding Schemes

Attack languages use different types of encoding schemes in representing attack scenarios. For example, some attack languages use rule-based system, some use colored Petri-net, regular expressions (or algebraic expressions), state transition diagrams, while the others use library of predicates. Each encoding scheme has its own strengths and limitations. A rule-based attack encoding scheme facilitates the usage of efficient algorithms of expert-based systems to analyze audit data. However, this approach is not suitable enough in terms of maintainability of the attack signature database. An attack scenario spans across several rules, and therefore, it is difficult to introduce changes to the existing attack signatures. Rule-based attack representations are difficult to read and write. Rule-based attack representations are procedural and, therefore, the attack specification not only defines what to detect but also specifies the way an attack is detected. On the other hand, attacks that are encoded in terms of states and transitions are easier to read, write, and make changes in future. This approach is more suitable for maintaining large attack signature database. However, too many states and transitions in an attack scenario can hamper the conciseness of the attack signature. The attacks represented using algebraic expressions are more concise. However, it is difficult to come up with a simple expression in case of a complex attack scenario.

Performance Evaluation

The performance of IDS largely depends on the quality of attack signatures they employ. Some of the performance criteria used for comparison are run time complexity, memory used, quantitative analysis regarding attack detection/identification. We indicate whether a particular IDS has carried out such an evaluation by providing a Yes (Y) or No (N) answer.

Interpretation of Attack Specifications

In order to detect intrusions as specified by the attack languages, the specification need to be translated to an operational form (a representation that shows the execution steps). Some of the approaches translate the specifications to the rules which are interpreted by the inference engines or C/C++ code that are compiled and linked with the run time systems of the IDS. The IDS which use regular expression-based attack languages build finite state machines from the specification and execute pattern matching algorithms to detect attacks.

EXTENDING SSL FOR ATTACK DESCRIPTION

Based on the study presented in the previous two sections, we have observed that SSL are used in the SDLC especially for functional requirement specifications, while in the operational phase, the current trend is to use attack languages for the purpose of intrusion detection. The same trend applies to other nonfunctional requirements (NFR) such as the specification of safety requirements. Delaying the incorporation of security aspects in the software design is a great obstacle to building secure software systems. Many researchers strongly believe that considering security aspects from the early stages of the SDLC can play a very important role in achieving secure software. One of the ways of achieving such secure software is to consider attack scenarios to which the software might be vulnerable to early in the SDLC. This helps to discover vulnerabilities in the system under design and fix those vulnerabilities before the software is deployed for clients. This approach is quite similar to 'learn from experience' approach. Although such attack information were not available in the past, many databases are maintained nowadays covering the different aspects of attacks and the vulnerabilities that they exploit (US-CERT, 2005). This information can be used to construct attacks against the systems, while they are still in the design phase. However, the SSL which are used during the SDLC are not expressive enough to represent attack scenarios. Some of the limitations of the SSL with respect to attack scenario specifications are briefly described in the following paragraphs using examples.

- Attack scenario specification requires a set of predicates and language constructs to express security relevant information.

For example, if we want to monitor TCP packets for a specific port number, a typical specification could be *TCPPacket.Port == 80*. Moreover, if we want to set a limit on the number of times Login failure event has occurred in the system (e.g., 3 times) it could be specified through *Repeat (Login-Failure,3)*. Most SSL lack these language features to express attack scenarios. They do not provide any library to access TCP/IP packets or audit logs in the system.

- Modeling attacks requires the specification of the events and the temporal relations that exist among the events. For example, consider a particular attack scenario that requires events *a, b,* and *c* occurring in that order, and where there should be at least 60 seconds delay between the events *a* and *b*. A sample specification can *be [a, b, and c] && Delay (a, b)>60*. Most SSL fail to express such requirements through their current language constructs.

The limitations of the SSL in specifying attack scenarios have been addressed through the introduction of attack languages that can encode attacks in a very concise and expressive way. However, we believe that the use of two sets of languages by the two sets of stakeholders of a project (developers and security professionals) introduces a gap in building a secure system. This gap can be minimized by extending the multipurpose SSL for the specification of attack scenarios. The benefit of this extension is twofold as explained below. It enables developers to have a clear idea on the security aspects of their systems and identify vulerabilities in their design. On the other hand, it enables the security professionals to learn about the system models and design the attacks accordingly. This extension is an effort towards unifying software and security engineering disciplines. The following subsections present some related work on extending example multipurpose SSL to capture features provided by the attack languages.

UMLintr

In Hussein et al. (2005), a specification-based framework for intrusion detection is presented. The framework utilizes and extends UML for the specification of intrusion scenarios. The new extension is called UMLintr. The UMLintr allows the developers to specify intrusion scenarios at various stages of the SDLC. In the requirements elicitation stage, intrusion scenarios are modeled as misuse-cases. In contrast to use-cases, misuse-cases show how actors abuse the services provided by the system. In the design stage, the developers use misuse-package, misuse-class, and misuse-state-machine diagrams to show the detailed information of the intrusion scenarios. In the implementation stage, code relevant elements of the misuse-class and misuse-state-machine diagrams are implemented. The resulted intrusion scenarios can be transformed into the intrusion signatures that are used by a misuse IDS.

AsmLx

In (Raihan, 2006), an intrusion detection framework for developing attack scenarios based on a software specification language abstract state machine language (AsmL) (Microsoft, 2005) is presented. The resulting language has been named AsmLx. The primary reason of choosing AsmL is that AsmL specifications are executable. Therefore, it is possible to test the system behaviors against the modeled attacks even before coding of the system begins. While the UMLintr focuses on attack specification that is easy to read and communicate with clients, the AsmLx targets a language that could be used to write even complex attack scenarios in an easy, declarative, concise, and expressive way. Attack specifications are written in the AsmLx as state-machines. The AsmLx has its own language constructs to specify the events related to an attack scenario, the intra-event conditions, and the temporal orderings of the events as well. The AsmLx has been designed in such a way that could capture different desirable features of attack languages as discussed in the previous sections. The AsmLx specifications are translated to AsmL scenario plugins which are compiled and linked with the run time system of the intrusion detection analysis engine.

CONCLUSION

As computer attacks are increasing, needs for securing software are escalating. Incorporating security mechanisms after developing the software has been proved to be a less effective approach. Unifying software engineering and security engineering, on the other hand, is a promising approach for developing secure software. The unification implies the handling of security requirements at every stage of a software security engineering process. Among different directions of this unification process, the chapter primarily focuses on extending SSL for the purpose of attack scenario specification.

SSL are introduced to model software in different levels of abstraction which makes exploring the software characteristics easier. Moreover, SSL facilitate the process of communicating software to customers and maintaining the software after the development. SSL also help in coding and test case generation. A classification of the SSL is presented. Along with the study on various SSL, the chapter presents a comprehensive view of the current state of the art of the attack languages. The study provides an overview of attack languages and their features. A number of criteria have been identified, and based on these criteria, a comparative study among the attack languages is presented. It shows that attack languages vary in purpose, expressiveness in attack description, and attack representation schemes.

Based on the study, we find that the multipurpose SSL have the potential to be extended for the specification of security requirements such as attack scenario descriptions that are currently expressed by attack languages. This extension, in our opinion, is an important step towards unifying software and security engineering. The chapter provides a brief overview of some research work in extending SSL for the specification of attack scenarios. Mostly, the current extensions focus on extending a specification language for misuse-based detection systems. In future, the extensions will be carried out for anomaly detection systems as well to build normal behavioral patterns by specifying the expected characteristics of the software.

REFERENCES

Abrial, J. (1996). *The b-book: Assigning programs to meanings.* Cambridge, UK: Cambridge University Press.

Allen, R., & Garlan, D. (1996). *The Wright architectural specification language* (Tech. Rep. CMUCS -96-TB). Pittsburgh, PA: Carnegie Mellon University, School of Computer Science.

Auernheimer, B. (1987). *RT-ASLAN: A specification language for real-time systems.* Unpublished doctoral dissertation, University of California, Santa Barbara.

Axelsson, S. (2000). *Intrusion detection systems: A survey and taxonomy* (Tech. Rep. No 99-15). Gothenburg, Sweden: Chalmers University of Technology, Department of Computer Engineering.

Bidoit, M., & Mosses, P. (2003). CASL user manual. *LNCS vol. 2900.* Springer Berlin.

Booch, G. (1991). *Object-oriented design with applications.* Redwood City, CA: Benjamin/Cummings.

Booch, G., Rumbaugh, J., & Jacobson, I. (1999). *The unified software development process.* Boston: Addison Wesley.

Bowenm, J. (1996). *Formal specification and documentation using Z: A case study approach.* International Thomson Computer Press.

CERT. (2005). *CERT/CC Statistics.* Retrieved December 2005 from http://www.cert.org/stats/

Chamberlin, D., & Boyce, R. (1974). SEQUEL: A structured English query language. *International Conference on Management of Data ACM SIGFIDET (now SIGMOD) Workshop on Data Description, Access and Control* (pp. 249-264).

Cheung, S., Lindqvist, U., & Fong, M. W. (2003). Modeling multistep cyber attacks for scenario recognition. *DARPA Information Survivability Conference and Exposition,* 284-292.

CIDF Working Group. (1999). *A CISL tutorial.* Retrieved December 2005 from http://www.isi.edu/gost/cidf/tutorial.html

Clements, P. (1996). A survey of architecture description languages. *ACM/IEEE International Workshop on Software Specification and Design,* 16-25.

Crosbie, M., Dole, B., Ellis, T., Krsul, I., & Spafford, E. (1996). *IDIOT – User's guide* (Tech. Rep. TR-96-050). West Lafayette, IN: Purdue University, Department of Computer Science, The COAST Project.

Cuppens, F., & Ortalo, R. (2000). LAMBDA: A language to model a database for detection of attacks. *International Workshop on Recent Advances in Intrusion Detection, 107,* 197-216.

Curry, D. (2000). *Intrusion detection message exchange format: Extensible markup language (XML) document type definition* (Intrusion Detection Working Group IETF Internet draft). Retrieved from http://xml.coverpages.org/draft-ietf-idwg-idmef-xml-01.txt

Deraison, R. (2000). *The Nessus attack scripting language reference guide.* Retrieved December 19, 2005, from http://www.nessus.org

Eckmann, S. T., Vigna, G., & Kemmerer, R. A. (2002). STATL: An attack language for state-based intrusion detection. *Journal of Computer Security, 10*(1/2), 71-104.

Finin, T., Fritzson, R., McKay, D., & McEntire, R. (1994). KQML as an agent communication language. *International Conference on Information and Knowledge Management,* 456-463.

Forrest, S., & Longstaff, T. A. (1996). A sense of self for Unix processes. *IEEE Symposium on Research in Security and Privacy,* 120-128.

Frolund, S., & Koistinen, J. (1998). *QML: A language for quality of service specification* (Tech. Rep. HPL-98-10). Hewlett Packard Laboratories.

Gabrielian, A., & Franklin, M. (1988). State-based specification of complex real-time systems. *Real-Time Systems Symposium,* 2-11.

Garvey, T. D., & Lunt, T. F. (1991). Model based intrusion detection. *National Computer Security Conference.* 372-385.

Habra, J., Charlier, B. L., Mounji, A.., & Mathieu, I. (1992). ASAX: Software architecture and rule-based language for universal audit trail analysis. *European Symposium on Research in Computer Security, 648,* 435-450.

Hewitt, C., Bishop, P., & Steiger, R. (1973). A universal modular ACTOR formalism for artificial intelligence. *International Joint Conference on Artificial Intelligence* (pp. 235-245).

Hofmann, P. (1996). *MHEG-5 and MHEG-6: Multimedia standards for minimal resource systems* (Tech. Rep.). Berlin, Germany: Technische Universitat Berlin.

Hussein, M., & Zulkernine, M. (2006). UMLintr: A UML profile for specifying intrusions. *IEEE International Conference and Workshop on the Engineering of Computer-Based Systems.* 279-286.

Ilgun, K. (1993). USTAT: A real-time intrusion detection system for Unix. *IEEE Symposium on Security and Privacy,* 16-28.

Jackson, M. (1983). *System development.* Englewood Cliffs, NJ: Prentice Hall.

Jacobson, I., Christerson, M., Johnsson, P., & Overgaard, G. (1992). *Object-oriented software engineering: A use case driven approach.* Boston: Addison Wesley.

Javits, H. S., & Valdes, A. (1994). *The NIDES statistical component: Description and justification* (Tech. Rep.). Menlo Park, CA: SRI International.

Jin, J., & Nahrstedt, K. (2004). QoS specification languages for distributed multimedia applications: A survey and taxonomy. *IEEE Multimedia, IEEE Computer Society Press, 11*(3), 74-87.

Ko, C., Ruschitzka, M., & Levitt, K. (1997). Execution monitoring of security critical programs in distributed systems: A specification-based approach. *IEEE symposium on security and privacy,* 175-187.

Kumar, S., & Spafford, E. H. (1994). A pattern-matching model for misuse intrusion detection. *National Computer Security Conference,* 11-21.

Larsen, P. G., & Pawlowski, W. (1995). The formal semantics of ISO VDM-SL. *Computer Standards and Interfaces,* 17(5/6), 585-602.

Lindqvist, U., & Porras, P. (1999). *Detecting computer and network misuse with the production-based expert system toolset (P-BEST).* Oakland, CA: IEEE Computer Society Press.

Lipner, S., & Howard, M. (2005). *The trustworthy computing security development life cycle.* Retrieved December, 2005, from http://msdn.microsoft.com/security/default.aspx?pull=/library/en-us/dnsecure/html/sdl.asp

McCanne, S., Leres, C., & Jacobson, V. (1998). *Tcpdump 3.4 documentation.* Retrieved December 19, 2005, from http://tcpdump.org

Meier, M., Bischof, N., & Holz, T. (2002). SHEDEL – A simple hierarchical event description language for specifying attack signature. *IFIP TC11 17ʰ International Conference on Information Security: Visions and Perspectives,* 559-571.

Michel, C., & Mé, L. (2001). ADeLe: An attack description language for knowledge-based intrusion detection systems. *IFIP TC11 International Conference on Information Security,* 353-368.

Microsoft. (2003). *Windows 2000 security event descriptions.* Retrieved December 2005, from http://support.microsoft.com/default.aspx?scid=kb;EN-US;299475#kbl

Microsoft. (2005). *The abstract state machine language.* Retrieved December 2005, from http://research.microsoft.com/fse/asml/docu.aspx

Naur, P., & Randell, B. (1969). Software engineering: Report of a conference sponsored by the NATO Science Committee, Garmisch, Germany, 1968. Brussels, Belgium: NATO, Scientific Affairs Division.

Nielsen, B., Ren, S., & Agha, G. (1998). Specification of real-time interaction constraints. *International Symposium on Object-Oriented Real-Time Distributed Computing,* 206-214.

OMG. (2004). *Common object request broker architecture (CORBA) specification* (Tech. Rep. version 3.0.3). Needham, MA: Object Management Group.

OMG. (2005). *OCL 2.0 specification* (Tech. Rep. version 2). Needham, MA: Object Management Group. Ostroff, J. S. (1992). Formal methods for the specification and design of real-time safety critical systems. *Journal of Systems and Software, 18*(1), 33-60.

Paxson, V. (1998). Bro: A system for detecting network intruders in real-time. USENIX Security Symposium, San Antonio, TX. *Computer Networks, 31*(23-24), 2435-2463. Elsevier.

Porras, P. A., & Kemmerer, R. A. (1992). Penetration state transition analysis- A rule-based intrusion detection approach. *Annual Computer Security Applications Conference,* 220-229.

Porras, P. A., & Neumann, P. G. (1997). EMERALD: Event monitoring enabling responses to anomalous live disturbances. *National Information Systems Security Conference,* 353-365.

Pouzol, J. P., & Ducassé, M. (2001). From declarative signatures to misuse IDS. *International Symposium on Recent Advances in Intrusion Detection, 2212,* 1-21.

Raihan, M. (2006). *AsmLx based intrusion-aware software systems.* Unpublished master's thesis, Queen's University, Kingston, Ontario, Canada.

Ranum, M. J., Landfield, K., Stolarchuck, M., Sienkiewicz, M., Lambeth, A., & Wall, E. (1997). *Implementing a generalized tool for network monitoring.* Systems Administration Conference, USENIX Association.

Rumbaugh, J., Blaha, M., Premerlani, W., Eddy, F., & Lorensen, W. (1991). *Object-oriented modeling and design.* Englewood Cliffs, NJ: Prentice Hall.

Ptacek, T. (1998). *Custom attack simulation language (CASL)* (Tech. Rep.). Retrieved December 2005, from http://www.sockpuppet.org/tqbf/casl.html

Roesch, M. (1998). *Writing Snort rules: How To write Snort rules and keep your sanity.* Retrieved December 2005, from http://www.snort.org/docs/snort_htmanuals/htmanual_2.4/snort_manual.html

Sekar, R., & Uppuluri, P. (1999). Synthesizing fast intrusion prevention/detection systems from high-level specifications. *USENIX Security Symposium, (pp. 63-79).* Berkley.

Smith, G. (2000). The Object-Z specification language. *Advances in Formal Methods* (vol. 1).Kluwer Academic.

Sun Microsystems Inc. (1991). *Installing, administering, and using the basic security module* (Tech. Rep.). Mountain View, CA.

Templeton, S. J., & Levitt, K. (2000). A requires/provides model for computer attacks. *Workshop on New security paradigms,* 31-38.

US-CERT. (2005). *US-CERT vulnerabilities notes.* Retrieved January 2006 from *http://www.kb.cert.org/vuls/*

Vaccaro, H. S., & Liepins, G. E. (1989). Detection of anomalous computer session activity. *Symposium on Research in Security and Privacy,* 280-289.

Van Deursen, A., Klint, P., & Visser, J. (2000). Domain-specific languages: An annotated bibliography. *ACM SIGPLAN Notices, 35*(6), 26-36.

Van Eijk, P., Vissers, C., & Diaz, M. (1989). *The formal description technique LOTOS.* Elsevier Science.

Vigna, G., Eckmann, S. T., & Kemmerer, R. A. (2000). Attack languages. *IEEE Information Survivability Workshop,* 163-166.

Wieringa, R. (1998). A survey of structured and object-oriented software specification methods and techniques. *ACM Computing Surveys (CSUR), 30*(4), 459-527.

Zulkernine, M., & Ahamed, S. (2005). Software security engineering: Towards unifying software engineering with security engineering. In M. Warkentin & R. Vaughn (Eds.), *Enterprise information systems assurance and system security: Managerial and technical issues* (pp. 215-233). Hershey, PA: Idea Group.

Chapter XVII
Dynamic Management of Security Constraints in Advanced Enterprises

R. Manjunath
Bangalore University, India

ABSTRACT

Providing security for the content that gets exchanged between physically and geographically different locations is challenging. The cost and resources to be used to meet this challenge has to be linked to the degree of security demanded by the content. In this chapter, the security associated with the transfer of the content is quantified and treated as a quality of service parameter. The user is free to select the parameter depending up on the content being transferred. As dictated by the demanding situations, a minimum agreed security would be assured for the data at the expense of the appropriate resources over the network.

INTRODUCTION

The growth of business at any facility or location has created a need of relocation of some of the functional units at physically and geographically different locations. This calls for the seemless secure and quality-based exchange of data among these units, paving the path for the growth of mobile enterprises.

Until recently, the quality of service (QoS) over the network and the security were two separate domains in the field of networking. Recently, it has been found out that the attack on a network drastically affects the service parameters. (Aurrecoechea, Campbell, & Hauw, 1996). Conversely, nonconformance to the service parameters results in errors in the recovered information. As one of the definitions of secure transmission encompasses the recovery of the replica of the transferred signal at the receiver, the errors in recovery may be attributed to the security failure. Moreover, any deviation in the observed service parameter could lead to a suspected attack on the network. For example, abnormal increase in the delays, sudden dropout in the packets may be due to the re transmission or interceptions from an intruder. Integration of these two technologies provides a single unified platform for the users to fight against the attacks on the network.

In this chapter, a scheme is suggested to extrapolate the service parameters to be observed at a later point of time. A large deviation of these parameters would indicate a possible attack on the network. Thus, it would be possible to detect the attack the earliest. A differentially fed neural network may be used for the extrapolation operation. The deviation in turn may be captured as a security service parameter.

QoS enforcement over a network has to first detect the type of the flow that exist on the network and subsequently allocate the network resources and the bandwidth depending on the priority. Some of the flows have to be contended with the available bandwidth. It provides enormous power for these traffic shapers and controllers in identifying the type of the traffic, using which it would be possible to detect the abnormalities in the traffic easily. A packet shaper can provide information about where abnormally large traffic connections are coming from. Intelligent elements are required to shape this traffic to fit in to the bandwidth making use of several optimization techniques. Such constraints and control on the network traffic would certainly reduce the proliferation of viruses over the network providing a better damage control and ample time for precautions in the other parts of the network.

One of the applications where both the QoS and the security are to be given serious look is the Voice over IP. It is an architecture and implementation for the real time transfer of the voice signals over the Internet protocol. In VOIP traffic, the voice packets are to be identified and assigned a higher priority over the data, as it has to meet the real time constraints. This segregation activity will be performed by an intelligence element present in the Firewall. The traffic will now flow in to the appropriate queues in the network depending up on the priority bits. The classification has to happen in real time, at the cost of dropping or rate controlling the other flows. The usage of a neural network to provide feed back to the source to reduce the packet transfer rate is the topic of discussion in this chapter.

BACKGROUND

The increased delay in the packets would provide an opportunity for the hacking or piracy software to duplicate, copy, or corrupt the packets. The converse is also true. The presence of malicious codes or attack on the network would result in increased packet delays. These malicious software needs some processing time over the data to corrupt them. It will have fallout on the service parameters of the connection.

The service parameters largely depend up on the status of the underlying network. To meet the service quality stringently, the end user feed back is often required. With this feedback it would be possible to adjust the data rates in such a way that the service quality is met. For example, in the transfer of video over the network, the delay and jitter constraints are to be stringently maintained. If these parameters exceed the upper limits set, a feedback signal originating from the end user equipment should be sent to the data source so that it can reduce the data rate by increasing the quantization step size. The reduced data rate reduces resource contention and the available bandwidth would be good enough to support the required data rate without building up the queue or delay. Thus user feed back plays an important role in meeting the required service.

When a feedback signal, specifically a differential feedback signal, is provided to a system, it would start exhibiting interesting properties as explained in (Manjunath & Gurumurthy, 2002). The differential signal may be generated computing the difference between consecutive samples in discrete time domain. In continuous time domain the signal would be subtracted with its delayed version. Higher ordered differentials would be generated in the same way.

If higher ordered differentials are used as additional inputs to a system for decision-making, the predictability of the system increases and the results would be future proof or more accurate. Throughout this chapter, such a system is referred as differentially fed artificial neural network (DANN).

Consider the estimation or merging problem where a set of DANNs each with a different degree of differential feedback is used for estimation. Each of them would out put a certain value inferred by its decision. The actual output would be the weighted sum of all these outputs. In is interesting to see that, as the order of the differential associated with the estimator increases, the output closely matches with the actual output.

The different estimator output different abstract levels of the actual information. The fusion of all these abstract representations would provide the total and true information. The representation forms a hierarchy of abstractions. Each level in the hierarchy is the dimensional superset of the other level, with the extra dimension originating from the next order differential term. Each level in the hierarchy is called "hyper plane." Hence, to control the rate of transfer of information, the appropriate hyper plane needs to be used. When the resources are abundant, more information may be transferred and when they are in dearth, more abstract data would be transferred to meet the service quality constraints.

The introduction of security as service parameters would have impact on the other service parameters. In the process of meeting the agreed service quality, the security software would start peeping in to the packets for possible viruses and consumes some processing time. It increases delay and obviously the queue length. The other service parameters would get a hit. It is as though the number of flows have increased in the network, as though the buffer size has shrunk. The use of a DANN for handling the resources in a network using differential feedback is given in Manjunath and Gurumurthy (2005a).

A broker can take the responsibility of providing the pre negotiated quality data to the end user. The user would be free from the network related issues. The constraint on the brokers is to meet the relative service parameters with minimal utilization of resources and minimum loss or rejection due to nonconformance to these security parameters. It is interesting to observe that the data gets dropped when the security constraints are not met at the broker. The broker may also drop them if the resources are full and no place to hold the data.

The architecture that makes use of the broker for meeting the service quality is based on feed forward and feedback paths. The feed forward path consists of the actual information or data or commodity flow departing from the source. The feedback signal comprises of the position and status of the information at the destination as seen by the agent. The differentially fed neural network sits as a controller, as a part of the loop comprising of the source, the forward path, the destination and the feedback path. The controller has to generate the appropriate feedback signals based on the information as seen by the agent.

The feedback information from the controller results in reduction/increase in the source operation rate, which in turn helps in proper scheduling. Based on the congestion status, different congestion control algorithms are used. Each one of them may be thought of as an estimator. A DANN with higher degree of differential feedback works as an ideal estimator to replace all of them.

Since the differentially fed neural network is a part of the loop, its presence has profound effect on the traffic in the loop. Traffic here refers to the movement of the commodity data. The DANNs make use of a large number of previous samples for decision making. Decisions thrown out by such a system contributes to Long-range dependency in the traffic. The abstract levels of hyper planes of DANN contribute to self-similarity of network traffic when observed over different time scales.

In essence, insertion of DANN in the traffic loop makes the entire network to behave as a differentially fed neural network, manifesting all its properties. The network here refers to the forward and feedback paths. Hence DANNs play a role more than replacing the conventional neural networks in traffic shaping. The traffic shaping involves maintaining the schedules, reduction in the delays and reduction in stranded times or reschedules while keeping up the agreed service parameters.

A multibit closed loop feedback mechanism is assumed here, with the bits representing the packet loss probability and express congestion status of the network. The notification signal or feed back signal is time shifted to get better performance. This algorithm is called random early prediction (REP) (Manjunath, 2006). Feedback based control is in widespread use in systems that need precise adaptive control. Although there is feedback and an accurate model is not needed (only one that captures the 'dominant' behavior of the system), careful design of the controller is necessary. Otherwise it leads to instability.

The relative service parameters are defined when the different classes of the flow contend for the common resources such as the operating path, buffering space that tend to get choked and required to maintain a fixed ratio of the flow members.

When the optimization problem does not yield a solution, meaning that it is impossible to satisfy all service guarantees simultaneously, some of the QoS guarantees are selectively ignored, based on a precedence order specified a priori. Due to the form of the constraints, the optimization problem is a nonlinear optimization, which can only be solved numerically. The computational cost of solving a nonlinear optimization upon each arrival to the link under consideration may be prohibitive to consider an implementation of an optimization-based algorithm at high speeds. A simple solution making use of DANN may be used. The DANN is basically a nonlinear control technique. It makes use of a prediction based feedback control to achieve proportional delay differentiation. Absolute differentiation is expressed in terms of saturation constraints that limit the range of the controller. The control loop around an operating point is made stable through differential feedback and a stability condition is derived on the linearised control loop. The stability condition gives useful guidelines for selecting the configuration parameter of the controller. The proposed closed-loop algorithm is an effective approximation of the optimization-based algorithm.

The REP algorithm is effective at providing proportional and absolute per-class QoS guarantees for delay and cancellation/reschedule. The closed-loop algorithm reacts immediately when the routes are going from under load to overload and reacts swiftly when the routes go from overload to under load. This indicates that the delay feedback loops used in the closed-loop algorithm are stable. Proportional delay differentiation does not match the target proportional factors when the route is under loaded, due to the fact that the algorithms are work conserving, and therefore cannot artificially generate delays when the load is small.

Results for ratios of delays indicate that proportional loss differentiation (i.e., schedule cancellation is achieved when the outbound route is overloaded and traffic is dropped). However, it is not met in any of the algorithms when the queue falls to 0. This implies that the algorithms basically manipulate the queue of the flow members and scheduling of the members to meet the relative delay and loss guarantees. The REP feedback loops used in the closed-loop algorithm appear to be robust to variations in the offered load. In addition, the results of the REP closed-loop algorithm are found to be better than the one without any shift.

The delays and losses experienced by classes are monitored, which allows the algorithm to infer a deviation compared to the expected service differentiation. The algorithm then adjusts service rate allocation and the drop rates to attenuate the difference between the service experienced and the service guarantees.

ISSUES AND SOLUTIONS

One of the issues in the integration of the security products with the QoS products is the interoperability. The Firewall will have its own standard database. It can store directory data in one type of file while the QoS agents can have their own architecture for the databases. These directories or databases cannot talk to each other so easily. A common directory schema is on the way of implementation.

The VOIP is highly sensitive for attacks. A virus can effectively publicize the confidential conversations. Repeatedly opening sessions to the same port may prevent even the legitimate users to access the port. The repetitions of the sessions that finally result in spasm are to be blocked.

Providing security in a wireless channel is challenging. The intruders would be immersed in the signals they want to hack. The hacking happens when the data gets transferred between the wireless device and the router. The hacker can regenerate the packets through a sniffer device. Wireless equivalent privacy (WEP) has been proposed in standards such as 802.11a that make use of wireless channel.

The data that gets exchanged between the wireless device and the router make use of a shared key for encryption. For every packet sent, the shared key together with another key called initialization vector would encrypt the packet. The WEP key and initialization vector are combined to get the encryption key. Then RC4 or CRC-32 (or a combination of both) encryption algorithm may be used to encrypt the data. As the initialization key would be included in the packet, it would be prone to attacks. In addition, there are only a limited number of 16,777,216 initialization vectors. It means the vectors start repeating after sometime and the hacker can easily identify the repeating patterns with the help of some intelligence.

To address the security issues associated with WEP, IEEE has come out with a new wireless security standard 802.11i. It makes use of the temporal key integrity protocol. Provision of using the wireless channel would be provided only for the authorized users through the remote authentication dial in user service (RADIUS) authentication. During wireless connection, user name and password are to be provided in order to access the wireless network. The data may be encrypted optionally using the advanced encryption standard (AES) algorithm. The standard provides the feature of Key caching. Here the login and the password details are stored in a cache so that the user need not re enter them after an intermittent break. The drawback with the standard is that the implementation and the equipments are costly. However it is worth to pay for the security it provides.

A combination of these algorithms or standards may be provided for the user as a choice for his security option. With the security service quality being parameterized, the users can set a value for the same. Depending on the value one of the algorithms may be invoked. A Bayesian network may be used to merge these algorithms and evolve with a security policy that gets adapted to the available resources and the other service parameters.

In a large enterprise, the databases get changed dynamically. As the database gets updated with changes, metadata keeps track of the same. Sophisticated, user centric languages such as XML are used to capture the metadata. The metadata contains information about the source, context and the time. With the context, the data gets converted in to useful information. The metadata is useful in describing the data quality and used in business intelligence applications (Gartner Report, 2005). The meta data provides useful information about the data abstraction in an enterprise.

The updated standard in encoded data exchange XACML provides the security fused to XML. XACML is the amalgamation of several security rules and policies that compete or overlap. This is known as combining. A DANN readily combines a set of rules and learns the combined one with Bayesian learning (Manjunath & Gurumurthy, 2004). A DANN can thus implement the XACML data exchange security model with rapid learning algorithm.

FUTURE TRENDS

A new form of attack on the network could be denial of service attack. Here the network may be virtually hijacked and the service would be denied to the end user. The malicious code can replicate the service requests to such an extent that the network would soon get overloaded and choked. Worst, the hijacker would get the data from the source while the intended user would be still negotiating with the service qualities.

Firewalls are generally used to detect the attack in the form of virus or malicious code. They can identify some of the fields in the IP header where the service parameters reside. However, some times they fail.

Integrated version of the security and QoS (Chatterjee, Sabata, & Sydir, 1998) products have started appearing in the market. The integration has entered deep in to the routers. Security prod-

ucts such as intrusion detection system (IDS) that can detect the intrusion and alert the QoS system to treat the traffic as per a set of rules are on the way. A Bayesian network can be conveniently used for learning the rules. An IDS keeps monitoring the traffic streams for the malicious codes in the background. Foe any suspicious traffic, the firewall would deny access to the WAN.

Another relation between the network security and the QoS is that the variation in the service parameters can indicate the place where the network attack has been originated and helps in network forensics. This information would be useful for fixing the problem with the infected site by shutting down or alerting the site users.

QoS products provide a kind of interim protection to the network. Once the virus is known, its presence can be checked in the stream in the background. It can apply patches to the host system. An effective communication interface and mechanism has to be in place to integrate the security with the QoS. The security protocols need to take the responsibility of assuring end-to-end QoS and vive versa. It is only then a safe communication can be ensured with agreed quality. The protocols need to come up.

Another interesting instance where the QoS and the security aspects interact is during the transfer of encryption key. It is highly sensitive and has to meet both the security as well as the service quality parameters. When the packets are encrypted, the QoS agents would find it difficult to peep in to the packets and classify the same. It calls for the effective integration of security benefits of the encryption and the performance benefits of QoS. The security constraints are (to be) stringent over the WAN. Hence, before entering in to the WAN, the priority bits or the information from the IP header are extracted and placed outside the encryption. This happens at the interface at the edge of the network. Alternatively, priority of the traffic flows are done first and then the encryption could be applied.

The emerging IPV6 has a lot of new features that may be exploited for the integration of the security and the service quality. It provides end-to-end or point-to-point transfer without a translation in the IP address. The network address translation (NAT) creates serious security and performance issues because of the usage of lengthy tables and translation overhead time resulting in increased jitter and the delay. IPV6 has to enable the VOIP packets to penetrate through the firewalls without compromising for the security. The presence of NAT on the other hand has a unique advantage,. The internal topology will not be exposed to the network and to the hackers.

Viruses may be embedded as payloads on the RTP traffic. The firewall can easily detect most of them. However, it takes some time and imparts delay and jitter in to the traffic. The jitter component comes in to picture since the packets that do not have virus need not be cleaned saving some processing time. The usage of random early prediction (REP) technique explained would reduce the delay ands the jitter. The RTP stream insertion attacks can also result in buffer overflows and subsequently in to cell loss.

Isolation of the genuine calls from the call set up attacks or the spasm is a task involving a lot of built in intelligence. A feedback from the end user to the data source can help in isolating these calls. The source reduces the transmission rates as a result of feedback in the genuine call. The duplicate calls create as Spam do not have these features and are classified as bad flows and subsequently get eliminated.

In the enterprise scenario, the security of data transfer can be changed adaptively depending up on the feedback from the QoS agents. If there is any suspicion of the attack or intrusion, a more complicated key may be used for encryption. The intruder cannot break the key immediately. Before he could access the actual data, the transfer would get over or the problem of intrusion gets fixed. The keys may be agreed in advance or transferred during runtime over a separate route.

However, the complicated encryption algorithms call for reduced service qualities. To retain the same quality for parameters such as delay or jitter, the differential feed back provided to the source has to reduce the data rate adaptively in such a way that the parameters are well in the range as much as possible.

Like any other service parameters, users will have options to select security constraints. More stringent constraints may be required for the transfer of very confidential information such as financial transactions. Some relaxation may be accepted for other information transactions such as confidential conversations depending up on the context. The stringent constraints mean equivalent overhead in terms of resources and commercial impact. It throws open several business models. Hence security parameters need to be defined and parameterized accurately and carefully in lines with the other service parameters. The client software has to provide options for the user to select these parameters appropriately.

One major advantage of integrating the QoS with the security ids that it provides a predictable usage of network resources. It converts security from a constant performance obstacle in to a performance constraint depending on the context.

The other interesting outcome of the integration is that it would be possible to exchange the other service parameters for security (i.e., there would be a free tradeoff among the service parameters in an attempt to share the underlying resources). Parameterization of the security provides an indication of to what extent the other parameters can be compromised without the violation of the service parameters. The stringent security constraints probably require the peeping in or examination of all the packets for the presence of all possible virus samples while the packets travel over the network. Naturally it takes more time and increases the delay in the packets. The delay may be reduced by reducing the target virus sample set while processing the packets over the network. The REP method retains the relative service parameters with in a flow to be held constant in spite of the presence of other bad flows (i.e., the increased security checks in a way decrease the delay). It happens through reduced flow rate. If the relative ration of service qualities among the different flows are to be held constant, the same techniques may be used.

In the audio or video data, a certain redundancies are associated with the data. More over, the human psycho acoustic and psycho visuals permit a certain loss of information. Any way it would not get perceived. Hence some of the packets may be dropped to meet the security constraints. More intelligence would be required to take a decision as to which packet has to be dropped. For example, a B-frame in the picture may be readily dropped compared to the I-frame. If the information is arranged in hierarchical form, some of the hierarchies or abstractions may be dropped and the time and processing power may be used for virus scan over the packets, compromising for the quality to meet the security constraints.

Another division of information is to partition the same in to structured and unstructured parts (Manjunath & Gurumurthy, 2005b). The unstructured parts come in various abstractions and generated by providing differential feedback. For the content provider, the data mapping on to various service parameters are mapped in advance over the different levels of abstractions. Depending on the user preferences and the network conditions, the appropriately matching abstraction level would be put on the network. The abstraction is actually fictitious. The data is basically stored at one point. The fabrication or run time linking would bring out the differences.

The hierarchical organization of the data in to abstract levels has a say over the query results. The user can enjoy different priorities over a query. Search engines based on the user permissions/authentication can provide the results as appropriate. The query results would correspond to different levels of abstractions of the data. For example, the key word "Q1 report" in an organization can

just provide a few curves to a general user while the milestones, itemized expenditures to an executive and the individual salary expenditures to a finance guy. The common user would get the total salary expenditures and not the salaries of the individuals. The vice-president of the organization may get all this information in a single Web page as appropriate. All these different data are basically pointing tom different databases with in the organization. Here the abstraction is totally artificial and is brought out in the way of linking the databases. Rather than telling, "access denied", the different category of the people would get some results depending up on their access privileges. During the runtime, it may be required to integrate the different databases as appropriate and depict the result. A matured Web technology can generate Web pages dynamically and provide multiple views. However, with the existing technologies, the different Web pages corresponding to the multiple abstractions may be generated in advance over off line and depicted depending up on the user privileges.

In a modern enterprise, multimedia data would be streamed across the different business units. It is especially required in videoconferences, trade shows, product demos, corporate training, and so forth. The streams are prone to attack over the network as they carry highly sensitive and crucial information of the organization. In addition, the organization can sell some of its products such as software, IPs, ideas on line. The digital movie or songs distributors have started selling their products online. In these cases, it is required to ensure that the data should not get hacked on the line. They stream the products to the end user over the network. The sale could be on the per download basis, or usage for a fixed duration.

CONCLUSION

Meeting security constraints for the data that gets transferred over the networking has been challenging ever since the data transfer over the network started. Though tools and techniques were developed to counter attacks on the network, new methodologies were developed by the attackers exploiting the loopholes in the technology. Day by day, the intrusion and attacks are coming with more harm and impact. In the enterprise scenario, more confidential data gets exchanged across the different operational units calling for everlasting research on the secure transfer of the data.

The security of data can be ensured only when it gets processed or scanned in the runtime during the passage over the network. This processing results in delays and severely affects the service qualities of the transferred data.

In this chapter, the security IDs treated as a service and clubbed with the other service parameters. The advantages are explored. The security services are linked to the data organization. A hierarchical data organization with multiple degrees of abstraction is proposed. Depending up on privileges, the users can enjoy the different databases that map on to the different levels of abstraction.

REFERENCES

Aurrecoechea, C., Campbell, A., & Hauw, L. (1996). A survey of quality of service architectures (Special issue). *Multimedia Systems Journal.*

Chatterjee, S., Sabata, B., & Sydir, J. (1998). *ERDoS QoS architecture* (Tech. Rep. ITAD-1667-TR-98-075). Menlo Park, CA.

Gartner report. (2005). *Maintaining data quality.* Retrieved from http://www.ebizq.net/views/download_raw? metadata_id =6210&what=feature

Manjunath, R. (2006). *Compact architecture for the analysis and processing of subnet signals using differentiators as building blocks.* Unpublished doctoral dissertation, University of Bangalore, India.

Manjunath, R., & Gurumurthy, K. S. (2002). *System design using differentially fed Artificial Neural networks.* TENCON'02.

Manjunath, R., & Gurumurthy, K. S. (2004). *Hyperplanes Generation Through*

Convolution With Gaussian Kernals. IICAI.

Manjunath, R., & Gurumurthy, K. S. (2005a). *Bayesian estimator with differential feedback.* MWSCAS.

Manjunath, R., & Gurumurthy, K. S. (2005b). Learning algorithm with DANN. In *Encyclopedia of Database Technologies and Applications.* Hershey, PA: Idea Group.

Chapter XVIII
Assessing Enterprise Risk Level:
The CORAS Approach

Fredrik Vraalsen
SINTEF, Norway

Tobias Mahler
Norweigan Research Center for Compuers and Law, University of Oslo, Norway

Mass Soldal Lund
SINTEF, Norway

Ida Hogganvik
SINTEF, Norway

Folker den Braber
SINTEF, Norway

Ketil Stølen
SINTEF, Norway

ABSTRACT

This chapter gives an introduction to the CORAS approach for model-based security risk analysis. It presents a guided walkthrough of the CORAS risk analysis process based on examples from risk analysis of security, trust and legal issues in a collaborative engineering virtual organisation. CORAS makes use of structured brainstorming to identify risks and treatments. To get a good picture of the risks, it is important to involve people with different insight into the target being analysed, such as end users, developers, and managers. One challenge in this setting is to bridge the communication gap between the participants, who typically have widely different backgrounds and expertise. The use of graphical models supports communication and understanding between these participants. The CORAS graphical language for threat modelling has been developed especially with this goal in mind.

INTRODUCTION

Businesses face an increasing number of security risks in the online world, not limited to those of a technical nature. At the enterprise level, technical aspects of security are tightly interwoven with other aspects such as trust and legal issues. This is particularly true for the new breed of networked, virtual organisations. A virtual organisation (VO) can be understood as a temporary or permanent coalition of geographically dispersed individuals, groups, organisational units or entire organisations that pool resources, capabilities and information to achieve common objectives (Dimitrakos, Goldby, & Kearney, 2004).

Virtual organisations' dependency on information and communication technology for performing their daily work leads to a number of risks related to security, trust and legal issues. One area where VOs face risks is the protection of intellectual property (IP) and confidential information, which is the focus of the case study presented in this chapter. Confidentiality is the property that information is not made available or disclosed to unauthorised individuals, entities or processes (ISO/IEC 13335, 2004). The individual stakeholders in a VO desire to protect their IP and maintain confidentiality of information, but at the same time they need to share some of this information with the other partners in the VO in order to fulfil common objectives as well as specific obligations laid down in a co-operation contract. The risks are exacerbated by the international nature of many VOs, as well as their dynamic nature where participants can join and leave the VO at any point during its lifetime.

There is no general international legal framework for the establishment and operation of virtual organisations, and legal issues in relation to VOs are still a topic for research. A strategic roadmap for advanced virtual organisations points out that the analysis of legal risks arising from operating VOs, and the development of legal strategies to overcome them, is an important research task in order to support collaborative networked organisations (Camarinha-Matos et al., 2004). Such legal strategies for VOs should focus both on the contracts that need to be put into place and on the technology that may be utilised in order to facilitate and support the collaboration. When drafting the VO collaboration contract, parties need to identify and address risks that may arise from the collaboration. This risk analysis should preferably follow a clear methodology. Some approaches have considered project risk management in a more general setting (Baccarini & Archer, 1999; Raz & Michael, 1999), focusing mainly on the risk of project failure. However, collaborators also need to assess risks to their own assets.

To reduce the risks involved with establishing, joining and operating a VO, an approach for analysing and managing enterprise security risks is needed which takes into account both technical and nontechnical aspects. The collaboration of different experts, like computer scientists and lawyers, is necessary when analysing what may go wrong in a co-operation (Heymann, 2005; Müller-Hengstenberg, 2005). The CORAS model-based risk analysis approach facilitates the integration of these different perspectives, and focuses also on incorporating the context of the system into the analysis, that is, the organisations, processes and people which interact with the system.

CORAS is a framework for model-based security risk analysis. This framework consists of a method, a language, and a computerised tool. The method integrates aspects from different risk analysis techniques with state-of-the-art system modelling methods based on UML 2.0 (OMG, 2005), the de facto standard modelling language for information systems. The CORAS graphical language for threat modelling is an extension of the UML 2.0 specification language. It is defined as a UML profile (Lund, Hogganvik, Seehusen, & Stølen, 2003), and has recently become part of an OMG standard (OMG, 2006).

The goal of this chapter is to make the reader familiar with the CORAS method for model based risk analysis as well as the graphical language used for threat modelling, and explain how they may be employed in the analysis of VOs. The next section provides more background on the CORAS approach, followed by a walkthrough of the CORAS risk analysis process. Finally, we present some concluding remarks.

The example case is based on a risk analysis which was performed in the TrustCoM IST project (*http://www.eu-trustcom.com/*) using CORAS (Mahler, 2005). The analysis focuses on a collaborative engineering project in the aerospace industry, where a group of companies establish a VO to collaborate on the upgrade of an airplane design. The focus of the analysis is on intellectual property rights (IPR) and confidentiality issues in relation to the sharing of trade secrets between the partners of the virtual organisation. Hence, the analysis is also an attempt to contribute to the investigation of methods for legal risk management, which are "in their infancy" (Burnett, 2005).

THE CORAS APPROACH

The CORAS risk management method is based on the AS/NZS 4360 standard for risk management (AS/NZS 4360, 2004). *Risk management* is the sum of the culture, processes and structures that are directed towards effective management of potential opportunities and adverse effects. The *risk management process* consists of systematic application of management policies, procedures and practice to the tasks of establishing the context and identifying, analysing, evaluating, treating, monitoring and communicating risks. Risk management thus covers the entire life cycle of the system or organisation, and may include several risk analyses with different focus areas and abstraction levels as the system or organisation and its surroundings evolve over time.

Risk analysis requires a clear understanding of the system or organisation to be analysed. This can only be achieved through the involvement of stakeholders and other interested parties with different backgrounds and knowledge about the system or organisation (e.g., decision makers, security experts, legal experts, system owners, developers, and users). These participants are involved in the identification and evaluation of risks and treatments through structured brainstorming sessions.

The effectiveness of such sessions depends on the extent to which the participants are able to communicate with and understand each other. The CORAS graphical language for threat modelling (den Braber, Lund, Stølen, & Vraalsen, 2005) has been designed to mitigate this problem within the security domain. The CORAS language covers notions like asset, threat, risk and treatment, and supports communication among participants with different backgrounds through the definition of easy-to-understand symbols associated with the modelling elements of the language. A recent study has shown that the graphical symbols allow the participants to understand and read the diagrams more quickly (Hogganvik & Stølen, 2005). Recent work has also focused on application of the CORAS language and method to the analysis of security, trust and legal issues (Brændeland & Stølen, 2004; Mahler & Vraalsen, 2005; Vraalsen, Lund, et al. 2005), as well as continuous improvements of the language based on experiences from use and empirical investigations.

Figure 1 shows the main elements of a risk analysis and gives examples of the graphical symbols used by the CORAS language. The *target* is the system or organisation, or parts thereof, which is the focus of the analysis. *Assets* are the parts or features of the target which have value to the client commissioning the analysis, such as physical objects, know-how, services, software and hardware, and so on. A *vulnerability* is a weakness of the system or organisation. A *threat* may exploit a vulnerability and cause an *unwanted incident*, an event which reduces the value of one or more of the assets. A *risk* is an unwanted incident along with its estimated likelihood and

Figure 1. Elements of a risk analysis

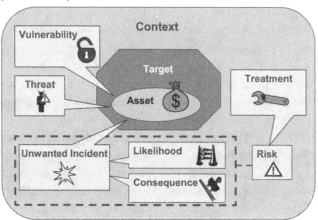

Figure 2. CORAS meetings

Meeting 1: Introduction
* Clients present the system or organisation they wish to analyse
* Identify the focus and scope for the analysis
* Set up analysis plan

Meeting 2: High-level analysis
* Risk analysts present their understanding of the target of analysis
* Identify assets
* Establish initial threats and vulnerabilities

Meeting 3: Approval
* Target of analysis documentation
* Assign values to assets
* Identify risk evaluation criteria

Meeting 4: Risk identification
* Identify risks through structured brainstorming

Meeting 5: Risk estimation and evaluation
* Estimate likelihood and consequence of risks
* Evaluate risks with respect to risk evaluation criteria

Meeting 6: Risk treatment
* Identify and evaluate treatments

Meeting 7: Finalisation meeting (if necessary)
* Present results and get any missing input

consequence values. *Treatments* represent various options for reducing risk.

The CORAS risk analysis process is typically organised as a set of meetings, as summarised in Figure 2. Between the meetings, the risk analysts need time to process the collected information,

gather additional necessary documentation, and prepare for the next step of the analysis.

The meeting schedule should be tailored to the needs of each individual risk analysis. Not all activities need to be conducted as face-to-face meetings, but may be performed through for ex-

Figure 3. The CORAS tool

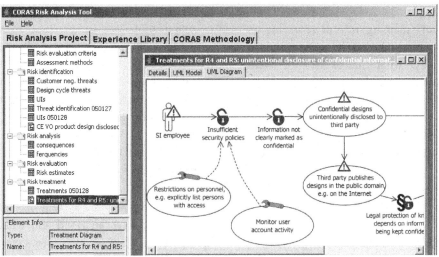

ample phone or video conferences or via e-mail discussions. Some meetings may be combined to save time or costs. For instance, in several cases we have combined meetings four through six into a two or three day workshop in order to reduce travel costs for the involved participants. This requires careful planning and preparation, however, as well as scheduling time during the workshop to give the analysts a chance to process the output, for example at the end of each day. On other occasions, additional meetings are needed, for example if new information comes up during the analysis which necessitates extra risk identification work to properly identify all the relevant risks.

Risk analysis is an elaborate and prolific process which involves many different types of documentation from different sources, such as UML models, tables with analysis data, and natural language descriptions of the target of analysis. All this information needs to be organised and accessible. In addition, it is important to maintain consistency between all the elements to prevent errors, and we also wish to be able to reuse elements from previous analyses where appropriate to avoid starting from scratch every

time. Computerised support for documentation, maintenance and reuse of analysis results is thus of high importance.

The CORAS Tool (Vraalsen, den Braber, Lund, & Stølen, 2005) is a Java-based risk analysis tool which is publicly available as open source (*http://coras.sourceforge.net/*). The client-server architecture of the tool enables multiple risk analysts to collaborate on the risk analysis projects. The risk analyst uses the CORAS client application to create new analysis projects, document and edit risk analysis results in tables and diagrams, generate analysis reports, and manage and reuse experiences from previous analyses. Information can be imported from various modelling and risk analysis tools used by the analyst through standardised data exchange formats, such as XMI for UML. The tool also contains a built in diagram editor for the CORAS graphical language. Help is provided to the user in the form of integrated online versions of the CORAS method and user guides. A screenshot of the CORAS client application is shown in Figure 3.

In the following sections, we will present the risk analysis meetings and activities in more detail. This will be illustrated with examples taken from the TrustCoM risk analysis.

INTRODUCTORY MEETING

The introductory meeting aims at achieving an initial understanding of what the client wishes to have analysed and what kind of risks the client is most concerned about. Some of the questions that should be answered include:

- For whom is the analysis carried out?
- For what purpose do we perform this analysis?
- What do we want to protect?
- What is the scope?

An in-depth analysis can be a time consuming and costly process, and the client typically has limited resources available for risk management. By clearly characterising the target and focus of the study, including identifying what falls outside the scope of the analysis, the available resources can be utilised in the most effective and efficient manner.

During a risk analysis, we make several assumptions and choices with regard to the system or organisation under analysis as well as its surroundings. Documenting these choices and assumptions is necessary in order to determine in which contexts the analysis results are valid. As the system or organisation and its surroundings change over time, these assumptions may no longer hold true. In this case, the analysis may need to be updated to determine whether the risk level of any of the previously identified risks has changed and to identify any new risks which may have arisen. Mechanisms thus need to be put in place to monitor the risks and assumptions and determine when a new risk analysis is necessary.

The introductory meeting should include the risk analysts and the client of the analysis, typically represented by a person with decision making powers with respect to the system or organisation being analysed. The meeting may also involve other stakeholders or parties who have an interest in or knowledge about the system or organisation.

The risk analysts should give a brief presentation of CORAS to familiarise the client with the risk analysis process and some of the methods and techniques which may be used, such as structured brainstorming and the graphical language.

Client Presents System or Organisation

The client presents the system or organisation they wish to have analysed and what kind of incidents they are most worried about. This presentation will typically include a mix of text (prose, tables, etc.), informal diagrams, such as rich pictures (Checkland & Scholes, 1990), and models describing the system or organisation to be analysed. Depending on what the client wishes to analyse, this presentation would normally cover a number of different areas, such as business goals and processes, users and roles, contracts and policies, hardware and software specifications, network layout, and so on.

SI is a company specialising in the integration of different aircraft subsystems. SI wants to win a contract with an airliner for the upgrade of their business jets with a new feature–an in-flight entertainment system. In order to be able to fulfil this objective, it joins a group of aerospace companies to form a virtual organisation in order to pool their resources and know-how and have a better chance of winning the contract. However, before joining the VO, SI wants to perform a risk analysis in order to determine the potential risks involved in this venture, and hires a consultant company to carry out the analysis.

The three main actors in this business scenario are:

- The airliner that operates a fleet of business jets.

- The proposed collaborative engineering VO (CE VO) which has the technical expertise to specify, design and integrate systems into complex products, and which may also manufacture the solution for the customer. Three partners would be involved in this VO; an avionics manufacturer, an in-flight system entertainment provider, and the aforementioned system integrator (SI)—the client of the risk analysis.
- An analysis consultancy which support design activities within engineering companies by performing general analysis work across engineering and scientific sectors.

Figure 4 shows a diagram presented by SI, depicting the actors and their relationships. The various subsystem designs and integrated designs produced and shared during the design process are stored in the product design database (PDD).

Characterise Focus and Scope of the Analysis

The client and the risk analysts should characterise the focus and scope of the analysis. Characterising the focus and scope is important to ensure both a common understanding of the problem at hand and to ensure an efficient use of the available resources by focusing on the aspects of the system or organisation that are of real importance to the client. This includes defining the borders between what is to be part of the analysis (target) and what is to be left out. Part of defining the scope is selecting which security properties are to be considered in the analysis, such as confidentiality, integrity, and availability, as well as other aspects of interest. The risk analysts should interact with the client to clarify any questions or uncertainties with regards to the target of analysis to avoid misunderstandings later on.

The system integrator is particularly concerned about loss of intellectual property and confidential information and the possibility of industrial espionage in connection with exchange of information with other partners, both internal and external to the VO. Retaining confidentiality of the design information communicated with the partners and stored in the Product Design Database is therefore of utmost importance. To prevent other companies from competing with the CE VO proposal, it is also important to protect the confidentiality of the requirements which have been gathered from the airline through the discussions and initial design meetings.

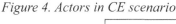

Figure 4. Actors in CE scenario

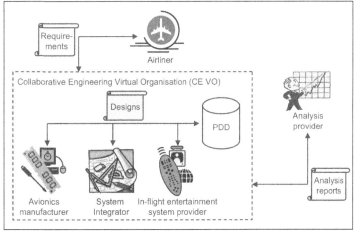

To limit the size of the analysis, other aspects such as data integrity issues, for example, malicious modification or deletion of information because of industrial sabotage or for example virus attacks, are left outside the scope of this particular analysis.

Plan the Analysis

Finally, the rest of the risk analysis should be planned in more detail, including identifying participants and meeting times and venues, based for example on the suggested meeting schedule presented in Figure 2. To achieve continuity in the risk analysis process it is important that the core group of participants commit to the risk analysis and are able to participate during the whole process so that the risk analysts do not have to interact with new and different people at every meeting. Additional persons may be involved in the different meetings based on the competence which is required.

The risk analysis team typically consists of one or two risk analysts who perform the actual risk analysis. One risk analyst should be responsible for leading the risk analysis sessions, and an additional person may act as a secretary during the sessions, recording the results and assisting the risk analysis leader when necessary.

The analysis team should include a representative of the client with decision making power with regards to the target of analysis. In addition, it should include other stakeholders, domain experts, and other interested parties with knowledge about the target of analysis, such as system managers, developers, users, lawyers, security experts, and so on. The goal is to involve people with different backgrounds and different insight into the problem at hand in order to elicit as much relevant information about potential risks as possible. If the risk

Table 1. Risk analysis roles

Role	Name	Organisation	Background/Expertise
Risk analysis leader	Thomas	CORAS Ltd.	Risk analysis, security
Risk analysis secretary	Frank	CORAS Ltd.	Risk analysis, security
Target owner	David	AirFrame Inc.	Aerospace industry
Domain expert	Peter	EngiCorp	Engineering & design
Domain expert	Irene	U. of Oslo	Intellectual property law
Domain expert	Claire	U. of London	Socio-economy and trust

Table 2. Risk analysis plan

Date	Tasks	Participants
29th November	Target identification Asset identification	Analysis leader & secretary, legal expert
11th January	High-level analysis	Analysis leader & secretary, legal expert
27th January	Approval Risk identification	Whole risk analysis team
28th January	Risk estimation and evaluation Risk treatment	Whole risk analysis team
2nd February	Cleanup of results Risk analysis report	Analysis leader & secretary, legal expert

analysis team becomes large, it may be beneficial to split it into smaller groups during parts of the process (e.g., the brainstorming sessions described below). The point is to give everyone a chance to participate and feel useful, as well as to be able to control the group when necessary.

The risk analysis team consisted of two risk analysts with backgrounds in security. The risk analysis team also included two representatives from the client company, the project leader for the aircraft upgrade project and an engineer with good knowledge of the engineering design processes. In addition, it involved an IP lawyer and an expert on socio-economy and trust. The participants of the risk analysis are documented in the risk analysis roles table as shown in Table 1.

The risk analysis for SI was performed over the course of 2½ months. Because the participants were spread across several countries, the main part of the analysis was performed during a two day workshop involving the whole analysis team. Other activities were performed in smaller groups and through phone conferences and e-mail discussions. The plan for the analysis is summarised in Table 2.

HIGH-LEVEL ANALYSIS

One of the goals of the second meeting is to ensure a common understanding of the focus and scope of the analysis, as well as to identify the client's main assets in the system or organisation. Assets are central to the CORAS risk analysis method and help guide the entire risk analysis process. The assets are used to assist in identifying risks and estimating their consequences in terms of loss of (monetary) value of the different assets. A high level analysis of threats, vulnerabilities and unwanted incidents is performed to help identify what the client is most worried about happening, and thus to ensure a correct characterisation of the focus and scope of the analysis.

Risk Analysts Present Target of Analysis

Based on the background documentation from the client and the presentations and discussions from the introductory meeting, the risk analysts start by presenting their understanding of the target of analysis, inviting comments and cor-

Figure 5. Target of analysis

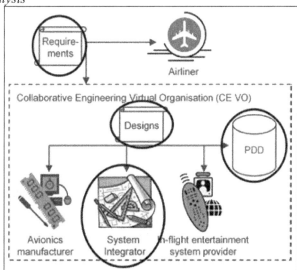

Figure 6. High-level CE VO design process

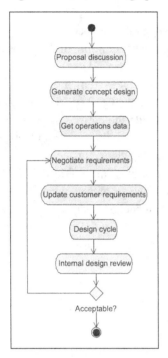

and customer requirements in relation to interaction between the partners of the CE VO and other external partners. The product design database (PDD) is central to the exchange of designs between the different CE VO partners and is regarded as a main focus point for the analysis. The target of the analysis is highlighted in the "rich picture" provided by the client of the VO and its partners, as shown in Figure 5.

The documentation provided by the client also contains descriptions of the main business processes related to the aircraft design process. A few of these are selected for analysis, based on where exchange of confidential information between the different participants occurs. The processes are modelled using UML activity diagrams, such as the high-level design process shown in Figure 6.

The legal expert and risk analysts also perform an analysis of the potential contractual obligations and rights of the VO and VO partners. It can be assumed that a number of different contracts will govern the internal and external relations and activities of the CE VO. These will most probably include at least three types of contracts:

rections from the client. This is done to ensure a common understanding of what is to be analysed and what is to be considered outside the scope of the analysis. The target is characterised using for example UML diagrams or other types of models to specify the target and its relations with the surroundings.

Based on SI's concerns, the focus of the risk analysis is defined as confidentiality of designs

- Consortium agreements, which establish a consortium of organisations with a common goal.
- Services or goods related contracts, e.g. outsourcing contracts, which govern the

Figure 7. Contracts in CE VO scenario

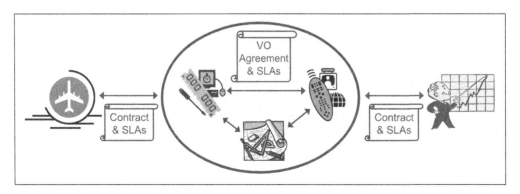

provision of services or the purchase of goods without establishing a consortium.

- Service level agreements (SLAs), that is, (mostly electronic) contracts that deal with the specific rules that partners in an operational business process are bound to.

An overview of these contracts and agreements are shown in Figure 7.

Identify Assets

Assets are the parts or features of the target of analysis that have value to the client and that the client wants to protect, such as physical objects, key personnel, services, software and hardware, or more intangible things such as know-how, trust, market share, and public image. By directing the analysis towards the assets of highest value to the client, one ensures that the available resources are spent on identifying the risks of highest impact on these assets. If the system or organisation does not contain any assets of value to the client commissioning the analysis, there is nothing that can be harmed and lose value for the client, and hence no point in a risk analysis.

The risk analysts typically perform an initial identification of assets based on the information provided by the client in presentations and target documentation. During the meeting, the list of assets is discussed and updated together with the client. To limit the size of the analysis, the number of assets should not grow too large; typically the four to six most important assets suffice.

As mentioned in the target characterisation, the integrated aircraft designs and customer requirements were identified as the most important IP from the viewpoint of the system integrator. In addition, based on the discussion, it becomes clear that the system integrator is also concerned about its public image and how trust may be affected, both the trust of the other VO partners and the trust of customers of the system integrator. The identified assets are shown in the asset diagram in Figure 8.

High-Level Risk Analysis

Sometimes it may be difficult to determine exactly what should and should not be included in the risk analysis. For instance, identifying the most important assets may be hard without also looking at the relevant risks at the same time. Furthermore, the client is often tempted to include as much as possible. However, the result of this may be an inability to analyse anything at all in sufficient detail due to lack of time and resources for the analysis.

A preliminary high-level analysis of the target may be performed to identify the most important assets, threats, vulnerabilities and unwanted incidents to ensure that the focus of the analysis

Figure 8. Asset diagram

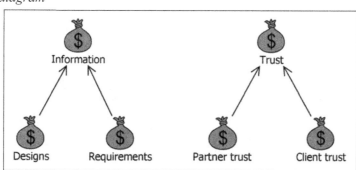

will be on the risks that the client is most worried about. The results of this analysis may help refine the focus and scope of the analysis and also serve as a starting point for the risk identification activity, where the results may be further refined and expanded upon.

This high-level analysis can thus be seen as a first iteration of the risk analysis. The same techniques for risk identification as described in the following sections may be utilised, but more informally. For example, one could use structured brainstorming as described in the section on risk identification below to identify focus areas but leave out the more detailed analysis of likelihood and consequence of the identified risks. The results of the high-level analysis are documented in a table such as the one below.

APPROVAL MEETING

The goal of the approval meeting is to ensure that the background documentation for the rest of the

analysis, including the target, focus and scope as characterised by the risk analysts, is correct and complete as seen by the client of the analysis. The documentation of the target of analysis, assets and risk evaluation criteria must be approved by the client.

The client does not have unlimited resources to implement risk reducing measures. We therefore need a mechanism to prioritise the risks and select risks for further attention and treatment. To facilitate this, we must identify the level of risk that the client is willing to tolerate, in terms of loss of asset value over a given time interval. In order to assess the potential loss, we also need to determine the value of the assets.

This meeting should also include people who will be involved in the following risk meetings, such as domain experts, users, and so on, in order to give them an introduction to the analysis.

In preparation for the approval meeting, the risk analysts need to clean up the documentation of the target of analysis and assets. CORAS diagrams should be created for the results of the

Table 3. High-level analysis table

Threat (deliberate)	Threat (accidental)	Threat (non-human)	Threat scenario — Unwanted incident — Asset		Vulnerability
Who/what causes it?			How? What is the incident? What does it harm?		What makes this possible?
...			...		...

Table 4. CE VO analysis asset table

Asset ID	Description	Asset category	Asset value
Designs	SI's share in the designs of the passenger aircraft	Information	Very high
Requirements	The requirements of the VO's customer	Information	High
Partner trust	The VO partner's trust in SI	Other	High
Client trust	The client/customer's trust in SI	Other	Very high

high-level analysis. The resulting documentation should be sent to the client for perusal prior to the meeting.

Documentation of Target of Analysis

The documentation of the target of analysis, i.e. the system or organisation being analysed and the focus and scope of the analysis, forms the basis for the rest of the analysis activities. It is therefore essential that it correctly describes the target of analysis and captures the aspects that the client is most concerned about. A walkthrough is conducted of the documentation, and any errors or omissions are pointed out and recorded. Changes may be performed on the fly or by the risk analysts later on.

Asset Values

After identification, the assets should be ranked according to value or importance to the client, in order to facilitate selection of the most important assets and also prioritising the risks later on. Not all assets can be measured in monetary value, such as human life and health. In these cases, other criteria for risk evaluation may be needed. The

assets should be documented in an asset table, as shown in Table 4.

Risk Evaluation Criteria

The goal of this activity is to determine what level of risk the client is willing to accept, in terms of what losses can be tolerated over a given period of time. Risk level is expressed in terms of likelihood, that is, what are the chances of this risk occurring, and consequence, what is the loss with regards to the asset which is affected by the risk. The likelihood and consequence values can be expressed in terms of quantitative values, such as statistical probability or amount of money lost. However, often we do not have the necessary data needed to calculate accurate values. Instead, we may use qualitative values for likelihood and consequence (e.g., low, medium, high), together with examples illustrating what these values mean. The values used for likelihood and consequence can be documented in a value definition table, such as the one shown in Table 5.

The risk evaluation criteria specify what level of risk the client is willing to accept, and should be expressed in terms of the likelihood and consequence values defined above. Based on the

Table 5. Value definition table from CE VO analysis

Value type	Values	
Likelihood	Rare:	Less than once per ten years.
	Unlikely:	Less than once a year.
	Possible:	About once a year.
	Likely:	2-5 times a year.
	Certain:	More than 5 times a year.
Consequence	Insignificant:	No impact on business. Minor delays.
	Minor:	Loss of profits. Lost project phases.
	Moderate:	Loss of project/client.
	Major:	Loss of business sector. Close department.
	Catastrophic:	Out of business

consequence and likelihood, a risk may either be accepted, or selected for further evaluation and treatment. Typically, this is done by setting up a matrix which shows the mapping of consequence and likelihood values to either "accept" or "evaluate," as shown in Table 6. Note that not all risks that end up in the "evaluate" region will necessarily be treated, depending on the availability and cost of effective treatments. Likewise, risks which end up in the "accept" region may still be treated if simple and inexpensive treatments are available.

RISK IDENTIFICATION

This meeting seeks to identify the risks to be managed, i.e. where, when, why and how incidents could prevent the achievement of objectives or reduce the value of an asset. The activity makes use of selected techniques and elements of conventional risk analysis methods which have been adjusted to fit the model-based approach of CORAS. The risk identification session is organised as a structured brainstorming, inspired by HazOp–Hazard and Operability Analysis (Redmill, Chudleigh, & Catmur, 1999).

The goal is to involve people with different backgrounds and different insight into the problem at hand in order to elicit as much relevant information about potential risks as possible. In addition to the risk analysts and the client, the meetings should include people with an interest in and knowledge of the system or organisation under analysis, such as security experts, lawyers, users, system managers, and so on.

Based on the identified assets, models describing the target, and the threats and weaknesses identified by the high-level analysis, the risk analysts should prepare the session by first selecting suitable models as a basis for the analysis, such as use cases, network diagrams, and so on, that match the desired level of abstraction. These should be illustrated using e.g. UML class, sequence or activity diagrams. The risk analysis leader should also prepare for vulnerability identification by selecting suitable checklists. The background documentation, in the form of models, checklists, and so on, should be sent out to the whole risk analysis team prior to the meeting.

Structured Brainstorming

The risk identification activity is organised as a structured brainstorming. The risk analysis team tries to identify scenarios describing how threats exploit vulnerabilities, leading to unwanted incidents which may reduce the value of one or more assets. The risk analysis leader uses the assets of highest value in conjunction with the diagrams of the target to guide the identification process, e.g. by asking relevant questions to the risk analysis team. The use of graphical diagrams also facilitates understanding and communication between the participants. The identification of threats and vulnerabilities may be supported with the use of

Table 6. Risk matrix from CE VO analysis

		Consequence					
		Insignificant	Minor	Moderate	Major	Catastrophic	
Likelihood	Rare					(Evaluate)	□ Accept risk
	Unlikely				(Evaluate)	(Evaluate)	
	Possible			(Evaluate)	(Evaluate)	(Evaluate)	▨ Evaluate risk
	Likely		(Evaluate)	(Evaluate)	(Evaluate)	(Evaluate)	
	Certain		(Evaluate)	(Evaluate)	(Evaluate)	(Evaluate)	

Figure 9. Model-based structured brainstorming

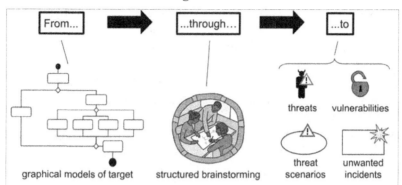

pre-defined questionnaires and checklists. This process is illustrated in Figure 9.

Vulnerabilities can be thought of as control mechanisms that ideally should be in place, but for some reason are missing or not sufficiently robust. Using this metaphor, vulnerabilities can be regarded as unsatisfactory controls, or exceptional circumstances that have not been planned for or that nullify the effect of existing, satisfactory, controls. Vulnerabilities can also be system characteristics that are impossible to treat; an internet connection that is crucial to the system, for example. Identifying new vulnerabilities is often a matter of finding the "blind spot". It is usually necessary to consider all aspects of the target (e.g., the organisational, judicial, physical, and computational characteristics) and compare these findings with the relevant policies.

During the meeting, one person from the risk analysis team should have the responsibility to record and document the results of the structured brainstorming. Following the risk identification meeting, the risk analysts structure the results and document the findings in diagrams using the CORAS graphical language for threat modelling. These diagrams are used later on as a basis for estimating the risk level as well as for identification of treatments. In the CORAS language, a threat (e.g., a disloyal employee or a computer virus) is related to a threat scenario, which is a sequence

of events or activities leading to an unwanted incident. A vulnerability may be attached to this relation. An unwanted incident is an event resulting in a reduction in the value of the target asset. Furthermore, an unwanted incident may initiate or lead to other unwanted incidents, forming chains of events.

The risk analysts should also assess the need for further threat or vulnerability identification. For each unwanted incident the risk analysts should decide whether it is described at an appropriate level of abstraction, or whether additional analysis is required. The reason for the latter could be the need for more detailed incidents to make the assignment of frequencies feasible, or that the unwanted incident seems to require a higher priority than originally assigned. Additional information may be elicited from the client or other participants of the risk identification session, or the risk analysis leader may determine that an additional risk identification meeting is needed, but this time focusing on a smaller part of the target of analysis.

As a basis for the analysis, a number of models of the business processes in the organisation were selected. Figure 6 shows a high-level view of the iterative design process used by the CE VO. This process includes a lot of collaboration between the different VO partners, as well as interaction with the airliner at a number of points, such as in the concept and requirements phases.

The identified risks relate to different IPR issues, including the protection of confidential information (i.e., know-how and trade secrets), the ownership of IP, and liability for IPR infringements by other VO partners. The internal collaboration in the CE VO and its cooperation with the analysis company and the airliner, respectively, implies that confidential information is shared or otherwise disclosed to VO partners or to external parties. This involves the risk that such confidential information is disclosed to third parties or used by VO members for purposes that are not related to the VO.

Figures 10, 11 and 12 show use of the CORAS graphical language for describing some ways in which confidential information can be disclosed along with potential consequences this disclosure may have. For example, an employee may have access to confidential information which he/she could disclose to a third party, either willingly or by mistake. This disclosure could lead to the information being used for competitive purposes, or it could reach the public domain and thereby lose its legal protection and value as a trade secret.

RISK ESTIMATION AND EVALUATION

As mentioned in the approval meeting section, the client does not have unlimited resources to implement risk reducing measures. We therefore need to prioritise the risks and select a subset of them for further attention and treatment. Risk estimation is the systematic use of available information to determine how often specified events may occur and the magnitude of their consequences. A *risk* is an unwanted incident along with its estimated likelihood and consequence values. These values are the basis for risk evaluation. The goal of the risk evaluation is to prioritise the risks and identify which ones are in need of treatment by

Figure 10. Hacker steals designs and sells them to competitor

Figure 11. Unfaithful employee discloses customer requirements

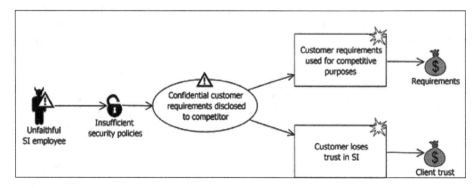

Figure 12. Loss of legal protection for know-how

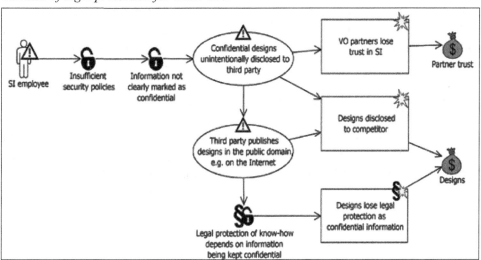

comparing against the preestablished risk evaluation criteria.

Estimate Risk Level

The goal of this activity is to estimate the level of risk for the identified unwanted incidents. This consists of evaluating the likelihood and consequence of the incident. The consequence is a measure of loss of asset value when the incident occurs, while the likelihood is a measure of how often an unwanted incident occurs. The diagrams output by the risk identification activity are used as a basis for the likelihood and consequence evaluation. These document the identified threat scenarios, and may also contain consequence values which have been provided by the risk analysis team during the risk identification.

The methods chosen for consequence and likelihood evaluation depend on the results from the risk identification, the historical and statistical information available, and the analysis group's ability to assign consequence and likelihood values. In many cases, estimates are elicited from the client, domain experts or other people with knowledge of the target of analysis. If statistical

Table 7. Consequence and likelihood table

Risk	Asset	Unwanted incident	Consequence	Likelihood
R1	Designs	Designs disclosed to competitor	Moderate	Unlikely
R2	Requirements	Customer requirements used for competitive purposes	Moderate	Unlikely
R3	Client trust	Customer loses trust in SI	Major	Unlikely
R4	Partner trust	VO partners lose trust in SI	Major	Possible
R5	Designs	Designs lose legal protection as confidential information	Moderate	Possible

or historical data is available, more sophisticated methods may be used, for instance Fault Tree Analysis (IEC 61025, 1990) for calculating the frequency of an incident.

The risk analysis leader presents the CORAS diagrams. For each diagram, consequence and likelihood values are estimated for the different threat scenarios and unwanted incidents, based on expert judgements made by the system owner in collaboration with the risk analysis team. Some of the risks identified in the CE VO analysis are listed in Table 7 along with their consequence and likelihood values.

An example of how calculation of the likelihood of risk R1 could be performed using fault tree analysis is shown in Figure 13. For each event, a probability is given for it occurring during a time period of one year. The resulting probability of 0.28 fits the likelihood category 'unlikely' ("less than once a year").

Fault trees may also be used as a mechanism to decompose and structure scenarios and events without necessarily needing to perform the probability calculations.

Evaluate Risks

The risk evaluation compares the estimated risk level against the pre-established criteria which were identified in the approval meeting. This enables a prioritisation of risks, which is the basis for the subsequent decision about which risks should be targeted for treatment. Note that we may not be in a position to treat all risks, depending on the resources available for establishing risk reducing measures.

Prior to the evaluation, risks may be grouped or categorised. This categorisation can be done according to different concerns, for instance grouping risks which affect the same assets or which stem from the same vulnerability. This may reduce the work necessary for treatment identification and evaluation as the different risks in a category can often be treated using the same approach. An example based on the CE VO risk analysis is shown in Figure 14.

We then apply the risk evaluation criteria specified earlier during the approval meeting.

Figure 13. Fault tree

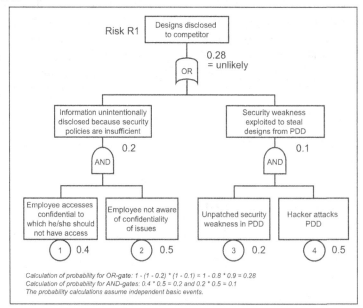

Figure 14. Risk category

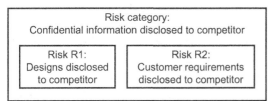

After estimating the likelihood and consequence of the risks, they are plotted into the preestablished risk matrix, as shown in Table 8. As can be seen, risks R3, R4 and R5 need further evaluation, whereas risks R1 and R2 are accepted and may only need to be monitored to see if their risk level changes in the future. In the evaluation of R3-R5 it was decided that they are all in need of treatment.

RISK TREATMENT

This phase aims at treating the nonacceptable risks by developing and implementing specific cost-effective strategies and action plans for reducing the risk level.

Identify Treatments

For each risk which is not accepted, potential treatment options are explored in a similar manner to the structured brainstorming used for risk identification. This session typically involves the same participants as the risk identification. A walkthrough is performed of the CORAS diagrams created from the risk identification sessions, and the participants are asked to come up with suggestions for different ways to reduce the risk.

There are four main approaches to risk treatment:

- Reduce the likelihood of the incident occurring.
- Reduce the consequence if the incident should occur.
- Transfer the risk to another party (e.g., through insurance or outsourcing).
- Avoid the activity leading to the risk.

The outcome of the treatment identification is documented using the CORAS graphical language by adding treatments to the existing diagrams.

For each of the risks which were not accepted during risk evaluation, potential treatments are explored by the risk analysts and the other participants. A selection of treatments to the risks described above is shown in the CORAS diagrams in Figure 15 and Figure 16. The figures show some threat scenarios from Figure 11 and Figure 12 and some options for treating them.

The aim in the CE VO analysis was to develop an integrated set of treatments, where legal and

Table 8. Risks plotted into risk matrix

		Consequence				
		Insignificant	Minor	Moderate	Major	Catastrophic
Likelihood	Rare					
	Unlikely			R1, R2	R3	
	Possible			R5	R4	
	Likely					
	Certain					

☐ Accept risk

▨ Evaluate risk

other measures are seen together. In this context, the focus was on proactive legal mechanisms, which try to solve legal issues before they arise. Various access rights policies can be imposed via contractual clauses in the agreement between the CE VO partners as well as with the analysis provider (e.g., requiring that access is limited to only those people involved in the project), as well as requiring that access to the confidential information is monitored to allow for auditing. This is shown as two treatments in the figures below, which reduce the likelihood that some of the vulnerabilities from Figure 11 and Figure 12 will be exploited.

Furthermore, if the technology is available, a VO-internal enterprise digital rights management (DRM) system could also reduce the risk of confidential information being disclosed, particularly if some of the contractual obligations could be enforced through technological means. Information security mechanisms like limitations to storage time and the deletion of data after use were also identified as possible treatments.

Evaluate Treatments

To determine the best expenditure of the resources available for risk reducing measures, the identi-

Figure 15. Treatments for risk R3

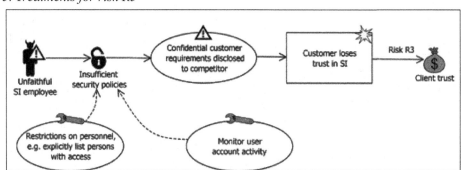

Figure 16. Treatments for risks R4 and R5

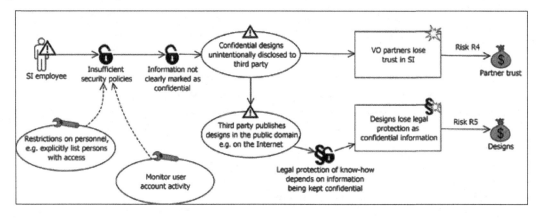

fied treatments are evaluated with respect to their usefulness. The degree to which the treatment reduces the level of risk is estimated, and a cost/benefit analysis is performed. Table 9 shows some examples of treatment evaluations from the CE VO analysis. Based on these results, the treatments can then be prioritised and implemented based on the available resources.

FINALISATION MEETING

For the risk analysis to have value, the findings of the risk analysis also need to be communicated to the relevant stakeholders to raise awareness and to ensure that relevant measures are put in place to prevent harmful events from occurring. In addition, the results may provide important input to future analyses, serving as a starting point and avoiding the need to start analysing from scratch every time.

The content of this meeting, and whether it is held at all, depends on how the client wants the findings of the risk analysis to be presented. To cut down on costs, the client may forego a written report in favour of a slide presentation of the main findings. Other clients want a written report, or a combination of both.

CONCLUDING REMARKS

In this chapter we have presented the CORAS method for model based security risk analysis and the CORAS graphical language. The risk analysis process has been illustrated with results from the analysis of a collaborative engineering VO scenario, where a number of risks and treatments were identified. The focus of this scenario was an integrated analysis of security, trust, and legal issues. The risk analyses conducted in the TrustCoM project indicate how legal risks, such as the loss of protection of confidential information, can be treated by an integrated solution, including contractual elements, trust management and security management (Mahler, 2005; Vraalsen, 2006). Interestingly, many of the relevant contractual treatments are also included in a general manner in the ALIVE contract template for VOs (ALIVE, 2002a). The risk analyses provide indications about how these rules can be adapted to the specific target under analysis. Since the graphical representation implies a simplification, a lawyer would have to integrate analysis results into the contractual document in an appropriate way, taking into account the terminology and the system of the contractual template.

Table 9. CE VO treatment evaluation

Risk	Unwanted incident	Asset	Treatment	Risk reduction	Cost
R3	Customer loses trust in SI	Client trust	Monitor user account activity	Major → Moderate	Low
R3	Customer loses trust in SI	Client trust	Access restrictions	Major → Moderate	High
R4	VO partners lose trust in SI	Partner trust	Monitor user account activity	Major → Moderate	Low
R4	VO partners lose trust in SI	Partner trust	Access restrictions	Major → Moderate	Medium
R5	Designs lose legal protection as confidential information	Designs	Monitor user account activity	No	N/A
R5	Designs lose legal protection as confidential information	Designs	Access restrictions	No	N/A

The analysis results presented in this chapter were generated during a number of brainstorming sessions involving participants with varied backgrounds, including law, computer science, engineering, economics, and formal methods and languages. Based on our experiences, the graphical models can indeed facilitate the communication and understanding with respect to security and legal issues in a multidisciplinary context, and this is also supported by other studies (Hogganvik & Stølen, 2005).

As a result of experiences and feedback from the risk analyses conducted in TrustCoM and other research projects, a number of improvements have been made both to the CORAS method and the graphical language (Vraalsen, 2006). Some of these improvements have been aimed at better support for legal risk analysis (Vraalsen, Lund, et al., 2005). Facilities have been added to enable modelling of legal risks and treatments, and reusable elements have been created in the form of e.g. checklists for legal risks. A number of general improvements have also been made. For instance, users were confused by the different types of lines and arrows in the diagrams, and these have now been cleaned up.

Current work focuses on updating the CO-RAS Tool with support for the new method and graphical language features. The built-in diagram editor has been extended with the new language facilities to support modelling of legal risks and treatments. Work is also being done on improving the reporting facilities in the tool and on updating the integrated online method handbook and tutorials.

ACKNOWLEDGMENT

The developments presented in this chapter were partly funded by the European Commission through the IST programme under Framework 6 grant 001945 to the TrustCoM Integrated Project and partly financed under the Research Council of Norway through the projects SECURIS (152839/220) and ENFORCE (164382/V30).

We would like to acknowledge the work done by David Goldby from BAE Systems, who has defined the collaborative engineering scenario for TrustCoM. We would also like to thank David Goldby, Xavier Parent and Claudia Keser for participating in the risk analysis sessions.

REFERENCES

AS/NZS 4360. (2004). *Risk management*. Standards Australia/Standards New Zealand.

ALIVE IST Project. (2002a). *Intellectual and industrial property rights (Tech. Rep. D13)*. Retrieved June 5th, 2006, from http://www.vive-ig.net/projects/alive/docs.html

ALIVE IST Project. (2002b). *VE model contracts (Tech. Rep. D17a)*. Retrieved June 5th, 2006, from http://www.vive-ig.net/projects/alive/models.html

Baccarini, D., & Archer, R. (2001). The risk ranking of projects: A methodology. *International Journal of Project Management, 19*, 139-145.

den Braber, F., Lund, M. S., Stølen, K., & Vraalsen, F. (2005). Integrating security in the development process with UML. In M. Khosrow-Pour (Ed.), *Encyclopedia of information science and technology* (pp. 1560-1566). USA: Information Resources Management Association.

Brændeland, G., & Stølen, K. (2004). Using risk analysis to assess user trust – A net-bank scenario. In C. Jensen, S. Poslad, & T. Dimitrakos (Eds.), *Proceedings of the Second International Conference on Trust Management (iTrust 2004)* (pp. 146-160). Oxford, England: Springer LNCS 2995.

Burnett, R. (2005). Legal risk management for the IT industry. *Computer Law & Security Report, 21*, 621-67.

Camarinha-Matos, L., Afsarmanesh, H., Löh, H., Sturm, F., & Ollus, M. (2004). A strategic roadmap for advanced virtual organizations. In L. Camarinha-Matos & H. Afsarmanesh (Eds.), *Collaborative networked oganizations: A research agenda for emerging business models.* New York: Springer.

Checkland, P., & Scholes, J. (1990). *Soft systems methodology in action.* New York: Wiley.

Dimitrakos, T., Goldby, D., & Kearney, P. (2004). Towards a trust and contract management framework for dynamic virtual organizations. In *E-Adoption and the knowledge economy: eChallenges 2004.* Vienna, Austria: IOS Press.

Heymann, T. (2005). Outsourcing in Deutschland – eine Bestandsaufnahme zur Vertragsgestaltung. Die Grundtypen des Outourcing und ihre Konsequenzen für die Vertragsgestaltung. *Computer und Recht, 10,* 706-710.

Hogganvik, I., & Stølen, K. (2005). On the comprehension of security risk scenarios. In *Proceedings of the 13ᵗʰ International Workshop on Program Comprehension (IWPC 2005)*, 115-124.

IEC 61025. (1990). *Fault tree analysis (FTA).* International Electrotechnical Commission.

ISO/IEC 13335. (2004). *Information technology – Security techniques – Management of information and communications technology security – Part 1: Concepts and models for information and communications technology security management.* International Organization for Standardization/ International Electrotechnical Commission.

Lund, M. S., Hogganvik, I., Seehusen, F., & Stølen, K. (2003). *UML profile for security assessment* (Tech. Rep. STF40 A03066). Oslo, Norway: SINTEF Telecom and Informatics.

Mahler, T. (Ed.). (2005). *Report on legal issues* (Tech. Rep. D15). Oslo, Norway: TrustCoM EU IST Project 01945.

Mahler, T., & Vraalsen, F. (2005). Legal risk analysis with respect to IPR in a collaborative engineering virtual organization. In *Proceedings of the 6ᵗʰ IFIP Working Conference on Virtual Enterprises (PRO-VE 2005).* Valencia, Spain.

Müller-Hengstenberg, C. D. (2005). Der Vertrag als Mittel des Risikomanagements. Ein Plädoyer für die dynamische Projektbegleitung im Vertrag. *Computer und Recht, 5,* 385-392.

OMG. (2006). *UML profile for modeling quality of service and fault tolerance characteristics and mechanisms, available specification* (OMG Document: ptc/2005-05-02) Author.

OMG. (2005). *Unified modeling language: Superstructure, version 2.0* (OMG Document: formal/2005-07-04).

Raz, T., & Michael, E. (1999). Use and benefits of tools for project risk management. *International Journal of Project Management, 19,* 9-17.

Redmill, F., Chudleigh, M., & Catmur, J. (1999). *HazOp and software HazOp.* Wiley.

Vraalsen, F. (Ed.). (2006). *Methods and Tools for legal risk management* (Tech. Rep. D17). Oslo, Norway: TrustCoM EU IST Project 01945.

Vraalsen, F., den Braber, F., Lund, M. S., & Stølen, K. (2005). The CORAS tool for security risk analysis. In P. Herrmann, V. Issarny, & S. Shiu, (Eds.), *Proceedings of the 3ʳᵈ International Conference on Trust Management (iTrust 2005)* (pp. 402-405). Paris: Springer LNCS 3477.

Vraalsen, F., Lund, M. S., Mahler, T., Parent, X., & Stølen, K. (2005). Specifying legal risk scenarios using the CORAS threat modelling language – experiences and the way forward. In P. Herrmann, V. Issarny, & S. Shiu (Eds.), *Proceedings of the 3ʳᵈ International Conference on Trust Management (iTrust 2005)* (pp. 45-60). Paris: Springer LNCS 3477.

Compilation of References

Abad, C., Taylor, J., Sengul, C., Yurcik, W., Zhou, Y., & Rowe, K. (2003). Log correlation for intrusion detection: A proof of concept. In *Proceedings of the 19ᵗʰ Annual Computer Security Applications Conference (ACSAC 2003)*. Los Alamitos, CA: IEEE Computer Society Press.

Abiteboul, S., & Hull, R. (1988). Data functions, datalog and negation. In *Proceedings of the ACM-SIGMOD Conference*.

Abrial, J. (1996). *The b-book: Assigning programs to meanings*. Cambridge, England: Cambridge University Press.

ActivCard. (2005). *How to catch a phish*(White paper). Retrieved July 1, 2006, from http://wp.bitpipe.com/resource/org_975950994_468/Phishing_WP.pdf

Agudo, I., Lopez, J., & Montenegro, J. A. (2005, December). A representation model of trust relationships with delegation extensions. *Lecture Notes in Computer Science, 3477,* 116-130.

ALIVE IST Project. (2002a). *Intellectual and industrial property rights (Tech. Rep. D13)*. Retrieved June 5ᵗʰ· 2006, from http://www.vive-ig.net/projects/alive/docs.html

ALIVE IST Project. (2002b). *VE model contracts (Tech. Rep. D17a)*. Retrieved June 5ᵗʰ· 2006, from http://www.vive-ig.net/projects/alive/models.html

Allen, R., & Garlan, D. (1996). *The Wright architectural specification language* (Tech. Rep. CMUCS -96-TB). Pittsburgh, PA: Carnegie Mellon University, School of Computer Science.

Almgren, M., & Jonsson, E. (2004). Using active learning in intrusion detection. In *Proceedings of the 17ᵗʰ IEEE Computer Security Foundations Workshop (CSFW'04)*. Los Alamitos, CA: IEEE Computer Society Press.

Anderson, J. P. (1980). *Computer security threat monitoring and surveillance* (Tech.l Rep.). Fort Washington, PA: James P. Anderson.

Anonymous. (2005). *Malware report: The impact of malicious code attacks.*Retrieved on July 7, 2006, from http://www.computereconomics.com/article.cfm?id=1090

Anti-Phishing Working Group. (2005, November). *Phishing activity trends report.* Retrieved July 1, 2006, from http://antiphishing.org/reports/apwg_report_Nov2005_FINAL.pdf

Apt, K. (1990). Logic programming. In J. van Leeuwen (Ed.), *Handbook of theoretical computer science*. Elsevier.

APWG. (2005, July). *APWG phishing activity report.* Retrieved October 7, 2005, from http://anti-phishing.org/APWG_Phishing_Activity_Report_Jul_05.pdf

Ars Technica. (2005). *Malware: What it is and how to prevent it.* Retrieved October 2005 from http://arstechnica.com/articles/paedia/malware.ars/1

AS/NZS 4360. (2004). *Risk management.* Standards Australia/Standards New Zealand.

Atluri, V., Chun, S. A., & Mazzoleni, P. A (2001). Chinese wall security model for decentralized workflow systems. In *Proceedings of the Eighth ACM conference on Computer and Communications Security,* 48-57.

Auernheimer, B. (1987). *RT-ASLAN: A specification language for real-time systems.* Unpublished doctoral dissertation, University of California, Santa Barbara, CA.

Aurrecoechea, C., Campbell, A., & Hauw, L. (1996). A survey of quality of service architectures (Special issue). *Multimedia Systems Journal.*

Authentication Guidance. (2005, October). *Authentication in an Internet banking environment.* Retrieved January 26, 2006, from ww.ffiec.gov/pdf/authentication_guidance.pdf

Axelsson, S. (2000). *Intrusion detection systems: A survey and taxonomy* (Tech. Rep. No 99-15). Gothenburg, Sweden: Chalmers University of Technology, Department of Computer Engineering.

Baccarini, D., & Archer, R. (2001). The risk ranking of projects: A methodology. *International Journal of Project Management, 19*, 139-145.

Bace, R., & Mell, P. (2001). *Intrusion detection systems.* NIST special publication in intrusion detection systems. Retrieved from http://csrc.nist.gov/publications/nistpubs/800-31/sp800-31.pdf

Bailey, D. (2006). Versatile appliance guards branches. *IT Week, 9*(4), 27.

Bank of America. (n.d.). *Here's how sitekey works.* Retrieved September 29, 2005, from http://www.bankofamerica.com/privacy/passmark/

Barkan, E., Biham, E., & Keller, N. (2003). Instant ciphetext-only cryptoanalysis of GSM encrypted communication. *CRYPTO 2003*, 600–616.

Barken, L. (2004). *How secure is your wireless network?* Upper Saddle River, NJ: Prentice Hall.

Barker, S. (2000). Data protection by logic programming. *Lecture Notes in Computer Science, 1861*, 1300-1314.

Barwinski, M. A. (2005). *Taxonomy of spyware and empirical study of network drive-by-download.* Unpublished doctoral dissertation, Naval Postgraduate School, Monterey, California.

Basel II. (2005). *International convergence of capital measurement and capital standards: A revised framework.* Basel Committee on Banking Supervision.

Becker, E., Buhse, W., Günnewig, D., & Rump, N. (Eds.). (2003). Digital rights management, technological, economic, legal and political aspects. *LNCS, 2770.*

Bertino, E., Bonatti, P. A., & Ferrari, E. (2001). TRBAC: A temporal role-based access control model. *ACM Trans. on Information and System Security, 4*(3), 191-233.

Bertino, E., Catania, B., Ferrari, E., & Perlasca, P. (2001). A logical framework for reasoning about access control models. In *Proceedings of the Sixth ACM Symposium on Access Control Models and Technologies (SACMAT)*, 41-52.

Bertino, E., Ferrari, E., & Atluri, V. (1999) The specification and enforcement of authorization constraints in workflow management systems. *ACM Transactions on Information and System Security (TISSEC), 2*(1), 65-104.

Beznosov, K. (2004). *On the benefits of decomposing policy engines into components.* Third Workshop on Adaptive and Reflect Middleware, Toronto, Canada.

Bidoit, M., & Mosses, P. (2003). CASL user manual. *LNCS vol. 2900.* Springer Berlin.

Biometrics Research homepage. (n.d.) Retrieved February 5, 2006, from http://biometrics.cse.msu.edu/

Blaze, M., Feigenbaum, J., & Lacy, J. (1996). Decentralized trust management. In *Proceedings of the IEEE Symposium on Security and Privacy*, 164-173.

Blaze, M., Feigenbaum, J., Ioannidis, J., & Keromytis, A. (1999). The KeyNote trust-management system version 2. *RFC, 2704.*

Blaze, M., Ioannidis, J., & Keromytis, A. (2000). DSA and RSA key and signature encoding for the KeyNote trust management system. *RFC, 2792.*

Blaze, M., Ioannidis, J., & Keromytis, A. (2003, May). Experience with the KeyNote trust management system: Applications and future directions. In *Proceedings of the First International Conference on Trust Management*, 284 - 300.

Blobel, B. (2001). The European TrustHealth project experiences with implementing a security infrastructure. *International Journal of Medical Informatics, 60*, 193-201.

Blobel, B. (2004). Authorisation and access control for electronic health record system. *International Journal of Medical Informatics, 73,* 251-257.

Blobel, B., Hoepner, P., Joop, R., Karnouskos, S., Kleinhuis, G., & Stassinopoulos, G. (2003). Using a privilege management infrastructure for secure Web-based e-health applications. *Computer Communication,* 26(16), 1863-1872.

Bluetooth SIG. (2006). *The official Bluetooth wireless info site.* Retrieved February 5, 2006, from http://www. bluetooth.com

Bonatti, P., & Samarati, P. (2002). A unified framework for regulating access and information release on the Web. *Journal of Computer Security, 10*(3), 241-272.

Booch, G. (1991). *Object-oriented design with applications.* Redwood City, CA: Benjamin/Cummings.

Booch, G., Rumbaugh, J., & Jacobson, I. (1999). *The unified software development process.* Boston: Addison Wesley.

Bosworth, S., & Kabay, M. E. (2002). Computer security handbook (4th ed.). Wiley.

Boukhonine, S., Krotov, V., & Rupert, B. (2005). Future security approaches and biometrics. *Communications of AIS, 16*(48), 937-966.

Bowenm, J. (1996). *Formal specification and documentation using Z: A case study approach.* International Thomson Computer Press.

Bradley, W. B., & Maher, D. P. (2004). The NEMO P2P service orchestration framework. In *Proceedings of the 37th Hawaii International Conference on System Science.*

Brændeland, G., & Stølen, K. (2004). Using risk analysis to assess user trust – A net-bank scenario. In C. Jensen, S. Poslad, & T. Dimitrakos (Eds.), *Proceedings of the Second International Conference on Trust Management (iTrust 2004)* (pp. 146-160). Oxford, England: Springer LNCS 2995.

BS7799-2:1999. (1999). *British standard - Specification for information security management system.*

Buchheim, T., Erlinger, M., Feinstein, B., Matthews., G., Pollock, R., Betser, J., et al. (2001). Implementing the Intrusion detection exchange protocol. In *Proceedings of 17th Annual Computer Security Applications Conference (ACSAC'01), IEEE Press,* 32-41.

Buchheim, T., Feinstein, B., Gupta, D., Matthews, G., & Pollock, R. (2001). *IAP: Intrusion alert protocol, Internet engineering task force, draft-ietf-idwg-iap-05.*

Burkholder, P. (2002). *SSL man-in-the-middle attacks (SANS report).* Retrieved January 30, 2006, from http://www.sans. org/rr/whitepapers/threats/480.php

Burnett, R. (2005). Legal risk management for the IT industry. *Computer Law & Security Report, 21,* 621-67.

Camarinha-Matos, L., Afsarmanesh, H., Löh, H., Sturm, F., & Ollus, M. (2004). A strategic roadmap for advanced virtual organizations. In L. Camarinha-Matos & H. Afsarmanesh (Eds.), *Collaborative networked oganizations: A research agenda for emerging business models.* New York: Springer.

Cantor, S., Kemp, J., Philpott, R., & Maler, E. (2005). *Security assertion markup language (SAML V2.0).* Retrieved March 15, 2005, from http://docs.oasis-open.org/security/ saml/v2.0/

Carey, N., Mohay, G., & Clark, A. (2003). Attack signature matching and discovery in systems employing heterogeneous IDS. In *Proceedings of the 19th Annual Computer Security Applications Conference (ACSAC 2003).* Los Alamitos, CA: IEEE Computer Society Press.

CERT. (2005). *CERT/CC Statistics.* Retrieved December 2005 from http://www.cert.org/stats/

CERT. (2005). *Denial of service attacks.* Retrieved October 2005 from http://www.cert.org/tech_tips/denial_of_service. html

CFCU. (2005, January 24). *CFCU credit union says customers received "phishing" scam e-mails.* Retrieved January 26, 2006, from http://today.14850.com/0124cfcuscam.html

Chadwick, D., et. al. (2003, March-April). Role based access control with X.509 attribute certificates. *IEEE Internet Computing,* 62–69.

Chamberlin, D., & Boyce, R. (1974). SEQUEL: A structured English query language. *International Conference on Management of Data ACM SIGFIDET (now SIGMOD) Workshop on Data Description, Access and Control,* 249-264.

Chatterjee, S., Sabata, B., & Sydir, J. (1998). *ERDoS QoS architecture* (Tech. Rep. ITAD-1667-TR-98-075). Menlo Park, CA:

Checkland, P., & Scholes, J. (1990). *Soft systems methodology in action.* New York: Wiley.

Cheswick, W. R., Bellovin, S. M., & Rubin, A. D. (2003). *Firewalls and Internet security: Repelling the wily hacker.* Addison-Wesley.

Cheung, S., Lindqvist, U., & Fong, M. W. (2003). Modeling multistep cyber attacks for scenario recognition. *DARPA Information Survivability Conference and Exposition,* 284-292.

Christodorescu, M., & Jha, S. (2003, August). *Static analysis of executables to detect malicious patterns.* Proceeds of the Usenix Security Symposium.

CIDF Working Group. (1999). *A CISL tutorial.* Retrieved December 2005 from http://www.isi.edu/gost/cidf/tutorial.html

CipherTrust. (n.d.). *Sender policy framework statistics.* Retrieved January 29, 2006, from http://www.ciphertrust.com/resources/statistics/spf_stats.php

Clements, P. (1996). A survey of architecture description languages. *ACM/IEEE International Workshop on Software Specification and Design,* 16-25.

Collberg, C. & Thomborson, C. (2002, August). Tamperproofing, and obfuscation - tools for software protection. *IEEE Transactions on Software Engineering* 701-746.

Collberg, C., Thomborson, C., & Low, D. (1997, July). *A taxonomy of obfuscating transformations* (Tech. Rep. 148).

Commite Europen de Normalisation ENV 13606 Standard. (2002). *Extended architecture.*

Commite Europen de Normalisation ENV 13729 Standard. (2002). *Secure user identification.*

Computer Network Defence Ltd. (2006). *Network intrusion detection systems product descriptions.* Retrieved from http://www.networkintrusion.co.uk/N_ids.htm. Last access: 2006/07/13

Convolution With Gaussian Kernals. **IICAI.**

CORAL. (2004). Coral consortium corporation. Retrieved January 26, 2006, from http://www.coral-interop.org/

Coull, S., Branch, J., Szymanski, B., & Breimer, E. (2003). Intrusion detection: A bioinformatics approach. In *Proceedings of the 19th Annual Computer Security Applications Conference (ACSAC 2003.,* Los Alamitos, CA: IEEE Computer Society Press.

Cox, B. (1994, September). Superdistribution. *Wired Magazine,* pp 89-92.

Cox, B. (1996). *Superdistribution objects as property on the electronic frontier.* Addison-Wesley.

CRAMM. *CCTA risk analysis and management method (version 5).* Retrieved from http://www.cramm.com/

Crampton, J., Loizou, G., & O'Shea, G. (2001). A logic of access control. *The Computer Journal, 44,* 54-66.

Cremonini, M., Damiani, E., De Capitani di Vimercati, S., Samarati, P., Corallo, A., & Elia, G. (2005). Security, privacy, and trust in mobile systems and applications. In M. Pagani (Ed.), *Mobile and wireless systems beyond 3G: Managing new business opportunities.* USA: IRM Press.

Crosbie, M., Dole, B., Ellis, T., Krsul, I., & Spafford, E. (1996). *IDIOT – User's guide* (Tech. Rep. TR-96-050). West Lafayette, IN: ,Purdue University, Department of Computer Science, The COAST Project.

Crutchfield, S. (n.d.). Outsmarting the malware. *EDPACS, 2006*(33), 18-20.

CSI Publications. (2005). CSI/FBI computer crime and security survey. Retrieved from *http://www.GoCSI.com*

Cuppens, F., & Miège, A. (2002). Alert correlation in a cooperative intrusion detection framework. In *Proceedings of the 2002 IEEE Symposium on Security and Privacy (S&P 2002).* Los Alamitos, CA: IEEE Computer Society Press.

Cuppens, F., & Ortalo, R. (2000). LAMBDA: A language to model a database for detection of attacks. *International Workshop on Recent Advances in Intrusion Detection,107,* 197-216.

Curry, D. (2000). *Intrusion detection message exchange format: Extensible markup language (XML) document type definition* (Intrusion Detection Working Group IETF Internet draft). Retrieved from http://xml.coverpages.org/draft-ietf-idwg-idmef-xml-01.txt

Damiani, E., De Capitani, S., Paraboschi, S., Samarati, P., & Violante, F. (2002). A reputation-based approach for choosing reliable resources in peer-to-peer networks. *Ninth ACM Conference on Computer and Communications Security.*

Damianou, N., Dulay, N., Lupu, E., & Sloman, M. (2001). The Ponder policy specification language. In *Proceedings of the International Workshop on Policies for Distributed Systems and Networks (POLICY),* 18-38.

De Capitani di Vimercati, S., & Samarati, P. (2001). Access control: Policies, models, and mechanism. In R. Focardi & F. Gorrieri (Eds.), *Foundations of security analysis and design - tutorial lectures* (vol. 2171 of LNCS). Springer-Verlag.

de Haas, J. (2005, Septemeber15-16). *Symbian phone security.* Presentation on T2'05 Conference, Helsinki, Finland. Retrieved October 9, 2005, from http://www.symternals.com/downloads/T2-Symbian-Security-v1.1.pdf

Debar, H., Curry, D., & Feinstein, B. (2005). *The intrusion detection message exchange format, IETF, RFC Draft, draft-ietf-idwg-idmef-xml-14.*

Del Fabbro, B., Laiymani, D., Nicod, J. M., & Philippe, L. (2004). A data persistency approach for the DIET metacomputing environment. *International. Conference on Internet Computing, IC'04,* Las Vegas, NV, pp. 701-707.

den Braber, F., Lund, M. S., Stølen, K., & Vraalsen, F. (2005). Integrating security in the development process with UML. In M. Khosrow-Pour (Ed.), *Encyclopedia of information science and technology* (pp. 1560-1566). USA: Information Resources Management Association.

Denning, D. E. (1987). An intrusion-detection model. *IEEE Transactions on Software Engineering, 13*(2).

Deraison, R. (2000). *The Nessus attack scripting language reference guide.* Retrieved December 19, 2005, from http://www.nessus.org

DevX Portal. (2006). *Wireless application security: What's up with that?* Retrieved February 6, 2006, from http://www.devx.com/Intel/Article/18013/0/page/1

Dhamija, R., & Tygar, J. D. (2005, **July 6-8**). The battle against phishing: Dynamic Security Skins. In *Proceedings of the 2005 Symposium on Usable Privacy and Security, Pittsburgh, PA.*

DIGIA Inc. (2003). *Programming for the series 60 platform and Symbian OS.* England: Wiley.

Dimitrakos, T., Goldby, D., & Kearney, P. (2004). Towards a trust and contract management framework for dynamic virtual organizations. In *E-Adoption and the knowledge economy: eChallenges 2004.* Vienna, Austria: IOS Press.

DMCA. (1998a). *H.R.2281 Digital Millennium Copyright Act (enrolled as agreed to or passed by both house and senate).* Retrieved January 26, 2006, from http://thomas.loc.gov/cgi-bin/query/z?c105:H.R.2281.ENR:

DMCA. (1998b). *The Digital Millennium Copyright Act of 1998 - U.S. copyright office summary.* Retrieved January 26, 2006, from http://www.copyright.gov/legislation/dmca.pdf

DMP. (2003). *Digital media project.* Retrieved January 26, 2006, from http://www.dmpf.org/

DMP. (2005). *Digital media project (Approved document No 3).* Retrieved January 26, 2006, from http://www.dmpf.org/open/dmp0653.zip

Douglas, D. (2004). *Windows mobile-based devices and security: Protecting sensitive business information.* Retrieved October 9, 2005, from http://download.microsoft.com/download/4/7/c/47c9d8ec-94d4-472b-887d-4a9ccf194160/6.%20WM_Security_Final_print.pdf

Duham, K. (2006). The problem with P2P. *EDPACS, 2006*(33), 9-13.

Duncan, M. V., Akhtari, M. S., & Bradford, P. G. (2004). Visual security for wireless handheld devices. *JOSHUA, 2.*

EBIOS. (2004, February). *Expression of needs and identification of security objectives.* Retrieved from http://www.ssi.gouv.fr/fr/confiance/ebiospresentation.html

Eckmann, S. T., Vigna, G., & Kemmerer, R. A. (2002). STATL: An attack language for state-based intrusion detection. *Journal of Computer Security, 10*(1/2), 71-104.

Egan, M. (2005). *The executive guide to information security.* Indianapolis, IN: Addison-Wesley.

Ellison, C. (1999). *SPKI Certificate Theory, RFC, 2693.*

Ellison, C., Frantz, B., & Lacy, J. (1996). *Simple public key certificate.* Internet draft available online from draft-ietf-spki-cert-structure-06.txt

Ellison, C., Frantz, B., Lampson, B., Rivest, R., Thomas, B. M., & Ylonen, T. (1999, September). SPKI certificate theory. *IETF RFC, 2693.*

EMCC Software. (2005). *Symbian OS v9 - Advances in Symbian OS.* Retrieved October 12, 2005, from http://www.newlc.com/article.php3?id_article=959

Emigh, A. (2005). O*nline identity theft: Phishing technology, chokepoints and countermeasures (ITTC report on online identity theft technology and countermeasures).* Retrieved on July 14, 2006, from http://www.anti-phishing.org/Phishing-dhs-report.pdf

Erbeschloe, M. (2005). *A computer security professional's guide to malicious code.* Oxford, England: Elsevier.

Erdos, M., & Cantor, S. (2002) *Shibboleth-architecture.* Retrieved May 2, 2002, from http://shibboleth.internet2.edu/docs/draft-internet2-shibboleth-arch-v04.pdf

EURESCOM P1207 OPERA. (2002). *Overview of state-of-the art DRM systems and standardisation activities.* Retrieved January 26, 2006, from http://www.eurescom.de/public/projectresults/P1200-series/P1207-TI.asp

EURESCOM P1207 OPERA. (2003). *An open DRM architecture.* Retrieved January 26, 2006, from http://www.eurescom.de/public/projectresults/P1200-series/P1207-D2.asp

Everett, C. (2005). Ready for take-off? *Infosecurity Today, 2*(6), 44-5.

Ewalt, D. M. (2005). *Citigroup blames UPS for customer data loss.* Retrieved January 26, 2006, from http://www.forbes.com/facesinthenews/2005/06/06/0606autofacescan09.html

Feinstein, B., Matthews, G., & White, J. (2002). *The Intrusion detection exchange protocol (IDXP), Internet engineering task force, RFC Draft, draft-ietf-idwg-beep-idxp-07.*

Feng, H. H., Giffin, J. T., Huang, Y., Jha, S., Lee, W., & Miller, B. P. (2004). Formalizing sensitivity in static analysis for intrusion detection. In *Proceedings of the 2004 IEEE Symposium on Security and Privacy (S&P'04),* Los Alamitos, CA: IEEE Computer Society Press.

FFIEC Guidance. (2005, October 12). *Authentication in an Internet banking environment (FIL-103-2005).*Retrieved January 25, 2006 from http://www.fdic.gov/news/news/financial/2005/fil10305.pdf

Finextra.com (2005). *Phishers target Nordea's one-time password system.* Retrieved January 24, 2006, from http://www.finextra.com/fullstory.asp?id=14384

Finin, T., Fritzson, R., McKay, D., & McEntire, R. (1994). KQML as an agent communication language. *International Conference on Information and Knowledge Management,* 456-463.

Fluhrer, S., Mantin, I., & Shamir, A. (2001). Weaknesses in the key scheduling algorithm of RC4. In S. Vaudenay & A. Youssef (Eds.), *Selected areas in cryptography* (pp. 1-24). Springer.

Forrest, S., & Longstaff, T. A. (1996). A sense of self for Unix processes. *IEEE Symposium on Research in Security and Privacy,* 120-128.

Foster, I., & Kesselman, C. (1998). The globus project: A status report. In *Proceedings of the IPPS/SPDP '98 Heterogeneous Computing Workshop,* pp. 4-18.

Foster, I., Kesselman, C., Tsudik, G., & Tuecke, S. (1998). A security architecture for computational grids. In *Proceedings of the Fifth ACM Conference on Computer and Communications Security Conference,* pp. 83-92.

Franke, H., Hochschild, P., Pattnaik, P., & Snir, M. (1994) An efficient implementation of MPI. *International Conference on Parallel Processing.*

Frolund, S., & Koistinen, J. (1998). *QML: A language for quality of service specification* (Tech. Rep. HPL-98-10). Hewlett Packard Laboratories.

F-Secure. (2004, December). *The malware attack against mobile phones is mounting.* Retrieved December 19, 2005, from http://www.f-secure.com/news/items/news_2004122200.shtml

F-Secure. (2005a). *F-secure virus description database.* Retrieved November 2005 from http://www.f-secure.com/v-descs/

F-Secure. (2005b). *F-Secure virus description: P2P worm.* Retrieved October 2005 from http://www.f-secure.com/v-descs/p2pworm.shtml

F-Secure. (2005c). *F-Secure virus description: Worm.* Retrieved October 2005 from http://www.f-secure.com/v-descs/worm.shtml

Fulton, J. (2006). Saving users from themselves. *EDPACS, 2006*(33), 20-21.

Gabrielian, A., & Franklin, M. (1988). State-based specification of complex real-time systems. *Real-Time Systems Symposium,* 2-11.

Garfinkel, S. L., Margrave D., Schiller, J. I., Nordlander, E., & Miller, R. C. (2005, April 2-7). How to make secure e-mail easier to user. In *Proceedings of the ACM Conference on Human Factors in Computing Systems, Portland, OR.*

Gartner report. (2005). *Maintaining data quality.* Retrieved from http://www.ebizq.net/views/download_raw? metadata_id =6210&what=feature

Gartner Study. (2004). *Gartner study finds significant increase in e-mail phishing attacks.* Retrieved January 17, 2006, from http://www.gartner.com/5_about/press_releases/asset_71087_11.jsp

Garvey, T. D., & Lunt, T. F. (1991). Model based intrusion detection. *National Computer Security Conference.* 372-385.

Geer, D. (June 2005). Security technologies go phishing. *IEEE Computer, 38*(6), 18-21.

Gelfond, M., & Lifschitz, V. (1988). The stable model semantics for logic programming. In Kowalski R., & Bowen, K. (Eds.), *Proceedings of the Fifth International Conference on Logic Programming (ICLP'88),* 1070-1080.

Gelfond, M., & Lifschitz, V. (1991) Classical negation in logic programs and disjunctive databases. *New Generation Computing, 9,* 365-385.

Georgakopoulos, D., Hornick, M. F., & Sheth, A. P. (1995, April). An overview of workflow management: From process modeling to workflow automation infrastructure. *Distributed and Parallel Databases 3*(2), 119-153.

Germain, M., & Ferrero, A. (2006). English translation Michèle Germain. Les réseaux particuliers – La sécurité des réseaux sans fil. In La Sécurité à l'usage des décideurs (pp. 154 to 166). Paris: © Éditions tenor 2006.

Gilliland, A. (2006). Understanding the IM security threat. *EDPACS, 2006*(33), 1-7.

Gopalakrishna, R., Spafford, E. H., & Vitek, J. (2005). Efficient Intrusion detection using automaton inlining. In *Proceedings of the 2005 IEEE Symposium on Security and Privacy (S&P'05).* Los Alamitos, CA: IEEE Computer Society Press.

Gordon, S. (2006). Fighting spyware and adware in the enterprise. *EDPACS, 2006*(33), 14-18.

Goth, G. (2005, January). Phishing attacks rising, but dollar losses down. *IEEE Security & Privacy Magazine, 3*(1), 8.

Grami, A., & Schell, B. H. (2005). *Future trends in mobile commerce: Service offerings, technological advances and security challenges.* Retrieved January 15, 2005, from http://dev.hil.unb.ca/Texts/PST/pdf/grami.pdf

Grance, T. (2004). *Computer security incident handling guide* (Special Publication 800-61). U.S. Department of Commerce, National Institute of Standards.

Grance, T., Hash, H., & Stevens, M. (2004). *Security considerations in the information development life cycle* (NIST

Special Publication 800-64 Rev.1). National Institute of Standards and Technology.

GSM Security Portal. (2006). Retrieved February 5, 2006, from http://www.gsm-security.net/

Gupta, M. (2002). *Building a virtual private network.* Premier Press.

Habra, J., Charlier, B. L., Mounji, A.., & Mathieu, I. (1992). ASAX: Software architecture and rule-based language for universal audit trail analysis. *European Symposium on Research in Computer Security, 648,* 435-450.

Hantz, F., & Guyennet, H. (2005). HiPoP: Highly distributed platform of computing. In *Proceedingss of the IEEE Joint Internationa Conference on Autonomic and Autonomous Systems (ICAS'05) and International Conference on Networking and Services (ICNS'05).* Tahiti, French Polynesia.

Hantz, F., & Guyennet, H. (2006). A P2P Platform using sandboxing. *WSHPCS (Workshop on Security and High Performance Computing Systems) in conjunction with the 20th European Conference on Modelling and Simulation (ECMS 2006),* Bonn, Germany, pp. 736-739.

Heath, C. (2006). *Symbian OS platform security: Software development using the Symbian OS security architecture.* England: Wiley.

Hewitt, C., Bishop, P., & Steiger, R. (1973). A universal modular ACTOR formalism for artificial intelligence. *International Joint Conference on Artificial Intelligence,* 235-245.

Heymann, T. (2005). Outsourcing in Deutschland – eine Bestandsaufnahme zur Vertragsgestaltung. Die Grundtypen des Outourcing und ihre Konsequenzen für die Vertragsgestaltung. *Computer und Recht, 10,* 706-710.

Hickey, R. A. (2005, November). *Loss, theft still no. 1 threat to mobile data.* Retrieved December 17, 2005, from http://searchmobilecomputing.techtarget.com/originalContent/0,289142,sid40_gci1143983,00.html

Hicks, S. (2005). *Mobile and malicious.* Retrieved December 17, 2005, from http://www.ciostrategycenter.com/darwin/Threat/threat_strategies/mobile_malicious/

Hoanca, B. (2006, Spring). How good are our weapons in the spam wars? A systems analysis of spam fighting techniques. *IEEE Technology and Society Magazine, 25*(1), 22-30.

Hoanca, B., & Mock, K. (2005, June 20-24). *Screen oriented technique for reducing the incidence of shoulder surfing.* Paper presented at Security and Management (SAM'05), Las Vegas, NV.

Hoefelmeyer, R. (2004). Malicious code: The threat, detection and protection. In H. F.Tipton & N. Krause (Eds.), *Information security management handbook.* Raton, FL: CRC Press.

Hofmann, P. (1996). *MHEG-5 and MHEG-6: Multimedia standards for minimal resource systems* (Tech. Rep.). Berlin, Germany: Technische Universitat Berlin.

Hogganvik, I., & Stølen, K. (2005). On the comprehension of security risk scenarios. In *Proceedings of the 13th International Workshop on Program Comprehension (IWPC 2005),* 115-124.

Hong, J. I. (2005, December). Minimizing security risks in ubicomp systems. *Computer,* 118-119.

Hopper, N., & Blum, M. (2000). *A secure human-computer authentication scheme (CMU Tech. Rep. CMU-CS-00-139).* Retrieved October 5, 2005, from http://reports-archive.adm.cs.cmu.edu/anon/2000/CMU-CS-00-139.pdf

Hussein, M., & Zulkernine, M. (2006). UMLintr: A UML profile for specifying intrusions. *IEEE International Conference and Workshop on the Engineering of Computer-Based Systems.* 279-286.

I Am Not A Geek. (2005). *Spyware removal guides.* October 2005 http://www.iamnotageek.com/a/spyware.php

IAIK. (2005). *AES lounge.* Retrieved from http://www.iaik.tu-graz.ac.at/research/krypto/AES/

IBM Report. (2006). *IBM Report: Surge in CRIMINAL-DRIVEN CYBER ATTACKS Anticipated in 2006.* Retrieved January 26, 2006, from http://www-03.ibm.com/press/us/en/pressrelease/19141.wss

IEC 61025. (1990). *Fault tree analysis (FTA).* International Electrotechnical Commission.

Ilgun, K. (1993). USTAT: A real-time intrusion detection system for Unix. *IEEE Symposium on Security and Privacy,* 16-28.

INDICARE. (2004). *The Informed dialogue about consumer acceptability of DRM solutions in Europe.* Retrieved January 26, 2006, from http://www.indicare.org/

Information Systems and Information Technology Solutions. (n.d.). *Sao Paolo University report.* Retrieved June 10, 2006, from http://www.virtual.epm.br/material/healthcare/B01.pdf

Intertrust. (2004). *Octopus principles of operation* (Internal memo).

Intertrust. (2005). *Reference technology.* Retrieved January 26, 2006, from http://www.intertrust.com/main/research/reference.html

Intoto Inc. (2005), *iGateway SSL-VPN.* Retrieved January 21, 2006, from http://www.intoto.com/product_briefs/iGateway%20SSL%20VPN.pdf

ISO 15048. (1999). *Information technology–Security techniques–Evaluation criteria for IT security* (common criteria). International Organization for Standardization.

ISO 15408. (2004). *Information technology—Security techniques—Evaluation criteria for IT security (Common Criteria), International Organization for Standardization (version 2.2, ISO 15408).* Retrieved from http://www.commoncriteriaportal.org

ISO 17799. (2000). *Code of practice for information security management* (ISO/IEC 17799:2000). International Organization for Standardization.

ISO/IEC 13335. (2004). *Information technology – Security techniques – Management of information and communications technology security – Part 1: Concepts and models for information and communications technology security management.* International Organization for Standardization/International Electrotechnical Commission.

ISO/IEC 9000:2000. (1999). *Quality management systems–Fundamentals and vocabulary.* ISO/IEC 9000:2000, International Organization for Standardization.

ISO/IEC. (2002). Risk management–Vocabulary–Guidelines for use in standards. *ISO/IEC Guide, 73.*

ISO17799. (2000). *Code of practice for information security management.* International Organization for Standardization.

ITU-T Recommendation X.509. (1997, June). *Information technology–*Open systems interconnection–The directory: Authentication framework.

ITU-T Recommendation X.509. (2000, March), *Information technology–*Open systems interconnection–The directory: Public-key and attribute certificate frameworks.

ITU-T Standard X. 509. (1995, October 24). *Information technology-Open systems interconnection-The directory: Public-key and attribute certificate frameworks.* Directive of the European Parliament and of the Council of 1995 on the protection of individuals with regard to the processing of personal data and on the free movement of such data. Retrieved January 10, 2006, from http://www.dsv.su.se/jpalme/society/eu-personal-privacy-directive.html

Jackson, M. (1983). *System development.* Englewood Cliffs, NJ: Prentice Hall.

Jacobson, I., Booch, G., & Rumbaugh, J. (1999). *The unified software development process.* Addison Wesley Longman.

Jacobson, I., Christerson, M., Johnsson, P., & Overgaard, G. (1992). *Object-oriented software engineering: A use case driven approach.* Boston: Addison Wesley.

Jammalamadaka, R. C., Mehrotra, S., & Venkatasubramanian, N. (2005, November 11). Pvault: A client server system providing mobile access to personal data. In *Proceedings of the 2005 ACM International Workshop on Storage Security and Survivability, Fairfax, VA.*

Jansen, W. A. (2003, May 12-15). *Authenticating users on handheld devices.* The 15th Annual Canadian Information Technology Security Symposium (CITSS), Ottawa, Canada. Retrieved July 11, from http://csrc.nist.gov/mobilesecurity/publications.html#MD

Javits, H. S., & Valdes, A. (1994). *The NIDES statistical component: Description and justification* (Tech. Rep.). Menlo Park, CA: SRI International.

Jin, J., & Nahrstedt, K. (2004). QoS specification languages for distributed multimedia applications: A survey and taxonomy. *IEEE Multimedia, IEEE Computer Society Press, 11*(3), 74-87.

Jones, A. K., & Lin, Y. (2001). Application intrusion detection using language library calls. In *Proceedings of 17th Annual Computer Security Applications Conference (ACSAC'01)*. Los Alamitos, CA: IEEE Computer Society Press.

Joshi, J., et. al. (2004, November–December). Access control language for multidomain environments. *IEEE Internet Computing*, 40-50.

Kang, M. H., Park, J. S., & Froscher, J. N. (2001). Access control mechanisms for interorganizational workflow. In *Proceedings of the Sixth ACM Symposium on Access Control Models and Technologies*, 66-74.

Kaplan, M. A. (1996). *IBM cryptolopesTM, superdistribution and digital rights management.* Retrieved December 1996, from http://www.research.ibm.com/people/k/kaplan

Karkimo, A. (2005, October 13). Kännykkää tunnistaa kantajansa askelista. *Tietokone computer science magazine on-line news.* Retrieved February 1st, 2006, from www.tietokone.fi

Kaspersky Security for PDAs. (n.d.) Retrieved June 30, 2005, from http://anti-virusi.com/kaspersky/kaspersky_pda.html

Kaspersky. (2005). *IRC worms.* Retrieved October 2005 from http://www.avp.ch/avpve/worms/irc.stm

Katsikas S., Spinellis D., Iliadis J., Blobel B., 1998, Using trusted third parties for secure telemedical applications over the WWW: The EUROMED-ETS approach, *Intern. Journal of Medical Informatics*, Elsevier, No.49, pp. 59-68

Kay, J. (2005). Low volume viruses: New tools for criminals. *Network Security, 2005*(6), 16-18.

Kazienko, P., & Dorosz, P. (2004). *Intrusion detection systems* (IDS) Part 2 – Classification; methods; techniques (White paper).

Kirda, E., & Kruegel, C. (2005, July, 26-28) Protecting users against phishing attacks with AntiPhish. In *Proceedings of the 29th Annual International Conference on Computer Software and Applications, Edinburgh, Scotland.*

Kizza, J. M. (2005). *Computer network security.* Springer.

Knight, W. (2005, July). Caught in the net. *IEE Revie,w 51*(7), 26-30.

Ko, C. (2000). *Logic induction of valid behavior specifications for intrusion detection.* Los Alamitos, CA: IEEE Press.

Ko, C., Ruschitzka, M., & Levitt, K. (1997). Execution monitoring of security critical programs in distributed systems: A specification-based approach. *IEEE symposium on security and privacy,* 175-187.

Kohl, U., Lotspiech, J., & Kaplan, A. (1997). *Safeguarding digital library contents and users protecting documents rather than channels.* Retrieved from http://www.dlib.org/dlib/september97/ibm/09lotspiech.html

Kormann, D., & Rubin, A. (2000). Risks of the Passport single signon protocol. *Computer Networks, 33,* 51-58.

Koshutanski, H. (2005). *Interactive access control for autonomic systems.* Unpublished doctoral dissertation, University of Trento, Italy.

Koshutanski, H., & Massacci, F. (2007). A negotiation scheme for access rights establishment in autonomic communication. *Journal of Network and System Management (JNSM) 15*(1), 117-136. Springer press.

Krebs, B. (2006). *Citibank phish spoofs 2-factor authentication.* Retrieved July 23, 2006, from http://blog.washingtonpost.com/securityfix/2006/07/citibank_phish_spoofs_2factor_1.html

Kruegel, C., Mutz, D., Robertson, W., & Valeur, F. (2003). Bayesian event classification for intrusion detection. In *Proceedings of the 19th Annual Computer Security Applications Conference (ACSAC 2003).* Los Alamitos, CA: IEEE Computer Society Press.

Kruegel, C., Valeur, F., Vigna, G., & Kemmerer, R. (2002). Stateful intrusion detection for high-speed networks. In *Proceedings of the 2002 IEEE Symposium on Security and Privacy (S&P.02)*. Los Alamitos, CA: IEEE Computer Society Press.

Kumar, S., & Spafford, E. H. (1994). A pattern-matching model for misuse intrusion detection. *National Computer Security Conference*, 11-21.

Lampson, B. (2004). Computer security in the real world. *IEEE Computer Society Press, 37*(6), 37, 46.

Landesman, M. (2005, November). Best defenders. *PC World*.

Larsen, P. G., & Pawlowski, W. (1995). The formal semantics of ISO VDM-SL. *Computer Standards and Interfaces*, 17(5/6), 585-602.

Le, V., & Guyennet, H. (2002). IPSec and DNSSEC to support GRID Application Security. *Workshop Security in the Second IEEE/ACM International Symposium on Cluster Computing and the GRID, CCGrid2002*, Berlin, Germany, pp. 405-407.

Le, V., & Guyennet, V. (2003). A scalable security architecture for grid applications. *GridSec, Second Workshop on Security and Network Architecture*, Nancy, France, pp 195-202.

Li, J., Li, N., & Winsborough, W. H. (2005). Automated trust negotiation using cryptographic credentials. In *Proceedings of the 12th ACM conference on Computer and communications security*, 46-57.

Li, N., & Mitchell, J. C. (2003) Datalog with constraints: A foundation for trust management languages. In *Proceedings of the Fifth International Symposium on Practical Aspects of Declarative Languages*.

Li, N., & Mitchell, J. C. (2003). RT: A role-based trust-management framework. In *Proceedings of the Third DARPA Information Survivability Conference and Exposition (DISCEX III)*, 201-212.

Li, N., Grosof, B. N., & Feigenbaum, J. (2003). Delegation logic: A logic-based approach to distributed authorization. *ACM Transactions on Information and System Security*

(TISSEC), 6(1), 128-171.

Li, N., Mitchell, J. C., & Winsborough, W. H. (2002). Design of a role-based trust management framework. In *Proceedings of IEEE Symposium on Security and Privacy (S&P)*, 114-130.

Li, Z., & Das, A. (2004). Visualizing and identifying intrusion context from system calls trace. In *Proceedings of the 20th Annual Computer Security Applications Conference (ACSAC'04)*. Los Alamitos, CA: IEEE Computer Society Press.

Liberty Alliance Project. (2003). *Liberty Alliance & WS-Federation: A comparative overview* (White Paper). Retrieved October 14, 2003, from http://www.liberty.org

Licari, J. (2006). Protecting the information workplace. *EDPACS , 2006*(33), 13-20.

Lindqvist, U., & Porras, P. (1999). *Detecting computer and network misuse with the production-based expert system toolset (P-BEST)*. Oakland, CA: IEEE Computer Society Press.

Lindqvist, U., & Porras, P. A. (2001). *eXpert-BSM: A Host-based intrusion detection solution for Sun Solaris*. Los Alamitos, CA: IEEE Press.

Lininger, R., & Vines, R. D. (2005). *Phishing: Cutting the identity theft line*. Indianapolis, IN: Wiley.

Lipner, S., & Howard, M. (2005). *The trustworthy computing security development life cycle*. Retrieved December, 2005, from http://msdn.microsoft.com/security/default.aspx?pull=/library/en-us/dnsecure/html/sdl.asp

Liska, A. (2002). *The practice of network security: Deployment strategies for production environments*. Prentice Hall .

Litan, A. (2005a). *Findings from Credit Reporting Agency: Authentication Practices* (Gartner Rep. G00136618).

Litan, A. (2005b). *Increased phishing and online attacks cause dip in consumer confidence* (Gartner Rep. G00129146).

Liu, W., Guanglin, H., Liu, X., Zhang, M., & Xiaotie, D. (2005, May 10-14). *Detection of phishing Web pages based on visual similarity.* Special Interest Tracks and Posters of the 14ᵗʰ International Conference on World Wide Web, Chiba, Japan.

Lu, W. W. (2002). *Broadband wireless mobile, 3G and beyond.* USA: Wiley.

Lund, M. S., Hogganvik, I., Seehusen, F., & Stølen, K. (2003). *UML profile for security assessment* (Tech. Rep. STF40 A03066). Oslo, Norway: SINTEF Telecom and Informatics.

Lymberopoulos, L., Lupu, E., & Sloman, M. (2003). An adaptive policy based framework for network services management. *Plenum Press Journal of Network and Systems Management, 11*(3), 277-303.

Mahler, T. (Ed.). (2005). *Report on legal issues* (Tech. Rep. D15). Oslo, Norway: TrustCoM EU IST Project 01945.

Mahler, T., & Vraalsen, F. (2005). Legal risk analysis with respect to IPR in a collaborative engineering virtual organization. In *Proceedings of the 6ᵗʰ IFIP Working Conference on Virtual Enterprises (PRO-VE 2005).* Valencia, Spain.

MailFrontier. (2005). *MailFrontier Phishing IQ Test II.* Retrieved October 5, 2005, from http://survey.mailfrontier. com/survey/quiztest.html

Man, S., Hong, D., & Matthews, M. (2003). A shoulder-surfing resistant graphical password scheme – WIW. In *Proceedings of the International Conference on Security and Management,* 105-111.

Man, S., Hong, D., Hayes, B., & Matthews, M. (2004). A password scheme strongly resistant to spyware. In *Proceedings of the International Conference on Security and Management,* 94-100.

Manjunath, R. (2006). *Compact architecture for the analysis and processing of subnet signals using differentiators as building blocks.* Unpublished doctoral dissertation, University of Bangalore, India.

Manjunath, R., & Gurumurthy, K. S. (2002). *System design using differentially fed Artificial Neural networks.* TENCON'02.

Manjunath, R., & Gurumurthy, K. S. (2004). *Hyperplanes Generation Through*

Manjunath, R., & Gurumurthy, K. S. (2005a). *Bayesian estimator with differential feedback.* MWSCAS.

Manjunath, R., & Gurumurthy, K. S. (2005b). *Learning algorithm with DANN.* In Encyclopedia of Database Technologies and Applications. Hershey, PA: Idea Group.

Mannan, M., & van Oorschot' (2005, November). On instant messaging worms, analysis and countermeasures. In *Proceedings of the 2005 ACM Workshop on Rapid Malcode.*

Markovski, J., & Gusev, M. (2003, April). Application level security of mobile communications (pp. 309 – 317). In *Proceedings of the 1ˢᵗ International Conference Mathematics and Informatics for Industry MII 2003.* Thessaloniki, Greece.

Marlin, J. D. A. (2005). *CE and DRM technology leaders to create a DRM toolkit for consumer devices.* Retrieved January 26, 2006, from http://www.intertrust.com/main/news/2003_2005/050119_marlin.html

Matsumoto, T. (1996, March). Human-computer cryptography: An attempt. In *Proceedings of the Third ACM Conference on Computer and Communications Security,* 68-75.

McCanne, S., Leres, C., & Jacobson, V. (1998). *Tcpdump 3.4 documentation.* Retrieved December 19, 2005, from http://tcpdump.org

MEDIS technical report. (n.d.). Retrieved September 28, 2005, from http://www.imp.bg.ac.yu/dokumenti/MEDIS-TechnicalReport.doc

MEHARI. (2004, December). *Harmonized method for risks analysis: Principles and mechanisms (CLUSIF, version 3).* Retrieved from http://www.clusif.asso.fr/fr/production/mehari

Meier, M., Bischof, N., & Holz, T. (2002). SHEDEL – A simple hierarchical event description language for specifying attack signature. *IFIP TC11 17ᵗʰ International Conference on Information Security: Visions and Perspectives,* 559-571.

Merwe, A. V. D., Loock, M., & Dabrowski, M. (2005). Characteristics and responsibilities involved in a phishing attack.

In *Proceedings of the Fourth International Symposium on Information and Communication Technologies*, 249-254.

Meyer, U., & Wetzel, S. (2004, September 5-8). *On the impact of GSM encryption and man-in-the-middle attacks on the security of interoperating GSM/UMTS networks.* The 15th IEEE International Symposium on Personal, Indoor and Mobile Radio Communications (PIMRC 2004), Barcelona, Spain. Retrieved February 5, 2006, from http://www.cdc.informatik.tu-darmstadt.de/~umeyer/UliPIMRC04.pdf

Michel, C., & Mé, L. (2001). ADeLe: An attack description language for knowledge-based intrusion detection systems. *IFIP TC11 International Conference on Information Security,* 353-368.

Microsoft and IBM white paper. (2005). *Security in Web service world: A proposed architecture and roadmap.* Retrieved September 28, 2005, from http://www-128.ibm.com/developerworks/webservices/library/ws-secmap

Microsoft. (2002). *NET Passport: Balanced authentication solutions.* Retrieved December 1, 2002, from http://www.passport.com

Microsoft. (2003). *Windows 2000 security event descriptions.* Retrieved December 2005, from http://support.microsoft.com/default.aspx?scid=kb;EN-US;299475#kb1

Microsoft. (2004). *NET Passport review guide.* Retrieved January 1, 2004, from http://www.passport.com

Microsoft. (2005). *The abstract state machine language.* Retrieved December 2005, from http://research.microsoft.com/fse/asml/docu.aspx

Microsoft. (2005).Retrieved on July 7, 2006, from http://www.microsoft.com/athome/security/spywarewhat.msx

Microsoft. (2005, November) *Microsoft developer network library.* Retrieved November 2005 from http://msdn.microsoft.com/library/

Microsoft. (2006). *Network Security for the Windows Mobile Software Platform.* Microsoft White Paper. Retrieved July 17, 2006, from http://www.microsoft.com

Milito, R. A. (2006). The inside-out approach to infection control. *EDPACS, 2006*(33), 9-14.

MobileCloak™ Portal. Retrieved July 20, 2006, from http://www.mobilecloak.com/

Mori, R., & Kawahara, M. (1990, July). Superdistribution: The concept and the architecture. *Transaction of the IEICE, E73*(7), 1133-1146.

Mori, R., & Tashiro, S. (1987, January). The concept of software service system (SSS). *Transaction of the IEICE, J70*(D1), 70-81.

Morin, J.-H., & Pawlak, M. (2005a, December 11). Towards a global framework for corporate and enterprise digital policy management. In *Proceedings of the SoftWars Conference on Protecting the Intangible Organizational Assets, Las Vegas, NV.*

Morin, J.-H., & Pawlak, M. (2005b, December 10). A credential based approach to managing exceptions in digital rights management systems. In *Proceedings of Fourth Pre-ICIS Academic Workshop AIM on New trends in IT and New Challenges in IT Regulation, Las Vegas, NV.*

MPEG-21. (2002). *MPEG-21 multimedia framework.* Retrieved January 26, 2006, from http://www.chiariglione.org/mpeg/standards/mpeg-21/mpeg-21.htm

MPEG-RDD. (2004). *Multimedia framework (MPEG-21)–Part 6: Rights data dictionary.* Retrieved January 26, 2006, from http://www.iso.ch/iso/en/CombinedQueryResult.CombinedQueryResult?queryString=21000-6

MPEG-REL. (2004). *Multimedia framework (MPEG-21)–Part 5: Rights expression language.* Retrieved January 26, 2006, from http://www.iso.ch/iso/en/CombinedQueryResult.CombinedQueryResult?queryString=21000-5

Muller, T. (1999). *Bluetooth Security Architecture.* White Paper. Retrieved July 20, 2006, from http://www.bluetooth.com/Bluetooth/Apply/Technology/Research/Bluetooth_Security_Architecture.htm

Müller-Hengstenberg, C. D. (2005). Der Vertrag als Mittel des Risikomanagements. Ein Plädoyer für die dynamische Projektbegleitung im Vertrag. *Computer und Recht, 5,* 385-392.

Mutz, D., Vigna, G., & Kemmerer, R. (2003). An experience developing an IDS Stimulator for the black-box testing of network intrusion detection systems. In *Proceedings of the 19th Annual Computer Security Applications Conference (ACSAC 2003).*Los Alamitos, CA: IEEE Computer Society Press.

Nanny. (2004, March 18). *Police investigation of nanny widens.* Retrieved January 30, 2006, from http://www.sfgate.com/cgi-bin/article.cgi?file=/chronicle/archive/2004/03/18/BAG6S5MUEO1.DTL

Naur, P., & Randell, B. (1969). Software engineering: Report of a conference sponsored by the NATO Science Committee, Garmisch, Germany, 1968. Brussels, Belgium: NATO, Scientific Affairs Division.

Nevis Network. (2006). *Stopping malware spread from untrusted hosts.* Retrieved July 7, 2006, from http://www.nevisnetworks.com

Nielsen, B., Ren, S., & Agha, G. (1998). Specification of real-time interaction constraints. *International Symposium on Object-Oriented Real-Time Distributed Computing,* 206-214.

Nilsson, U., & Maluszynski, J. (2000). *Logic, Programming and prolog* (2nd ed.).

OASIS. (1993). *Organization for the advancement of structured information standards.* Retrieved March 28, 2006, from http://www.oasis-open.org/

OCP. (2005). *The secure video processor (SVP) initiative–SVP open content protection system: Technical overview.* Retrieved January 26, 2006, from http://www.svpalliance.org/docs/e2e_technical_introduction.pdf

OCTAVE. (1999, June). *Operationally critical threat, asset and vulnerability evaluation (version 2.0).* Retrieved from http://www.cert.org/octave/methods

ODRL. (2002). *The open digital rights language (ODRL) initiative.* Retrieved January 26, 2006, from http://www.odrl.net/

Olzak, T. (2005). *Wireless Handheld Device Security.* Retrieved October 12, 2005, from http://www.securitydocs.com/pdf/3188.PDF

OMA. (2002). *Open mobile alliance.* Retrieved January 26, 2006, from http://www.openmobilealliance.org/

OMA. (2004). *Open mobile alliance.* Retrieved January 26, 2006, from http://www.openmobilealliance.org/release_program/drm_v1_0.html

OMA. (2006a). *Open mobile alliance.* Retrieved January 26, 2006, from http://www.openmobilealliance.org/release_program/drm_v2_0.html

OMA. (2006b). *Open mobile alliance.* Retrieved January 26, 2006, from http://www.openmobilealliance.org/release_program/drm_v2_0.html

OMC. (2005). *Open media commons.* Retrieved March 28, 2006, from http://www.openmediacommons.org/

OMC. (2006a). *Open media commons FAQ's.* Retrieved March 28 , 2006, from http://www.openmediacommons.org/faqs.html

OMC. (2006b). *Open media commons releases specifications and source code for open, royalty-free digital rights management.* Retrieved March 28, 2006, from http://www.openmediacommons.org/news/03212006-omcworkshop_press_release.html

OMG. (2004). *Common object request broker architecture (CORBA) specification* (Tech. Rep. version 3.0.3). Needham, MA: Object Management Group.

OMG. (2005). *OCL 2.0 specification* (Tech. Rep. version 2). Needham, MA: Object Management Group. Ostroff, J. S. (1992). Formal methods for the specification and design of real-time safety critical systems. *Journal of Systems and Software, 18*(1), 33-60.

OMG. (2005). *Unified modeling language: Superstructure, version 2.0* (OMG Document: formal/2005-07-04).

OMG. (2006). *UML profile for modeling quality of service and fault tolerance characteristics and mechanisms, available specification* (OMG Document: ptc/2005-05-02) Author.

Open Mobile Alliance (2006). *WAP Forum.* Retrieved February 6, 2006, from http://www.wapforum.org/

Oram, A. (2001). *Peer-to-peer: Harnessing the power of disruptive technologies.* O'Reilly.

Origins of the Word. (n.d.). *Origins of the word "phishing."* Retrieved January 5, 2006, from http://www.antiphishing.org/word_phish.html

OTP. (1998). RFC 2289 - *A one-time password system.* Retrieved October 5, 2005, from http://www.faqs.org/rfcs/rfc2289.html

PalmSource, Inc. (2006). *PalmSource portal.* Retrieved July 17, 2006, from http://www.palmsource.com.

Paquette, J. (2000). *A history of viruses. Retrieved July 7, 2006, from http://www.securityfocus.com/infocus/1286*

Park J. S. (2005). Security analyses for enterprise instant messenger (EIM) systems. *EDPACS, 2005*(32), 8-24.

PassMark. (n.d.). *PassMark security: Two-factor two-way authentication.* Retrieved September 29, 2005, from http://www.passmarksecurity.com/main.jsp

Paulk, M. (2001). Extreme programming from a CMM perspective. *IEEE Software, 18*(6), 19–26.

Paulk, M. C., Curtis, B., Chrissis, M. B., & Weber, C. V. (1993). *Capability maturity model* (SE, version 1.1). Software Engineering Institute.

Paxson, V. (1998). Bro: A system for detecting network intruders in real-time. USENIX Security Symposium, San Antonio, TX. *Computer Networks, 31*(23-24), 2435-2463. Elsevier.

Perelson, S., and Botha, R. (2004). *A*n Investigation Into Access Control for Mobile Devices. In H. S. Venter (Ed.), J. H. P. Eloff (Ed.), L. Labuschagne (Ed.), M.M. Eloff (Ed.), ISSA 2004 Enabling Tomorrow Conference. *Peer-reviewed Proceedings of the ISSA 2004 Enabling Tomorrow Conference. Information Security South Africa* (ISSA).

Peter, M. (2005). *Guide to malware incident prevention and handling* (Special Publication, pp. 800-83). U.S. Department of Commerce, National Institute of Standards.

Plamer, G. (2005). De-peremetrization: Benefits and limitations. *Information Security Technical Report 2005*(10), 189-203.

PMI. (2000). *A guide to the project management body of knowledge.* Author.

Pohlman, N., & Crothers, T. (2002). *Firewall architecture for the enterprise.* Wiley.

Porras, P. A., & Kemmerer, R. A. (1992). Penetration state transition analysis- A rule-based intrusion detection approach. *Annual Computer Security Applications Conference,* 220-229.

Porras, P. A., & Neumann, P. G. (1997). EMERALD: Event monitoring enabling responses to anomalous live disturbances. *National Information Systems Security Conference,* 353-365.

Pouzol, J. P., & Ducassé, M. (2001). From declarative signatures to misuse IDS. *International Symposium on Recent Advances in Intrusion Detection, 2212,* 1-21.

Price, G. (2005). Editorial: The security perimeter. *Information Security Technical Report, 2005*(10), 185.

Primode. (2005). *Information security glossary.* Retrieved July 7, 2006, from www.primode.com/glossary.html

Privacy Rights Clearinghouse. (2005). *A chronology of data breaches reported since the ChoicePoint incident.* Retrieved May 31, 2006, from http://www.privacyrights.org/

Ptacek, T. (1998). *Custom attack simulation language (CASL)* (Tech. Rep.). Retrieved December 2005, from http://www.sockpuppet.org/tqbf/casl.html

Pulkkis, G., Grahn, K., Karlsson, J., Martikainen, M. & Daniel, D.E. (2005). Recent Developments in WLAN Security. In Pagani, M. (Ed.), *Mobile and Wireless Systems Beyond 3G: Managing New Business Opportunities.* USA: IRM Press

Quisquater, J-J., Quisquater, M., Quisquater, M., Quisquater, M., Guillou, L. Guillou, M. A., et al. (1990). How to explain zero-knowledge protocols to your children. In G. Brassard (Ed.), *Advances in cryptology* (vol. 435, pp. 628-631). Springer-Verlag.

Rabek, C., Lewandowski, M., Khazan, I. & Cunningham, K. (2003). Detection of injected, dynamically generated, and obfuscated malicious code. In *Proceedings of the 2003 ACM Workshop on Rapid Malcode.*

Raihan, M. (2006). *AsmLx based intrusion-aware software systems.* Unpublished master's thesis, Queen's University, Kingston, Ontario, Canada.

Rankl, W. & Effing, W. (2003). *Smart Card Handbook.* (3ʳᵈ ed), USA: John Wiley & Sons.

Ranum, M. J., Landfield, K., Stolarchuck, M., Sienkiewicz, M., Lambeth, A., & Wall, E. (1997). *Implementing a generalized tool for network monitoring.* Systems Administration Conference, USENIX Association.

Raz, T., & Michael, E. (1999). Use and benefits of tools for project risk management. *International Journal of Project Management, 19,* 9-17.

Redmill, F., Chudleigh, M., & Catmur, J. (1999). *HazOp and software HazOp.* Wiley.

Reichertz, P. (in press). Hospital information systems—Past, present, future. *International Journal of Medical Informatics.*

Rittinghouse, J.W. & Ransome, J.F. (2004). *Wireless Operational Security.* Amsterdam. Elsevier Digital Press.

Rivest, R., & Lampson, B. (1996). *SDSI - A simple distributed security infrastructure* (Working document). Presented at CRYPTO '96.

RMS. (2003). *Microsoft Windows rights management services (RMS) for Windows server 2003.* Retrieved May 31, 2006, from http://www.microsoft.com/rms

Roberts, P. (2004, September 13). *Symantec launches antiphishing service.* Retrieved January 25, 2006, from http://www.infoworld.com/article/04/09/13/HNsymanti-phishing_1.html

Roesch, M. (1998). *Writing Snort rules: How To write Snort rules and keep your sanity.* Retrieved December 2005, from http://www.snort.org/docs/snort_htmanuals/htmanual_2.4/snort_manual.html

Rose, M. (2001). RFC 3080: The blocks extensible exchange protocol core. *Internet Engineering Task Force.*

Rosenblatt, B., Trippe, B., & Mooney, S. (2001). *Digital rights management: Business and technology.* New York: Hungry Minds/Wiley.

Ross, B., Jackson, C., Miyake, N., Boneh, D., & Mitchell, J. C. (2005). Stronger password authentication using browser extensions. In *Proceedings of the 14ᵗʰ Usenix Security Symposium.*

Ruan, C., & Varadharajan, V. (2003). A formal graph based framework for supporting authorization delegations and conflict resolutions. *International Journal of Information Security, 1*(4), 211-222.

Ruan, C., & Varadharajan, V. (2004). A weighted graph approach to authorization delegation and conflict resolution. *Lecture Notes in Computer Science, 3108,* 402-413.

Ruan, C., Varadharajan, V., & Zhang, Y. (2002) Logic-based reasoning on delegatable authorizations. In *Proceedings of the 13ᵗʰ International Symposium on Methodologies for Intelligent Systems,* 185-193.

Ruan, C., Varadharajan, V., & Zhang, Y. (2003). A logic model for temporal authorization delegation with negation. In C. Boyd & W. Mao (Eds.), *Proceedings of the Sixth International Conference on Information Security (ISC), 2851,* 310-324.

Rubin, S., Jha, S., & Miller, B. P. (2004). Automatic @sis of NIDS attacks. In *Proceedings of the 20ᵗʰ Annual Computer Security Applications Conference (ACSAC'04).* Los Alamitos, CA:. IEEE Computer Society Press.

Rubin, S., Jha, S., & Miller, B. P. (2005). Language-based generation and evaluation of NIDS signatures. In *Proceedings of the 2005 IEEE Symposium on Security and Privacy (S&P'05).* Los Alamitos, CA:. IEEE Computer Society Press.

Rumbaugh, J., Blaha, M., Premerlani, W., Eddy, F., & Lorensen, W. (1991). *Object-oriented modeling and design.* Englewood Cliffs, NJ: Prentice Hall.

SAML. (2004). *Security assertion markup language (SAML).* Retrieved from http://www.oasis-open.org/committees/security

Sandhu, R., Coyne, E., Feinstein, H., & Youman, C. (1996). Role-based access control models. *IEEE Computer 39*(2), 38-47.

Sarbanes-Oxley Act of 2002, 116 Stat. 745 (2002).

Savage, S., & Voelker, G. M. (2004). *NSF cybertrust center proposal: Center for Internet epidemiology and defenses.*

Saxena, N., Tsudik, G., & Yi, J. H. (2003). Admission control in peer-to-peer: Design and performance evaluation. *ACM Workshop on Security of Ad Hoc and Sensor Networks (SASN). USA*

Schneier, B. (April 2005). Two-factor authentication: Too little, too late. *Communications of the ACM, 48*(4), 136.

Schoderbek, P., Schoderbek, C., & Kefalas, A. (1990). *Management systems–Conceptual considerations* (4th ed.). Irwin.

Seamons, K., Winslett, M., & Yu, T. (2001). Limiting the disclosure of access control policies during automated trust negotiation. In *Network and Distributed System Security Symposium.* San Diego, CA.

Sekar, R., & Uppuluri, P. (1999). Synthesizing fast intrusion prevention/detection systems from high-level specifications. *USENIX Security Symposium, (pp. 63-79).* Berkley.

Setec Portal. (2006). Retrieved February 5th, 2006, from http://www.setec.fi

Shackman, M. (2005). *Platform Security: A Technical Overview.* Retrieved October 11, 2005, from http://www.symbian.com/developer/techlib/papers/plat_sec_tech_overview/platform_security_a_technical_overview_v1.1.pdf

Shanahan, M. (1989). Prediction is deduction but explanation is abduction. In *Proceedings of IJCAI'89* (pp. 1055-1060). Morgan Kaufmann.

Shankar, U., & Paxson, V. (2003). Active mapping: Resisting NIDS evasion without altering traffic. In *Proceedings of the 2003 IEEE Symposium on Security and Privacy (SP.03).* Los Alamitos, CA:. IEEE Computer Society Press.

Sibert, O., Bernstein, D., & Van Wie, D. (1995, July 11-12,). The DigiBox: A self-protecting container for information commerce. In *Proceedings of First USENIX Workshop on Electronic Commerce, New York, NY.*

Siezen, S. (2005). *Symbian OS Version 9.1, Product Description.* Retrieved July 20th, 2006, from http://www.symbian.com/files/rx/file6965.pdf

Silva, P. F., & Westphall, C. P. (2005, July, 17-20). A model for interoperability of answers in intrusion detection systems. *CD-ROM Proceedings of the Advanced International Conference on Telecomunications (AICT 2005),* Lisbon, Portugal.

Silver, C. (2005). *Time Warner employee data missing.* Retrieved January 26, 2006, from http://money.cnn.com/2005/05/02/news/fortune500/security_timewarner/?cnn=yes

Slade, R. M. (2004). Malware and computer viruses. In H. F. Tipton & N. Krause (Eds.), *Information security management handbook.* Raton, FL: CRC Press.

Slewe, T., & Hoogenboom, M. (2004, May). Who will rob you on the digital highway? *Communications of the ACM, 47*(5), 56-60.

Sloman, M., & Lupu, E. (1999). Policy specification for programmable networks. In *Proceedings of the First International Working Conference on Active Networks,* 73-84.

Smirnov, M. (2003). Rule-based systems security model. In *Proceedings of the Second International Workshop on Mathematical Methods, Models, and Architectures for Computer Network Security (MMM-ACNS),* 135-146.

Smith, G. (2000). The Object-Z specification language. *Advances in Formal Methods* (vol. 1).Kluwer Academic.

Smulders, T. H. (2004). *Security threats of executing malicious applications on mobile phones.* Masters thesis. Technische Universiteit Eindhoven, Department of Mathematics and Computer Science, Netherlands. Retrieved July 20th, 2006, from http://www.win.tue.nl/~ecss/internships/reports/TSmulders2004.pdf

Sobrado, L., & Birget, J.-C. (2002). *Graphical passwords.* Retrieved April 14, 2005, from http://rutgersscholar.rutgers.edu/volume04/sobrbirg/sobrbirg.htm

Sobrado, L., & Birget, J.-C. (2005). *Shoulder surfing resistant graphical passwords.* Retrieved October 5, 2005, from http://clam.rutgers.edu/~birget/grPssw/srgp.pdf

Sommerville, I. (2004). *Software engineering* (7th ed.). Addison Wesley.

Sonnenreich, W., Albanese, J., & Stout, B. (2006, February). Return on security investment (ROSI)–A practical quantitative model. *Journal of Research and Practice in Information Technology, 38*(1), 99.

SPKI. (1999). SPKI certificate theory. *IETF RFC,* 2693. Retrieved from, http://www.ietf.org/rfc/rfc2693.txt

SSE-CMM Project. (2003). *Systems security engineering capability maturity model* (version 3.0).

Stefik, M. (1996). Letting loose the light: Igniting commerce in electronic publication. In M. Stefic (Ed.), *Internet dreams: Archetypes, myths and metaphors.* Cambridge, MA.

Stevens, M. (2006). UTM: One-stop protection. *Network Security, 2006*(2), 12-14.

Stubblefield, A., Ioannidis, J., & Rubin, A. (2001). *Using the Fluhrer, Mantin, and Shamir attack to break WEP.* (Tech. Rep. TD-4ZCPZZ). AT&T Labs.

Sucurovic, S., & Jovanovic Z. (in press). *Java cryptography & attribute certificate management.* San Francisco: Dr. Dobb's Journal.

Sucurovic, S., & Jovanovic, Z. (2005, February). *Java cryptography & X.509 authentication.* San Francisco: Dr. Dobb's Journal.

Sun Microsystems Inc. (1991). *Installing, administering, and using the basic security module* (Tech. Rep.). Mountain View, CA.

Sun Microsystems. (2005). *Sun Microsystems president Jonathan Schwartz shares project dream.* Retrieved January 26, 2006, from http://www.sun.com/smi/Press/sunflash/2005-08/sunflash.20050822.2.html

Sun, J., Howie, D., Koivisto, A., & Sauvola, J. (2001). Design, implementation, and evaluation of Bluetooth security. In *Proceedings IEEE International Conference on Wireless LANs and Home Networks,* Singapore, 121 - 130.

Sunderam V. S. (1990). A framework for parallel distributed computing. *Concurrency: Practice and Experience, 2*(4), 315-339

Sung, A. H., Xu, J., Chavez, P., & Mukkamala, S. (2004). Static analyzer for vicious executables (SAVE). In *Proceedings of 20th Annual Computer Security Applications Conference (ACSAC),* 326-334.

Sunner, M. (2005). E-mail security best practice. *Network Security, 2005*(12), 4-6.

SVP. (2004). *The secure video processor (SVP) initiative.* Retrieved January 26, 2006, from http://www.svpalliance.org/

Symantec Corporation. (2005). *Symantec security response.* Retrieved November 2005 from http://securityresponse.symantec.com/avcenter/

Symantec Corporation. (2006). *Symantec mobile security for Symbian.* Retrieved January 15, 2006, from http://www.symantec.com/Products/enterprise?c=prodinfo&refId=921 and http://eval.veritas.com/mktginfo/enterprise/fact_sheets/ent-factsheet_mobile_security_for_symbian_04-2005.en-us.pdf

Symantec. (2005). *Wireless handheld and smartphone security.* Retrieved December 16, 2005, from http://enterprisesecurity.symantec.com/Products/products.cfm?MenuItemNo=2&productID=663&EID=0

Symbian OS Version 9.3 (2006). Retrieved July 20th, 2006, from http://www.symbian.com/files/rx/file7999.pdf

Symbian OS: Overview To Security (2006). Version 1.1, Retrieved January 26th, 2006 from http://sw.nokia.com/id/5e713b29-fe0e-488d-8fc6-b4dd1950f3c2/Symbian_OS_Overview_To_Security_v1_1_en.pdf

Symbian Signed Portal. Retrieved January 30th, 2006 from http://www.symbiansigned.com

Symbian. (2006). *Symbian OS: The mobile operating system.* Retrieved January 26th, 2006 from http://www.symbian.com

Szor, P . (2005). *The art of computer virus research and defense.* Upper Saddle River, NJ: Addison-Wesley.

Talukder, A. K. (2005). Clean and tidy. *Communications Engineer, 3*(4),38-41.

Talukder, A. K., Rao V. B., Kapoor, V., & Sharma, D. (2004). Artificial hygiene: A critical step towards safety from e-mail viruses. In *Proceedings of the IEEE INDICON 2004*, 484-489.

Taylor, L. (2004-2005). *Handheld Security, Part I-V*. Retrieved October 9, 2005, from http://www.firewallguide.com/pda.htm

Templeton, S. J., & Levitt, K. (2000). A requires/provides model for computer attacks. *Workshop on New security paradigms*, 31-38.

TimeWarner. (2005). *Time Warner statement on lost employee data tapes*. Retrieved January 26, 2006, from http://www.timewarner.com/corp/newsroom/employee_data_tapes/press_release.html

Tombini, E., Debar, H., Mé, L., & Ducassé, M. (2004). A serial combination of anomaly and misuse IDSes applied to HTTP traffic. In *Proceedings of the 20th Annual Computer Security Applications Conference (ACSAC'04)*. Los Alamitos, CA:. IEEE Computer Society Press.

Ullman, J. D. (1988). *Principles of database and knowledge-base systems: Vol. I.* Computer Science Press.

Ullman, J. D. (1989). *Principles of database and knowledge-base systems: Vol. II.* Computer Science Press.

US-CERT. (2005). *US-CERT vulnerabilities notes*. Retrieved January 2006 from *http://www.kb.cert.org/vuls/*

Vaccaro, H. S., & Liepins, G. E. (1989). Detection of anomalous computer session activity. *Symposium on Research in Security and Privacy*, 280-289.

Van Deursen, A., Klint, P., & Visser, J. (2000). Domain-specific languages: An annotated bibliography. *ACM SIGPLAN Notices, 35*(6), 26-36.

Van Eijk, P., Vissers, C., & Diaz, M. (1989). *The formal description technique LOTOS*. Elsevier Science.

Van Wie, D., Sibert, O., & Horning, J. (1997, October 7-10). Panel on the InterTrust commerce architecture. In *Proceedings of the 20th National Information Systems Security Conference*, Baltimore, MD.

VASCO. (2005, December). *Avoid phishing – Use strong authentication*. Retrieved July 1, 2006, from http://www.firewalls.com.au/docs/nophishing.pdf

VeriSign. (2005, December). *Unified authentication tokens*. Retrieved July 1, 2006, from http://www.verisign.com/products-services/security-services/unified-authentication/usb-tokens/index.html

Vigna, G., Eckmann, S. T., & Kemmerer, R. A. (2000). Attack languages. *IEEE Information Survivability Workshop*, 163-166.

Vigna, G., Gwalani, S., Srinivasan, K., Belding-Royer, E. M., & Kemmerer, R. A. (2004). An intrusion detection tool for AODV-based ad hoc wireless networks. In *Proceedings of the 20th Annual Computer Security Applications Conference (ACSAC'04)*. Los Alamitos, CA:. IEEE Computer Society Press.

Viveros, S. (2005). Changing malware threats- AV vendors's view. *Network Security, 2005*(12), 16-18.

Vraalsen, F. (Ed.). (2006). *Methods and Tools for legal risk management* (Tech. Rep. D17). Oslo, Norway: TrustCoM EU IST Project 01945.

Vraalsen, F., den Braber, F., Lund, M. S., & Stølen, K. (2005). The CORAS tool for security risk analysis. In P. Herrmann, V. Issarny, & S. Shiu, (Eds.), *Proceedings of the 3rd International Conference on Trust Management (iTrust 2005)* (pp. 402-405). Paris: Springer LNCS 3477.

Vraalsen, F., Lund, M. S., Mahler, T., Parent, X., & Stølen, K. (2005). Specifying legal risk scenarios using the CORAS threat modelling language – experiences and the way forward. In P. Herrmann, V. Issarny, & S. Shiu (Eds.), *Proceedings of the 3rd International Conference on Trust Management (iTrust 2005)* (pp. 45-60). Paris: Springer LNCS 3477.

Waker, J. (2005). The extended security perimeter. *Information Security Technical Report, 2005*(10), 220-227.

Wan, T., & Yang, X. D. (2000). *IntruDetector: A software platform for testing network intrusion detection algorithms.*

Webopedia, (2005). Trojan horse. Retrieved October 2005 from http://www.webopedia.com/TERM/T/Trojan_horse. html

Weeks, S. (2001). Understanding trust management systems. *IEEE Symposium on Security and Privacy.*

Wei, Z., & Meinl, Z. (2004). *Implement role based access control with attribute certificates, ICACT 2004.* International Conference on Advanced Communication Technology, Korea.

Welch, V., Foster, Y., Kesselman, C., Mulmo, O., Pearlman, L., Tuecke, S., et al. (2004). X.509 proxy certificates for dynamic delegation. *Third Annual PKI R&D Workshop.*

WEPCrack. Retrieved March 3, 2004, from http://webcrack.sf.net

Wetzel, R. (2005, February). Tackling phishing. *Business Communications Review*, pp. 46-51.

Whalley, I. Arnold, B., Chess, D., Morar, J., Segal, A., & Swimmer, M (2000). *An environment for controlled worm replication & analysis (Internet-inna-box).* Retrieved from http://www.research.ibm.com/anti-virus/SciPapers/ VB2000INW.pdf

Whitman, M. E., & Mattord, H. J. (2004). Management of information security. *Course Technology.*

Wieringa, R. (1998). A survey of structured and object-oriented software specification methods and techniques. *ACM Computing Surveys (CSUR), 30*(4), 459-527.

Wieslander, J., Boldt, M., & Carlsson, B. (2003). Investigating spyware on the Internet. In *Proceedings of the Seventh Nordic Workshop on Secure IT Systems, Norway.*

Wi-Fi Alliance Portal. (2006). Retrieved February 5th, 2006, from http://www.wi-fi.org

Wi-Fi Alliance. (2003). *Enterprise solutions for wireless LAN security.*

Wikipedia. (2005). The free encyclopedia. Retrieved on July 7, 2006, from http://en.wikipedia.org/wiki/Mobile_code

Wildstrom, S. H. (2005, March 3). New weapons to stop identity threat. *Businessweek.*

Winsborough, W., & Li, N. (2004). Safety in automated trust negotiation. In *Proceedings of the IEEE Symposium on Security and Privacy,* 147-160.

Wood, M., & Erlinger, M. (2002). *Intrusion detection message exchange requirements, IETF, RFC Draft, draft-ietf-idwg-requirements-10.*

WordSpy-Phishing. (n.d.). *Phishing.* Retrieved January 23, 2006, from http://www.wordspy.com/words/phishing.asp

WS-Security. (2006). *Web services security* (WS-security). Retrieved from http://www.oasis-open.org/committees. wss

Wu, M., Miller R. C., & Garfinkel, S. L. (2006). *Do security toolbars actually prevent phishing attacks?* Retrieved July 14, 2006, from http://groups.csail.mit.edu/uid/projects/ phishing/chi-security-toolbar.pdf

Wu, Q., & Shao, Z. (2005). Network anomaly detection using time series analysis. In *Proceedings of the Joint International Conference on Autonomic and Autonomous Systems and International Conference on Networking and Services (ICAS/ICNS 2005).*Los Alamitos, CA:. IEEE Computer Society Press.

Wu, Y.-S., Foo, B., Mei, Y., & Bagchi, S. (2003). Collaborative intrusion detection system (CIDS): A framework for accurate and efficient IDS. In *Proceedings of the 19th Annual Computer Security Applications Conference (ACSAC 2003).* Los Alamitos, CA:. IEEE Computer Society Press.

X.509. (2001). The directory: Public-key and attribute certificate frameworks. *ITU-T Recommendation X.509:2000(E) | ISO/IEC 9594-8:2001(E).*

XACML. (2004). *eXtensible Access Control Markup Language (XACML).* Retrieved from http://www.oasis-open. org/committees/xacml.

XrML. (2000). *eXtended rights markup language.* Retrieved March 28, 2006, from http://www.xrml.org/

XrML. (2002). XrML 2.0 (Technical Overview Version 1.0). Retrieved March 28, 2006, from http://www.xrml. org/Reference/XrMLTechnicalOverviewV1.pdf

Ye, T. S. and Cheang, A.. (2005, September). *The Mobility Threat*. Retrieved December 18, 2005, from http://cio-asia. com/ShowPage.aspx?pagetype=2&articleid=2535&pubid= 5&issueid=63

Ye, Z., Smith, S., & Anthony, D. (2005). Trusted paths for browsers. *ACM Transactions on Information and System Security, 8*(2), 153-186.

Yoshihisa, I., Miharu, S., Shihong, L., Masato, K. (2005). Face Recognition on Cellular Phone. Demo *Proceedings of the 10th IEEE International Conference on Computer Vision (ICCV2005)*, Beijing, China, October 15-21, 2005. Demo Nr 13

Yu, T., & Winslett, M. (2003). A unified scheme for resource protection in automated trust negotiation. In *Proceedings of the IEEE Symposium on Security and Privacy*, 110-122.

Yu, T., Winslett, M., & Seamons, K. E. (2003). Supporting structured credentials and sensitive policies through interoperable strategies for automated trust negotiation. *ACM Transactions on Information and System Security (TISSEC), 6*(1), 1-42.

Zuccato, A. (2004). Holistic security requirement engineering for electronic commerce, *Computers & Security, 23*(1), 63–76.

Zuccato, A. (2005). *Holistic information security management framework for electronic commerce.* Unpublished doctoral dissertation, Karlstad University Studies, Sweden.

Zulkernine, M., & Ahamed, S. (2005). Software security engineering: Towards unifying software engineering with security engineering. In M. Warkentin& R. Vaughn (Eds.), *Enterprise information systems assurance and system security: Managerial and technical issues* (pp. 215-233). Hershey, PA: Idea Group.

Zviran, M., & Erlich, Z. (2006). Identification and authentication: Technology and implementation issues. *Communications of AIS, 17*(4), 90-105.

About the Contributors

Djamel Khadraoui received his PhD from Blaise Pascal University of Clermont-Ferrand (France). He is a senior researcher in the domains of enterprise IT security, intelligent systems, and software architectures. Dr. Khadraoui is also active in the domain of Web-centric and interactive multimedia applications. His recent interests are related to multi-agents systems dealing with negotiation and arbitration applied to the domains of trusted e-contracting. Khadraoui is managing EUREKA projects in the area of telecom and security (BUGYO, RED, €-Confidential, CARLINK, AUTOTRUST). He is the representative of the Security and Trust Management ERCIM working group as well as of the Trust and Security working group of NESSI. He was a general chairman of AISTA04. He is member of ISO JTC1/SC27/WG2 related to IT security techniques/security techniques and mechanisms. He gives lectures at the University of Metz (France) and the Luxembourg University in the area of security.

Francine Herrmann received a PhD in computer science from PARIS-VI University. She worked at CNET Research Center from 1985 to 1988. In 1989, she joined the Computer Science Department of Metz University and the LITA computer science laboratory. She is now the director of the computer science department and manages the master of computer security of Metz. Her main research areas are parallel and distributed algorithms, parallel constraints and security in parallel computations.

* * *

Isaac Agudo received an MS in mathematics in 2002 from the University of Malaga, where he is working on his doctoral thesis. In 2002 he started working with the Computer Science Department at the University of Malaga. He has participated in the IST Project CASENET (Computer-Aided solutions to Secure ElectroNic commercE Transactions), included in the 5th Framework Programme and in the PRIVILEGE project, financed by the Spanish government. In 2003, he spent 3 months in the Fraunhofer Institute for Secure Information Technology (SIT), as part of the CASENET project. His principal research interests are authorization and delegation and their associated formal models. He has participated in several international conferences on these topics and in security courses.

Indranil Bose is an associate professor of information systems at the School of Business, The University of Hong Kong. He holds a PhD in management from the Krannert School of Management, Purdue University, an MS in industrial engineering from Purdue University, an MS in electrical and computer engineering from University of Iowa, and a BTech in electrical engineering from the Indian Institute of Technology. He is an active researcher and teacher in the fields of telecommunication and networking, information security, data mining, and supply chain management. His research has been supported by grants from several agencies including the Hong Kong Research Grants Council and Lucent Technologies. He has more than 40 publications in various scholarly and interdisciplinary journals, proceedings of international conferences, and chapters of books.

Folker den Braber holds an MSc in computer science from the University in Leiden, The Netherlands. He has been working as a research scientist at SINTEF Information and Communication Technology since 2001 with the Department for Quality and Security Technologies. His main research interests are in semiformal modeling, system architecture and development, and security analysis and architecture.

Patrick Chavez is currently a doctoral student in computer science at New Mexico Tech and a research assistant with New Mexico Tech's Institute for Complex Additive Systems Analysis. His research interests are information security, network security, malware analysis, honey pots, and data mining.

Alexis Ferrero graduated in 1987 from Sup Télécom (ENST), Paris. After 20 years in the telecommunication industry, Ferrero is currently the IT director at RTL Radio France. He has authored seven books on telecommunications, in English and French, and many articles in technical magazines. He is occasionally a teacher or trainer for different French universities.

Mário M. Freire is the head of the Department of Computer Science, University of Beira Interior, Covilhã, Portugal, where he is also the director of the MSc programme in computer science and engineering. He is an associate professor of computer science at the University of Beira Interior. His main research interests include network architectures and protocols, network and information security, multimedia networking and P2P systems, and Semantic Web and Web services. He has been the co-editor of two books and has authored or co-authored approximately 90 papers in international refereed journals and conferences. Presently, he teaches courses in computer networks, security and systems management, and multimedia networks.

Eric Garcia is an assistant professor at the University of Franche-Comté. He received a PhD in computer science in 2001. He is now working in the Network and Distributed Systems Group at the LIFC, the research laboratory for computer science at the university. He is the head of the InterregIII European Project DECOPREME/Teledermatology.

Sophie Gastellier-Prevost works as an associate professor at the French National Institute of Telecommunications INT, in which one she is in charge of the security-dedicated master-grade and post-grade programs of the engineering school. She is a member of the research group VIS, and her main topics of interest are related to network security (security architectures, firewalls, access control, vpns) and ip-based protocols (IP multicast, routing protocols). Previously, she worked in the industry as a presales engineer (SE) at CISCO SYSTEMS, and after she joined ERICSSON as a product specialist (data products : Juniper routers), then as a global solutions architect both on fixed and mobile solutions (including dial-up and xDSL access, GPRS and UMTS, Multimedia over IP, VPNs and network security, IP/ATM/MPLS, backbones).

Michèle Germain was graduated engineer in 1968 from the Institut Supérieur d'Electronique de Paris (ISEP). For Matra Communication and EADS, she participated in large telephone and radio communication projects. She intervenes now as a consultant in telecommunication domain. She is co-author of several books on the new technologies of information and communication, and she lectures courses on secured radio communications in several engineer high schools.

Kaj J. Grahn, DrTech, is presently senior lecturer in telecommunications with the Department of Business Administration, Media, and Technology at Arcada Polytechnic, Helsinki, Finland. His current research interests include mobile and wireless networking and network security.

Hervé Guyennet is a professor in computer science at the University of Franche-Comté. He is working on distributed systems: load balancing, collaborative work, distributed platform, multimedia, and QoS. He is the head of the Network and Distributed Systems Group at the LIFC. He has been the scientific advisor for 12 theses. He is the Franche-Comté representative of the ITEA European project proteus/telemaintenance.

Fabien HANTZ is a thesis student in computer science at the University of Franche-Comté. He is member of the distributed systems Group (LIFC) and particularly works on the design of secured desktop-computing platforms. He is the author of the HiPoP platform.

Bogdan Hoanca is an assistant professor of management information systems at the University of Alaska Anchorage (UAA). Before joining UAA, he co-founded, started up and sold a company that builds components for fiber optic communications. He also helped start and consulted with a number of other startup companies in optical fiber communications. Hoanca received a PhD in electrical engineering from the University of Southern California in 1999. His current research interests revolve around technology, in particular e-learning and societal implications of technology, as well as privacy and security.

Ida Hogganvik received an MSc in computer science from the Norwegian University of Science and Technology (NTNU) in 2003. Since then she has worked on her PhD in the Cooperative and Trusted Systems Group at SINTEF ICT, where she is developing a graphical approach to risk identification for use in structured brainstorming in security analysis.

Mohammed Hussein is a doctoral student at the School of Computing at Queen's University, Canada. He received a BSc degree in computer science from Sharjah University, UAE (2004). He received his MSc in computer science from Queen's University, Canada (2006). During his MSc program, Hussein was a member of the Queen's Reliable Software Technology group.

Jonny Karlsson has a BSc in information technology from Arcada Polytechnic, Helsinki, Finland. Since May 2002, he has been working in Arcada Polytechnic as a course assistant and course teacher in programming and network security related courses and as a research assistant. His current research interests include wireless and mobile network security.

Jouni Karvo received an MSc (Tech.) and DrSc (Tech.) at Helsinki University of Technology (TKK) (1997 and 2002, respectively). Currently, he is working as a researcher at Networking Laboratory of TKK, his research interests including wireless and mobile networks, and ad hoc networks. He lectures courses on basics of data communications and mobile networks. Dr. Karvo has published numerous scientific articles on recognized international journals and conferences.

Halim M. Khelalfa received an MS in computer sciences from The American University in Washington, DC (1980), and a PhD from the Illinois Institute of Technology (1985). He is currently an associate professor in the College of Information Technology, University of Wollongong in Dubai. Previously, he directed the Basic Software Laboratory at CERIST, Algiers, Algeria. Prior to this, he was a member of the technical staff with AT&T Bells Labs, networking division. His current research interests include: performance evaluation of networks, anonymity and privacy, inference control in data mining, software protection, and intrusion prevention.

Hristo Koshutanski received an MSc in mathematics from Plovdiv University "Paisii Hilendarski" in 2001 and a PhD in computer science and telecommunications from University of Trento in 2005. He won the E-NEXT SATIN award (The European Doctoral School of Advanced Topics In Networking) for doctoral research in 2005. He was an invited speaker at ESSLLI'05 summer school in August 2005. Dr. Koshutanski has just won the EU Marie Curie Fellowship. Dr. Koshutanski's research interests include distributed system security, trust management, access control models and authorization policies. He has published a number of scientific papers at international conferences and workshops.

J.-Christophe Lapayre is a professor in computer science at the University of Franche-Comté. He is a member of the Network and Distributed Systems Group (LIFC). His research area includes multimedia collaborative work. He is interested in applying distributed algorithms theories to manage concurrency accesses in collaborative work. He is the head of the InterregIII European project TeNeCi/Teleneurology.

Maryline Laurent-Maknavicius, PhD, works as a professor in the French National Institute of Telecommunications INT, and is the head of the research group VIS (towards a secure infrastructure). She is member of the French CNRS UMR 5157 SAMOVAR. Her main topics of interest both in research and master-grade/post-grade courses are related to network security, including the following areas: mobile IPv6, mesh/ad hoc networks, public key infrastructures, and access control. She is involved in the IETF standardization. She was co-chair of the SAR conference on Security and Network Architectures, Batz sur Mer, France, June 2005, and she is program committee member of several conferences (IEEE/ASWN, SAR, ECUMN).

Javier Lopez received an MS and PhD in computer science (1992 and 2000, respectively) from the University of Malaga. From 1991 to 1994 he worked as a systems analyst in the private sector, and in 1994 he joined the Computer Science Department at the University of Malaga, where he is an associate professor. His research activities are mainly focused on information and network security, leading some Spanish and EU research projects in those areas, and part of his research has been developed while been a visiting researcher at several universities, namely, Wisconsin-Milwaukee and Yale in the United States, Tsukuba in Japan, and QUT in Australia. Prof. Lopez is the co-editor-in-chief of Springer's *International*

Journal of Information Security (IJIS), member of the editorial boards of *Information Management and Computer Security Journal* and *International Journal of Internet Technology and Secured Transactions,* Spanish representative of the IFIP TC-11 WG (Security and Protection in Information Systems), and member of the steering committee of ERCIM's Working Group on Security and Trust Management.

Mass Soldal Lund holds a CandScient (MSc) degree in computer science from the University of Oslo, specializing in formal methods. Currently he is employed as a research scientist at SINTEF Information and Communication Technology, where he has been working with risk analysis and threat modelling since 2001, and at the University of Oslo, where he is writing a PhD. With his co-workers he has authored several papers on model-based risk analysis and he made substantial contributions to the OMG standard "UML Profile for Modeling Quality of Service and Fault Tolerance Characteristics and Mechanisms." His main research interests are formal and semi-formal specification techniques and languages, model-based testing, risk analysis and threat modeling.

Ref. jur. Tobias Mahler LLM, is a research fellow at the Norwegian Research Center for Computers and Law (NRCCL) at the Faculty of Law, University of Oslo. Mahler holds a German law degree and a LLM degree in computers and law from the European Legal Informatics Study Program (EULISP) from the Universities of Hannover and Oslo. Mahler's is a doctoral research on risk analysis of relations involving legal and trust aspects is funded by the Research Council of Norway under the research project ENFORCE. Mahler is leading the legal research in the European research project TrustCoM (www.eu-trustcom.com) under the European Commission's IST program. He is also participating in the European research project LEGAL-IST (www.legal-ist.org), mainly focusing on business collaborations, identity management and data protection law. He is a member of international conference program committees, focusing on privacy, security and trust.

R. Manjunath is a research scholar from the university Visveswaraiah College of Engineering, Bangalore University, India. He was born in 1971 in Kolar, India. His doctoral thesis spans signal processing, neural networks, data transfer over the network, and data integration. He has published about 55 papers in international conferences and journals in diverse areas involving the applications of signal processing. He has chaired many international conferences. His research interests include networking, signal processing, and supply chain, database architecture. He has industrial and academic experience over 11 years in various fields, including signal processing, data transfers, data organization, and neural networks.

Fabio Massacci is a full professor in informatics at the Universita' di Trento and guest scientist at SINTEF (NO). He was visiting researcher at IRIT Ð Toulose (FR), assistant professor at the University of Siena and got a PhD at the University of Roma I "La Sapienza" in 1998. His main research interests are computer security, formal verification, and requirements engineering. He published a number of articles on international conferences and journals. He coordinates an international EU project on security of mobile code, is a site leader of a project on security engineering and two basic research projects on security protocol verification and security requirements for organizations. He is rectors' delegate for ICT procurements and services for 4MÛ/yearly budget. He is member of ACM and IEEE and a chartered engineer since 1995.

Kenrick Mock received his PhD in computer science from the University of California, Davis, in 1996. He currently holds the position of associate professor of computer science at the University of Alaska Anchorage. His research centers on complex systems, information management, artificial intelligence, computer security, and technological innovations in education. Mock has previously held positions as a research scientist at Intel Corporation and as CTO of an Internet startup company, Unconventional Wisdom.

Jose A. Montenegro received an MS and PhD in computer science (2001 and 2006, repectively) from the University of Malaga. In 1998, he started working with the Computer Science Department at the University of Malaga, where he is an assistant professor. He has participated in several security projects, including a Framework for the Secure Communication between Public Administrations and Citizens through Internet, and the IST Project CASENET (Computer-Aided solutions to Secure ElectroNic commercE Transactions), included in the 5th Programme. His principal research interests are authorization, authentication and modelling security requirements in UML. He has participated in several international conferences on these topics, and security courses as the Fifth European Intensive Programme on Information and Communication Technologies Security (IPICS 2002).

Jean-Henry Morin is an associate professor at Korea University Business School. He holds a PhD and a degree in information systems from University of Geneva, where he has been Chargé de Cours in the Object Systems Group since 2000. He is co-founder of PebbleAge SA, a Geneva-based company specialized in corporate performance management solutions, where he was director of research and development until 2004. He has published in international conferences and journals and has worked on many European research projects. His research interests include digital rights and policy management (DRM/DPM), corporate information asset management, compliance, corporate governance, electronic commerce and services, peer-to-peer computing, mobile objects (agents), electronic publishing and information services over open networks.

Srinivas Mukkamala is a senior research scientist with New Mexico Tech's Institute for Complex Additive Systems Analysis and adjunct faculty at the Department of Computer Science New Mexico Tech. He is a technical manager of the Information Assurance Research Group, New Mexico Tech. Mukkamala received a BE in computer science and engineering from University of Madras in 1999, an MS in computer science, and PhD from New Mexico Tech.

Michel Pawlak holds a DEA in management and technology of information systems and a degree in information systems of the economics and social sciences faculty from the University of Geneva. Since 2001 he is research assistant in the Object Systems Group (OSG) of the Centre Universitaire d'Informatique (CUI) at the University of Geneva where he is currently completing his PhD. His research interests cover free and open source software (F/OSS) process improvement, digital rights and policy management, secure mobile agents, as well as issues related to interoperability and alignment.

Göran Pulkkis, DrTech, is presently senior lecturer in computer science and engineering at the Department of Business Administration, Media, and Technology at Arcada Polytechnic, Helsinki, Finland. His current research interests network security, applied cryptographic and quantum informatics.

Mohammad Raihan completed his Master of Science from the School of Computing, Queen's University, Canada. His primary area of interest is software security. At present, he is working as a software developer in Eyeball Networks Inc. located in West Vancouver, Canada.

Ketil Stølen is chief scientist and group leader at SINTEF. Since 1998 he has been a professor in computer science at the University of Oslo. Stølen has broad experience from basic research (4 years at Manchester University; 5 years at Munich University of Technology, 8 years at the University of Oslo) as well as applied research (1 year at the Norwegian Defense Research Establishment; 3 years at the OECD Halden Reactor Project; 6 years at SINTEF). He did his PhD "Development of Parallel Programs on Shared Data-structures" at Manchester University on a personal fellowship granted by the Norwegian Research Council for Science and the Humanities. At Munich University of Technology, his research focused on the theory of refinement and rules for compositional and modular system development—in particular, together with Manfred Broy he designed the Focus method, as documented in the Focus-book, published in 2001. At the OECD Halden Reactor Project he was responsible for software development projects involving the use of state-of-the-art CASE-tool technology for object-oriented modelling. He led several research activities concerned with the modelling and dependability-analysis of safety-critical systems. He has broad experience from research projects—nationally as well as internationally—and from the management of research projects. From 1992-96 he was project-leader under Sonderforschungsbereich 342 "Methodik des Entwurfs verteilter Systeme" at Munich University of Technology. From 2001-03 he was the technical manager of the EU-project CORAS which had 11 partners and a total budget of more than 5 million EURO. He is currently managing three major Norwegian research projects focusing on issues related to security, privacy and trust.

Snezana Sucurovic is a leading researcher in Institute Mihailo Pupin, Belgrade, Serbia. She received a BSc in electronics and an MSc in computer sciences from the Faculty of Electrical Engineering, Belgrade, Serbia. She is preparing her PhD thesis at the same faculty. She got several national awards for scientific papers. Her research interests include advanced EHCR architecture and data protection.

Antonins Sulaiman is currently a PhD student in computer science at New Mexico Tech. His research interests are information security, network security, malware analysis, and data mining.

Andrew H. Sung is currently professor and chairman of the Computer Science Department of New Mexico Tech, and a founding coordinator of the school's new Information Technology Program. He is also the associate director for education and training of ICASA (*Institute for Complex Additive Systems Analysis*, a statutory research division of New Mexico Tech performing work on information technology, information assurance, and analysis and protection of critical infrastructures as complex interdependent systems). Sung received a BS in electrical engineering from National Taiwan University in 1976, an MS in mathematical sciences from the University of Texas at Dallas in 1980, and a PhD in computer science from the State University of New York at Stony Brook in 1984.

Nhat Dai Tran is a BSc student in information technology at Arcada Polytechnic, Helsinki, Finland. He is currently working at Arcada Polytechnic as a research assistant. His research interests include wireless and mobile network security.

Fredrik Vraalsen received his Cand. Mag. (BSc) in informatics and mathematics from the University of Oslo in 1999. In 2001 he received an MSc in computer science from the University of Illinois at Urbana-Champaign. During his graduate studies he worked on performance monitoring and analysis of Grid computing systems, and was also a research assistant in the Pablo research group. Since 2001 he has been employed as research scientist in the Cooperative and Trusted Systems group at SINTEF, where he has been working on projects involving mobile systems and technologies, systems architecture and design, security risk analysis, and system development.

Albin Zuccato received an MSc in economics and computer science from the Technical University, Austria, and a PhD in computer science from Karlstad University, Sweden. He worked at the Austrian bank Erste Bank between 1997 and 2001 as a project and security manager. For the present, he is member of the Privacy and Security Group (PriSec) at Karlstad University where he works with security and privacy management. He also teaches courses in computers security and software engineering.

Mohammad Zulkernine is a faculty member of the School of Computing of Queen's University, Canada, where he is leading the Queen's Reliable Software Technology (QRST) research group. He received a BSc in computer science and engineering from Bangladesh University of Engineering and Technology in 1993. Dr. Zulkernine received an MEng in computer science and systems engineering from Muroran Institute of Technology, Japan in 1998. He received a PhD from the Department of Electrical and Computer Engineering of the University of Waterloo, Canada, in 2003, where he belonged to the university's Bell Canada Software Reliability Laboratory. Dr. Zulkernine's current research focuses on software engineering (software reliability and security) and network security (intrusion detection). His research has been funded by a number of provincial and federal funding agencies and industry: Bell Canada, Canada Foundation for Innovation (CFI), Ontario Ministry of Economic Development and Trade (MEDT), National Science and Engineering Research Council of Canada (NSERC), and Mathematics of Information Technology and Complex Systems (MITACS), Canada. He has been very active in the international research community as a conference program committee member, paper and grant application reviewer, session chair, and invited speaker. Dr. Zulkernine is also cross-appointed in the Department of Electrical and Computer Engineering of Queen's University, and a licensed professional engineer of the province of Ontario, Canada. He is a member of the IEEE, ACM, and the IEEE Computer Society.

Index

certification authority (PKCA) 110
infrastructure (PKI) 4, 42, 154
registration authority (PKRA) 110

Q

qualification authentication authority (QAA) 110
quality
of service (QoS) 302
of service modeling language (QML) 290

R

radio waves 77
random early prediction (REP) 308
registration authority 110
RegQueryValueEx function 207
regular expression over events (REE) 294
release-of-information credential (CRoI) 123
remote authentication dial in user service (RA-DIUS) 4, 86, 306
reporting languages 292
reproduction 244
response languages 292
return
on investment (ROI) 263
on security investment (ROSI) 7, 18
rights
delegation 23
management services (RMS) 175
risk
management 261
role
-based access control (RBAC) 111
based trust management framework (RT) 159
model 155
root
component 112, 114
rootkits 239

S

scanners 207
script-viruses 243
secondary care provider (SCP) 112
secure
electronic transactions (SET) 51
socket layer (SSL) 4, 214
video processor (SVP) 176

security
architecture 2, 7, 15, 19
constraints 1, 19
education training and awareness (SETA) 247
identifier (SID) 39
policy 5, 7
sensitive servers 9, 10, 17
service level agreements (SLAs) 321
Shibboleth
attribute requester (SHAR) 157
Indexical Reference Establisher (SHIRE) 157
short message service (SMS) 35
simple
hierarchical event description language (SHEDEL) 294
mail transfer protocol (SMTP) 3
single
sign-in (SSI) 156
sign on (SSO) 24, 28
social engineering 211
software
development life cycle (SDLC) 286
key loggers 224
specification languages (SSL) 286, 287
usage monitor (SUM) 174
source of authorization (SOA) 155
SSH server 26
SSL protocol 24
stealth 244
storage protection 31
structured query language (SQL) 290
subscriber identity module (SIM) 42
Symbian
-based mobile computing devices 31
application 54
based mobile devices 32
devices 31
OS 31, 35
architecture 31
platforms 33
security 36
root certificate 38
security 32
synchronized random dynamic (SRD) 214
system integrator (SI) 317

T

temporal key integrity protocol (TKIP) 86